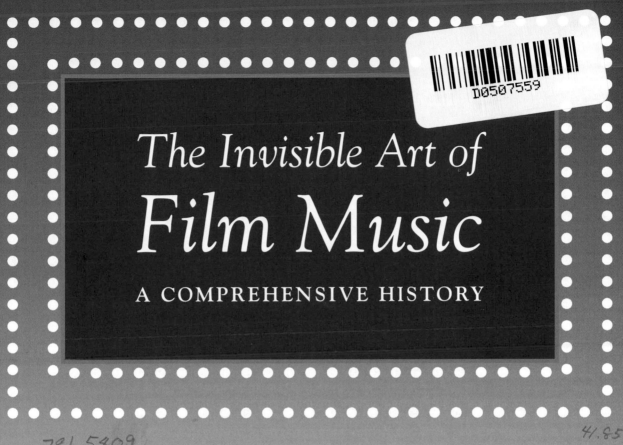

The Invisible Art of
Film Music
A COMPREHENSIVE HISTORY

Laurence E. MacDonald

MOTT COMMUNITY COLLEGE

ARDSLEY HOUSE, PUBLISHERS, INC., NEW YORK

ARDSLEY HOUSE

Published in the United States of America
Ardsley House
4501 Forbes Boulevard, Suite 200
Lanham, Maryland 20706

To the two most influential women in my life:

*My mother, Mildred Robinson MacDonald, who first
introduced me to movies and to music at a very young age;*

*and my wife, Rose Ann, without whose tireless support and
loving encouragement this book would not have been possible*

Contents

1950–59

4 • • • • • • *The Decline of the Studio System* • • • • • •113

1980–89

7 • • • • • *The Influence of Synthesized Sound* • • • • • 277

List of Biographical Sketches

Preface

As a professor of music history and a longtime film and music critic, I decided many years ago to write a book on the history of film music, a subject about which at that time very little had been written. After I conducted some initial research, my commitment to promoting film music led to the radio program "Music from Movies," which made its debut in October 1976 on the Flint, Michigan public radio station, WFBE. As a volunteer producer, I conceived a series of hour-long programs devoted to film-music pioneers, which profiled, among others, Max Steiner, Alfred Newman, and Miklos Rozsa. Over the years, the presentations on composers and their scores that I prepared for the radio show, along with the interviews I conducted with film composers, increased my determination to write a book on film music.

As a preliminary step, I produced a chronological outline of film music history, which took as its starting point the introduction of synchronized sound. There have been some changes in the structure of this book since its inception, though its basic idea remains the same: *The Invisible Art of Film Music* celebrates the contributions of musicians to the medium of motion pictures. Arranged as a chronological survey, this book includes biographical sketches of many of the most important film composers, including accounts of how they became involved in the highly complex art of scoring movies. This book is also about the many films themselves, how their scores came to be written, and what types of music these films contain.

It is inherently difficult to describe in words a medium that depends so totally on aural experience. I nonetheless hope the descriptions of this text will serve to elucidate the nature of film music and the ways in which music enhances the film-viewing experience. I also hope the brief outlines preceding each chapter—which collectively profile the media of recording, broadcasting/telecasting, and film for the decades from the 1920s to the 1990s—will help the reader place in perspective the achievements of film composers through the years since the introduction of synchronized sound.

Regrettably, one cannot convey the entire history of film music within a single volume. I have made many difficult decisions concerning which films and composers to include, and, admittedly, many potential discussions of significant scores have been bypassed for lack of space. Owing to the chronological organization of this volume, the works of some composers are scattered throughout the text; this is especially true of the music of composers of particular longevity, such as Miklos Rozsa and Jerry Goldsmith.

It is my hope that this adherence to a historically structured account of the development of film music will enhance the reader's appreciation for the evolutionary process of music in films.

One aim of *The Invisible Art of Film Music* is to introduce film music to the general student, the film historian, and the aspiring creator of new cinematic work. In order to facilitate its accessibility, no examples of musical notation are included. This book also targets the film-music enthusiast, whom I hope will become better informed concerning some noteworthy but lesser known film composers.

Finally, I hope this effort will shed light on some of the unsung heroes of film music, whose career achievements deserve to be understood, and whose scores deserve to be heard.

Acknowledgments

During the years through which this book has evolved, many people have helped me in various ways. First of all, I would like to acknowledge Forrest Alter, former head of the Art, Music, and Drama Department of the Flint Public Library. When I began my research on film music in the 1970s, Mr. Alter allowed me to peruse new books as soon as copies came in; his encouragement has been invaluable in terms of my commitment to this project.

I wish to express my deepest gratitude to the memory of Tony Thomas (1927–97), whose writings on film music have been a true source of inspiration, and to Kenneth M. Siegel (1945–97), whose friendship and courage helped make the writing of this book a labor of love.

Additionally, there are many others who have given assistance. John Waxman helped, not only with the biographical material on his father, but also in directing me to many other informed sources who subsequently read sections of the book and gave helpful input. Thanks go to Nicholas Rozsa and Nina Rota for checking the sections on their fathers, and to Leslie Korngold for reading the biographical material on his grandfather. Fred Karlin also assisted me by locating sources of composer photos and by giving helpful advice. Professor Michael T. Coolen of Oregon State University read an early version of the manuscript and offered many valuable suggestions. Many others read sections of the manuscript and made helpful comments. Michael Kamen contributed some thoughtful insights, as did Hans Zimmer and Elliot Goldenthal. Stacy Allyn, of the Ronni Chasen Agency, deserves my eternal thanks for setting up telephone interviews for me with each of these three composers. Elia Kazan helped clear up some matters with regard to the composers who worked on his films. Others, such as David Raksin and Elmer Bernstein, expressed encouragement along the way. Margaret Adamic, of the Disney Publishing Group, and Scott Shukat, of the Scott Shukat Agency, both helped with materials relating to Disney films. The faculty and staff of Mott Community College also deserve thanks for helping in various ways. Their efforts are deeply appreciated.

Many others deserve to be thanked for helping with the collecting of pictures for this book. Stephanie Ogle, of Cinema Books (Seattle), and Jerry Ohlinger, of Jerry Ohlinger's Movie Material Store Inc. (New York), were of great assistance in locating film stills and publicity shots. Mary Corliss and her staff at the Film Stills Archive of the Museum of Modern Art (New York) helped a great deal with some rare photos, as did Dace Taube, of the University Libraries at the University of Southern California. Thanks also go to Katy Bennett, Vice President for Marketing, The Detroit Symphony, for the use of the Aaron Copland photo; to Pearl Wexler for the picture of Maurice Jarre; and to the following: April Biggs, Ronni Chasen, Olivia Tiomkin Douglas, Thomas Jaehnig, Brian Loucks, Jeannie Poole (of the Film Music Society), David Sneed—and especially, Gay Goodwin Wallin, who went well out of her way to assist me. All of the above have earned my lasting gratitude for helping make a dream into a reality.

Martin Zuckerman, of Ardsley House, deserves recognition for his patience and guidance during the three years that this book has evolved from a series of loosely connected essays into its present form. In the production of the book, Laura Jones has proved to be of great assistance, not only with the typesetting, but also with her generosity and patience. Karen Bernath deserves credit for her ingeniously creative book design that has transformed a pile of typewritten pages into something visually appealing.

INTRODUCTION

*Music
and the Birth of Film*

Ever since filmmaking began, music has been a vital aspect of the cinematic art. According to Charles Hofmann in his book *Sounds for Silents*: "Since the earliest days of the movies there has really been no such thing as a 'silent film.' Music was always an integral part of the showing of motion pictures, inseparable from the visual, indispensable as accompaniment to films."[1]

During the final years of the nineteenth century, silent films became a popular form of entertainment in the United States and in many other countries. The "flickers," as these early films were known, were short one-reelers that appealed to a broad cross-section of viewers from various social classes and ethnic backgrounds. Without any dialogue these films contained no language barriers; they began to attract audiences that enjoyed viewing a make-believe world filled with action and physical comedy. Edwin S. Porter's *The Great Train Robbery* (1903), with a cast of forty and almost twelve minutes long, was an early milestone.

The first flickers were shown in either vaudeville theaters, music halls, or penny arcades. In theaters designed for live entertainment, house musicians were often called upon to accompany both live shows and screenings of silent films.[2] As the film medium gained in popularity, additional screening facilities were needed. This need brought about the emergence of the first movie theaters.

THE EVOLUTION OF MOVIE THEATERS. The first movie houses, which were little more than converted storefronts, first appeared in European cities as early as 1896. The first permanent movie theater in the United States was Thomas H. Tally's Electric Theater in Los Angeles, which

Nickelodeon theater, Pittsburgh.

The Museum of Modern Art/Film Stills Archive

opened in 1902. The Nickelodeon Theater, the name of which reflected its five-cent admission charge, opened in Pittsburgh in 1905. The name "nickelodeon" eventually became a generic term by which early movie houses were identified.[3]

As the American film industry continued to expand, neighborhood theaters were opened in many cities across the country by 1912. Soon after, larger ones, like the Strand in New York City, which opened on Broadway in April 1914, became the prototype of the gaudily decorated movie palaces that were built in many American cities by the beginning of the 1920s.[4]

MUSIC FOR SILENT FILMS. Since many of the earliest movie houses were of the storefront variety, with neither permanent seating nor any type of acoustical sound treatment, music was needed to enhance the viewer's enjoyment of the screen's soundless images. The music for silent films generally ranged from the sounds of an upright piano in a small movie house to those of a pipe organ, equipped with all sorts of sound effects, in a larger theater. In a few of the largest theaters, a full symphony orchestra was sometimes employed (provided there was a big enough orchestra pit).

The earliest musical accompaniments for films consisted of collages of previously composed material, played by musicians with variable amounts of training and skill, who ultimately decided what sort of music should be played. According to Charles Hofmann:

> The house musician usually played what he liked, or what he already knew. Lively music to a solemn scene was a common experience during those first years. More often the same music was heard for every picture and there was little differentiation between one film and another. It was as if the musicians never watched the screen![5]

Another insight into the nature of early film music comes from film historian Arthur Knight, who describes silent film music as follows:

> When the big downtown theaters began to spring up after 1914, most of them had large pit orchestras to play at least for the evening shows. Afternoon performances might be accompanied either by a smaller ensemble or by the organ . . . the standard equipment included a mighty Wurlitzer, that behemoth of mechanical sound with its banks and banks of gleaming keys and special effects . . . the purpose of such accompaniment was twofold: to provide suitable mood music for the picture, and to blot out for the patrons such distractions as the whir of the projectors, the banging of chairs and (above all) the noises of other patrons.[6]

Eventually, the choice of musical selections for the accompaniment of films began to be made by the filmmakers themselves, who provided listings of musical selections that were recommended for use with their films. The first listings, which emanated from the Edison Company in 1909, were referred to as "musical suggestion sheets." The next year, the term "cue sheet" began to be used. By the 1920s, film companies regularly distributed cue sheets along with their films, in order to guarantee a better consonance between the visual imagery and the music.

As film began to evolve into an art form, the composition of original scores as musical accompaniment was probably inevitable. Evidence suggests that the earliest original scores came from Europe, where many illustrious composers began receiving commissions to write film scores. According to the author of *70 Years at the Movies*:

> The composer [Camille] Saint-Saëns was asked to write a special score for the prestigious film production *L'assassinat du Duc de Guise* in 1908, and after that it became customary for any feature-length film to have a specially composed or compiled musical accompaniment. Music, therefore, was an important branch of the silent film business.[7]

D.W. GRIFFITH. The musical score began to be perceived as an integral part of American filmmaking through the creative genius of film director D. W. Griffith. After acting in some of Edwin S. Porter's films, Griffith began working as a staff director for the Biograph Company. In 1911, Griffith stretched the boundaries of the medium by producing films that were two reels long. By 1913, he had completed the first four-reel American film, *Judith of Bethulia*, and it was one year later that he made the American screen's first major epic, *The Birth of a Nation*, a lavish twelve-reel drama about the Civil War and its aftermath.[8]

For this monumental film Griffith hired composer/conductor Joseph Carl Breil (1870–1926) to produce a symphonic score. The result, for the most part, consisted of passages from works by Richard Wagner, Peter Ilyich Tchaikovsky, Franz Liszt, and a potpourri of other nineteenth-century composers. What Breil could not achieve by borrowing, he resolved by composing new musical themes. The final product was then assembled into a permanent score, which ultimately consisted of 226 separate cues. Orchestral parts were circulated with the film, accompanied by a conductor's score on which the cues were marked for proper synchronization with the film. During the film's opening engagements, this score was played by a seventy-piece orchestra.[9]

The Birth of a Nation, while of epic dimensions, caused considerable controversy because of its sympathetic portrayal of white supremacy in the South following the Civil War. Despite public protests against the film, there was little equivocation about its music: the film score had truly arrived!

Griffith subsequently hired Breil to score several other films, including *Intolerance* (1916), which many regard as Griffith's masterpiece. However, this film was not nearly as successful at the box office as its predecessor, and Griffith's career began to falter.

Meanwhile, other filmmakers began to commission composers to write original scores for their films, as they became aware of the value of specially designed music.

COMBINING SOUND AND FILM. During the early years of filmmaking, many experiments took place, both in the United States and in Europe, in an attempt to develop a mechanism for combining recorded sound with film. As early as 1889, Thomas Edison's assistant, W. K. Laurie Dickson, demonstrated a device called the Kinetophone, which used a kind of stethoscope to add sound accompaniment to the Kinetoscope, the motion-picture machine that formed the main attraction at peep-show parlors.[10]

Later experiments involved the use of discs, but there was little means of sound amplification for these audio recordings. This problem prevented any widespread application of the device, especially with the evolution of the mammoth movie palaces of the 1920s.

A major advancement in the possibility of sound films came with the experiments of Lee De Forest (1873–1961), the self-proclaimed "Father of Radio." In 1906, De Forest patented a means of sound amplification known as the audion tube. With this invention he became a pioneer in radio broadcasting, and he subsequently applied his sound amplification device to the medium of motion pictures.

EIGHT DECADES OF FILM MUSIC. The text that follows is, above all, an attempt to celebrate the story of film music during the past eight decades. The careers of both the pioneers of film music and the more recent composers have been included, in an effort to acknowledge the efforts of the many creative musicians who have provided exciting and vibrant musical accompaniments for the flickering images on the silver screen.

This chronological narrative concerns a part of the motion-picture medium which, though it cannot be seen, can be powerfully felt. The invisible art of film music is a subject about which all too little has been written, even though music has complemented the film medium's projected images throughout the history of the motion picture.

Endnotes

1. Charles Hofmann, *Sounds for Silents* (New York: DBS, 1970), p. 1. (Note: No page numbers are given in the book; this page number represents the first page following the Foreword.)

2. Ibid., p. 2.

3. David Cook, *A History of Narrative Film* (New York: W. W. Norton & Co., 1981), p. 28.

4. Arthur Knight, *The Liveliest Art*, Rev. ed. (New York: MacMillan, 1978), p. 40.

5. Hofmann, p. 2.

6. Knight, p. 125.

7. Ann Lloyd, ed., *70 Years at the Movies* (New York: Crescent Books, 1988), p. 84.

8. Ephraim Katz, *The Film Encyclopedia*, 2d ed. (New York: HarperCollins, 1994), pp. 559–60.

9. Roger Manvell, ed., *International Encyclopedia of Film* (New York: Crown, 1972), p. 371.

10. Barry Norman, *The Story of Hollywood* (New York: New American Library, 1987), p. 9.

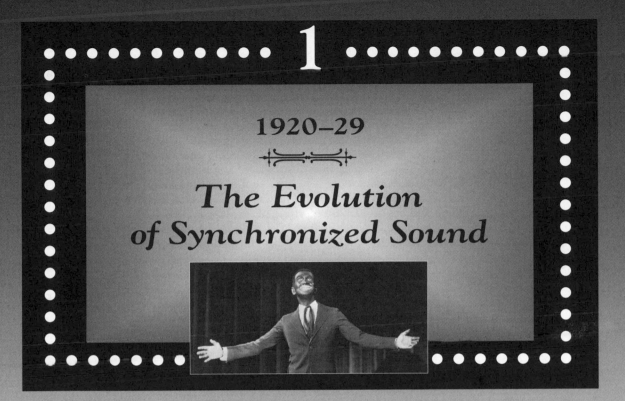

1

1920–29

The Evolution of Synchronized Sound

In order to fully appreciate the revolutionary developments in the medium of film during the 1920s, we must understand the forces that shaped the spirit of free enterprise in the United States during the decade that has come to be known as the "Roaring Twenties." In the wake of World War I, the American automobile industry achieved an unprecedented success, with Henry Ford's company continuing to mass-produce the Model T, reaching the one-million mark by December 1915, and twenty-seven million units by 1927.[1] Also fanning the flames of the economic boom was a reckless mood on Wall Street, with stock market indexes climbing to dangerously high levels. Investors were unaware of the risks involved, as they poured millions of dollars of personal wealth into the purchase of shares of the various commodities.

The optimistic mood of the 1920s was also enhanced by the spread of jazz, which provided a rhythmically upbeat musical accompaniment to the free-flowing bootleg booze of innumerable speakeasies. So much jazz was played during this decade that author F. Scott Fitzgerald referred to it as the "Jazz Age." Whether known as the "Roaring Twenties," the "Jazz Age," or the "Era of Prohibition," the period following World War I was a devil-may-care decade in which the movies gained their "voice" through the work of a number of intrepid inventors who continually experimented with various types of machinery in order to bring sound to the motion picture.

RADIO. The revolution in sound technology that eventually led to the development of "talkies" began with the radio and recording industries. The advent of radio broadcasting started when the first regular licensed program was broadcast on station WWJ in Detroit on August 20, 1920.[2] By 1922, there were already five hundred stations operating in the United

States. In 1926, the National Broadcasting Company (NBC) was founded by Dr. David Sarnoff; soon several rival networks, including the Columbia Broadcasting System (CBS) and the Mutual network, were in operation. By the end of the decade, radio had become firmly established as one of the nation's principal forms of in-home entertainment.

POPULAR MUSIC. During the 1920s, the recording industry also went through a period of tremendous progress. Although the Victor Talking Machine Company had first introduced the Victrola record player in 1906, it took many years before a million-selling recording was reached. That milestone came in 1919 with bandleader Ben Selvin's recording of "Dardanella." Paul Whiteman's 1920 recording of "Whispering," backed by "The Japanese Sandman," went even further, with sales of two million copies. By the middle of the '20s, the million-seller became common, with total annual record sales approaching the level of 130 million.[3]

MOVIES. In the midst of the dual entertainment boom created by technological advances in both the radio and the recording media, the motion picture industry entered a period of unprecedented change. The evolution of the talking motion picture, or "talkie," as it was originally called, involved the creative efforts of many talented individuals. These efforts ultimately led to a series of drastic changes in moviemaking during the late 1920s. It was precisely these changes that facilitated the creation of the musical scores that have accompanied many of the noteworthy films of the past several decades and that have become a vital part of our collective cinematic experience.

THE MOVIE INDUSTRY GOES WEST. By 1920, not only had America gained world domination in filmmaking, but the movie medium in the United States had become dominated by a small number of companies that had moved from the East Coast to California during the past decade. Hollywood no longer had a small-town atmosphere; it was now a bustling community. Paramount Pictures, having grown through a merger in 1916 to become the largest film studio, was turning out an annual average of 120 feature-length films in the period 1917–22.[4]

Other studios also thrived: Universal Pictures was founded in 1912; the Fox Film Corporation was started in 1915 and merged with 20th Century Pictures in 1935; Loew's Inc. was begun in 1910, was enlarged in 1920 through the takeover of the Metro Company, and amalgamated into Metro-Goldwyn-Mayer (MGM) in 1924; and United Artists was established as a producing, releasing, and distributing company in 1919 by Douglas Fairbanks and his wife Mary Pickford, along with Charlie Chaplin and D. W. Griffith.

The newest studio in town was the CBC Sales Company, which began its existence in 1920. Under its later and more familiar name, Columbia Pictures, it would be acquired in 1924 by Harry Cohn, the company's cofounder, who became the head of production.

Meanwhile, the four Warner brothers, who had moved their filmmaking operations to the West Coast in 1919, set up their first Hollywood studio on Sunset Boulevard; but from 1920 through 1922, they had funds to produce only two or three features per year. Despite the expansion of the company

Warner Brothers'
West Coast studio,
with cameos of the
four brothers.

The Museum of Modern Art/Film Stills Archive

into Warner Bros. Inc. in 1923, they had a long way to go before achieving any lasting success in filmmaking. That would take some ingenuity, and a gamble on the financial viability of "talkies."

VALENTINO'S TANGO. Although motion pictures of the early 1920s were still silent, that fact didn't prevent Hollywood filmmakers from shooting scenes involving music and dance. A case in point is the biggest hit of 1921, Metro's *The Four Horsemen of the Apocalypse*, which features a dance scene in an Argentinian bar that made both the tango and the actor who danced it overnight sensations.

Born in Italy in 1895, Rodolfo Guglielmi arrived in New York in 1913, where he soon began a show-business career as a nightclub dancer, giving himself the stage name of Rudolph Valentino. Soon he found his way to California, where he managed to get small parts in several films, usually as a dancer. But in 1921, screenwriter June Mathis recommended him for the starring role of Julio in the film version of Spanish author Vicente Blasco-Ibañez's antiwar novel about the decline of a noble Argentinian family during World War I.[5] The resultant film, with its sensuous dance scene, made Valentino a major star, and soon thereafter he signed a contract with

Paramount, where his appearance in the title role of *The Sheik* made him the screen's first great lover. Sadly, his life would end five years later, before audiences had a chance to hear him speak on film; but words could not have enhanced the image he had created in that single tango scene.

D.**W. GRIFFITH: *DREAM STREET*.** The year 1921 is also notable for the experimental use of recorded sound in a feature film. D. W. Griffith's *Dream Street*, which opened in New York on April 12, was a critical and box-office failure, but it remains historically important as the first feature film to contain a song. According to Miles Kreuger, noted authority on film musicals:

> Wendell McMahill, president of Kellum Talking Pictures, Inc., was planning a program of talkies for New York's new civic center, Town Hall. Eager to exploit the name Griffith on his marquee and certain that the director would be willing to recoup some of his losses on his recent fiasco, McMahill suggested the addition of sound to *Dream Street*. On Wednesday, April 27, the picture's star, Ralph Graves, went to the Kellum studios and recorded a lone song to fit a scene already in the picture. The feature was trimmed in length and opened on May 1 with several musical and dramatic short subjects.[6]

The sound system used in *Dream Street* was one of many that had been developed in Europe before World War I. These early sound systems all had one thing in common: they required either a disc or a cylinder, which meant that a technician had to attempt to synchronize a separate recording device with the projection of the film. The clumsiness of this technique proved to be a setback for the development of sound motion pictures. Even so, in the years ahead, the enterprising Warner brothers, in a desperate attempt to save their financially teetering studio, would gamble with everything they had on this admittedly imperfect sound-on-disc setup.

EARLY SOUND-ON-FILM SYSTEMS. While silent films enjoyed a prosperity that seemed to increase with each year, by 1922 there was a noticeable flurry of activity with regard to the introduction of recorded sound into the motion picture medium. In 1922, both in several European cities and in the United States, there were a number of noteworthy experiments by intrepid sound engineers who were attempting to break through the movie sound barrier. In Berlin, for instance, the first sound-on-film productions to be exhibited in public were shown at the Alhambra Kino on September 17. These films used a process called Tri-Ergon, developed by three Germans, Josef Engl, Joseph Massolle, and Hans Vogt. Their system was similar to that of Frenchman Eugene Lauste, who in 1910 had succeeded in recording speech on film, employing an electromagnetic recorder and a string galvanometer.[7] Unfortunately, the havoc wreaked by World War I had prevented Lauste from getting the financial backing to proceed.

Meanwhile, in the United States Dr. Lee De Forest, who had invented the audion tube in 1906, began leasing a sound-on-film system developed by Theodore Case and Earl Sponable of Auburn, New York. In November 1922, De Forest organized a company called the De Forest Phonofilm Corporation and also, at about that time, he created a second company, the De Forest Patent Holding Company. According to film historian Harry Geduld, "[This company] controlled his patents in the field of sound recording and reproducing (more than 70 patents were involved)."[8]

Lee De Forest, sitting next to one of his numerous inventions.

The Museum of Modern Art/Film Stills Archive

De Forest benefited from the support of Dr. Hugo Riesenfeld, who provided New York's Rivoli Theater as a screening facility for De Forest's film creations, which were given the name "Phonofilms." Riesenfeld also offered to assist De Forest by locating a production studio, plus the technicians and musicians needed for the project. De Forest began to produce a series of short talking features at the Norma Talmadge studio on East 48th Street in New York. The cameraman for the De Forest Phonofilms was Harry Owens, who had been sent by Riesenfeld to help in the project. In the next three years, De Forest would produce several short features each week. This production pattern clearly anticipated the work that would eventually begin at the Warner studio when their sound-on-disc system was adopted.

LEE DE FOREST'S PHONOFILMS. The first group of Lee De Forest's Phonofilms to be exhibited was introduced on April 15, 1923, at the Rivoli Theater. The program also included the silent feature film *Bella Donna*, which starred the popular Polish actress Pola Negri in her first American film. Advertised as "films that actually talk and reproduce music without the use of phonographs," these Phonofilms were one-reelers that featured many of the most popular musical stars of the 1920s, such as Eddie Cantor, Harry Richman, Sophie Tucker, and George Jessel.[9]

In technical terms, however, the De Forest shorts were not produced on a very sophisticated level. The photography of Harry Owens, for instance, consisted primarily of a static one-camera setup. Nevertheless, De Forest vigorously continued the production of his film novelties in the rented space of the Norma Talmadge Studio. There he produced close to a thousand short films between 1923 and 1927.[10] Among the more noteworthy of these films is the first motion picture recording of a United States president, Calvin Coolidge. Other speakers in De Forest's Phonofilms included Senator Robert La Follette and George Bernard Shaw.

The musical performances heard in most of the Phonofilms were adapted from a variety of vaudeville acts. Occasionally, an instrumental group would be featured, with such orchestra leaders as Ben Bernie, Paul Sprecht, and Otto Wolf Kahn. Perhaps the most significant of all of De Forest's works is *Love's Old Sweet Song*, which lays claim to being the first dramatic talkie film to be released commercially.[11]

THE SOUND OF SILENTS. The public as a whole continued to embrace silent pictures; in 1923, the most celebrated film was Paramount's *Covered Wagon*, an epic Western that featured a score by Hugo Riesenfeld (1879–1939). As the printed example included in Charles Hofmann's *Sounds for Silents* clearly indicates, Riesenfeld's musical score begins with an Indian motif that segues into a grandiose rendition of "The Star Spangled Banner," with a bit of "The Girl I Left behind Me" thrown in. Cue 26, an original theme in $\frac{6}{8}$ time, has a marchlike flavor and is heard intermittently throughout the film.[12]

Riesenfeld held the position of musical director at three New York movie houses, the Rialto, the Rivoli, and the Criterion. It was part of his job to arrange all the scores for pictures that played at those theatres, and to conduct a seventy-piece orchestra in the pit. According to Gillian Anderson, whose book, *Music for Silent Films 1894–1929*, is the definitive guide on the subject of silent-movie scores, four conductors worked under Riesenfeld; his library of film music consisted of six thousand orchestral scores plus thousands of unorchestrated pieces suitable for pianists or organists.[13]

Samuel L. "Roxy" Rothafel was an early devotee of film music. As manager of the Strand (1914–19) and Capitol (1919–25), he hired full-sized orchestras to provide background music. At the Roxy, which he built and managed from 1927 to 1932, he not only hired an orchestra but also had a five-manual Kimball theater organ installed.[14]

Not every theater owner had Rothafel's taste (or budget), but clearly the business of providing music for films was an arduous task and required the talents of a great many people. The Loew's theater chain alone, at the peak of the silent era, employed six hundred orchestral musicians and two hundred organists (with half the organists working in New York). The Loew's library consisted of fifty thousand scores, a phenomenal quantity of music by anyone's standards.[15]

Many renowned classical musicians got their start in movie houses. One celebrated example is Eugene Ormandy, who, having just arrived in the United States from his native Hungary in 1921, was hired by Rothafel to work at the Capitol Theater in New York. Ormandy served first as a violinist in the orchestra, and later moved up to conductor.[16]

The determination of inventors like Lee De Forest meant that the silent era could not last forever. Movies with recorded background scores would jeopardize the livelihoods of thousands of hard-working musicians, whose labors had given enjoyment to millions of moviegoers.

PHONOFILM FIRSTS (AND LASTS). When Lee De Forest successfully showed his Phonofilms in April 1923, he became the first person to exploit talking motion pictures commercially. As soon as his photographer, Harry Owens, completed the sound installations at several East Coast theaters in 1924, De Forest set out on a tour with his films. Although Phonofilms proved to be quite popular, De Forest lacked the entrepreneurial skills of Thomas Edison. Not only did he rent out the sound equipment to each theater for the meager sum of $150 per week, but he seemed to be indifferent to the financial possibilities of his Phonofilms, since he never bothered to have any of them copyrighted.[17]

Still, given the novelty of this new medium and the determined efforts of De Forest to produce and exhibit his Phonofilms, one has to wonder why he didn't experience a greater degree of success. Perhaps the explanation lies with the Hollywood moguls, who maintained a skeptical attitude toward talking pictures because these novel films were expensive to produce and because sound installations in theaters were costly. The ultimate failure of Phonofilms proved to be a lasting disappointment to De Forest, who would eventually lose his license to the Case-Sponable system, which involved a new sound-reproducing device that could be added to existing projectors. Subsequently, De Forest left the motion picture business.

ERNO RAPEE: MOTION PICTURE MOODS. Despite all these efforts, silent films were far from a thing of the past. In fact, Erno Rapee (1891–1945), one of the most famous silent-film composers, who had a long career as principal conductor of orchestras at several New York theaters—the Rivoli; the Capitol; the Roxy; and, later, the Radio City Music Hall—produced a 674-page manual for silent-film musicians, the full title of which is *Motion Picture Moods for Pianists and Organists, a Rapid Reference Collection of Selected Pieces Adapted to Fifty-Two Moods and Situations*. According to Charles Hofmann, this book's publication in 1924 was considered a blessing from Heaven by the many movie-house musicians who had to select and arrange music for two or three different features a week. In the preface, Rapee explained his purpose for the book: "I tried to create the necessary bridge between the screen and the audience which is created in the larger motion picture houses by the orchestra."[18]

Rapee's book, with its encyclopedic approach to the subject, was a serious attempt to enhance the musical backgrounds for silent films. Surely no art form thought to be on the point of extinction would have had such an exhaustive effort as this produced on its behalf. However, within five years, Rapee's manual would have little value, since the silent film was headed for oblivion.

RIVAL SOUND SYSTEMS. Silent movies enjoyed a banner year in 1925 due to the huge success of *Ben-Hur* and *The Big Parade*, which were produced by MGM during its first full year of operation. However, a race was on between rival motion picture companies to market the first viable sound-recording system. Theodore Case, having become frustrated with De Forest's lack of foresight and business sense, withdrew De Forest's license in September 1925 and soon began negotiating with William Fox, head of the Fox Film Corporation, who eventually would purchase rights to both the Tri-Ergon and the Case-Sponable systems.[19]

Western Electric developed an alternate sound-recording system, which used a sound-on-disc device. Although most of the major film companies failed to express much enthusiasm for the process, Sam Warner convinced his three brothers that sound films could turn their fledgling company into one of the giants of moviemaking. After Western Electric granted Warner Bros. exclusive rights to their process in June 1925, a period of experimentation began. With Sam Warner as supervisor, sound equipment was installed in the old Vitagraph studio in the Flatbush section of Brooklyn. Initially, problems emerged with the sound experiment. As Jack Warner later wrote: "No matter how carefully they sound-proofed the studio, there were always mysterious noises on the playbacks—whirring sounds, coughs, a small boy's shout, a squeaking chair, an unidentifiable rumbling."[20]

One by one, the problems were solved. The rumbling sound was eventually found to be coming from the subway, which at that point ran aboveground about a block from the studio. This forced a move to the vacated Manhattan Opera House, where sound experiments continued into 1926.

1926

WARNER BROS. AND THE BIRTH OF VITAPHONE. The race toward sound motion pictures intensified considerably during the spring of 1926, especially with the founding of the Vitaphone Corporation. This is the name Warner Bros. chose for its new subsidiary company, formed on April 20, 1926, in which it entered into partnership with Western Electric, the parent company of Bell Laboratories. The intention was to produce sound pictures using the Western Electric sound-on-disc equipment.[21] With Sam Warner installed as president, the Vitaphone Corporation assumed managerial control of the filmmaking experiments taking place at the Manhattan Opera House. In the next few months, several one-reel musical featurettes were filmed there. The already financially strapped studio risked everything on this venture, spending a total of three million dollars in a single year on its attempt to break the motion-picture sound barrier.

Hugh Stoller and
Hugh Pfannenstiehl,
standing in front of their
sound-on-disc invention,
similar to the Vitaphone,
c. 1925.

Warner Bros.' painstaking efforts with the Vitaphone process culminated in one of the most historic events in the history of motion pictures: the gala premiere of *Don Juan*. This first feature-length sound film was initially shown to the public on the evening of August 6, 1926 at the Warners' Theatre in New York City. It became the talk of the industry because of its revolutionary use of a prerecorded soundtrack; but it was technically a silent film since there was no spoken dialogue. Its musical score was the joint work of three composers, William Axt, David Mendoza, and Major Edward Bowes. The score was recorded on a series of large discs, each of which contained the exact amount of music needed to coincide with an entire reel of film (approximately ten minutes).[22] These discs were designed for play at 33⅓-rpm, and had to be changed by the projectionist at the end of each reel. In addition to the score, which was recorded by the New York Philharmonic under conductor Henry Hadley, the New York premiere showing was accompanied by synchronized sound effects, including the clashing of swords and the chiming of bells.

Don Juan is a lavishly produced adventure epic that stars John Barrymore as the notorious Spanish nobleman whose boudoir activities create quite a stir in Rome at the time of the powerful and ruthless Borgias. The style of the music is decidedly old-fashioned, with a symphonic sweep that helps to establish the decadent atmosphere. There are a number of musical themes scattered throughout the score, including a Spanish-flavored main-title tune, plus a habanera-style piece that is associated with Don Juan. This theme is first heard when the young Juan accompanies his father, Don José (also played by Barrymore) to the banquet hall in their villa. Following the death of José from a stab wound inflicted by one of his

Don Juan, palace scene, with Estelle Taylor and Montagu Love.

jealous lovers, the scene shifts to Rome, where Juan, now an adult, becomes notorious for his amorous adventures. During the Roman scenes, several additional musical ideas are introduced into the score. One theme, which prominently features flutes, accompanies dancers who provide entertainment for guests at a variety of social gatherings.

The film's most famous scene is a duel between Juan and Count Donati (Montagu Love) over the affections of the virtuous Adriana (Mary Astor). During the duel, besides the rambunctious orchestral accompaniment, there is also the sound of clanking swords. In the final reel Juan rescues Adriana from the clutches of the evil Borgias and then singlehandedly fights off a dozen pursuers, while the synchronized score continues to provide a rousing musical background.

As successful as the screening of *Don Juan* was, many members of the audience were even more impressed by a program of Vitaphone short subjects that preceded the film. These shorts featured a number of musical performances, including a Wagner overture played by the New York Philharmonic, operatic arias sung by Giovanni Martinelli and Marion Talley, and a banjo solo played by Roy Smeck.[23] There was also an introductory speech by Will Hays, president of the Motion Picture Producers and Distributors of America. All in all, with the combination of musical and talking short subjects plus the sound of *Don Juan*'s robustly romantic score, the evening was a huge success. This program ran for eight weeks in New York, and then had highly profitable engagements in Chicago, Los Angeles, Boston, Detroit, St. Louis, and even some European cities.[24] As David Cook reports in his comprehensive work *A History of Narrative Film*: "The critics were unanimous in their praise of the Vitaphone system, describing it as 'uncanny in its excellence,' 'impossible to imagine,' and 'the eighth wonder of the world.' "[25]

Exactly two months after the premiere of the first Vitaphone feature, Warner Bros. launched a second synchronized-sound program with the film *The Better 'Ole*, starring Syd Chaplin (Charlie Chaplin's brother). A program of Vitaphone shorts was again included, with musical material featuring Broadway stars Al Jolson and George Jessel, and also several vaudeville acts.[26] Again the public and critical reaction was favorable.

Despite the enthusiastic public response to the revolutionary Vitaphone process, Warner Bros. was faced with an enormous financial risk. In order to show Vitaphone productions on a wider basis, a massive sound-equipment installation had to be set in motion. The new head of the company, Harry Warner, traveled around the United States in 1926 in an attempt to convince theater owners to invest in the equipment. An indication of the theater owners' reluctance is the fact that, even by the end of 1927, there were fewer than two hundred American movie houses equipped for sound.[27]

WILLIAM FOX AND THE CASE-SPONABLE SYSTEM. With the premiere of *Don Juan*, the rivalry between Warners and Fox heated up. On September 23, 1926, only six weeks after the public unveiling of Vitaphone, William Fox paid Theodore Case a reputed million dollars for the patents and development of the Case-Sponable system; as a result the Fox-Case Corporation was formed.[28] Fox was later sued by De Forest, who claimed (with righteous indignation) that this sound process was actually Phonofilm (which it was). Eventually, Fox became embroiled in lengthy litigation over the alleged patent infringement.[29] However, that didn't stop the company from pressing ahead with sound-on-film experiments. Thus, the second launching of synchronized sound in motion pictures was about to take place, with the announced name of Fox Movietone.[30]

INTRODUCING THE **M**OVIE **T**HEME **S**ONG: **"C**HARMAINE.**"** Erno Rapee, in addition to his manual for pianists and organists, had written music before coming to the United States, including a 1913 tune that he adapted as the melody of "Charmaine." This song formed the basis of his score for the 1926 Fox film *What Price Glory?*, which became the year's biggest box-office hit. According to David Shipman, "Dolores Del Rio played the heroine, Charmaine, and Fox distributed a copy of a song of that name to be played as an accompaniment to the film."[31] "Charmaine" became the first hit song to emanate from a film score. The theme song was on its way to becoming an important, if often abused, element in film scoring.

THE **F**IRST **T**ALKIE: *THE JAZZ SINGER.* The event that changed the movies forever was the premiere of *The Jazz Singer* at the Warners' Theatre in New York City on October 6, 1927. After the success of *Don Juan*, Warner Bros. purchased the film rights to Samson Raphaelson's stage play, *The Jazz Singer*, which had starred George Jessel. Although Jessel was initially asked to repeat his stage role of Jakie Rabinowitz, the cantor's son who wants to be a Broadway performer, he held out for more than the $30,000 offered. Subsequently, Eddie Cantor was offered the role, but declined it. However, he suggested Broadway star Al Jolson for the part. Interestingly enough, when Jolson agreed to do the film, he wound up getting more than twice what Jessel had been offered.[32]

The Jazz Singer was basically a musical film, with a synchronized background score recorded by the Vitaphone Orchestra, conducted by Louis Silvers. Several vocal numbers sung by Jolson were interpolated into the picture. The background score, composed by Silvers, consists of original themes combined with bits of borrowed classical melodies, in the usual manner of the silent-film score. A recurring theme is from Tchaikovsky's *Romeo and Juliet*; there are also instrumental arrangements of such standards as "Sidewalks of New York." The songs heard in the film include some of Jolson's vaudeville hits, including "Toot, Toot, Tootsie," "My Mammy," and "Blue Skies." The only song composed specifically for the film, "Mother, I Still Have You," was written by Jolson along with Louis Silvers.

Al Jolson as
The Jazz Singer.

alternative silent versions; at the same time sound effects and music were patched on to silent films to prolong their commercial life. Nevertheless, the silent cinema, with all the art and sophistication it had perfected over the last three decades, had instantly become archaic.[45]

By the spring of 1928, it had become clear that even the very worst sound film would make more money than the best silent picture. Warner Bros. continued to lead the pack with its production of *Lights of New York*, which, upon its release on July 7, 1928, was hailed as "the first 100 percent all-talking picture."[46] Basically a cheaply made gangster thriller with a running time of only fifty-seven minutes, *Lights* became so popular that Jack Warner took several films that were currently in production and added talking sequences to them to increase their market value.[47]

An even bigger hit was Al Jolson's second film, *The Singing Fool*, which was released in September 1928. With such songs as "Sonny Boy" and "It All Depends on You," *The Singing Fool* includes more singing and dialogue than *The Jazz Singer* but is still only a part-talkie, with about one-third of its length still done in the old silent format, with intertitles. Even so, *The Singing Fool* was Warners' highest grossing movie of the 1920s, with a worldwide gross of $5.9 million (in fact, no movie after it would make as much until the release of *Gone with the Wind* in December 1939).[48]

The Singing Fool, in which Jolson plays an aspiring singer with an unfaithful wife and a terminally ill child, is even more maudlin than Jolson's prior film. The song "Sonny Boy" was written at Jolson's request by the team of Buddy De Sylva, Lew Brown, and Ray Henderson to replace an Irving Berlin tune that Jolson considered unsuitable for his voice. "Sonny Boy" was intended as a satire on the type of sentimental ballad that was so popular during the 1920s, but Jolson took it seriously and sang it in his typically over-emotional style. As a result, the song became hugely successful, with sheet-music sales topping the three-million mark.[49]

THE SOUND-ON-FILM SYSTEM. More than any other film made in the late 1920s, *The Singing Fool* demonstrated beyond a doubt that a new era in filmmaking had truly arrived. As a result of its success, by the end of 1928 approximately eighty features with sound had been produced by Hollywood studios.

To simplify and regulate the production of sound films, a committee had already been formed by producer Adolph Zukor in December 1926. For fifteen months, this group, which included representatives from six production companies, studied various sound processes, including Vitaphone, Movietone, RCA's Photophone, and Western Electric's new sound-on-film system. Finally, in May 1928, the six companies entered into an agreement with Western Electric to adopt its sound-on-film system as an industry standard. Even Warner Bros. soon adopted this system (although the company retained the name Vitaphone).[50]

Now that a compatible system had been adopted, the film companies could proceed to reequip their production facilities. By the end of 1928, the rush for sound was in full swing. Two major talkies opened late that year: Paramount's *Interference* in November, and Fox's *In Old Arizona* in December. Starring Warner Baxter as the Cisco Kid (a role for which he won the Academy Award), *In Old Arizona* was billed as "the first 100% all-talking drama filmed outdoors."[51] This movie, which used the Movietone system, proved unequivocally the superiority of the sound-on-film process over Vitaphone's unreliable sound discs.

Meanwhile, Walt Disney, an industrious young filmmaker of animated short subjects, took advantage of the synchronized sound phenomenon by adding a soundtrack to his animated short subject *Steamboat Willie*, the third animated film featuring Mickey Mouse. Disney had created Mickey's character earlier that year and decided to hold back the previously completed *Plane Crazy* and *Gallopin' Gaucho* in favor of adding sound to *Steamboat Willie*. The resulting seven-minute short subject, featuring the songs "Steamboat Bill" and "Turkey in the Straw," was first shown at the Colony Theater in New York City on November 18, 1928, on the same bill as an early talkie called *Gang War*.[52] *Steamboat Willie* was an unqualified success.

The sound-on-film system Disney used was a close approximation of Movietone. It was called "Powers Cinephone" after the often unscrupulous producer with whom Disney was associated, Pat Powers, who had actually based his system on the patented inventions of others.[53] Numerous animated shorts with synchronized sound were soon produced by a number of animation studios, including those at Warner Bros. and Paramount; but Disney himself remained the single most important figure in film animation, with a continuing series of Mickey Mouse cartoons, and, beginning in 1929, a series of musical cartoons called *Silly Symphonies*. Although Disney's early animated efforts are crudely drawn, they are important because of their careful synchronization between picture and sound. Walt Disney understood, perhaps better than anyone, the full value of the revolutionary talkie.

By the end of 1928, sound installations had been completed in approximately one thousand of the more than twenty thousand movie houses in America.[54] This number, although significantly higher than that of the preceding year, was still only five percent of the total number of theaters. Within another year, the number would rise to about four thousand; by the end of 1930, more than thirteen thousand theaters would be wired for sound. Clearly, the sound revolution was under way.

THE BROADWAY MELODY: ALL TALKING! ALL SINGING! ALL DANCING! The early talkies with their songs and dances had more of an impact on musical films than they had on dramatic films with instrumental underscoring. Musicals became so popular in the early days of sound films that the word "talkies" seems almost inappropriate; a more accurately descriptive term would be "singies."

When MGM released *The Broadway Melody* in February 1929, another milestone in the sound revolution was reached. Advertised as "all-talking, all-singing, all-dancing," *The Broadway Melody* features a plot device that would be repeated ad nauseum in years to come: the backstage drama involved in the staging of a musical show. Interspersed with the dialogue are several songs that became major hits: "The Wedding of the Painted Doll," "You Were Meant for Me," and the title song "Broadway Melody," all composed by Nacio Herb Brown and Arthur Freed.

Although there were perhaps better films released in 1929 than *The Broadway Melody*, none captured the public's interest more completely. Because of this picture's success, every major Hollywood star was expected to make his or her talkie debut in a musical film. At this point the careers of many silent film stars came into jeopardy as new faces appeared on the scene. Many of these new actors were recruited from the Broadway stage, where the required singing and dancing skills were taken for granted.

The Broadway Melody is innovative in a number of ways. First, its score consists primarily of original songs, rather than the familiar standards that had been used in Al Jolson's films. Second, the "Painted Doll" sequence was shot in early two-tone Technicolor, which had been used to some extent during the silent-film days of the early '20s, but would now be used to decorate musical sequences in many early talkies. *The Broadway Melody* was also the first talking motion picture that most American audiences had the chance to see since only a select few theatres had previously been equipped to show the sound versions of the earlier talkies.

A **DELUGE OF MUSICAL MADNESS.** *The Broadway Melody* helped to open the floodgates to a deluge of musicals, including MGM's *Hollywood Revue of 1929*, in which Brown and Freed's classic "Singin' in the Rain" was introduced, and Fox's *Movietone Follies of 1929*, which had the distinction of being the first film to use Fox's 70-mm Grandeur System —a forerunner of the many widescreen processes that would begin to emerge in the 1950s.

Meanwhile, Warner Bros. produced two film revues in 1929, *On with the Show!* and *The Show of Shows*, in the first of which Ethel Waters is seen and heard singing her classic rendition of "Am I Blue?" This film includes over a dozen other comedic and musical skits featuring well-known stage and screen performers. It is also distinguished for being the first talkie shot entirely in two-color Technicolor. *The Show of Shows*, although not nearly as memorable, does have some entertaining moments, especially comedienne Winnie Lightner's rendition of the delightful "Singin' in the Bathtub."

Paramount jumped into the musical arena with two films starring Maurice Chevalier, *Innocents of Paris* and *The Love Parade*. In the former, Chevalier introduced "Louise"; the latter presented Jeanette MacDonald in her film debut. The much-acclaimed *Love Parade*, which was nominated for six Academy Awards in 1930, also signifies the talkie debut of director Ernst Lubitsch, whose innovative techniques would create a new genre of American films through the next decade.

Besides Al Jolson and Maurice Chevalier, the only other stage stars of the '20s to have a lasting success in talkies were the Marx Brothers, who made their film debut for Paramount in 1929 in the film version of their stage hit *The Cocoanuts*. Combining a zany brand of verbal humor with their considerable musical talents, the Marx Brothers were naturals for the new medium of film musicals. They would continue to appear in successful movies with interspersed musical episodes into the 1940s.

Using the combination of sound, music, and color (and occasionally widescreen images), all the movie studios tried to capitalize on the musical craze. Over fifty musical films were released in 1929, and another hundred films each featured a song or two.[55]

In addition to the many musical feature films, dozens of animated musical short subjects were released in 1929, including Walter Lantz's first Oswald the Rabbit cartoon, *Ozzie of the Circus*; Paul Terry's first *Aesop's Fable*; the first in a series of *Screen Songs* drawn by Dave Fleischer; and the first of Columbia's Krazy Kat cartoons. Walt Disney continued to lead the animation parade with his *Silly Symphonies*, beginning with *The Skeleton Dance*, a graveyard frolic set to the music of Edvard Grieg ("March of the Dwarfs," from the *Lyric Suite*, opus 54).[56]

THE **FIRST OSCARS.** Despite the furor over talking pictures, the talkies were shut out of the first annual Academy Awards ceremony, held on May 29, 1929, since the governing board of the Academy of Motion Picture Arts and Sciences felt that it would not be fair to place silent films and talkies in competition with each other. With an eligibility year extending from August 1927 through July 1928 and with *The Jazz Singer* declared ineligible for the Best Picture award, the first film to win the prize was Paramount's *Wings*, a lavishly produced epic of aviators in combat during World War I.[57] Although *Wings* was a silent film, it used recorded sound effects; there was color for the aerial battles plus a widescreen process called "Magnascope."

In the second year of Academy voting, which covered films released between August 1928 and July 1929, talkies were eligible and managed to dominate the awards. *The Broadway Melody* won the Best Picture award at the ceremony held on April 30, 1930.

REINVENTING **THE CRAFT.** In a space of less than three years, between 1926 and 1929, the physical operation of the entire motion picture industry was overhauled. From *Don Juan* to *The Broadway Melody*, the techniques of filmmaking changed so drastically that the craft of making movies had to be reinvented. As Chapter Two will show, no one in Hollywood was really quite prepared for the sound revolution. In the years ahead, cinematic experimentation would continue and would lead to the making of films as artistically accomplished as some of the finest achievements of the silent film era, with accompanying musical scores of comparable quality.

Endnotes

1. Charles Van Doren and Robert McHenry, eds., *Webster's Guide to American History* (Springfield, MA: G. & C. Merriam Co. 1971), p. 376.

2. Ibid., p. 410.

3. David Ewen, *All the Years of American Popular Music* (Englewood Cliffs, NJ: Prentice-Hall, 1977), pp. 278–80.

4. Joel W. Finler, *The Hollywood Story* (New York: Crown, 1988), p. 19.

5. Ephraim Katz, *The Film Encyclopedia*, 2d ed. (New York: HarperCollins, 1994), p. 1400.

6. Miles Kreuger, "The Birth of the American Film Musical," *High Fidelity*, vol. 22, no. 7 (July 1972), p. 43.

7. Patrick Robertson, *Guinness Film Facts and Feats*, new ed. (Middlesex, England: Guinness Superlatives,1985), pp. 138–39.

8. Harry M. Geduld, *The Birth of the Talkies: From Edison to Jolson* (Bloomington: Indiana University, 1975), p. 95.

9. Kreuger, p. 43.

10. Ibid.

11. Robertson, p. 139.

12. Charles Hofmann, *Sounds for Silents* (New York: DBS, 1970), p. 9.

13. Gillian B. Anderson, *Music for Silent Films 1894– 1929: A Guide* (Washington, D.C.: Library of Congress, 1988), p. xxiv.

14. Neal Gabler, *An Empire of Their Own: How the Jews Invented Hollywood* (New York: Anchor Books, 1988), pp. 95–100. Rothafel, who dropped the "p" from his name (originally "Rothapfel"), later managed the Radio City Music Hall, which opened in December 1932. Failing health thereafter began to take its toll of Rothafel, who died in 1936 at the age of fifty-three.

15. Anderson, p. xxiv.

16. Ibid., p. xxviii.

17. Kreuger, p. 43.

18. Hofmann, p. 19.

19. Kreuger, p. 43.

20. Jack Warner, in *The Warner Bros. Golden Anniversary Book,* with a critical essay by Arthur Knight (New York: Film and Venture Corp., 1973), p. 11.

21. Kreuger, p. 43.

22. Arthur Knight, *The Liveliest Art*, rev. ed. (New York: Macmillan, 1978), p. 127. Knight estimates that the Vitaphone discs ranged between thirteen and seventeen inches in diameter.

23. Ted Sennett, *Warner Brothers Presents* (New York: Castle Books, 1971), p. 11.

24. David Cook, *A History of Narrative Film* (New York: W. W. Norton & Co., 1981), p. 238.

25. Ibid.

26. *Warner Bros. Golden Anniversary Book*, p. 11.

27. Knight, p. 128.

28. Ann Lloyd, ed., *70 Years at the Movies* (New York: Crescent Books, 1988) p. 85.

29. Cook, p. 241.

30. Ibid.

31. David Shipman, *Cinema: The First Hundred Years* (New York: St. Martin's, 1993), p. 92.

32. *Warner Bros. Golden Anniversary Book*, p. 12.

33. Robertson, p. 141.

34. Cook, p. 240.

35. Kreuger, p. 44.

36. Cook, p. 241.

37. Ibid.

38. Kreuger, p. 44.

39. Cook, p. 241.

40. Ibid.

41. *Warner Bros. Golden Anniversary Book*, p. 12.

42. Kreuger, p. 44.

43. Ewen, p. 276.

44. Ibid.

45. Lloyd, p. 95.

46. Sennett, p. 22.

47. *Warner Bros. Golden Anniversary Book*, p. 12.

48. Richard Barrios, *A Song in the Dark: The Birth of the Musical Film* (New York: Oxford University, 1995), p. 49.

49. Edwin M. Bradley, *The First Hollywood Musicals: A Critical Filmography of 171 Features, 1927 through 1932* (Jefferson, NC: McFarland & Co., 1996), p. 13.

50. Lloyd, p. 85.

51. Knight, p. 129.

52. Richard Hollis and Brian Sibley, *The Disney Studio Story* (New York: Crown, 1988), p. 17.

53. Ibid.

54. Thomas W. Bohn and Richard Stromgren, *Light and Shadow: A History of Motion Pictures* (Port Washington, NY: Alfred, 1975), p. 212.

55. Tony Thomas, *Harry Warren and the Hollywood Musical* (Secaucus, NJ: Citadel, 1975), p. 21.

56. Hollis and Sibley, p. 18.

57. Charles Matthews, *Oscar A to Z: A Complete Guide to More Than 2,400 Movies Nominated for Academy Awards* (New York: Doubleday, 1995), p. 441.

2

1930–39

The Dawn
of the Golden Age

Despite the devastating economic impact of the Great Depression, many significant cultural and technical developments occurred during the 1930s. The radio, recording, and film media all enjoyed a period of remarkable growth as a collective entertainment industry which helped to lift the spirits of a depressed society.

RADIO. Millions of Americans found solace in the comedy programs anchored by such personalities as former vaudevillians Freeman Gosden and Charles Correll, who provided the voices of "Amos 'n' Andy." This program enjoyed an uninterrupted run of over thirty years (1928–60) and remains the highest rated program in radio history. Right behind "Amos 'n' Andy" in the all-time ratings is "Fibber McGee and Molly," played by Marian and Jim Jordan, which began in 1931 and lasted until 1952.[1]

Besides such other comedy personalities as Jack Benny, Fred Allen, Bob Hope, George Burns and Gracie Allen, Fanny Brice (as Baby Snooks), and Edgar Bergen (with his alter ego Charlie McCarthy), radio was the stamping ground for many popular singers, including Kate Smith, Eddie Cantor, and Alice Faye. With the record industry booming, radio became a lively source of song promotion throughout the 1930s, especially for the many recording stars who hosted their own shows. Perhaps the most famous singing star of radio was Bing Crosby, who took over the hosting duties from Al Jolson on NBC's "Kraft Music Hall" in 1936. Even after becoming a top star of musical films, Crosby continued to perform on radio.[2]

POPULAR MUSIC. Radio's prosperity did much to elevate the recording industry, especially with the new swing craze. Although the dance bands of the 1920s had already started to use jaunty swing rhythms, it was not until 1932 that the term "swing" began to catch on, with such hit songs as Duke Ellington's "It Don't Mean a Thing (If It Ain't Got That Swing)."

Benny Goodman became known as the "King of Swing," a title he was awarded in a 1936 *Time* magazine article about the Goodman band's engagement at the Congress Hotel in Chicago.[3] His hit recording of "Sing, Sing, Sing," also in 1936, led to a job offer that would become a sought-after commodity in the careers of popular 1930s dance bands: a featured role in a Hollywood movie.

MOVIES. Benny Goodman's appearance in Paramount's *Big Broadcast of 1937* helped to usher in a new era for film musicals. With Goodman's growing fame and the rise to stardom of such former band singers as Bing Crosby, films that featured popular musical crazes of the day proliferated in the 1930s. In fact, several studios had competing series of musical films. Warner Bros. led the way with its series of *Gold Diggers* movies. The best was *Gold Diggers of 1933*, which featured a tuneful score that included such Harry Warren and Al Dubin songs as "We're in the Money" and "The Shadow Waltz." Later editions, also with songs by Warren and Dubin, were produced in 1935, 1937, and 1938.

MGM went back to its very first talkie musical for inspiration when *Broadway Melody of 1936* was filmed, with songs by Nacio Herb Brown and Arthur Freed, who had provided songs for the original 1929 film. Later editions of this series were produced in 1938 and 1940.

The most popular musical-film stars of the 1930s usually appeared as couples. Fred Astaire and Ginger Rogers, became known for their elegant dance routines in such films as *The Gay Divorcee* (1934) and *Top Hat* (1935); "America's Singing Sweethearts," Jeanette MacDonald and Nelson Eddy, entertained with their versions of such classic operettas as *Naughty Marietta* (1935) and *Rose Marie* (1936). Still another costarring couple that charmed the decade's moviegoers resulted from the pairing of crooner Dick Powell with dancer Ruby Keeler. Powell and Keeler appeared together in seven Warner Bros. musicals, beginning with *42nd Street* (1933).

The most popular film star of the 1930s was Shirley Temple, who made her feature film debut at the age of four in *Red-Haired Alibi* (1932), and in 1934 became a star at Fox with such charming films as *Little Miss Marker*. With a remarkable string of successful movies, she was rated the top box-office star for four consecutive years, from 1935 to 1938. With the single exception of Bing Crosby in the 1940s, no one has ever equaled or surpassed that record.[4]

THE ADVENT OF FILM UNDERSCORING. By the beginning of the 1930s, the conversion from silent movies to talkies was almost totally complete. Furthermore, the battle over the rival sound processes was ended, with the sound-on-film system nurtured by William Fox (through his Movietone newsreels) winning the day. By 1931, virtually all film-sound technicians, even those employed by Warner Bros., the company that had championed the Vitaphone sound-on-disc system, were using this more reliable process. Although Warner Bros. would continue to market its sound films with the Vitaphone logo, the disc process used for *The Jazz Singer* and *The Singing Fool* was basically abandoned because of the unreliability of its synchronization of sound and picture.[5]

Despite steady advances in sound technology, the practice of assigning composers to write dramatic underscoring in the talkie era came about after much resistance on the part of most filmmakers. Ironically, at the beginning of the 1930s, the early talkies became more silent than the silent movies themselves. Without the benefit of the live musicians who had accompanied the screenings of silent films, music was almost totally absent from the early talkies, except for the musicals. For instance, in such esteemed films as *Cimarron* and *Arrowsmith* (both 1931), there is almost no score, with music inserted mainly during the opening and closing credits. Apparently, filmmakers were concerned that a background score would distract the audience from hearing the dialogue, which in the case of such early talkies as *Disraeli* (1929), was virtually nonstop. The overabundance of dialogue was enhanced by the fact that many early talkies, including *Disraeli*, were adapted from the Broadway stage.

This reluctance to use underscoring eventually waned after film-music pioneer Max Steiner proved that music could enhance a dialogue scene. In 1932, with the approval of David Selznick, then vice president of production at RKO (the film production branch of the Radio-Keith-Orpheum company), Steiner scored several pictures, including *Symphony of Six Million* and *Bird of Paradise*. His success in these endeavors would lead to his landmark score for *King Kong* (1933), the music of which helped pave the way for all of the composers who worked in film during the Golden Age of Hollywood, a period that lasted from the mid-'30s until 1950.

In the pages that follow, many of the composers who thrived during the Golden Age of Hollywood are profiled; with their stories are included commentaries about some of the most significant musical works written for films. Beginning with Steiner's *King Kong* in 1933, there are several featured scores for each year that represent important contributions to the art of film music. Beginning with 1936, there is also a section at the end of each annual segment entitled "Short Cuts," often containing general commentary on the year's film music as well as brief profiles of additional scores. This chronological approach to the history of film music is intended as a means of highlighting the most memorable scores that have been written for films since the advent of synchronized sound.

T**HE THREE GODFATHERS OF FILM MUSIC.** Several talented musicians whose dedication to film qualifies them to be regarded as "godfathers" of the film-music art found employment in Hollywood by 1930.

Max Steiner. The first to arrive was Max Steiner (1888–1971), whose career prior to his coming to America in 1914 was that of a highly regarded theatrical composer and conductor, both in his native Vienna and in London. Steiner was raised in a theatrical family and considered a musical prodigy. As the only child of Gabor and Marie Steiner, Max was named after his famous grandfather, Maximilian Steiner, who was the impresario of the Theater an der Wien. Max's father was both a theatrical producer and an inventor; he was known for building the giant Ferris wheel known as the Riesenrad.[6] Max's mother was a dancer in several of his grandfather's productions.

Following several years of piano lessons, Max enrolled at the age of sixteen at the Conservatory of Music and Performing Art in Vienna, where he

Max Steiner.

studied numerous instruments, including piano, organ, violin, double bass, and trumpet. He also pursued courses in harmony, counterpoint, and composition, while gaining experience outside the classroom as a conductor of musical productions. While still in his teens, Steiner wrote the book, words, and music for several operettas, including *The Crystal Cup*, *The Merry Widower*, and *The Beautiful Greek Girl*; in 1907, he conducted the premieres of the last two of these productions at the Orpheum Theater in Vienna.[7]

In 1909, Steiner emigrated to England, where he was hired by a producer named George Dance first as a rehearsal pianist and then as a conductor for stage musical productions in London. He continued his career in England for several years as a composer of theatrical and symphonic music and continued to conduct a variety of theatrical productions.

In 1914, at the outbreak of World War I, Steiner received emigration papers, which allowed him to come to America. In New York he resumed his career as music director for stage musicals. In 1915, he was noticed by Samuel Rothafel, who hired him to conduct the orchestra at the Riverside Theater for showings of silent films. But soon, Steiner resumed working as an orchestrator and conductor of Broadway musicals, including those with scores by such renowned composers as Victor Herbert, George Gershwin, Jerome Kern, and Vincent Youmans. Steiner continued to work on Broadway productions throughout the '20s.

With the advent of sound films, Steiner was invited to Hollywood in December 1929 to orchestrate the songs for RKO's film version of Harry Tierney's Broadway hit *Rio Rita*, for which Steiner had served as both orchestrator and conductor. Once Steiner arrived in Hollywood, there would be no turning back, thanks to RKO vice president William LeBaron, who liked Steiner's work on *Rio Rita* so much that he was immediately offered a contract to work at the studio's newly formed music department. By October 1930, Steiner assumed the directorship of RKO's music wing. Working on a shoestring budget, he was given the use of a ten-piece orchestra and a limit of three hours to complete a scoring session on each film.[8] Fortunately, within a few years, Steiner was able to convince his bosses to allow him more budgetary expenditures on the fledgling business of creating film scores.

Alfred Newman. Another promising young musician who began working in Hollywood at this time was Alfred Newman (1901–70). Like Steiner, Newman was working on Broadway when his call came from Hollywood. Alfred Newman was the eldest of ten children who were born and raised in New Haven, Connecticut. His father was a produce dealer; his mother was passionately fond of music and sent her eldest son to a local piano teacher when he was six. The young Newman's piano-playing skills developed so rapidly that by the age of nine he was sent to New York to study with Sigismond Stojowski and Alexander Lambert. He also took lessons in composition. Performing as a pianist, by the age of twelve he was supporting his entire family by giving five shows a day for Gus Edwards at the Harlem Opera House.[9]

Newman played the piano for singer Grace La Rue on the vaudeville circuit when he was thirteen, and two years later he became pianist for the show *Hitchy-Koo*, in which La Rue costarred with Raymond Hitchcock

Alfred Newman.

and Irene Bordoni. This led to other shows, many of which went on tour. It was while he was traveling with the road companies of these shows that Newman was given conducting opportunities. His ambition to become a conductor of musicals was furthered by William Daly, an experienced Broadway music director, who taught Newman the basics of the craft. Between the ages of fifteen and seventeen, Newman often conducted matinee performances. This experience led to a full-time job as a music director on Broadway.

From 1920 to 1930, Newman conducted a number of major shows that appeared on the New York stage. Among these were *George White's Scandals of 1920*, *Funny Face*, and *Treasure Girl*, all of which featured the music of George Gershwin. He also conducted *Spring Is Here*, *Criss Cross*, and *The New Moon*. In 1930, Irving Berlin asked Newman to come to California to work on *Reaching for the Moon*, an original film musical with Berlin's songs, which was being produced by Joseph Schenck, head of United Artists. According to author Jack Jacobs:

> Newman arrived in Hollywood early in '30 only to find that *Reaching for the Moon* was not ready to be scored. To save paying Newman's salary, Schenck lent him to Sam Goldwyn, who had just produced *One Heavenly Night*, a romantic comedy with Evelyn Laye, that had songs by Nacio Herb Brown, Bruno Granichstaden and Edward Eliscu. . . . Goldwyn liked his score for *One Heavenly Night*, gave him a contract, and recommended him to other producers.[10]

Although Newman had not considered himself a composer, the next few years would afford him the opportunity to become one of the leading creative men in film music. In the words of Tony Thomas:

> As soon as [*Reaching for the Moon*] was completed, Samuel Goldwyn asked Newman to stay and arrange the music for several of his pictures. In agreeing to do so, Newman set the course of his life's work. So continuously busy did Newman become that he was never able to return to Broadway or [to realize] his ambition of becoming a symphonic conductor. Newman found himself challenged and intrigued by the possibilities for music opened up by the coming of sound. He had a keen ear for sound and thought in terms of high fidelity recording long before it became standard practice.[11]

Dimitri Tiomkin.

Dimitri Tiomkin.

Dimitri Tiomkin (1894–1979) was born in the Ukraine. He spent his youth in St. Petersburg, where he was enrolled for seven years at the St. Petersburg Conservatory. There he studied with the esteemed piano professor Felix Blumenthal, who was noted for training such outstanding concert pianists as Vladimir Horowitz. To make ends meet, Tiomkin played the piano in silent-movie theaters while still enrolled as a student. This was his first taste of the improvisation of musical sounds to accompany the flickering images on the silver screen.

After the Russian Revolution in 1917, Tiomkin left his homeland and went to Berlin, where his father started a successful medical practice. Dimitri met there another Russian pianist, Michael Kariton, who helped him get piano training, with Ferruccio Busoni. Working as a duo, Tiomkin and Kariton played many concerts. Tiomkin got his first opportunity to come to the United States when the duo received an offer to perform in America in 1925.[12] It was on this first American tour that Tiomkin met the woman he would marry: Austrian dancer and choreographer Albertina

Rasch. For a while after the marriage, Tiomkin continued to concertize and his wife went on with her career as a ballet impresario. But the Wall Street crash in October 1929 changed the Tiomkins' fortunes, since their services were no longer in demand.

Because musical films were all the rage in 1929, Tiomkin accompanied his wife to MGM, where she choreographed ballet sequences for such early talkie musicals as *The Rogue Song*. MGM accepted her suggestion that her husband be allowed to compose the music for her ballets. Thus began Tiomkin's career in film music.

THE DECLINE OF THE MUSICAL. Following the huge success of such early movie musicals as *The Broadway Melody* and *Gold Diggers of Broadway*, Hollywood producers managed to keep the musical tide flowing into 1930, with approximately seventy-five more musical films produced in that single year. This represents the high-water mark of the musical flood, which soon began to ebb. Studio executives learned that, as the quantity of musical films increased, so did the public's apathy. Even Al Jolson, the first talkie superstar, failed to match the success of his earlier films when he starred in three Warner Bros. musicals in 1929 and 1930: *Say It with Songs*, *Mammy*, and *Big Boy*.

Perhaps if more time and money had been spent on some of the early talkie musicals, the public's appreciation of them might have been longer-lasting; but with the Great Depression settling in, there were inevitable budget cutbacks. Another problem was that there just weren't that many really good singing actors. Many of the silent era's biggest stars did not adapt well to sound, especially those who did not have a musical background. The supply of Broadway players eager to become Hollywood stars had been pretty much exhausted by 1930, and many of the actors who were available weren't big enough names to attract large numbers of moviegoers. In addition, the supply of good musical material was quickly exhausted, with practically every major Broadway musical of the 1920s being adapted for the screen within three years of the release of *The Jazz Singer*. As the Broadway well began to run dry, Hollywood producers began commissioning new scores, by such esteemed composing teams as Sigmund Romberg and Oscar Hammerstein II, who were signed by Warner Bros. to compose four original screen operettas in 1930—but these films ultimately met with little box-office success.[13]

EARLY DRAMATIC FILM SCORES. By 1931, the bottom fell out of the musical market. Only eleven musical films were produced in 1931, and only ten more were released in 1932. It became evident to Hollywood's studio moguls that this form of moviemaking was on the way out. With public acceptance of song-and-dance films on the wane, only one new musical movie, Ernst Lubitsch's *Smiling Lieutenant*, with Maurice Chevalier and Claudette Colbert, received much critical acclaim upon its release in 1931. As the popularity of film musicals continued to decline, however, scores for dramatic films began to emerge.

MAX STEINER: CIMARRON. While under contract at RKO, Max Steiner wrote his first original score for *Cimarron*, which won the 1931 Oscar for Best Picture. Steiner's score consists mostly of an overture to this rambling saga of the Oklahoma territory in the years following the land rush of

1889. As the film's titles appear, there is a dramatic fanfarelike bit of music with pounding drums, which soon gives way to a more melodious pair of tunes. The first of these is a rhythmically buoyant theme, whereas the second is set in the style of a leisurely paced march, with a melody of noble character. In the first scene, the music fades as a bugle sounds the beginning of the historic land rush. From this point on, there is no further contribution from Steiner until the last reel, in which the aging Sabra (Irene Dunne) is feted upon her election to Congress. At the conclusion of a banquet, the march theme is heard in a slow tempo as Sabra is being congratulated. At the very end of the film, as a statue of Sabra's late husband Yancy Cravat (Richard Dix) is unveiled, a short bit of the march theme returns once more. From this beginning, Steiner went on to compose music for over 120 RKO features released between 1931 and 1936.[14]

ALFRED **N**EWMAN: *STREET SCENE.* Alfred Newman, who had been hired the preceding year as chief executive of producer Samuel Goldwyn's music department, solidified his film-music career during 1931 with the movie version of Elmer Rice's play *Street Scene,* which features an extended piece of music that describes a typical day on a street on the Lower East Side of New York City. With its clever combination of jazzy and sentimental styles, the music of *Street Scene* is uncomfortably close to George Gershwin's *Rhapsody in Blue,* which was composed seven years earlier, especially in its bluesy main theme. However, there are faster passages in which Newman attempted, with remarkable success, to describe the hectic pace of Lower East Side life.

Not only would Newman's musical depiction of New York City influence the style of other film scores, but *Street Scene*'s blues theme would actually be borrowed for many subsequent films. In several of these, scored by Newman himself, it typically accompanied vistas of the Manhattan skyline. The composer's 1940s scores at 20th Century-Fox that feature this theme include *The Dark Corner* (1946) and *Kiss of Death* (1947).[15] *Street Scene*'s music was also used as a prelude to the second CinemaScope film, *How to Marry a Millionaire* (1953), in which Newman appears on screen conducting the 20th Century-Fox studio orchestra. Although Newman abridged the work for this occasion, the music of *Street Scene* benefits from the glorious stereophonic sound used for the new recording. With the many wide-screen panoramas of the New York skyline included in the short travelogue with which the film opens, the *Street Scene* score serves as a singularly appropriate musical accompaniment.

DIMITRI **T**IOMKIN: *RESURRECTION.* Next to the pioneering efforts of Max Steiner and Alfred Newman in 1931, the early contributions of Dimitri Tiomkin are perhaps less noteworthy. Because of the sudden demise of the musical, Tiomkin found little work as a composer of dance music for the filmed ballet numbers choreographed by his wife. With his Russian background, however, he was considered the logical choice to compose the music for Universal's film version of Tolstoy's *Resurrection.* Although this score, which is infused with the sounds of Russian folk songs, is considered a minor effort in comparison with his later work, it represents the beginning of a long and illustrious career.

Thus, in the space of a single year, each of these three composers—Steiner, Newman, and Tiomkin—produced his first original background score for a film. As a consequence, the three became spiritual godfathers to the new medium of motion-picture scoring. All that remained was for producers to become convinced that background music would not drown out the dialogue. Since almost every dramatic or comedy film of the early 1930s was virtually scoreless, except for the music heard during the opening and closing credits, opportunities for film composers were extremely limited. One man's gamble would soon bring about drastic changes in film scoring and open up a world full of musical possibilities.

MAX STEINER: MUSIC FROM WALL TO WALL. David Selznick, who became vice president of production at RKO in June 1931, allowed Steiner to score several films made in 1932. The first concerns a young doctor in New York City who lets success go to his head. This film, *Symphony of Six Million*, which includes music in forty percent of the footage, helped to establish the precedent that, given the right dramatic situation, background music was not only allowable, but could, in fact, enhance the dramatic impact of a film.

Even more Steiner underscoring is present in *The Most Dangerous Game*, in which Joel McCrea and Fay Wray play shipwreck survivors on an island where the deranged Count Zaroff (Leslie Banks) hunts humans for sport. There is music sporadically through the first part of the film, including Steiner's waltz theme for Zaroff, who demonstrates his musical skills by playing this piece on the piano. The music is virtually nonstop in the closing scenes, with a lengthy chase episode which is driven by a steadily pulsating drum sound.

In *A Bill of Divorcement*, based on a popular stage play, Steiner refrained from underscoring the dialogue but composed a romantic theme for the end of the last reel. In this scene a shell-shocked World War I veteran and his estranged daughter (played by John Barrymore and Katharine Hepburn, respectively) are reunited through music. Seated side-by-side at a piano, the daughter begins playing a piece her father had once started to compose but never finished. He joins in and suddenly figures out an ending. This piano duet, which brings the film to its happy conclusion, lasts under two minutes. Steiner later recorded an expanded version called "Unfinished Sonata," and included it in a 1956 RCA album of his film music.[16]

Before the end of 1932, Steiner finally got the opportunity to score an entire film: the South Seas romance, *Bird of Paradise*, which had an exotic locale (it was shot in Hawaii). This film allowed Steiner free rein to create a continuous musical commentary. As a result, *Bird of Paradise* contains the first truly "wall-to-wall" score. The main theme consists of a romantic melody for strings, with Hawaiian guitar added for exotic flavor, and there is also a great deal of music for tribal dancing, plus some native chanting. Steiner even devised a five-note jungle call for Johnny (Joel McCrea), the American sailor who goes native, and his beloved Luana (Dolores Del Rio), the tribal princess.

In 1932, Steiner worked on approximately twenty-five pictures. Because of limited time and tight budgets, he usually devised music for the titles only, but occasionally, as in *Bird of Paradise*, where he perceived the need for a continuous musical accompaniment, he stubbornly fought for the time and money necessary to accomplish the score that he envisioned.[17]

While Steiner's work at RKO was breaking new ground in film scoring, neither Alfred Newman nor Dimitri Tiomkin had yet had an opportunity to compose a full-length score, although the United Artists pictures *Rain* and

Bird of Paradise,
with Joel McCrea
and Dolores Del Rio.

Mr. Robinson Crusoe had exotic locales and thus allowed Newman to invade Steiner territory with atmospheric main-title themes. It was Steiner alone who had the studio backing needed to subsidize extensive musical experimentation at this time.

KONG **C**OMES **C**ALLING. The single most outstanding film-music accomplishment of the early 1930s was the score for *King Kong.* Merian C. Cooper and Ernest B. Schoedsack combined their filmmaking talents to produce and direct a fantastic story about a giant ape, discovered on an uncharted island, who is captured, brought back to New York, and ultimately destroyed because of a beautiful woman. It was the classic "Beauty and the Beast" story, updated to include enough visual thrills to delight Depression-era moviegoers with escapist entertainment.

The president of RKO had doubts about the film even before the music was added, because of the considerable money that had already been spent. Max Steiner was assigned the relatively easy task of assembling a score by using previously composed materials. Cooper intervened by instructing Steiner to compose an original score, and said that he himself would pay for the use of the orchestra.[18] Eight weeks later, the score had been written and recorded by an orchestra of some forty-six players. This was one of the largest ensembles ever gathered up to that time for a film-score recording. It added $50,000 to the film's overall cost, but the result was a historic advance in film music.[19]

Kong's score has several stylistic roots, some of which demonstrate Steiner's ability to build on the work he had done the preceding year. In response to the film's exotic jungle locales (not to mention the presence of Kong himself), Steiner utilized an adventurous harmonic vocabulary that he had experimented with in the chase scenes of *The Most Dangerous Game.* For the tribal dance scenes Steiner created rhythmically driven themes that expanded on the style of music he had employed for the native-ritual episodes in *Bird of Paradise.* In his use of unresolved dissonances, Steiner also tended to emulate the French Impressionistic style of Claude Debussy, whose harmonic patterns often defy traditional rules of chord progression.

King Kong. Kong and Fay Wray atop the Empire State Building.

Perhaps the single most noteworthy aspect of Steiner's score for *King Kong* is the split-second synchronization of music with visual movement. Nowhere in the film is this more apparent than in an early scene on the island, when unannounced visitors are spotted by the tribal chief, who then abruptly halts a ceremony that has been taking place. As he takes several steps toward the visitors, the music follows every move he makes, with a tuba boldly sounding out a series of successively lower tones in imitation of his downward stepping. When he stops walking, the music also stops, and when he begins to move forward again, the music also starts up once more.

As background music, the score of *King Kong* is not always melodious, but in its incessant rhythms and weird chords, combined with its ingenious synchronization of music with the visuals, it represents a milestone in the history of film music. For many moviegoers, *Kong* was probably the first film to contain a noticeable musical underscore. With its many scenes in which the music is unimpeded by dialogue, this film gave Steiner an unprecedented opportunity to demonstrate the power of music to create feelings of excitement and nervous anticipation.

The linkage between music and visual imagery that Steiner demonstrated so capably in his *King Kong* score became known in the industry as "mickey mousing," probably because, in the animated Disney shorts, the music tends to carefully mimic the action. Steiner was taken to task for this technique by other film composers, but there is no denying that in situations like the ones depicted in *King Kong*, the connection between sight and sound strongly enhances the film's impact.

In *King Kong*, Steiner produced what he felt was one of his few modernistic film scores, and it remained one of his personal favorites. The score proved to be extremely useful for other films made in subsequent years, including *The Last Days of Pompeii* (1935) and *The Last of the Mohicans* (1936), both of which were scored by Roy Webb (1888–1982). Bits of *Kong*'s music reappeared in both of these films, as well as in other films scored by Steiner himself; one of these is *Son of Kong*, which was rushed into production immediately after *King Kong*'s sensational debut. Few scores in the history of the motion picture have had an impact as immediate as Steiner's ingenious work on *King Kong*.

THE RETURN OF THE MUSICAL. Besides the emergence of Max Steiner as a major force in dramatic film scoring, 1933 is also noteworthy for a pair of musicals that feature Steiner's orchestral arrangements. With the release of RKO's *Flying Down to Rio*, Fred Astaire and Ginger Rogers became major box-office stars. Although only supporting players in

Rio, they made cinema history with their dancing to the song "The Carioca." They were quickly offered starring roles in their next film, *The Gay Divorcee*. Their popularity ultimately helped to elevate the film musical to an even higher pinnacle than it had attained in the first years of the talkies.

HARRY WARREN: *42ND STREET*. The musical film that really put the genre back on track was Warner Bros.' *42nd Street*, which established Dick Powell and Ruby Keeler as motion picture stars and featured innovative choreography by the ingeniously talented Busby Berkeley. This film also helped to launch the film song-writing career of Harry Warren, who had written movie songs previously. With *42nd Street*, he moved into a spectacularly successful phase of his career. Later that year, Warren's songs added tunefulness to two other Warner Bros. musicals, *Gold Diggers of 1933* and *Footlight Parade*. In the next five years, Warren would create the melodies for such additional Warner Bros. hits as *Dames*, *Wonder Bar* (with Al Jolson), and three more *Gold Diggers* films.

With lyricist Al Dubin, Harry Warren helped to create some of the most memorable songs in Hollywood history at Warner Bros. in the period 1933–38. He then moved on to work with a succession of talented lyricists at three other studios, including 20th Century-Fox, MGM, and Paramount, where he would continue writing songs—almost four hundred in all—into the 1960s.[20]

THE FIRST OSCARS FOR MUSIC. It was in 1934 that the Motion Picture Academy first began to recognize the efforts of film musicians. Two new categories were added to the 1934 Oscar nominations: Best Song and Best Score. Unfortunately, the Academy citations failed to distinguish between original background scores and those that consisted of song adaptations or arrangements of borrowed thematic materials.

Of the three score nominees, only one, *The Lost Patrol*, by Max Steiner, represents an original score. The other two, *The Gay Divorcee*, also by Steiner, and *One Night of Love*, consist mainly of song arrangements. When *One Night of Love* was announced as the winner, the award went not to the film's composers, Victor Schertzinger and Gus Kahn, but to Louis Silvers, head of the music department at Columbia Pictures, which had produced the film. The practice of citing the music-department head instead of the composer would continue until 1938, when wisdom prevailed and the Academy changed the rules so that the composer was personally cited in the nomination process. Moreover, two separate scoring categories were established in 1938 to distinguish between the use of original musical themes and adaptations of borrowed materials.[21]

SERGEI PROKOFIEV: *LIEUTENANT KIJÉ*. The most remarkable film score of 1934 is the work of Sergei Prokofiev (1891–1953). The renowned Russian composer, who had lived and worked abroad for fifteen years, accepted this film-scoring assignment, his first, shortly after relocating to his homeland in 1933. The result was a delightful score for Alexander Feinzimmer's *Lieutenant Kijé* (U.S. title: *The Czar Wants to Sleep*) by a musician whose name is associated more often with concert music than with film scoring.

Lieutenant Kijé's satirical premise involves the fabrication of heroic deeds by military personnel, who try to conceal from the vain Czar Paul I the fact that the supposedly heroic Lieutenant Kijé really does not exist at all. Prokofiev's score cleverly combines elements of romance, adventure, and comedy with just a tinge of melancholy regarding the stupidity of blind loyalty to an all-powerful ruler. Prokofiev gave this "hero," who was created out of a clerical error on a military roster, a strong musical presence in the score. A solo cornet, which has the role of Kijé's musical "voice," is first heard in a ghostly fanfare that recurs throughout the film, and later is featured in sprightly wedding music.[22]

The original film score consists of sixteen brief musical numbers, with several songs that were modeled, according to Prokofiev biographer Harlow Robinson, on "urban songs" of the eighteenth century.[23] Prokofiev reworked the score in 1934 to produce a concert suite, fashioning five movements out of the score material. He considerably rearranged and reorchestrated the music, and made a provision that the song themes used in the second and fourth movements could be either sung or played instrumentally.[24]

The *Lieutenant Kijé Suite* may be considered the first important concert piece to be adapted from a film score. After conducting the first performance on December 21, 1934, Prokofiev would move on to many other musical projects, including film music composed in collaboration with director Sergei Eisenstein. Meanwhile, the *Lieutenant Kijé Suite* began to gain favor with audiences worldwide, and in the years since its composition, it has become one of the most frequently recorded of all of Prokofiev's works.

ALFRED NEWMAN: *OUR DAILY BREAD*. Despite the large number of films that both Max Steiner and Alfred Newman worked on in 1934, only a small number of extensive musical scores were composed for films made that year. One of the most noteworthy is the exciting music composed by Newman for King Vidor's *Our Daily Bread*. Especially memorable is the sequence in which a group of desperate workers dig an irrigation ditch in an effort to bring water down a hill to the crops below. As the water surges down the newly dug trench, Newman's music greatly enhances the exhilaration of the scene.

JEANETTE MACDONALD FILMS. In 1934, Jeanette MacDonald made her first films under the MGM banner. After leaving Paramount, where she had successfully costarred with Maurice Chevalier in three films, including the inventive *Love Me Tonight* (1932), MacDonald was cast in the screen adaptation of Jerome Kern's *Cat and the Fiddle* (1934), in which she costarred with Ramon Novarro. After this, she was again paired with a somewhat reluctant Chevalier (and again directed by Ernst Lubitsch) in *The Merry Widow* (also 1934), the film that established her as one of the studio's leading stars. All that remained was for a more willing costar to be found, which happened the next year, when she and Nelson Eddy were signed to costar in *Naughty Marietta*.

THE GOLDEN AGE BEGINS. By 1935, with the New Deal in place, the devastating impact of the Great Depression was beginning to wane, and American filmmakers embarked on a new era of prosperity. Since the onset of the Depression, many local theater owners had been luring movie audiences by lowering ticket prices and giving away free merchandise ("dish nights" were common). Box-office figures improved in 1935 and would continue to rise during the rest of the decade.[25]

Now that Hollywood had successfully weathered the economic storm, the studios began lavishing attention on more expensive films, with such elaborate production values as color photography and outdoor scenery. The Technicolor era began in 1935 with Rouben Mamoulian's film *Becky Sharp* —the first ever shot with the new three-strip color process developed by the Technicolor Corporation. Shooting on location also became more common, as in the 1935 Oscar-winning film *Mutiny on the Bounty*. Thus, the groundwork was laid for a remarkable era in motion picture history which has become known as the "Golden Age of Hollywood."

The Golden Age, which film historians have designated as the period 1935–50, features some of the most creative work by many of the great film composers, including the pioneers Max Steiner, Alfred Newman, and Dimitri Tiomkin. With the exception of Tiomkin, who remained independent throughout his career, most successful film musicians worked under contract at major movie studios. Besides the actors, writers, directors, and technicians, full staffs of music personnel, including composers, arrangers, copyists, and players, were all in place. In this supportive environment, composers such as Steiner and Newman thrived.

MAX STEINER: *THE* INFORMER. One of the most outstanding film scores of 1935 was Max Steiner's atmospheric work for John Ford's masterpiece *The Informer*, based on a novel by Liam O'Flaherty, set in Dublin during the Irish rebellion of 1922. The film was a money-losing gamble for RKO, but it inspired Steiner to demonstrate his mastery in a medium he had helped to establish. His synchronizing skill is especially noteworthy in a scene in which the movement of Gypo (Victor McLaglen) seems to have been choreographed to the music. When he is walking toward British headquarters to inform on a fellow Irish rebel named Frankie, Steiner's heavily accented chords follow each footstep.

In a famous scene which occurs later in the film, Gypo is in a jail cell, with water dripping on him. In Steiner's words:

> I had a certain music effect I wanted to use for this. I wanted to catch each of these drops musically. The property man and I worked for days trying to regulate the water tank so it dripped in tempo and so I could accompany it. This took a good deal of time and thought because a dripping faucet doesn't always drip in the same rhythm. We finally mastered it, and I believe it was one of the things that won me the [Academy] award.[26]

For the final sequence of the film, Steiner composed a lovely choral piece, "Sancta Maria," which is sung by a choir in a church where the dying Gypo has gone to ask for forgiveness from the mother of the man whose death he caused.

In addition to Steiner's original music, there are several borrowed melodies in the score. To enhance the Irish flavor, Steiner included "Danny Boy," "Rose of Tralee," "The Wearing of the Green," and "Minstrel Boy"; for the hated British officials he used a minor-key variant of "Rule Britannia."

The Informer is an absorbing drama of betrayal, guilt, and atonement, with a Steiner score that is an early example of the use of the Wagnerian leitmotif, a melodic concept in which each character in the story is represented by a separate motif or theme. Steiner's personal affection for Richard Wagner's music may have contributed to this thematic approach in his film scores. In any case, with *The Informer* Steiner established techniques that would be in use throughout the Golden Age of Hollywood.

Although MGM's *Mutiny on the Bounty* won the Best Picture Oscar for 1935, *The Informer* also won several awards, including Best Actor (Victor McLaglen), Best Director (John Ford), Best Screenplay (Dudley Nichols), and Best Score (Max Steiner). This was the first of three Oscars that Steiner would win, in a career spanning almost four decades.

ARTHUR BLISS: *THINGS TO COME.* Another film-music milestone of 1935 is the extensive symphonic score written by English composer Arthur Bliss (1891–1975) for the Alexander Korda production *Things to Come*, based on the story by H. G. Wells. The author acted as consultant and also as adapter of his own story. Korda went along with Wells's suggestion to use Bliss to score the film, and even agreed to let Bliss compose much of the score before the shooting took place, so that many of the film's key scenes were timed to fit the music. As a result, *Things to Come* is an extraordinary example of film and music synchronization.[27]

When the film was finally released in early 1936, it was regarded as a failure. Consequently, despite the concert suite that Bliss later prepared, the music has never received the recognition that it so richly deserves. As a symphonic portrait of a futuristic war and its aftermath, Bliss's lush orchestrated score, which includes several brilliant marches and choral pieces, ranks among the finest film music achievements of all time.

THE ADVENT OF ERICH WOLFGANG KORNGOLD. The year 1935 is also significant as the time when two European composers—Erich Wolfgang Korngold and Franz Waxman—came to Hollywood and established themselves as important contributors to the film-music medium.

Erich Wolfgang Korngold.

Courtesy of Leslie Korngold

Korngold (1897–1957) was a child prodigy in his native Austria and a veteran opera composer by the age of twenty. Actually, Korngold's early career resembles that of Wolfgang Amadeus Mozart, after whom he was named.[28] Korngold began tinkering with the piano at the age of three and was playing the instrument fluently when he was seven. By the age of ten, he was performing his own pieces for some of the most prominent musicians in Europe, including Gustav Mahler, who acknowledged the child to be a genius. The young Korngold completed the music for a ballet, *Der Schneemann*, in 1908, when he was only eleven. In the next few years he began to conquer the operatic stage; he completed his first two operas, *The Ring of Polykrates* and *Violanta*, at the age of sixteen, and when he was twenty-three he introduced what has generally been regarded as his masterpiece, *Die tote Stadt* (*The Dead City*).

Throughout his youth Korngold was guided, as Mozart had been, by an authoritarian father. Dr. Julius Korngold was the most influential music critic in Europe in the early part of the twentieth century. In 1902, when young Erich was five, his father succeeded the renowned Edward Hanslick as music critic of the Viennese newspaper *Die Freie Presse*; he held the post until 1934. Since he was in such a position of power, both he and his young son came under fire. According to Rudy Behlmer:

> Young Korngold became the talk of musical circles everywhere, and enemies of his father were quick to accuse the critic of using his influence to promote an artificially created "child prodigy." They even charged that the boy had been given the name Wolfgang only after his musical talent developed, in order to suggest an analogy with Wolfgang Mozart.[29]

Eventually the criticism subsided, and the young composer was recognized as a genuine prodigy. Richard Strauss said the following about Korngold's music, which he conducted on more than one occasion: "This firmness of style, this sovereignty of form, this individual expression, this harmonic structure—it is really astounding."[30]

In 1924, the twenty-seven-year-old composer married Luise von Sonnenthal, the granddaughter of the manager of the Hofburg Theatre in Vienna. They had two sons, Ernst (1925–96) and George (1928–87), who became a producer at RCA Victor Records. Meanwhile, Korngold's operatic career continued with *The Miracle of Heliane* (1927). Two years later, he began a collaboration with the renowned theatrical producer Max Reinhardt, which initially resulted in a revised version of Johann Strauss, Jr.'s *Die Fledermaus*. Also in 1929, Korngold arranged an operetta score, based on Strauss's waltzes, that evolved as *Waltzes from Vienna*. Five years later, this show was produced on the New York City stage under its new title, *The Great Waltz*.

That same year, Reinhardt brought Korngold to Hollywood to arrange Mendelssohn's music for the Warner Bros. film version of Shakespeare's *Midsummer Night's Dream*. After completing this assignment, Korngold returned to Vienna to work on his fifth opera, *Die Kathrin*; but dire events in Europe soon caused the Korngold family, who were Jewish, to seek refuge in America. The immediate reason for their leaving was the cancellation of the planned premiere of *Die Kathrin*, by Nazi orders. Because his younger son was ailing and needed a warmer climate, Hollywood, which also afforded plentiful employment opportunities, was chosen as the Korngold home until the end of World War II.

In 1935, Korngold wrote his first two original film scores. His first score was for the Paramount musical *Give Us This Night*, starring Gladys Swarthout. Unfortunately, despite some lovely music, this film was a box-office failure when belatedly released in 1936. Korngold fared better with his second original score, a sweepingly romantic background for Errol Flynn's first big Hollywood adventure film, *Captain Blood*. This film was a box-office hit and won a nomination for Best Picture of 1935. Korngold's music so impressed Warner Bros. executives that they offered him a contract. His situation became unique in that he made several unusual demands, all of which were agreed to by Warner Bros.; his film work would be confined to two pictures per year, he would have more than the usual four to six weeks allotted for a single score, and his name would be listed separately in the opening credits.[31] This last stipulation is quite remarkable in that in the early 1930s, composers often received no credit whatsoever; when they did get credit, their names were crowded in with those of such other technicians as editors and cinematographers.

Once this contract was in place, Korngold became the highest paid composer in Hollywood, with the additional advantage of being able to choose the films he would agree to score.[32] Thus was cemented one of the most extraordinary, if short-lived, careers in the history of the movies.

FRANZ WAXMAN: *THE BRIDE OF FRANKENSTEIN.* Franz Waxman (1906–67) had worked on several films in his native Germany, including *The Blue Angel* (1930), as well as on a French film, *Liliom* (1934). He first came to the United States to adapt the score of Jerome Kern's *Music in the*

The Bride of Frankenstein,
with Elsa Lancaster
and Boris Karloff.

Air (1934) for Fox. James Whale next hired Waxman to score the sequel to *Frankenstein*, which was eventually called *The Bride of Frankenstein*.

Never again would a Universal horror film contain such a rich musical background, filled with exotic orchestral colors and unusual harmonies, including a daring amount of dissonance. Waxman's principal melodic motifs include a chilling five-note idea for the monster (played by Boris Karloff, in a reprise of his 1931 role) and a weirdly romantic three-note idea for his bride (Elsa Lanchester)—coincidentally, the song "Bali Ha'i," from Richard Rodgers and Oscar Hammerstein II's 1949 musical, *South Pacific*, begins with a three-note pattern identical with this bride motif. In the climactic "Creation" sequence, both of these principal motifs are heard, along with an ongoing kettledrum tone that produces an eerie heartbeat effect.

Waxman's imaginative score still enhances the impact that *The Bride of Frankenstein* has on viewers today. In addition, through a series of recent recordings, this innovative music has finally begun to achieve the recognition that it so richly deserves.[33]

THE FORMATION OF STUDIO MUSIC DEPARTMENTS. By 1935, all the major American film companies had fully developed music departments, and many noteworthy composers and arrangers had accepted studio contracts. Film production was done on an assembly-line basis, with as many as five hundred films produced in America in a single year; thus, most Hollywood musicians were given very tight schedules. For this reason a majority of film composers relied on orchestrators to assist them in completing their scores by the studio-imposed deadlines. The amazing thing is that, despite the short amount of time generally allotted for the scoring of each film, usually no more than four to six weeks, such a vast quantity of fine music was produced during the Golden Age of Hollywood.

The sound motion picture had now outgrown the label of "talkie" and had evolved into a skillfully produced form of commercial entertainment. The seven major Hollywood studios, Warner Bros., MGM, Paramount, Universal, Columbia, RKO (established in 1928), and the newly formed 20th Century-Fox, were on the brink of creating some of the finest filmmaking achievements of all time. The high quality of these films would inspire some highly memorable film music.

THE STUDIO SYSTEM. By the mid-1930s, most of the films made in America were produced under what has become known as the "studio system." Actors, writers, directors, technicians, and musicians were all placed under contract in order to facilitate the movie-making assembly line. By 1936, the roster of musicians at each studio included several composers and arrangers, plus a full orchestra for the recording sessions.

Among the major studios, Warner Bros. had the distinction of having the finest music department in Hollywood. Leo Forbstein (1892–1948) had served as music director ever since being appointed to that position in 1928. His signing of both Max Steiner and Erich Wolfgang Korngold to Warner Bros. contracts in 1936 virtually guaranteed the quality of that studio's scores. With such additional composers and arrangers as Hugo Friedhofer (1902–81), who worked on the orchestration of almost all of Korngold's film scores, the Warner Bros. music department sanctioned wall-to-wall scoring of almost every picture, and in the process facilitated the advancement of the art of film scoring throughout the Golden Age.

MAX STEINER: *THE CHARGE OF THE LIGHT BRIGADE.* Max Steiner's first Warner Bros. score, for *The Charge of the Light Brigade*, a big-budget action film inspired by Alfred Lord Tennyson's epic poem, concerns the exploits of a British regiment, the 27th Lancers, with Errol Flynn in the heroic role of Captain Geoffrey Vickers. This episodic picture doesn't get around to the suicidal charge described by Tennyson until late in the film, after many other battles, set mostly in India, have already taken place.

The Charge of the Light Brigade, with Errol Flynn.

The villainous Surat Khan (C. Henry Gordon) escapes from his native India and joins the Russians, who are embroiled in the Crimean War, against Turkey, England, and France. Vickers, the Khan's mortal enemy, conceives the idea of having the Lancers charge the entire Russian army, thereby allowing more time for the rest of the English soldiers to advance.

Steiner's score is built primarily on a stately march theme ("Forward the Light Brigade"), which appears in various tempos and orchestral guises throughout the film. During the climactic charge, this theme, now faster than ever before, is combined in musical counterpoint with "Rule Britannia" and the Russian anthem "God Save the Czar." The music dramatically enhances the visual imagery of the relentless charge of the six hundred who ride into the Valley of Death, only to be felled by an endless volley of cannon fire.

Steiner was honored with a 1936 Oscar nomination for the score of *Light Brigade*. He also received a nomination that year for the romantic themes he composed for David Selznick's early Technicolor film *Garden of Allah*; but it is clearly the *Light Brigade* score that has been the more acclaimed of the two.

ERICH **W**OLFGANG **K**ORNGOLD: **A**NTHONY **A**DVERSE. After rushing to complete the score for *Captain Blood*, for which he was given just three weeks because of its previously announced release date, Korngold embarked on one of the longest and most thematically involved scores in Hollywood history: the sweepingly romantic music for *Anthony Adverse*. This Mervyn LeRoy-directed adaptation of Hervey Allen's mammoth bestselling novel of the same name (1933) is an expensively mounted costume drama with dozens of characters and a very episodic plot, in which Fredric March appears as the adult Anthony and Olivia de Havilland is his beloved Angela. To accompany Anthony's turbulent adventures, Korngold fashioned a lavish score, which can be heard almost continuously throughout the film's extensive length (about 2 hours and 20 minutes), with forty-three separate musical motifs for the various characters and situations.

When Korngold's music won the Oscar for Best Score of 1936, Leo Forbstein, the head of the Warner Bros. music department tried to give the Oscar to Korngold after the ceremony, but the composer politely refused to accept it.[34] Only years later did this Oscar deservedly come into Korngold's possession, long after the bizarre practice of awarding the scoring Oscar to the studio music department had been discontinued.

CHARLIE **C**HAPLIN: **M**ODERN **T**IMES. Although Charlie Chaplin (1889–1977) was certainly not an accomplished musician, he nevertheless had remarkable musical instincts, which he demonstrated by personally conceiving the music for all his feature-length films, released by United Artists, beginning with *The Circus* (1928). His modus operandi was to hum or whistle tunes to professional musicians, who wrote down the tunes and arranged them into scores under Chaplin's personal supervision.

For his 1936 film *Modern Times*, Chaplin created several notable melodies which, together with a few borrowed themes, were arranged into a complete score by David Raksin and Eddie Powell. Alfred Newman conducted the finished product for the recording sessions.[35]

Since *Modern Times*, like its direct predecessor *City Lights* (1931), is basically a silent film with synchronized sound effects and music, there is an almost continuous concert of background score. Machinelike music accompanies the opening scenes of hapless Charlie, at war with the Machine Age, attempting to tighten bolts on an assembly line. He suffers a nervous breakdown, and performs a hilariously choreographed ballet with his wrenches, tightening anything (and everything) that moves.

For the central episodes, in which Charlie's character befriends a young girl of the streets (played by Paulette Goddard), Chaplin conceived a theme that later became known as the melody of "Smile," the lyrics for which were written in 1954 by John Turner and Geoffrey Parsons. To this day, "Smile" remains one of the most famous songs to emerge from a film score.

SHORT CUTS ■■■■ **Alfred Newman.** Beginning in 1936, Alfred Newman began to excel as music director for Samuel Goldwyn's films. With director William Wyler also under contract, Goldwyn assigned Newman to compose scores for two Wyler-directed films made that year, *These Three* and *Dodsworth*, plus another film that Wyler codirected, *Come and Get It*. Although these scores are not as lushly orchestrated as the later ones Newman did at 20th Century-Fox, they are interesting nonetheless. The tender theme used throughout *These Three*, one of Newman's loveliest, again proved useful ten years later, when it became the love theme of *The Razor's Edge*. There is less scoring in *Dodsworth*, in which one principal lyrical theme is used to accompany several scenes. Also heard is an exotic melody that was used for the Atlantic crossing scene early in the picture. A year later, Newman used this tune again in *The Hurricane*, where it became known as "The Moon of Manakoora."

Come and Get It, which Wyler completed after director Howard Hawks walked off the picture because of a dispute with Samuel Goldwyn, features remarkable music. Largely based on the old song "Aura Lee," this score foreshadows the lavish backgrounds that would regularly accompany the later films Newman worked on at 20th Century-Fox. Twenty years later, Elvis Presley would immortalize this melody when it was borrowed for the title song of his first film, *Love Me Tender*.

■■■■ **Virgil Thomson.** One other 1936 film score of significance is the music written by distinguished American composer Virgil Thomson (1896–1989) for Pare Lorentz's documentary short subject, *The Plow That Broke the Plains*. Under sponsorship of the U. S. Department of the Interior, Lorentz, a former journalist and film critic, helped to raise public consciousness about the plight of the farmers in Oklahoma's Dust Bowl through this poetically structured work. Thomson's evocative score includes a variety of short musical pieces in which he used several familiar melodies, such as "I Ride an Old Paint" and "The Streets of Laredo." Thomson also fashioned a six-movement orchestral suite from the score, and a year later he did the same with his music for Lorentz's 1937 documentary *The River*, which also was produced with U. S. government funds. The score for *Plow* was the first film music by an American composer to be arranged as a concert work for symphony orchestra.

MYTHICAL PLACES AND EXOTIC LOCALES. Shangri-La, Manakoora. Ruritania. These are but a few of the faraway mythical places to which movie audiences could be escorted by popular films released in 1937. The respective films that magically transported filmgoers to these exotic locales—*Lost Horizon*, *The Hurricane*, and *The Prisoner of Zenda*— brought both pleasure and thrills to moviegoers looking for escapist entertainment. In addition to these three 1937 box-office hits, two expensively mounted MGM films, *Captains Courageous* and *The Good Earth*, also took film audiences to remote regions: the former is set primarily on a fishing vessel at sea; the latter takes place in China.

Another acclaimed film of 1937 is set in the mythical world of Hollywood itself: David Selznick's *A Star Is Born*, in which Janet Gaynor plays a small-town girl who dreams of becoming a movie star. *A Star Is Born* candidly reveals the inner workings of a movie studio, while it also provides a cautionary tale about the price of success. This film represents Tinseltown holding up a mirror to itself, and revealing the ruthless methods used in creating (and destroying) careers.

Alongside the foregoing fictional films, most of which were adapted from highly acclaimed novels, the scripts of some other films released in 1937 were based on factual material. Chief among these is William Dieterle's *Life of Emile Zola*, the second in Warner Bros.' series of biographical films which had begun the previous year with *The Story of Louis Pasteur*. With Paul Muni buried under makeup as Zola, and with an evocative score by Max Steiner, *The Life of Emile Zola* walked off with the Oscar as Best Picture of 1937. This marked the second consecutive year that a biographical film won the big prize (following *The Great Ziegfeld* in 1936).

DIMITRI TIOMKIN: LOST HORIZON. For *Lost Horizon* Tiomkin composed his first masterwork, and perhaps the best score of his career. Director Frank Capra chose Tiomkin, a personal friend, over more established film composers because he wanted "new, fresh, novel music."[36]

James Hilton's popular 1933 novel, on which the movie is based, is primarily set in a mythical place—called Shangri-La—located in the Valley of the Blue Moon, which is surrounded by the towering Himalayas. The surprisingly mild climate in this valley allows the inhabitants to live a very long time, without outward signs of aging. To this magical valley come several travelers who have been rescued from a plane crash. Among the survivors is Robert Conway (played by Ronald Colman), an English adventurer, who becomes so fascinated with Shangri-La that he doesn't want to leave, even after learning that his coming there was no accident.

Lost Horizon's score is filled with exotic elements, including a wordless choral effect, which is introduced during the picture's opening credits to augment the strings in the exotic Shangri-La theme, one of Tiomkin's most inspired melodies. In stark contrast to this lyrical beginning is the film's opening sequence, which vividly depicts a riot at the Baskul airport in China, while Conway is attempting to help refugees board planes that will take them to safety. This almost frantic scene is accompanied by furiously dramatic music, and is scored for lots of brass and drums.

After the plane carrying Conway crashes on a snowy mountainside, the score takes on a much more Oriental tone, as a group of Asian rescuers finds the crash victims, bundles them warmly, and escorts them by foot to a safe haven. At this point Tiomkin's score features such metallic instruments as gongs and a variety of small bells to accompany their march. The colorful words of Kurt Sven provide an apt description of this music:

> This ponderous march movement builds, the many dissonances serve to emphasize something of the strangeness of the journey, so far removed is its purpose from the normal range of human experience. A huge climax is reached, but the music suddenly evaporates; only the chiming of monastery bells is heard in the distance, for the travelers have come in sight of the Celestial City. And here, as Conway looks on the clear sunlit valley, there occurs one of the most magical moments in the film. Myriad voices sound from afar. The sound of massed voices singing or murmuring wordlessly in the distance has a mystical quality. . . . Here is the essence of Shangri-La, an earthly paradise whose walls are splayed with centuries-old vines flaunting their fragrant blossoms; whose broad stairway beckons to the great portico of the lamasery; whose acres of flat white roofs shimmer in the sun; . . . a cloistered Eden where people live to unheard-of ages.[37]

With the shift of locale to Shangri-La, the score abandons the rhythmically charged patterns that have propelled the story thus far in favor of an ingeniously unstressed flow. When the travelers first enter the enchanted Valley of the Blue Moon, Tiomkin's music achieves a magical effect. A new Oriental-style theme is first performed by the choir without instrumental accompaniment; a harp and strings eventually join in. Kurt Sven's words again aid in describing the music of Shangri-La:

> Toward the end of this sequence voices and bells are raised in a chant based on the Chinese pentatonic, or five-note scale . . . which, like the main Shangri-La theme, conforms to no Western standards of metrical regularity; it has rather the cold and tranquil beauty of ancient Chinese lacquers or pearl-blue Sung ceramics.[38]

In the central section of the film, when Conway becomes interested in the pretty schoolteacher Sondra (Jane Wyatt), Tiomkin's music features a love theme that was hinted at in the opening-credit music. In one scene the score features a rapid-paced scherzo as the two go riding together through the valley. When they approach a waterfall, the music becomes more passionate, as strings, harps, flutes, and celesta join in an upward-rising spiral of sound. There is also a musical piece in this section entitled "Chinese Children's Scherzo," for the group of children Sondra is teaching.

For the funeral procession that follows the death of the High Lama, Tiomkin's main theme, with wordless voices, is heard once again, in counterpoint with a new melody used as a slow, ceremonial marching theme. The music in this scene is augmented by a unique conglomeration of metallic and drumlike instruments, performed by twenty-two players. The roster of instruments includes a xylophone, a vibraphone, a marimba, five glockenspiels (orchestra bells), three sets of tubular bells, two sets of

Lost Horizon, with Jane Wyatt, Ronald Colman, and Margo.

large chimes, a set of tuned cymbals, four tuned Tibetan gongs, three other gongs of different sizes, and a Tibetan rata drum.[39] As this theme continues, the orchestration of strings, woodwinds, and brass gradually builds up. Unfortunately for the music, Conway, who has been observing the procession from his apartment, closes the window midway through this scene, at his brother's insistence. As a result, from this moment on, the volume of the music is severely reduced.[40]

At the conclusion of this sequence, the score's main theme swells up to a terrifically dramatic level as Sondra runs toward the entrance to the valley in hopes of finding Conway before he has a chance to get away. As she repeatedly yells, "Bob! Bob!," Tiomkin's theme maintains the same highly charged level of emotion until Sondra breaks down in tears when she finds that Conway and his party have already ascended the snowy mountain.

Lost Horizon failed to impress those who saw it at previews, but Capra's decision to shorten the film by removing the two original opening reels (a full twenty minutes of film) helped to save the picture. Tiomkin's musical contribution to this film cannot be overestimated. Without his richly romantic score the wondrous Shangri-La would not have come to life so vividly on the silver screen.

ALFRED NEWMAN: *THE HURRICANE* AND *THE PRISONER OF ZENDA.* Like Tiomkin, Newman demonstrated in the film music he composed in 1937 a growing mastery of the medium. *The Hurricane*, one of nine motion pictures Newman worked on that year, is Samuel Goldwyn's elaborate version of the Charles Nordhoff and James Norman Hall novel of the same name, about ill-fated lovers on the isle of Manakoora. Skillfully directed by John Ford, *The Hurricane* introduced two then-unknown actors, Jon Hall and Dorothy Lamour, as the newlywed native couple Terangi and Marama, who are separated when he gets into a fight and lands in jail.

The real star of this film is the huge storm, which was filmed on a Hollywood sound stage by assistant director James Basevi. Sound effects for the storm precluded the need for music, which is primarily confined to the more romantic moments of the film. The principal theme, later known as "The Moon of Manakoora," with lyrics by Frank Loesser, is one of Newman's most memorable pieces of film music.[41]

Newman's scoring plays a relatively greater role in *The Prisoner of Zenda* (based on the 1894 novel of the same name by Anthony Hope), which contains a number of robustly romantic themes for this often-filmed tale of political intrigue set in the mythical kingdom of Ruritania. For the coronation scene, in which Rudolf is persuaded to impersonate his cousin (both characters played by Ronald Colman), the ailing heir to the throne, Newman borrowed a theme from George Frederick Handel's "March" from the oratorio *Judas Maccabeus*; additionally, the ballroom music consists of a waltz theme from Johann Strauss, Jr.'s *Artist's Life*. Newman's original score includes a royal march, heard as Rudolf and Flavia (Madeleine Carroll) descend a series of staircases to the ballroom, and the love theme, which is heard periodically throughout the film.

This is Newman's finest film-music achievement of the 1930s and the only score he did for Selznick, who routinely hired Max Steiner. This one time, he gambled on Newman (with Steiner's recommendation), and the result illustrates that, as with the groundbreaking music for *King Kong* four years earlier, Selznick knew exactly what he was doing.

RULE CHANGES FOR MUSIC OSCARS. In 1937, the Motion Picture Academy changed the rules for music nominations in order to give credit to a greater number of musicians. Beginning then and continuing through 1945, every studio was virtually guaranteed a nomination for Best Score. All that was necessary was for executives of each studio to choose a score and submit their selection to the Academy. This explains why in 1937 there were fourteen of these nominations.[42]

Despite this change the Oscar was still awarded, as it had been since the music categories were established in 1934, to the music department head. When Charles Previn, head of Universal's music department, was awarded the 1937 scoring Oscar for *One Hundred Men and a Girl*, there was not even a mention of the actual composer (whose name, in fact, has never been identified).[43] This awkward practice would fortunately be stopped with another rule change in 1938, which stipulated that the composer would personally be cited.

Another change that was enacted with the 1938 Oscars brought about a splitting of the scoring nominations into two categories: Best Score and Best Original Score. Thus, the Academy began to recognize the difference between composing scores and arranging them. A peculiarity of this new ruling was that the same score could be nominated in both categories; this happened in 1938 with Franz Waxman's music for *The Young in Heart*; it also happened with Aaron Copland's scores for *Of Mice and Men* and for *Our Town*, in 1939 and 1940, respectively.[44]

Other rule changes would occur in the 1940s, which would clarify the scoring categories. In 1941, the classifications became listed as "Scoring of a Dramatic Picture" and "Scoring of a Musical Picture." The first of these was further refined the next year when it was redesignated "Scoring of a Dramatic or Comedy Picture."[45] With this realignment of the nonmusical category and with the paring down of the list of nominees (in 1946) to at most five scores in each class, the music Oscars would remain somewhat constant until the 1960s, when the Academy started playing around again with the categories, creating yet more confusion.

SHORT CUTS ⬛⬛⬛⬛ **Max Steiner.** For *A Star is Born*, Max Steiner composed a tuneful score with a number of original themes for this inside look at Hollywood. Most prominent is a lilting waltz theme, associated with Esther Blodgett (Janet Gaynor), who wants to be a movie star and eventually becomes one (as the renamed Vicki Lester). For the scene in which Esther first arrives in Los Angeles, the score includes an appropriately apt borrowing of the melody "California, Here I Come," as trains, planes, and automobiles all bring the hopeful to the West Coast. Although not on the same creative level as Steiner's more innovative *Kong* and *Informer* scores, *A Star Is Born* is a melodious foreshadowing of the epic score that he would compose two years later for Selznick's monumental *Gone with the Wind*.

⬛⬛⬛⬛ **Erich Wolfgang Korngold.** Warner Bros. kept Korngold busy in 1937 by offering him the opportunity to score two more films starring Errol Flynn. *Another Dawn*, a triangular love story set against an exotic desert backdrop, brought out Korngold's lyrical side, with a rhapsodic love theme that later became the opening melody of his Violin Concerto, opus 35.

The Prince and the Pauper afforded Korngold the opportunity to create an altogether charming and lighthearted score. Set in Tudor England, this delightful Mark Twain adaptation features Flynn in the role of Miles Hendon, who saves the day by rescuing the endangered young crown prince and helping him become the rightful king. Korngold's music for *The Prince and the Pauper* is an unexpected departure from the heroic style of *Captain Blood*. Here he confined his scoring to predominantly lightweight orchestrations, which allowed the amusing aspects of the story to shine through the dark shadows of political intrigue. Korngold perfectly matched the tone of Mark Twain's story with one of his most ingratiating works.

■■■ **Herbert Stothart.** For *The Good Earth*, which Irving Thalberg was planning before his untimely death in 1936, MGM composer Herbert Stothart (1885–1949) created a score that effectively complements the simple events in the everyday lives of Chinese peasants. The score has an appropriately Oriental sound, with melodies based on the pentatonic scale, and with instruments that produce authentic Chinese sounds added to the traditional orchestration. There is nothing innovative about this score, though, like most of Stothart's work (all of which was done for MGM), it is perfectly competent.

■■■ **Franz Waxman.** In 1937, Franz Waxman, who had departed from Universal the year before for a stint as a contractual composer at MGM, began to get some major scoring assignments. The best of these was *Captains Courageous*, based on Rudyard Kipling's novel about a spoiled rich boy who learns some valuable life lessons from Manuel, a Portuguese sailor (Spencer Tracy), while aboard a fishing ship. In addition to a heroic main theme, Waxman included a Catalan folk tune for Tracy's character. This score is a harbinger of the great things Waxman would accomplish later in his career.

■■■ **Victor Young.** A new name in 1937 film scoring was that of Victor Young (1900–56), who had signed on with Paramount the preceding year and who spent most of his career in Hollywood working for that studio. Although his initial scoring opportunities were generally for such lightweight fare as *Swing High, Swing Low* and *Vogues of 1938*, his inimitable song-writing talent would eventually be demonstrated with a variety of movie theme songs that have become classics.

■■■ **Miklos Rozsa.** Another 1937 newcomer was the thirty-year-old Hungarian composer Miklos Rozsa (1907–95), who was already a published composer of several symphonic and chamber music works when producer Alexander Korda hired him to create the score for *Knight without Armor*, a romantic thriller with Marlene Dietrich and Robert Donat. Set in Russia during the Bolshevik revolution, *Knight without Armor* has music that features a dramatic main theme, plus several other melodies based on borrowings from Russian folk songs. The film's most impressive music is a rhapsodic love theme that foreshadows the ardent lyricism of Rozsa's later film-composing style.

■■■ *Snow White and the Seven Dwarfs.* A special achievement in film music came from an unexpected source: Walt Disney's first feature-length animated film, *Snow White and the Seven Dwarfs*. With a lilting score, consisting of songs by Frank Churchill and Larry Morey, and background music by Leigh Harline and Paul J. Smith, *Snow White* became an instant classic. Among its eight songs, which gracefully punctuate the action, are "Someday My Prince Will Come" and "I'm Wishing." Two others, "Whistle While You Work" and "Heigh Ho," made the Hit Parade between February and May 1938.[46] *Snow White*'s songs helped set the stage for the rich musical contribution to be made by later Disney composers.

1938

RUSSIAN FILM MUSIC. Although the number of films produced in Russia since the advent of synchronized sound is small compared with the vast quantity of American films made during the same period, many significant film scores have been written by Russian composers.

DMITRI SHOSTAKOVICH: A LONG CAREER. Dmitri Shostakovich (1906–75), who spent his entire career in the Soviet Union, scored thirty-five films between 1928 and 1971, and was working on another when he died. Among his most noteworthy film scores is the music for the silent film *New Babylon* (1929), the manuscript of which was discovered in the Lenin State Library shortly after he died.[47] In the decade following *New Babylon*, Shostakovich scored a dozen films, including three from 1938: *A Great Citizen*, *The Man with a Gun*, and *Volochayevsk Days*. Unfortunately, none of these films have ever been widely seen outside of Russia.[48]

SERGEI PROKOFIEV: ALEXANDER NEVSKY. Unlike Shostakovich, Sergei Prokofiev, whose *Lieutenant Kijé* music was described on pages 33–34, wrote only a handful of film scores. All are highly significant.

A gifted child prodigy, Prokofiev entered the St. Petersburg Conservatory at the age of thirteen; for his audition he brought along manuscripts of four operas, two sonatas, a symphony, and several piano pieces.[49] After making his professional debut as a pianist at the age of nineteen, Prokofiev became known as the *enfant terrible* of Russian music.[50] He enjoyed being an avant-garde musician since it brought him attention that he might not otherwise have received.

After the Russian Revolution, Prokofiev received permission to leave his homeland. He spent the next fifteen years abroad, but did not find fulfillment, especially not in the United States, where New York critics were hostile to his music. His reception was somewhat better in Chicago, where his opera *The Love for Three Oranges* was first performed in 1921. Ultimately, he returned to Europe and spent several years in Paris. Finally, at the end of 1932, he decided to return to Russia, with the hope of reestablishing himself as a leading composer of modern Russian music.

Since his return was voluntary, the Soviet leaders eventually accorded him many honors. Even so, his final twenty years, between 1933 and 1953, were difficult in the sense that he had to rein in his penchant for modern dissonance and harmonic experimentation. One of his first projects upon resettling in the USSR was the score for Alexander Feinzimmer's *Lieutenant Kijé*. After completing a concert suite based on his *Kijé* music in 1934, Prokofiev began a collaboration with director Sergei Eisenstein, whose earlier *Battleship Potemkin* (1925) and *October* (1928) remain among the most acclaimed films of all time.

Sergei Prokofiev.

Hearst Newspaper Collection/ University of Southern California

Alexander Nevsky,
with Nikolai Cherkassov
(on the right).

For *Alexander Nevsky* (1938), Eisenstein's first sound film, Prokofiev composed one of the masterworks of film music. In a significant departure from the way in which most American films were scored in the late 1930s, Nevsky's opening credits are shown in total silence. The first music is heard when title cards are shown, explaining the thirteenth-century conflict between the Russians and the German Crusaders. This sets the stage for Eisenstein's dramatic opening scene, which features the capture of Pskov by the Teutonic knights and the subsequent emergence of Alexander from his place of seclusion to take command of the Russian army. There is a call to arms and a general mobilization of volunteers to repulse the advancing Germans, followed by a battle on ice, which takes place on frozen Lake Chud. By the end of the day the German knights and their heavily armored horses have fallen through the cracking ice to a watery grave. In the aftermath of the battle the camera scans the rows of bodies, as a Russian girl searches for two young men who have been competing for her affection. This sequence leads to the film's final scene, featuring Alexander's triumphant liberation of Pskov.

The original recording of the score was dismally substandard. Nevertheless, the music remains a powerful commentary on the film's action.[51] Several choral pieces are included, among the most stirring of which is "Arise, Ye Russian People," which is first heard as Alexander assumes his leadership role.

For the central battle scene on the frozen lake, which lasts over thirty minutes, Prokofiev wrote an extended symphonic piece that consists of several musical ideas connected by a driving rhythmic pulse. Not only is there is a unique sense of audiovisual integrity about the battle scene and its aftermath, but the film as a whole benefits from the high degree of collaboration between director and composer, since Eisenstein agreed to let Prokofiev compose much of the score even before the relevant sequences were filmed.[52]

In 1939, Prokofiev arranged seven segments of the *Nevsky* score as a cantata. The work includes both choral numbers and a song for solo soprano (a eulogy for those who died in battle). It is in this form that listeners have come to appreciate Prokofiev's outstanding achievement, through live concert performances and excellent recordings by several major orchestras. In addition, a 1993 film restoration project, with a completely new recording of the film's score, has led to a release of both the film (on videotape and laser disk) and the restored soundtrack. At last, Prokofiev's music can be properly appreciated in the context of the original film.

Prokofiev and Eisenstein subsequently worked together again on a film trilogy, *Ivan the Terrible*, based on the life of Czar Ivan IV. Music from the two completed films (a third was scripted but never shot) has also been arranged as a concert work.

MAX **STEINER:** *JEZEBEL.* The American film-music scene was dominated throughout 1938 by Warner Bros. composers. Of the ten pictures Max Steiner scored that year, *Jezebel* is especially noteworthy since it not only marked the beginning of a fruitful period in the career of Bette Davis, who won her second Oscar for the role of Julie, a selfish Southern belle, but also featured Henry Fonda, in one of his first starring roles, as Pres Dillard, a prosperous young banker in 1852 New Orleans. The film's memorable music includes a sensuous waltz, which Steiner uses for the film's titles and also for the ballroom scene in which Julie appears wearing a red dress, even though the custom of the time is for all unmarried young ladies to wear white.

Steiner's waltz theme is transformed into dramatic underscoring for the closing scene. Julie, who has matured in the course of the film, helps to transport Pres, who is seriously ill with yellow fever, out of a quarantined New Orleans. The music, in a much slower tempo than before, builds to a thrilling climax as the film ends.

ERICH **WOLFGANG** **KORNGOLD:** *THE ADVENTURES OF ROBIN HOOD.* The 1938 Oscar for Original Score went to Korngold's magnificent music for Warner Bros.' epic filming of *The Adventures of Robin Hood.* Although Korngold had initially declined to do the score on the grounds that the film had more action than he felt comfortable with, he later agreed to do it, and created a classic film score.[53]

Several factors contributed to the success of *Robin Hood.* First, there is the inspired casting: Errol Flynn in the title role, Claude Rains as the conniving Prince John, Basil Rathbone as the prince's fellow conspirator Sir Guy of Gisborne, and Olivia de Havilland as Maid Marian. Then there is the gorgeous Technicolor photography by Tony Gaudio and Sol Polito and the fast-paced direction by Michael Curtiz and William Keighley. Most of all, there is Korngold's glorious music.

From the rousing march heard during the opening titles, Korngold's score unfolds with a continuing stream of melodic ideas that flow through each successive segment of the film. Korngold's steady stream of melodic ideas helped both to humanize the drama and to enhance its romantic qualities, while at the same time setting a rhythmic pace for the entire picture.

The *Robin Hood* score is not as epic in scale as much of Prokofiev's *Alexander Nevsky* music; still it managed to establish the symphonic style for the scores of most of the action films made during Hollywood's Golden Age and for almost all later adventure epics, including the scores by John Williams for the *Star Wars* and *Indiana Jones* trilogies.

SHORT **C**UTS. Although *Alexander Nevsky* was probably seen by only a handful of American moviegoers during its initial release, several other European films did extremely well in the United States in 1938.

■ ■ ■ **Arthur Honegger.** Arthur Honegger (1892–1955) was one of Les Six, a group of modern musicians who were brought together in Paris around 1918 through the influence of the eccentric French composer Erik Satie. Because of their opposition to the gargantuan Germanic orchestrations of Richard Strauss and Gustav Mahler, these six composers became known as Neoclassicists. Besides Honegger (who was born of Swiss parents in Le Havre), other prominent members of this group include Darius Milhaud (1892–1974), Francis Poulenc (1899–1963), and Georges Auric (1899–1983). Honegger and Milhaud had composed music for a number of silent films in the 1920s.

Honegger's music for *Pygmalion*, based on the George Bernard Shaw play in which Professor Henry Higgins (Leslie Howard) wagers that he can teach flower seller Eliza Doolittle (Wendy Hiller) to be a proper English lady, humanizes the characters and softens the satire. Using basically a small group of solo players, Honegger fashioned a jaunty and at times humorous musical accompaniment, which shows up most noticeably in the scenes where Eliza is practicing her diction with the help of Higgins's machines.

■ ■ ■ **Joseph Kosma.** Another contender for the 1938 Oscar was Jean Renoir's *Grand Illusion*, a gripping World War I drama starring Jean Gabin, with Erich von Stroheim as a German prisoner-of-war (POW) commander. Its young composer, Joseph Kosma (1905–69), a native of Hungary, worked in France throughout a career that spanned more than three decades. Kosma's score is featured in only a few scenes. Among the most noteworthy is the sequence in which three POWs are being transported by train to a prison fortress. Here the music includes a rhythmically driven idea played by strings. After *Grand Illusion*, which was only his third film score, Kosma worked with Renoir on two more films, including the classic *La regle du jeu*—English title: *Rules of the Game* (1939).

MAX **S**TEINER: GONE WITH THE WIND. No film made in the late 1930s was more eagerly anticipated than the movie version of Margaret Mitchell's Pulitzer Prize–winning novel, *Gone with the Wind*. David O. Selznick had purchased the rights to the book in July 1936, one month after the novel first appeared; but it was almost three and a half years before the film was ultimately completed.

Actually, Selznick almost passed up the opportunity to film Mitchell's blockbuster novel. According to movie historian Herb Bridges:

Gone With the Wind was not David Selznick's discovery. It was first brought to his attention by Katharine Brown, the head of his New York story office. Macmillan had sent advance copies of the novel to leading movie studios, including Selznick International Pictures. After reading it Katharine immediately cabled to Selznick in Hollywood, saying: "I beg, urge, coax, and plead with you to read it at once. . . . I know that after you do you will drop everything and buy it."[54]

Selznick's initial reluctance stemmed from the fact that there had not been a successful movie with a Civil War setting since *The Birth of a Nation.* Furthermore, without an actress to play the lead role of Scarlett O'Hara, there could be little chance of making a decent film. Katharine Brown persisted, however, and on July 30, 1936, Margaret Mitchell was paid $50,000 for the film rights to her book.[55]

Fashioning a workable screenplay from Mitchell's 1,037-page novel was a daunting task which ultimately involved the efforts of several writers. According to Susan Sackett:

> At least 10 writers worked on the screenplay. Although Sidney Howard [who died of a farming accident before the film's premiere] was credited and received the Oscar for Best Screenplay, other drafts were written by F. Scott Fitzgerald, Jo Swerling, Ben Hecht, John Balderston, John Van Druten, and Michael Foster. Selznick himself did the final rewrites.[56]

Gone with the Wind, with Clark Gable and Vivien Leigh.

As with all of his other films, Selznick took painstaking efforts in every aspect of the production, including the casting. The choice of Clark Gable to play Rhett Butler was made rather easily, since Gable was the public's choice. MGM acquired the distribution rights and 50 percent of the profits in exchange for the loan of Gable. Selznick also wound up getting $1.25 million from his father-in-law, Louis B. Mayer, for this extravagant production. The movie eventually cost almost $4 million, which was $1.5 million over its original budget.[57]

The selection of an actress to play Scarlett O'Hara, on the other hand, was anything but easy. The process took over two years and entailed a nationwide talent search, with a total of 1,400 actresses interviewed. Many movie historians have reported on this search, with estimates of the number of actual screen tests varying from thirty-one to possibly one hundred. Again Sackett enlightens us on this painstaking process: "The most extensive screen tests in the history of motion pictures were made for this role. Sixty actresses tested, with 165,000 feet of film shot, costing $105,000 (enough to shoot a minor film in those days)."[58] Many of Hollywood's top female stars, including Bette Davis, Joan Bennett, and Norma Shearer, coveted the role, but the part eventually went to the relatively unknown British actress Vivien Leigh.

For the other two principal roles, Olivia de Havilland campaigned hard to be chosen for the part of Melanie, whereas Leslie Howard had to be prodded into taking the role of Ashley Wilkes by the promise of producing and starring in Selznick's next film, *Intermezzo*.

Selznick also experienced difficulties with his technical crew. Lee Garmes, the Oscar-winning cinematographer, left the production over a disagreement about the look of the film when Selznick wanted to display more vivid colors. Ernest Haller then took over and gave the film the rich palette that would eventually lead to an Oscar for color cinematography.

There was also trouble concerning Selznick's choice of a director. George Cukor shot several scenes, but three weeks into the filming he left the production. One version of why he left is that Gable considered Cukor a woman's director, and thus wasn't happy to be working under him. Another version suggests that Cukor was frustrated trying to deal with Selznick's dictatorial control. Victor Fleming, who was currently finishing MGM's *Wizard of Oz*, was called in to take over, but after four months, he suffered a nervous breakdown. The final quarter of the film was directed for the most part by Sam Wood, with contributions from Sidney Franklin, William Wellman, and even Selznick himself. Fleming eventually returned after a four-week absence, and directed scenes shot in the afternoon, while Wood worked in the morning.[59] Since Fleming did the major part of the work, he received sole credit and was singled out for the Oscar as the film's director.

About halfway into the shooting, Selznick had already decided upon Max Steiner as composer of the score. In March 1939, Selznick sent a memo to Henry Ginsberg, his general manager, in which he made his first mention about the music for his film:

> I think that whoever is going to do the score on *Gone With the Wind* ought to know about it now so that he can be spending whatever time he has free in study of the music of the period and generally doing preparatory work. . . . My first choice for the job is Max Steiner.[60]

Selznick's choice of Steiner is not difficult to believe since they had worked together at RKO in the early 1930s. Almost all of the films that Selznick made independently in the late '30s were scored by Steiner, with the significant exception of *The Prisoner of Zenda*, for which Alfred Newman, through Steiner's personal recommendation, supplied the music.

Once Steiner agreed to do the score of *Gone with the Wind*, his services could only be procured by obtaining permission of the executives at Warner Bros., with whom he had contracted in 1936. Permission was granted, but Steiner's heavy work load at Warner Bros. prevented him from keeping up the pace that Selznick demanded. Shrewdly, Selznick let it be known that Herbert Stothart, MGM's top composer, was enthusiastic about doing the score himself; Selznick also implied that he might even consider having two composers coproduce the score. This idea offended Steiner, who then worked out a schedule to allow the time necessary for him to complete this monumental project.[61]

Steiner spent twelve weeks on *Gone with the Wind*'s music; it was the longest period he ever spent on a single score, and was by far the lengthiest film score he ever attempted to write. A team of five orchestrators was employed: Hugo Friedhofer (who worked with Steiner regularly at Warner Bros.), Maurice de Packh, Bernard Kaun, Adolph Deutsch, and Reginald Bassett. According to Rudy Behlmer, a noted authority on Selznick, Steiner composed three hours of music, two hours and thirty-six minutes of which were used in the final release print of the film.[62]

A lengthy analysis of Steiner's score could take up an entire book, but Behlmer points out some of the score's principal attributes:

> The four principal characters have their own motifs, as well as the main supporting characters—Mammy (Hattie McDaniel), Scarlett's father (Thomas Mitchell), Scarlett and Rhett's daughter Bonnie (Cammie King) and Belle Watling (Ona Munson). There are two dominant love themes, one associated with the spiritual, sensitive love of Ashley and Melanie, the other a subtle depiction of Scarlett's continuous passion for Ashley and his wavering feelings towards her.[63]

Steiner's score consists of ninety-nine separate pieces of music, based on eleven primary motifs, with sixteen additional ideas taken from folk and patriotic sources. Notably, there is no Scarlett and Rhett love theme, and Scarlett's theme is based on Stephen Foster's song "Katie Belle" (presumably because Katie is Scarlett's first name).[64] Among the score's most noteworthy melodies is the "Mammy" theme, which, perhaps because the character was a slave, was cast in the style of a ragtime tune. For Rhett Butler, Steiner decided to reflect the character's military background by creating a march theme.

By far the most famous melody of the score is "Tara," named for the O'Hara family's Georgia plantation. Its fame was elevated in the early 1940s when it became the musical basis of the song "My Own True Love," with lyrics by Mack David. When heard today, more than a half century after the making of *Gone with the Wind*, this bold and heroic theme immediately conjures up images of the film. It is not only the best remembered of all of Steiner's countless movie themes, but also one of the most enduring musical compositions ever written for a film.

An exhaustive list of all of the borrowed melodies used in Steiner's scoring would take up too much space, but such other Stephen Foster tunes as "Louisiana Belle," "Dolly Day," "Ring De Banjo," "Beautiful Dreamer," and "Old Folks at Home" should be mentioned. Dan Emmet's "Dixie" also appears prominently, as does Henry C. Work's "Marching through Georgia" and the traditional tunes "Garry Owen" and "Bonnie Blue Flag."[65]

Because of the pressure of completing the score on time, Steiner found it necessary to involve Friedhofer and Deutsch, along with fellow Warner Bros. orchestrator Heinz Roemheld, in composing small bits of material based on Steiner's thematic ideas. In addition, two short cues (of less than a minute in duration), one by Franz Waxman and the other by William Axt, were extracted from scores found in the MGM library.[66]

The finished musical score, under Steiner's name alone, was dubbed into the completed film, which received a gala premiere at the Loew's Grand Theater in Atlanta on December 15, 1939. When Oscar time came in early 1940, *Gone with the Wind* won an unprecedented nine awards, including Best Picture. Steiner's score, though nominated, failed to win, that honor going to Herbert Stothart for his original score for *The Wizard of Oz*. The music of *Gone with the Wind* may not be the best work of Steiner's Hollywood career, but in terms of its sheer scope it is a remarkable achievement.

AARON COPLAND: *THE CITY* AND *OF MICE AND MEN*. Aaron Copland (1900–1990), who was growing in stature as a serious American composer of symphonic works throughout the 1930s, wrote his first film score in 1939, for a forty-four-minute documentary film *The City*, which was produced by Ralph Steiner and Willard Van Dyke specifically for the New York World's Fair.

Copland's first Hollywood score was written shortly thereafter, for the film version of John Steinbeck's *Of Mice and Men*, a grim story of two drifters, George (Burgess Meredith) and Lennie (Lon Chaney, Jr.), who find employment on a California ranch, but dream of starting up their own spread. There is sparse use of underscoring in the film, but Copland understood how to enhance the dramatic moments, such as a confrontation scene in which Curley (Bob Steele), the ranch owner's son, taunts the hulky and mentally slow Lennie, who finally grabs the man's gloved hand in mid-air. The wrenchingly dissonant chord that accompanies the closeup shot of the two interlocked hands produces a great sense of tension that is sustained until Lennie lets go, whereupon Curley collapses on the floor.

Copland subsequently produced a concert work entitled *Music for Movies*, a five-movement suite that incorporates music from both *The City* and *Of Mice and Men*, together with a theme from his 1940 film score of *Our Town*. Copland followed in the footsteps of Sergei Prokofiev and Virgil Thomson by demonstrating that a worthy concert-hall composition could be fashioned from film music.

SILVESTRE REVUELTAS: *LA NOCHE DE LOS MAYAS*. Silvestre Revueltas (1899–1940), born in Mexico but educated mostly in the United States, composed seven film scores between 1935 and his untimely death five years later at the age of forty. The best of these scores is his music for the 1939 Mexican film *La noche de los Mayas* (*The Night of the Mayas*). Due to the failure of the film, it was many years before this music was widely heard. Only in 1961 was a four-movement orchestral suite fashioned from the score; in this form the work has been performed and recorded numerous times.

The work's principal theme is heard at the outset of the opening movement, in which a large brass ensemble boldly proclaims a repeated series of three-note motifs, accompanied by string chords. Melodically, the music has an almost primitive effect, with patterns of tones that continually repeat the same pitches and then move upward or downward within a small range. The last movement, "Night of Enchantment," is a set of rhythmic variations that includes an ingenious assemblage of percussion instruments played by a dozen musicians. One of the most unusual sound effects in this work is produced by a conch shell which, when blown into, produces a mellow, hornlike sound. *Mayas* is filled with overlapping rhythms that help to create a uniquely pulsing effect. In its symphonic form this is a brilliant work that deserves a permanent place in the repertoire.

SHORT CUTS. Sometimes regarded as the greatest year in the history of the movies, 1939 witnessed the release of many other highly acclaimed films, including such classics as *Goodbye, Mr. Chips*, *Ninotchka*, *Stagecoach*, *Mr. Smith Goes to Washington*, *Wuthering Heights*, *The Women*, *Dark Victory*, and *The Wizard of Oz*.

■ ■ ■ **Richard Addinsell.** *Goodbye Mr. Chips*, which includes Robert Donat's Oscar-winning performance, has an attractive score by British composer Richard Addinsell (1904–77), who would achieve his principal movie-composing fame a few years later for *Warsaw* Concerto (written for the 1941 film *Dangerous Moonlight*). A highlight of the *Chips* score is the stirring theme used as the school song for Brookfield, the private boys' school where Mr. Chipping spends his entire teaching career. (The boys' nickname for him is "Mr. Chips.")

■ ■ ■ **Werner Heymann.** The music for *Ninotchka*, Greta Garbo's first comedy, was composed by German-born Werner Heymann (1896–1961), who came to the United States in 1933 and specialized in scores for comedies. He worked with such major directors as Ernst Lubitsch (on *Ninotchka*) and Preston Sturges (on *Hail the Conquering Hero*, 1944). Although *Ninotchka*'s music is sparse, the main theme, a tuneful waltz, is played exuberantly during the opening credits.

■ ■ ■ **Herbert Stothart:** *The Wizard of Oz.* Stothart's Oscar-winning score for MGM's lavish filming of L. Frank Baum's *Wonderful Wizard of Oz* (1900) includes numerous musical quotations from works by others. The score didn't really qualify for the category of Best Original Score, but somehow the Oscar voters overlooked that bit of music irregularity. Most prominent among the borrowed materials is the Harold Arlen–E. Y. Harburg song "Over the Rainbow." Not only is this song featured instrumentally during the opening credits, but it appears many times in the underscore. Two other notable tunes that appear are Robert Schumann's piano piece "The Happy Farmer" (which is associated with Dorothy's dog, Toto), and Modeste Mussorgsky's *Night on Bald Mountain* (for the chase scenes at the witch's castle). Several MGM studio arrangers and orchestrators assisted Stothart on the score. These include George Stoll, George Bassman, Bob Stringer, Murray Cutter, Paul Marquardt, Leo Arnaud, and Conrad Salinger. Strangely, only Stothart received a screen credit.

■ ■ ■ **Dimitri Tiomkin.** Among the most acclaimed films of 1939 is Frank Capra's *Mr. Smith Goes to Washington*. The patriotic score is by Tiomkin, who scored the picture with several borrowed American folk tunes, including "Red River Valley," "When Johnny Comes Marching Home," and especially "Yankee Doodle," which is heard during the opening credits and is associated thereafter with James Stewart's character.

■ ■ ■ **Alfred Newman.** Samuel Goldwyn's production of Emily Brontë's *Wuthering Heights* features sensitive direction by William Wyler, fine performances by Laurence Olivier as the tormented Heathcliff and by Merle Oberon as the fragile Cathy, plus a haunting score by Alfred Newman. The most prominent melody is "Cathy's Theme," which is heard during the film's romantic episodes. Because of the episodic nature of the film, which uses the novel's framing device to tell the tragic story of Cathy and Heathcliff in flashbacks, Newman's music is essential for connecting the various elements of the story into a coherent whole. This score reveals a fully mature style, and clearly points to the many exceptional works that Newman would create at 20th Century-Fox, where he signed on as music director in 1939.

■■■■ **Erich Wolfgang Korngold.** Two exceptional Korngold scores appeared in 1939 as accompaniments for colorful historical dramas. For *The Private Lives of Elizabeth and Essex,* Korngold created lush backgrounds, with a rousing march theme for Essex (Errol Flynn) and one of his most noble and heroic melodies for Elizabeth (Bette Davis). For *Juarez,* a slow-moving but atmospheric drama that features an almost unrecognizable Paul Muni as the Mexican revolutionary leader, Korngold produced a more subdued background, with a lovely romantic theme for Empress Carlotta (Bette Davis) and the borrowed Mexican tune "La Paloma" for Emperor Maximilian (Brian Aherne). Korngold did his homework well before composing this score; "La Paloma" was Maximilian's favorite song.

■■■■ **Richard Hageman.** One other exceptional 1939 film that deserves mention for its music is John Ford's *Stagecoach,* which elevated John Wayne to stardom. Often hailed as the "granddaddy" of all later Westerns, this movie features a pastiche of American popular songs, arranged by Dutch-born composer Richard Hageman (1882–1966). The resultant music, which won the Oscar for Best Score, includes "Rio Grande" (which is heard whenever the stagecoach is en route), "At the River" (Doc's theme, for the hard-drinking medic played by Thomas Mitchell in a portrayal that won him an Oscar), and "I Dream of Jeannie with the Light Brown Hair" (for Lucy, the young female passenger played by Louise Platt). This is a rousing score, but it is not worthy of the prize it won, considering the competition, which included Copland's *Of Mice and Men* and Korngold's *Elizabeth and Essex.*

POSTLUDE

THE **T**ALKIES **C**OME **OF** **A**GE. When the first full decade of talking pictures began, because of the constraints of sound synchronization, movies were primitively photographed productions, having to be shot almost entirely on indoor sets; the closing of the decade witnessed large-scale epics that were increasingly filmed on outdoor locations. Likewise, during the 1930s, film scores evolved from sparsely written accompaniments, which were confined to the opening and closing credits, to almost continuous musical commentaries, which underscored practically every scene.

As the 1940s loomed ahead, with the Nazi war machine wreaking havoc throughout Europe, Hollywood filmmakers were prospering. Many new faces were emerging, both in front of and behind the camera, and such major musical talents as Bernard Herrmann and Miklos Rozsa would soon arrive in Hollywood. Despite the world's troubles, American moviemaking was in the midst of a glorious period that was rich in terms of both productivity and artistic achievement.

Endnotes

1. Frank Buxton and Bill Owen, *The Big Broadcast: 1920–1950* (New York: Viking, 1972), p. 14.

2. Ibid., p. 171.

3. David Ewen, *All the Years of American Popular Music* (Englewood Cliffs, NJ: Prentice-Hall, 1977), p. 324.

4. Joel W. Finler, *The Hollywood Story* (New York: Crown, 1988), p. 102

5. David Cook, *A History of Narrative Film* (New York: W. W. Norton & Co., 1981), p. 245.

6. Tony Thomas, *Film Score: The Art and Craft of Movie Music* (Burbank, CA: Riverwood, 1991), p. 56.

7. James V. D'Arc and John N. Gillespie, *The Max Steiner Collection* (Provo, UT: Brigham Young University, 1996), p. 24.

8. Tony Thomas, *Music for the Movies* (South Brunswick, NJ: A. S. Barnes and Co., 1973), p. 113.

9. Jack Jacobs, "Alfred Newman," *Films in Review*, vol. X, no. 7 (August–September, 1959), p. 403.

10. Ibid., p. 404.

11. Thomas, *Film Score*, pp. 221–22.

12. Thomas, *Music for the Movies*, p. 65.

13. Edwin M. Bradley, *The First Hollywood Musicals: A Critical Filmography of 171 Features, 1927 through 1932* (Jefferson, NC: McFarland & Co.), p. 200.

14. Harry Haun and George Raborn, "Max Steiner," *Films in Review*, vol. XII, no. 6 (June–July, 1961) p. 343.

15. Page Cook, Liner notes for *Captain from Castile: The Classic Film Scores of Alfred Newman*, RCA CD, 0184-2-RG.

16. *Great Love Themes from Motion Pictures*, with Max Steiner and His Orchestra, RCA Victor LP, LPM-1170.

17. Thomas, *Film Score*, p. 59.

18. Ibid., p. 68.

19. Fred Steiner, Liner notes for *King Kong*, Original 1933 Motion Picture Score, Southern Cross Records CD, SCCD 901.

20. Ephraim Katz, *The Film Encyclopedia*, 2d ed. (New York: HarperCollins, 1994), p. 1432.

21. Anthony Holden, *Behind the Oscar: The Secret History of the Academy Awards* (New York: Simon and Schuster, 1993), p. 551.

22. This melody, along with several other Prokofiev film themes, was used as the background score of Woody Allen's 1975 film *Love and Death*. More recently, the wedding theme was featured in Carter Burwell's score for *Doc Hollywood* (1991).

23. Harlow Robinson, *Sergei Prokofiev: A Biography* (New York: Viking, 1987), p. 278.

24. Israel V. Nestyev, *Prokofiev* (Stanford: Stanford University, 1960), p. 251.

25. Martin Quigley, Jr. and Richard Gertner, *Films in America 1929–1969* (New York: Golden, 1970), p. 61.

26. Thomas, *Film Score*, p. 78.

27. Kenneth Von Gunden and Stuart H. Stock, *Twenty All-Time Great Science Fiction Films* (New York: Arlington House, 1982), p. 11.

28. Jessica Duchen, *Erich Wolfgang Korngold*, (London: Phaidon, 1996), p. 17.

29. Rudy Behlmer, "Erich Wolfgang Korngold," *Films in Review*, vol. XVIII, no. 2 (February 1967), pp. 87–88.

30. Ibid.

31. Behlmer, *Films in Review*, vol. XVIII, no. 2, p. 90.

32. Thomas, *Music for the Movies*, p. 124.

33. Of the many recordings of Waxman's music, the most comprehensive is a reconstruction by Tony Bremner and Soren Hyldgaard, which was recorded by the Westminster Philharmonic Orchestra, under Kenneth Alwyn, and released on a Silva Screen CD, SSD 1028, in 1993.

34. Behlmer, *Films in Review*, vol. XVIII, no. 2, p. 91.

35. Thomas, *Film Score*, p. 197.

36. Frank Capra, *The Name above the Title* (New York: Macmillan, 1971), p. 218.

37. Kurt Sven, Liner notes for *Lost Horizon: The Classic Film Scores of Dimitri Tiomkin*, on an RCA CD, 1669-2-RG, pp. 9–10.

38. Ibid., p. 10.

39. Ibid., p. 11.

40. One of the distinct advantages of modern film score recordings is that they afford the opportunity to hear a score as it might have sounded if the film's dramatic situation had not interfered. While the final portion of the funeral procession music is all but obliterated in the film of *Lost Horizon*, on the Gerhardt recording the music's volume is kept at a higher level; this allows the listener to feel the full impact of Tiomkin's creativity.

41. As mentioned earlier, this theme appears briefly in a shipboard scene in *Dodsworth*, which Newman scored a year before doing the music for *The Hurricane*.

42. Holden, pp. 550–51.

43. Ibid.

44. Ibid., pp. 551–52.

45. Ibid., pp. 553–56.

46. Elston Brooks, *I've Heard Those Songs Before: The Weekly Top Ten Tunes for the Last Fifty Years* (New York: William Morrow and Co., 1981), pp. 76–78.

47. Royal S. Brown, Liner notes for *The New Babylon*, a new recording of the 1928–29 silent film score performed by an ensemble of soloists from the Moscow Philharmonic, conducted by Gennady Rozhdestvensky, on a Columbia Records LP, M34502. This was recorded by Melodiya in the USSR and released in the United States in 1977.

48. Vincent J. Francillon and Steven C. Smith, *Film Composers Guide*, 2d ed. (Los Angeles: Lone Eagle, 1994), p. 207.

49. Joseph Machlis, *Introduction to Contemporary Music*, 2d ed. (New York: W. W. Norton and Co., 1977), p. 217.

50. Ibid., p. 218.

51. John Goberman, Liner notes for the 1993 soundtrack recording of the restored version of *Alexander Nevsky*, released on RCA Victor CD, No. 61926-2. For the new soundtrack, the score was performed by the St. Petersburg Philharmonic and conducted by Yuri Temirkanov.

52. Robinson, p. 351.

53. Fred Karlin, *Listening to Movies: The Film Lover's Guide to Film Music* (New York: Schirmer Books, 1994), p. 190.

54. Herb Bridges and Teryl C. Boodman, *Gone with the Wind: The Definitive, Illustrated History of the Book, the Movie and the Legend* (New York: Simon and Schuster, 1989), p. 9.

55. Ibid.

56. Susan Sackett, *The Hollywood Reporter Book of Box Office Hits* (New York: Billboard Books, 1990), p. 16.

57. Bob Thomas, "The Story of Gone with the Wind," included as a booklet with the record album of the original soundtrack released in 1967 on an MGM Records LP, SIE-10 ST.

58. Sackett, p. 16.

59. Bridges and Boodman, p. 187.

60. Rudy Behlmer, Liner notes for the studio recording of *Gone with the Wind* by the National Philharmonic Orchestra, conducted by Charles Gerhardt, RCA Victor CD, 0452-2-RG.

61. Thomas, *Music for the Movies*, p. 116.

62. Behlmer, Liner notes for GWTW, RCA 0452-2-RG.

63. Ibid.

64. Ibid.

65. Thomas, *Film Score*, pp. 60–65. For a complete listing of all of the music cues used in *GWTW*, Tony Thomas's *Film Score: The Art and Craft of Movie Music* is a reliable source, since Thomas consulted the sheets prepared for the 1947 rerelease of the film. In this six-page listing, there is a complete reel-by-reel breakdown of the music, with both titles and composers listed.

66. Behlmer, Liner notes for *GWTW*, RCA 0452-2-RG.

3

1940–49

World War II and Its Aftermath

Although World War II caused worldwide turmoil, the decade 1940–49 represents a period of great artistic achievement in film music. A brief look at the entertainment media of this turbulent decade will provide a useful background.

RADIO. Throughout the Depression, radio had experienced such an unparalleled popularity that by the beginning of the 1940s, the home radio set was the average person's window on the world. There was at least one radio in virtually every home. Listeners could enjoy a wide variety of programming, including news broadcasts, sporting events, and especially a large number of variety and drama programs. Such perennial favorites as "Amos 'n' Andy" and "Fibber McGee and Molly" continued to entertain millions of listeners, while popular stars like Bing Crosby, Bob Hope, and Jack Benny hosted variety programs with a large number of guest stars, comedy skits, and musical numbers. Many of the most popular recording stars of the 1940s either hosted or made guest appearances on radio, and thus listeners could get a steady diet of the currently popular songs.

TELEVISION. Despite the continuing popularity of radio, however, the rise of television in the closing years of the decade would eventually challenge the older broadcasting format. With the establishment of such network variety shows as those hosted by Milton Berle (on NBC) and Ed Sullivan (on CBS) in the fall of 1948, soon the major singing stars of radio would make their way onto the small TV screen.

POPULAR MUSIC. Meanwhile, many of the leading recording artists of the 1930s enjoyed continuing popularity during the World War II years and beyond. Bing Crosby, who appeared regularly both on radio and in the movies, was the favorite singing star of the 1940s. With worldwide sales of twenty-five million copies,[1] the crooner's rendition of Irving Berlin's "White Christmas," which he introduced in Paramount's *Holiday Inn* (1942), remained the all-time top-selling recording, until Elton John's 1997 rendition of "Candle in the Wind." In 1944, Crosby's popularity received another boost when he played the singing priest Father Chuck O'Malley in Leo McCarey's sentimental hit *Going My Way*. With this role, for which he was awarded an Oscar, Crosby became the top box-office star from 1944 to 1948.

Several new faces burst upon the music scene during the war years, but none had a more sensational impact than Frank Sinatra, who had begun in the late 1930s as a vocalist with the Harry James and Tommy Dorsey bands. When Sinatra went on his own to become a solo singer and film star in 1942, he led the way for other band singers. By the end of World War II, most of the bands had broken up, and thus the path was paved for the singing careers of Perry Como, Frankie Laine, Billy Eckstine, Dick Haymes, and Nat "King" Cole.

Women singers—Dinah Shore, Peggy Lee, Margaret Whiting, Ella Fitzgerald, Sarah Vaughan, and especially Doris Day—also benefited from the demise of the dance bands. Following her smash success with "Sentimental Journey" as a front singer with Les Brown's band, Day went on to Hollywood stardom at Warner Bros., where she made her debut in *Romance on the High Seas* (1948) and soon became a top box-office attraction.

The record industry itself made great strides during the 1940s, especially with the arrival of the long-playing (LP, $33\frac{1}{3}$-rpm) record album, which was introduced by Columbia in 1948. Not to be outdone, RCA almost concurrently introduced the seven-inch 45-rpm disc, which within a few years would become the standard format for pairs of songs, as a replacement for the old 78-rpm record. By the beginning of the 1950s, both of these new formats would achieve widespread popularity, especially for the release of original cast albums of Broadway shows and original movie soundtracks. By midcentury, recordings of film music could easily be obtained at local record shops or in the music departments of major department stores. Along with this availability came a new phenomenon: the soundtrack collector, who could savor the sounds of a film score long after seeing the movie.

MOVIES. While many 1940s films either provided glimpses of World War II or tackled any number of other significant issues, this was the decade in which Technicolor came into wide usage, and nowhere was color more evident than in the musical film. Throughout the early years of the decade, most of the major Hollywood studios presented colorful escapist entertainments that helped moviegoers forget about the war for a couple of hours.

A few musical extravaganzas reminded audiences that there was a war going on. Paramount's *Star Spangled Rhythm* (1942), MGM's *Thousands Cheer* (1943), and Warner Bros.' *Hollywood Canteen* (1944) featured all-star casts made up of contract players from their respective studios, playing themselves as entertainers who were usually brought together to put on a show to boost the morale of the men in uniform. Undoubtedly the most patriotic of the forties musicals was Warner's *This Is the Army*, which Irving

Berlin updated in 1943 from his old World War I stage revue. Not only was this the most profitable film of the year, but it was among the biggest movie hits of the entire decade.

Meanwhile, Judy Garland made a string of successful films at MGM, including the charming *Meet Me in St. Louis* (1944), in which she sang the now-classic Ralph Blane–Hugh Martin hit "The Trolley Song," and *The Harvey Girls* (1946), which contains a rousing score by Harry Warren. Helped by Judy's enthusiastic vocal performance, Warren's "On the Atchison, Topeka and the Santa Fe" went on to win the 1946 Oscar for Best Song. Judy also costarred with Mickey Rooney in ten MGM musicals, including *Babes in Arms* (1939), *Strike Up the Band* (1940), *Babes on Broadway* (1942), and *Girl Crazy* (1943). The remarkable chemistry of this duo made them both audience favorites, although it was actually Mickey who was voted top box-office star for the years 1939–41, largely on the basis of his successful *Andy Hardy* pictures. In 1948, Judy made a pair of remarkable films: *Easter Parade*, in which she provided Fred Astaire with a lively dance partner, and *The Pirate*, in which she held her own against Gene Kelly's balletic flair. *The Pirate*, however, was a box office dud, and in only two more years her MGM career would come to an abrupt end, after only two more films, *In the Good Old Summertime* (1949) and *Summer Stock* (1950).

Judy Garland became too ill to costar with Fred Astaire in *The Barkleys of Broadway* (1949). Although the dance team of Fred Astaire and Ginger Rogers had been apart since 1939, Rogers was coaxed into costarring with her former dance partner for old time's sake. This film proved to be a most nostalgic endeavor, especially when Fred and Ginger danced to the strains of George Gershwin's "They Can't Take That Away from Me," a song they had introduced twelve years earlier (in *Shall We Dance*). But their reunion was short-lived, and they went their separate ways again.

The other great duo of the 1930s, Jeanette MacDonald and Nelson Eddy, made three more films together for MGM at the beginning of the forties: *New Moon* (1940), *Bitter Sweet* (1940), and *I Married an Angel* (1942). However, the chemistry on display in their earlier movies was not so evident in these films, the last of the eight pictures to feature the team that has been called the "most successful singing partnership in musical film history."[2]

Music played a strong role in several films made by Walt Disney in the early 1940s. Following upon the sensational success of *Snow White and the Seven Dwarfs* (1937), a pair of animated Disney films won Oscars for their music. *Pinocchio* (1940) won Academy Awards for not only its original score but also for the song "When You Wish Upon a Star," while *Dumbo* (1941) won the Oscar in a newly created category, Scoring of a Musical Picture.

In between these two films came the original release of Disney's most unique musical production, *Fantasia* (1940), a concert film with eight pieces of classical music accompanied by animation. The music was recorded by the Philadelphia Orchestra under the direction of Leopold Stokowski in 1938, using experimental sound equipment referred to by Leonard Maltin in his book *The Disney Films* as "sound cameras."[3] The resultant sound, dubbed "Fantasound," had a multidirectional effect, since the Disney sound engineers played around with the levels obtained from the nine different microphones used in the recording sessions. Despite the time and expense that went into its creation, *Fantasia* received a mixed critical and public reaction, and did not turn a profit until it was rereleased several times.

Many of the almost three hundred musical films made during the 1940s were enormously popular, but with the arrival of TV variety shows by the end of the decade, the popularity of movie musicals began a steady decline. Although some fine film adaptations of Broadway musicals would appear in the years ahead, never again would there be in Hollywood the rich pool of talent that had collaborated in the production of so many entertaining examples of the musical genre.

ERICH **W**OLFGANG **K**ORNGOLD: *T*HE *S*EA *H*AWK. Following the success of *The Adventures of Robin Hood* and *The Private Lives of Elizabeth and Essex*, Erich Wolfgang Korngold took on Merrie Olde England for a third time, with Warner's 1940 filming of Rafael Sabatini's novel *The Sea Hawk*. This book was seen as a perfect vehicle for Errol Flynn, the swashbuckling star of the two preceding films.

In fact, most of the credits for *The Sea Hawk* look like a carbon copy of those two films. Again Michael Curtiz directed, Hal B. Wallis produced, Sol Polito did the cinematography, and Seton Miller, who had coscripted *Robin Hood*, cowrote the screenplay along with Howard Koch. And once again, it was Korngold who did the music.

Though Warner had already filmed this novel in 1924, the new version of *The Sea Hawk* cannot really be considered a remake. The only thing the novel and the 1940 film have in common is the title. Seton Miller had written a story entitled *Beggars of the Sea*, which told of the exploits of Sir Francis Drake; with the war raging in Europe, this story was deemed a

The Sea Hawk,
with Errol Flynn.

perfect vehicle for demonstrating pro-British patriotism. The Spanish villains of the story who plot an invasion of England can be seen as a parallel to the Nazis. The character of Drake was fictionalized as Geoffrey Thorpe, who captains the *Albatross* and plunders Spanish ships that pose a threat to the English fleet. Because of his vigilance Thorpe and a small group of other English sea captains are referred to as "sea hawks."[4]

At thirty-one Errol Flynn was in fine shape physically, and thus capable of performing some of the gymnastic stunts required by the script, including swinging from ropes and engaging in rambunctious swordplay. Although a double was used in the dueling scenes for the long shots, a lot of what appears on film is actually Flynn himself, who seems to have enjoyed every minute of the elaborately staged action.

One significant departure from the filming of Flynn's two previous historical epics is the use of black-and-white photography. The decision was a cost-cutting one. Other money-saving measures included the recycling of sets and costumes from *Elizabeth and Essex* and the use of relatively minor supporting actors. Instead of Bette Davis as Queen Elizabeth, in *Sea Hawk* Flora Robson assumed the role. And Brenda Marshall, instead of Olivia de Havilland, was given the role of Thorpe's sweetheart, Doña Maria. Nevertheless, the film still managed to cost $1,700,000, which by 1940 standards was a considerable sum.

At two hours and six minutes, *The Sea Hawk* is one of the longest films that Korngold ever worked on, and it includes symphonic scoring in all but twenty minutes of its final running time. This was his tenth original score in less than six years, and it was completed in seven weeks (more than twice the time allotted for *Captain Blood*). Four orchestrators shaped the music from Korngold's highly detailed sketches, including Hugo Friedhofer (who worked on almost all of Korngold's film projects), Ray Heindorf, Milan Roder, and Simon Bucharoff. The finished product was recorded over a period of weeks rather than in continuous recording sessions. According to the composer's younger son, George Korngold:

> A total of 58 hours was spent over a period of weeks to record the music with the Warner orchestra, which in this case numbered 54 men. During the Panama sequence scoring, additional percussionists were called in to play tambourine, timbales, marimba, temple blocks and other exotic instruments unusual to Korngold. When there was one percussionist short, Ray Heindorf, who had orchestrated the sequence, ran around the studio filling in on one instrument and then another. I recall he was wearing beltless trousers and almost dropped them twice while dashing about the stage.[5]

As with many of Korngold's other film scores, the opening credits are at first accompanied by a robust fanfare, which then segues into a slower-paced romantic theme. The fanfare music later returns for the scene in which Thorpe and his men escape captivity in Panama and prepare to set sail for England. As the ship embarks, a chorus is heard singing the song "Strike for the Shores of Dover," which is directly based on the fanfare melody. The romantic theme is used for the scenes between Thorpe and Doña Maria, whose uncle, the villainous Don José (Claude Rains), has been conspiring with King Philip of Spain to launch the Armada against England. Yet another lilting tune is sung by Doña Maria as she tends roses in a garden; this song was later published along with a group of Korngold art songs as his opus 38.[6]

In the climactic duel between Thorpe and the traitorous Lord Wolfingham (Henry Daniell), who tries to prevent Thorpe from informing the queen of plans for the Spanish Armada, Korngold's breathlessly fast-paced music helps to make this one of the most exciting swordfights in cinema history.[7]

The "Jungle March" to which George Korngold referred in his interview is a surprisingly contemporary piece of music, with saxophones and piano in addition to a large battery of percussion instruments. At first, this music may seem a bit out of place in the score, but it does capture the dramatic mood of the scene in which Thorpe's men march through the Panamanian jungle in search of Spanish gold, only to be ambushed by Spanish soldiers.

With this music, Korngold bade farewell to the action and adventure movies that had sparked his imagination for the previous five years.

CHARLIE CHAPLIN: *THE GREAT DICTATOR.* For Charlie Chaplin's first talking picture, *The Great Dictator*, as for his previous films *City Lights* and *Modern Times*, he insisted on creating the melodic motifs himself and hiring someone who could arrange them into a background score. This time around, songwriter Meredith Willson (1902–84) accepted the assignment and received an Oscar nomination in the Original Score category.

Strangely enough, there isn't much original thematic material in *The Great Dictator*'s score. Themes by two famous German composers were borrowed for the film; these include Richard Wagner's Prelude from *Lohengrin* and Johannes Brahms's "Hungarian Dance no. 5," each of which figures in a prominent scene. To the sound of intoxicatingly sweet strings playing the *Lohengrin* music, Hynkel (Chaplin's maniacally funny imitation of Hitler) dreams of world conquest while taking a globe off its stand and performing a ballet atop his desk with it. He repeatedly bounces the globe into the air as though it were a balloon while the soothing strains of the Wagner theme continue to sound.

The other scene with a noteworthy use of borrowed music is probably the most hilarious in the entire film. It features a Jewish barber (Chaplin in his other role) shaving a customer to the strains of Brahms's "Hungarian Dance," which is being broadcast over the radio. Each move of the razor is carefully synchronized to the rhythmic movement of the music, as the barber's movements speed up or slow down to keep time with the beat. There has perhaps never been a more delightful pantomime-with-music in film than this ingeniously choreographed scene.

SHORT CUTS In addition to *Gone with the Wind*, which was just beginning its wide release in 1940, several other significant literary adaptations appeared on screen at the beginning of the new decade.

■■■■ **Alfred Newman.** Chief among these was John Ford's screen adaptation of *The Grapes of Wrath*, which followed *Of Mice and Men* as the second film in as many years based on a John Steinbeck novel. Brilliantly adapted by Nunnally Johnson, the film stars Henry Fonda in one of his best screen roles, as Tom Joad. Tom is the wayward son who returns from prison just as his family is being evicted from their Oklahoma farm. The subsequent trek west in a dilapidated truck along Route 66 is accompanied by Alfred Newman's jaunty music, which is largely based on the folk song "Red River Valley." In many scenes the tune is played on the accordion with no other instrumentation. It is a simple yet effective musical accompaniment.

■■■■ Aaron Copland and Other Symphonic Composers.

Following *Of Mice and Men*, Aaron Copland scored Sam Wood's film version of *Our Town*, Thornton Wilder's acclaimed stage play of life and death in the fictional town of Grovers Corners, New Hampshire. Although the film's literalness in terms of its sets goes against the play's imaginative avoidance of props and staging, Copland's lyrical music is a worthy compensation. His main theme, which he later used as part of his *Our Town* Suite and which he also incorporated into the orchestral suite *Music for Movies* (along with themes from both *The City* and *Of Mice and Men*), is a slow-moving piece. Based on a five-note idea, it uses the tones of the major triad in the pattern C-G-E-C-C. Though he never worked steadily in the film medium, Copland understood the emotional language of film music and successfully achieved the right resonance in his music to match the on-screen imagery.

Copland is one of a small number of composers of symphonic music who found occasional work in Hollywood during the 1940s. Among the others were Werner Janssen (1899–1990), who scored a dozen American-made films, mostly for United Artists; Mario Castelnuovo-Tedesco (1895–1968), who composed a dozen film scores during the 1940s, mostly for Columbia; and Alexandre Tansman (1897–1986), who contributed music for four 1940s films.

■■■■ Franz Waxman.

David O. Selznick followed up the hugely successful *Gone with the Wind* with a film adaptation of Daphne du Maurier's romantic mystery *Rebecca*. To direct the picture, Selznick recruited Englishman Alfred Hitchcock to come to America for the first time. Since England was embroiled in the war, this offer turned out to be particularly fortuitous for Hitchcock, whose penchant for suspense and intrigue resulted in many successful thrillers.

To score *Rebecca*, Selznick employed Franz Waxman, who had been working at MGM since 1936. For this single picture he was loaned to Selznick. Waxman's music propels the viewer into the film with a wonderfully romantic theme that accompanies the opening credits. For the closing scene, in which Manderley, the lavish estate of Max de Winter (Laurence Olivier) and his young second wife (Joan Fontaine), is destroyed in a huge blaze, Waxman ingeniously contributed an ascending series of ominous chords that help to convey a great sense of drama as the camera moves in ever closer to a pillow on Rebecca's bed, on which an embroidered "R" is being encircled by the creeping flames.

■■■■ Miklos Rozsa.

Miklos Rozsa came to America in 1940. His film-composing career had begun in England in 1937 with the score for Alexander Korda's *Knight without Armor*. Evidently Korda was pleased with Rozsa's work, for he began using him regularly. Thus, when Korda relocated his London film company to America in 1940 to complete the filming of *The Thief of Bagdad*, Rozsa came along. Given the resources of a full-scale symphony orchestra, Rozsa created a series of melodious motifs for the assorted characters in this colorful Arabian Nights fantasy. Included in the score are several songs: "I Want to Be a Sailor," sung by Abu (Sabu), and the love song sung by the Princess's old nurse are the most noteworthy. With its gorgeous Technicolor photography, beautiful sets, and impressive visual effects, *The Thief of Bagdad* won Academy Awards in these three categories, and also won Rozsa his first Oscar nomination.

■ ■ ■ ■ **Max Steiner.** Max Steiner began the new decade with several fine scores, including melodious backgrounds for two Bette Davis dramas, *The Letter* (for which he received an Oscar nomination) and *All This and Heaven Too*. Although he would remain productive, he would never again write the sheer numbers of scores that he had created in the 1930s.

B**ERNARD** H**ERRMANN**: R**AISING** K**ANE.** Few film enthusiasts will argue with the critical appraisal that *Citizen Kane* is one of the finest films ever made, even though of the nine Oscars for which it was nominated, it garnered only one (Best Original Screenplay).

For the production of *Citizen Kane*, two extraordinarily talented young men arrived in Hollywood for the first time—Orson Welles, who directed, produced, cowrote, and starred in the film, and Bernard Herrmann, one of the most gifted and dedicated composers ever to work in motion pictures.

Herrmann, a native New Yorker who was born on June 29, 1911, showed musical promise at a young age, despite the fact that neither of his parents was musically inclined. By the age of thirteen he had already won a songwriting contest; during his years at DeWitt Clinton High School, he continued to take music lessons on a private basis. He subsequently became a composition major at New York University, but a fellowship award led him to Juilliard, where he spent two years studying composition with Bernard Wagenaar and conducting with Albert Stoessel.[8]

While at Juilliard, Herrmann got his first taste of scoring for the theater, with a ballet number that he wrote for a Broadway musical called *Americana* (1932). Around this time he also formed the New Chamber Orchestra, which was devoted to the performance of rarely heard music; this was his first regular stint as a conductor.

The next phase of his career is explained by Tony Thomas:

> At the age of 22, Herrmann was hired by the Columbia Broadcasting System to write and conduct music for their serious and educational programs. A year later, in 1933, he was given the post of staff conductor of the CBS Orchestra, which included the production of most of their music programming.[9]

In the fall of 1933, Johnny Green (1908–89) signed a contract with CBS for a radio series called "Music in the Modern Manner." Because Green did not have enough time to handle all his duties, Herrmann, who was recognized by Green as a young talent, became a CBS employee.[10]

By 1934, Green had involved Herrmann in composing original background music for the "Modern Manner" series. The first of Herrmann's original CBS scores was the music for a reading of John Keats's poem "La belle dame sans merci," which was aired that May. Many other Herrmann scores followed for various continuing programs. He managed to juggle the duties of arranging, conducting, and composing for radio with writing music for the concert hall. From 1934 to the end of the decade, several premieres of Herrmann works took place in New York; such works as the *Currier and Ives* Suite were produced during this time.

In 1935, Herrmann became a staff conductor at CBS and began working on the "School of the Air" program; he also served on a project that brought him into contact with the prodigiously talented actor/writer/director Orson Welles. For a series called "Columbia Workshop," Welles adapted William Shakespeare's *Hamlet*, casting himself in the title role; Herrmann was the composer of the incidental score. The two collaborated again two years later on another Shakespearean project—a radio adaptation of *Macbeth*, which aired in two parts on May 2 and 9, 1937.[11]

In 1938, Welles and Herrmann began to collaborate on a regular basis, when CBS invited Welles to bring his Mercury Theatre, a stage company that produced both classic and new works, to radio. On July 11, 1938, "The Mercury Theatre on the Air" premiered with an adaptation of Bram Stoker's *Dracula*. Herrmann was musical director for the show, with a twenty-seven-piece orchestra. Although this program was originally planned as a summer replacement for "The Lux Radio Theatre," it proved to be popular enough to be continued as a Sunday evening offering into the fall.

Thus it was that on Sunday, October 30, 1938, Welles and company aired what has been regarded as the most famous radio broadcast of all time—an adaptation of H. G. Wells's *War of the Worlds*. An updated script by Howard Koch turned the story into what seemed to be a news broadcast. "War of the Worlds" created a sensation.

On August 21, 1939, Welles signed a sixty-three-page contract with RKO, which gave him complete artistic control for two film projects. Subsequently, CBS decided to move the production team of Welles's radio program, now called the "Campbell Playhouse,"[12] to the West Coast so that Welles could continue as both radio producer and filmmaker. As Welles gave more and more attention to possible film projects, however, the CBS series, despite the general excellence of the programs, came to an end on March 31, 1940, with a radio performance of *Jane Eyre*.[13]

After several false starts, screenwriter Herman J. Mankiewicz came up with an original story about a wealthy newspaper tycoon, which became the prototype for the screenplay of a cinematic masterpiece. July 30, 1940, marks the official starting date of principal photography on *Citizen Kane*; Welles served as director while the camera work was supervised by Gregg Toland. Shooting continued until October 23, after which Welles spent the rest of the year working with editor Robert Wise and visual-effects consultant Vernon Walker.[14]

Orson Welles and Bernard Herrmann at a recording session of *Citizen Kane*.

Welles had Bernard Herrmann in mind for the score of *Citizen Kane* even before the film was shot. In fact, Welles sent Herrmann a telegram on July 18, 1940, in which he gave the composer the following instructions:

> Opera sequence is early in shooting, so must have fully orchestrated recorded track before shooting. Susie sings as curtain goes up in the first act, and I believe there is no opera of importance where soprano leads with chin like this. Therefore suggest it be original . . . by you—parody on typical Mary Garden vehicle. . . . Here is a chance for you to do something witty and amusing—and now is the time for you to do it.[15]

The opera sequence, which Welles suggested should be called *Salammbô*, with an ancient Roman setting, is one of several elements in *Citizen Kane* that gave Herrmann exceptional musical opportunities. To understand Herrmann's score, a short synopsis of *Citizen Kane* is necessary.

The film opens with a long-distance shot of an ominously dark castle that stands on an imposing hilltop. In a succession of brief shots, the camera closes in on the window of an upstairs bedroom, where an elderly man lies bedridden. Soon this man expires after uttering one last word—"Rosebud." The life of this man, multimillionaire Charles Foster Kane, is then summarized by means of a newsreel entitled "News on the March," with voice-over narration and music. Shadowy figures are then seen in a projection room, where those in attendance express puzzlement over the meaning of Kane's life. Jerry Thompson (William Alland), one of the reporters present, is ordered to find out the significance of "Rosebud."

From this point on, Kane's life is revealed in a series of loosely connected flashbacks that are framed by Thompson, who first reads the memoirs of Kane's childhood guardian, the wealthy banker Walter Thatcher (George Coulouris). Thompson then embarks on a series of personal interviews with those who knew Kane, including his second wife, Susan Alexander (Dorothy Comingore), who has descended from opera star to hard-drinking lounge singer; Thompson also seeks out two people who formerly worked at the *Inquirer* (the first newspaper in Kane's journalistic empire), Jed Leland (Joseph Cotten) and Mr. Bernstein (Everett Sloane); the final interview is with Kane's butler, Raymond (Paul Stewart).

Through the flashbacks that accompany each interview, the life of Kane is presented like pieces of a jigsaw puzzle, with bits of the story revealed as each of the people questioned gives his or her personal slant. By the end of the film, Kane has been shown as ambitious and charming, but also as ultimately selfish and pitiable, a man incapable of giving love, but always trying to be loved. His political aspirations are destroyed as a result of his flirtation with Susan, who becomes his second wife after the accidental death of his first wife and their son. Kane's later years are spent in accumulating expensive art objects at Xanadu, his palatial estate in Florida. His second marriage ends when Susan, hopelessly frustrated and bored, walks out on

Citizen Kane, with Orson Welles.

him. Kane thereafter lives on in seclusion until his death as a lonely old man. The final scene includes shots of dark smoke rising from one of Xanadu's chimneys, as much clutter is thrown into a furnace. In one of the last closeups, Kane's boyhood sled is revealed, as flames begin to scorch it. At last, we finally understand the meaning of "Rosebud," as we see the name imprinted on the sled.

Stylistically, Herrmann's score shifts many times during the course of the film. Starkly dramatic chords both open and close the film. The music becomes much more romantic for some of the flashbacks, especially for the scene of young Charlie playing with his sled in the snow, and for the first part of the breakfast montage, which is Leland's reminiscence about Kane and his first wife, Emily (Ruth Warrick).

In six short vignettes, the Kanes are seen at breakfasts that span at least ten years. The music shifts from a lilting waltz played by strings to a jaunty tune for woodwinds, and then it shifts again to a darker brass sound. In contrast with the loving and playful conversation of the newlyweds, heard at the outset of the montage, the final breakfast clip shows the more mature couple eating in silence. Their alienation is suggested by Mrs. Kane reading the *Chronicle*, a rival to her husband's newspaper. By this time, the music has shifted back to strings, which play a slower rendition of a bit of the waltz heard earlier. Repeated tones on the harp accompany this passive moment, when no further arguments are likely between the estranged couple.

A variety of marches and other up-tempo tunes, including a ragtime number, are used for the scenes that revolve around Kane's adventures as a newspaper publisher. These lighthearted moments are in striking contrast with the darker music with which the film begins and ends.

The grandest music in the film is the aria composed for the opera *Salammbô*, which is slated as his second wife's operatic debut. Although the aria is weakly sung in the film, due to Susan's inability to demonstrate any strength as a soprano, it is quite a powerful piece. Herrmann revealed the weakness of Susan's singing voice by setting the music in too high a key for the voice used on the soundtrack. If one can get past the inadequacy of the singing, there is in the accompaniment of this aria some of the most glorious and powerful instrumentation that Herrmann ever composed.

Herrmann's biographer, Steven C. Smith, includes the following comments about *Kane*'s music in his book *A Heart at Fire's Center*:

> With *Citizen Kane*, a musical revolution took place. Undeniably Neo-Romantic in style, Herrmann's score was nonetheless unique in its blend of dramatic scoring and its incorporation of indigenous American music, its innovative orchestration and its pioneering use of bridging musical device. . . . Rejecting the then-prevalent Hollywood practice of scoring a film with virtually nonstop music . . . Herrmann instead composed brief aural "bridges" that signaled a quick temporal or scenic transition in the film.[16]

Herrmann, in a lecture given a few years before his untimely death, had the following to say about his score for *Citizen Kane*:

> I decided that I would use the old musical form of the leitmotiv [sic], in other words a theme that is transferred incessantly. So the very first bars I wrote are a series of few notes that dominate the entire film, no matter what's happening. In my mind it was a sort of variant on the ancient hymn "Dies Irae," and seems to suggest to me what the subject of *Kane* was, which is "All is vanity."[17]

Herrmann went on to describe the score's other primary motif, which is first presented as a four-note theme on the vibraphone as Charlie plays in the snow with his sled. "Musically, the prelude tells you what the whole film is about. . . . This second theme tells everybody what Rosebud is, even though they soon forget about it. But the music has told them right away."[18]

Not all the music in the film is by Herrmann. The accompaniment for the newsreel is a collage of previously composed bits of music, including Anthony Collins's "Belgian March" from *Nurse Edith Clavell* (1939), which was used for the newsreel's titles; Alfred Newman's *Gunga Din*, which is heard as Xanadu is shown; plus fragments from the RKO music library, including Roy Webb's music for the RKO films *Reno* (for Kane's growing newspaper empire) and *Five Came Back* (for the clip of Mr. Thatcher).[19]

Some of the musical backgrounds consist of source music, including the 1933 blues tune "In the Mizz," by Charles Barrett and Haven Johnson, which introduces an inebriated Susan Alexander; and Rodgers and Hart's "This Can't Be Love," which is interpolated into the lavish party scene that occurs during a bizarre picnic in the Florida Everglades.[20] Last, there is the Herman Ruby song "Oh Mr. Kane," which is used as Kane's campaign music. The final composite of scoring is as much a jigsaw puzzle as the film's very structure, but the music is consistently appropriate and plays a significant role in elevating the film to the level of a genuine classic.

However remarkable *Citizen Kane* is in every respect, the film's chances for box-office success were severely hampered by the powerful opposition of the Hearst newspaper chain, which not only refused all advertising connected with the film but also threatened to cancel all advertising for any theater which dared to show it. The difficulty arose when William Randolph Hearst was informed by Louella Parsons, the well-known gossip columnist who worked for the Hearst newspapers, that Welles's film was an unflattering fictionalized version of Hearst's life. Despite Welles's public disclaimers about the derivation of the film's screenplay, Hearst wielded his considerable power and tried to block the film's release. RKO boss George Schaefer was doggedly determined to allow *Kane* to be shown, even though other studio heads, wanting to appease Hearst, made offers such as the one proposed by Louis B. Mayer, who made a substantial bid to buy the original film negative.[21] Ultimately, *Citizen Kane* was released on May 1, 1941, after several delays, but no major theater chain would screen the film; therefore it played in only a limited number of independently owned movie houses.

Many Motion Picture Academy members were acquaintances of William Randolph Hearst, who had been a film producer since before 1920. The Academy members were keenly divided on the artistic merits of *Kane* and refused to accord it any Oscars except the writing award, which was really earned by Mankiewicz, who conceived the script, with Welles getting involved only with later drafts.

Bernard Herrmann emerged from the Oscar ceremony for 1941 with a golden statuette, but not for his *Kane* music. Soon after completing the scoring of *Citizen Kane*, he received an offer from RKO to score the film version of Stephen Vincent Benet's *The Devil and Daniel Webster*. Compared to the controversy that surrounded *Kane* as it was being prepared for release, there was little difficulty with this production, except for its title. Because censors objected to the word "Devil" in the title, the film was renamed *All That Money Can Buy*, by which name it was officially entered in the Oscar race. The film was eventually exhibited under several different titles, including *Daniel and the Devil, Here Is a Man,* and *A Certain Mr. Scratch.*[22]

The name "Mr. Scratch" refers to the character of the Devil who, in Benet's story, appears in New Hampshire farmer Jabez Stone's barn when the latter swears he would be willing to sell his soul if he could bring in a healthy crop. Mr. Scratch (Walter Huston) soon produces a seven-year contract, which Stone (James Craig) dutifully signs. Stone has a prosperous seven years, but eventually enlists the legal aid of local hero Daniel Webster (Edward Arnold) to extricate himself from the contract. A most unusual trial then takes place, in which famous persons from the past serve as the jury. Not only does the eloquence of Webster's defense persuade the jury to rule in Stone's favor, but Mr. Scratch is permanently banished from New Hampshire.

Herrmann's fanciful music includes several old fiddler's reels, including "The Devil's Dream," which is heard at a barn dance, and "Pop Goes the Weasel," when Mr. Scratch stirs the dancers into a frenzy. According to Steven C. Smith, the frantic sound of the violin in the latter piece was accomplished by the overdubbing of four separate violin tracks.[23] There is also some eerie ghost music, which accompanies several scenes, including those involving Mr. Scratch and the mysterious Belle (Simone Simon), the beguiling maid Mr. Scratch provides for the newly affluent Stones in their country mansion.

Daniel Webster might be considered a minor scoring effort as compared to *Citizen Kane,* but it won for Herrmann the only Oscar he would ever receive in his illustrious career as composer of some of the most ingenious and original film scores in the history of the motion picture.

ALFRED NEWMAN: *HOW GREEN WAS MY VALLEY.* Based on the warmly nostalgic novel of the same name by Richard Llewellyn, 1941's Oscar-winning film, *How Green Was My Valley,* is a moving portrait of a Welsh mining family, which was actually shot in the hills surrounding California's San Fernando Valley, where a crew of one hundred men labored diligently to construct a facsimile of a Welsh mining town.[24] The finished product looks wonderfully realistic, as shot by cinematographer Arthur Miller, who gave this film a convincingly gritty look. John Ford's skilled directorial hand also played a significant role in highlighting the poignant drama of the Morgan family, whose youngest son Huw (Roddy McDowall), tells the story as a memoir.

To capture the soul of the miners, many Welsh hymns were included in the film. The Welsh Eisteddfod Chorus was brought in to lend them authenticity, as in the opening credits, which are accompanied only by a cappella singing. Alfred Newman, as composer of the film's score, cleverly combined the Welsh tunes with his own original background themes. Most prominent of these themes is an impassioned melody that is first played in ethereal fashion by high strings, accompanied by wordless voices. It is heard several times, including the scene where Huw begins to walk again after a long illness. A borrowed Irish tune called "The Sixpence" provides a soft lyrical accompaniment for scenes between Huw's sister Angharad (Maureen O'Hara) and the local preacher (Walter Pidgeon).

A darker sound prevails in some of the mining scenes, especially the film's climactic mine explosion, when Huw's father (Donald Crisp) is trapped by falling beams and is finally brought up on the elevator, mortally wounded. Throughout the film, Newman's score helps the viewer to maintain a strong sense of emotional attachment to the story, so that *How Green Was My Valley* emerges as an absorbing family chronicle.

MIKLOS ROZSA: FILMS ABOUT WOMEN.

Following *The Thief of Bagdad*, Alexander Korda remained in the United States, where he produced two films in 1941 and a third in 1942. Miklos Rozsa composed the scores for all three films.

The first was *That Hamilton Woman*, the story of the English naval hero Lord Nelson and his relationship with Lady Hamilton, the wife of the English ambassador to Naples. Set against a background of the Napoleonic wars, this film was a thinly disguised morale booster for the Allied forces. The idea for the film was apparently suggested to Korda by Winston Churchill himself, who later spoke of this as his favorite film. The story is a bit slow-paced but maintains interest chiefly because of its two stars, Laurence Olivier and Vivien Leigh. Their portrayal of the famous adulterous lovers carries with it the conviction of their own off-screen affection, and Miklos Rozsa's score is suitably romantic, with a love theme that ranks as one of his loveliest creations. In this lyrical music, a solo violin and a solo cello carry on an intimate dialogue that creates a musical representation of the two lovers, who are not fated to find lasting happiness together.

Another lyrical Rozsa score accompanies Korda's second 1941 film, *Lydia*. Merle Oberon (Korda's wife at the time) appears in the title role of a woman who is reunited for a nostalgic evening with four men from her past. The story is one of irony since three of the men, Michael, Frank, and Bob, remember her fondly, but Richard, whom she considers the great love of her life and whose return she has awaited for forty years, doesn't remember her at all. The musical score includes a pair of memorable themes; the first is a lilting waltz for Lydia, while the other is a love theme that reveals the un-requited nature of her passionate feelings for the one man she truly wanted.

In addition to these two themes, a remarkable set of piano improvisations is played by Frank, a concert pianist who, blind himself, works at a school for the blind run by Lydia. In the scene where he introduces himself to her when he applies for a job, he demonstrates how he can help the children "see" through his music. As he plays, he verbally describes a number of situations with appropriate music. It is obvious from the look on Lydia's face that she is charmed by Frank and his piano playing. In the next scene, which takes place at a school Christmas party, he plays two more pieces: the first, a vivid description of the sea, with the sun setting over the water followed by a storm, and the second, a playful piece about a clown.

SHORT CUTS ■■■■ Franz Waxman.

Following the success of *Rebecca*, Alfred Hitchcock again employed one of its stars, Joan Fontaine, and its composer, Franz Waxman. In *Suspicion*, Lina (Fontaine) is attracted to Johnnie (Cary Grant) and marries him without knowing much about him. She begins to have doubts about him, and eventually believes that he plans to murder her. What could have been a cliché-ridden melodrama emerges as a portrait of gradually accelerating terror, thanks to Fontaine's Oscar-winning performance and Waxman's skillful underscoring, which begins during the opening credits with a swirlingly romantic main theme.

For the most part, Hitchcock kept this film relatively low-key, and Waxman wisely refrained from overaccenting the drama. Only in the final scenes, when Lina is convinced that her husband has caused the death of his best friend and is about to kill her, does the music become intense. In the film's climactic scene, Lina rides in a car with her husband up a steep and winding road. The music becomes increasingly dramatic as he continues to accelerate. Tension mounts as the music provides an exciting crescendo of sound. Ultimately, *Suspicion* is weakened by its fabricated and somewhat implausible ending, but it remains a worthy film.

■■■■ **Meredith Willson.** Set in the Deep South in 1900, Lillian Hellman's play *The Little Foxes*, adapted for the screen by William Wyler, revolves around the cold and heartless Regina Giddens (Bette Davis), whose family runs the town in which they live. She alienates her daughter Alexandra (Teresa Wright), and willfully allows her husband to die. The scene in which Regina's husband Horace (Herbert Marshall) has a heart attack while Regina sits motionless in a chair is chilling to watch. Regina's hardened stare is seen in closeup while Horace gropes for his medicine in the background. There is no music until the moment he falls; then Regina jumps out of the chair, with a dramatic musical outburst.

This film, masterfully photographed by Gregg Toland, who again used the deep-focus style he had employed for *Citizen Kane*, contains such heavy theatrics that a throbbing musical score would have been oppressive. Producer Samuel Goldwyn commissioned songwriter Meredith Willson to write the score, and the result is a sparse accompaniment that relies on spirituals, sung a cappella, for the opening and closing credits. Orchestral music is used only in select moments, most notably when Horace collapses, and later when Alexandra confronts her mother. Very strange, modernistic music is heard as the camera moves in on the hardened face of Regina, who watches from an upstairs window as Alexandra defiantly leaves home.

Although there had already been a few films about various aspects of World War II in Europe and in the Pacific, it was in 1942 that Hollywood filmmakers began in earnest to use the film medium to boost the morale of both the fighting men overseas and the millions of Americans at home who waited anxiously for their return.

HERBERT STOTHART: MRS. MINIVER. MGM led the parade of patriotic films with *Mrs. Miniver*—winner of six Oscars, including Best Picture and Best Director (William Wyler)—which paid tribute to the indomitable British, who suffered long and hard through the Nazi bombing raids during the Battle of Britain in 1940. Although there isn't much actual war footage in the film, the calamitous effect of the bombings on the lives of the residents of a small village near London, where the Miniver family resides, is clear. Through each and every ordeal the Minivers persevere, mostly due to Mrs. Miniver (Greer Garson), who is a pillar of strength to those around her, including her husband (Walter Pidgeon) and her son (Richard Ney), both of whom go off to fight, and her daughter-in-law, Carol (Teresa Wright), who is mortally wounded by flying shrapnel. There is much sentiment in the film, provided especially by the kindly Mr. Ballard (Henry Travers), who wins the annual flower-growing contest in the village with his newest hybrid rose, named the "Miniver Rose," in honor of the protagonist.

Herbert Stothart wisely refrained from smothering this film with too much music. There is an understated violin theme for Mrs. Miniver; but what stands out most is Stothart's borrowing of such familiar musical materials as the hymns "O God Our Help in Ages Past" and "Onward Christian Soldiers," both of which are sung in a church that gets heavily damaged as the film progresses. Also heard is the familiar second theme from Sir Edward Elgar's *Pomp and Circumstance* March no. 1 (also known as "Land of Hope and Glory"), which adds a patriotic flavor to the film.

MORE PATRIOTIC FILMS. Besides *Mrs. Miniver*, more than one hundred other films released in 1942 are clearly patriotic in nature. *Forty-Ninth Parallel* (U.S. title: *The Invaders*) includes the first film score by esteemed English composer Ralph Vaughan Williams (1872–1958). It marks an auspicious but belated debut into film composing, since he was already sixty-nine when he began the score. He would continue to compose film music through the end of the decade, in the course of which he would write a genuine masterpiece of film music, the score for *Scott of the Antarctic* (1948).

Warner Bros. also paid homage to the war effort with *Yankee Doodle Dandy*, in which James Cagney won an Oscar for playing Broadway composer and star George M. Cohan. *Dandy* begins with the elderly Cohan's arrival at the White House for a meeting with President Franklin D. Roosevelt. Cohan expects to be scolded for playing the president in the 1937 Broadway musical *I'd Rather Be Right* but instead receives the Congressional Medal of Honor. It is while awaiting the President that Cohan recalls his long and illustrious career in a flashback that features performances of many Cohan songs, including "Over There," the most popular song during World War I.

Several feature-length documentaries were also released to theaters in 1942. Many major filmmakers, who had enlisted in the armed services after the attack on Pearl Harbor, were put in charge of military film production. Their efforts resulted in some exceptional films, including John Ford's *Battle of Midway* and Frank Capra's *Prelude to War*. These two films won 1942 Oscars in the same category since, for that year only, the usual rules were suspended; four Oscar winners were declared in the Documentary category, which had a total of twenty-five nominees.[25]

BERNARD HERRMANN: THE MAGNIFICENT AMBERSONS. Among the major scores of 1942 is Bernard Herrmann's charming music for Orson Welles's atmospheric version of Booth Tarkington's novel *The Magnificent Ambersons*, which unfortunately was taken out of Welles's hands and considerably altered from its original form. The changes that RKO sanctioned include a new ending and several additional scenes that were shot without either Welles's or Herrmann's participation. In this hybrid state and with a running time that was changed from its original two-hour length to a mere eighty-eight minutes, the picture still managed to receive several Oscar nominations, including citations for both Best Picture and Best Score.

There is a marked contrast between the scores of *Citizen Kane* and Welles's second picture. Where *Kane* is endowed with flamboyantly dramatic music, *Ambersons* consists of a delicate score, largely based on Emil Waldteufel's waltz "Toujours ou jamais." This melody is used as the basis of a clever set of variations in the film's opening sequence, in which Welles's voice is heard narrating the history of the once proud Amberson family of Indianapolis and how their fortune declined over time.

Regrettably, more than half of Herrmann's original score was discarded when the film was reedited. Replacement music by Roy Webb was used for the new scenes shot by RKO studio personnel. Herrmann subsequently demanded that his name be removed from the film's credits. Thus, in the closing-credit sequence, which is announced by Welles without the aid of printed titles, Herrmann's name is conspicuously absent.

ERICH WOLFGANG KORNGOLD: *KINGS ROW.* As skillfully adapted by Casey Robinson, Sam Wood's absorbing drama based on Henry Bellamann's novel *Kings Row* is an episodic saga of several people who grow up in the small Midwestern town of Kings Row. The central figure in the story is Parris Mitchell (Robert Cummings), who befriends the town ne'er-do-well Drake McHugh (Ronald Reagan in his best film role). While Parris becomes a dedicated psychiatrist, Drake marries Randy (Ann Sheridan), and works for the railroad, until an accident leaves him crippled. In one of the film's most memorable scenes, Drake awakens to discover the loss of his legs, which have been needlessly amputated by the sadistic Dr. Gordon (Charles Coburn).

Erich Wolfgang Korngold's main theme is a majestic and noble melody that immediately grabs the viewer's attention during the opening credits. It becomes more lighthearted when Parris, Drake, and their friends are first

Kings Row, with Robert Cummings, Ann Sheridan, and Ronald Reagan.

seen as children. In this score Korngold moved even further away from the romantic style of his late 1930s swashbucklers, which he first abandoned when he created the modernistic musical background for *The Sea Wolf* in 1941. Especially dissonant is the eerie-sounding theme for Louise Gordon (Nancy Coleman), who is troubled by a growing awareness of her father's brutality. The music helps the viewer sense her mental anguish as she tells Parris about what happened to Drake. In the penultimate scene, to assuage Drake's bitterness, Parris tells him how he became crippled. Then Parris races to the home of his sweetheart, while the triumphant main theme returns, this time with a choir added in a lavish arrangement of Ernest Henley's *Invictus.*

MIKLOS ROZSA: *THE JUNGLE BOOK.* Following the fanciful *Thief of Bagdad,* Alexander Korda decided to film Rudyard Kipling's *Jungle Book* with his teenage star Sabu as Mowgli, who is raised by wolves and grows to know the ways and language of animals. Beautifully photographed in Technicolor by Lee Garmes, with brilliant set designs (constructed around Lake Sherwood, just north of Los Angeles), *The Jungle Book* is nevertheless not as entertaining as *The Thief of Bagdad.* Sabu, who had a high-pitched voice and rather limited acting abilities, was part of an ensemble cast in the previous picture but here was the central character. Another problem was the casting of non-Indian actors in key supporting roles; their presence did little to provide a properly authentic atmosphere.

The movie's biggest problem is its script, which features Mowgli's story as a tale told to English travelers by an old villager. If the plot had concentrated on Kipling's stories themselves, the film might have been enchanting, but it is spoiled by a subplot in which three greedy fortune seekers, with Mowgli's help, find a lost city with a hidden treasure. The film descends into formulaic melodrama as one hunter kills the other two. The subsequent forest fire, though colorfully filmed and exciting, adds little to the film.

However faltering *The Jungle Book* may be as drama, Miklos Rozsa's score remains a masterwork. For each animal character, Rozsa devised a separate theme with a particular timbre of orchestral color; for example, the lumbering elephant tune is played by trombones and tubas and the wolves are portrayed by horns.

The music of *The Jungle Book* became the first symphonic film score to be released on records. Shortly after the film was completed, Rozsa conducted the RCA Victor Symphony in an adaptation of the score, with Sabu providing a narration that introduces the various animals (and the instruments of the orchestra which represent them). This historic recording was originally released on a three-record set of 78s, was eventually rereleased on a long-playing record, and has been subsequently reissued many more times. In the late 1950s, Rozsa conducted a new recording of the score with the Frankenland State Symphony Orchestra, with narration by Leo Genn.[26]

MAX STEINER: NOW, VOYAGER. Max Steiner's work at Warner during 1942 comprises a total of seven scores, including a rousing effort for Errol Flynn as George Armstrong Custer in *They Died with Their Boots On* and music for two Bette Davis films, *In This Our Life* and *Now, Voyager*. Not only does *Now, Voyager* feature one of Davis's finest acting showcases, but it includes one of Steiner's most melodious scores, which deservedly won for him the second of his three scoring Oscars.

Seldom has a composer's penchant for lyrically romantic melodies been better demonstrated than in *Now, Voyager*. Basically an extended soap opera, *Voyager* continually soars as Steiner's lush, fully orchestrated strains escort the viewer through a series of episodes in which Charlotte Vale (Bette Davis) undergoes psychiatric treatment to repair the damage done by her domineering mother (Gladys Cooper), whose control of her daughter causes Charlotte to suffer a nervous breakdown.

With intensive treatment, Dr. Jaquith (Claude Rains) helps Charlotte find herself, and as part of his therapy she goes on a cruise, where she attracts the attention of the lonely, albeit married Jerry (Paul Henreid). Love blossoms, but the two go back to uncertain fates in their respective domestic situations, she with her mother and he with his unloving wife. Eventually, they meet again, through Jerry's adolescent daughter Tina. Tina is being treated at the sanitarium to which Charlotte returns, following her mother's death. The balance of the film involves Charlotte's attempts to free the introverted Tina of her shyness, since she sees Tina as a carbon copy of herself at that age. The film ends with Charlotte and Jerry making a pledge to remain close friends, if nothing more.

Now Voyager is an engrossing drama, largely due to its impressive cast, but Steiner also deserves credit for giving the film so much dramatic credibility. The love theme, which is heard several times, is one of Steiner's most inspired creations, with some very unusual harmonic shifts. This melody was later used by Steiner for a song entitled "It Can't Be Wrong," in which form the *Now, Voyager* theme became familiar to millions of listeners who had never seen the film. A popular recording was released in early 1943, which stayed on the charts for nineteen weeks.[27]

SHORT CUTS ■■■■ **Alfred Newman.** Following his lovely, Welsh-flavored score for *How Green Was My Valley*, Alfred Newman stepped into Erich Wolfgang Korngold territory for the robust scores of *The Black Swan* and *Son of Fury*. Although not on the same level as Korngold's *Sea Hawk*, the music of *The Black Swan* is consistently pleasing, with a number of colorfully orchestrated themes that keep the tale of privateer Jamie Waring (Tyrone Power) moving at a brisk pace. Especially memorable is the choral music used during the main title. Elsewhere, an exotic motif that is reminiscent of Newman's score for *The Hurricane* is heard several times. Used throughout the film is a high-sounding trumpet motif which punctuates almost every scene. The climactic battle is completely under-scored, with a marchlike theme that helps sustain a mood of excitement.

Almost as successful is Newman's melodious score for John Cromwell's *Son of Fury*. As in *The Black Swan*, there is a dramatic fanfarelike first theme, played by trumpets, and an exotic love theme that again bears similarities to Newman's "Moon of Manakoora," from *The Hurricane*. This second theme, set in triple meter, is most memorably heard in an unaccompanied choral arrangement that underscores the scene in which Ben (Tyrone Power) prepares to leave his place of refuge on a tropical island (and the native girl played by Gene Tierney) and return to England. As he bids fare-well, the lilting choral music adds to the tenderness of the scene.

■■■■ **Dimitri Tiomkin.** *The Moon and Sixpence*, which was adapted from H. Somerset Maugham's novel inspired by the life of painter Paul Gauguin, contains one of Tiomkin's most lyrical scores. The main-title theme, in a richly romantic idiom, includes a rising melodic line that gradually builds in intensity.

Once the painter Charles Strickland (George Sanders) reaches Tahiti, the score takes on an exotic flavor, with native drums that are heard in several scenes. The lullaby melody Strickland's native wife hums to their baby is based on one of the motifs introduced during the opening credits. The score is seldom prominent, except at the end, after the artist's death, when his wife, acting upon her husband's prior instructions, sets fire to their home. As Charles's art collection goes up in flames, Tiomkin's music celebrates the end of the painter's life in almost majestic fashion.

■■■■ **Richard Hageman.** *The Shanghai Gesture* may be one of Josef von Sternberg's lesser films, but with some atmospheric production values plus an unusually effective score by Richard Hageman, the film sur-mounts its plot shortcomings. In this movie, Hageman's style is far removed from the Western style of his Oscar-winning music for *Stagecoach*. Since most of the film takes place inside a Shanghai casino run by Madame Gin Sling (Ona Munson), Hageman's score strives to create an atmosphere of romance mixed with intrigue. When Poppy (Gene Tierney) becomes a com-pulsive gambler, the score conveys a sense of restlessness and danger, with lots of woodwind trills used to supply dramatic tension.

■■■■ **Frank Churchill and Edward Plumb.** Following the song-filled *Pinocchio* and *Dumbo*, Disney shifted gears with the animated film version of Felix Salten's 1923 novel *Bambi, a Life in the Woods*. Instead of creating a musical film in which the animal characters would actually sing the songs, the composers of *Bambi*'s score included several vocal numbers which were intended as background music. A choir is heard at various points in the film, including the opening credits, in which the score's main theme, "Love Is a Song," is featured.

The musical score of *Bambi*, which was composed by Frank Churchill and Edward Plumb, is intricately synchronized with the animation, especially in the scene that includes the song "Little April Showers." At first, a solo oboe provides the sound of raindrops. At the height of the storm, a wordless choir contributes a wind effect, while cymbals and timpani convey the sounds of lightning and thunder. There are many charming moments in this score, which deservedly won an Oscar nomination.

1943

ALFRED NEWMAN: *THE SONG OF BERNADETTE*. In his forty-year career as a film musician, Alfred Newman's name is listed in the credits of over 250 films. After a decade of working for Samuel Goldwyn, every score that he wrote between 1942 and 1960 was for 20th Century-Fox, where he was in charge of the music department.

Newman has the distinction of being the most Oscar-nominated film composer ever, with forty-five citations, and the only film musician to win nine of the golden statuettes. Although the vast majority of those Oscars were for musical films, Newman also won the award for his inspired original score for the 1943 religious drama *The Song of Bernadette*.

When Fox decided to film Franz Werfel's novel based on the story of Bernadette Soubirous, the French teenager who claimed she actually saw a vision of the Blessed Mother in a grotto near a dump site outside Lourdes in 1858, the studio gambled that audiences could accept the unexplainable aspects of the story without scoffing. To lessen the possibility of alienating non-Catholics, the identity of the Blessed Mother was never once mentioned. Instead, she was referred to as a "beautiful lady." Nonetheless, only the most naive moviegoers would not connect this story with the reported apparitions.

The Song of Bernadette, with Jennifer Jones.

The film's producers also gambled on their choice of a leading lady. The selection of Jennifer Jones, then twenty-four, proved to be an inspired bit of casting. By lifting her voice out of its normal register, Jones was able to convince audiences that Bernadette was only a teenager at the time of the apparitions. Her performance also impressed members of the Motion Picture Academy, who voted her the Oscar as Best Actress of 1943. She was surrounded by a stalwart supporting cast of veteran character actors, including Anne Revere as her mother, Charles Bickford as a parish priest, and Gladys Cooper as a nun who remains skeptical about Bernadette's visions.

Though the film is extremely long for that era (156 minutes), George Seaton's excellent script, Henry King's sensitive direction, and Arthur Miller's Oscar-winning cinematography sustain the viewer's interest. But the real glue that holds this picture together is Alfred Newman's poignant music.

The score is richly orchestrated, with a women's chorus added for the apparition scenes. Especially noteworthy is the music for the scene of Bernadette's first vision, which begins visually with a little gust of wind and the rustling of leaves. The music starts softly with the strings, and as the wind increases in velocity, the music begins to swell to a dramatic climax. When the "beautiful lady" appears, the music becomes very ethereal, with high tones on the violins. Although only Bernadette can see the lady, we in the viewing audience are allowed to share in the mystic moment because we see her too.

The music of *Bernadette* became the second film score to be commercially recorded. Newman, who like Victor Young was under contract to Decca Records, used a performing ensemble simply identified as "Alfred Newman and His Orchestra" to record score excerpts that were released on a set of 78s. Like Rozsa's *Jungle Book*, the *Bernadette* score has been re-released many times. Regrettably, the sound of the strings on the original recording was very strident, and that tone quality has prevailed on all subsequent releases.[28]

Max Steiner: *Casablanca*. No film shown during 1943 was more topical than Warner Bros.' *Casablanca*, which features a microcosmic view of World War II. The story of how this film came about is almost as interesting as the movie's plot, for many casting and script changes were made along the way. Due to the popularity of *Kings Row*, Warner Bros. was apparently planning to reunite Ronald Reagan and Ann Sheridan in the roles of Rick Blaine, proprietor of the Café Americain, and Ilsa Lund, wife of Czech underground leader Victor Laszlo. But Humphrey Bogart became the final choice for Rick and Ingrid Bergman was borrowed from the Selznick studio to play Ilsa. The unique chemistry of these two makes it difficult to conceive of other actors in the roles.

The screenplay, which was based on an unproduced play by Murray Burnett and Joan Allison called *Everybody Goes to Rick's*, went through several revisions. The Epstein brothers, Julius and Philip, prepared an early draft, which was later revised by Howard Koch, whose previous claim to fame was the radio script for Orson Welles's *War of the Worlds*.

Most of the story takes place inside the Café Americain, which is owned by Rick, a disillusioned American expatriate. He has come into possession of two stolen letters of transit which would provide safe passage out of Casablanca, a city that is carefully guarded by the Germans. When Victor Laszlo (Paul Henreid) brings his wife Ilsa into the nightclub one evening, Rick immediately recognizes her as the woman with whom he had an affair in Paris when the German occupation began. Rick is now Laszlo's only hope of leaving Morocco.

As the shooting of the movie progressed, even the stars did not know how the movie was supposed to end. Several versions were filmed by director Michael Curtiz before the film's final denouement was decided upon.

Despite the disarray in the production of *Casablanca*, there has never been a movie with so much often-quoted dialogue. Ironically, the film's most famous line, "Play it again, Sam," is an inaccurate quote; the word "again" is not spoken. When Ilsa recognizes Sam, the piano player, who used to play a song for Rick and her in Paris, she tells him, "Play it once, for old time's sake . . . play it, Sam. Play 'As Time Goes By.'"

The Herman Hupfeld song "As Time Goes By" had been decided upon by the screenwriters without conferring with Max Steiner, who had been assigned the background score. Steiner argued strenuously in favor of an original song of his own composition, but the scene between Ilsa and Sam had already been shot, with Bergman humming a few bars of "As Time Goes By." By the time Steiner began working on the score, Bergman had already had her hair cut short for *For Whom the Bell Tolls* and any reshooting of her scenes in *Casablanca* was thereby rendered impossible.[29]

Steiner may not have been happy with the situation, but he still managed to make meaningful use of the melody of "As Time Goes By" whenever

Bergman and Bogart were on-screen together. It connects them musically and reinforces the audience's belief that they still care deeply for each other, despite her avowed devotion to her husband and his work.

Steiner's score includes several borrowings besides the Hupfeld song. "La Marseillaise," the French national anthem, represents the Allied cause, whereas two German songs, "Deutschland über alles" and "Die Wacht am Rhein," are simultaneously interpolated for the Nazis who have military control over Casablanca. The resulting score is heavily laden with melodic references to these tunes; Steiner's ingenious use of them results in a score that not only enhances the dramatic situations, but also plays heavily on the viewer's sympathies for the Allies. The emotional impact of this film is so remarkably undimmed by the passage of time that, after more than fifty years, *Casablanca* remains a vivid portrayal of human conflict.

MIKLOS ROZSA: *FIVE GRAVES TO CAIRO.* Miklos Rozsa's affiliation with London films was terminated when Alexander Korda decided, upon the completion of *The Jungle Book*, to move his company back to England. Rozsa liked working in Hollywood and subsequently signed with Paramount, where he met a director with whom he would collaborate several times over the next thirty-five years—Billy Wilder.

Rozsa's first project at Paramount, *Five Graves to Cairo*, was the first film that Wilder and Charles Brackett did together with Wilder as director, Brackett as producer, and the two as coauthors.

Five Graves to Cairo was a timely spy thriller because of its North African setting. With the fall of Tobruk in the autumn of 1942, Field Marshal Erwin Rommel was on the verge of conquering the entire northern part of the Dark Continent. In *Five Graves*, a British soldier (Franchot Tone), after falling out of his tank, finds his way on foot to a French outpost. He becomes a spy and assumes the identity of a waiter who has been sympathetic to the German cause. By gaining Rommel's confidence, he learns the whereabouts of five underground fuel storage depots (the "five graves" of the title).

Rozsa's music begins with a dark-hued march theme, very dramatic in its minor-key harmony. There is also stirring music for the concluding battle, and there is a tender theme for the British soldier's visit to the grave of the young Alsatian woman (Anne Baxter), who had assisted him in his efforts to learn the Nazis' military secrets.

Although Wilder and Brackett were pleased with Rozsa's music, Paramount's music director became enraged about Rozsa's refusal to remove a few dissonant tones. Wilder intervened and told the music director to stop interfering with Rozsa's score.[30]

SHORT CUTS ■■■ Dimitri Tiomkin. Another creative association that began in 1943 was that of Dimitri Tiomkin with Alfred Hitchcock. Tiomkin's first Hitchcock score was for the atmospheric thriller *Shadow of a Doubt*, in which Joseph Cotten plays a supposedly suave relative who comes back to the small California town of Santa Rosa, where he is idolized by his niece (Teresa Wright), until she discovers that he is the notorious "merry widow" murderer.

Starting with the opening credits Tiomkin provides the viewer with a musical clue to Cotten's villainy by using Lehar's waltz theme from *The Merry Widow*. In the course of the film, this lilting melody is subjected to some stark dissonance and some brash orchestration. Tiomkin's cleverness in this score seems a perfect match for Hitchcock's bizarre sense of humor.

■ ■ ■ **Erich Wolfgang Korngold.** In 1943, Erich Wolfgang Korngold did just one score—the beautiful music for *The Constant Nymph*, in which Joan Fontaine plays a frail young musician whose love for a composer (Charles Boyer) is initially thwarted by his infatuation with a well-heeled socialite (Alexis Smith). Eventually, the two musicians merge their creative talents to compose a piece of music which is performed at the film's conclusion. The work, entitled "Tomorrow," is an extended cantata-like composition for solo contralto, women's choir, and orchestra. The rich romanticism of Korngold's music for this film is in striking contrast to the ebullient theatricality of his 1930s scores for epic adventure films.

■ ■ ■ **Franz Waxman.** Meanwhile, Franz Waxman left MGM in 1943, after a term of seven years, and joined the ranks at Warner Bros. Among the distinctive works created during his first year there is *Old Acquaintance*, the first Bette Davis film in several years not to have a Max Steiner score. His other work for Warner Bros. that year includes patriotic backgrounds for *Air Force* and *Edge of Darkness*.

■ ■ ■ **Victor Young.** Victor Young's dramatically charged music for Sam Wood's film version of Ernest Hemingway's *For Whom the Bell Tolls* is one of the best efforts of his career. None of his other scores so fully captures the range and scope of the film it accompanies. Young's music underscores the story of an American professor who joins a group of Loyalist guerrillas during the Spanish Civil War and agrees to blow up a strategic bridge. Robert Jordan (Gary Cooper), the American, finds their constant quarreling hard to bear, but is soothed by Maria (Ingrid Bergman), who has been rescued from a brutal confinement, during which time her head was shaved.

The plot is long and rambling, but Young's music, which shifts back and forth between dramatic pseudo-Spanish music and a sensual love theme, prevents the film from becoming dull. The movie is also aided immeasurably by the chemistry of the starring duo, and by the dynamic screen presence of Katina Paxinou, who plays Pilar, a fiery guerrilla leader.

■ ■ ■ **Edward Ward.** In Universal's Technicolor remake of the silent classic *Phantom of the Opera*, Claude Rains plays Enrique Claudin, a talented Parisian composer, who strangles a music publisher for stealing his piano concerto. Claudin is then disfigured when the publisher's employee, who had watched the strangling, throws acid on his face. Combining operatic scenes with macabre melodramatics, *Phantom* contains an interesting score by Edward Ward (1896–1971). Ward arranged an entire operatic sequence for the film by adapting parts of Tchaikovsky's Symphony no. 4. Other borrowings include various Chopin melodies, which were incorporated into an operatic vocal scene entitled "Amour et gloire." Ward contributed one main theme of his own composition which serves both as the principal melody of the Phantom's piano concerto and as an operatic number. Ward's score provides the film with a romantic sound, which is appropriate in view of the story's nineteenth-century setting. In the final analysis, with the robust singing of Nelson Eddy and company and the beautiful sets and costumes, this version of *Phantom* works better as a musical than as a horror story.

1944

David Raksin.

Courtesy of David Raksin

DAVID RAKSIN: *LAURA*. David Raksin (b. 1912) got an early taste for the cinema from his father, who conducted scores for silent films at the Metropolitan Opera House in his native Philadelphia.

The younger Raksin began studying the piano at an early age, and also taught himself the organ and percussion. From his clarinet-playing father he learned about the woodwinds. At the age of twelve, he organized his own dance band, and by fifteen, he was a member of the local chapter of the musicians' union.[31]

Raksin subsequently got a degree in music at the University of Pennsylvania, and then headed for New York, where he made arrangements for various dance bands, including that of Benny Goodman. He also played piano for many such groups and thus expanded his already growing feel for jazz. He spent two years as an arranger for the Harms music publishing company. After making some valuable contacts with other arrangers, such as Eddie Powell and Herbert Spencer, he got his first call to come to Hollywood. In fact, it was because of a recommendation from Powell and Spencer that Alfred Newman decided, in 1935, to take a chance on David Raksin as his associate on the Chaplin film *Modern Times*. According to Tony Thomas:

> Newman would conduct the score but hadn't time to arrange Chaplin's music. Raksin's job was to make musical logic from the humming and whistling of Chaplin. . . . [T]he job spread out over a period of five months, a rough baptism but one which enabled Raksin to confirm his ambition to compose for the screen.[32]

In the late 1930s, Raksin arranged, adapted, and collaborated on scores of a large number of features, shorts, cartoons, and documentaries. At Fox he worked with David Buttolph and Cyril J. Mockridge on the music for several films between 1938 and 1940. In the early 1940s, he began to get solo scoring stints; by the time Newman assigned him *Laura* in 1944, Raksin was primed for the job.

Often a producer or director will give specific instructions about the type of music he wants for a film. In the case of *Laura*, Otto Preminger, who was both producer and director, had in mind a familiar song which would serve as a theme for the mysterious Laura Hunt (Gene Tierney), who is thought to have been murdered. After unsuccessfully attempting to secure the rights to George Gershwin's "Summertime," Preminger decided upon Duke Ellington's "Sophisticated Lady." Raksin met with Preminger on a Friday, and objected that the Ellington song was too familiar and would elicit wrong associations from the audience. Preminger gave Raksin until the following Monday to produce his own theme.

A weekend of struggle ensued, during which no usable ideas came to mind. Finally, on Sunday night, as Raksin was rereading a letter from his wife that he had received the day before, he began to realize that she was going to seek a divorce. In a state of mental anguish, he sat down at the piano, and the first phrase of the *Laura* theme came to him spontaneously. Thus was born, in a state of sorrow, one of the most hauntingly beautiful compositions ever written for a film.[33]

Based on a Vera Caspary story, *Laura* is a murder mystery with numerous plot twists. In the investigation that follows the murder of Laura Hunt, detective Mark McPherson (Dana Andrews) becomes infatuated with a portrait of Laura that hangs on a wall in her apartment, where the murder occurred. He also meets two men who were involved with her, a snobbish columnist and radio personality named Waldo Lydecker (Clifton Webb) and her fiancé (Vincent Price). Midway through the film, the mystery cleverly shifts gears, as the body thought to be Laura's turns out not to be.

Connecting the loose threads of the film is David Raksin's music, which is almost exclusively based on the theme that he composed during his fateful weekend. The music is especially noteworthy in the scene where Mark looks around Laura's apartment and can't take his eyes off her portrait. Here the *Laura* theme begins with a haunting piano line accompanied by strings; it then builds to a lushly orchestrated statement. Without a single line of dialogue, Raksin's music ingeniously conveys McPherson's feelings for the supposedly dead Laura. This is one of the most powerful moments in the film, and one that is completely dependent on music to set the mood and convey the emotions of the character on screen.

Despite the studio's lack of publicity for this film, due to the channeling of all available resources into the promotion of *Wilson*, *Laura* was a box-office success and the theme went on to become a popular hit. Woody Herman's recording debuted on *Your Hit Parade* on April 21, 1945, and spent fourteen weeks among the nation's top ten recordings, reaching the top spot on June 2.[34] Eventually, Johnny Mercer added lyrics to the theme and several vocal versions were recorded.

Laura, with Clifton Webb and Dana Andrews, plus portrait of Gene Tierney.

From 1937 until 1946, each studio and production unit was guaranteed an automatic Oscar nomination in every music category, but only one nominee could be submitted from each company. Thus, because *Wilson* was

Darryl F. Zanuck's pet project and therefore Fox's official entry in the 1944 Academy Awards, *Laura*'s music never stood a chance of being nominated.[35]

MAX STEINER: *SINCE YOU WENT AWAY.* Max Steiner's most exemplary score of the year, which won for him a third Oscar, was written for David Selznick's sentimental film about the home front during World War II, *Since You Went Away.* This score has more melodic material than any other Steiner score with the exception of *Gone with the Wind.* A stirring string theme is heard during the opening credits. There are specific themes for characters, including a bluesy theme for the maid (Hattie McDaniel); a sprightly theme for Brig (Shirley Temple), the younger daughter of Anne Hilton (Claudette Colbert); and even a comic theme, played by contrabassoon, for Soda, the family's English bulldog. One of the film's more prominent themes is a borrowed one, namely the lilting waltz from *A Star Is Born,* which is heard in scenes involving Anne and Lieutenant Tony Willet (Joseph Cotten). Another theme, which closely paraphrases the 1943 song "I'll Be Home for Christmas," is used for scenes between Anne's older daughter Jane (Jennifer Jones) and her boyfriend Bill (Robert Walker). This melody is heard most effectively in the memorable scene at a station in which Jane tearfully chases the train that is transporting her sweetheart off to war. Though this scene was much mimicked in comedy films of the 1980s, the original, which is paced by a gradually accelerating tempo that suggests the increasing velocity of the train, still retains a powerful emotional quality.

SHORT CUTS ■■■■ **Miklos Rozsa.** With a brilliant script by Raymond Chandler and the film's director, Billy Wilder, *Double Indemnity,* the movie adaptation of James M. Cain's lurid novel of the same name, contains incisive dialogue for Phyllis Dietrichson (Barbara Stanwyck) and Walter Neff (Fred MacMurray), especially in the scene of their first meeting, which sets this dark tale of deception and murder into motion. The tense, dramatic music of *Double Indemnity* was composed by Miklos Rozsa, whose score for Wilder's earlier film, *Five Graves to Cairo,* impressed the director so much that Rozsa was virtually guaranteed the job of scoring the new film.

The ominous funeral march that accompanies the opening credits immediately establishes an atmosphere of impending doom. There is also an agitated string melody that is repeated throughout the film as a scene-connecting device; this idea also conveys an aura of suspense and helps to propel the story forward. This score made Rozsa the quintessential musical voice for the film noir, a genre that became increasingly popular as the decade continued.

■■■■ **Bernard Herrmann.** Bernard Herrmann's collaboration with Orson Welles continued with *Jane Eyre,* although here Welles's involvement was limited to acting (as Edward Rochester). *Jane Eyre* features one of Herrmann's most atmospheric scores. Long-sustained melodic tones help to define the repressed feelings of Jane (Joan Fontaine) and the dark secret about the mysterious presence in Thornfield Hall's tower.

■■■■ **Victor Young.** Victor Young produced the music for the romantic ghost story *The Uninvited,* in which the character played by Ray Milland composes a piano piece for the young lady who formerly owned the supposedly haunted house in which he lives. Since her name is Stella, he gives his music the title "Stella by Starlight." With lyrics later added by Ned Washington, this beautiful theme is an undeniable asset to the film in which it was introduced.

MIKLOS ROZSA AND THE THEREMIN. Like so many other composers who worked in Hollywood during the Golden Age, Miklos Rozsa had a European background.

He was born in Budapest in 1907, where he spent his first eighteen years. Although his industrialist father had no great interest in music, Rozsa's mother was a talented pianist. At age five, the young Miklos began studying the violin, and at seven, he composed a march and also performed a Mozart violin concerto while dressed as the great child prodigy, complete with powdered wig.[36] After finishing high school in 1925, he enrolled at the University of Leipzig, but switched to the Conservatory of Music the next year. By the time he turned twenty-one, Rozsa not only had graduated with high honors, but also had been put under contract by the music-publishing firm of Breitkopf and Haertel.

Rozsa's career as a composer of concert-hall music developed steadily thereafter, with several published pieces of chamber music. He remained in Leipzig as an assistant to his composition professor Hermann Grabner until 1931, when he moved to Paris. In 1934, his orchestral work Theme, Variations and Finale brought him international recognition when it was introduced by Charles Munch. It was Arthur Honegger, one of *Les Six*, who gave Rozsa the idea of composing music for movies. However, there was little film employment available in Paris for a composer who had not done film music before. Rozsa moved to London in 1935, where further orchestral scores increased his name recognition. His ballet score *Hungaria* proved to be the work that got him his first film-scoring assignment. Director Jacques Feyder heard *Hungaria*, invited Rozsa to dinner, and subsequently hired him to score *Knight without Armor*, which Feyder was directing for Alexander Korda's company, London Films. When this movie was released in 1937, Rozsa's career as a film composer was launched.

Despite this success, Rozsa never thought of himself as a film composer per se. Rather, he wished to be considered simply a composer because of his keen interest in both music for the concert hall and film scoring. Throughout his active career Rozsa would never withdraw from either of these musical pursuits. As late as the 1980s, he continued to score films while still managing to find the time to complete a series of solo sonatas, including works for the violin, the clarinet, the guitar, and the oboe.

Rozsa's fame as a film composer eventually eclipsed his recognition as a composer of symphonic, chamber, and choral works, thanks to his long-term working relationships with filmmakers such as Alexander Korda and Billy Wilder. It was Korda's production of *The Thief of Bagdad* that brought Rozsa to the United States for the first time, when the entire production crew of this fantasy film was uprooted from London in 1940 because of the Nazi air raids. The filming was completed in Hollywood, where Rozsa wrote the score at a studio that Korda rented for his production staff. After his work on this film was finished, Rozsa remained in America. In 1943, he began a term of employment at Paramount. Billy Wilder's *Five Graves to Cairo* was the first of eight films he would score for that studio over a five-year period.

Miklos Rozsa.

Courtesy of Nicholas Rozsa

With Wilder's next film, *Double Indemnity*, Rozsa embarked on what was to become one of the most celebrated phases of his film-music career. With its daringly dissonant music, the score of *Double Indemnity* caught the attention of several filmmakers; but the one person who seems to have truly revered this score was Alfred Hitchcock, who at the time was directing *Spellbound*, a film that attempted to break new ground in its use of psychotherapy and hypnosis as plot devices. Hitchcock requested that Rozsa find a "new sound" that could represent an amnesia victim's paranoia about a murder he fears he has committed. Rozsa responded by incorporating in his orchestration one of the world's first electronic instruments, the theremin.

The theremin is a revolutionary device that was named by its Russian inventor, Leon Theremin, when he first demonstrated it in 1920. It consists of two rods that project, one vertically and one horizontally, from a rectangular wooden cabinet. The vertical rod controls the pitch, and the horizontal one, the volume. When the instrument is activated, an electromagnetic field is set up between the two rods, and as the player's hands move between the rods, a humming sound is produced. At no time do the hands come into physical contact with the instrument. It is possible to create a variety of pitches by moving the hands around, and a rapid waving motion produces a vibrato effect.

Although *Spellbound* has the distinction of being the first motion picture to use electronically produced sounds in a prominent way, this film actually represents Rozsa's third attempt to incorporate electronic effects into his film music. In 1940, he had wanted to use the *ondes martenot*, a French electronic keyboard instrument that is capable of producing single tones with a vibrato effect similar to that of the theremin, for the genie sequences in *The Thief of Bagdad*; but Maurice Martenot, the instrument's inventor and sole performer, was called up to fight for France and thus was unavailable. In 1941, with Martenot still at war, Rozsa thought again about using Leon Theremin's device, since both producer Walter Wanger and director Henry Hathaway wanted him to use an eerie sound in his score for the war film *Sundown*. Neither was interested in spending the money to import a theremin from Europe, so Rozsa resolved the problem by using a musical saw.[37]

Leon Theremin, with the prototype of his invention, the theremin, circa 1929.

With *Spellbound*, Rozsa's desire to incorporate actual electronic sounds into a film score would finally meet with success. In the film, Gregory Peck appears as "J. B.," an amnesia victim who arrives at a private sanitarium posing as its new director, Dr. Edwardes. He soon learns that the man he pretends to be has recently been murdered, and he is the most likely suspect in that person's death. Ingrid Bergman plays Dr. Constance Peterson, a member of the psychiatric staff, who takes more than a casual interest in this troubled man. Believing him to be innocent of any wrong-doing, she surreptitiously attempts to help him regain his memory through hypnosis, and before long a personal relationship develops.

Rozsa's score includes a romantic main theme that conveys the passionate feelings of

Hearst Newspaper Collection/University of Southern California

Spellbound, with Gregory Peck and Ingrid Bergman.

the doctor for her patient; a more light-hearted and faster-paced melody is used for the scenes in which the two of them are traveling in search of people and places that might help to jog his memory. The third principal theme is the most unusual since it represents the paranoia of Gregory Peck's character, who has flashbacks and troubling dreams. For these moments, including dream sequences ingeniously designed for the film by Salvador Dali, Rozsa assigned the melodic line to the theremin. Dr. Samuel Hoffman, who became known in Hollywood for his ability to play this novel instrument, performed Rozsa's melodic line for the film's soundtrack.[38]

As a result of *Spellbound*'s revolutionary score, Rozsa was asked to use the theremin several more times, but he agreed to its further use on only three occasions, the first of which came immediately after the completion of *Spellbound.* For *The Lost Weekend,* Billy Wilder's film version of Charles Jackson's harrowing novel of the same name, about a frustrated writer's alcohol addiction, Rozsa employed the theremin for scenes in which the story's principal character, Don Birnam (Ray Milland), is under the influence of the bottle. In one of the film's most memorable scenes, Birnam is desperately trying to get some cash by pawning his typewriter, but since it is Yom Kippur, all the pawn shops along New York's Third Avenue are closed. The music vividly expresses the inner voice of Birnam's mind, which goes from thirst to anxiety to sheer panic, through the repeated use of a four-note idea, the first two tones of which are a rising octave. The theremin projects this idea with a pseudovocal timbre that becomes truly frightening as it repeats the tones with a gradually increasing volume.

The film's most frightening scene comes later, as Birnam experiences delirium fits. In his hallucinations he observes a bat giving chase to a mouse and eventually biting it, with streams of blood trickling down the wall. Again the theremin's unique sound conveys the writer's rising panic, which comes to a climax with a shattering force as he screams loudly and repeatedly, to the accompaniment of Rozsa's gripping music.

When the Academy Awards for 1945's eligible films were announced, *The Lost Weekend* emerged as the big winner, with Oscars for Best Picture, Best Actor (Milland), Best Director (Wilder), and Best Screenplay (Charles Brackett and Wilder). Although Rozsa was nominated for his score, he did not win for *The Lost Weekend*; instead, it was his score for *Spellbound*, also nominated, that brought him his first Oscar.

Rozsa later commented that he would have preferred to win for *The Lost Weekend* because he felt that Billy Wilder's picture had the stronger score. However, *Spellbound*'s music has proved to be extremely popular, in the concert arrangement of the score that Rozsa made at the request of Broadway composer Jerome Kern, who was part owner of the Chappell Publishing Company. Chappell had previously published the *Warsaw* Concerto, which Richard Addinsell had arranged from his score for *Dangerous Moonlight* in 1941. The immense popularity of that symphonic work convinced executives at Chappell that a concert piece based on *Spellbound*'s music could have similar success. The parallel between the two scores even extended to their titles, with Rozsa's work to be named *Spellbound* Concerto. When Rozsa protested that, without a prominent solo part, the work really didn't qualify to be called a "concerto," Kern told him to ignore such technicalities, saying "Oh, never mind that."[39]

Rozsa complied with the publishers by arranging an orchestral suite of *Spellbound*'s principal themes. Later, he rearranged the music and included a prominent solo piano part, and in this revised version the *Spellbound* Concerto has become a popular concert piece. The premier performance was given by Rozsa's long-time friend, pianist Leonard Pennario, for whom Rozsa later wrote his Piano Concerto, opus 31 (1967). In the 1980s, Rozsa greatly enlarged the *Spellbound* Concerto by producing a new version for two pianos and orchestra. This arrangement was given its world premiere in Salt Lake City in July 1984, and was subsequently recorded by Varese Sarabande, with Elmer Bernstein conducting.[40]

Following his celebrated use of the theremin in 1945, Rozsa was strongly urged to use the instrument several more times, but he steadfastly resisted, for fear of being typecast as Hollywood's resident theremin composer. In 1947, however, he did use the theremin a third time, to convey a mysterious secret in Delmer Daves's *The Red House*. After that, he again refused to use it, despite being asked by many filmmakers, including William Wyler, who thought it would be ideal for the Christ theme in his 1959 remake of *Ben-Hur*. Rozsa resisted Wyler's suggestion and wound up using an organ instead of the wavy-toned theremin.

When Carl Reiner made the clever comedy *Dead Men Don't Wear Plaid* in 1981, he interspersed new footage of Steve Martin and Rachel Ward with clips from several 1940s films that had originally been scored by Rozsa. Reiner hired Rozsa to compose a score that would incorporate the music contained in the various bits and pieces of old footage. Since the new film was supposed to both look and sound like a film noir, Rozsa decided to use the theremin one more time. The task of making this patchwork quilt into a cohesive whole was Rozsa's final film-music assignment.

Little other use of the theremin was made in film music, except for a few films such as Robert Siodmak's *Spiral Staircase* (1946) and Robert Wise's *Day the Earth Stood Still* (1951). Bernard Herrmann employed the theremin in the latter film to convey the ominous presence of Gort the robot. Most recently, the theremin has been featured in a few film scores of the 1990s, including the music by Howard Shore for *Ed Wood* (1994), Tim Burton's affectionate tribute to the director of several films that are widely acknowledged to be among the worst ever made. The wavy tones of the theremin seemed appropriate for this film, with its black-and-white photography, which attempted to emulate the look of Wood's own films. A year later, Elliot Goldenthal used the theremin in his rambunctious accompaniment for the third of the Warner Bros. Batman films, *Batman Forever*.

BERNARD HERRMANN: *HANGOVER SQUARE*. One of the most fascinating characters in 1940s films is the murderous pianist portrayed by Laird Cregar in *Hangover Square*. Based on the novel of the same name by Patrick Hamilton—whose best-known literary work, *Angel Street*, was the source of two films, including MGM's glossy thriller *Gaslight* (1944)—*Hangover Square* is the story of George Harvey Bone, a talented but troubled young musician. Though the man's life is seemingly devoted to teaching the piano and creating beautiful music, at times he suddenly becomes violent and commits murder, after which he remembers nothing. As the murders by strangulation continue, a trail of evidence leads the police to suspect Bone, who is composing a piano concerto for a concert performance. In the climactic scene, one of Bone's piano students, a young woman, begins playing his concerto, accompanied by an orchestra. The police surround the hall, which accidentally catches on fire. In the ensuing chaos, everyone escapes from the burning building except Bone himself. Going to the piano, he resumes playing his music at the point where his student left off when she joined the orchestra in a hasty departure, and he finishes the piece alone as the entire hall becomes engulfed in flames.

Herrmann scored the concerto to reflect the dramatic situation in this last scene; thus the last section of the work is for piano solo, without orchestral accompaniment. This is perhaps the only piano concerto ever written with such a peculiar ending, and yet the last moments of this work, with its powerfully somber bass chords, are among its most effective. The opening of the work, which Herrmann named *Concerto Macabre*, contains a strikingly rhythmic motif for solo piano, with a descending pair of strong bass octaves followed by a sharply accented chord that is repeated four times. This pattern forms the rhythmic and harmonic background for the concerto's main theme, which features a dramatic, rhythmically charged melodic idea. This music, which also serves as the accompaniment for the picture's opening titles and as the motif for Bone following each of his murderous acts, leads to a more romantic second theme, in which Herrmann created some of his most passionate music. Ironically, this theme is based on a rather cheap music-hall tune that is sung by a stage performer (Linda Darnell) who eventually becomes one of Bone's murder victims. The middle section of the concerto, which is the fastest paced part of the work, is based on the episodes in which Bone is in the midst of his murderous stalkings.

Thus, Herrmann not only created a vibrant piece of music for the film's denouement, but cleverly incorporated into the concerto various bits of thematic material that already served as part of the film's underscore. Although the picture was not a huge box-office hit, over the years *Hangover Square* has become a cult favorite, especially for fans of Bernard Herrmann, who regard this score as one of his supreme creative accomplishments.

SHORT CUTS. With the war winding down, the mood of most of the world might have been more optimistic in 1945 than in previous years, but the mood in the movies was getting progressively darker.

■■■■ **Max Steiner.** Beginning with *Double Indemnity* in 1944, James M. Cain's novels began to be adapted for the screen; in the process moviegoers were introduced to more hard-edged characters, including greedy businessmen, conniving wives, and vulnerable drifters, all of whom could get sucked into schemes of betrayal and murder. With Joan Crawford in the title role, Cain's novel *Mildred Pierce* was made into one of 1945's most popular films, about a long-suffering woman who tries to give her daughter everything, even at the expense of her own marriage. In the role of Veda, Ann Blyth gave new meaning to the phrase "spoiled rotten" through her portrayal of the self-seeking, destructive daughter.

Max Steiner's music is properly melodramatic most of the time, with a main theme that surges like the waves that wash away the film's opening titles. However, for the romantic scenes between Mildred and her husband Monte (Zachary Scott) Steiner used the love theme from *Now, Voyager*, which by the mid-1940s had become popularly known as the melody of the song "It Can't Be Wrong."

■■■■ **Herbert Stothart and Mario Castelnuovo-Tedesco.** Another author of dark tales whose fiction made an imprint on Hollywood in 1945 was Oscar Wilde, whose story *The Picture of Dorian Gray* became one of MGM's top films of the year. The film had wonderfully atmospheric photography and a fascinatingly cold performance by Hurd Hatfield in the title role—a man who never ages, but whose sinful ways are revealed in his portrait, which progressively changes until it has a completely grotesque facade. The background score is credited to Herbert Stothart; however, according to Miklos Rozsa in his autobiography *Double Life*, most of the score was written by Mario Castelnuovo-Tedesco (1895–1968), who worked in Hollywood for thirty years without ever receiving any real acclaim.[41] Despite the inclusion of original scoring, the film's most notable music is not by either of these composers. For scenes of Dorian playing the piano, the last of Chopin's Preludes, opus 28, was chosen. Its haunting main theme permeates the film with an aura of melancholy and conveys a beauty of spirit otherwise sorely lacking in the man whose fingers repeatedly play this piece.

■■■■ **Frédéric Chopin, as Arranged by Miklos Rozsa.** The year 1945 was also a good one for film biographies of famous musicians. First came a highly fictional version of Frédéric Chopin's life, *A Song to Remember*, with a rather robust Cornel Wilde inappropriately cast as the frail Polish pianist and composer. Although this film is of little worth as history, it does provide filmgoers with a generous sampling of Chopin's music. José Iturbi furnished masterful piano interpretations for the soundtrack as Cornel Wilde mimicked the playing on camera. Miklos Rozsa took time out from creating original scores to make orchestral arrangements of several Chopin themes, and even composed some original music in a Chopinesque style to knit various bits of Chopin's music together into a background score. Besides being beautifully photographed in Technicolor, this picture brought to the 1940s filmgoing public an appreciation of some of the loveliest music ever composed for the piano.

■■■■ **George Gershwin, as Arranged by Max Steiner and Ray Heindorf.** Warner Bros.' *Rhapsody in Blue* is a rather superficial film biography of George Gershwin, who is played by a debonair but bland Robert Alda. As with the Chopin film, there is a lot of contrivance in the screenplay, but the producers of this film were successful in rounding up a number of notable musicians who had known Gershwin, and who portrayed themselves in the picture. Gershwin's long-time friend, pianist Oscar Levant, played lengthy portions of Gershwin's works on camera, including the original *Rhapsody in Blue* and the Concerto in F. Also on hand were Al Jolson, Paul Whiteman, George White, and Hazel Scott. These performers lent the film an air of authenticity in the handling of the musical excerpts. Max Steiner and Ray Heindorf did the requisite orchestral arrangements.

These two films were progenitors of many other film biographies of well-known musicians that would be made in the next several years. While the Hollywood treatment usually negates any historical value, the musical sequences in these films are of almost uniformly outstanding quality, due to the involvement of so many talented performers and arrangers.

•••••••••
1946
•••••••••

HUGO FRIEDHOFER: *THE BEST YEARS OF OUR LIVES.* The name Hugo Friedhofer (1902–81) may seem somewhat obscure to the average moviegoer, but to the serious cinema devotee, Friedhofer ranks as one of the most creative artists of the medium.

As the son of a cellist, the San Francisco–born Friedhofer began studying cello at age thirteen; however, in his early years he leaned toward a career as a painter. After dropping out of high school at age sixteen, he went to work as an office boy, while taking painting courses at night at the Mark Hopkins Institute. At age eighteen, Friedhofer's interests turned toward music; after two years of intensive study on his instrument, he began playing with various orchestras. In 1925, he gained a position in the orchestra at the Granada Theatre, which he later described as "one of that decade's most ornate film cathedrals."[42]

Friedhofer soon became more interested in composing and arranging music than in playing. He studied harmony, counterpoint, and composition with the Italian composer Domenico Brescia, who had studied alongside Ottorino Respighi at the Conservatory of Bologna. After five years of study, he set aside the cello to become an arranger for stage bands. Synchronized sound had arrived by this time, and in 1929, he was offered a job at the Fox studio by a violinist friend, George Lipschultz, who had become music director for Fox.[43]

Friedhofer's career during the early days of the talkies consisted of orchestrating scores composed by others; among the films he worked on was the musical *Sunny Side Up*, which denotes the talkie debut of Janet Gaynor and Charles Farrell. Friedhofer's employment at Fox lasted until 1935, when he lost his job due to the studio's merger with Darryl F. Zanuck's 20th Century Pictures. He worked for a few months as a freelance arranger, and then was offered a contract by Leo Forbstein, head of the Warner Bros. music department. Friedhofer began his work there by arranging two scores: Korngold's music for *Captain Blood* and Steiner's score for *The Charge of the Light Brigade*. He was routinely called upon to orchestrate the creative works of others, including fifteen of Korngold's scores and fifty of Steiner's.

Hugo Friedhofer, seated, with Emil Newman.

Hearst Newspaper Collection/
University of Southern California

If it hadn't been for Alfred Newman, Friedhofer might have been stuck forever in the role of orchestrator. Twice Samuel Goldwyn asked Newman to recommend a composer, and on both occasions Newman suggested Friedhofer. The first of these recommendations led to Friedhofer's first full-length score, *The Adventures of Marco Polo* (1938), which starred Gary Cooper. Despite Friedhofer's success with this project, Forbstein was reluctant to lose his most capable arranger. But in 1946, when Goldwyn approached Newman for a second time, Friedhofer seized an opportunity that severed his ties with Warner Bros. and launched him on a two-decade film-composing career, during which he composed many outstanding scores.

The film that transformed Friedhofer's career was *The Best Years of Our Lives*, not only the most critically acclaimed motion picture of 1946 but also the most successful at the box office. The film follows three World War II veterans as they return to their families in Middle America, planning to pick up the pieces of the lives they had left behind. At the annual Oscar ceremony in early 1947, *Best Years* collected seven awards, including one for Best Picture; one for its director William Wyler; and another for Friedhofer's score, perhaps the finest of his career.

Like Aaron Copland's earlier scores for *Of Mice and Men* and *Our Town*, Friedhofer's music for *The Best Years of Our Lives* demonstrates a stylistic simplicity that is a far cry from the lush wall-to-wall sound of most other scores composed during Hollywood's Golden Age. Director Wyler encouraged Friedhofer to avoid the typical Hollywood sound, although Wyler later complained that the score should have resembled Alfred Newman's music for *Wuthering Heights*. Apparently, Samuel Goldwyn didn't much appreciate the score either, although after the Oscars were awarded, his attitude became considerably more approving.

Thematically, Friedhofer's score is based on six principal melodic motifs that function in the same way as Richard Wagner's operatic leitmotifs, serving to identify various characters and situations. Of these ideas, by far the most important is the one which first appears in the music that accompanies the opening titles. Instead of being a fully developed theme in the style of such Golden Age composers as Korngold or Steiner, Friedhofer's idea features a repeated use of the tones of the C-major triad. As the theme continues, a number of ascending octaves are heard; these bold melodic intervals help to impart an air of hope and confidence to the film.

The second motif, a lively idea that utilizes triad patterns, is first heard when the three veterans are in a cargo plane taking them to their hometown. A third motif, the score's slowest music, is heard as each man reaches his destination.

In Robert Sherwood's screenplay, based on MacKinlay Kantor's novel *Glory for Me*, the three veterans represent different social classes. Al Stephenson (Frederic March), a successful banker with a devoted wife and two nearly adult children, returns to his old job, but incurs the anger of his boss when he authorizes noncollateral loans to war veterans. Fred Derry (Dana Andrews) is a former soda jerk whose wife Marie (Virginia Mayo), whom he married only twenty days before his induction, has been unfaithful. Homer Parrish (Harold Russell), the youngest of the three, is returning to his lower-middle-class home (and the girl next door) with hooks in place of his hands, which were severely burned. The plights of these three men form the focus of the film, which moves episodically back and forth among them.

The Best Years of Our Lives, with Harold Russell, Teresa Wright, Dana Andrews, Myrna Loy, Hoagy Carmichael, and Fredric March.

Friedhofer composed themes for two of the female characters, Homer's sweetheart Wilma (Cathy O'Donnell) and Al's daughter Peggy (Teresa Wright), but he did not specifically create individual themes for each of the returning veterans. Instead, he used bits of the three main melodic motifs heard at the beginning of the film to unite them in a common struggle to become reconnected with their families and to move on in their respective lives. In the course of the film, the score's main thematic elements are combined in various ways that tie all the plot situations together and provide a musical accompaniment of unusual force and beauty.

Though the film runs almost three hours, there isn't an excessive amount of music. Friedhofer confined his efforts to scenes that he felt needed musical support, such as the moment when Homer invites Wilma to observe his helplessness at bedtime. Friedhofer's tender music beautifully underscores Wilma's feelings. Her love cannot be stopped by Homer's handicap, even though he fears she only pities him. Taken as a whole, the score is an American classic, the product of a composer whose celebrity may not equal that of his contemporaries Miklos Rozsa, Bernard Herrmann, and Franz Waxman, but whose work is unmistakably that of a master craftsman.

ERICH WOLFGANG KORNGOLD: DECEPTION. The music of *Deception* is the last of Korngold's Hollywood scores (although the belated 1947 release of *Escape Me Never* makes *Deception* the penultimate Korngold score to be heard in theaters). Basically a soapy melodrama with a musical motif, *Deception* benefits greatly from Korngold's lush score, which includes themes that make up the melodic material of a cello concerto that is performed toward the end of the film. As in Franz Waxman's scoring of *Humoresque* (discussed under "Short Cuts"), much classical music by various composers is performed during the concert-hall sequences, which involve the film's principal characters: Alexander Hollenius (Claude Rains), a temperamental conductor; Karel Novak (Paul Henreid), a virtuoso cellist, who has just returned to America following a term of incarceration in a European POW camp; and Christine Radcliffe (Bette Davis), a talented pianist whose prior affair with the cellist causes the conductor, with whom she is currently involved, to become insanely jealous.

The cello concerto is a crucial plot element since it is an original work of the cellist. Novak is scheduled to play the concerto's solo part, with Hollenius as conductor of the accompanying orchestra. Before the fateful event, a lot of histrionic behavior takes place, as Christine tries to prevent Hollenius from unnerving Novak and causing him to be replaced by another cellist. Various sections of the concerto are heard as background music, including some small bits that were recorded at the piano for the film's soundtrack by Korngold himself.[44] Due to the composition's length, the film's climactic performance scene includes a truncated version of the work. Later, Korngold prepared an expanded version which became the Concerto in C for Cello and Orchestra, opus 37. Consisting of a single movement, the work includes three main sections, an opening allegro, an adagio section, and a lively closing section in the form of a fugue.

Regrettably, most of the prints of *Deception* that show up on television suffer from badly processed sound, which causes the music to have a wavering pitch. Whether this was a purposeful effect, supposed to emulate the then-trendy sound of the theremin is unclear. The result, however, is more annoying than effective, especially with regard to the slow section of the concerto, in which the cello's wobbly tone is truly painful to listen to.

ROY WEBB: MUSIC FOR THRILLERS. From the time Max Steiner left RKO in 1936, Roy Webb (1888–1982) was the composer of almost every film made at that studio over the next twenty years. Although many of his efforts were limited by the low budgets of many of RKO's releases, occasionally he had the opportunity to create scores of full symphonic breadth. Two thrillers made at RKO in 1946, Alfred Hitchcock's *Notorious* and Robert Siodmak's *Spiral Staircase*, provide a study in contrast.

Coming right after *Spellbound*, with Rozsa's full-bodied symphonic accompaniment, *Notorious* is noticeably lacking in musical underscoring. Webb's music consists mainly of a melodious main-title theme which conveys the sensual character played by Ingrid Bergman. An American secret agent, played by Cary Grant, engages Bergman's character, the daughter of a Nazi sympathizer, in a spying operation for the United States. The plot involves her marrying an avowed Nazi (Claude Rains) living in Rio de Janiero. Most of the film's dialogue scenes have no music at all.

In contrast with *Notorious*, *The Spiral Staircase* afforded Roy Webb one of his richest scoring opportunities. This film, based on Ethel Lina White's novel *Some Must Watch*, has all the typical trappings of a melodramatic thriller: a big house with long, dark passageways, lots of stormy weather, and a psychopathic killer on the loose. Dorothy McGuire plays Helen, a mute young woman whose inability to speak has been caused by the traumatic experience of watching her parents burn to death in a fire. Helen works in the household of an elderly invalid, Mrs. Warren (Ethel Barrymore), who has an uncanny psychic sense and predicts dire things. The old lady fears for Helen's life, since several young women with various physical ailments have recently been murdered.

Webb's score is noteworthy for its inclusion of the theremin's eerie sounds, the first of which occurs during the opening titles, where a humming tone is utilized to produce a spooky effect. In the scene that follows, while a silent movie is being projected in the downstairs hall of a hotel, a murder is about to take place upstairs. A partially crippled young woman is being observed by a stalker concealed in a closet in her room. The camera zooms in until the eye of the intruder is seen in stark closeup. Here the wavy sound of the theremin is heard again; it is heard several more times as accompaniment to similar closeups of the murderer's eye.

Background music is practically wall-to-wall, except for a few moments when a howling storm's fury is the only background sound. One of the most effective scenes is Helen's fantasy, in which she daydreams that she is about to be married to the young doctor who is looking after the bed-ridden Mrs. Warren. She sees herself dancing with the doctor at a fancy ball, while a lilting waltz is being played. When the minister asks her to say the wedding vows, she is unable to speak. At this point the music shifts from a romantic style to a much more dissonant one. Throughout the film, Webb's music creates tension and sustains a dramatic rhythm. Together with Robert Siodmak's skillful direction, Webb's musical contribution is a great asset to *The Spiral Staircase*, one of the classic thrillers of all time.

SHORT CUTS ■■■ **Miklos Rozsa.** Rozsa was nominated for an Oscar for *The Killers*, a rather stark melodrama based on the Ernest Hemingway short story, that features the film debut of Burt Lancaster in the role of Swede, a boxer mixed up with racketeers who send two of their hit men to a small town to kill him. Rozsa's main theme, built on a dramatic four-note motif, clearly anticipates the familiar *Dragnet* music of Walter Schumann, who used a similar "dum-de-dum-dum" pattern for the theme of the popular radio and TV series. In fact, the similarity of the *Dragnet* motif caused Rozsa's publisher, Robbins Music, to file a lawsuit. Although Schumann contended that any plagiarism was unintentional, an out-of-court settlement was negotiated.[45]

■■■ **Bernard Herrmann.** Also nominated was Herrmann's evocative percussion-inflected score for *Anna and the King of Siam*, a dramatic version of Margaret Landon's book of the same name, concerning the relationship between an English governess and the stubborn Siamese king. This film was made by 20th Century-Fox, the same studio that a decade later would film the glorious Rodgers and Hammerstein musical *The King and I*, based on the same story. Excerpts from the score of the earlier film were only recorded in 1995, and thus Herrmann's music has not been much appreciated until recently.

■■■ **Franz Waxman.** The score of Warner's music-filled drama *Humoresque* earned Franz Waxman a nomination. In this film John Garfield plays Paul Boray, whose career as a concert violinist is complicated by his relationship with a married socialite named Helen Wright (Joan Crawford), who is emotionally unstable. For one of the scenes in which Paul is performing onstage, Waxman borrowed his own *Carmen* Fantasy (based on themes from Bizet's opera), which he had written as a concert piece for Jascha Heifetz earlier in 1946. Isaac Stern, who is credited as music advisor for *Humoresque*, recorded the violin solos that Garfield mimics onscreen. The film's title is taken from Dvorak's "Humoresque," opus 101, no. 7, which is heard during the opening credits, in an arrangement for violin and orchestra.

The most compelling use of music in the film occurs in the final reel, where Helen becomes distraught upon hearing Paul play Wagner's "Liebestod" (from *Tristan und Isolde*) on a radio broadcast. As the music continues, Helen walks from her beach house toward the ocean and soon disappears into the surf. There isn't much original music in *Humoresque*, but Waxman expertly handled the adaptations of the numerous classical works which are featured in the film.

■■■■ **William Walton.** The one remaining musical score nominee for 1946 has become a classic. When Laurence Olivier decided to film Shakespeare's *Henry V* in 1944, he enlisted the services of renowned English composer William Walton (1901–83) for the score. When the film opened in America two years later, it won all kinds of accolades from critics and wound up as a Best Picture nominee. Walton's score is a fine example of this very gifted composer's serious approach to film music. A concert suite of excerpts from the score was subsequently recorded by Walton, and several other recordings have appeared in recent years, including an hour-long work entitled *Henry V: A Musical Scenario after Shakespeare*, which was arranged by Christopher Palmer. With the addition of a narrator, this concert work provides a fine introduction to the works of Walton, who deserves to be ranked among the finest composers of the twentieth century.

■■■■ **Alfred Newman.** An example of how much a composer can improve on his own work is readily demonstrated by Alfred Newman's richly romantic score for Darryl F. Zanuck's film of W. Somerset Maugham's *Razor's Edge*. The beautiful love theme, heard in the film's early scenes with Tyrone Power and Gene Tierney in Paris, had been originally written by Newman for *These Three* (1936). The difference between the two versions indicates how much change had occurred in the ten years that separate the two scores. Whereas the typical orchestra for a 1936 film-score recording usually included fewer than thirty players, by 1946 the major Hollywood studios used as many as eighty players, in order to produce a full symphonic sound. The powerful effect that many of Newman's 20th Century-Fox scores achieve owes a lot to the lushness of the orchestrations, which were usually handled by Eddie Powell, one of the geniuses of film-score arranging. An additional asset is the frequent use of 20th Century-Fox concertmaster Louis Kaufman, who contributed greatly with his sweetly expressive tone in moments scored for the solo violin.

■■■■ **Dimitri Tiomkin.** Dimitri Tiomkin's career had faltered somewhat after his spectacular success with *Lost Horizon* in the late 1930s. Perhaps his steadfast refusal to align himself with other composers who accepted studio contracts cost him some of the better scoring assignments. However one views his decision in this regard, a look at his credits for the 1940s indicates that many of his scores were written for low-budget films, including several composed from 1943 to 1945 for Monogram, a small company devoted to Westerns and serials. He also scored over a dozen military-financed documentaries. Several of these were produced by Frank Capra, who invited Tiomkin to join him at the Army Film Center in Hollywood.

In 1946, Frank Capra, just back from World War II, returned to making feature films and hired Tiomkin to do the score for the Christmas fantasy *It's a Wonderful Life*, starring Jimmy Stewart, also just back from the war.

This rather grim tale of George Bailey and his fateful Christmas Eve plays like a modern variation on Dickens's *Christmas Carol.* Tiomkin composed a wonderfully dramatic score, in parts of which he included variations on the Gregorian chant melody "Dies irae." Capra later reedited the film and moved much of the music around. Tiomkin refused to work for Capra again!

David Selznick's mammoth Western *Duel in the Sun* provided Tiomkin with a happier experience, although in its initial stages this scoring project alienated several of Hollywood's top musicians. The controversy began when Selznick invited six composers to audition for the film by having each one score a scene; then he planned to evaluate the six entries and choose a composer to do the entire picture. Among the insulted composers was Miklos Rozsa, who expressed his outrage by informing Selznick that he never wanted to hear his name mentioned again.[46] Apparently, Tiomkin was willing to cooperate with the strong-willed producer, who eventually hired him. The resulting score gets positively Wagnerian in the last sequence, in which former lovers Jennifer Jones and Gregory Peck shoot each other, then die with their hands touching in a last loving gesture. Where else but in Hollywood could a composer create music for such visual histrionics?

BERNARD HERRMANN: *THE GHOST AND MRS. MUIR.* After working at 20th Century-Fox as a guest composer for the past three years, at the invitation of Alfred Newman, Bernard Herrmann received a film-scoring assignment that resulted in the enchanting score of Joseph L. Mankiewicz's *Ghost and Mrs. Muir.*

Described by Tony Thomas as "the least frightening ghost story ever filmed," this movie is really a romance, but one with a most unusual twist: one of the two lovers is dead.[47] As scripted by Philip Dunne from the novel of the same name by R. A. Dick, *The Ghost and Mrs. Muir* is an atmospheric period piece, set in pre–World War I England. The story concerns Lucy Muir (Gene Tierney), a youthful widow with a young daughter, who moves into Gull Cottage, an old seaside house, despite the real estate agent's warnings about the house being haunted. Almost from the moment she moves in, the spirit of the house's former resident, Captain Daniel Gregg (Rex Harrison), becomes a bothersome presence. When Lucy demands that the spirit reveal himself, the captain appears, and the two subsequently become friends.

To alleviate her financial difficulties, the captain assists her by dictating his memoirs to her. The resulting book, a series of colorful adventures, is published and brings her a comfortable income. Through a chance meeting at the publisher's office with a well-to-do author, Miles Fairley (George Sanders), a romance develops, despite Captain Gregg's objections. Lucy plans to marry Miles, but inadvertently learns that he already has a wife. The captain has already decided that he must not stand in Lucy's way, and his visitations cease.

In the film's magical last scene, Lucy, now grown quite elderly, is sitting in a chair with a glass of milk in her hands. When the glass tips over and the milk spills out, we know that she is dead. At this point, Captain Gregg reappears and offers her his hand. A suddenly younger Lucy rises from the chair, and the happily reunited couple walk out the door and into eternity, hand in hand.

Such a fanciful tale as this could have been ludicrous if the mood of the film had not been right. Bernard Herrmann's inspired score establishes the right ambiance from the very outset, with music that combines aspects

The Ghost and Mrs. Muir,
with Gene Tierney
and Rex Harrison.

of mystery, melancholy, and romance. The score is based on several motifs that are introduced early in the film. For the opening titles, Herrmann uses a sea motif that consists of two parts, the first a restlessly rising line played by woodwinds and harp, and the second a calmer, descending, three-note figure played by strings. The melody that follows is a four-note idea that begins with an ascending seventh followed by two descending tones. Playing against this idea is a series of four arpeggiated chords for woodwinds and harp; the first note of each arpeggiated figure provides a descending motif. This pattern becomes crucially important in the film's concluding scene, when the entire orchestra takes up the idea in a glorious final crescendo. This same descending figure relates melodically to Lucy's theme, which consists of the same tones, but with an additional one inserted in the middle of the pattern. In this way, Herrmann ties together many of the film's melodic elements and has them play off each other. In the course of the story several other motifs are introduced, including one for Captain Gregg and another for the romance of Lucy and Miles. Taken together, these short patterns amount to a wellspring of ideas which Herrmann ingeniously utilized to create a richly melodic musical tapestry.

There are fleeting moments when the music has loud outbursts, but for the most part the score consists of subtly orchestrated moments that play underneath the story and sustain a mood of prevailing melancholy, perhaps suggestive of the impossible gulf that separates Lucy from the spectral sea captain. Only in death can she totally give herself to him. When her death does occur, the music bursts forth with a majestic proclamation of the descending pattern that is identified both with Lucy and with Gull Cottage, the enchanted place which has fatefully brought them together. There have been happy endings in Hollywood films before and since *The Ghost and Mrs. Muir,* but never has there been such a transcendentally beautiful reunion of two souls as that which provides this film its exultant ending, buoyed so magnificently by Herrmann's triumphant closing chords.

MIKLOS ROZSA: CRIME FILMS. With his music for mid-1940s films about amnesiacs, alcoholics, and gangsters, Miklos Rozsa became typecast as a composer of agitated and often dissonant music for the hard-edged modernistic melodramas that have been categorized as film noir. The seven scores that Rozsa completed in 1947 suggest that many Hollywood producers placed their projects in his capable hands, in hopes that his music would raise both the quality and the box-office potential of their films.

The most noteworthy of these scores emerged as Rozsa's second Oscar winner—the music for George Cukor's film *A Double Life*, in which stage actor Anthony John (Ronald Colman) becomes overly involved in his theatrical performances. After taking on the murderous role of *Othello*, he kills a young woman (Shelley Winters) during a mental blackout. Although the role of the tormented actor was a far cry from the heroic parts that had made him an international star, Colman won his only Oscar for this portrayal.

The score begins with a modernistic, dramatic musical style but later takes on a more archaic flavor in order to create an atmosphere appropriate for Shakespeare's play. The music heard during the *Othello* scenes is not in the style of Shakespeare's time; in fact, the on-stage music bears a striking resemblance to the brass music of Venetian composer Giovanni Gabrieli, who lived in the late seventeenth century. The decision to use Gabrieli's style came from director Cukor, who felt that this majestic ceremonial music would be ideal for the *Othello* scenes since much of the play takes place in Venice.[48] Frequently, the music heard during an on-stage performance is carried over into the ensuing scenes. This subliminally suggests that Anthony John cannot easily step out of his stage role.

Long stretches of the film, especially the last reels, have little underscoring. The sections of the film that do use Rozsa's music are by far the most effective, in that they keep the tragic overtones of the story from becoming too dominant.

Another exceptional film with a strong Rozsa score is Delmer Daves's *Red House*, for which the composer utilized the eerie sounds of the theremin for the third time. In this small-budget but tense drama, Edward G. Robinson plays a farmer who harbors a terrible secret concerning a small house in the woods. When a young farmhand (Lon McAllister) gets too curious about the red house, dire things happen. As it had done previously, the theremin enhanced Rozsa's ability to convey mental disturbance, with its wavy, almost voicelike sounds. The score is characterized by the same sort of rich orchestration and by the same frequently impassioned style that are found in both *Spellbound* and *The Lost Weekend*.

Rozsa's 1947 output also includes the music for two films featuring Burt Lancaster. In *Desert Fury* (which was actually filmed prior to *The Killers*) and *Brute Force*, Rozsa's rhythmically punctuated musical backgrounds aided considerably in enhancing Lancaster's growing reputation as an on-screen "tough guy."

SHORT CUTS ■ ■ ■ ■ Max Steiner. Max Steiner conceived a delightful score for the film version of the Broadway hit *Life with Father*, in which William Powell played the tyrannical banker Clarence Day, who lives with his wife and four sons in a Madison Avenue brownstone toward the end of the nineteenth century. His patient but strong-minded wife Vinnie (Irene Dunne) discovers that her husband has never been baptized and then persuades him to receive the sacrament.

Beginning with a quotation of "Sweet Marie" (Mr. Day's favorite song), the music behind the opening credits also features an exuberant up-tempo theme that perfectly captures both the humor and the warmth of this story. This theme continues as the film opens. Annie, the new maid, goes out to the milk wagon for Mr. Day's specially prepared milk container, and then helps to serve breakfast in their New York brownstone. As usual in Steiner's scores, the "mickey-mousing" effect is used to good advantage. When the breakfast tray is put into the dumbwaiter and while it is being pulled up to the next floor, the music climbs the scale right along with it. In the final scene, when the Days leave their home in a horse-drawn carriage to go to church for Mr. Day's long-delayed baptism, the opening theme is heard in a gloriously robust arrangement. Steiner's music was among the five nominees in the category Scoring of a Comedy or Dramatic Picture.

■■■■ **Erich Wolfgang Korngold.** Erich Wolfgang Korngold's richly romantic score for *Escape Me Never*, composed in 1945, was not heard until the film's belated release in late 1947. While the film itself is far from memorable, Korngold composed for it a melodious theme that became the only "pop" song he ever wrote for a film, "Love for Love," which features lyrics by Ted Koehler.

Except for some arrangements of Wagner's music which he provided for the Richard Wagner biographical film *Magic Fire* in 1953, *Escape Me Never* represents Korngold's Hollywood swan song. The death of his father in 1945 and his own heart attack in 1947 convinced him to withdraw from the film-composing scene. He did, however, complete several concert works. One of these, the Violin Concerto in D Major, opus 35, first performed by Jascha Heifetz in 1947 and subsequently recorded by RCA Victor, features several melodic ideas that were derived from the scores of *Anthony Adverse*, *Another Dawn*, *Juarez*, and *The Prince and the Pauper*. Although many critics derided Korngold's use of film materials in the composition of this concert piece, its beauties cannot be denied.

■■■ **Franz Waxman.** Of the eight scores Franz Waxman produced in 1947, two were for the Humphrey Bogart films *The Two Mrs. Carrolls* and *Dark Passage*. The first of these is especially dramatic and musically compelling. Bogart's role as a psychopathic painter allowed the actor to overact outrageously. Waxman, on loan to Selznick, produced a lovely score for the Hitchcock-directed film *The Paradine Case*. Although long stretches of the film, set primarily in a British courtroom, have no scoring, there was sufficient music for Waxman later to arrange his Rhapsody for Piano and Orchestra, based on the film's principal themes. Although this work has never achieved the popularity of other 1940s film compositions such as the *Warsaw* Concerto and the *Spellbound* Concerto, Waxman's Rhapsody is a worthy companion to those more familiar pieces.

■■■■ **Alfred Newman.** At 20th Century-Fox, Alfred Newman did not get much of a scoring opportunity with either *Gentleman's Agreement* or *Call Northside 777*, both of which are unique for the time in that they totally lack background music except for their opening and closing credits. On the other hand, Newman's rousing score for *Captain from Castile*, with a lavish full-symphonic background, accompanies this colorful but overlong film about the Spanish exploration of the New World, with Tyrone Power as Pedro De Vargas, a young soldier who joins the expedition of Hernando Cortez. This very melodious score has a number of romantic themes. The beautiful love theme for Pedro and Catana (Jean Peters) begins with shimmering strings accompanying a high violin melody that has an ethereal, almost impressionistic quality, in the style of Claude Debussy. The thrilling "Conquest" theme, heard at the conclusion, is scored for a full symphony orchestra complemented by a military band. This exciting march music is heard while the camera shows a panoramic view of the entire expeditionary force making its way through a Mexican river valley. Newman garnered one of his forty-five Oscar nominations for this score, which became his second to be recorded.

■ ■ ■ **David Raksin.** David Raksin continued in the ranks of guest composers at 20th Century-Fox with his marvelously crafted score for the controversial *Forever Amber*. Kay Windsor's best-selling novel, about a seventeenth-century English lass who uses her beauty to climb England's social ladder and eventually becomes King Charles II's mistress, was initially considered too racy for the screen. However, after a discreet trimming of some of the story's steamier elements, *Forever Amber* achieved a wide release and became one of the year's most popular films.

Although panned by critics, *Forever Amber* contains some of Raksin's best work, including a lovely minor-key theme for Amber (Linda Darnell), and two very exciting musical sequences. The first accompanies the scenes of the Great Plague of 1665, with a dramatic funeral march that is heard as scores of bodies are carted through the streets of London. The second is a fast-paced contrapuntal piece heard during the subsequent Great London Fire, which nearly destroyed the city in 1666. A rising orchestral tumult momentarily brings this portion of the film to life, with rich Technicolor photography to enhance the fire scenes. The film soon slips back into a plodding and rather bland tale. At times, only the lavish production values and Raksin's richly textured musical backgrounds keep this film from being a crashing bore.

RALPH VAUGHAN WILLIAMS: SCOTT OF THE ANTARCTIC. Among the prominent composers who scored the many major films produced in postwar England were Arthur Bliss, Arnold Bax (1883–1953), Brian Easdale (1909–1995), William Walton, and the most celebrated of all, Ralph Vaughan Williams.

Born in Gloucester, England, on October 12, 1872, Vaughan Williams, in the first years of the new century, began to achieve recognition for his works, many of which were influenced by English folk song. In 1910, he composed a pair of masterworks, *A Sea Symphony* (Symphony no. 1) and *Fantasia on a Theme by Thomas Tallis*.[49] Vaughan Williams's fame spread widely in the second decade of the twentieth century, when he composed a number of important orchestral works. *A London Symphony* (Symphony no. 2) brought him to the front ranks of English composers at the time of its premiere in 1913. After a stint in the military during World War I, he created a variety of symphonic works, most of which, in their post-Romantic idiom, bear more than a little similarity to the style of Korngold's theatrical works, which were being introduced around the same time in Vienna. Vaughan Williams did not have the opportunity to compose a film score until he was almost seventy, but finally, in 1941, he produced a score for *The Invaders*. Five other film scores followed between 1942 and 1946.

Scott of the Antarctic, with
John Mills.

Vaughan Williams's most outstanding score was the
the 1948 film *Scott of the Antarctic*, a grim, meticulously
crafted reenactment of an ill-fated 1911–12 expedition
to the South Pole. Led by British explorer Robert Falcon
Scott, the expedition reached the South Pole in January
1912, only to discover the Norwegian flag already in
place. Tragically, Scott and the other four members of
his team all died on the return trip, due to the severity of
the weather.

Beginning with massively ominous orchestral chords,
the music for the film's opening credits consists of a
slow-paced noble theme. Actor John Mills's voice is first
heard as Captain Scott begins to record his thoughts in a
journal of the trek. The camera scans the barren Antarctic
wilderness, accompanied by the eerie sounds of a solo
soprano voice and strings. The combination of sight and
sound makes one truly feel the intensity of the Antarctic
cold. Vaughan Williams's music suggests the courage of
these men, who know only too well that they might not
survive the journey home.

To evoke the frozen environment that Scott and his
fellow adventurers encounter on their trek to the South
Pole, Vaughan Williams devised an ingenious instrumentation. Included, besides the large-scale symphony
orchestra, are a wordless solo soprano and female chorus,
plus a wind machine, a piano, a celesta, orchestra bells,
and a vibraphone. Together, these vocal/instrumental effects chillingly convey the icy expanse of the landscape.

Of the emotionally moving music written for this film Tony Thomas
writes: "Vaughan Williams' score for *Scott of the Antarctic* is one of the greatest achievements in film music. It transcends mere pictorialism and delves
into the mystery of man's compulsion to adventure in forbidding places."[50]

BRIAN EASDALE: *THE RED SHOES*. Born in Manchester in 1909,
English musician Brian Easdale studied at the Royal College of Music,
and then worked as a conductor and composer. In the early 1930s, he
began writing orchestral tone poems such as *The Sixth Day*, which was
premiered in a concert conducted by Sir Malcolm Sargent. In 1934, Easdale
made the fortuitous acquaintance of Benjamin Britten, who engaged him in
working with Brazilian filmmaker Alberto Cavalcanti on a series of documentary films. After eight years of scoring these productions, Easdale
switched to feature films in the mid-1940s. He was recommended to filmmakers Michael Powell and Emeric Pressburger by Carol Reed. Thus, he had
the opportunity to score both *Black Narcissus* in 1947 and *The Red Shoes*,
his magnum opus, the following year.

Despite a rather obvious story and some uneven acting, *The Red Shoes*
is perhaps the best ballet movie ever made. The film is notable for its outstanding color photography, for its memorable dance choreography, and for
Brian Easdale's evocative Oscar-winning music. The plot concerns the plight
of Vicki, a young ballerina (Moira Shearer), who is torn between her love for
Julian (Marius Goring), a young and ardent composer, and her devotion to

both dancing and her impresario, Lermontov (Anton Walbrook). Vicki is scheduled to star in a new ballet based on Hans Christian Andersen's tale "The Red Shoes," with music that is being composed by Julian. Lermontov tries to disrupt the budding romance by persuading Vicki that her love for dancing must come before everything else. The resultant conflict eventually leads to the film's tragic conclusion.

In the first portion of the film there is practically no underscoring. Music is reserved for the ballet theater, where we see and hear excerpts from several famous ballets, including *Swan Lake*, *Giselle*, and *Les Sylphides*. Easdale's original music is built around the ballet score that Julian is composing. The music for *The Red Shoes Ballet* consists of a dramatic overture and several separate dance scenes. The ballet, with its surreal fantasy atmosphere, is quite modern but also quite enchanting. Its musical style combines both elements of romanticism and a more modernistic harmonic idiom, with occasional dissonances that contribute greatly to the score's effectiveness. The ballet music is used dynamically in the film; not only do we hear the finished product toward the end of the film, but we also first encounter the score as it is being composed, when Julian tries out some of his ideas on a piano.

The most ingenious use of music occurs at the end of the film, when Vicki is hopelessly torn between her two loves. Julian has also written a new opera, *Cupid and Psyche*. While Julian's opera is being broadcast on the radio, Lermontov tries to persuade Vicki to go on with her dancing career, which she has decided to abandon in favor of marriage to Julian. The music seems to assault her senses. In a panic she runs out of the room and desperately jumps from a balcony into the path of a fast-moving train.

The Red Shoes, with Moira Shearer.

MAX **S**TEINER: **J**OHNNY **B**ELINDA AND **T**HE **T**REASURE OF THE **S**IERRA **M**ADRE. The music for *Johnny Belinda* and *The Treasure of the Sierra Madre* is the work of Max Steiner, who had a really productive year in 1948, with ten scores.

His Oscar-nominated score for *Johnny Belinda* helps to humanize a story that, in the wrong hands, could have seemed sordid and distasteful. Skillfully directed by Jean Negulesco, *Johnny Belinda* is set in a small fishing village in Nova Scotia. A concerned physician (Lew Ayres) tries to help a deaf mute, Belinda MacDonald (Jane Wyman), by teaching her sign language. Soon, a relationship develops; but Belinda is raped by Locky, a local fisherman (Stephen McNally), and becomes pregnant. The townspeople start whispering about the doctor being the father of the child, and although the doctor and Belinda do get married, their troubles do not end there.

The score begins with a heroic-sounding theme, which segues into a series of Scottish-flavored tunes to represent the residents of Nova Scotia, who are predominantly of Scottish ancestry. The most dramatic music occurs when Belinda is raped. The sounds of an out-of-tune violin are incorporated into the score as Locky fumbles with a violin to entice Belinda, who is fascinated by the instrument even though she can only feel its vibrations. Midway through the film, when Belinda gives birth to little Johnny, Steiner introduces the score's most memorable melody, a tender lullaby, which becomes the film's principal theme from this point on.

John Huston's *Treasure of the Sierra Madre* wound up among the year's nominees for Best Picture, and is now one of the most acclaimed films of the 1940s, despite the fact that it was initially a box-office flop. Humphrey Bogart's unsympathetic portrayal of Fred C. Dobbs was a far cry from his hard-boiled detective roles, and Walter Huston played the old prospector without teeth (he actually had them removed for the film) to lend his fast-talking character a certain authenticity.

Steiner's score for this wonderfully acted melodrama begins with a rousing fanfare, followed by an excitingly paced dramatic theme that has a Spanish accent. Once the Mexican locale of the story has been established, however, Steiner's score exhibits no further Hispanic qualities. The decision not to carry the Spanish theme throughout the film was possibly made because the three prospectors (Bogart, Huston, and Tim Holt) are all Americans. The choice of musical style also seems to suggest the universality of greed.

The principal "trek" theme is heard several times, in a gradually slower tempo as the movie progresses; this suggests the cumulative weariness of the three adventurers as they plod onward into the Mexican hill country. For the gold that the prospectors discover, Steiner devised a jingling motif, which is played by an unusual combination of instruments, including two vibraphones, two harps, two pianos, a celesta, orchestra bells, a triangle, and suspended cymbals. This special sound effect is used most prominently when, near the end of the film, the spilled bags of gold are blown away during a fierce windstorm.

SHORT **C**UTS ■ ■ ■ ■ **Alfred Newman.** *The Snake Pit* includes one of Alfred Newman's finest scores. Instead of the romantic lyricism of such earlier scores as *The Song of Bernadette* (1943) and *The Keys of the Kingdom* (1945), here Newman established a mood of mental fragility for Virginia (Olivia de Havilland), a troubled young woman who spends time in a mental institution.

Newman's other 1948 scores are on the lighter side, especially the music for *Sitting Pretty*, in which Clifton Webb first portrayed the eccentric Mr. Belvedere. For the Gregory Peck Western *Yellow Sky*, Newman did no background scoring except for a rousing main-title march theme played by brass. This theme, which Newman had already used in *Brigham Young* (1940), became a standard piece of musical accompaniment for many subsequent films, including several other Western films produced by 20th Century-Fox.

■■■■ **Miklos Rozsa.** Rozsa concluded his short stint at Universal studios in 1948 with five more scores for tense thrillers, including *Criss Cross*, *Kiss the Blood off My Hands*, and a partial score for *The Naked City*, the final film produced by Mark Hellinger, who died of a heart attack while the film was being edited. Because of a moved-up release date, Frank Skinner was assigned the scoring of the dialogue scenes, while Rozsa scored the outdoor sequences. These scenes, including the final chase sequence, were shot on location in New York City. Rozsa composed a particularly impressive concluding piece for the film, which he called "Epilogue: The Song of a Great City." He intended this piece as a musical tribute both to New York City and to Mark Hellinger himself; it is one of Rozsa's most dramatically compelling compositions.

■■■■ **Daniele Amfitheatrof.** Russian-born Daniele Amfitheatrof (1901–83), came to the United States in 1937 as an orchestral conductor, and was signed by MGM two years later. Amfitheatrof's tenure as a studio composer was short-lived, however, and by 1948, he was freelancing. Max Ophuls's *Letter from an Unknown Woman* provided him with an excellent opportunity to create a richly romantic musical background.

This story of a woman's unrequited love for a pianist features two principal musical themes. The first, based on Franz Liszt's concert etude "Un Sospiro," is first heard during the opening credits and then in its original form as a piano piece which is being practiced by pianist Stefan Brand (Louis Jourdan). Brand has just moved into an apartment building in Vienna, and Lisa Berndl (Joan Fontaine), then only fourteen years old, quickly develops a crush on him. Some years later, she has a very brief affair with him. The second melody appears when Stefan and Lisa, spending an evening together, dine in a restaurant. The restaurant's orchestra plays a lilting waltz theme. Stefan goes to a piano and plays an elaborate series of variations on the waltz melody. Both themes are used in the underscoring of the later scenes in this atmospherically produced film, which, despite its melancholy ending, remains one of the most romantic movies of all time.

■■■■ **Virgil Thomson.** No perusal of the 1948 film-music scene would be complete without mention of Virgil Thomson's evocative music for Robert Flaherty's *Louisiana Story*. Produced by Standard Oil, this film shows, in a series of beautifully photographed scenes, the arrival of oil-drilling equipment at a Louisiana bayou, as observed by a fourteen-year-old boy. A native of the region, the boy watches as the outside world invades the bayou with huge machinery; eventually oil is tapped, the oil pump is sealed off, and the engineers depart. Dispensing with narration, Robert Flaherty, whose 1922 *Nanook of the North* is one of the earliest and best examples of the documentary art, allowed the camera, assisted by Thomson's music, to tell the story. With a score largely based on Acadian songs and dances, *Louisiana Story* is a richly atmospheric visual poem. Thomson, who arranged each of his scores for the late 1930s documentaries *The Plow That Broke the Plains* and *The River* into orchestral suites, arranged parts of his score for *Louisiana Story* into two separate orchestral works. The first, *The Louisiana Story Suite*, consists primarily of original themes. The second, *Acadian Songs and Dances*, consists of seven sections, each of which features material borrowed from a collection of French folk songs, edited by Irene Therese Whitfield.[51]

AARON COPLAND: THE BROOKLYN STRAVINSKY. The career of Aaron Copland parallels those of several European composers, such as Sergei Prokofiev, Dimitri Shostakovich, and Ralph Vaughan Williams. Each of these renowned composers of symphonic music considered the composing of film music to be similar to the writing of music for a ballet or an opera. All four used their consummate imagination and skill in writing film scores.

Copland, who was born in Brooklyn on November 14, 1900, got a rather late start in music, when he began taking piano lessons at the age of fourteen. His progress, however, was so rapid that, within three years, he began studying harmony with famed composer/teacher Rubin Goldmark. Throughout his early years, Copland was never particularly drawn to the idea of a university education, but he did study at the newly founded School of Music for Americans at Fontainebleau, outside Paris, in 1921. There he came into contact with a woman who had a profound impact on many young composers—Nadia Boulanger. He was so impressed with her that he stayed on in Paris and continued to study with her on a private basis, until his return to America in 1924. His career as a symphonic composer was launched with the Symphony for Organ and Orchestra, and Nadia Boulanger played the organ part for the premier performance.

For a time, Copland's music was filled with jazz harmonies and rhythms, but by the end of the decade he had moved into a much more dissonant phase of his career with such esoteric works as the Piano Variations (1930). It was this piece, with its startling accents and its percussiveness, that helped earn for Copland the label "the Brooklyn Stravinsky."[52]

By the mid-1930s, Copland had begun to rethink his position as an elitist among modern American composers. Realizing that audiences felt removed from his harshly modernistic style, Copland resolved to modify his melodic and harmonic language. In the words of David Ewen:

> Dissatisfied with his failure to please audiences, and feeling that he had been working in a sort of vacuum, Copland now made a conscious effort to speak "in the simplest possible terms." Not only did he simplify his writing, but he also adopted a speech which he felt was more easily assimilable.[53]

Commencing with the symphonic piece *El Salón México* in 1936, Copland's music became laden with popular song melodies and a generally more diatonic melodic and harmonic style. In the next few years, he created the scores of several ballets, including *Billy the Kid* (1938), *Rodeo* (1942), and *Appalachian Spring* (1944).

Copland also began writing music for films, beginning with the score of the documentary *The City*, which was shown at the New York World's Fair in 1939–40. Like Virgil Thomson, Copland worked in film music on a very sporadic basis. In fact, in the decade following the masterful scores he composed in quick succession for *Of Mice and Men* (1939) and *Our Town*

Aaron Copland.

(1940), Copland composed the music for only a few more films. In 1943, Samuel Goldwyn hired him to write the score for Lewis Milestone's *North Star*, an ambitious film set in Russia during World War II. In 1945, Copland did the score for *The Cummington Story*, a documentary produced by the U.S. Office of War Information. Next in his film career came two Hollywood projects that were filmed within a single year: Milestone's *Red Pony* and William Wyler's *Heiress*, both released in 1949.

The Red Pony, which was actually filmed and scored in 1948, is the second film adaptation of a John Steinbeck story with music by Copland (the first being *Of Mice and Men*). Whereas the earlier Steinbeck adaptation features a lean and tensely dramatic score that appears only sparsely in the film, *The Red Pony* features a lush and richly orchestrated accompaniment for a boy's impressions of life on a California ranch.

The opening closeup shots of various birds and animals convey a sense of a child's view of nature, full of mystery and wonder. This scene, which leads directly into the opening credits, is accompanied by the voice of an unseen narrator and by Copland's sweet and gentle background music. The score's main theme first appears as accompaniment for the titles, with a "do-mi-so" pattern that is one of Copland's simplest, yet most effective, tunes, perfectly suited for the simple story of a boy, Tom (Peter Miles), who idolizes a ranch foreman, Billy Buck (Robert Mitchum), and receives as a gift a new-born colt.

One of the score's highlights is the "Walk to the Bunkhouse" music, which accompanies an early scene in which Tom follows Billy to the bunkhouse, where Billy keeps old clippings of his championship days as a rodeo rider. The sprightly syncopations of this walking music (a Copland trademark, which appears also in his ballet scores for both *Billy the Kid* and *Rodeo*) has been much imitated in Western film scores by such composers as Elmer Bernstein and Jerry Goldsmith.

Two other noteworthy sections of the *Red Pony* score involve daydreams that Tom experiences in the early part of the film. In the first, which occurs as he is walking to school, he picks up a stick and starts banging on his lunchpail. As he turns around and starts walking backward, kicking up clouds of dirt, he imagines himself and Billy outfitted in armor, riding on horseback in front of an army of soldiers, with a castle in the background. The music suddenly becomes majestic, with stately chords that fittingly describe this magical moment.

The second daydream occurs later that day, after Tom returns from school and begins to do his chores. As he feeds the chickens in the pen, he starts turning around, and suddenly the chickens become horses in a circus ring. Again the music shifts into a different mode, this time including brassy orchestrations of a raucous circus march.

These three musical episodes, plus the score's opening and closing music and two other sections, were included by Copland in an orchestral suite that he arranged shortly after his completion of the film's score. This concert piece premiered with the Houston Symphony on October 30, 1948.[54] In the intervening years, it has become one of Copland's most popular works; many recordings by major orchestras were released in the early 1990s.

In contrast to the cheerful nature of *The Red Pony*'s music, Copland's score for *The Heiress* contains sounds of a considerably darker coloration.

The Heiress, with
Montgomery Clift
and Olivia de Havilland.

This exquisitely filmed adaptation of Henry James's novel *Washington Square* tells of a wealthy spinster's desperate love for a young man whom her father (rightfully) suspects is a fortune hunter.

Prominently featured in the score is the French song "Plaisir d'amour," which is used as the theme for Catherine Sloper (Olivia de Havilland), who becomes smitten with the dashing but penniless Morris Townsend (Montgomery Clift). This melody, with its lilting waltz rhythm, conveys the depth of Catherine's love at several points in the film, but most particularly in the scene where Catherine's domineering father, Dr. Sloper (Ralph Richardson), is taking her on board a ship bound for Europe, in the hope that Catherine would get over her infatuation. The sweet sounds of the violins convey Catherine's undaunted feelings for Morris, who shows up at the pier to give her a parting gift.

One of the most memorable scenes occurs after Catherine and her father have returned from Europe. The two have had a bitter confrontation, during which her father threatens to cut off her inheritance if she marries Morris. Catherine defies her father and, with the help of her meddling aunt (Miriam Hopkins), makes plans to elope. Morris fails to arrive at the prescribed hour of nine o'clock in the evening, and Catherine's mood changes from happy expectation to bitter feelings of rejection. Copland's music for this scene was originally of a lighter texture, but as he himself pointed out in later interviews, the preview audiences laughed at Catherine when she lugged her bags back into the house. His subsequent rethinking of the music for this scene resulted in a grippingly dramatic musical background that featured slow-paced, sustained string tones with a widely arching melody line, accompanied by dark-tinted chords.[55]

Further changes in the score were made, but unfortunately Copland himself was not involved in making them. Before the film's official premiere, the music for the opening credits was drastically altered by a Paramount studio musician, at Wyler's request. As a result, Copland's original title music, which was strikingly dramatic, was replaced by a rather pedestrian arrangement of the "Plaisir d'Amour" melody. Copland was understandably incensed at this change and requested that his name be removed from the credits; but it was too late, since the film was already in theaters. In one of the eternal ironies of the film-music business, he won an Oscar for the score, even though he was not responsible for the final version.

Perhaps because of the unkind manner in which his music for *The Heiress* was treated by Wyler and Paramount executives, Copland refrained from scoring films for the next twelve years. He composed only one further film score, and that was for a low-budget film *Something Wild*, which flopped when released in 1961. He later salvaged some of its music by incorporating it into an orchestral suite entitled *Music for a Great City*, an evocative set of four mood pictures that celebrate life in New York City.

In view of the high quality of the scores Copland composed for films, it is regrettable that there are so few of them. Of all the serious symphonic composers of the twentieth century (with the possible exception of Sergei Prokofiev), Copland seems to have best understood the special requirements and challenges imposed on the composer by the film medium.

THE **T**HREE **G**ODFATHERS: **S**TILL **S**CORING AFTER **A**LL **T**HESE **Y**EARS. As the end of the 1940s neared, the three godfathers of film scoring—Max Steiner, Alfred Newman, and Dimitri Tiomkin—were all still very active. Steiner was producing scores for Warner Bros. at the rate of nine or ten annually, while Newman was not far behind, with six or seven scoring projects per year at 20th Century-Fox, not counting musicals. Tiomkin continued to find work as a freelance artist, at the rate of five or six film scores a year. A careful look at the end-of-the-decade accomplishments of each of these composers indicates that all three were still at the height of their creative powers.

Among Max Steiner's achievements during 1949 were four scores. Despite his Oscar nomination for the ill-fated *Beyond the Forest*, which features the last of Bette Davis's starring roles at Warner Bros., Steiner did better work on behalf of three other films, including *White Heat*, which ends with bombastic closing music, as Cody Jarrett (James Cagney), about to blow himself up along with the oil truck on which he is standing, yells "Top of the world, Ma!" In *The Fountainhead*, based on the Ayn Rand novel, Steiner created a powerfully modernistic main theme for the architect Howard Roark (Gary Cooper). Roark's theme begins with a series of ascending melodic leaps, and there is also an eloquent love theme for Howard Roark and Dominique Wynand (Patricia Neal). Best of all of Steiner's 1949 scores is the ebulliently romantic score of *The Adventures of Don Juan*, in which Errol Flynn proved, after a long layoff from action roles, that he could still cross swords with skill and finesse. Obviously written in the Korngold vein, Steiner's music consists of a steady stream of tuneful melodic ideas, from the rousing opening march theme to the lovely serenade that accompanies several of the Don's romantic escapades. There is also a lilting theme with a habanera rhythm.

From 1934 through 1949, Steiner achieved a distinction no other musician in Hollywood could claim: he was nominated in every single Oscar race, starting with the initiation of the music categories in 1934. During those sixteen years he won three Oscars, more than any other Hollywood musician in that span of time except for Alfred Newman.

Alfred Newman himself has the distinction of receiving the most Oscar nominations ever for a musician; he received a total of forty-five nominations, spread over a thirty-four-year period. He wasn't nominated for a score in 1949 (he did receive a nomination, however, for his Gregorian chant-inflected song "Through a Long and Sleepless Night," in *Come to the Stable*), even though he had produced a number of strong scores. Of these, *Twelve O'Clock High* is probably the best, with its dramatic opening theme played by soaring violins. Otherwise, there is not much music in the film, and none whatsoever in the scenes of bombing missions, where the sound effects provide the only audio background.

Another Newman score of 1949, that of *Down to the Sea in Ships*, contains an attractive use of sea chanteys, which he employed similarly to the way he used Welsh songs to flavor his score for *How Green Was My Valley*. In his continuing position as head of the music department at 20th Century-Fox, Newman was ever ready to assign such talented composers as

Bernard Herrmann, David Raksin, and Hugo Friedhofer to some of the best films produced at that studio.

In the late 1940s, Dimitri Tiomkin experienced a few lean years during which he was hired for some low-budget films of dubious distinction; in 1949, he obtained some first-rate projects, including *Home of the Brave* and the Oscar-nominated *Champion*, which features Kirk Douglas in the unsympathetic role of Midge Kelly, an ambitious boxer who uses everyone around him to get to the top of his profession. Tiomkin's music skillfully mirrors Douglas's hard-edged acting portrayal by eschewing the use of strings. For the training sequences at the gym, Tiomkin used a Steineresque mickey-mousing effect, with woodwinds, brass, and cymbals, to create an almost comical background, as Midge does a dancelike training routine with his boxing partner. There is even a hint of jazz in this score, in which saxophones and muted trumpets are often used. In rejecting the standard symphonic arrangements of themes, this score clearly anticipates the sound of the 1950s, in which jazz harmonies, rhythms, and instrumental colors would play an increasingly significant role.

S**HORT** C**UTS** ■■■■ **Miklos Rozsa.** In his first year under contract at MGM, Miklos Rozsa wrote several scores, the best of which is his lushly orchestrated music for Vincente Minnelli's *Madame Bovary*, based on Gustave Flaubert's famed novel of marital discord. Rozsa's score ingeniously captures the tormented spirit of Emma Bovary (Jennifer Jones), the unhappy wife of a French provincial doctor; her frustration leads to infidelity and ultimately to her death. To represent Emma, Rozsa created a throbbingly dramatic theme that also accompanies the film's opening credits. For the film's pivotal ballroom scene Rozsa devised a sensuous waltz, the melody of which swirls around while the various couples dance. As Emma is spun in circles by an admirer (Louis Jourdan), the music gradually swells in intensity until the mood becomes overwhelmingly sensuous. Rozsa's music comes to a powerful climax when servants are seen smashing windows so that Emma can breathe. This score marked an auspicious debut for Rozsa at MGM, the studio that would be his professional home for the next decade, during which he would create some of his finest film music.

■■■■ **Louis Gruenberg.** The 1949 Oscar-winning film, *All the King's Men*, a strongly acted drama adapted from Robert Penn Warren's fictional version of the career of Huey Long, is noteworthy for having a musical score by Louis Gruenberg (1884–1964), a Russian-born composer who lived in the United States throughout his active career. He became celebrated as the composer of the 1933 opera *The Emperor Jones*, based on the Eugene O'Neill play. Between 1940 and 1950, Gruenberg composed ten film scores, of which the most noteworthy are his scores for *The Commandos Strike at Dawn* (1943), which won for him the third of his three Oscar nominations, and *All the King's Men*.[56]

The opening-title music of *All the King's Men* shares with Aaron Copland's work the use of strikingly dramatic themes and vibrant rhythms. Unlike the standard Hollywood film, with its wall-to-wall score, *All the King's Men* includes little background score. Music is limited principally to scene changes, where it acts as a connecting bridge. There are short bits of lively music as newspaper headlines are flashed on the screen, announcing the latest accomplishments in the career of Willie Stark (Broderick Crawford), the Huey Long figure. In the film's climactic assassination scene, when Willie is gunned down on the state capitol's steps, all that is heard as accompaniment is the sound of snare drums. As Willie dies, dramatic chords bring *All the King's Men* to a downbeat conclusion. In this film, it isn't the music itself so much as the lack of it that is noteworthy, since so few Hollywood films of the 1940s dared to let the dialogue speak for itself. It was a sign of changing times that director Robert Rossen avoided the standard practice by letting this film be released with so little background music.

POSTLUDE

THE END OF THE GOLDEN AGE. As filmmaking neared midcentury, the Golden Age of Hollywood was clearly coming to an end. After World War II, there were few swashbucklers such as those that had been made before and during the war. Instead, a new type of contemporary, realistic drama was gaining momentum, with on-location shooting lending more authenticity to the visual design. In many of these films, including Elia Kazan's Oscar-winning *Gentleman's Agreement* (1947), as well as Henry Hathaway's *Call Northside 777* (1948), there was virtually no underscoring. As these films demonstrate, the wall-to-wall symphonic background was no longer considered a regular fixture.

The stylistic innovations found in such late-1940s film scores as *Champion* suggest not only the closure of the Golden Age but also the imminent demise of the studio system that had helped to foster the Golden Age in the first place. After 1950, with an increasingly international approach to filmmaking, Hollywood would no longer be the production base for the American film industry. Instead, the name "Hollywood" would conjure up cherished memories of a once-glorious time when the legendary stars of the silver screen not only left impressions on the sidewalk in front of Grauman's Chinese Theatre, but also left indelible imprints on the collective memory of an adoring public which flocked to theaters week after week in search of the romance, thrills, and laughter that the movies offered as an alternative to the real world outside.

Endnotes

1. Susan Sackett, *Hollywood Sings! An Inside Look at Sixty Years of Academy Award–Nominated Songs* (New York: Billboard Books, 1995), p. 51.

2. Ephraim Katz, *The Film Encyclopedia*, 2d ed. (New York: HarperCollins, 1994), p. 865.

3. Leonard Maltin, *The Disney Films*, abridged and updated ed. (New York: Popular Library, 1978), p. 93.

4. Tony Thomas, *The Great Adventure Films* (Secaucus, NJ: Citadel, 1976), p. 106.

5. Rudy Behlmer, Liner notes for *The Sea Hawk* CD, Varese Sarabande VSD-47304, from an interview with George Korngold.

6. Ibid.

7. Thomas, *The Great Adventure Films*, p. 110.

8. Page Cook, "Bernard Herrmann," *Films in Review*, vol. XVIII, no. 7 (August–September, 1967), p. 398.

9. Tony Thomas, *Film Score: The Art and Craft of Movie Music* (Burbank, CA: Riverwood, 1991), p. 172.

10. Steven C. Smith, *A Heart at Fire's Center: The Life and Music of Bernard Herrmann* (Berkeley: University of California, 1991), pp. 43–44.

11. Orson Welles and Peter Bogdanovich, *This Is Orson Welles* (New York: HarperCollins, 1992), p. 337.

12. Ibid., p. 349.

13. Ibid., p. 360.

14. Ibid., pp. 360–61.

15. Ibid, pp. 56–57.

16. Smith, p. 77.

17. Ibid., p. 78.

18. Ibid., p. 79.

19. Ibid.

20. Welles and Bogdanovich, pp. 55–56.

21. Smith, p. 84.

22. Martin Quigley, Jr. and Richard Gertner, *Films in America 1929–1969* (New York: Golden, 1970), p. 113.

23. Smith, pp. 86–87.

24. Bob Dorian and Dorothy Curley, *Bob Dorian's Classic Movies* (Holbrook, MA: Bob Adams, 1990), p. 82.

25. Mason Wiley and Damon Bona, *Inside Oscar: The Unofficial History of the Academy Awards*, 10th anniversary ed. (New York: Ballantine Books, 1996), p. 129.

26. The original RCA recording of *The Jungle Book* was released on an Entr'Acte LP, ERM-6002, in 1979. The later remake, with Leo Genn's narration, was issued in England on a United Artists LP, UAS 29725. Both are in monaural sound. The English album has the bonus of an extended suite from Rozsa's *Thief of Bagdad*.

27. Elston Brooks, *I've Heard Those Songs Before: The Weekly Top Ten Tunes for the Last Fifty Years* (New York: William Morrow and Co., 1981), pp. 117–18.

28. The following commentary appears on the back cover of the 1979 Varese Sarabande LP reissue of the original 1943 recording: "The excessive shrillness particularly evident in the strings on all previous issues of *Song of Bernadette . . .* is an unfortunate distortion that occurred at the original recording sessions."

29. Frank Miller, *Casablanca: As Time Goes By . . . 50th Anniversary Commemorative* (London: Virgin Books, 1993), p. 160.

30. Miklos Rozsa, *Double Life* (New York: Wynwood, 1989), p. 131.

31. Tony Thomas, *Music for the Movies* (South Brunswick, NJ: A. S. Barnes and Co., 1973), pp. 160–61.

32. Ibid.

33. David Raksin, Liner notes for the album *David Raksin Conducts His Great Film Scores*, RCA LP, ARL-1-1490.

34. Brooks, pp. 133–35.

35. Wiley and Bona, p. 1029.

36. Ken Doeckel, "Miklos Rozsa," *Films in Review*, vol. xvi, no. 9 (November 1965), p. 536.

37. Rozsa, p. 146.

38. Albert Vincent Glinsky, *The Theremin in the Emergence of Electronic Music* (unpublished Doctoral Dissertation, New York University, 1992), p. 272. Dr. Hoffman apparently played the theremin part of the *Spellbound* Concerto score numerous times, including for later concert performances. In 1958, Hoffman was given credit on the album cover of a studio recording of *Spellbound* made by Ray Heindorf and the Warner Bros. Studio Orchestra, released on the Warner Bros. label (WB 1213). This recording has been reissued twice—first as an LP in 1974 on Rod McKuen's Stanyan label (SRQ 4021), and then in the 1980s as a Stanyan Compact Disc (STZ 116-2).

39. Rudy Behlmer, Liner notes for *Spellbound: The Classic Film Scores of Miklos Rozsa*, a 1975 RCA recording, ARL1-0911 (LP format), reissued as an RCA CD (0911-2-RG).

40. It should be noted that for this recent recording the theremin has been replaced by the *Ondes Martenot* (Varese Sarabande CD, VCD-47226). It seems that there are few theremins in existence and thus the similar-sounding *Ondes*, with its attached keyboard, has been used to render a reasonable facsimile of the original theremin sounds. It should also be noted that synthesizers can also produce thereminlike tones, and have been called upon to reproduce the theremin parts of Rozsa's film scores for recordings made since 1970, including those with Charles Gerhardt conducting the National Philharmonic, released by RCA as part of the Classic Film Score Series.

41. Rozsa, p. 207.

42. Tony Thomas, "Hugo Friedhofer," *Films in Review*, vol. XVI, no. 8 (October 1965), p. 497.

43. Ibid.

44. George Korngold, Liner notes for *Elizabeth and Essex: The Classic Film Scores of Erich Wolfgang Korngold*, issued as part of the RCA Classic Film Score series (0185-2-RG, CD format).

45. Jon Burlingame, *TV's Biggest Hits* (New York: Schirmer Books, 1996), pp. 16–17. According to Burlingame, Walter Schumann had been at Universal when the score of *The Killers* was being recorded; so he couldn't deny having heard Rozsa's theme. Despite the financial settlement, which awarded Rozsa half of all future royalties for "Dragnet" music, Rozsa never received any screen credit for this most famous of all TV police-show themes.

46. Rozsa, pp. 147–48.

47. Tony Thomas, *The Films of the Forties* (Secaucus, NJ: Citadel, 1975), p. 198.

48. Rozsa, p. 156.

49. David Ewen, *The World of Twentieth Century Music* (Englewood Cliffs, NJ: Prentice-Hall, 1968), p. 856.

50. Thomas, *The Great Adventure Films*, p. 131.

51. Ewen, *World of Twentieth Century Music*, p. 836.

52. Arthur Berger, *Aaron Copland* (New York: Oxford University, 1953), p. 42.

53. Ewen, *World of Twentieth Century Music*, p. 161.

54. Ibid., p. 170.

55. Aaron Copland, interviewed for the TV documentary *Aaron Copland: A Self Portrait* (1985). Copland explains that Paramount executives, following a disastrous preview at which the audience laughed at this crucial scene, prevailed on him to "save the picture." So he made the music darker and the scene worked.

56. Ewen, *World of Twentieth Century Music*, pp. 328–29.

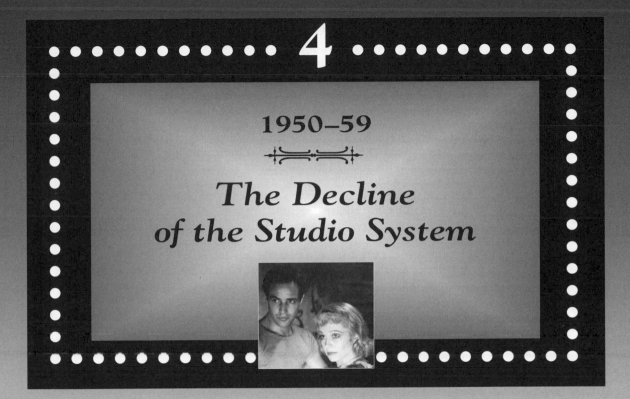

4

1950–59

The Decline of the Studio System

PRELUDE

The decade that is now popularly known as the "Fabulous Fifties" is historically significant as a time of innovation in the entertainment media. For example, color programs were first introduced on network television, and stereophonic sound emerged in the recording industry. Above all, a new type of music, called "rock-'n'-roll," arrived on the scene. This was also a turbulent decade in the motion picture industry; the established studio system began to wane, and independent film production became increasingly common.

POPULAR MUSIC. On the popular-music front, at the beginning of the decade tuneful ballads were being recorded in vast numbers, with many former band singers now gaining fame as solo recording artists. Doris Day, who had the advantage of being a popular movie star, introduced several of her hit songs in her films. Such is the case with "Secret Love," which Doris introduced in the title role of *Calamity Jane* (1953). The song spent eighteen weeks on "Your Hit Parade" in early 1954 and won the Oscar that spring as the best movie song of 1953. Almost as big a hit was her recording of "Whatever Will Be, Will Be," from Hitchcock's thriller *The Man Who Knew Too Much.* This too was an Oscar-winning song (for 1956), and it spent sixteen weeks on the Top Ten charts.[1]

Frank Sinatra had a blossoming career as both a film and a recording star in the 1950s. Though he was dropped by Columbia Records in 1952, he soon began a long association with Capitol Records. His recording of "Young at Heart" replaced "Secret Love" as number one on "Your Hit Parade" on April 17, 1954, and shortly thereafter became the title song of Warner's musical remake of the 1938 classic *Four Daughters,* with Sinatra and Doris Day in the roles originally played by John Garfield and Priscilla Lane.[2]

Throughout the 1950s, many song hits came from Hollywood films. In most of these years, at least one film song rose to the top of the charts. Among the most noteworthy movie songs of the decade were "My Foolish Heart" and "Mona Lisa" (both 1950), "Song from *Moulin Rouge*" and "That's Amore," from *The Caddy* (both 1953), "Unchained Melody" (1955), "Moonglow and Theme from *Picnic*" (1956), and "Tammy" and "April Love" (both 1957).[3]

The advent of rock-'n'-roll led to some tremendous changes in the popular music of the mid-1950s. Bill Haley and the Comets became trendsetters with such hits in 1954 and '55 as "Shake, Rattle and Roll" and "See You Later, Alligator." Their signature tune was "Rock around the Clock," a song that had not done well when first released. However, when it was used in Richard Brooks's popular movie *The Blackboard Jungle* (1955), a dramatically charged film about troubled teens at an inner-city high school, the song became a huge hit and signaled the beginning of a new era in pop music. "Rock around the Clock" developed into a teenage anthem, a song that was adopted as the theme of the younger generation. The popularity of this song led to the recording of thousands of other songs aimed directly at teenagers, who now represented a significant new market for record companies. Soon almost every popular recording artist began to record songs with a rock beat.

The performer who brought rock-'n'-roll to a position of lasting importance was Elvis Presley, a country singer from the Memphis area who signed with RCA in early 1956. His recordings of "Heartbreak Hotel," "Hound Dog," and "Don't Be Cruel" soon made him the world's most successful recording artist. Despite the popularity of such black performers as Fats Domino, Little Richard, Chuck Berry, and the Platters, plus competition from other such rising pop stars as Pat Boone and Ricky Nelson, Presley dominated the record charts for the balance of the 1950s. Indeed, rock-'n'-roll was here to stay, and Elvis was its king.

TELEVISION. In the world of broadcasting the 1950s were notable for the replacement of radio as the principal means of in-home entertainment by network television. This replacement was a gradual process. In 1944, the first TV stations beamed a signal to a few Eastern cities like New York and Philadelphia; but it was several years before there was an actual network of local stations that could carry the video signals on anything approaching a national basis.

At first there were four TV networks: the National Broadcasting Company (NBC), the Columbia Broadcasting System (CBS), the American Broadcasting Company (ABC), and DuMont; the leader in the fledgling TV industry was clearly NBC, which announced the beginning of a network of TV stations in early 1948.[4] In June of that year, "The Texaco Star Theatre" began a long-running Tuesday evening variety hour, with Milton Berle as host. CBS followed within a month by starting the Sunday evening program "The Toast of the Town," hosted by newspaper columnist Ed Sullivan. Berle emerged the immediate victor in the network rivalry, with a phenomenal ratings share in his early-evening time slot. Ed Sullivan, with his limited skill as an entertainer, took longer to become a ratings success.[5]

The number of TV sets in American homes increased at a dramatic rate, with a total of four million being reached by 1950. This was the first year that the number of TV viewers in New York and other Eastern cities matched the number of radio listeners.[6] Also in that year, NBC introduced "Your Show of Shows," with the fine comedic ensemble of Sid Caesar, Imogene Coca,

Carl Reiner, and Howard Morris, and brought "Your Hit Parade" from radio to the nation's TV screens.[7]

Another CBS program that began in the fall of 1951 became the standard by which all other 1950s situation comedies would be judged. "I Love Lucy," which featured Lucille Ball and her husband at that time, Desi Arnaz, became America's favorite TV show for six seasons and helped CBS to become the top-rated network.

A second comedy phenomenon of 1950s television was Jackie Gleason, whose Saturday evening variety program made its debut on CBS in the fall of 1952 and soon became one of TV's most watched shows, with an ensemble cast that often appeared in the "Honeymooners" skits. These were later spun off into a separate series that would eventually become as enduringly popular in syndicated reruns as the "I Love Lucy" episodes.

Another 1952 TV debut that had a great impact on the future of the medium was that of "Dragnet," which had started on radio in 1949 with Jack Webb as Sergeant Friday. The televised version became the first popular police show on TV, with one of the most recognizable musical themes of the decade. By the end of the 1950s, many crime-solving TV programs would emerge, such as "Perry Mason," "M Squad," and "Peter Gunn," the last of which would benefit greatly from the jazz-inflected music of Henry Mancini.

Television enabled people to watch major events unfold. Thus, millions viewed the Senate investigation of organized crime in 1951, and even more people were glued to their TVs during the Army-McCarthy hearings of 1954.

MOVIES. Even before Senator Joseph McCarthy took on the U.S. Army, the suspicion of communist infiltration of the movie industry led to hearings by the House Committee on Un-American Activities (HUAC). Many actors, writers, and directors were blacklisted as a result of the Hollywood "witch hunt," which persisted into the mid-1950s.

Blacklisting endangered the film industry at a critical time, in view of the rise of television. Statistics showed that ever since the arrival of network TV, the number of moviegoers was steadily diminishing. By 1953, box-office receipts fell to the lowest level in nearly a decade.

To counteract this downward trend, film producers sought to promote movie-theater attendance by almost any means available. One method used to lure audiences into theaters was the proliferation of signs that proclaimed the slogan "Movies Are Better Than Ever."[8]

Many 1950s film included daring subject matter. Even though the production code prohibited such topics as drug addiction and illicit sex, these adult themes appeared with increasing frequency. Otto Preminger challenged the code with his films *The Moon Is Blue* (1953) and *The Man with the Golden Arm* (1955). Meanwhile, the plays of Tennessee Williams, with their earthy and often sexually obsessed characters, were brought vividly to life on the screen. *A Streetcar Named Desire* (1951) and *Baby Doll* (1956), both directed by Elia Kazan, achieved notoriety. In *Streetcar*, Marlon Brando's bare-chested display of raw sexuality helped him become a major star; Carroll Baker's provocative performance as a thumb-sucking teenage bride led to the condemnation of *Baby Doll* by the Catholic Church's censorship board, The Legion of Decency.

The sexiest star of the 1950s was Marilyn Monroe, who was catapulted to stardom through her alluring presence in the 20th Century-Fox films *Niagara* (1952) and *Gentlemen Prefer Blondes* (1953). Soon, several other curvaceous blondes were given the star treatment in a seemingly endless effort to duplicate Marilyn's success.

Epic films offered movie audiences a thrilling experience they could not get at home. MGM led the parade of splashy spectacles with *Quo Vadis* (1951) and closed the decade with *Ben-Hur* (1959). Other studios followed suit, with Warner's *Land of the Pharaohs* (1955) and Paramount's *Ten Commandments* (1956), the last—and most expensive—film to be directed by Cecil B. DeMille.

Before the end of 1952, two revolutionary photographic processes were introduced, in a further attempt to attract moviegoers. The first was the premiere at New York's Broadway Theater of the wide-screen film *This Is Cinerama*. The second was the Hollywood premiere of *Bwana Devil*, which had been shot in a three-dimensional process called Natural Vision. Although *Bwana Devil* created only a short-lived boom in 3-D movies (a process hampered by the inconvenience of wearing polaroid eyeglasses in cardboard frames), *This Is Cinerama* had a far-reaching impact on the look and sound of movies.

In conjunction with the novelty of an extra-wide curved screen, the producers of Cinerama enlisted the services of sound experts to design a stereophonic system to enhance the wraparound visual effect. Hazard E. Reeves, director of one of the largest sound laboratories in the Eastern United States, was commissioned to design an innovative sound system to accompany Cinerama's visual projection. The system Reeves devised utilized a magnetic recording process with seven separate sound tracks. Five of these tracks were used to power speakers located behind the enormous triple-width screen, while a sixth could be channeled into any of the speakers mounted on walls around the theater. A seventh was designed as a control track, the purpose of which was to guide the movement of sound in a stereophonic manner, so that the viewer could differentiate left from right.[9]

In 1953, Hollywood studios attempted to supply new equipment to thousands of theaters. As part of a general upgrade, theaters were rewired to accommodate stereophonic sound and larger screens were installed so that wide-screen films could be shown.

Since the Cinerama projection system was too costly for all but a select few theaters, a simpler, less expensive process needed to be found. In 1952, 20th Century-Fox bought up the patent rights to a French process using an anamorphic lens, which was capable of squeezing a wide image onto standard 35-mm film. When projected, this squeezed image would return to wide angle and produce a picture that had a width-to-height ratio of over two to one. Under the name CinemaScope, this process was put to commercial use when 20th Century-Fox launched a series of wide-screen films, beginning with a spectacular version of Lloyd C. Douglas's novel *The Robe*.

While Fox invested millions of dollars in its CinemaScope films, several other wide-screen processes were hurriedly developed by other studios. Paramount introduced VistaVision in 1954; Todd-AO, WarnerScope, Technirama, and other similarly named processes were introduced shortly thereafter.[10] Eventually, most of these wide-screen techniques were abandoned in favor of Panavision, which was first introduced in 1959. Even the original Cinerama process was eventually changed, in favor of a single-projector system, which eliminated the annoying vertical lines that appeared between the converging frames on the oversized screen.

Despite all the gimmicks—wide screens, 3-D images, and stereophonic sound—the movie industry never wholly regained the sheer numbers of filmgoers who had attended theaters on a regular basis before the arrival of network television programming. Only with a select few extravagantly budgeted movie spectaculars could Hollywood hope to draw future audiences in large numbers. For good or ill, the blockbuster mentality that came into being during the 1950s has remained in force ever since.

After a quarter-century, musical films began a period of decline. Although MGM continued to have successes in the early part of the decade with such hits as *An American in Paris* (1951), *Singin' in the Rain* (1952), and *Seven Brides for Seven Brothers* (1954), profits began to dwindle with such later efforts as *Kismet* (1955), *Les Girls* (1957), and *Silk Stockings* (1957). These last two films, which starred Gene Kelly and Fred Astaire, respectively, were the last musical movies that either of these two graceful dancers would ever star in.

In the 1950s, the wall-to-wall score became almost obsolete. Fewer films had continuous background music; occasionally, as in Robert Wise's *Executive Suite* (1954), there was no musical score whatsoever. Although Max Steiner, Alfred Newman, and Dimitri Tiomkin, among others, continued to score films throughout the 1950s, fewer movies employed the symphonic style that these film-music pioneers had used so successfully in previous decades. Many 1950s film scores used jazz, including Alex North's groundbreaking score for *A Streetcar Named Desire* (1951). Soon many other films were scored in a more modernistic style. The most drastic departure from traditional scoring came with MGM's *Forbidden Planet* (1956), for which Louis and Bebe Barron conceived an entire score of "electronic tonalities."[11]

Although the Golden Age was past, Hollywood studios continued to employ composers on a full-time basis. Max Steiner contributed prolifically to Warner Bros. films throughout the decade, while Alfred Newman achieved some of his best work at 20th Century-Fox and Miklos Rozsa began a series of epic scores for historical romances at MGM. Victor Young continued working at Paramount, although he increasingly accepted outside assignments, such as the one that finally won him an Oscar, Mike Todd's *Around the World in Eighty Days* (1956).

Meanwhile, freelance composing in Hollywood was on the increase, with Franz Waxman joining the independent ranks of Dimitri Tiomkin, Bernard Herrmann, and Hugo Friedhofer. All of these composers contributed some exceptional scores during the 1950s. Tiomkin created an especially innovative Western score for *High Noon* (1952), in which the song "Do Not Forsake Me" was woven into the background score. The success of this music had a tremendous impact on film scoring, since producers became convinced that commercial recordings of film songs could help promote films prior to their release. Consequently, title songs became a fad in the mid-1950s; their mention by radio disc jockeys helped advertise the films.

From *Cinderella* (1950) to *Alice in Wonderland* (1951), *Peter Pan* (1953), and *Lady and the Tramp* (1955), Disney composers contributed a number of tuneful songs that have continued to charm viewers young and old through the many subsequent reissues of these films and their eventual release on videotape. The last Disney animated film of the decade, *Sleeping Beauty* (1959), which has one of the most interesting Disney scores, is based on the music Tchaikovsky composed in 1890 for the ballet *The*

Sleeping Beauty. Tchaikovsky's lilting "Sleeping Beauty Waltz" became the melody of the song "Once upon a Dream," while other themes from the ballet score were also transformed into a number of charming songs. Additionally, much of Tchaikovsky's music was borrowed for the dramatic background scoring, which won for George Bruns (b. 1914) an Oscar nomination.

Hollywood at midcentury was a far cry from what it was in the early days of filmmaking. With the advent of sound in the 1920s, the glitter and glamour of the movies had become an increasingly significant part of American culture; but by 1950, the Golden Age of studio production was coming to an end. The post–World War II trend toward increased realism led filmmakers to look beyond studio sets and go to the streets for added authenticity. With this more realistic visual approach, many producers began to reject the concept of the traditional wall-to-wall background score for fear that music might create an atmosphere of romantic escapism that would be at odds with the visual realism they were attempting to create.

FRANZ **W**AXMAN: *S*UNSET *B*OULEVARD. Just as the efficacy of continuous underscoring was being questioned, German-born composer Franz Waxman proved that a strong musical score, with perhaps a touch of modernism in its harmony, rhythm, and instrumentation, could heighten the dramatic impact of a film such as Billy Wilder's *Sunset Boulevard.*

Long before Waxman arrived in the United States and worked with renowned directors like Wilder and Hitchcock, he grew up surrounded by classical music, as had many other European film composers before him. The youngest of seven children raised in a middle-class Jewish family in Upper Silesia, young Franz Wachsmann at first received little encouragement for his musical studies. Despite Franz's talent for playing the piano, his father arranged for him to work as a bank teller when he was only sixteen. A year later, in 1923, against his father's wishes, Franz enrolled in the Dresden Music Academy. Soon he transferred to the Berlin Music Conservatory, where he studied composition and conducting. As a rebellious youth he had no financial backing from his family and thus had to support himself by playing in the evening in cafés. This led to an offer to become the pianist for the Weintraub Syncopaters, one of the most popular jazz bands in Europe.[12]

According to Page Cook, one of the composers who worked with the band had a strong influence on young Wachsmann:

> Some of its music was written by Friedrich Hollaender, who was older than Waxman. He recognized the latter's seriousness about music, encouraged him, and introduced him to Gretl Walter. Her father was Bruno Walter, one of our day's most talented conductors, and he accelerated, and deepened, the musical education of Franz Waxman.[13]

Hollaender (1896–1976), who later came to Hollywood and became a respected film composer under the name Frederick Hollander, left the Syncopaters to write background scores for producer Erich Pommer at the Universum Film Aktiengesellschaft (UFA) studio in Berlin. In 1930, he arranged for Wachsmann to get a job orchestrating and conducting scores for films made in Berlin. One of his first tasks was the orchestration and conducting of Hollaender's music for *The Blue Angel*, which made Marlene Dietrich an international star. During the next three years, Wachsmann

Franz Waxman.

Photo by and courtesy of John W. Waxman

got the opportunity to write his own music for films; he also made friends of Fritz Lang, Billy Wilder, and Peter Lorre, and met his first wife, Alice Schlachmann. In 1933, shortly before their marriage, he was beaten up by a gang of Nazis on a Berlin street. He and Alice then moved to Paris, where Erich Pommer and Fritz Lang had also gone to evade the Nazis. There, in 1934, Wachsmann scored *Liliom*, which was produced and directed by Lang. Soon thereafter, Pommer was offered a producing job at the Fox studio in Hollywood, and he hired Wachsmann as music director for the film version of Jerome Kern's *Music in the Air*. Upon arriving in the United States, Franz simplified the spelling of his name to its present form.

Waxman's first original score for an American film came in 1935, when he was hired by James Whale to write the innovative music of *The Bride of Frankenstein*. He continued to labor for many years as a studio musician, first at Universal (1935–36), then at MGM (1936–43), and finally at Warner Bros. (1943–47). Much of his early work is set in either a romantic or a comedy idiom, in such films as *The Young in Heart* (1938) and *The Philadelphia Story* (1940). His atmospheric Hitchcock scores, such as *Rebecca* (1940) and *Suspicion* (1941), are a different type of film music, conveying a sense of mystery and suspense. In this genre his work somewhat prefigures that of Miklos Rozsa. In subsequent years, Waxman produced some of the finest film music of his career. Throughout the 1950s, he was a potent advocate of full symphonic scoring. His first major score of the new decade came almost immediately, with Billy Wilder's *Sunset Boulevard*. With his writing collaborators Charles Brackett and D. M. Marshman, Jr., Wilder fashioned the screenplay for *Sunset Boulevard*, a searing drama that looked at Hollywood from the inside.

In the film's scenario, former movie queen Norma Desmond (Gloria Swanson) lives in a run-down, but still ornate mansion on Hollywood's Sunset Boulevard. She is patiently looked after by her butler Max (Erich von Stroheim), who also happens to be her former director and first husband. Norma hires Joe Gillis (William Holden), a financially strapped young screenwriter, to edit and polish her script based on the Biblical character Salome, a role which she hopes to enact as her comeback. A strange attraction draws Norma and Joe together. The once-famous Norma basks in the glories of her earlier career, while the opportunistic Joe lives in the dreams of his future successes. Each feeds off the other until an inevitable clash occurs, with tragic consequences for both.

Sunset Boulevard's script, which has some of the best movie dialogue ever written, provided an actor's field day, especially for Gloria Swanson, who was not Wilder's first choice for the role (he wanted Mae West). As a Paramount contract player, William Holden got his big film break here.[14]

Waxman's score contains two principal melodic motifs. The first, a busy, modernistic theme, is heard during the opening credits; thereafter it is used as traveling music when Joe is being chased by car repossessors and winds up with a flat tire in the driveway of Norma's mansion. The second is an exotic melody associated with Norma, which is heard whenever she discusses her plans to return to the screen as Salome. It is also used effectively in the studio scene, where she hopes to discuss her comeback. When she drops in on Cecil B. DeMille, he is at work shooting *Samson and Delilah*. Norma is invited by DeMille to sit in his director's chair while he finishes shooting a scene. An elderly lighting technician recognizes her. As he turns

Sunset Boulevard, with
Gloria Swanson and
Cecil B. DeMille.

a spotlight on her, the "Salome" theme swells up gloriously. Later, when Joe starts packing his things and prepares to leave the mansion, Norma's increasingly unstable mental state is suggested by long-sustained, eerily wavering, high-pitched tones played by woodwinds and strings, which also make a subtle reference to the "Salome" theme.

It is in the final scene, in which Norma fatally shoots Joe, who falls into the swimming pool, that her big comeback moment finally arrives. Max, comprehending her totally deranged condition, gets the police to back off so that he can try to coax her to come downstairs from her room, where she has gone. He instructs the news photographers to roll their cameras, and sets up a scene with Norma as Salome, letting her know that she is to greet the people at her palace as she descends a grand staircase.

Waxman's choice of harmony and instrumentation at the beginning of this scene seems to convey the feeling that Norma is all wrong for the part of Salome, with an alto saxophone providing at one point an anachronistic bit of melody. Although the matter of her being too old to play Salome is never discussed, it is made clear by Waxman's music that Norma's obsession with the Biblical character is a clear indication of her madness. As she moves forward, with her arms extended, the rich orchestration suggests that Norma Desmond has now truly become Salome. As the film ends, she walks directly toward the camera for her long-awaited closeup, accompanied by powerful closing chords.

For Waxman, this Oscar-winning score marked the beginning of a creatively fertile decade, during which he would create some of the best scores of his entire film-music career.

DIMITRI TIOMKIN: CYRANO DE BERGERAC AND D.O.A. Dimitri Tiomkin created most of his film music in 1950 for independent producers who released their films through United Artists. For Stanley Kramer, with whom he had worked the preceding year on *Champion*, Tiomkin

scored two new films, *The Men* and *Cyrano de Bergerac. Cyrano* provided him an opportunity to create a Baroque-period orchestration, in which a harpsichord provides an atmospheric harmonic background.

The main-title theme, heard periodically throughout the film, begins with a bright fanfare melody. In one of the courtship scenes, Cyrano (José Ferrer) speaks for Christian (William Prince), who has solicited his friend to assist him in his attempt to woo Roxanne (Mala Powers). Here a solo violin, accompanied by harp and strings, plays a romantic theme. For the battle scenes, Tiomkin provided a dissonant accompaniment, filled with jarring brass chords. During much of the film, an a cappella choir is heard singing wordlessly behind the dialogue. The use of voices, a staple in Tiomkin's orchestrations, harks back to the music of *Lost Horizon*, his first important film score. At the end of the movie, as Roxanne listens to Cyrano reciting from memory a letter that she has worn on a chain around her neck for years and which she has long assumed to have been written by Christian, strings are combined with wordless voices. As Cyrano dies, the music swells and bells begin to toll, followed by a robust closing statement of the opening fanfare melody.

One other 1950 Tiomkin score of note is *D.O.A.*, a small-budget film in which Edmond O'Brien plays a man who goes into a police precinct to report his own murder prematurely. During the opening credits, as we see the man's legs moving in steady marchlike fashion toward the building and then inside toward the front desk, Tiomkin's music is cleverly synchronized, in mickey-mouse fashion, with each move the man makes. Although this Steiner-inspired technique has often been overemphasized, in *D.O.A.* its use is quite effective.

ALFRED NEWMAN: *ALL ABOUT EVE.* At 20th Century-Fox, Alfred Newman entered into the new decade with several new scores, including those for *The Gunfighter*, *No Way Out*, and *Panic in the Streets*. The 1950 film score for which he is best remembered is the music for the movie that beat out *Sunset Boulevard* as the year's Oscar-winning picture—Joseph L. Mankiewicz's *All about Eve*.

As a writer and director, Mankiewicz was something of a Hollywood *wunderkind*. To this day, he is the only person ever to win back-to-back Oscars as both writer and director—for *A Letter to Three Wives* in 1949 and for *All about Eve* in 1950. In *All about Eve* he created a fascinating picture of Broadway actors and the people who surround them. When Claudette Colbert, the original choice, injured her back, she was forced to give up the role.[15] Bette Davis inherited the part of the aging stage star Margo Channing. Davis's unforgettable performance is immensely enhanced by Mankiewicz's acutely tailored dialogue, which is laced with an acerbic wit.

Although Newman's music is heard during less than a third of the film's total running time, what he created is memorable. The main-title music consists of two ideas, first a majestic brass fanfare, and then a marchlike melody that begins with a boldly rising octave played by violins, with brass chords and timpani used as a driving rhythmic accompaniment. The march theme later reappears in a slower tempo, played by strings alone. As emotionally moving as any melody Newman ever created, this theme is associated with Eve Harrington (Anne Baxter), the catalyst who brings the characters of the story into conflict.

When Karen Richards (Celeste Holm) takes star-struck Eve backstage to meet her idol Margo Channing, Eve at first appears sincere in her desire to be in the presence of such a star. Soon it becomes clear that her motives are much more calculated. Eve soon lets Karen know that she wants to star in the new play that Karen's husband Lloyd (Hugh Marlowe) has written with Margo in mind. How Eve succeeds in getting the role takes up much of the film, as told in flashbacks by several characters, including acid-tongued critic Addison De Witt (George Sanders), who figures out Eve's self-serving agenda and outsmarts her in the film's ironic conclusion. As part of the final irony, Eve, who has become an award-winning Broadway star, meets young Phoebe (Barbara Bates), whose seeming admiration of Eve repeats the earlier scenario. In the concluding scene, as Phoebe stands in front of a wardrobe mirror, wearing Eve's coat and handling Eve's newly won acting trophy, Newman's soaring main-title music returns for a final triumphant statement.

SHORT CUTS ■■■■ Victor Young.

Victor Young's majestic score for *Samson and Delilah*, Cecil B. DeMille's lavish version of the Old Testament story, was among the music nominees in 1950. His colorful score begins in dramatic fashion, with a three-note idea that arches upward by a seventh, then drops back down in pitch. This is followed by an exotic main theme and by another melody that later appears as the love theme. The use of a tonal pattern that resembles a minor scale with a raised fourth step helps to give these melodies a pseudo-Hebraic flavor. There is much dance music in the film, including a bacchanal scene at the temple. All of Young's themes, which convey the spirit of Hollywood's Golden Age, make it patently clear that DeMille had no desire to abandon his old-fashioned style of filmmaking.

■■■■ Max Steiner.

At Warner Bros., Max Steiner found an opportunity to create a historically flavored score with his rousing music for the medieval romance *The Flame and the Arrow*. With Burt Lancaster and his old circus partner Nick Cravat performing a dazzling series of acrobatic stunts, this film afforded Steiner the chance to create lighthearted music, including a fast-moving main theme played by mandolins. A dramatic fanfare is used periodically to punctuate the action; but in the concluding sword-fight, with its clanging swords and crashing furniture, there is no music.

The absence of music in one of *The Flame and the Arrow*'s key scenes is indicative of a new approach to film scoring in the 1950s. This revisionist way of thinking about the presence of music in film is an important factor in the movement toward realism, in which American filmmakers of the '50s began to emulate the style of such eminent Italian directors as Vittorio De Sica and Roberto Rossellini, in whose post–World War II films music is used much more sparingly than in American films of the same period.

■■■■ Anton Karas.

The music for Carol Reed's *Third Man* was performed on the zither. The single melody that is repeated throughout the film has become one of the most popular movie themes of all time.

Its composer, Anton Karas (1906–85), was a prominent Viennese zither artist who was discovered while the film was being shot on location in Vienna. The music that Karas recorded for *The Third Man*, his only film work, was not so much composed as improvised, with its now-familiar theme. As a score, Karas's work doesn't contribute very much to the tension of Graham Greene's mystery story. Rather, the twangy music serves as an almost disinterested bystander that goes about its business while the intriguing story of Harry Lime (Orson Welles) and his faked funeral unfolds. Karas could be criticized for a lack of variety in his film composing, but then the zither itself has a rather limited range of sounds.

1951

Perhaps it is purely coincidental that, with the rise of independent film production in the 1950s and the concomitant decline of the old studio system, several new faces emerged on the film music scene. Many of these composers would have a considerable impact on the style of film music.

ALEX NORTH: *A STREETCAR NAMED DESIRE.* Among the most talented and influential of the new composers working in Hollywood in the early 1950s was Alex North (1910–91), who was forty years old when Elia Kazan invited him to come to Hollywood to score the film version of Tennessee Williams's celebrated play *A Streetcar Named Desire.* For this candidly adult drama of sexual longing, set in New Orleans, Kazan wanted the musical background to include jazzy rhythm and instrumentation, which North introduced into the film's music.[16]

Photo by Gay Goodwin Wallin

Alex North.

Little in North's educational background suggests that he had a long-term interest in jazz. Having studied the piano as a youngster, he attended the Juilliard School in New York. He spent the school year of 1933–34 as a student at the Moscow Conservatory; upon his return to the United States he studied composition with Ernst Toch. With the help of Aaron Copland he received commissions for several ballets.

North entered the Army in 1942 and worked for the Office of War Information, wherein he was assigned, as was Dimitri Tiomkin, to the task of scoring documentary films, one of which was *A Better Tomorrow.*[17]

The first hint that North might be interested in jazz was a work commissioned by Benny Goodman, which North wrote when he was off duty. The resulting composition, Revue for Clarinet and Orchestra, was introduced by Goodman, with Leonard Bernstein conducting the City Symphony Orchestra, on November 18, 1946.[18] About his interest in jazz North once wrote, "It is my opinion that jazz, as source material, has been sadly neglected by our serious contemporary American composers."[19]

After World War II, North's career as a composer continued to blossom, with several commissions and even a Guggenheim fellowship, which led to the writing of his Symphony no. 1 (1948).[20] Meanwhile, he continued to score documentary films for various governmental agencies, including the State Department, the Health Department, and the Agriculture Department. In all, he scored about eighty short films, ranging in length from about fifteen to thirty minutes, with wall-to-wall music.[21]

As early as 1939, North began writing music for Broadway plays, the most celebrated of which was Arthur Miller's 1949 Pulitzer Prize-winning *Death of a Salesman,* directed by Elia Kazan. The Broadway production of *A Streetcar Named Desire* was also directed by Kazan, who persuaded his bosses at Warner Bros. to hire North to do the score for the film.

What North accomplished in his *Streetcar* music was a groundbreaking use of the jazz idiom for film music. Jazzy rhythms and chords had been used in many 1940s film musicals, but never before had the language of jazz been central to the background score of a dramatic film.

North's main-title music emphasizes a blues style. A slow string theme is accompanied by jazzy brass chords, with a solo piano added for background

A Streetcar Named Desire,
with Marlon Brando
and Vivien Leigh.

effect. This segues directly into an upbeat-style swing piece that accompanies Blanche DuBois (Vivien Leigh) as she arrives in the city and looks for the streetcar to take her to her sister Stella's downstairs apartment in a rather old section of New Orleans.

For the character of Stella's husband, Stanley Kowalski, which Marlon Brando skillfully recreated from his exciting Broadway stage performance, North's theme used an alto saxophone. This instrument had not been used very often in previous film scores, but after it was used in *Streetcar* (and also in Franz Waxman's music for *Sunset Boulevard* and for *A Place in the Sun*), it came into prominence.

North utilized an old waltz tune, which Blanche refers to as the "Varsouviana" (the same melody as that of "Put Your Little Foot Right Out"), for scenes in which Blanche remembers the music the band played at the Moon Lake Casino on the night her husband shot and killed himself. This melody, with tinkly, bell-like tones provided by the celesta, represents echoes from Blanche's past and also provides an indication of her fragile mental state. In the film's final scene, as the emotionally distraught Blanche is to be taken away by two mental-health officials, the score assumes a poignant quality, with strings providing a dramatic minor-key theme that strongly hints at the degree of madness to which Blanche has been driven by her brutish brother-in-law's sexual assault on her.

Overall, music is used sparingly, so as not to overemphasize the emotions of Tennessee Williams's text. The result is a score that doesn't draw undue attention to itself, but is always there to enhance the film.

For a first film score, North's accomplishment with *Streetcar* cannot be overpraised. His music helps the viewer feel the impending tragedy of

Blanche DuBois unfold. In that final scene, it is both North's music and Vivien Leigh's heartrending portrayal that evoke empathy.

After *Streetcar*, North immediately scored two other projects: Otto Preminger's *Thirteenth Letter* and the film version of *Death of a Salesman*. In the 1951 Oscar race North was nominated for both *Streetcar* and *Salesman*, but failed to win. Despite thirteen additional nominations over the next four decades, Alex North, one of the supreme composers of film music, would never win in the competitive music categories; his sole Oscar came in 1986, when he was awarded an honorary lifetime-achievement award.

BERNARD HERRMANN: *THE DAY THE EARTH STOOD STILL.* The year 1951 marks Bernard Herrmann's return to film scoring after a three-year hiatus, during which time he completed the opera *Wuthering Heights*. His return is significant because his highly innovative scores for Robert Wise's *Day the Earth Stood Still* and several other futuristic films helped usher in a new vogue for science-fiction movies.

This film attempted to portray an alien visitation in a serious manner, without elaborate hardware (the notable exception being the giant robot named Gort). Herrmann's music involves an unconventionally creative orchestration; it consists of thirty brass instruments augmented by four pianos, four harps, and some unusually eerie electronic effects provided by an electric violin and an electric bass, plus two theremins, which were played for the film's soundtrack by Dr. Samuel Hoffman, the man who had performed the theremin parts of Miklos Rozsa's scores in the mid-1940s.[22] Especially noteworthy in this score is Herrmann's ominous brass writing for the scenes involving Gort. Whenever the robot appears, several long-sustained brass chords, combined with the wavering tones of the theremin, create a truly ominous feeling. Elsewhere in the film, as in the opening scene in which the flying saucer is tracked by radar, Herrmann creatively combines fast-moving bass notes on two of the pianos with rapid high notes on the other keyboards to create a feeling of nervous anticipation.

DIMITRI TIOMKIN: *FROM SCI-FI FILM TO THRILLER.* To create an eerie musical background for Howard Hawks's film *The Thing from Another World*, Tiomkin employed a large ensemble made up of low-pitched instruments, including double basses combined with a large number of woodwinds and low brass; to these he added several percussion instruments, including two sets of timpani, a flexatone, a wind machine, two pianos, three harps, an electric organ, a pipe organ, and a theremin. These instruments were divided into five groups.[23]

The score begins in dramatic fashion. Chords of gradually intensifying volume are heard while the title of the movie is progressively revealed by beams of light that penetrate a dark surface to reveal the illuminated letters. The music for *The Thing* is among the least melodic of all of Tiomkin's scores; its emphasis is on ominous chord patterns which are heard at periodic points in the film, first when an air force team stationed at the North Pole approaches the landing site where a flying saucer lies buried beneath the ice, and later when the creature they have discovered in the ice thaws out and begins stalking the military compound.

There are two especially dramatic scenes with boldly dissonant music. The first involves an attempt to incinerate the alien and the second is the film's chilling climax. When the creature is destroyed by electrocution, the score's instrumental effects are joined together in a grand splash of sound.

Although the theremin's wavy tones are less prominently used in *The Thing* than in *The Day the Earth Stood Still*, they still manage to convey an uneasy feeling. If Tiomkin's music may be ultimately less original in substance than Herrmann's masterful score, it still manages to enhance one of the most terrifying films of the early 1950s.

Tiomkin also wrote the dramatically charged music for Alfred Hitchcock's *Strangers on a Train*. In this ingenious thriller, Robert Walker plays Bruno Antony, a smooth-talking sociopath, who suggests to Guy Haines (Farley Granger), a tennis pro whom he meets on a train, that they swap murders. Although Guy thinks Bruno is only kidding, the body of Guy's estranged wife is discovered at an amusement park and Guy becomes the prime suspect.

Tiomkin's music accelerates in tempo as the film progresses. For a wonderfully edited scene in which Guy plays a tennis match while Bruno tries to retrieve an incriminating cigarette lighter that has fallen into a storm drain, Tiomkin's music carefully follows the crosscutting between the two simultaneous situations. The score switches back and forth between fast-moving music for the tennis volleys and a slower, more ominous background for the closeups of Bruno's hand reaching down into the storm drain.

Music also plays an important role in the climactic struggle between Bruno and Guy, on a carousel at the park to which Bruno has returned to plant the fateful lighter. When the carousel's operator is shot and accidentally falls on the gears, the music speeds up as the carousel starts to spin wildly out of control.

Tiomkin's scoring is seldom subtle, but for highly dramatic scenes such as those in *Strangers on a Train*, his rhythmic and passionate music provides the viewer with a heightened sense of excitement.

SHORT CUTS ■■■■ Miklos Rozsa.

At MGM, Miklos Rozsa got his first golden opportunity to accompany an epic film set in ancient times when he scored the expensively mounted *Quo Vadis*. Basically a love story with a spectacular setting, the scenario of this film includes the burning of Rome, gladiatorial combat, and several impressive crowd scenes for which Rozsa provides a number of Roman marches. Also included in the score are melodies that resemble Gregorian chants, such as the minor-key theme heard in the film's opening titles. A more romantically styled theme is the beautiful melody devised for the character of Phrygia (Deborah Kerr), who is the love interest for the story's principal character, Marcus Vinicius (Robert Taylor). There is also a purposefully mundane tune for Nero (played by the scene-stealing Peter Ustinov), which he sings as he plucks the strings of his lyre while Rome goes up in flames. One of the films's positive contributions to historical accuracy is having Nero pluck the lyre rather than play the fiddle, which may not have existed then.

■■■■ **Franz Waxman.** The score that won the 1951 Oscar was Franz Waxman's romantically tinged music for George Stevens's *Place in the Sun*, an updated version of Theodore Dreiser's *American Tragedy* (1925). By moving Dreiser's novel from the 1920s to the contemporary period, Stevens's screenwriters lost some of the social significance of the story in terms of the American class struggle of the earlier period.

George Eastman (Montgomery Clift), a humble factory worker, becomes romantically involved with a fellow worker, Alice Tripp (Shelley Winters), who soon gets pregnant. By the time the pregnancy is revealed, George has already met another woman, Angela Vickers (Elizabeth Taylor), whose wealthy family invites him to the country club, where he gets a taste of a better lifestyle. Soon George finds himself torn between two worlds.

Franz Waxman's background score is not completely original. In one of the early sequences, when George takes Alice out on a date, the Jay Livingston and Ray Evans song "Mona Lisa" is heard, followed shortly thereafter by Johnny Green and Edward Heyman's "Out of Nowhere." Later, a second rendition of "Out of Nowhere" emanates from a radio, this time performed with a Latin beat. Waxman's original music consists primarily of two themes, which are used for George's two relationships. A purposefully clumsy tune signifies his uneasiness when he is with Alice, whereas the theme for George's courtship of Angela consists of an insinuatingly sexy tune which features the alto saxophone. As these two melodies alternate, so also does the direction of George's thoughts and feelings spin back and forth.

A throbbing rhythmic idea is used to convey George's confused thoughts when he contemplates killing Alice, who has threatened to expose his duplicity to the Vickers family if he doesn't marry her. Following the fateful scene at the lake where the rowboat capsizes and Alice drowns, there is more dramatically charged music. The police seek George for questioning in the matter of Alice's death. As he eludes them, a rhythmically energized string idea begins, and several overlapping lines are added in the manner of a fugue. The music gradually builds in intensity until the moment when George is apprehended.

DIMITRI TIOMKIN: *HIGH NOON.* Fred Zinnemann's *High Noon* is the rather ordinary story of a crisis for Will Kane, the marshal of a small Western town, who had once arrested and helped imprison a gunman, Frank Miller. Now Miller has been pardoned and he's coming on the noon train. With the help of three members of his gang, who are at the train station awaiting his arrival, Miller plans to settle an old score with Kane.

News of Miller reaches Will as he resigns his job and is about to leave town with the young woman he has just married. Everyone encourages him to leave, especially his pacifist wife, whose Quaker upbringing compels her to avoid a violent confrontation. Will's conscience, however, will not let him abandon his post in a cowardly manner. With little more than an hour till the train arrives, he tries to round up some help for his cause, but everyone he approaches turns him down. Thus, he must face the enemy alone.

As Will Kane, Gary Cooper evinces the dogged determination of a rather humorless man, about whom we basically know very little. What we do know is that he has integrity and that he never runs away from trouble.

Visually, *High Noon* resembles many B-pictures of the 1950s. This black-and-white film has a no-frills set that consists primarily of a main street in a frontier town, bordered by rows of typical buildings: a hotel, a saloon, a barber shop, and a jail.

Two things ultimately separate *High Noon* from the average movies of its day. One is Carl Foreman's script, which includes psychological insights into even the most minor characters. Not only did this film become the prototype of the "adult Western," but also Foreman devised the story to take place on a single day—in fact, in the span of eighty-five minutes, the same as the film's total running time. The other factor is Dimitri Tiomkin's music, which in keeping with the grim aspects of the story, features no violins in the string section, and even the low strings are subordinated to the sounds of low woodwinds, brass, and piano.

The music is predominantly based on the title song, subtitled "Do Not Forsake Me." This song, with lyrics by Ned Washington, was recorded for the film's soundtrack by the renowned country singer and Western film actor Tex Ritter. With only guitar, accordion, and a thumping drum sound for instrumental background, Ritter's voice is heard over the film's opening credits, while we watch Miller's gang meet outside Hadleyville and ride into town toward the train station. No other sounds are heard, not even the clopping of horse hooves. The song fades at the sounding of a church bell, which announces the beginning of a Sunday morning service. Tiomkin's underscore starts at this point. On the screen we see the three gang members being recognized by the townsfolk, who react with fear because they sense an imminent violent confrontation. In the early scene in which Will and his bride Amy (Grace Kelly) begin to ride out of town, the theme is heard in a lyrical arrangement featuring strings and harmonica. The song makes several subsequent reappearances, as Will, who has taken Amy to the hotel to wait for him, unsuccessfully tries to round up deputies. As he walks from the marshal's office to the saloon, then to the church, the song continues, with lyrics that help to explain the story.

High Noon, with Gary Cooper and Grace Kelly.

As the film progresses, the orchestration of the theme takes on a much more menacing quality. The camera continually shows clocks in closeup, a reminder that noon is drawing ever closer. Since the passing of time in the film is equivalent to real time, clocks assume a very significant role as film props. Tiomkin's music begins to reflect the importance of time early on in the film; clock-ticking sounds played on a harp permeate several scenes. These repeated tones add a subliminal effect, as if to say that Will is being reminded by the film's music that time is running out. As noon draws ever closer, the music builds up dramatically. One minute before noon, a pendulum wall clock is seen in full closeup, accompanied by music that has been carefully synchronized with the movement of the pendulum. A few seconds before noon, pounding timpani and loudly accented brass chords are heard as rhythmic punctuation, with a bit of Tiomkin's song melody thrown in. The relentless buildup continues until noon is shown on the clock face, at which point the music abruptly stops and an ominous train whistle sounds.

After the train arrives and Frank Miller is reunited with his gang members, the music starts up again and assumes a tumultuous marchlike quality as the four gunmen begin their hike into town. In the ensuing gun battle, several variations on the song melody are heard, with a variety of bombastic orchestral effects. After the battle, in which Will triumphs (with his bride's help), and the two are reunited, they ride out of town for a second (and final) time, while Tex Ritter's voice is heard once again. The film ends with quiet music as the buckboard in which the couple are riding rounds a bend and heads out of the camera's view. This pianissimo ending is quite astonishing for its time, when almost every other film announced the end title with a blaring orchestral fanfare.

Although the music of *High Noon* now ranks as one of the most famous film scores of the early 1950s, few people thought Tiomkin's music appropriate when the film was first completed. Harry Cohn, head of Columbia Pictures, thought the whole film was so bad that he refused to have his company release it. Producer Stanley Kramer ultimately got United Artists to distribute the film.[24]

There are conflicting stories concerning the way in which the film wound up in its final form, with Tiomkin's song as background music. Elmo Williams, who shared an Oscar for editing the film, seems to have spread the story that, following a disastrous preview of the film, he came up with the idea of having the film reedited, with the addition of a song that would be interpolated at various points, and with the film's structure rearranged to reflect the passage of real time between Will Kane's wedding and the fateful showdown at noon.[25]

In his autobiography, director Fred Zinnemann supports the opposing view: that Carl Foreman's script was originally planned with an exact-time scheme. According to Zinnemann: "The entire action was designed by Foreman and Kramer to take place in the exact screening time of the film— less than ninety minutes."[26]

Another point of contention about *High Noon* concerns the derivation of the song itself. While Tiomkin claims in his autobiography that it was his idea to rescue the film by inserting a song that would be featured throughout the picture, Zinnemann again makes a claim to the contrary:

> Kramer had brilliant, original ideas about the musical style of the movie, especially the use of a theme song, which he insisted should be a Western ballad. He kept asking the composer, Dimitri Tiomkin, to try and try again, until he had come up with the tune to Ned Washington's lyrics "Do not forsake me, O my darling."[27]

Yet another point of contention concerns the lyrics. Not only does Tiomkin claim that it was his idea to insert the song, but he also asserts that he wrote the tune first, and then contacted Ned Washington in order to have lyrics added.[28]

For Dimitri Tiomkin, *High Noon* proved to be the spark that ignited his career. Although he had already been composing film scores for two decades, with this film he became firmly established as the composer *de rigueur* for Western movies.

Following the success of *High Noon*, virtually every producer in Hollywood began to rethink the role of music in films, with the idea of using songs to promote movies prior to their theatrical release. In a sense, *High Noon* had a negative impact on film scoring, for many subsequent films that would have benefited from a traditional symphonic approach to the main-title music wound up having songs instead of instrumental themes. With this fundamental change in film scoring, many composers began to feel threatened. In fact, Elmer Bernstein later wrote that the demand by movie producers for title songs contributed directly to the decline of the Golden Age:

> It is no secret that many title songs have made more money than the movies they came from. Movie companies suddenly became music publishing houses and recording firms so as not to allow any of the loot to slip by them. And in the process the serious composition of thoughtful film scores was given short shrift.[29]

VICTOR YOUNG: FROM *SCARAMOUCHE* TO *THE GREATEST SHOW ON EARTH.* Though Victor Young worked under contract at Paramount throughout his Hollywood career, he did some of his best work while he was on loan to other studios. Such is the case with *Scaramouche*, MGM's engaging film of Rafael Sabatini's novel, set in eighteenth-century France right before the revolution. Stewart Granger plays André Moreau, who seeks vengeance for the death of a dear friend who has been killed in a duel. The title is taken from the name Moreau adopts as a member of an acting troupe he joins to conceal his true identity (because there is a price on his head).

Victor Young's robust score consists mainly of a rousing main-title theme and a rhapsodic waltz tune. This is one of his few forays into the swashbuckler territory previously governed by Korngold; yet it is an immensely appealing score. Strangely, the climactic duel between Granger and Mel Ferrer, the longest in cinema history, is noteworthy for having no music at all; crowd noises and clanging rapiers provide sufficient sound effects that a musical background was deemed dispensable.

Also in 1952, the Irish-flavored score for John Ford's *Quiet Man* remains one of his most memorable works. There are several tuneful melodies in this score, including the boisterous music for the climactic fistfight between Sean Thornton (John Wayne) and Will Danaher (Victor McLaglen). However, for the love theme of Sean and Mary Kate (Maureen O'Hara), Young borrowed the melody of the 1949 song "The Isle of Innisfree," by Richard Farrelly. Young also employed the song "I'll Take You Home Again, Kathleen" as part of his underscore.

Young also composed the score for a Korean war melodrama, RKO's *One Minute to Zero*. Although the film is undistinguished, "When I Fall in Love," a song from the score, has become a classic. This lilting ballad was subsequently used in the Errol Flynn action film *Istanbul* (1957), in which Nat "King" Cole performs the song in a nightclub scene. More recently, this tune was incorporated into the romantic song score that accompanies Nora Ephron's *Sleepless in Seattle* (1993). Of Victor Young's many lyrical song melodies, "When I Fall in Love" is one of the most enduringly popular.

Of Young's three scores for Paramount that year, the most important was the song-filled score for DeMille's Academy Award-winning circus epic *The Greatest Show on Earth*. Although most of the music consists of traditional circus tunes, Young incorporated a few of his own melodies, including the music for a song entitled "Popcorn and Lemonade."

SHORT CUTS ■■■ **Georges Auric.** John Huston's *Moulin Rouge*, based on the life of French painter Henri de Toulouse-Lautrec, contains a charming score by French composer Georges Auric (1899–1983). For one of the scenes in the famed Parisian nightclub, Huston had Zsa Zsa Gabor appear as famed chanteuse Jane Avril. Although Gabor's voice was dubbed (rather poorly!), the "Song from Moulin Rouge" (also known as "Where Is Your Heart") became a hit, via the recording by Percy Faith and his orchestra, with vocalist Felicia Sanders. Because Huston barely made the deadline for Oscar qualification, most of the nation did not get to see *Moulin Rouge* until well into 1953. In fact, the song did not debut on "Your Hit Parade" until April 18, 1953. It remained among the top ten songs for twenty-five weeks, during eight of which it was number one.

Though Auric was overlooked in the Oscar race, his music for *Moulin Rouge* would remain his best-remembered work from a career that spanned four decades, during which he wrote scores for many renowned French films, including Jean Renoir's *Beauty and the Beast* (1946) and *Orpheus* (1950). Perhaps because of Auric's success with *Moulin Rouge*, William Wyler hired him to do the score of *Roman Holiday* (1953).

■■■■ **David Raksin.** Before making *Roman Holiday*, however, Wyler completed a film adaptation of Theodore Dreiser's *Sister Carrie*. The screen version, *Carrie*, concerns Hurstwood (Laurence Olivier), an affluent married man and his infatuation with a young actress, his subsequent fall from grace, and her rise to fame as a stage star. With Jennifer Jones in the title role, *Carrie* is continually lifted by a lovely musical score by David Raksin. Especially moving is the score's principal theme, which draws the viewer's sympathy to Hurstwood, whose obsessive behavior causes the breakup of his marriage and his financial ruin.

In addition to *Carrie*, Raksin scored Vincent Minnelli's film *The Bad and the Beautiful*, a fascinating fictional look inside the motion picture industry, as told by three prominent film people—a director (Barry Sullivan), a star (Lana Turner), and a writer (Dick Powell)—who have been summoned by their studio boss to discuss working again with producer Jonathan Shields (Kirk Douglas). In separate segments, the three explain how Jonathan has used and manipulated them and why they have no desire to work with him again. The film unfolds in a series of flashbacks that take us inside the world of moviemaking. Raksin's main theme, heard periodically throughout the film, features a sensuously romantic saxophone melody. This music, which was titled "Love Is for the Very Young," is every bit as memorable as his earlier "Laura" theme and has become a popular jazz standard through recordings by such renowned artists as Stan Getz.[30]

■■■■ **Bronislau Kaper.** Another theme that has become a standard is the haunting melody that Bronislau Kaper (1902–83) used in *Invitation*. Though this theme is now commonly identified by the film title, it was actually composed two years earlier for *A Life of Her Own*, which starred Lana Turner. Among Kaper's film compositions, the "Invitation" theme is second only to the classic music of *Green Dolphin Street* (1947) in the number of recordings that have been made of it by both pop and jazz artists.

■■■■ **Miklos Rozsa.** Miklos Rozsa provided scores for two colorfully filmed historical dramas made in 1952. For *Plymouth Adventure*, he used bits of old hymn tunes to create an appropriately Pilgrim-flavored musical background; for *Ivanhoe*, he created one of the many classic scores for historical romances that would keep him occupied throughout the 1950s.

The heroic main theme for *Ivanhoe*, with its trumpet fanfare melody, establishes at once the flavor of medieval England and the undaunted spirit of Sir Wilfred of Ivanhoe (Robert Taylor), who risks all to rescue Richard the Lion-Hearted from his imprisonment in Austria and help him to regain his throne.

Together, these two films afforded Rozsa the opportunity to do research on the music of earlier times. Although he had already painstakingly delved into the past to produce his excellent score for *Quo Vadis*, for these newer projects he was actually able to quote a variety of melodies, especially in *Plymouth Adventure*. For this score, he borrowed tunes from Henry Ainsworth's Psalter, which was published in Amsterdam in 1612 and is known to be the sole music book that accompanied the Pilgrims on their transatlantic voyage. For the film recording, a choir was employed to sing one of Ainsworth's hymns, "Confess Jehovah, Thankfully!"[31]

1953

ALFRED NEWMAN: *THE ROBE*. With the new CinemaScope process, 20th Century-Fox launched a series of wide-screen films, beginning with a spectacular version of *The Robe*, which premiered at Grauman's Chinese Theatre in Hollywood on September 24, 1953.[32]

Based on the 1942 novel by Lloyd C. Douglas, *The Robe* tells a fictional story built around the Crucifixion. Marcellus Gallio (Richard Burton) is a Roman tribune and a senator's son, whose defiance of the powerful Caligula

The Robe, with Jean Simmons, Jay Robinson (seated next to her), and Richard Burton (holding the robe).

(Jay Robinson), grandnephew of the emperor, causes him to be assigned to one of the least desirable of jobs, managing an army outpost in Palestine. The source of the conflict is a Greek slave named Demetrius (Victor Mature), who is bought by Marcellus at a slave market over the objections of Caligula, who wants the physically brawny slave for his own household.

Upon Marcellus's arrival in Palestine, he observes the citizenry celebrating the arrival in town of a young rabbi named Jesus. Within a few days, Jesus is arrested and sentenced to die. At the Crucifixion, Marcellus wins the condemned man's robe in a roll of dice, but when he attempts to wear the garment, he becomes horrendously distraught. Demetrius, horrified by the death scene he has just observed, runs off with the robe. Marcellus returns to Rome in a frail state of health. After he recuperates, he returns to Palestine in search of Demetrius, who has become a Christian. Ultimately, Marcellus becomes a Christian himself. Back in Rome once again, he defies Caligula one more time. With Diana, his sweetheart (Jean Simmons), Marcellus is condemned to die. Proudly, the two walk arm in arm out of the palace to embrace death and the glory beyond.

Although *The Robe* drew critical brickbats in certain quarters, about its music there is little question. Alfred Newman, who had already produced fine scores for over two decades, outdid himself with the marvelously dramatic music for this film. To coordinate the music with the use of CinemaScope and multichannel stereophonic sound, Newman composed a huge background score. Thunderously ominous opening brass chords, accompanied by a wordless choir, introduce the main-title theme. This music is heard again, with tremendously dramatic orchestration, during the Crucifixion scene.

For romantic moments between Marcellus and Diana, Newman created one of his most memorable themes, a lyrical minor-key melody that is played by strings, with an expressive solo cello added in several places. This is initially heard during the scene in which Marcellus first departs for Palestine. Although Diana is supposed to marry Caligula, her affections for Marcellus are made quite obvious by the sonorous beauty of this music.

In *The Robe*, as in other films set in Roman times, there are a number of marchlike pieces. The principal one of these accompanies Caligula and his soldiers as they enter the slave market at the beginning of the film. Also noteworthy is a lugubrious funeral march, based on the score's main-title theme, which accompanies the scene of Jesus carrying the cross to Calvary.

In contrast with these dramatic musical episodes are several that rely on a much smaller instrumentation, especially the music that accompanies the scene in which Marcellus arrives in Palestine on Palm Sunday. Here a choir sings wordlessly with a background consisting mostly of harp and percussion. In a later scene at a well, a young crippled woman sings a song with harp accompaniment. There is also an ethereal vocal piece, sans instruments, which is heard when Marcellus accepts Jesus as the Savior.

The final music in the film, which is one of the most inspired parts of Newman's score, features a chorus of "Hallelujahs" sung by a large choir, with full orchestra; this joyous music accompanies the closing moments of *The Robe*, as Marcellus and Diana courageously face their impending deaths.

Newman didn't even gain an Oscar nomination for the score of *The Robe* (an oversight that caused Franz Waxman to protest by resigning his Academy membership). Ironically, Newman did win a 1953 Oscar for the musical adaptation of Irving Berlin's songs in *Call Me Madam*.

BERNARD HERRMANN: THREE ACTION POTBOILERS. The three films that were offered to Bernard Herrmann at 20th Century-Fox in 1953, *White Witch Doctor*, *Beneath the Twelve-Mile Reef*, and *King of the Khyber Rifles*, are of interest today largely because of Herrmann's inventive musical backgrounds.

Of the three, *White Witch Doctor* has the most memorable score. The instrumentation includes a number of African instruments, many of which are heard in the opening music, entitled "Talking Drums." This segues directly into a frantically paced main-title theme with brass, native drums, and even a brake drum, which adds a clanging effect. A percussion-laden string theme is heard in the safari sequence in which a nurse (Susan Hayward) is being escorted to a jungle clinic by a fortune-hunting guide (Robert Mitchum). In a later scene, in which a deadly tarantula is placed inside her tent while she is sleeping, Herrmann's accompaniment features a serpent, a curved brass instrument that produces a growling tone (he liked this bizarre sound so much that he used it again, for the giant lizard sequence in *Journey to the Center of the Earth*).

At the emotional center of this score is one of Herrmann's loveliest themes, a nocturne for strings, harp, and woodwinds, with solos for oboe and clarinet. The melodic line is then taken up by the strings; this produces a gorgeously emotional effect.

Although neither of Herrmann's two other 1953 scores approaches the beauty of the *White Witch Doctor* score, both have instrumental features that distinguish them from the standard action-movie musical backgrounds. For *Beneath the Twelve-Mile Reef*, Herrmann devised a watery accompaniment featuring a large string orchestra with nine harps. This instrumentation provides an appropriately dreamlike effect for the scenes in which the CinemaScope cameras went underwater to film this story of sponge divers on Key West. In its soaring melodic motifs and richly romantic harmony, this music often alludes to the sound of the later Hitchcock scores, especially *Vertigo* and *Marnie*.

In the *Twelve-Mile Reef* score Herrmann experimented with dark brass sonorities for a scene in which fishermen are attacked by an octopus. This ingeniously menacing music prefigures Herrmann's later fantasy scores for *The Seventh Voyage of Sinbad* and *Jason and the Argonauts*.

While *King of the Khyber Rifles* may be the least memorable of the trio of action potboilers, at least one sequence provided him with an unusual musical opportunity. For a sequence entitled "Attack on the Mountain Stronghold," in which Indian insurrectionists charge a British-held fort, a wildly rhythmic background includes a pounding accompaniment that features fifteen timpani of various sizes, three gongs, and three bass drums, plus brass, woodwinds, and an organ.[33] As is often the case in Herrmann's film work, this score is not very melodic. In the context of the film, however, his acute awareness of the scene's dramatic essence led him to devise an instrumental conglomeration that has a compelling sensory impact.

MIKLOS ROZSA: THREE HISTORICAL DRAMAS. At MGM, Miklos Rozsa enjoyed a grand year, with five scores for a variety of colorfully produced films. Without doubt, the standout is the dramatic music for Joseph L. Mankiewicz's excellent version of Shakespeare's *Julius Caesar*. Rozsa's score is built on two contrasting themes; the one for Caesar is a majestic upward-rising idea, whereas the one for Brutus has a more tragic cast, with a melodic pattern that circulates around a central tone within a confined pitch range. Both ideas are featured in the Praeludium, which is played over the opening credits. (Rozsa also composed a grandiose overture, based on the "Brutus" theme, which was intended for use in theaters prior to the commencement of the film; but MGM rather foolishly rejected this music in favor of a performance of Tchaikovsky's *Capriccio italien*.) The score of *Julius Caesar*, which includes a variety of marches, fanfares, and processions that occur at various places in the film, won for Rozsa a richly deserved Oscar nomination.

Of Rozsa's other scores for 1953 films, *Young Bess* and *Knights of the Round Table* both contain exceptional music. For *Young Bess* Rozsa created an inspired score, which begins with a majestic trumpet fanfare. This is followed by a soaring theme for strings and French horns that represents Henry VIII's daughter Elizabeth (played as a young adult by Jean Simmons). Another prominent theme is a light-hearted tune for strings and woodwinds called "Hatfield," for Elizabeth's home during her childhood.

Knights of the Round Table, MGM's CinemaScope version of the Arthurian saga, includes a highly dramatic and lavishly orchestrated score. The main theme, heard during the opening credits, is a minor-key march for brass, strings, and pounding drums. Rozsa also devised a five-note motif that utilizes both rising and falling fourths. This melodic pattern appears in several guises, the most dramatic of which occurs during the film's elaborately staged battle scenes.

SHORT CUTS ■■■■ **Elmer Bernstein.** Some really low-grade films emanated during the height of the 3-D craze; among these, the nadir in terms of quality are two movies made by Astor films, *Cat Women of the Moon* and *Robot Monster*. Interestingly enough, Elmer Bernstein (pronounced Bern-STEEN), in his third year as a film composer, wrote the scores for both of these grade Z cheapies! While biding his time on the way to hopefully better things, Bernstein evidently had to ply his trade on whatever was available to him. Like many other film composers before and since these two ineptly produced sci-fi flicks, he at least got some practice in film scoring by working on them. *Robot Monster* does have an interesting score, in which blaring brass chords are used to stir up some thrills whenever the gorilla-suited alien with the fishbowl helmet shows up.

■■■■ **Dimitri Tiomkin.** Although Dimitri Tiomkin achieved an enormous success with his music for *High Noon*, none of the six scores he worked on during 1953 were for Westerns. Instead, he scored a number of contemporary dramas, the best of which were the Warner films *Blowing Wild* and *I Confess*. In *I Confess*, which reunited Tiomkin with Alfred Hitchcock for the fourth time, after a church caretaker admits to a murder in the privacy of the confessional, the priest (Montgomery Clift) who has heard the confession becomes the primary suspect. Tiomkin's repeated use of the doleful "Dies irae" melody from the Gregorian funeral Mass resulted in an unusually compelling score.

■■■■ **Victor Young.** By far the most noteworthy score that Young did during 1953 was the music for George Stevens's memorable Western film *Shane*, with Alan Ladd as a drifting gunfighter. The main theme, known as "The Call of the Faraway Hills," is a tuneful piece that conveys the expanse of the Western plains where the settlers depicted in this film set up homesteads, over the objections of the cattle ranchers. For Marian (Jean Arthur), wife of the settler played by Van Heflin, Young borrowed the same tune that Alex North had included in his *Streetcar Named Desire* score, where it is referred to as the "Varsouviana." Whereas North's use of the tune has psychological implications of Blanche DuBois's mental instability, here the melody takes on a warmer, more sentimental cast, as Young wished to convey the unwavering strength of this woman, whose loving husband and small boy depend on her supportive presence.

■■■■ **Bronislau Kaper.** One of MGM's top composers, Bronislau Kaper, won an Oscar for his charming score of *Lili*, the fanciful tale of a young orphaned girl (Leslie Caron), who joins a carnival and becomes involved with two men: a bitter, physically impaired puppeteer (Mel Ferrer) and a dashing magician (Jean-Pierre Aumont). The puppeteer can express his feelings for Lili only through his puppets, and she is drawn at first to the magician. Ultimately, she realizes that it is the puppeteer that she really loves. Kaper composed a beguiling tune for the film, "Hi-Lili, Hi-Lo," which is sung as part of the puppet-theater act. This deceptively simple little waltz tune is later incorporated into an innovative dream sequence that takes the form of a ballet in which Lili's feelings for the two men are worked out in a complex psychological pantomime. The dream sequence provides a remarkable musical finale for this enchanting film.

■■■■ **George Duning.** After receiving his first Oscar nomination in 1950 for *No Sad Songs for Me*, George Duning (b. 1908) began a series of noteworthy achievements as a staff composer at Columbia. One of the strongest of these was the score for Fred Zinnemann's marvelously acted version of James Jones's World War II novel *From Here to Eternity*, about American soldiers and their women in Hawaii around the time of the attack on Pearl Harbor. Duning's music gives this trenchant drama its humanity, especially in the sensually charged scene at the beach, with Sergeant Milt Warden (Burt Lancaster) and his commanding officer's wife, Karen Holmes (Deborah Kerr). Montgomery Clift, as the trumpet-playing soldier Prewitt, excelled in his scenes with Lorene (Donna Reed), who works at the New Congress Club. For their romantic scenes Duning used a theme composed by Fred Karger and Robert Wells. Although this theme was composed as a title song, it is never actually sung in the film. Another tune, "Reenlistment Blues," also by Karger and Wells, with additional lyrics by James Jones, is sung on two occasions. It is also used by Duning in the main-title music and is heard instrumentally toward the end, when Prewitt is accidentally shot by his own men following the fateful bombing raid.

There is a lot of borrowed music in the film. Several Hawaiian dance pieces are heard, in scenes set at the New Congress Club. In the final scene, where Karen and Lorene meet by chance on a boat taking them back to the American mainland, Duning incorporated the melody of "Aloha Oe" into the background score. With the racier elements of Jones's story toned down, *From Here to Eternity* was the deserving winner of eight Academy Awards, while Duning's score earned him his second nomination.

FOOTNOTE TO **1953.** After *The Robe*, almost all subsequent Cinema-Scope films released by 20th Century-Fox would have an extension of the familiar brass-and-drums music that Alfred Newman had composed as a studio logo in 1937. As head of Fox's music department, Newman created a soaring bit of music to accompany the announcement of the new wide-screen process. This logo extension was first heard at the beginning of *How to Marry a Millionaire*, in which it serves as a rousing introduction to Newman's *Street Scene*, a rhapsodic film theme from 1931 that forms a musical prologue to this second CinemaScope film.

•••••••••
1954
•••••••••

LEONARD **B**ERNSTEIN: *O*N THE *W*ATERFRONT. Between 1953 and 1955, a lot of money was spent on lavish Technicolor movies that used any of the various wide-screen processes. Thus, it is perhaps curious that, for each of these three years, the Oscar for Best Picture went to a black-and-white film that was photographed in conventional 35-mm. Elia Kazan's *On the Waterfront*, the Academy Award-winning film of 1954, is one of the three films, an outstanding drama that features on-location shooting in and around New York City. It has the distinction of being the only film for which Leonard Bernstein (pronounced Bern-STINE) (1918–90) composed an original score. Like his concert pieces and his Broadway productions, the music of *On the Waterfront* is an emotion-filled and often eloquent commentary.

When Bernstein was approached to do the score for this film, he was already an established star of the concert hall, both as composer and as conductor. His meteoric rise to fame had occurred in the early 1940s when, shortly after graduating from Harvard, he began an apprenticeship as a conductor under Serge Koussevitsky, music director of the Boston Symphony Orchestra. At the Tanglewood estate in the Berkshires of Massachusetts, Koussevitsky had begun a conductors' training school as part of the Boston Symphony's summer program. It was there that Bernstein first got the opportunity to conduct an orchestra. In 1943, he was appointed assistant conductor of the New York Philharmonic, and on November 14 of that year, he served as a last-minute replacement for Bruno Walter with the New York Philharmonic at Carnegie Hall. Bernstein's conducting, which included a performance of Miklos Rozsa's Theme, Variations and Finale, caused a sensation. According to Rozsa, four Philharmonic performances of the work had been scheduled for New York during November 1943, the last of which was to be broadcast.

Leonard Bernstein.

> Walter conducted the first three but due to sudden illness had to delegate the broadcast to one of his assistants, the young Leonard Bernstein. My piece came just before the interval and was splendidly performed; there was a youthful drive that not even Walter could have equaled, and a bravura that I have hardly heard since.[34]

After this sensational appearance, Bernstein's future as a conductor was assured. The offers to conduct, which began pouring in, included an invitation to lead the New York Philharmonic as a full-fledged guest conductor. Fifteen years later, in 1958, he would be appointed the first American-born music director of this illustrious orchestra.

In 1944, his ballet *Fancy Free*, with choreography by Jerome Robbins, helped to established him as a promising young composer. Later that year, he and Robbins collaborated with Betty Comden and Adolph Green on a Broadway musical adaptation of *Fancy Free*. With the title *On the Town*, this show opened on December 28, 1944, and ran for 463 perform-ances.[35] An unmistakable element in both the original ballet and the musical adapted from it is the inclusion of jazz rhythms. Much of Bernstein's creative work, whether in the form of a concert-hall piece or a Broadway musical, contains a brash, jazzy sound. It is this quality, combined with a strongly romantic melodic sense, that distinguishes his work from that of other modern American composers. Aaron Copland, who had used jazz elements in some of his early works, stated that Bernstein belongs to a modern school that can be linked with George Gershwin:

> Bernstein represents a new type of musician—one who is equally at home in the world of jazz and in the world of serious music. George Gershwin made something of an attempt to fill that role but Bernstein really fills it—and with ease.[36]

Following the success of *On the Town*, Bernstein created many other works which include jazz elements; two of these are *The Age of Anxiety* (Symphony no. 2), a work for piano and orchestra (1949), and Prelude, Fugue and Riffs (1949). For the stage he wrote music for a 1950 production of *Peter Pan* and, with the help once again of Comden and Green, the score of *Wonderful Town* (1953), a Broadway musical based on the play *My Sister Eileen*. With such snappy musical numbers as "Conga," "Swing," and "Wrong Note Rag," combined with such pretty ballads as "Ohio," "A Little Bit in Love," and "A Quiet Girl," *Wonderful Town* is convincing proof of Bernstein's ingenious musical gifts.

The popularity of *Wonderful Town* may have been the stimulus that inspired producer Sam Spiegel to hire Bernstein in 1954 to score Elia Kazan's *On the Waterfront*. This story of strife between unionized longshoremen and corrupt union bosses was filmed on location near Hoboken, New Jersey. Budd Schulberg's screenplay was based on his own story about union corruption and on a Pulitzer Prize-winning series of articles by Malcolm Johnson, a reporter for the *New York Sun*. In the film the New Jersey piers are under the iron-fisted control of Johnny Friendly (Lee J. Cobb), a corrupt union boss, who extracts money from the stevedores in exchange for their getting a day's work and silences anyone who talks to federal investigators.

In the film's opening scene a young dockworker, Joey Doyle, is thrown from the roof of his apartment building. Father Barry (Karl Malden), after administering the last rites to Doyle, attempts to find out the circumstances surrounding the man's death. His efforts are met with resistance because of the workers' fears of union reprisals.

The story's principal character, Terry Malloy (Marlon Brando), is a stevedore who at first doesn't question Johnny Friendly's authority. After Doyle's death, a homicide that Terry unknowingly helped set up, he begins to listen to his conscience. Complicating Terry's situation is his growing affection for Joey's sister Edie (Eva Marie Saint, in her film debut), who wants to know who killed her brother. Another problem for Terry is presented by his brother Charley (Rod Steiger), a crooked attorney who is one of Friendly's chief henchmen. In a taxi, a desperate Charley, under pressure from Friendly, tries to persuade Terry to take a gun and kill another man who has been targeted by the union. After Terry refuses, Charley himself is killed. This act of violence finally convinces Terry to come forward and testify. In a climactic fistfight, Terry, outnumbered by Friendly and two of his henchmen, is given a brutal beating. With Father Barry's subtle persuasion, Terry ultimately gets back on his feet in order to lead his fellow longshoremen back to work, over the protests of Johnny Friendly, whose unscrupulous

On the Waterfront,
with Eva Marie Saint
and Marlon Brando.

control of the union is finally thwarted. The film's conclusion may be a bit simplistic, but the moral victory of the workingman over the corrupt labor leader furnishes an emotionally satisfying ending.

Almost every element of the film received universal praise at the time of the film's release. The single element that received wide criticism was Leonard Bernstein's musical score. Bosley Crowther, in an appreciation of the film that appeared in the book *The Great Films: Fifty Golden Years of Motion Pictures*, mentions a few of the criticisms: "too bold, too brassy, too pretentious."[37] A lengthier criticism appears in Roy Prendergast's *Film Music: A Neglected Art*, where the author cites specific examples of how Bernstein's lack of experience as a composer of film music led to some misconceived moments in the film—moments in which the music either tries too hard or is inattentive to the dialogue by being overcomposed:

> Bernstein's lack of experience in the area of film composition tends to destroy the effect, in terms of the picture, of what is some very beautiful music. However, the same material as film music, becomes, in many places, intrusive and inept-sounding from a dramatic standpoint.[38]

A scene that Prendergast cites provides an example of how a composer can overwrite. When Terry asks Edie to go out for a beer, the love theme builds up to a gorgeously orchestrated big moment. Because of the dialogue, the music is suddenly deadened, where one feels it should be allowed to reach an emotional peak. Yet, if the music were to soar at this point, the dialogue would be drowned out. Prendergast points out that Kazan changed the scene in the final stages of editing, to have Brando's mumbled lines made more audible. This necessitated the reduction of the music's volume. Even so, the presence of a soaring statement of the film's love theme at this stage in Terry and Edie's relationship seems premature.

Putting aside these reservations about Bernstein's score in terms of its suitability for some of the scenes it accompanies, there are many fine aspects to *Waterfront*'s music. On its own terms the love theme is a lyrically inspired piece of music. When first heard in the film, it is played simply, by flute and harp. In the previously mentioned scene between Terry and Edie, the strings state the theme in a soaring statement that comes to a climax when a solo trumpet takes over the melodic line.

One of the chief assets of the score is the main-title theme, which is first heard during the opening credits in a simple statement for solo French horn. The upward-rising tones of this melody reflect the courage of Terry Malloy, who eventually stands alone against Friendly and his gang. This theme assumes truly heroic proportions in the film's closing scene, in which a brutally battered Terry staggers past rows of workers who are waiting for him to lead them back to the workplace.

Some turbulent, jazzy music, with saxophone and pounding kettle-drums, accompanies the first appearance of Johnny Friendly and his men as they set their plot against Joey Doyle into motion. The nervous motif that is heard here makes several subsequent appearances, which effectively underscore the conflict in the film.

Lastly, a dolorous string melody is heard in two very dramatic scenes: first, when Father Barry is coming up out of the hold of a ship with the body of Dugan (Pat Henning), a longshoreman, who has been killed by falling cargo; and second, when Terry and Edie discover the body of Charley, whose death occurs shortly after the memorable scene in the taxi, in which Terry refuses to do any more of Friendly's dirty work.

Leonard Bernstein's score, although nominated for an Oscar, lost to the more conventional Dimitri Tiomkin score for *The High and the Mighty*. This turn of events was not really surprising, in view of the fact that Tiomkin was a member of the Hollywood community, while Bernstein was an outsider. Bernstein's celebrity as a Broadway composer may have weighed against his winning an Oscar. In the 1950s, there seems to have been a marked resentment by Hollywood folk for New York-based actors, directors, and other technicians who came to film from the Broadway stage.

SHORT CUTS ■■■■ Alfred Newman and Bernard Herrmann.

At 20th Century-Fox Alfred Newman had an interesting year as a collaborator. For the musical *There's No Business Like Show Business*, he worked with his brother Lionel to produce arrangements of Irving Berlin songs; the lavish filming of Mika Waltari's best-selling novel *The Egyptian* required Newman to share the creative effort with Bernard Herrmann. Although *The Egyptian* was scheduled to be scored by Newman alone, Darryl F. Zanuck pushed up its release date. Newman, knowing that he could never finish the score for this two-hour-plus film by himself, accepted Herrmann's idea that they collaborate in order to speed up the project. The result is a surprisingly effective score, with each composer scoring approximately half of the music.[39] Herrmann's contributions are relegated to the portions of the film in which Sinuhe (Edmund Purdom) is infatuated with the beautiful but dangerous Nefer (Bella Darvi); Newman did the main-title theme plus the marches and various other required pieces. Though Newman and Herrmann demonstrated noticeably different compositional styles in their respective work, the two managed to pull together a score that fits the film—a feat that is all the more remarkable because they did not meet even once while the score was being composed.

■■■ **Max Steiner.** Another highlight of 1954 was Max Steiner's rousing score for Edward Dmytryk's *Caine Mutiny*, which is one of his few scores not written for Warner Bros. Its main theme has a tuneful marchlike quality that seems to propel the U.S.S. Caine as it sails in the Pacific Ocean during World War II. After a violent storm, during which Lieutenant Maryk (Van Johnson) relieves Captain Queeg (Humphrey Bogart) of his command in order to secure the safety of the ship and its crew, the march is heard again as the Caine passes under the Golden Gate Bridge en route to San Francisco, where the climactic court-martial of Maryk takes place.

■■■ **Dimitri Tiomkin.** Perhaps the most noteworthy of Dimitri Tiomkin's six new scores for 1954 was his Oscar-winning music for William Wellman's airplane-in-distress drama, *The High and the Mighty*. Tiomkin's catchy whistling theme for the airplane pilot played by John Wayne became one of the year's biggest pop hits, with two successful versions of the theme, one by Les Baxter, the other by Leroy Holmes. Both recordings became best-sellers, and the theme spent seventeen weeks on the Top Ten list.[40]

Tiomkin also contributed a throbbingly dramatic score for Hitchcock's *Dial M for Murder*. Though not as effective as his music for *I Confess*, this last of Tiomkin's Hitchcock scores is a worthy effort. This is especially true in the telephone scene, where Margo (Grace Kelly) is scheduled to be killed by an intruder while she answers the phone. The music builds to a histrionic level as Margo fends off her assailant with a fateful pair of scissors.

········
1955
········

There have been several composers since the end of Hollywood's Golden Age whose careers in film music have been sparked by the interest of a filmmaker. Four of Elia Kazan's films made between 1951 and 1956 share the common distinction of including the film-scoring debuts of their respective composers. Following *A Streetcar Named Desire*, which brought Alex North to Hollywood for the first time, Kazan directed *On the Waterfront*, which became Leonard Bernstein's only film-scoring accomplishment. Kazan then hired a pair of unknowns. The more noteworthy of these was Leonard Rosenman (b. 1924), who came to prominence as the composer of a highly original score for *East of Eden*. A year later, Kazan would offer the controversial *Baby Doll* as a first scoring opportunity for the jazz musician Kenyon Hopkins (1912–83).

LEONARD ROSENMAN: *EAST OF EDEN.* How Rosenman was offered the job of scoring *East of Eden* is an interesting story in itself.

Born in Brooklyn in 1924, he had early training as a painter; but when he returned from duty in the air force during World War II, he decided to study music. He became a theory and composition student under Arnold Schoenberg, one of the most avant-garde musicians of the twentieth century, who had moved to California from his native Austria in 1933. With Schoenberg's guidance, Rosenman came into contact with some of the most advanced compositional techniques in contemporary music, including the use of a twelve-tone row, which Schoenberg had first demonstrated in the 1920s.

While Kazan was beginning to shoot *East of Eden*, Rosenman was living in New York, where he gave piano lessons. Among his pupils was the aspiring young actor James Dean. After Dean was hired to play the lead

Leonard Rosenman.

Photo by Gay Goodwin Wallin

role of Cal in the film adaptation of Steinbeck's novel *East of Eden*, he took Kazan to a concert that Rosenman was giving at New York's Museum of Modern Art. Afterward, Dean introduced Rosenman to his director, who asked the composer if he was interested in scoring films.[41] Since Kazan was producing as well as directing *East of Eden*, he had some say in the choice of a composer; he selected Rosenman and gave him free rein to create whatever music he thought appropriate.

Steinbeck's sprawling novel, which has strong Biblical overtones, includes much more story than a single film could safely encompass. Thus, in Paul Osborne's screenplay only the last third of the book has been transferred to film. The setting is Salinas, California, in 1918, as Americans are getting ready to join in fighting World War I. Adam Trask (Raymond Massey) is a reputable, Bible-reading businessman and father of two teenage boys, Aron (Richard Davalos), who is a dutiful son, and Cal (James Dean), who is a ne'er-do-well. In the course of the story, Cal learns that his mother, Kate (Jo Van Fleet), who he was told had died shortly after he and his brother were born, lives in Monterey, a nearby town, and runs a bawdyhouse. Cal falls in love with his brother's girl, Abra (Julie Harris). He also practically destroys his family when he cruelly surprises his brother by taking him to Kate's establishment. Aron then gets drunk and enlists in the armed services. Adam, horrified because his favorite son has scorned him over the deception concerning their mother, suffers a paralyzing stroke. In the film's final scene, a remorseful Cal stays steadfastly by his father's bedside, and the two finally become reconciled.

The strongly emotional undertone and the frequent use of slanted camera angles in Kazan's film provided Rosenman with the inspiration to create an unusual score, filled with dissonance and unusual harmonic progressions. The score also has a lyrical melody in an altogether simpler musical idiom, which recurs several times in the film. It is first heard about halfway through the opening titles, when a beginning moment of weird dissonance gives way to this much more consonant music. It is next heard vocally, as a

East of Eden, with James Dean.

little tune that is hummed by Abra and Aron in the ice house, where she is cradling him in her arms. A fully orchestrated statement comes later in the film when Cal and Abra are on a Ferris wheel and they kiss for the first time. It is also present at the film's conclusion, which takes place at the Trask home, where Cal's bedridden father manages to speak a few words, and asks Cal to get rid of an annoying nurse and tend him personally. Cal obliges, and with Abra looking on, he pulls up a chair to begin a bedside vigil, now convinced that he has finally won his father's approval.

Occasionally, in the midst of the more modernistic music that Rosenman has devised, the first six notes of the main theme can be heard as a kind of Wagnerian leitmotif. It basically operates as a unifying element in the score, and suggests the growing affection of Cal for his brother's girl.

For the most part, the score is made up of fragmentary bits of music that do not lend themselves easily to a hearing apart from the film. Although the score's dissonant moments seem quite appropriate in the context of the film, it is Rosenman's lyrical melody that lingers in the mind of the viewer.

Shortly after completing his first scoring assignment, Rosenman was hired by producer John Houseman at MGM to compose music for *The Cobweb*, a Vincente Minnelli-directed film about doctors and their patients at a private mental institution. The dissonance of *East of Eden*'s music is mild by comparison with this score, which is basically atonal. In fact, *The Cobweb* is considered to be the first film score to contain a twelve-tone row.[42] The main-title music features two elements that return throughout the score: agitated figures for strings and glissandos on the kettledrums. These elements account for much of the impact of this score, which is understandably a difficult listening exercise for viewers.

Rosenman scored a third film during 1955, Nicholas Ray's *Rebel without a Cause*. In what is sometimes regarded as his quintessential performance, James Dean plays Jim Stark, a troubled youth trying to adjust to his new surroundings in suburban Los Angeles, including the high school he is attending for the first time. The leader of a hostile gang challenges him to a fight with switchblades. The conflict escalates into an automobile "chicken" race between Jim and Buzz (Corey Allen), the gang leader.

Instead of the atonality he used in *The Cobweb*'s music, Rosenman adopts a more jazz-inflected style in *Rebel*, especially in the film's main-title music, which begins with a blues tune that features a swing rhythm. This segues into a second theme, played by strings, which is more melodious in nature. As with Rosenman's two earlier film scores, there is a plentiful amount of dissonance, especially for scenes such as the switchblade fight and the "chicken" race.

Rosenman's three debut film scores share a common element: in each one a dissonant agglomeration of sound forms the final chord. With a dynamic piling up of tones played by full orchestra, from low brass on the bottom to shrill woodwinds on top, this mass of sound has become a signature chord in Rosenman's film scoring. Unfortunately, in later years he would lean on this harmonic procedure a bit heavily, so that some of his work is rather predictable in its use of this score-closing effect.

BERNARD HERRMANN: *THE TROUBLE WITH HARRY* AND TWO FAILURES.

Two of the three films Bernard Herrmann worked on in 1955 did not do particularly well at the box office. *Prince of Players*, Fox's first CinemaScope film to lose money,[43] featured Richard Burton as noted Shakespearean actor Edwin Booth, whose brother, John Wilkes Booth (John Derek) assassinated President Lincoln. Herrmann's music aims at nobility in the opening credits, with a theme consisting of a majestic brass idea that segues into a marchlike idea built on a five-note motif.

Another noble failure as a film was *The Kentuckian*, directed by its star, Burt Lancaster, whose lack of directorial experience proved to be a serious flaw in terms of this film's dramatic continuity. However, there is much to savor in Herrmann's background score, which begins with a rhythmically propelled idea that is passed back and forth between a French horn and an oboe, over the accompaniment of strings.

Herrmann's most ingenious score of 1955, the first in his legendary collaboration with director Alfred Hitchcock, was for *The Trouble with Harry*, a mordant comedy in which several New Englanders, including a little boy, have to decide what to do with a dead body (the "Harry" of the title).

Throughout the film, the music cleverly shifts in style as required by the story, with the result that the film achieves a beguiling mixture of moods. A sinister four-note motif played by French horns is heard at the beginning of the titles, followed by a tongue-in-cheek tune featuring staccato woodwinds and horns. In the opening sequence the autumnal beauty of Vermont is seen, accompanied by beautifully lyrical music played by a solo English horn that alternates with oboe, above a sustained string background.

When the little boy hears three gunshots and then discovers the body of Harry, the four-note motif from the titles returns. Thereafter, every time someone comes across the body, those same four notes are again sounded with a menacing quality by the French horns.

Although this film was only mildly successful at the box office and is a curio in the career of Alfred Hitchcock, perhaps because of its lighthearted story line, it nevertheless is a landmark, in that it represents the first fruits of a creative collaboration that would lead in the ensuing decade to some of the greatest musical scores ever written for films.

ELMER **B**ERNSTEIN: *T*HE *M*AN WITH THE *G*OLDEN *A*RM. Otto Preminger's *Man with the Golden Arm* was controversial at the time because it was denied a seal of approval by the Motion Picture Association of America. The source of the controversy was the film's candid portrayal of drug addiction, which involves the story's main character, a heroin-taking jazz drummer named Frankie Machine (Frank Sinatra). The role of Frankie was the most challenging of Sinatra's movie career, as the film includes painful scenes in which Frankie goes through withdrawal.

Although Elmer Bernstein had not done a jazz score prior to this film, Preminger trusted that he could create appropriate music for several performance scenes involving the use of jazz instruments. The resulting score is a bit of a hybrid, some of which has conventional symphonic scoring, whereas other parts are arranged for a jazz ensemble that includes some of the great names of jazz. Among the stellar players involved are trumpeter Pete Candoli; flugelhorn player Shorty Rogers; and drummer Shelly Manne, whose solos were mimicked on screen by Sinatra.

The most famous music in the score is the main-title theme. After an opening five-note idea for brass is sounded twice, accompanied by an insistent drum rhythm, the main melodic idea is sounded by trumpet and flugelhorn. This idea is coupled with a repeated five-note rhythmic figure, which propels the theme forward.

Several recordings were made of this music, including a Decca release of the film's soundtrack, which became a bestseller. Other recordings of the main-title theme were arranged and recorded by a variety of bandleaders, including Richard Maltby, Dick Jacobs, and Billy May. The McGuire Sisters even recorded a vocal version of this theme, called "Delilah Jones," which features lyrics by Sylvia Fine. During the months following the release of *The Man with the Golden Arm* in December 1955, these recordings helped to popularize the film. In the Oscar race for 1955, both Sinatra and Elmer Bernstein were nominated. For Bernstein, it would be the first of over a dozen Oscar nominations in a career of more than four decades.

GEORGE **D**UNING: *P*ICNIC. One of the best scores of 1955 was actually not widely heard until the national release of Joshua Logan's *Picnic* in the spring of the following year. Issued just in time to qualify for the 1955 Oscars, *Picnic* is a fine example of a stage adaptation that has been cinematically enhanced through the use of real locales (it was shot in a town in Kansas). William Inge's play, which takes place on Labor Day in a small town in the American heartland, deals with the emotional problems of several residents who are affected by the unexpected arrival of Hal, a former football hero and drifter (William Holden). Hal falls in love with Madge (Kim Novak), a restless young woman who is simply waiting for someone to come along and take her away from this town and its predictable plainness. Even though she is practically engaged to Alan (Cliff Robertson), the son of the town's wealthiest businessman, Madge is swept away by Hal's smooth talk and good looks. At the film's conclusion she runs off to join him, over the objections of her anguished mother.

George Duning's original music is highly dramatic, with enough dissonance to place it in contemporary times, but with an overriding romantic theme that captures the growing affection of its main characters. The film's most famous scene comes toward the end of the day-long picnic, when all are sitting on benches near a lake, with a band playing nearby. The old tune "Moonglow" starts to be played off-camera, and Hal and Madge begin to dance. As their bodies start swaying in time to the music, Duning's love theme becomes superimposed over "Moonglow," and the two tunes continue in simultaneous counterpoint. The resulting music, recorded by Columbia Pictures music director Morris Stoloff with a studio orchestra, was eventually edited into a shorter musical number and released as a single. As "Moonglow and Theme from *Picnic*," this recording became one of the best-selling records of 1956; a second version, arranged by Lawrence Welk's TV music director George Cates, was performed on Welk's TV show. The *Picnic* music climbed into the Top Ten on May 5, 1956, and remained on the charts for sixteen weeks, with six weeks spent as number one.[44]

W**ALTER** S**CHUMANN:** *T**HE** N**IGHT OF THE** H**UNTER.**** One of the outstanding film-music achievements of 1955 is the music by Walter Schumann (1913–58) for the atmospheric film version of Davis Grubb's Depression-era novel *The Night of the Hunter* (the only film ever directed by actor Charles Laughton). Though he had only one previous film to his credit (the 1954 film version of *Dragnet*), Schumann produced a magical score for this story of Harry Powell (Robert Mitchum), a deranged preacher who first marries and later kills a young widow named Willa Harper (Shelley Winters) for a cache of stolen money. He then stalks her two children, who know where the loot is hidden.

Schumann's score, which includes motifs for both voices and instruments, begins during the opening credits with several darkly ominous brass chords, followed by a female chorus singing the lullaby "Dream, Little One, Dream." Both of these motifs appear periodically throughout the film. The first is heard again when Willa's body is discovered, and then once more when the two youngsters seek refuge in a rowboat that takes them downriver while they sleep. In a beautifully shot scene, with the moon's rays causing trees and barns to be reflected in the water, a solo voice is heard in a sweet rendition of the lullaby tune.

Walter Schumann made an important contribution to *Night of the Hunter*, a film which has attained the stature of a classic. It is a pity that he did not live long enough to create any further film scores.

SHORT CUTS ■■■■ **Roy Webb and Harry Warren.** Despite the emphasis on color photography and wide-screen processes in films of the mid-1950s, small-budget pictures in black-and-white still managed to do well. Such is the case with Delbert Mann's *Marty*, which is based on a Paddy Chayevsky TV play. In this beguiling film, Marty Pilletti (Ernest Borgnine), who works at a butcher shop in the Bronx, is being pressured to find a wife. When he meets Clara (Betsy Blair), a lonely chemistry teacher, both his widowed mother and his friends object to his newfound relationship (for one thing, she is not Italian). Marty decides to ignore their objections and follow his feelings.

Marty includes one of the last scoring efforts by Roy Webb, who had been at RKO since the 1930s, but spent his last years in Hollywood as a freelancer. The principal melody in Webb's score comes from a song written for the film by Harry Warren, who was also in his final years as a Hollywood composer. Warren's catchy waltz tune, which is put through a series of clever variations, is first heard during the opening credits, and then frequently reappears as scene-connecting music. An especially spirited arrangement of the melody occurs in the scene where Marty accompanies Clara to her apartment house door. After they part, he runs down the street, hailing a cab; the swelling music helps to suggest the depth of Marty's feelings.

Webb's orchestral arrangements, which consist mostly of strings, woodwinds, and harp, add to the overall charm of this film, which won several prizes, both at the Cannes Film Festival and at the 1955 Academy Awards.

■■■■ *Pete Kelly's Blues.* What *Man with the Golden Arm* did for 1950s jazz, *Pete Kelly's Blues* did for Dixieland, in Jack Webb's colorful period film about a group of musicians during the Prohibition era. As in *Golden Arm*, a lot of music is performed on camera, with off-camera music dubbed by top jazz musicians. Jack Webb is seen playing the trumpet, but the sound is actually that of Dick Cathcart, a member of Matty Matlock's jazz band. Matlock provided the arrangements for the group known in the film as Pete Kelly's Big Seven. These is also a bluesy background theme by Warner's music chief, Ray Heindorf, that is heard during the opening credits (and is later sung, with lyrics by Sammy Cahn). "He Needs Me," by Arthur Hamilton, is sung in the film by Peggy Lee, who won an Oscar nomination for her role as a gangster's girlfriend who becomes a singer with the band, but tragically winds up in a mental institution.

■■■■ *Love Is a Many-Splendored Thing.* The title song from *Love Is a Many-Splendored Thing*, written by Sammy Fain and Paul Francis Webster, became enormously popular. Not only did the song win an Oscar, but so did Alfred Newman's lush background score, which was almost entirely built around this melody. A recording of the song by the Four Aces became a huge hit, with a twenty-week stay on the Top Ten list. In the years since the release of the film, several other movies have included interpolations of the melody, including Paul Mazursky's *Harry and Tonto* (1974).

■■■■ **Alex North.** One other film of 1955 that features a memorable romantic ballad is *Unchained*, a small-budget film about a California prison without walls. Alex North's poignant background theme, which was sung in the film as "Unchained Melody," became the only song in North's entire career to receive an Oscar nomination. This song continues to be one of the most famous of all movie-related tunes, thanks to the popularity of *Ghost*, a 1990 film which includes a recording of the song by the Righteous Brothers on the soundtrack.

VICTOR YOUNG: *AROUND THE WORLD IN EIGHTY DAYS*. *Around the World in Eighty Days* is the only movie produced by Mike Todd, a flamboyant producer of works for the stage in the 1940s. This colorful wide-screen version of Jules Verne's classic 1873 novel, which features a host of cameo appearances by familiar actors, is a delight from start to finish.

When *Around the World* opened in late 1956 on a reserved-seat basis in select theaters equipped with the 65-mm Todd-AO wide-screen system, it became one of the most acclaimed films of the year; its success led to the installation of wide-screen equipment in many additional theaters across the country. The picture, which made more at the box office than any of the Cinerama films, had one of the longest theatrical runs in motion picture history, with repeat bookings in many of the theaters that had shown it in its initial run. In some cities, despite the later arrival of such further Todd-AO pictures as *South Pacific* (1958) and *Porgy and Bess* (1959), *Around the World* was still being shown as the decade ended.

S. J. Perelman's adaptation of the Verne novel, while preserving the story's plot about a globe-encircling adventurer named Phileas Fogg who wagers that he can traverse the planet in eighty days, includes healthy doses of humor, most of which emanates from the casting of Mexican comedian Cantinflas as Fogg's trustworthy valet, Passepartout. While Fogg (David Niven) retains the stiff upper lip so crucial to his character, Passepartout is allowed to romp through the story, whether being chased by crowds of angry temple worshippers in Japan or being captured by Indians in the American West. If certain episodes in the film seem rather extraneous, especially the bullfight sequence, there is compensation aplenty in terms of the film's colorful locales. Seldom has a Hollywood film required the staggering effort that went into the filming of *Around the World*. Thirty-four assistant directors worked on 112 locations, with 140 sets constructed in 13 countries, to complete the filming.[45] Todd commissioned Hollywood veteran Victor Young to create the musical score.

The central problem in scoring Mike Todd's film was finding a way of bringing its disparate elements together to make a musically coherent whole. Young solved this problem by assigning to each of the major characters a theme that could travel with him around the globe. Fogg is represented throughout by "Rule Britannia," while Passepartout's theme is the first segment of "La Cucaracha," a Mexican tune that humorously conveys Cantinflas's nationality. Another recurring character is Inspector Fix (Robert Newton), who joins the global circumnavigation because he suspects that Fogg is the culprit who robbed the Bank of England on the very day Fogg departed on his journey. For this character, instead of composing a full-fledged theme, Young used one of the classic clichés of silent films, a theme that was generally used to announce the arrival of the villain.

There are a number of original melodies in the film, the most memorable of which is a waltz theme first heard when Fogg and his trusty servant depart from Paris in a hot-air balloon. As they soar over the French countryside in a southerly direction, the lilting strains of this theme are heard in a lovely string arrangement. Later, after the rescue in India of Princess

Around the World in Eighty Days, with Robert Newton, Cantinflas, Shirley MacLaine, and David Niven

Aouda (Shirley MacLaine), who is scheduled against her will to be burned to death alongside the body of her deceased royal spouse, this theme is used to suggest the budding romance between her and Fogg.

Another original theme that is heard in the early sequences of the film is interspersed with "La Cucaracha" as Passepartout is bicycling to an employment office where he first applies for the job of personal valet. This theme, incidentally, is cleverly incorporated into the background scoring of the prologue. In an opening sequence Edward R. Murrow discusses the history of man's attempts to travel around the world and even to the Moon. The short 1902 film by Georges Melies, *A Trip to the Moon*, which was also based on a Jules Verne story, is shown with commentary by Murrow and with accompanying piano music. As the old-fashioned silent-movie music continues, Young's theme appears briefly, in a style that seems to fit the vintage of the footage being shown.

Another original theme is heard for a scene aboard the train in which the travelers cross overland from Bombay to Calcutta. This music includes a beautiful cascading string idea, which then leads to a lyrical melody that is momentarily combined with "La Cucaracha" when Passepartout is looking out the train window at the Indian countryside.

Two other original ideas are used in the score for the American sequences. Another train theme seems similar to many old-time Western motifs, but works wonderfully to create a feeling of expansiveness as the train travels through scenic canyons. The other idea is a furious-paced string melody that is heard as the intrepid team is forced to use a make-shift vehicle which consists of a sidecar outfitted with a sail.

Several other borrowed melodies appear in Young's score. A French song called "Auprès de ma Blonde" is heard in an early scene in which Fogg and his companion arrive in Paris. Familiar melodies galore are heard during the American sequence, especially "The Bear Went over the Mountain," which is played by a marching band as part of a political campaign. Other familiar tunes include "Yankee Doodle," "The Girl I Left Behind Me," and "Shoo Fly." During the scene in which the U.S. cavalry comes to the rescue of Passepartout, the "Lone Ranger" segment of Rossini's *William Tell* Overture is humorously included.

Because of the nature of the prologue no opening credits appear. Thus, Young did not get an opportunity to compose main-title music; but this film is a landmark in its use of closing titles. In order to give credit to all the actors who appear in cameos, plus the legion of technicians who were in-volved in the making of the film, an extended sequence was devised by Saul Bass; it lasts over six minutes and includes a clever consolidation of the film's many sequences and locales. The names of the individual actors are shown on screen, accompanied by clever bits of animation that refer to scenes in which the actors appeared, plus short fragments of the music that had earlier been used with the scenes. Real inspirations are the use of a timepiece with legs for Fogg and a bicycle for Passepartout. At the end of the credits, the timepiece bursts open to reveal a heart. This is accompanied by a glorious final reprise of the waltz theme, with majestic closing chords.

All in all, this score is the crowning achievement of Victor Young's career. Sadly, it is also among the last scores that he composed. Less than four weeks after the opening of *Around the World*, Young succumbed to a fatal heart attack on November 10, 1956. When the Oscars for *Around the World* were handed out in early 1957, Victor Young became the first com-poser of a film score to win a posthumous award. It was a richly deserved tribute to one of the most gifted melodists in film-music history.

ELMER BERNSTEIN: *THE TEN COMMANDMENTS.* Several film ex-travaganzas released in 1956 have memorable music. The longest movie of the year, Cecil B. DeMille's *Ten Commandments*, is chiefly memorable today as the film that made Charlton Heston, as Moses, a superstar. It is also one of a trio of films released in 1956 in which Yul Brynner played his first starring roles. As Rameses, Pharaoh of Egypt and Moses' chief adversary in *The Ten Commandments*, Brynner demonstrated a sense of villainy that is in marked contrast with his other two roles of that year, the charming Russian general in *Anastasia* and the charismatic king of Siam in *The King and I* (for which he won the Oscar for Best Actor).

One other reason for remembering *The Ten Commandments* is Elmer Bernstein's majestic score. Coming from the same time period as his jazzy music for *The Man with the Golden Arm*, this score is one of the longest in cinema history. If it is also old-fashioned in its harmonic and melodic idiom, credit for that must go to DeMille himself, who encouraged Bernstein to create a score in the style of Hollywood's Golden Age.

The main-title music begins with a heroic fanfare, followed by a stirring main theme that is associated with Moses. A middle-Eastern flavor is apparent in the melody and harmony of this music, through the use of the chromatically raised fourth step of the scale. Bernstein also composed a love theme, which serves to connect the character of Moses with Nefretiri (Anne Baxter), who plans to marry Moses until he is found to be a Hebrew.

There are many spectacular sequences in the last hour of the film, among the most memorable of which is the Exodus scene in which thousands of Hebrews are assembled for their departure from Egypt. DeMille insisted that the music for this scene be fast-paced because he felt that the movement on screen was not otherwise going to have much dramatic impact. Bernstein complied, and the scene does seem to move much faster than it would have otherwise.

This score may not have been the most musically satisfying of Bernstein's early career, but the huge success of this film paved the way for him to become one of the most respected composers in Hollywood within the next few years.

DIMITRI TIOMKIN: *GIANT* AND *FRIENDLY PERSUASION*. For Dimitri Tiomkin, 1956 was a year of two golden opportunities. First, he scored George Stevens's epic version of Edna Ferber's novel *Giant*, and later that year William Wyler hired him to score the film version of Jessamyn West's novel *Friendly Persuasion*, about a Quaker family in Indiana. Both films received Best Picture nominations, and Tiomkin himself was nominated twice, for the score of *Giant* and for the title song of *Friendly Persuasion*.

Giant, the longest film of Tiomkin's film-scoring career, tells the story of the rich Benedict family and the crises they endure over a period of three decades. When young Texas rancher Bick Benedict (Rock Hudson) travels to Maryland in the early 1920s to purchase a horse from a prominent physician, he winds up getting not only the horse but also the doctor's spunky

Giant, with James Dean and Elizabeth Taylor.

daughter Leslie (Elizabeth Taylor). Almost from the moment he brings his bride to Texas to become first lady of the huge Reata ranch, sparks fly as her values clash with the Benedict family's deprecating attitude toward the many Mexicans who work on the ranch. Bick and Leslie eventually raise three children, none of whom turn out the way their parents have planned.

Complicating the Benedicts' lives is a hard-drinking ne'er-do-well named Jett Rink (James Dean), to whom Bick's sister has willed a small piece of the Reata property. When Jett strikes oil, he becomes a huge thorn in Bick's side. As World War II approaches, Jett, now a playboy millionaire, finally convinces Bick to drill for oil. The film winds up with the Benedicts as a middle-aged couple with grown children, one of whom has married a Mexican woman. Meanwhile, the younger of their two daughters (Carroll Baker) is infatuated with Jett, until her uncle (Chill Wills) proves to her that Jett is basically no good. In an ironic conclusion, Bick winds up fighting on behalf of his now part-Mexican family when they are refused service in a restaurant.

Central to Tiomkin's score is a rousing main theme that rises to emotional heights with a wordless chorus behind an instrumentation of brass and strings in the film's opening credits. This theme is later heard in a bombastic arrangement for brass and drums when Bick and Leslie set out by motorcar from the train depot to make the final fifty-mile trip to the Benedicts' Victorian mansion situated in the middle of Reata's grazing land.

Two other musical ideas figure prominently in the score. The first is a soaring love theme that accompanies the early scenes in which Leslie becomes infatuated with Bick and shows signs of turning his life upside down, even though they have just met. In the scene where her father waits to drive Bick to the station to catch a return train to Texas, Bick and Leslie look at each other so intently that they don't hear the train whistle. The string sonority beautifully suggests their blossoming relationship. The other idea is Jett Rink's theme, which is played by harmonica with strings and soft drum accompaniment. Its shuffling beat suggests Jett's laconic lifestyle, whereas its lilting melody gives voice to his feelings for Leslie, which become quite obvious as the film progresses.

The score also includes a rendition of "The Eyes of Texas Are upon You" and a jukebox recording of "The Yellow Rose of Texas," which at the time *Giant* was in production was the nation's number-one song. Strangely, the version in the film is not the hit recording by Mitch Miller but rather a very similar arrangement by the Warner Bros. music director, Ray Heindorf.

For the Indiana locale of *Friendly Persuasion*, Tiomkin created a beautiful theme that is first heard over the opening credits in a vocal rendition by Pat Boone, whose recording of the song was released before the film itself and became one of the nation's Top Ten tunes for six weeks at the end of 1956. This film runs the gamut from gentle comedy to intense melodrama as Jess Birdwell (Gary Cooper) tries to keep his Quaker family out of the Civil War. His son Josh (Anthony Perkins, in his film debut) has different ideas, however. Four other Tiomkin songs are heard in this score, which is one of the most tuneful of Tiomkin's career.

Short Cuts ■■■■ Alfred Newman.

Alfred Newman's score for *Anastasia* is primarily based on a minor-key theme that has a romantic sweep in its upward-climbing melody patterns. Newman composed lots of ballroom music for this film, in which the mentally troubled Anna Anderson

(Ingrid Bergman) is being tutored in impersonation, so that she can convince the dowager Empress (Helen Hayes) that she actually survived the massacre which wiped out the Russian royal family in 1918. A special feature of the score is the Russian Easter music that is heard in the film's opening scene. Also worth noting is a recording of the main theme by Pat Boone, with lyrics by Paul Francis Webster, who collaborated with noted film composers on dozens of movie songs. In this case the vocal version of the *Anastasia* theme is not actually heard in the film.

■■■■ **Alex North.** *The Bad Seed*, based on the Maxwell Anderson play about a murderous little girl, provided Alex North with the opportunity to create a score largely built around the French children's song "Au clair de la lune." Rhoda (Patty McCormack) is seen practicing this tune at the piano in her apartment; eventually, this melody is used in the orchestral background. It is featured most effectively during the film's concluding sequence when Rhoda, undeterred by a thunderstorm, walks briskly to a lakeside dock to retrieve a spelling-bee prize for which she had murdered a classmate. The music, which is played in a fast tempo but slightly off-key, ingeniously conveys Rhoda's scheming intentions.

■■■■ **Miklos Rozsa.** Miklos Rozsa composed an emotional score for the film biography of Vincent Van Gogh *Lust for Life*. With Kirk Douglas in a magnificent portrayal as the tormented painter, Rozsa's music captures both the yearning and the anguish that Van Gogh suffered in his short artistic career, which ended with his tragic suicide. Two extended sequences in the film are devoted to shots of the paintings, accompanied by some of the most dramatic music in the score. Elsewhere, the music stays at a more subdued level, and at times it is barely audible under the dialogue.

■■■■ **Louis and Bebe Barron.** The most unusual film score of 1956 is featured in MGM's *Forbidden Planet*, which has become a cult classic among sci-fi aficionados. Loosely based on Shakespeare's *Tempest*, this film is noteworthy for having the first completely electronic background ever devised for a motion picture. One might hesitate to call the accompaniment a "musical" score since so much of the time all that one hears is various beeps and squeaks, which are the collective work of the husband-and-wife team of Louis and Bebe Barron. While their unique score is not very listenable apart from the film, it works well in the picture. The film is set on a planet named Altair IV, where an American group of astronauts has landed in search of a long-missing scientist (Walter Pidgeon).

■■■■ **Bernard Herrmann.** Bernard Herrmann followed up his score for Hitchcock's film *The Trouble with Harry* with a second collaboration with the master of suspense. In 1956, Hitchcock remade one of his early films, *The Man Who Knew Too Much*, and greatly expanded the story. In Marrakesh, an American couple, Ben and Jo McKenna (James Stewart and Doris Day), unwittingly learn of an assassination plot. Their son Hank (Christopher Olson) is then kidnapped and taken to England, where a foreign diplomat is to be shot during a concert at Royal Albert Hall.

For the one and only time in his film career, Bernard Herrmann played himself on camera as conductor of the Royal Philharmonic, which is giving a performance of the *Storm Clouds* Cantata of Arthur Benjamin, a work that was originally composed for the earlier version of this story. As Herrmann conducts, the camera moves in ever closer to the percussionist, whose climactic cymbal crash is the cue for the intended assassination. As Ben runs frantically through the corridors in search of the gunman, Jo spots the assassin and lets out a terrific scream. The final moments of the cantata are almost completely overwhelmed by the ensuing chaos, as the audience runs for cover.

The Man Who Knew Too Much also features the Oscar-winning song "Whatever Will Be, Will Be" (by Jerry Livingston and Ray Evans). The McKennas have been invited to the British Embassy to be personally thanked by the diplomat who has survived the shooting, thanks to their intervention. Jo's singing alerts her son, Hank, who is being held by the conspirators in an upstairs room. When Jo and Ben hear Hank whistling this melody, they know that he is nearby, and they eventually rescue him.

Herrmann provided a very dramatic prelude, with blaring brass and pounding percussive effects, for the film's opening credits, but there isn't all that much original music in this film. His later Hitchcockian efforts would give him far richer scoring opportunities. In fact, three of the next four Hitchcock films, all made between 1957 and 1960, would have some of the finest music ever composed for films.

•••••••••
1957
•••••••••

FRANZ **W**AXMAN: **T**HE **P**INNACLE OF **H**IS **C**AREER. For Franz Waxman, the year 1957 marks the pinnacle of a career that spanned over thirty-five years and almost 150 original film scores. During that year he created three remarkable original scores, plus a fourth score that includes scintillating arrangements of previously composed themes.

First was the springtime release of Billy Wilder's film *The Spirit of St. Louis*, based on Charles Lindbergh's 1953 Pulitzer Prize–winning book about his daring solo flight across the Atlantic in May 1927. With the flight used as a framing device, Lindbergh's story is told in a series of flashbacks, as he remembers events in his earlier life, including stints as a barnstorming stunt pilot, aerial mail deliverer, and flight instructor. Comical scenes of his military service during World War I are also included.

The Spirit of St. Louis, with James Stewart as Charles Lindbergh.

Waxman's score consists of two principal melodic ideas. The first is a pattern consisting of several pairs of boldly ascending fifths that form the series C–G, E–B, G–D, B–F♯, D–A. The steep upward incline of this series suggests the idea of soaring to heights that no one has ever experienced before. The second principal idea is the flying theme, a melody that ascends stepwise until it falls back down after the seventh tone. The first of these ideas is dramatically presented in the film's opening credits, whereas the second is heard during a flashback scene in which Lindbergh is shown flying for the first time.

The foregoing comments refer to Waxman's original version of the score, as heard on the soundtrack album, not to the version heard in the final cut of the film. Jack Warner, head of

Warner Bros., wasn't impressed with Waxman's tense and often dissonant chords, which make the opening credits strikingly dramatic. Instead, he wanted a more melodious piece; so he assigned Ray Heindorf and Roy Webb the task of rewriting Waxman's opening music. The result is interesting in its own right, with a lovely statement of the flying theme introduced in place of the dissonant-chord passage with which Waxman ended the original main-title music. A curious feature of the rewritten credit music is the bit of "La Marseillaise" that is used as the credits come to an end.[46] Waxman did incorporate bits of the French national anthem into the score; but he didn't feature the tune until midway through the film, when Lindbergh finally takes off from Roosevelt Field on Long Island, en route to Paris.

With the flight taking up the entire last half of the film, music plays a significant role, since there isn't much in the way of dialogue, except for an amusing bit of business involving an unexpected passenger, a common housefly. Still more flashbacks, with clever musical accompaniment, are inserted into the film as Lindbergh daydreams about his youth during the tedious thirty-three-hour flight. In the climactic part of the film, as he fights back his exhaustion, after going two days without sleep, the music gets quite dramatic. The last leg of the trip, from the moment he sees fishing boats off the coast of Ireland to the triumphant landing at Le Bourget field in Paris, is accompanied by a soaring musical accompaniment. At several points in Waxman's score, the flying theme is superimposed by strings over the opening motif, which is usually played by brass. The cumulative effect is one of ever-increasing excitement and anticipation, a feeling that Waxman wisely utilizes throughout the film to capture the emotion of this story.

Waxman next worked on a completely different type of film about people in a small New England town who are caught in a variety of sexual situations. Based on the best-selling novel by Grace Metalious, Mark Robson's *Peyton Place* was one of the prestige productions of the year, wonderfully photographed in an actual town in Maine. With a terrific cast of young players and a convincing performance by Lana Turner in the role of Constance MacKenzie, mother of Allison (Diane Varsi), the protagonist, *Peyton Place* surpassed its origins and became one of 1957's best films.

Waxman's music helps this film enormously, from the opening motif that he used instead of Alfred Newman's 20th Century-Fox logo music, to the film's main theme, a slow-moving melody in three-quarter time that is built on a mostly ascending pattern of eight tones. This main theme is used in a variety of tempos to create many of the film's musical backgrounds. As the new high school principal, Michael Rossi (Lee Philips), comes motoring into town, the main theme is heard in a very up-tempo arrangement in which the strings are accompanied by a woodwind idea that forms a counterpoint against the main tune. This same theme, incidentally, was used by Waxman in the sequel, *Return to Peyton Place* (1961), and it also appeared as the main musical idea in the ABC prime-time series based on Grace Metalious's characters, which aired from 1964 until 1969.

There is a much darker musical background for the parts involving Selena Cross (Hope Lange), who is assaulted by her drunken stepfather (Arthur Kennedy) and becomes pregnant. In a very tense scene, he chases her through the woods, with dire results (she miscarries, but not before fatally wounding him with a club). The music here, extremely modernistic in its dissonance, effectively highlights the histrionics on screen.

Music of a much gentler nature accompanies Joshua Logan's filming of James Michener's *Sayonara*, about American fliers in Japan during the Korean war. For the main-title theme, Waxman was prevailed upon to use an Irving Berlin song that had been written (but not used) for a Broadway show. Whereas other composers of film scores have often resisted the idea of incorporating title-song themes into their background scores, Waxman utilized Berlin's melody ingeniously. The score has a deftly melodic character in which this borrowed tune figures prominently alongside several original ideas by Waxman himself. The two most prominent original melodies in the score are the theme for Katsumi (Myoshi Umeki), a young Japanese woman who becomes the wife of flyer Joe Kelly (Red Buttons) over the objections of his superior officer, and the theme for Eileen (Patricia Owens), who is engaged to another flyer, Major Lloyd Gruver (Marlon Brando), until he breaks off their relationship because of his infatuation with a Japanese entertainer, Hana-Ogi (Miiko Taka). Both melodies are lyrical creations; the Katsumi melody has a poignant quality that helps to define her relationship with Kelly, whose defiance of army regulations has tragic consequences.

In addition to these tuneful creations there is much native Japanese music, including an old tune called "Sakura Sakura" and music for the Kabuki theater, used in scenes featuring Ricardo Montalban in a surprising performance as a Japanese actor who becomes interested in Eileen. An extended sequence in the film consists of a theatrical performance by Hana-Ogi's dance company, the Matsubayashi Theatre. The Western-style music of this performance is in marked contrast with the Kabuki theater's Oriental-flavored music.

In its tangled romantic relationships *Sayonara* is a complex story with both happy and tragic overtones, buoyed along by an evocative score that, despite a large diversity of elements, succeeds in providing a dramatically cogent musical atmosphere.

Waxman's fourth effort of 1957 was for Billy Wilder's romantic comedy *Love in the Afternoon*, the score of which consists of arrangements of melodic materials both borrowed and new. The song "Fascination," which is based on the 1904 "Valse Tzigane" of F. D. Marchetti, provides the film's main romantic background melody.

During the film, "Fascination" is performed numerous times by a band of gypsy musicians who are routinely hired to play in the Parisian hotel suite of American millionaire Frank Flanagan (Gary Cooper). Flanagan seems to have a girl in every port (or at least in every hotel). The plot revolves around the relationship that develops between Flanagan and Ariane (Audrey Hepburn), the cello-playing daughter of a private detective (Maurice Chevalier) who has been shadowing Flanagan on behalf of a suspicious husband. When Ariane learns that her father's client plans to shoot Flanagan, she decides to warn him, but conceals her identity; in the process she becomes romantically involved with him. This leads to many comic complications, including Flanagan's unsuccessful attempts to learn her name.

The repeated use of "Fascination" leads to a pair of hilarious comments about music that occur incidentally in the witty script by Wilder and cowriter I. A. L. Diamond. After spending a romantic afternoon with Flanagan in his hotel room, Ariane can't stop humming "Fascination." Afterward, when fellow music student Michel (Van Doude) drops her off at her apartment and hands over her cello, he asks her to stop humming this song because, in his words, "it lacks any musical merit whatsoever."

Later, when Ariane returns home after attending a performance of a Wagner opera with Michel, she again hums "Fascination." Her father hears it, and asks what it is. She responds by saying that it's a Wagner tune. At first he wonders why, with his knowledge of Wagner, he doesn't recognize it, but then he concludes that it is probably someone else's tune and says, "Those composers, they all steal from one another."

In addition to "Fascination," the score of *Love in the Afternoon* includes arrangements of two other borrowed tunes, "C'est si bon" (music by Henri Betti, lyrics by Jerry Seelen) and "L'Âme des Poètes." Also, in the film are three pieces of music that are listed in the credits as being by Matty Malneck. These are a title song; a tune named after Audrey Hepburn's character "Ariane"; and finally "Hot Paprika," a lively pseudo-Hungarian piece that is featured in a couple of memorable scenes. In the first scene, John McGiver, as the jealous husband, storms into the hotel where his wife is dallying with Flanagan, while Ariane tries to sneak into the hotel room to warn Flanagan. This gypsy-flavored piece, with violin and cimbalom (a flat, shallow wooden tray with strings that are struck by small mallets), keeps the scene moving at a frantic pace. The second scene in which "Hot Paprika" is used occurs late in the film, when Frank begins to discover his true feelings for Ariane, despite her continued refusal to reveal her identity. As he repeatedly listens to a message she recorded on his dictaphone, the gypsy musicians play the song, although they take momentary breaks to drink the champagne that Frank keeps offering them from the room-service cart that is being rolled back and forth between rooms. The music continues until they all wind up in a drunken stupor.

Although Waxman's contribution to this film was relatively small, his arrangements of "Fascination" and the Malneck tunes add considerably to the charm of this cleverly scripted farce. Regrettably, *Love in the Afternoon* was the last collaboration between Waxman and Wilder. Although they had known each other since the days in Germany in the early 1930s, when they were both starting out in films, Wilder didn't hire Waxman until he did *Sunset Boulevard* in 1950, and only four of Wilder's directorial efforts would eventually be scored by Waxman. Fortunately, one of those four, the inspired score of *The Spirit of St. Louis*, can be acknowledged as a masterpiece of film music, one of the high-water marks of Waxman's entire career.

MALCOLM ARNOLD: *THE BRIDGE ON THE RIVER KWAI.* The Oscar-winning score of 1957 is the throbbingly dramatic music of *The Bridge on the River Kwai*, by the English symphonist Malcolm Arnold (b. 1921). The musical score is just one of several factors in the success of this film, which was the year's big winner at the Academy Awards, with seven Oscars going to this wide-screen drama about a Japanese prisoner-of-war camp in Burma (now Myanmar) during World War II. The story itself is based on the short novel *The Bridge over the River Kwai*, by the French author Pierre Boulle, who, contrary to the Oscar citation, is not the adapter of his own novel. The real adapter is, in fact, the blacklisted writer Carl Foreman, who did not claim its authorship until many years later.

The director of *Kwai*, David Lean, already had such distinguished British films as *Great Expectations* (1947) and *Oliver Twist* (1948) behind him when he decided to take on this ironic antiwar story about a captured British officer, Colonel Nicholson (Alec Guinness), who uses the job of constructing a bridge as a means of enhancing the morale of his fellow prisoners. The filming took place on Ceylon (now Sri Lanka) and involved months of combating junglelike conditions. There were also immense difficulties involved in filming the climactic scene, in which a supply train crashes into the gorge following the detonation of the bridge with dynamite that guerrilla commandos have rigged to the base of the wooden structure.

Above all else, it was the music that made *Kwai* an international success. Ironically, the "Colonel Bogey March," which figures so prominently in the film as the tune the prisoners whistle as they march toward the camp, was not the first choice for this scene. According to Lean's biographer Stephen Silverman, Lean originally had wanted a World War I song called "Bless 'Em All"; but when producer Sam Spiegel found out how much it would cost for the rights to this song, he told Lean they would have to come up with something else.[47] That's when Lean remembered the "Colonel Bogey" tune, which he had sung as a child.

At the time of the film's release, Mitch Miller's recording of the "Colonel Bogey March," which had been composed by Kenneth J. Alford (1881–1945) in 1914, became extremely popular.[48] This recording, in turn, helped the box-office prospects of the film and may have had something to do with the Oscar that Malcolm Arnold received, even though he wasn't the composer of *The Bridge on the River Kwai* theme. Actually, Arnold was partially responsible, because he did compose an original march theme as a counterpoint to the "Colonel Bogey" melody. Mitch Miller incorporated the two tunes in his recording, so that the final product is a hybrid of the Arnold and the Alford tunes.

Arnold's original music, with the exception of the "River Kwai March," is not very melodious. The opening credits unfold with a series of bombastic chords played by overlapping groups of trumpets, French horns, and trombones, accompanied by pounding kettledrums and other drums. This music continues for some time until a bit of melody appears in the strings; but this soon disappears as the dissonant brass chords return. Arnold's principal melody, a heroic theme that celebrates the endurance of the POWs, finally appears. This inspired tune gets short shrift through most of the score but finally emerges beautifully in the sunset scene late in the film, in which the bridge has been completed and the Japanese commander and Colonel Nicholson proudly survey the site.

SHORT CUTS ■■■■ Hugo Friedhofer.

Nominations for the Original Score Oscar of 1957 went to Hugo Friedhofer for *Boy on a Dolphin* and *An Affair to Remember*. The former score, composed for a scenic but otherwise routine drama about deep-sea diving for treasure off the coast of Greece, includes some atmospheric musical background, but is not as distinguished as many of Friedhofer's other late-1950s efforts. However, there are some pleasing romantic musical moments for the scenes featuring Alan Ladd and Sophia Loren. The most memorable musical ingredient in the score for *An Affair to Remember* is Harry Warren's romantic title song, which also received a nomination. The melody of this song was cleverly interwoven by Friedhofer into his background score for this second screen version of Leo McCarey's 1939 romantic drama *Love Affair*. The 1957 film benefits greatly from Friedhofer's lush orchestrations of Harry Warren's melody and from the chemistry between Cary Grant and Deborah Kerr.

■■■■ **John Green.** Even better than the two Friedhofer scores is John Green's brilliant music for MGM's wide-screen Civil War drama *Raintree County*. Long renowned for his arrangements for screen musicals, Green (1908–89) finally got the chance to prove his worth as a dramatic composer with this score, which combines action scenes of war with romantic episodes. The story involves young Johnny Shawnessy (Montgomery Clift), who is tricked into marrying Susannah (Elizabeth Taylor), a Southern belle who turns out to be emotionally unstable. Woven into the score is Green's own song, "The Ballad of Raintree County," which is performed during the opening credits by Nat "King" Cole and is thereafter heard instrumentally, with the help of a wordless chorus. The music is by far the best thing about this film, which failed to live up to MGM's expectations as a successor to Selznick's famed Civil War drama *Gone with the Wind*.

■■■■ **Paul Smith.** The final Oscar nominee is a real curiosity, the music of Walt Disney's *Perri*, a cute nature film about a squirrel. Its composer, Paul Smith (1906–85), was a Disney studio employee who had scored many earlier films, including *20,000 Leagues under the Sea* (1954) and several of the studio's *True-Life Adventures* series, including *Beaver Valley* (1950), *Nature's Half Acre* (1951), *The Olympic Elk* (1952) and *Water Birds* (1952). For all these films, Smith composed music that underscores each action in a mickey-mousing manner. The abundant use of strings makes these scores sound overly sentimental at times, but Smith was supremely skillful at matching the documentary footage with appropriate musical backgrounds. *Perri*, a departure from Disney's popular documentary-style nature films, was created as a *True-Life Fantasy*, in which nature footage is utilized to create a fictional story. In this case the story was an adaptation of a children's book by Felix Salten, whose most famous work is *Bambi*.[49] Although *Perri* is delightful for young audience members, there have been no further fantasy films made in this pseudodocumentary manner.

■■■■ **Mario Nascimbene.** Several Europeans produced memorable scores for American films released in 1957. Noted Italian composer and conductor Mario Nascimbene (b. 1913) began to gain esteem as a film musician with his dramatic score for David Selznick's expensively mounted remake of Ernest Hemingway's *Farewell to Arms*. As unfortunately flawed as the film is, largely due to the casting of Selznick's wife, Jennifer Jones, as the young English nurse who falls in love with an American ambulance driver (Rock Hudson), Nascimbene's score contains a hauntingly beautiful love theme, which deserves to have become more popular than it did. Prior to the film's release, Les Baxter recorded the theme with his orchestra for Capitol Records, but the tune did not do nearly as well as some of Baxter's other recordings, such as "Unchained Melody."

■■■■ **Richard Addinsell.** Another interesting score was by Englishman Richard Addinsell, whose lilting main-theme waltz elevates the opening credits of *The Prince and the Showgirl*. In this charming, if slight, comedy, Sir Laurence Olivier (who also directed the film) plays the Prince Regent of Carpathia, who tries to seduce an American stage entertainer, played by Marilyn Monroe. In contrast with such other British composers as William Alwyn and Malcolm Arnold, Addinsell produced relatively few film scores during the 1950s. Indeed, the creativity of Addinsell's later years may have been impeded somewhat by the overriding fame of his earlier *Warsaw Concerto* (from the 1941 film *Dangerous Moonlight*).

■ ■ ■ **Bronislau Kaper.** Polish-born Bronislau Kaper's charming music for Sidney Franklin's beautifully photographed Technicolor remake of *The Barretts of Wimpole Street* represents one of the year's scoring highlights. Much of Kaper's lyrical score is based on the song "Wilt Thou Have My Hand?" At one point in the film, this song is sung by all nine Barrett siblings, who have gathered for an evening of merriment while their tyrannical father is away. The catchy tune was actually written for the original 1934 version by that film's composer, Herbert Stothart. In the remake, Elizabeth (Jennifer Jones) plays the song on the piano as everyone sings.

■ ■ ■ **George Antheil.** One other significant score of 1957 is the work by George Antheil (1900–59) for Stanley Kramer's elaborate costume drama *The Pride and the Passion.* Although the two male stars, Cary Grant and Frank Sinatra, seem miscast in their respective roles of an English naval officer and a Spanish revolutionary, and Sophia Loren is too obviously Italian to be convincing as a Spanish girl, the production itself is stunningly beautiful, with a giant cannon as the movie's real star. Antheil, a formerly notorious avant-garde composer who had scored several epics for Cecil B. DeMille in the late 1930s, got this one last chance to score a major film, and he made the most of it. The score begins with a rousing main theme in the style of a Spanish bolero, which sets the story in motion. A small band of Spanish peasants enlist the help of an English military officer, Captain Trumbull (Grant), in order to surmount the logistical problems of lugging the cannon over the countryside to Avila for a showdown with Napoleon's army.

"Rule Britannia" is brought in to denote Captain Trumbull; Miguel (Sinatra) is represented by a lyrically expressive theme that speaks of his affection for Maria (Loren). A high point of the score comes in a scene in which the cannon has to be rescued from a gully into which it falls after its restraining ropes break. The bass line of the music consists of a quick-moving repeated pattern upon which a highly dramatic theme is built. Antheil's work greatly enhances the scene, which is entirely dependent on music for its emotional impact.

BERNHARD HERRMANN: GREAT COLLABORATIONS. There have been many successful collaborations between composers and filmmakers since the advent of the talkies. Some of the most outstanding include Tiomkin and Capra; Prokofiev and Eisenstein; Copland and Milestone; and, of course, Herrmann and Welles. Although the last of these collaborations was regrettably curtailed by the cancellation of Orson Welles's contract at RKO in 1942 after only two films had been completed, Herrmann went on to team up with two other filmmakers, with each of whom he produced some of his most strikingly original scores.

By 1958, Herrmann had scored three Hitchcock films. But these were merely appetizers compared to the full-course musical meal that Herrmann would serve up for Hitchcock's *Vertigo.* Based on the French novel *D'entre les morts,* by Pierre Boileau and Thomas Narcejac, *Vertigo* is among Alfred Hitchcock's bleakest films but also one of his most fascinating. The novel's original French setting has been changed to San Francisco. We first observe a predawn chase across rooftops, involving a fugitive who is pursued by a

Vertigo, with James Stewart
and Kim Novak.

uniformed policeman and a plainclothes detective, Scottie Ferguson (James Stewart). After the pursued man successfully leaps from one building to another, the policeman manages to make the same leap. Scottie, not so lucky, finds himself clinging to a gutter, dangling several stories above the street. At this point we come to realize his fear of heights, as the policeman tries to reach him. Tragically, in the process of trying to help Scottie, the cop loses his balance and falls to his death.

This is Hitchcock's unique way of introducing the film's real story, which involves Madeleine (Kim Novak), the wife of an old friend of Scottie. Because of Madeleine's inscrutable behavior, her husband hires Scottie to tail her. She spends hours in an art museum staring at the portrait of a Spanish woman named Carlotta Valdez. An apparent suicidal tendency is revealed when she unexpectedly jumps into San Francisco Bay. Scottie's rescue of Madeleine brings the two together, and he soon becomes enamored of her.

There is much more music in this film than in the three previous films that Herrmann scored for Hitchcock. The opening credits, cleverly designed by Saul Bass, include swirling abstract patterns that make the attentive viewer feel the dizziness that Scottie himself will later experience. The credits are musically accompanied by a repeated six-note motif for strings and harp that is periodically punctuated by menacing chords. String trills also contribute to the dizzying effect of the visual designs.

In the opening chase scene, the strings contribute a series of rapid-spinning patterns that propel the three men, who are first seen from a distance as shadowy figures set against the dim outline of the city. When Scottie is clinging to the gutter, the camera angle shifts to give the viewer an idea of what Scottie sees as he looks down. Through cinematographer Robert Burks's clever maneuvering of the lens, we get the feeling of moving both forward and backward; loud harp glissandos add to the vertigo effect. When the policeman plunges, the music punctuates his fall with a very dramatic sustained chord.

In the film's main story line, the mysterious Madeleine is represented by a theme in the style of a habanera, which musically connects her with the portrait of Carlotta. In the scene following Scottie's rescue of Madeleine, Herrmann clearly conveys Scottie's growing affection through a ravishingly lovely theme, one of the composer's most romantic compositions.

Though it was largely dismissed by critics at the time, in recent years *Vertigo* has garnered considerable acclaim and has even been listed among the greatest films of all time by some critics.

Shortly after completing work on *Vertigo*, his fourth Hitchcock film, Herrmann commenced another score that would result in a surprisingly meaningful collaboration. *The Seventh Voyage of Sinbad* was Herrmann's first score for producer Charles Schneer, who in the mid-1950s specialized in science fiction, but in 1958 turned his attention to creating films with magical or mythological settings. By hiring Herrmann for *Sinbad*, Schneer brought the composer into contact with one of the most ingenious special-effects masters in the history of cinema, Ray Harryhausen. The animation of a variety of mythological creatures for Schneer's *Sinbad* made this Harryhausen's most ambitious project to date.

Compared to the ominously modern atmosphere of *Vertigo*, the multicolored Arabian fantasy *The Seventh Voyage of Sinbad* might not seem to be the type of film suited to Herrmann's musical temperament, but on closer inspection this first of several fantasy films with Herrmann's music has quite a lot in common with his Hitchcock scores.

The opening-title theme is an altogether fresh Herrmann sound—a buoyant dancelike idea, constructed upon a rapidly repeated four-note rhythmic ostinato. Then the violins sweetly sound a lyrical melodic pattern that is later used for the film's love theme for Sinbad (Kerwin Matthews) and his bride-to-be, Princess Parisa (Kathryn Grant).

The score is filled with an orchestral exoticism that is reminiscent of Nicolai Rimsky-Korsakov's richly textured *Scheherazade*, but there is no direct copying of that composer's work. Instead, Herrmann found his own way to accompany this fantastic story in which the sinister magician Sokurah (Torin Thatcher) thwarts the nuptial plans of Sinbad and Parisa by shrinking her to the size of a doll. She can be restored only by a potion made from the eggshell of a giant roc that inhabits the Island of Colossa. Thus, Sinbad sets sail on a series of adventures in which he encounters such fantastic creatures as a giant cyclops, a two-headed roc, and a huge dragon.

Much of Herrmann's music is dramatic underscoring for scenes in which Sinbad and his crew are confronted by a variety of giant creatures. The most famous music in the film is the "Duel with the Skeleton," a dramatic piece for brass, castanets, xylophone, and drums, which accompanies the sword battle between Sinbad and a life-size skeleton that has been conjured up by Sokurah. The score is rich in melodic motifs, which Herrmann used to enhance this magical story.

JEROME MOROSS: *THE BIG COUNTRY*. Far more original than most of the other film music composed in 1958 is the memorable score by Jerome Moross (1913–83) for William Wyler's sprawling Western film *The Big Country*. Although Wyler originally wanted Aaron Copland to score this film, his final choice of Moross was an inspired one. Already known as a symphonic composer of many concert-hall works, Moross approached the task of scoring this film as though he were writing music for an opera.

Following an opening trumpet fanfare, which is accompanied by swirling string figures, the main-title theme emerges as a rousing and tuneful piece that vividly depicts the West with its open expanses. One of the more noteworthy features of this theme is Moross's repeated tendency to use syncopated accents, specifically a series of rhythmic emphases that occur behind the second beat of the four-beat metric pattern. This insistently accented feature is a foreshadowing of the boldly accented themes that would appear within a few years in the Western music of Elmer Bernstein, especially the main theme of *The Magnificent Seven*.

The score of *The Big Country* includes several other prominent themes, all of which feature the use of the pentatonic (five-tone) scale, which gives Moross's music a sense of stylistic coherence. Especially noteworthy among these themes is "The Welcoming," a tune that is introduced in the film's opening scene, when Jim McKay (Gregory Peck) is first reunited with his fiancée, Pat Terrell (Carroll Baker), whose father, Major Terrell (Charles Bickford), runs the Ladder Ranch. Another prominent theme is the lyrical tune identified as "The Big Muddy," a waterway which separates the Ladder Ranch from the property of Terrell's enemy, Rufus Hannessey (Burl Ives).

Several melodies in the score, even the opening fanfare, become transformed in the course of the film to provide additional melodic motifs in Moross's score, which remains one of the most remarkable of this composer's long and distinguished career. Although he had previously scored seven films and would go on to write nine more over the next decade, the score for *The Big Country* is his most memorable, and it is the only film work for which he received an Oscar nomination.

NEW KIDS ON THE BLOCK. Two young composers who became big names in film music as a result of scoring opportunities in 1958 were Henry Mancini and Johnny Mandel.

Although Henry Mancini (1924–94) had actually been working as a film composer and an arranger at Universal since 1952, the year 1958 represents a turning point in his career. Not only did he score Orson Welles's *Touch of Evil*, in which he created a haunting main theme featuring the piano in a jaunty waltz tune, but this was the year he became hugely successful as the composer of the NBC detective series "Peter Gunn." Mancini's hard-driving main theme, with its now-famous eight-note bass ostinato, was heard, along with several other catchy background tunes, on an RCA record album that became one of the most successful releases in the history of that label and the first TV soundtrack to become a million seller.[50] The popularity of this recording spawned a second album, which was released a few months later. The success of both "Peter Gunn" and the later "Mr. Lucky" series would eventually lead Mancini to start scoring feature films directed by the producer of both of these series, Blake Edwards. Soon Mancini would create renowned film melodies.

The other newcomer, Johnny Mandel (b. 1925), wrote his first film music in 1958, the jazzy score of *I Want to Live*, in which Susan Hayward won an Oscar for playing convicted murderess Barbara Graham. Mandel's background as a jazz trumpeter and a trombonist with Jimmy Dorsey, Buddy Rich, and Count Basie served him well, as did his arranging stint in the 1940s with the Artie Shaw band. For this film score Mandel served up a tasty mixture of jazz tunes, which were performed on the soundtrack by such noted artists as drummer Shelly Manne and trumpeter Jack Sheldon. The success of this effort would lead Mandel to become a film-scoring regular in the 1960s, during which time he would collect an Oscar for "The Shadow of Your Smile" (from *The Sandpiper*).

SHORT CUTS The list of Oscar nominees for music in 1958 does not reflect all the best scores of that year. Notably absent from the Scoring of a Dramatic or Comedy Picture category was Bernard Herrmann, whose scores for *Vertigo* and *The Seventh Voyage of Sinbad* were overlooked. By far the most deserving of the five nominees was Jerome Moross, whose music for *The Big Country* quickly became a film-music classic.

■■■■ Dimitri Tiomkin. The score that won the Oscar is Dimitri Tiomkin's understated music for John Sturges's *Old Man and the Sea*, based on Ernest Hemingway's short novel. The plot revolves around an elderly Cuban fisherman (Spencer Tracy), who goes out too far from his seaside village in his quest for a big catch. Large portions of the film are almost totally without dialogue. Tracy provided a voiceover narration that conveys the fisherman's thoughts during a two-day ordeal with a huge marlin. He kills the fish, but cannot fend off several hungry sharks. Tiomkin's music occasionally gets dramatic, especially when the marlin repeatedly leaps out of the water; otherwise, this is one of Tiomkin's more subdued scoring efforts.

■■■ **Oliver Wallace.** One of the other nominated scores is a rather curious choice: the music for *White Wilderness*, a film in Disney's *True-Life Adventure* series. The composer was Oliver Wallace (1887–1963), who was born in England but did almost all his film work for Disney, beginning with *Dumbo* in 1941. Like the film music of Paul Smith, who was nominated for *Perri* the year before, Wallace's work is in the tried-and-true tradition of the composers of scores for animated films, in which the music carefully mimics every action on the screen.

■■■ **David Raksin.** Although David Raksin's nominated music for Delbert Mann's *Separate Tables* is not on the same level as the score for *The Big Country*, Raksin still managed to compose a lyrical musical background about the residents of an English seaside hotel. In this loquacious but engrossing drama two one-act plays of Terence Rattigan have been merged into a single intertwined scenario. Raksin was prevented from writing main-title music because of the inclusion of a rather sentimental title song by Harry Warren.

■■■ **Hugo Friedhofer.** The last 1958 Oscar nominee is Hugo Friedhofer's eloquent score for Edward Dmytryk's *Young Lions*, based on Irwin Shaw's novel of three World War II soldiers, one of whom (Marlon Brando) is a German officer; the other two (Dean Martin and Montgomery Clift) fight on the Allied side. Friedhofer's main theme is a dramatically charged march, with an ominously powerful brass sound in the melody combined with pounding drums. In contrast with this turbulent music is a sweetly lyrical love theme associated with Christian (Brando) for his relationships with two women. With this score and that of *In Love and War*, also released in 1958, Friedhofer completed his "War Trilogy" of films about World War II that had begun with *Between Heaven and Hell* (1956).

■■■ **Bronislau Kaper.** Meanwhile, Bronislau Kaper created one of the year's best scores when he was assigned the task of creating musical backgrounds for *Auntie Mame*, the film version of the smash Broadway hit, with Rosalind Russell triumphantly recreating her hilarious stage role as the eccentric Mame Dennis. Instead of giving Mame a rousing and wildly comic musical accompaniment, Kaper concentrated on her nobility of character. The result is a soaring waltz theme that is introduced immediately in the opening credits and brought back many times thereafter. The one truly wild piece of music in the film is introduced when Mame goes to the Southern plantation where her fiancé, Beauregard Pickett Burnside (Forrest Tucker), introduces her to his staunchly anti-Yankee family. A fox hunt is given in her honor, during which she gets stuck to the saddle of an otherwise unridable horse, and crashes into an icehouse, ending up with the fox inside her coat. Kaper's boisterously rhythmic music propels this scene and meshes perfectly with the visual hilarity.

■■■■ **Elmer Bernstein.** One of the most productive film composers in 1958 was Elmer Bernstein, who, in fact, averaged four scores a year between 1954 and the end of the decade. Bernstein's work on behalf of *The Buccaneer* features a rousing fanfare theme for brass and a soaring love theme for strings. Meanwhile, Anthony Mann's film version of Erskine Caldwell's *God's Little Acre* includes a tuneful score infused with the sounds of gospel melodies, along with a jazz-oriented background. Delbert Mann's *Desire under the Elms*, adapted from the play by Eugene O'Neill, contains some of Bernstein's most brooding music, especially in the scenes in which Eben (Anthony Perkins) looks longingly at his father's new wife, Anna (Sophia Loren). Solo woodwinds such as oboe and clarinet, along with harps and strings, provide a melancholy, minor-key flavor that expresses musically the feelings that Eben is suppressing. There is also an ingenious use of counterpoint in the scene in which Eben's father, Ephraim (Burl Ives), celebrates the birth of a son while a fiddler churns out a lively dance tune. Simultaneously, much more somber string theme is heard as Eben stares at the newborn child, who is actually his son.

Bernstein's best work of the year is his rhythmically driven music for Vincente Minnelli's *Some Came Running*, based on James Jones's novel, in which Dave Hirsch (Frank Sinatra), a frustrated writer, returns to his Indiana home town after World War II. In contrast with the dramatic main-title music, there is considerable use of a blues theme for scenes with Ginny (Shirley MacLaine), a floozy who develops a crush on Dave. Meanwhile, Dave falls for Gwen Frence (Martha Hyer), a local college teacher who admires his writing. A lyrical theme for piano and strings accompanies a scene in which she reads one of Dave's unpublished stories. As she turns the pages, the theme becomes soaringly romantic; the music clearly indicates Gwen's growing feelings for not only the writing, but for the writer himself.

■■■■ **Mario Nascimbene.** Following *A Farewell to Arms*, Mario Nascimbene created a musically rich score for Richard Fleischer's beautifully photographed historical film *The Vikings*. This fictionalized account of a Viking prince (Tony Curtis) and his love for an English princess (Janet Leigh) features one primary melodic idea that begins with a boldly rising octave. This heroic theme, which is heard in a variety of tempos and moods, is Nascimbene's most distinguished film-music creation.

MIKLOS ROZSA: BEN-HUR. When MGM announced that it was going to remake the 1925 silent hit *Ben-Hur*, there was little doubt that Miklos Rozsa would be offered the scoring assignment.

For the past ten years, since he had started working under contract at MGM, Rozsa excelled as the master of films with historical settings. In both *Quo Vadis* (1951) and *Julius Caesar* (1953), he created musical tapestries which vividly evoke the pageantry of Ancient Rome. Having continued through the 1950s with colorful scores for other historical films, such as *Ivanhoe*, *Young Bess*, and *Diane*, Rozsa was ideally suited for *Ben-Hur*.

The new film, with a $15 million budget, was for a time the most expensive movie ever made. It was only the second film (after *Raintree County*) to utilize the panoramic wide-screen process called Camera 65. More than a year was required for filming. The chariot-race sequence took six months to plan and two months to shoot; at a cost of $1 million, these were at the time the most expensive eleven minutes of footage ever filmed.[51] With the exception of the chariot race, which was staged by action director Andrew Marton, *Ben-Hur* was directed by William Wyler, who had been a production assistant on the 1925 version.

Because of Wyler's painstaking efforts *Ben-Hur* became more than just a Biblical spectacle. More than anything else, it is a dramatically compelling drama of human conflict. Judah Ben-Hur (Charlton Heston), an aristocratic young Jew, seeks revenge against his boyhood friend Messala (Stephen Boyd), who has used an unfortunate accident as a pretext for imprisoning Judah's mother and sister and condemning Judah to be a galley slave. Judah fortuitously rescues the commander of the Roman fleet, becomes a prince of Rome, and returns to Judea; meanwhile, his mother and sister have become lepers. Thinking them dead and seeking vengeance, he forms an alliance with Sheik Ilderim (Hugh Griffith), who engineers a showdown between Judah and Messala in a chariot race in which Judah drives the sheik's white stallions. Despite Messala's death, which results from an accident that occurs during the race, Judah still cannot find peace. But then he offers water to the very man who had helped him when he was en route to a slave ship. The man is Jesus, who has been condemned to die on that day. During the storm that follows Jesus' death, Judah's mother, Miriam (Martha Scott), and his sister, Tirzah (Cathy O'Donnell), are miraculously cured of their leprosy. In a tearful reunion they all embrace, together with Esther (Haya Havareet), a longtime family friend whom Judah plans to marry.

The film was made in Rome at the Cinecitta studios; twenty-four reels of film were taken back to Hollywood, where it took nine months of editing to finish the film. In its final form, *Ben-Hur* had a running time of three hours and thirty-one minutes, just a few minutes less than that of Selznick's *Gone with the Wind.* The lengthy filming time of *Ben-Hur* was actually a blessing for Rozsa in that it gave him much more than the usual amount of time to write the score, the longest of his career. When the composition was finished, Rozsa had completed over two hours of musical cues. The actual recording of the score, with Rozsa conducting the MGM studio orchestra of one hundred players, took seventy-two hours of recording time, spread out over twelve separate sessions.[52]

The first segment of the film, which precedes the opening credits, features the Nativity, with the Magi following a star to the stable in Bethlehem. Rozsa's music for this sequence consists of two themes. The first, the "Star of Bethlehem" music, is a lovely piece for strings, woodwinds, and horns, with wordless voices. The second, the "Adoration of the Magi," has the lyrical simplicity of a folk song; female voices sing the melody wordlessly, with strings and flutes doubling them, while an accompanying effect in the low woodwinds conveys the mooing of a cow in the stable.

Then comes the sound of a ram's horn, followed by a dramatic brass fanfare, which leads directly into the main-title music. As the credits are spread across the wide screen, the first melody heard is the "Christ" theme, which is based on a four-note motif: G–F♯–D–E. This archaic-sounding music soon gives way to the "Judah" theme, which is boldly dramatic. Then comes the love theme, a soaring string melody with echoes of the Christ motif in the brass. All these ideas are featured prominently in the score and return several times, along with other dramatically inspired musical motifs.

Among the other notable pieces of music is a Roman march for Messala's arrival and a parade through the streets of Jerusalem. Then there is the music for the rowing of the galley slaves, in which the tempo begins slowly, with a pounding drumbeat; since the Romans want to test the skill of the slave rowers, the tempo increases gradually until ramming speed is attained. By this time, the music has become frantically fast and turbulent.

One of the most famous pieces in the score is the "Parade of the Charioteers," in which the nine teams of race participants parade around the Circus Maximus. In the midst of this music the "Judah" theme returns, as an indication that this is the fateful moment when Judah can finally avenge the wrong that Messala has done to him and his family. In the chariot race itself crowd noises, combined with the grinding of wheels, the cracking of whips, and the ripping sounds caused by Messala's protruding wheel spikes, make up a plentifully noisy soundtrack; thus music is absent.

The film's closing scenes, which revolve around the Crucifixion of Jesus, have very powerful music. The "Procession to Calvary" is a slow-paced theme that effectively accompanies Jesus as he carries the cross through the streets. After Jesus is nailed to the cross, the music takes on a mournful

Ben-Hur, with
Charlotn Heston

quality, which continues until the moment of his death. Then a fierce storm begins, during which Miriam and Tirzah realize that they are cured. As the rain falls, the full orchestra commences a dramatic statement of the "Christ" theme, in which the melody is treated in the form of a round, with the brass imitating the melodic patterns of the strings. While this theme continues, the camera follows the blood-stained puddle beneath the cross, as the water is washed away in the torrent. The blood and water from the cross form a small stream that then empties into a raging river, which in turn flows on toward the sea. The music finally calms down as the storm subsides. In the closing moment of the film, as Judah embraces his family, the music segues into a thrilling final statement of several of the score's principal ideas, including the "Judah" theme and the "Christ" motif, while a choir joyously sings the word "Alleluia."

The music of *Ben-Hur* is not only the high-water mark of Miklos Rozsa's career as a film composer but also one of the most exceptional film scores ever written. This score, which was selected for one of the eleven Oscars that *Ben-Hur* won, accompanies the last epic motion picture produced under the studio system. With this film Rozsa's tenure as a contract composer at MGM came to an end. Although his next score was composed for *King of Kings*, an MGM release, this film was independently produced by Samuel Bronston. In the 1960s, most of the studios would divest themselves of their vast properties, as a result of which they would remain corporate entities, but without the facilities to shoot films on their premises.

Even though *Ben-Hur* went on to become, for a time, the second among top-grossing films of all time (behind *Gone with the Wind*), few films would ever again invite the kind of symphonic background that Rozsa contributed to *Ben-Hur*. This film and its score stand as symbols of the final remnants of the Golden Age of Hollywood.

BERNARD HERRMANN: *JOURNEY TO THE CENTER OF THE EARTH AND NORTH BY NORTHWEST.* Herrmann had a field day with his score for the colorful adaptation of Jules Verne's *Journey to the Center of the Earth.* This engaging film has clever sets (including the use of the Carlsbad Caverns) and an attractive cast, with James Mason as Professor Lindenbrook, who leads an expedition into the Earth's interior. Among the group are young Alec (Pat Boone), one of the professor's students; a Swedish guide (Peter Ronson); and Carla (Arlene Dahl), the sole female member of the group, who eventually captures the professor's heart.

Herrmann's orchestration is highly unconventional; he dispensed with strings and concentrated instead on brass, woodwinds, and percussion, with five organs (four electric ones plus a giant pipe organ) used to convey the depths to which these intrepid travelers descend.

The main thematic material consists of a four-note trumpet idea first heard as the group descends into an extinct volcano. The score also includes a bombastic chordal idea featuring the organs, brass, and percussion. For the film's climactic sequence, in which the group is propelled up a volcanic shaft during an eruption, Herrmann devised a slowly rising musical idea that utilizes all his orchestral palette; unfortunately, the sound mixers allowed this music to be almost completely covered by the massive sound effects. Herrmann later gave a much better idea of how this music was supposed to sound on a recording entitled *The Fantasy Film World of Bernard Herrmann*, which also includes excerpts from three of his other film scores.[53]

The score for Alfred Hitchcock's *North by Northwest* is one of the most ingenious in the ongoing Hitchcock–Herrmann collaboration. The film is based on a typical Hitchcock situation in which an innocent man is wrongly suspected of being someone else—in this case, a spy who is pursued by counterspies (played by James Mason and Martin Landau). However, *North by Northwest* has a lighter tone than many of Hitchcock's other 1950s films. Coming right after the morbidly fascinating *Vertigo*, this film benefits greatly from the witty script by Ernest Lehman and from Cary Grant's incomparable acting in the role of Roger Thornhill, an advertising executive. In an early scene Thornhill innocently raises his hand in a restaurant, trying to flag a waiter; this gesture is interpreted as a wave at a group of spies, who think he is an agent. This simple act initiates a plot in which Thornhill finds himself in constant danger. He manages to survive both a wild downhill ride in a car without brakes and an encounter with a crop-dusting airplane.

Herrmann launches this film with a turbulent, if not very tuneful, opening-title piece that lets us know right away that this is going to be a thriller. The action stops long enough for a train sequence in which Roger first meets the mysterious Eve (Eva Marie Saint). Amid much snappy dialogue Herrmann introduces one of his most romantic themes, a lyrical idea that alternately features a solo clarinet and an oboe, sounded over a background of strings.

The film's most famous scene, in which Thornhill repeatedly has to avoid a cropduster plane, is surprisingly lacking in music until the moment when the plane crashes into the side of a tanker trunk. Only at this point do Herrmann's wrenchingly dissonant chords arrive to underscore the excitement of the horrific explosion that occurs.

North by Northwest is one of the most enjoyable of Hitchcock's films, with one of Herrmann's most masterful scores.

ADOLPH **D**EUTSCH: *S*OME *L*IKE *I*T *H*OT. Two of 1959's most memorable films—*Some Like It Hot* and *Anatomy of a Murder*—both incorporate the sounds of jazz. Billy Wilder's *Some Like It Hot*, which is set during the Roaring Twenties, involves a couple of Chicago musicians, Joe (Tony Curtis) and Jerry (Jack Lemmon), who inadvertently witness the St. Valentine's Day Massacre. In order to avoid being killed by the murderers, they hide out in drag as members of Sweet Sue's band, which is en route by train to Florida for a three-week engagement. Comic complications abound as both male musicians become attracted to the band's sexy singer, Sugar Kane (Marilyn Monroe), who seems to reciprocate their friendly interest, but does not know their true gender.

In the film there is a mixture of musical styles, including several Dixieland numbers. These were recorded by Matty Malneck, who had previously composed tunes for Wilder's *Love in the Afternoon*. Several well-known songs of the flapper era are sung by Marilyn Monroe, including "Runnin' Wild" and the classic "poo-poo-pa-doop" song "I Wanna Be Loved by You." There is also some lush scoring by Adolph Deutsch (1897–1980), who had worked at Warner Bros. alongside Max Steiner for many years before becoming an award-winning composer/arranger at MGM in 1948.

In the film's most memorable sequence, there is a clever juxtapositioning of two borrowed musical ideas. While Joe is impersonating a millionaire (replete with a hilarious Cary Grant accent) in order to woo Sugar aboard a yacht, Jerry, in his female guise as Daphne, is doing the town with Osgood (Joe E. Brown). The scene shifts back and forth between the two venues. For the moments with Joe and Sugar there is a lush arrangement for strings of the "Park Avenue Fantasy," which was written in 1935 by Matty Malneck and Frank Signorelli (but is better known as the melody of the 1939 song "Stairway to the Stars"). For the nightclub scenes with Jerry (as Daphne) and Osgood, "La Cumparsita" is heard as the two perform a hilariously athletic tango. Through clever editing, each of the two pieces of music fits exactly into the appropriate film footage, with continually delightful results.

DUKE ELLINGTON: ANATOMY OF A MURDER. The other notable jazz-oriented score from 1959 marks the debut of Duke Ellington (1899–1974) as a film composer. For Otto Preminger's *Anatomy of a Murder*, based on the best-selling novel by Robert Traver, Ellington devised an atmospheric musical background. Filmed in Michigan's Upper Peninsula, this engrossing courtroom drama features James Stewart as a defense attorney whose client, a military officer accused of murder, needs all the help he can get to fend off the crafty prosecutor (George C. Scott).

The jazz tunes in the score range from slow bluesy themes to much more swinging numbers. Like the zither music in *The Third Man*, Ellington's score here really doesn't comment very much on the film; on the contrary, the music primarily serves as flavoring for the scenes that take place outside the courtroom. As such, the music quite effectively establishes a lighter tone for the moments when the murder trial is in recess. Several prominent musicians are heard on the soundtrack, including Ellington himself (who appears briefly in the film as "Pie Eye"), and such other notables as Clark Terry, Johnny Hodges, and Shorty Baker. Although Ellington was sixty years old when he completed his first film score, his often sassy backgrounds have the freshness and youthful vitality of a composer half his age.

SHORT CUTS ■ ■ ■ ■ **Alfred Newman.** One of 1959's most prestigious films is George Stevens's moving wide-screen adaptation of the Broadway play *The Diary of Anne Frank*. Although critics were rather unkindly disposed toward some of the actors in this film, especially Millie Perkins in the pivotal role of Anne, there was little doubt that Stevens had captured on film the emotional center of this factual drama of the Frank family, who were forced to hide in the attic of a factory in Amsterdam during World War II. It was there that the teenage Anne recorded her thoughts and feelings in the diary that has become so famous.

In Alfred Newman's Oscar-nominated music, one of the most poignant scores in his long career, the violins play a crucial role both in the film's uplifting main theme and in the soaringly romantic love theme, with its continually ascending scale patterns.

Especially moving is a scene, late in the film, between Anne and Peter (Richard Beymer), who is the son of the Van Daans, the people who share the factory hiding place with the Franks. From a secret vantage point, they look out over the buildings below while the German police wagons come down the street with sirens blaring. The music begins softly, but as the two teenagers share a kiss, there is a tremendous surge in the orchestration. No one could convey better than Newman the idea of passionate young lovers just beginning to discover the depth of their feelings.

■ ■ ■ **Franz Waxman.** Franz Waxman's score for Fred Zinnemann's *Nun's Story* was also nominated for an Oscar. This is another inspired effort from a man whose strengths as a film composer kept increasing with age. Coming a quarter of a century after *The Bride of Frankenstein*, his American film-scoring debut, Waxman's music shows real empathy for Sister Luke (the radiant Audrey Hepburn). There are many moments of quiet but intense beauty in the film, especially in the long section that meticulously details the highly structured and rule-oriented daily routine of the postulants. In the scene in which Gabrielle is received into the order and becomes Sister Luke, there is much use of Gregorian chant melodies. These melodies influenced Waxman directly, since all the thematic material of the film is derived from Gregorian chants.[54]

■ ■ ■ **Frank De Vol.** The two remaining Oscar-nominated scores were composed by first-time nominees. Of the two, Frank De Vol (b. 1911) was cited largely on the basis of the overall charm of the film *Pillow Talk*, the first movie to feature Rock Hudson and Doris Day as a romantic comedy team. De Vol's work is clever, and it enhances the comedic nature of this story of a romantic deception; but it really isn't in the same league with the other nominees.

■ ■ ■ **Ernest Gold.** The one remaining nominee for 1959 was Ernest Gold (b. 1921), who was cited for the music of Stanley Kramer's depressing end-of-the-world film *On the Beach*, based on the Nevil Shute novel. Gold had scored films since the mid-1940s, but most of his scoring projects had been of the extremely low-budget variety. Kramer hired him to conduct George Antheil's score of *The Pride and the Passion* in 1957, and then used him as a composer for the first time on *The Defiant Ones* in 1958. It was *On the Beach* that really established Gold as a major film musician. Ironically, the tune that became well-known as a result of this film is not by Gold. Rather, it is the old Australian song "Waltzing Matilda," which was used because of the Australian setting of much of the film, in which the few survivors of the fallout that has resulted from a nuclear war prepare to die. The lilting strains of this tune are strangely at odds with the rest of this extremely downbeat film. The film is watchable principally because of its attractive cast, which includes Gregory Peck, Ava Gardner, and Fred Astaire.

■ ■ ■ **Max Steiner.** The most popular film music to emanate from a 1959 film was in Max Steiner's score for *A Summer Place*, a steamy Warner Bros. tale of illicit love. After three decades of work in Hollywood, Steiner was past his prime. By now, he was demonstrating little of the creative genius he had shown in such landmark scores as *King Kong* and *The Informer*. For this film, however, he shrewdly fashioned a lilting balladlike theme for the young lovers, played by Troy Donahue and Sandra Dee, whose parents are involved in adultery. The young lovers' theme is accompanied by an insistent triplet figure, a standard ingredient in rock-'n'-roll of the '50s. The trendiness of this music may have been contrived, but the result was magical. At the beginning of 1960, "The Theme from *A Summer Place*," as recorded by Percy Faith, climbed the *Billboard* charts, where it topped the list for nine weeks.[55]

POSTLUDE

TWO RISING STARS. Two film composers who would become masters of the art in the 1970s got their scoring starts at the end of the Fabulous Fifties, and both came to the medium of film after having written music for several TV shows. Jerry Goldsmith (b. 1929) composed his first film score for a low-budget Western named *Black Patch* in 1957, while John Williams (b. 1932), who at the time was known as Johnny Williams, did his first film score in 1959 for a feeble little crime drama called *Daddy-O*, which starred accordion player Dick Contino. It is worth noting that Leonard Maltin, in his *Movie and Video Guide*, gives these two films a "Bomb" rating. Like the film-music pioneers of the early years of the talkies, Goldsmith and Williams benefited from these maiden efforts. With a little luck and with the possibility of collaborating with talented filmmakers, these film composers would become two of the most respected musicians in Hollywood during the next three decades.

Endnotes

1. Elston Brooks, *I've Heard Those Songs Before: The Weekly Top Ten Tunes for the Last Fifty Years* (New York: William Morrow and Co., 1981), pp. 223–25.

2. Ibid., pp. 206–8.

3. Ibid., p. 197. These dates reflect the years when these songs were listed on the charts. In some cases, if a film opened at the end of a year, the song (or songs) from that film did not become popular until early in the following year; e.g., *Moulin Rouge* opened in a few cities during December 1952 in order to qualify for the Oscars. Its subsequent national release helped to promote the "Song from *Moulin Rouge*," which entered the Top Ten on April 18, 1953.

4. Harry Castleman and Walter J. Podrazik, *Watching TV: Four Decades of American Television* (New York: McGraw-Hill Book Co., 1982), p. 30.

5. Ibid., p. 36.

6. Ibid., p. 45.

7. Ibid., pp. 57–59.

8. Martin Quigley, Jr. and Richard Gertner, *Films in America 1929–1969* (New York: Golden, 1970), p. 187.

9. Patrick Robertson, *Guinness Film Facts and Feats*, new ed. (Middlesex, England: Guinness Superlatives, Ltd., 1985), p. 147.

10. David Cook, *A History of Narrative Film* (New York: W. W. Norton & Co., 1981), pp. 420–21.

11. On the soundtrack, released in 1978 on a Planet Records LP, the Barrons are credited with "electronic tonalities"; the beeps and squeaks of their synthesized sounds are never referred to as a "musical score."

12. Tony Thomas, *Film Score: The Art and Craft of Movie Music* (Burbank, CA: Riverwood, 1991), p. 35.

13. Page Cook, "Franz Waxman," *Films in Review*, vol. XIX, no. 7 (August–September 1968), p. 416.

14. Jeff Burkhart and Bruce Stuart, *Hollywood's First Choices (or Why Groucho Marx Never Played Rhett Butler): How Hollywood's Greatest Casting Decisions Were Made* (New York: Crown, 1994), pp. 11–17.

15. Ibid., pp. 4–5.

16. In a letter to the author dated September 8, 1987, Elia Kazan indicated that he wanted jazz elements to be used in the score of *Streetcar Named Desire*.

17. David Ewen, *American Composers Today* (New York: H. H. Wilson, 1949), p. 179.

18. Ibid.

19. Ibid., p. 180.

20. Ibid., p. 179.

21. Tony Thomas, *Music for the Movies* (South Brunswick, NJ: A. S. Barnes and Co., 1973), p. 181.

22. Steven C. Smith, Liner notes for the CD release of *The Day the Earth Stood Still*, Fox Film Scores, 11010-2.

23. Christopher Palmer, Liner notes for the RCA highlights recording *The Spectacular World of Classic Film Scores*, RCA 2792-2-RG (CD format), from an interview with Charles Gerhardt.

24. Fred Zinnemann, *A Life in the Movies: An Autobiography* (New York: Charles Scribner's Sons, 1992), p. 106.

25. Peter van Gelder, *That's Hollywood: A Behind-the-Scenes Look at 60 of the Greatest Films of All Time* (New York: HarperCollins, 1990), p. 153.

26. Zinnemann, p. 97.

27. Ibid., p. 108.

28. Dimitri Tiomkin and Prosper Buranelli, *Please Don't Hate Me* (New York: Doubleday & Co., 1959), p. 231.

29. Elmer Bernstein, "What Ever Happened to Great Movie Music?", *High Fidelity*, vol. 22, no. 7 (July 1972), p. 58.

30. A live recording from Tanglewood featuring Stan Getz with Arthur Fiedler and the Boston Pops was released by RCA in 1967 (LSC-2925). This recording also features Raksin's "Song after Sundown," from his score for the 1961 picture *Too Late Blues*.

31. Liner notes for the LP, which includes music from the soundtracks of *Ivanhoe*, *Plymouth Adventure*, and *Madame Bovary*, MGM E3507, released in 1957. This album was for the most part a reissue, since four tracks from each of the first two films had earlier appeared on two 1952 releases, a boxed set of 45s (MGM K179) and a 10-inch LP (MGM E-179).

32. Robertson, p. 146.

33. Palmer, Liner notes for *Spectacular World of Classic Film Music*.

34. Miklos Rozsa, *Double Life* (New York: Wynwood, 1989), pp. 131–32.

35. Paul Robinson, *Bernstein* (New York: Vanguard, 1982), pp. 19–20.

36. Aaron Copland, *Copland on Music* (New York: W. W. Norton & Co., 1963), pp. 172–73.

37. Bosley Crowther, *The Great Films: Fifty Golden Years of Motion Pictures* (New York: G. P. Putnam's Sons, 1967), p. 217.

38. Roy M. Prendergast, *Film Music: A Neglected Art*, 2d ed. (New York: W. W. Norton & Co., 1992), p. 130.

39. Steven C. Smith, *A Heart at Fire's Center: The Life and Music of Bernard Herrmann* (Berkeley: University of California, 1991), pp. 181–82.

40. Brooks, pp. 208–10.

41. Joseph McBride, ed., *Film Makers on Film Making: The American Film Institute Seminars on Motion Pictures and Television* (Boston: Houghton Mifflin, 1983), vol. 1, p. 115.

42. Thomas, *Film Score*, p. 310.

43. Smith, p. 185.

44. Brooks, pp. 222–24.

45. Susan Sackett, *The Hollywood Reporter Book of Box Office Hits* (New York: Billboard Books, 1990), p. 124.

46. Royal S. Brown, Liner notes for the Varese Sarabande CD rerelease of the original film soundtrack (VSD-5212), which appeared in 1989.

47. Steven M. Silverman, *David Lean* (New York: Harry M. Abrams, 1989), p. 125.

48. Stanley Sadie, ed., *The Norton/Grove Encyclopedia of Music* (New York: W. W. Norton & Co., 1988), p. 15. Alford is the *nom de plume* for a British military officer named Frederick Ricketts, who published many marches, of which "Colonel Bogey" became the most famous.

49. Leonard Maltin, *The Disney Films*, abridged and updated ed. (New York: Popular Library, 1978), p. 282.

50. Joseph Murrells, *Million Selling Records* (New York: Arco, 1984), p. 119.

51. Sackett, *Box Office Hits*, p. 140.

52. *The Story of the Making of "Ben-Hur"* (New York: Random House, 1959). This book was included with the first release of the film's score as part of a boxed set (MGM 1E1 and S1E1).

53. This album was originally released as a London Phase 4 LP, SP 44207. It later reappeared on CD as part of the *Cinema Gala* series, where it was entitled simply *Film Fantasy*, no. 421 266-2. Most recently, it appeared as part of another London CD, no. 443 899-2.

54. Liner notes for the Stanyan Records rerelease of the original soundtrack. Waxman is quoted regarding his trip to Rome to do the score; he studied Gregorian music, which led to his use of the many melodies in the score of *The Nun's Story* that are based on chant.

55. Elston Brooks, p. 251.

5

1960–69

The Changing of the Guard

PRELUDE

In many ways the decade of the 1960s was one of the twentieth century's most turbulent, a time that began with the optimistic ascendancy of John F. Kennedy to the White House and ended with the horrifying reality of Vietnam. In between there were several assassinations of political and religious leaders, plus racial tensions in America's largest cities that led to full-blown riots in the summers of 1964 through 1967. In this decade there were tumultuous developments in the world of entertainment, not only in popular music but also in the TV and film industries.

POPULAR MUSIC. In popular music the 1960s can be characterized as the decade of the "British Invasion." When the Beatles arrived in New York on February 7, 1964, the four Liverpudlians were greeted by thousands of screaming young fans, who caused riotous outbreaks at the sites of their first American concerts, including one at Carnegie Hall.[1] The notoriety of the Beatles was enhanced by two appearances on the Ed Sullivan TV show. With Beatles songs broadcast live into millions of American homes, parents found themselves on the opposite side of the generational fence from their teenage children. The Beatles craze grew to even greater proportions with the release of the film *A Hard Day's Night* that summer.

Although Beatlemania continued throughout the decade, the Beatles themselves remained a group for only a few years. Their last live concert took place in 1966, and by 1970 John, Paul, George, and Ringo went their separate ways, never again to reach the level of acclaim that they had achieved together as the "Fabulous Four." Other English rock groups like the Rolling Stones, The Who, and Led Zeppelin, gained millions of loyal fans; but no matter how successful these groups became, none ever eclipsed the Beatles.

Even the Broadway stage was not immune to the sounds of rock-'n'-roll. Despite the popularity of such traditionally conceived musicals as *Hello, Dolly!* (1964) and *Funny Girl* (1964), which made Barbra Streisand a major singing star, one of the most influential stage musicals of the 1960s was *Hair*, with music by Galt MacDermot, which was advertised as "an American tribal love-rock musical" when it first opened Off-Broadway in late 1967. Six months later, a revamped and enlarged production reached the Broadway stage and caused a sensation because of its rebellious attitude toward the war in Vietnam, its frankness about sex, and a nude scene. *Hair* provided a number of songs that became popular, especially "Aquarius" and "Let the Sunshine in," both of which became hits through a recorded medley made by one of the decade's most popular singing groups, the Fifth Dimension.

In the late 1960s, the Beatles as well as other performers got caught up in a countercultural phenomenon based on such drugs as heroin and LSD. By 1969, when the first Woodstock music festival took place on a farm in New York State, millions of young people were part of the drug culture, which accompanied the antiwar protests then going on. Such dynamic performers as Janis Joplin, Jimi Hendrix, and The Doors' Jim Morrison, all of whom eventually succumbed to their drug addiction, were among the icons who rebelled against American entanglement in an unpopular war.

TELEVISION. Paralleling the turbulence in popular music, TV comedy during the 1960s began to reflect a broad spectrum of cultural attitudes. In contrast with such pioneering sitcoms of the '50s as "I Love Lucy" and "The Honeymooners," many of the newer comedies concentrated on fantasy; this was the case with "Bewitched" (1964–72); "Gilligan's Island" (1964–67); and "I Dream of Jeannie" (1965–70). Homespun humor was represented by "The Andy Griffith Show" (1960–68) and "The Beverly Hillbillies" (1962–71). Some 1960s sitcoms were aimed at a more sophisticated audience; this is especially true of "The Dick Van Dyke Show" (1961–66), which introduced one of TV's most enduring comediennes, Mary Tyler Moore. This show also set a standard for strong ensemble casts, with support from Morey Amsterdam, Rose Marie, and Carl Reiner, who created the series.

With the Vietnam War continuing to escalate throughout the 1960s, several television programs began to acknowledge world events by subjecting viewers to strong doses of political satire. The first was "That Was the Week That Was," which lasted less than two seasons (from January 1964 to May 1965), to be followed by "The Smothers Brothers Comedy Hour."

The most successful comedy show at the end of the decade was "Rowan & Martin's Laugh-in," which brilliantly spoofed everything in America and beyond through a quick series of blackouts and short skits. With its rampant one-liners and nonstop gags, this show's irreverence was in stark contrast to the dire events being reported in the nightly news.

"The Carol Burnett Show," though not politically motivated, provided viewers with diversion from newscasts through a variety of entertaining skits and musical numbers. One of TV's finest comedy ensembles, which included Carol Burnett herself, Harvey Korman, Tim Conway, Vicki Lawrence, and Lyle Waggoner, created great hilarity.

Although comedy seemed to dominate prime-time TV during the 1960s, a few dramatic programs were successful. In addition to the Westerns such as

"Gunsmoke," "Bonanza," and "The Virginian," ABC's "The Fugitive" (1963–67) offered an engrossing series of episodes in which Dr. Richard Kimble (David Janssen) attempted to elude capture as he hunted for a one-armed man whom he believed to be his wife's murderer. Two series with hospital settings, "Dr. Kildare" and "Ben Casey" (both 1961–66), also furnished viewers with something more substantial than comic relief. In both shows the dramatic content was enhanced by strong background musical themes, provided in the first instance by a neophyte (Jerry Goldsmith) and in the other by a veteran (David Raksin).

The most influential sci-fi series in TV history was "Star Trek," which began in 1966 and lasted for three seasons in prime time. Following its cancellation the show began to attract a cult following. "Trekkies" held nostalgic conventions, and by the end of the 1970s, Paramount would launch several feature-length films that reunited most of the original cast members. Additionally, three syndicated TV series would eventually be spun off from the original show.

In stark contrast with most of the popular TV programs of the decade is CBS's "Sixty Minutes," which debuted in 1968 (and is still extant as of this writing), with a number of top news correspondents among the show's regular reporters. Other developments included the transition from live broadcasts to either filmed or videotaped shows and the addition of network showings of theatrical films. By early 1967, each network was broadcasting two nights of movies per week. Because of the high cost of buying broadcast rights to major films, movies began to be made specifically for television. By the end of 1966, NBC had struck a deal with Universal to produce a series of original films, which were to be broadcast without prior theatrical showing.

With the rise of made-for-TV movies, a greater amount of work became available to film composers who could work within the tight time lines and budgets of these productions. Only on rare occasions would musicians be granted the time and the budget to create works on a scale as elaborate as their scores for theatrical films. Even within the restrictions required by this hybrid film genre, many composers contributed some genuinely fine work.

MOVIES. As the 1960s began, the major movie studios had already started to divest themselves of almost all their production facilities. They remained as corporate entities to oversee the financing of films and often acted as releasing companies for independently produced movies.

Without the rigid controls of the old studio system, feature films made in the 1960s often cost more than $10 million apiece. Because of the impressive box-office returns of such 1950s epics as *The Ten Commandments* and *Ben-Hur*, Hollywood producers often fell victim to a belief in "the bigger, the better." A number of expensive 1960s films drove movie studios to the brink of bankruptcy. Especially ruinous was 20th Century-Fox's production of *Cleopatra*, which cost about $40 million, and which failed to show a profit even when its TV rights were sold.[2]

The 1960s may be regarded as the beginning of the end for the screen musical; but, even though song-and-dance films were pretty much a thing of the past, four of the Oscar-winning pictures of the '60s were musical films. The fact that all four were adapted from highly acclaimed and long-running stage musicals may have contributed to their success. In any case,

West Side Story (1961), *My Fair Lady* (1964), *The Sound of Music* (1965), and *Oliver!* (1968) were all big hits at the box office, with *The Sound of Music* becoming the all-time box-office champion (until *The Godfather* surpassed it in 1972).

So few movies were being shot in black-and-white that the Oscar categories were changed in 1967 to remove any distinction between color and black-and-white filming (which affected the areas of cinematography, art direction, and costuming). Meanwhile, CinemaScope and other processes were replaced as the favored wide-screen technique by Panavision in the early part of the decade. The Cinerama process, used by MGM for two feature films in the early 1960s, was subsequently simplified to a single-projector technique, but was still phased out of existence by the end of the decade.

The 1960s are noteworthy for the arrival of adult films which presented a challenge to the old motion picture production code. When Mike Nichols directed the film version of Edward Albee's controversial play *Who's Afraid of Virginia Woolf?* in 1966, the code was already outmoded. In 1968, the Motion Picture Association of America replaced the old code with a system of self-regulation, which gave ratings to all forthcoming films. Once this new policy was in place, films with bold, adult themes could be released without fear of being suppressed. Thus, another weapon in the ongoing media war was put in place, as Hollywood began making films that could not be shown uncut on network TV.

For film composers, the 1960s represents the changing of the guard, with some of the noted film pioneers—in particular the three godfathers—composing their last scores during those years. Max Steiner's declining health, including failing eyesight, forced him to retire in 1965, after thirty-five years of film scoring. His last scores did little to enhance his reputation, and when he died on December 28, 1971, he would be chiefly remembered for the scores of the many exceptional films of the 1930s and '40s that had given him the opportunity to develop the technique of film scoring to such a high level of artistry. Dimitri Tiomkin composed his last original film score in 1968, for the forgettable comedy *Great Catherine*. His last involvement with film scoring was arranging the music for the biographical movie *Tchaikovsky* (1971), which he coproduced in Russia. He lived in retirement for the last years of his life, and died on November 11, 1979. Meanwhile, although Alfred Newman never officially retired, he reached the final chapter in his illustrious film career with the score of *Airport*, whose release coincided with the composer's death on February 17, 1970.

Franz Waxman, younger than these three pioneers of film scoring, nevertheless preceded all of them in death. Having composed several masterful film scores in the first three years of the decade, including the powerful music of *Taras Bulba* (1962), he was not much in demand from 1963 on. He succumbed to cancer in 1967 at the age of sixty.

Two other composers, Bronislau Kaper and André Previn (b. 1929), whose film-scoring careers came to an end in the 1960s, had both been affiliated with MGM for most of their Hollywood years. Although Kaper wrote a magnificent score for his last MGM picture, the expensive remake of *Mutiny on the Bounty* (1962), he began to lose interest in the profession in which he had been involved for almost three decades. He composed six scores between 1964 and 1968, but then turned his attention to other musical pursuits. Although he lived on until cancer claimed him on April 25, 1983, he would make no further contributions to film music.

André Previn's disdain for the Hollywood atmosphere has been well-documented in a number of books, including his own *No Minor Chords*, an often witty 1991 memoir in which he vividly describes the lack of musical insight shown by Hollywood producers. The title itself alludes to a frequently repeated anecdote about Irving Thalberg, who, having been informed by an assistant that the problems with his newest film stemmed from the composer's use of minor chords, sent an interoffice memo to the MGM music department in which he instructed all of that studio's music employees henceforth to avoid the use of minor chords in their scores.[3] Despite his increasingly negative attitude, Previn still managed to create some masterful scores for films made in the '60s, including *Elmer Gantry* (1960) and *Dead Ringer* (1964). Previn did four scores for Billy Wilder films between 1961 and 1966, but during this period he began to concentrate on orchestra conducting in the concert hall.

A few efforts in the jazz vein appeared in the 1960s, by composers as divergent as André Previn (*The Subterraneans*, 1960), Elmer Bernstein (*Walk on the Wild Side*, 1962), Quincy Jones (*The Pawnbroker*, 1965), Chico Hamilton (*Repulsion*, 1965), Herbie Hancock (*Blow-Up*, 1966), and Michel Legrand (*The Picasso Summer*, 1969). Because of an increasing tendency toward scores of a jazz or pop sound, the majority of film scores of the '60s no longer needed composers with a symphonic background. For this reason such masters of the art of film music as Bernard Herrmann and Miklos Rozsa found themselves being employed less often as the '60s progressed. Alfred Hitchcock hired Bernard Herrmann for several films in the early '60s, but by 1965 their relationship ended abruptly with a rift that led Herrmann to leave Hollywood altogether, though he subsequently composed several excellent scores for films made in Europe.

ELMER BERNSTEIN: *THE MAGNIFICENT SEVEN*. The rousing music that Elmer Bernstein composed for John Sturges's *Magnificent Seven*, an Americanization of Akira Kurosawa's classic film *The Seven Samurai*, has been widely imitated.

Bernstein's background is in sharp contrast to the settings of the Western movies which he scored. Born in New York City on April 4, 1922, he had early interests in both painting and dancing, but his talent centered primarily on the piano. Hoping to become a concert pianist, he entered the Juilliard School of Music, where he trained with Henriette Michelson, who was impressed with his improvisational skills. She took him to meet Aaron Copland, who arranged for Bernstein to study with one of Copland's pupils, Israel Sitowitz. Bernstein subsequently received scholarships for study with the renowned composers Roger Sessions and Stefan Wolpe, and enrolled at New York University, where he majored in music education while still aiming to become a concert pianist.[4]

Bernstein's aspirations were interrupted by World War II. In 1943, after joining the Army Air Corps, he was assigned to compose music for radio programs; he also worked as an arranger for Glenn Miller, who had formed the U.S. Army Air Corps Band. Despite the experience as composer and arranger garnered during his three years of military service, when he reentered civilian life he found few opportunities to utilize his newly developed skills. Once again, he pursued a solo performing career; but a series of fortuitous events soon paved his way to Hollywood. According to Tony Thomas:

Elmer Bernstein.

In 1949, he [Bernstein] was offered the job of writing a score for the United Nations Radio Service for a program concerning the armistice achieved by the UN in Israel. The program was carried by NBC and was heard by the writer-producer Norman Corwin, who engaged Bernstein to write a score for one of his dramatic productions. This in turn was heard by a Columbia Pictures executive who invited Bernstein to Hollywood to write the scores for two pictures, *Saturday's Hero* and *Boots Malone*, both in 1951.[5]

In 1952, Bernstein gained recognition for an unusually modernistic score which he wrote for *Sudden Fear*. It differed from the typical film score both in its dissonant harmony and in its sparse instrumentation. This score should have cemented Bernstein's reputation in Hollywood, but a few years would pass before he became established. In the meantime, he scored whatever projects came his way. Perhaps 1953 marks the low point of his film-music career, with scores for two cheap productions, *Robot Monster* and *Cat Women of the Moon*. Fortunately, Bernard Herrmann recommended him as composer for the 1955 CinemaScope drama *The View from Pompey's Head*, which, in turn, helped to influence Cecil B. DeMille to choose him to replace the ailing Victor Young as composer for *The Ten Commandments*.

It was after he did this epic score, and his jazzy, Oscar-nominated music for Otto Preminger's *Man with the Golden Arm*, that Bernstein finally began to find recognition. By the end of the 1950s, offers for film scores began to come regularly, with several directors, including Delbert Mann, Anthony Mann, Robert Mulligan, and Vincente Minnelli, utilizing his creative talent to good effect. Among Bernstein's earlier scores were three for Western films: *Battles of Chief Pontiac* (1952), *Drango* (1957), and *The Tin Star* (also 1957). It was John Sturges's remake of the Kurosawa classic that elevated Elmer Bernstein to the front ranks of Hollywood composers.

When Sturges decided to remake Kurosawa's film, for which he paid a small fee for the rights and received the Japanese director's blessing, he obtained backing from the Mirisch Brothers at United Artists, but with the provision that he cast a known star in the lead role. Despite his middle-European accent, Yul Brynner was perceived as being a strong, silent presence and thus suitable for the role of Chris, who aids the villagers against a small army of bandits that continually pillages their supplies. Sturges began filming *The Magnificent Seven*, with its setting shifted from medieval Japan to late-nineteenth-century Mexico. Once Bernstein was hired to do the score, the obvious question was whether there should be a Tiomkin-style ballad. Tiomkin was then the accepted master of the Western genre, having scored *High Noon* and Sturges's own *Gunfight at the O.K. Corral* (1957). The decision to eschew a song as a vocal background was wise because of this film's episodic structure. Bernstein's main-title music sweeps the viewer into a world of roisterous adventure. After some boldly syncopated opening chords, the main theme is heard, with a rising pattern of fifths that is used several times over a continually hard-driving rhythmic accompaniment. This theme, which is heard periodically throughout the film, is associated with Chris and the other six gunmen who have been hired to ward off the bandits. The second most prominent theme is a dramatic idea for brass and drums which begins with three repeated tones, followed by five more that move in a confined melodic range. This music is associated with Calvera (Eli Wallach), the bandit leader.

The Magnificent Seven, with (left to right) Robert Vaughn, Steve McQueen, Charles Bronson, Yul Brynner, Brad Dexter, Horst Buchholz, and James Coburn.

Though most of the score is up-tempo, especially during the many riding scenes where Bernstein's music purposefully plays at a faster tempo than the leisurely movement on screen, there are also moments of a quieter and calmer nature. One especially effective moment occurs when one of the gunfighters, Vin (Steve McQueen), engages Chris in a philosophical discussion of the latter's motives for helping the villagers. Here the main theme is played more slowly, with an oboe carrying the melody over a background of strings and harp. Elsewhere there are dance pieces for the villagers, as they celebrate moments of respite from Calvera's attacks. Guitar music can be heard prominently in some of the film's quieter moments.

Tony Thomas's evaluation of the film is particularly apt:

> *The Magnificent Seven* should not be made the subject of academic discussions. It's an adventure yarn with some fine action sequences, good color photography by Charles Lang, Jr. of rugged Mexican settings and most conspicuously a music score by Elmer Bernstein that is not so much background as up-front. The music is an integral part of the spirit of the picture and its rhythmic, lilting main theme—later used on television commercials as the Marlboro Country music—remains one of the most popular tunes ever written for the movies, and deservedly so.[6]

Elmer Bernstein wrote scores for three other films in 1960, each different from the others. These include a score for the documentary *Israel*, with strains of Jewish music, which was written and produced by Leon Uris, author of the best-selling novel *Exodus*, and the jazz-flavored music for Robert Mulligan's *Rat Race*, in which Bernstein was able to further his interests in contemporary jazz sounds for which he had shown so much flair in *The Man with the Golden Arm* and *Sweet Smell of Success* (1957). Last, Bernstein composed the romantic background music for the film version of John O'Hara's *From the Terrace*. Curiously, the sweepingly lyrical main theme begins with a melodic pattern that is similar to the beginnings of both Jule Styne's title song from *Three Coins in the Fountain* and the love theme of Bernard Herrmann's score of *North by Northwest*. Despite the similarities, Bernstein's theme soars in a romantic direction that is all its own. Taken together, these scores indicate Elmer Bernstein's enormous talent as a film composer, and also show him to be one of the most versatile musicians in Hollywood.

SCORES FOR HISTORICAL EPICS.

The year 1960 was a big one for lavishly produced wide-screen historical dramas that contain memorable background music. For *The Alamo*, John Wayne's sprawling epic about the ill-fated Texan stand against a Mexican attack, Dimitri Tiomkin produced a beautiful score with a lot of choral backgrounds. The song "The Green Leaves of Summer," which Tiomkin wrote for this film, is heard toward the end of the film in an extended arrangement for a cappella voices. Considering the bombastic nature of much of Tiomkin's music, his understatement in this sometimes meandering but always watchable film is laudable.

Another lavish film is Stanley Kramer's *Spartacus*, in which Alex North's music brilliantly depicts the notable slave revolt against the Roman Empire in 73 B.C. Kubrick later disowned his work on *Spartacus*; but what cannot be denied is the astonishingly detailed action sequences, such as the scene wherein Spartacus (Kirk Douglas) brings together hundreds of fellow ex-slaves in a march to the sea and a final escape from the pursuing Roman army. Alex North's dramatic score, one of his finest, combines moments of classical beauty with elements of contemporary dissonance. The brilliant piling up of brass tones during the marchlike main theme provides a strong hint of the overall quality of this score. Two additional pieces of exceptional beauty are the love theme for Spartacus and Varinia (Jean Simmons) and a lyrical serenade for strings and mandolin, which is heard during a peaceful interlude in the camp, where ex-slaves and their families have congregated. This score is arguably the pinnacle of North's career, though he would continue to write excellent film accompaniemts for almost three more decades.

ANDRÉ PREVIN: *ELMER GANTRY.*

Richard Brooks's dramatically compelling adaptation of *Elmer Gantry*, Sinclair Lewis's provocative novel about Bible-toting evangelists during the 1920s, features a powerful performance by Burt Lancaster in the title role. For *Gantry*, composer André Previn produced one of the most modern of film scores in terms of its dissonant harmony. The dramatically charged main theme, which is based on a seven-note motif, appears throughout the film in a variety of guises. Previn's music mainly serves to sum up Elmer's hyperkinetic personality and his impact on the crowds that flock to the tent to hear him preach. The harmony is especially dissonant during the film's opening credits, where the seven-note idea is accompanied by a series of powerful brass chords.

Among the score's other original themes, especially noteworthy is the blues tune that is associated with Elmer's former girl friend-turned-prostitute, Lulu Bains (Shirley Jones). For the several revival meetings, old gospel songs, such as "Stand Up for Jesus" and "At the River," are sung by Patti Page, who plays Sister Rachel. Finally, when Elmer makes romantic advances toward the evangelist Sister Sharon (Jean Simmons), his motif is slowed down to become less bold and, at the same time, more lyrical.

S HORT CUTS ■■■■ **Ernest Gold.** The Academy Award-winning score of 1960 was Ernest Gold's dramatic music for Otto Preminger's lengthy modern epic *Exodus.* Based on Leon Uris's novel, *Exodus* presents a fictionalized version of the events that led to the formation of the modern state of Israel. Its soaring main theme permeates the score with its heroic melody, which is associated with Ari (Paul Newman), Uris's fictional hero. There is also a lovely theme for the tragic Karen (Jill Haworth) and an occasional reference to "Hatikvah," the Israeli national anthem.

■■■■ *The Apartment.* Billy Wilder's Oscar-winning movie *The Apartment* includes one of the year's most popular musical themes. The score's composer, Adolph Deutsch, cannot be given credit for this theme since it is based on a 1949 piano piece "Jealous Lover," by British composer Charles Williams. According to the film's star, Jack Lemmon, Wilder had a great memory for old songs, even though he couldn't carry a tune. He remembered this music when *The Apartment* was being shot, and suggested that it be used as the romantic background theme. It took United Artists some time to track it down. Both *The Apartment* and the *Exodus* themes became enormously popular in 1960 through a pair of recordings made by the piano duo of Arthur Ferrante and Louis Teicher for United Artists Records.

■■■■ **Bernard Herrmann.** For Alfred Hitchcock's *Psycho*, with Anthony Perkins as Norman Bates, Bernard Herrmann's often imitated "black-and-white" music, written for strings only, begins with a rhythmically charged idea associated with Marion (Janet Leigh), who flees Phoenix with a bundle of money and drives to California, where she winds up at the Bates Motel. In the film's most famous sequence, the shower scene, Herrmann devised a series of screechy violin sounds that suggest repeated stabbings with a butcher knife, as Marion is brutally attacked by a shadowy figure. This same music is also used for the second murder, when the investigator, Mr. Arbogast (Martin Balsam), goes snooping around the old house on the hill behind the motel. High-pitched violin harmonics are heard as Arbogast ascends the stairs. When Mrs. Bates jumps out of her bedroom armed with a butcher knife, the screechy sounds return.

■■■■ **Manos Hadjidakis.** A new sound in film scoring that became immensely popular in the early 1960s emanated from the background score of Jules Dassin's *Never on Sunday.* The film features Dassin's wife, Melina Mercouri, as Ilya, the fun-loving prostitute of Piraeus, who takes Sundays off so she can read the great Greek plays. The Oscar for Best Song went to the vocal version of this catchy tune, which made Manos Hadjidakis (1925–94) a composer to be reckoned with. With this infectious score, the Greek bouzouki became an established film-music instrument; it would be heard from several more times, especially in 1964, with Hadjidakis's music for *Topkapi* and his fellow countryman Mikis Theodorakis's flavorful score for *Zorba the Greek.*

1961

Henry Mancini.

THE HENRY MANCINI–BLAKE EDWARDS COLLABORATION. Of the many long-term collaborations that have existed in the movie business between composers and directors, none has lasted longer nor resulted in more film scores than the thirty-seven-year partnership of composer Henry Mancini and director Blake Edwards.

Born in Cleveland in 1924, Mancini decided at an early age that he wanted to compose movie scores. He describes the very day of his decision in his autobiography, *Did They Mention the Music?* After seeing Cecil B. DeMille's *Crusades* in Pittsburgh at the age of eleven, his already fertile musical imagination was fired.[7] Subsequent studies at Carnegie Tech and Juilliard involved his taking up the flute as a performance instrument, plus courses in composing and arranging. Mancini eventually landed a job at Universal as a member of the music staff. He describes in his book the many tasks assigned to him and to others on the staff. Universal music director Joseph Gershenson would farm out segments of films to a number of different people, all of whom would submit their work without receiving any screen credit, unless they did the whole project themselves.[8]

> The music department consisted of Joe Gershenson; his assistant, Milt Rosen; composers Frank Skinner and Hans Salter, who were given complete pictures to score; and, at my level, composers who were assigned the overflow, several of us working on various parts of the same picture. It also included an excellent orchestrator named David Tamkin, who in working on our scores gave us all lessons in orchestration, and a music librarian named Nick Nuzzi.[9]

Mancini describes the method by which he and fellow staff member Herman Stein were assigned their film-scoring projects:

> Joe Gershenson would call in Herman Stein and me to look at a picture. Herman and I would decide where the music would go and discuss it with Joe—or with the producer, if he came around. . . .I would get my five reels and Herman his five. If the love theme fell in his half of the picture, he'd write it. And if he used it in the first half of the picture, I would use it in the second half, and vice versa. The theme, whichever of us wrote it, would be just a melody line, which we would then arrange and give to David Tamkin for orchestration.[10]

Mancini also writes that, because most of Universal's releases were low-budget pictures, many of the scores were compiled by cribbing the music of earlier Universal pictures. Since the studio owned the rights to its movie scores, the original composer had no say in the matter. Mancini describes the recycling process as follows:

> Assigned to one of the Francis the Mule or Kelly the Dog pictures (Kelly was one of the animals that never made it at Universal), you'd go to the library and tell Nick Nuzzi, "Give me the music from so-and-so and so-and-so"— pictures you thought might have some things you could use. You'd get a big stack of music by eight or ten different composers and proceed to create a score out of it.[11]

One score from Mancini's salad days at Universal that stands out is the jaunty musical background for Orson Welles's *Touch of Evil* (1958). Even though the film was taken away from Welles and reedited, with its music shifted around, Mancini remembers it as being one of his proudest moments in film scoring.[12]

Toward the end of his six-year stint at Universal, Mancini worked on three pictures made by Blake Edwards. Edwards and Mancini got on well together, and when Edwards subsequently went to NBC with his "Peter Gunn" project, Mancini scored the series with swingy, jazz-inflected background music. The series debuted in the fall of 1958 and became an immense hit; the music itself became an even bigger success. Mancini produced two albums of "Peter Gunn" music and won the first of several Grammys. These successes ultimately led to his return to feature-film scoring—as an accomplished composer of first-class film music.

Breakfast at Tiffany's, based on the Truman Capote novella about Holly Golightly, a young, free-spirited woman living in New York, was planned by Paramount as a vehicle for Audrey Hepburn. Blake Edwards, who was hired to direct the film, had Henry Mancini in mind for the score.

The first problem Mancini faced was to convince the producers that he should be allowed to compose a song needed for a scene with Audrey. At the time it was customary to farm out such song-writing jobs to more experienced musicians, but Edwards managed to talk his producers into letting Mancini write it himself. Since Audrey Hepburn was not a trained singer, there was the built-in problem of composing something that she could handle. In his book Mancini tells how he skirted this issue:

> Audrey was not known as a singer. There was a question of whether she could handle it. Then, by chance, I sat watching television one night when the movie *Funny Face* [1957] came on, with Fred Astaire and Audrey. It contains a scene in which Audrey sings "How Long Has This Been Going On?" I thought, You can't buy that kind of thing, that kind of simplicity. I went to the piano and played the song. It had a range of an octave and one, so I knew she could sing that. I now felt strongly that she should be the one to sing the new song in our picture—the song I hadn't written yet. . . . It took me a month to think it through. . . . One night at home, . . . [I] sat down at the piano, and all of a sudden I played the first three notes of a tune. . . . I built the melody in a range of an octave and one. It was simple and completely diatonic: in the key of C, you can play it entirely on the white keys. It came quickly. It had taken me one month and half an hour to write that melody.[13]

Breakfast at Tiffany's,
with Audrey Hepburn.

Thus was born one of the great movie songs of all time, "Moon River." Johnny Mercer's lyrics, with the enchanting line "Waitin' 'round the bend, my huckleberry friend," made the song even more memorable.

The score of *Breakfast at Tiffany's* depends mightily on the melody of "Moon River," which is first heard in an instrumental version during the opening credits, where it is played by a solo harmonica, with guitar, strings, and wordless voices. It is also used in a couple of dramatic scenes to add an emotional quality, especially when Holly tells her upstairs neighbor Paul (George Peppard) how she left home at fourteen. Later it comes in again to underscore the emotional scene where Doc Golightly (Buddy Ebsen), who still thinks he's married to Holly although the marriage was annulled long ago, gets on a bus to go back to Texas.

She tells him that she's not Lula Mae anymore (that's her real name!), and that she has a new life in New York. The most crucial use of "Moon River" occurs in the scene, to which Mancini alludes in his book, where Holly is sitting on her window sill; while accompanying herself on the guitar she sings a serenade for Paul, who listens from an upstairs window.

There is much more to the music, such as the up-tempo jazz numbers and a cha-cha tune for the extended party scene in Holly's apartment, which ends abruptly when her Japanese landlord Mr. Yunioshi (Mickey Rooney, in a hilarious role) calls the police. Then there's the "walking" theme, a catchy tune for wordless voices, strings, and xylophone, which accompanies Holly and Paul as they traipse around Manhattan. First they go to Tiffany's, then to a library, and finally to a dime store, where they shoplift a pair of Halloween masks, put them over their faces, and then slowly walk out of the store without being detected.

One of the score's most noteworthy features is a stinger chord (one that draws the viewer's attention) which punctuates several scenes, with a vibrato effect created by the use of vibraphone plus several other instruments, including piano and harp. The score of *Breakfast at Tiffany's* succeeds in capturing the many moods of New York, with an instrumentation that would lead to other scores in which the conventional orchestration would be replaced by a jazzier, swing-band type of sound.

The two Oscars Mancini won, for the film's score and for "Moon River," guaranteed him a long-lasting career in Hollywood. He continued to write film scores for the next three decades, during which he collected two more Oscars (for the 1962 title song of *Days of Wine and Roses* and for the song score of the 1982 *Victor/Victoria*). Perhaps the most successful fruits of the Mancini–Edwards collaboration began with *The Pink Panther* (1964), which spawned a series of films featuring Peter Sellers as the bumbling Inspector Clouseau. In all, Mancini composed the scores for eight *Pink Panther* films.

MIKLOS ROZSA: SCORING SAMUEL BRONSTON'S EPICS.

Because of the slow but steady decline of the studios during the 1950s, combined with the gradual dissolution of the studio music departments, the selection of composers to score films became the independent producer's responsibility by the beginning of the 1960s. This development would ultimately hurt film scoring because those holding the purse strings were often not musically informed. One master composer who still did get called on was Miklos Rozsa, who scored *King of Kings* and *El Cid*, both produced by Samuel Bronston in 1960–61. The music of *King of Kings* is marked by a direct, emotional approach to the Christ story, with a stirring main theme that ties the various episodes of the picture together. Unlike Rozsa's earlier *Ben-Hur* score with its spectacular brass scoring, this film score primarily features strings.

For *El Cid*, starring Charlton Heston as the legendary Spanish hero, Rozsa traveled to Madrid to do research. He later described this experience:

> There was research to do, because I knew nothing of Spanish music of the Middle Ages. The historical adviser on the film was the greatest authority on the Cid, Dr. Ramon Menendez Pidal, aged ninety-two. It was he who introduced me to the twelfth-century Cantigas of Santa Maria, in one of what must have been at least ten thousand books in his vast and beautiful library. . . . I spent a month in intense study of the music of the period. I also studied the

Spanish folk songs which Pedrell had gone about collecting in the early years of this century. With these two widely differing sources to draw upon, I was ready to compose the music. As always, I attempted to absorb these raw materials and translate them into my own musical language.[14]

The finished product is a masterpiece of symphonic film music that harks back to the Golden Age. The prelude, used for the opening credits, is a showcase for two of the score's principal themes. The first is an upward-arching melody that conveys the heroic character of Rodrigo Diaz de Vivar, known in legend as "El Cid," or *Cid Campeador* (Lord Conqueror). The second is an inspired love theme, which compares with the many lyrical themes Rozsa composed for his earlier epic scores, such as for *Quo Vadis* and *Ben-Hur*. Scattered throughout the film's background music are several majestic fanfares, played by an expanded brass section, and dramatic marches, including the "El Cid March" and "Entry of the Nobles." With this epic score and the dramatic *King of Kings* music, Rozsa rightfully regarded 1961 as "the climax and watershed of my film career."[15]

ELMER **B**ERNSTEIN: **B**OTH IN AND OUT OF THE **S**ADDLE. Continuing in his Western vein, Elmer Bernstein created a rousing background for Michael Curtiz's last film, *The Comancheros*, with John Wayne as a Texas Ranger. While this score's principal melodic idea resembles the previous film's famous "Marlboro Theme" stylistically, it avoids being a carbon copy.

Bernstein's other film-music accomplishments in 1961 include a romantic-styled background for *By Love Possessed*; the rhythmically driven modernistic music for the potent hospital drama *The Young Doctors*, and his best score of the year, the Oscar-nominated music for Peter Glenville's film adaptation of Tennessee Williams's *Summer and Smoke*.

This last film, a colorfully produced period drama set in a small Mississippi town in 1916, concerns the sexual frustration of Alma Winemiller (Geraldine Page), a minister's daughter who cannot openly express her feelings for her neighbor John Buchanan (Laurence Harvey), a restless medical student who feels pressured to follow in his physician father's footsteps. Bernstein's main theme features a melody that defines the character of Alma. Over a restless harmonic background Bernstein designed a widely arching melodic line which features tones that leap upward, only to fall back down in pitch. The prevailingly downward spiral of this melody conveys an unavoidable sense of melancholy—a key to the underlying tragedy of the frustrated love that causes the destruction of Alma's fragile personality. A series of solemn brass chords with accompanying pairs of soft woodwind tones is also featured as punctuation for this theme, the various elements of which add poignancy to Williams's story. The depth of Bernstein's perception of Alma may be heard throughout this emotionally moving score.

SHORT **C**UTS ■■■ **Bernard Herrmann.** The Charles Schneer–Ray Harryhausen film *Mysterious Island* features a turbulent Bernard Herrmann score. Although the resulting music isn't as tuneful as his *Seventh Voyage of Sinbad*, there are stunningly dramatic moments featuring an expanded brass section of eight horns and four tubas, plus lots of percussion. The prelude is a bombastic piece consisting of long, sustained chords played by brass and woodwinds, with punctuating drums and cymbal crashes. The opening scene, in which a small group of fugitives escapes from a

Confederate prison in an observation balloon, features a wildly rhythmic piece, with swirling woodwind figures in triplet rhythm accompanying heavy brass chords and percussion effects.

The most ingenious parts of the score accompany scenes on an uncharted island in which gargantuan species are encountered: for a giant crab, the music features the eight horns plus more pounding chords by brass and percussion; for a giant bee, the orchestra becomes a buzzing machine, with string tremolos, woodwind trills, and flutter-tonguing in the brass; and for a giant bird there is a Baroque-style fugue that begins in the low woodwinds and eventually features several different instrumental colors in a wildly inventive orchestral romp.

■ ■ ■ **Dimitri Tiomkin.** One of the biggest box-office hits of 1961 was the World War II action adventure *The Guns of Navarone*, the first and best of several films based on stories by Alistair McLean. Dimitri Tiomkin, in a respite from Western films, gave this score a very driving beat, as in the main-title music, known as the "Legend of Navarone," in which the trumpets boldly proclaim an emotionally stirring marchlike melody, followed by a second theme of heroic character featuring soaring strings.

■ ■ ■ ■ **Hugo Friedhofer.** The troubled Marlon Brando film *One-Eyed Jacks* emerged as a major disappointment in 1961, despite some fine acting moments; but Hugo Friedhofer produced one of his finest scores on its behalf, with a main theme of noble character played by trumpets over a background of strings. Friedhofer, one of the most underrated of all film composers, would only write six film scores in the entire decade.

■ ■ ■ ■ **Laurence Rosenthal.** One of the younger composers in films, Detroit native Laurence Rosenthal (b. 1926), wrote a fine score for Daniel Petrie's memorable film version of Lorraine Hansberry's stage play *A Raisin in the Sun*. Rosenthal produced a highly sympathetic accompaniment for the plight of a proud black woman, Lena Younger (Claudia McNeil), who wants to use the insurance money left behind by her late husband to move her family from their cramped Chicago apartment. Rosenthal's principal theme features a melody of noble simplicity, which climbs upward by thirds (C–E–G–B flat) before returning down the scale. The upward reaching of the pitches is an indication of Lena's dogged determination to make a better life for her family.

THE NEW WAVE. At the end of the 1950s, a group of young French filmmakers, known as *La Nouvelle Vague* (The New Wave), including François Truffaut, Claude Chabrol, Jean-Luc Godard, Eric Rohmer, and Louis Malle, favored a more personal, free style of filmmaking, as opposed to the older, more formally structured films. By the early 1960s, many of these directors' films were shown on American screens, and although the strong creative spirit of the New Wave soon began to dissipate, the influence of these filmmakers would last for a long time.

One of the effects of the New Wave was the creation of musical scores by several French composers, some of whom had scored documentary short subjects in the early 1950s, but by the end of the decade had made the transition to scoring feature-length films. Among these were four who became internationally famous during the 1960s: Georges Delerue (1925–92),

Michel Legrand (b. 1932), Francis Lai (b. 1932), and Maurice Jarre (b. 1924), each of whom eventually won at least one Oscar for an original film score. To date, Maurice Jarre has collected three Academy Awards.

MAURICE JARRE: LAWRENCE OF ARABIA.

Maurice Jarre was born in Lyons, the son of André Jarre, a technical director for a local French radio station.

Maurice Jarre.

Maurice had no formal introduction to music until age sixteen when he wanted to play in a music ensemble. Because percussion instruments could be learned more quickly than others, he entered the National Conservatory of Music as a percussion student; he also studied composition there with the renowned Arthur Honegger, who had been a member of the group known as *Les Six*. Eventually, Jarre became a timpanist with the Paris Radio and Symphony orchestras. He also got a taste of the theater by playing in the orchestra of the Jean Louis Barrault theater company, and became their arranger and conductor. But composing was his real love.

In 1951, French actor Jean Vilar founded a national theater company, and asked Jarre to compose scores for live theatrical productions. Jarre wrote music for such plays as *Richard II*, *Don Juan*, and *Macbeth*. The next year, he composed his first film score—a short antiwar documentary *Hôtel des Invalides*. The director of this film, Georges Franju, retained Jarre's services throughout the rest of the decade, during which time Jarre composed music for several ballets, and also wrote a number of concert works, including his Concerto for Percussion and Strings (1956).

By 1960, Jarre had moved from composing scores for documentaries to scoring feature films, among which were *La Tête contre les Murs* (1958) and his first English-language movie, *Crack in the Mirror*, starring Orson Welles. Shortly thereafter, Jarre scored the film *Sundays and Cybele*, which won the 1962 Oscar for Best Foreign Language Film. His music for this film so impressed producer Sam Spiegel that he invited Jarre to take part in composing the score for Spiegel's epic saga about T. E. Lawrence.

The Hollywood producer informed Jarre that there were going to be three composers working on the score of this British film, *Lawrence of Arabia*, with newcomer Peter O'Toole as the enigmatic title character. The famed Russian composer Aram Khachaturian, who was born in Armenia, was to write the Arabian music, and Benjamin Britten was to compose the British music. Spiegel wanted Jarre to compose the dramatic music for the balance of the film. Jarre was perplexed by this arrangement; he was later pleased to learn that neither Khachaturian nor Britten was available.[16]

Spiegel had yet another composer up his sleeve—Richard Rodgers, with limited dramatic underscoring experience. When the film had been edited down from the forty hours of rough cut to its final running length of just under four hours, Spiegel gathered together Lean, Jarre, and a pianist, who was called upon to demonstrate some of Rodgers's themes. When Lean expressed his dislike for this music, Jarre was asked to demonstrate his own music. Lean was so pleased with the grandiose main theme for *Lawrence* that he urged Spiegel to give Jarre the entire job. There were only four weeks remaining before the premiere. Jarre remembers the exhausting task of completing the project: "Working like crazy, day and night, I barely survived this experience, having to do everything in such a short time. I was only sleeping two or three hours per night."[17]

Lawrence of Arabia, with
Peter O'Toole and
Omar Sharif.

The most obvious thing about *Lawrence of Arabia's* music is its sheer
size. To construct a score which would have a sense of grandeur comparable to the wide-screen images of the desert vistas, Jarre employed an
enlarged orchestra, plus the electronic *ondes martenot,* the eerie sounds of
which were used to suggest the eternal mystery of the Arabian desert expanse. He also used an old string instrument called the "kithara," which is a
type of lyre, the string tones of which contribute an exotic flavor to the score.

The main theme, which makes repeated use of a descending fourth
(C–G), lends a romantic aura to Lawrence's adventures as a British soldier
sent into the Arabian desert in 1916 in order to organize the Arabs against
the Turkish army. Although Robert Bolt's script never quite solves the riddle
of who Lawrence really was, Jarre's music, with its combined British and
Arabic elements, indicates that he had divided loyalties. The British flavor
is brought out in the "Home" theme, which suggests his British roots. The
Arabic flavor comes across in the "Arab" theme, which suggests middle-
Eastern music through the use of scales with lowered tones. As a nod to
the British flavor, Jarre was persuaded to incorporate a borrowed march
theme, "The Voice of the Guns," written by Kenneth J. Alford.

Spiegel insisted on using famed conductor Adrian Boult to lead the
London Philharmonic in the recording sessions for the film; but Boult conducted only the overture, with Jarre doing the rest. In the film's credits,
Boult is listed as the conductor of the entire score, whereas, on the film's
soundtrack recording, Jarre is listed as the sole conductor.

Even before the release of *Lawrence*, Jarre became involved with an-other wide-screen epic, Darryl Zanuck's meticulously staged recreation of the D-day invasion, *The Longest Day*, the most expensive black-and-white film in history, at $8.5 million.[18] Although the main march theme is based on a song composed for the film by one of its costars, Paul Anka, Jarre was commissioned to compose additional music and to do the orchestral arrange-ments of Anka's tune. The result was an appropriately patriotic score.

Because of the combined box-office successes of *The Longest Day* and *Lawrence of Arabia*, plus *Lawrence*'s seven Oscars (including Best Picture, Best Director, and Best Music Score—Substantially Original), Jarre was virtually assured of receiving additional major scoring projects. In the years following *Lawrence*, he scored films made in France and the United States. (His first trip to America occurred in 1965, when he was hired by William Wyler to score *The Collector*.) Meanwhile, his friendship with David Lean led to his writing one of the most renowned movie scores of all time, the music of *Doctor Zhivago* (1965). This collaboration lasted for only four films (these were the last movies directed by Lean, who died in 1991), but in terms of their sheer size, these films all demanded major scoring efforts. If Jarre were remembered only for the music of David Lean's movies, he would still be considered a major film composer.

TWO BY ELMER BERNSTEIN. One of the finest scores of the 1960s is from Robert Mulligan's film of Harper Lee's autobiographical Pulitzer Prize-winning novel *To Kill a Mockingbird*. Elmer Bernstein's lyrically in-spired, often gentle music reflects the childlike wonder that is at the heart of this story of two small children in Alabama during the Depression and their reactions to the dire events that occur around them. Especially serious is the trial of a black man, falsely accused of raping a white woman. He is de-fended by the children's father, Atticus Finch (Gregory Peck).

Although there are some melodramatic plot turns, including an assault on the children by one of the white townspeople, the score is filled with charming moments. The main-title theme is a lilting waltz tune played by

To Kill a Mockingbird, with Gregory Peck, Mary Badham, John Megna, and Philip Alford

piano and strings, with a solo flute. For the scene in which one of the children, who is playing with an automobile tire, rolls right up to the porch of the house where the feared Boo Radley lives, the music has a Coplandesque flavor, with many syncopated chords and sudden pauses. The music conveys a great sense of compassion for the children in this film, which is narrated by Scout, the younger of the two, as an adult. This is a film full of wondrous things, not the least of which is Bernstein's memorably eloquent music.

Bernstein also composed a noteworthy score for a film set in New Orleans, *Walk on the Wild Side*, the main theme of which, with lyrics by Mack David, received an Oscar nomination as Best Song. It is most memorably heard in a bluesy instrumental version played over the film's clever opening credits, during which several cats are seen slowly prowling about. The jazz score of *Walk on the Wild Side* is a worthy companion to such earlier Bernstein scores as those for *The Man with the Golden Arm* and *Sweet Smell of Success*.

AND TWO BY BERNARD HERRMANN. Herrmann's score for J. Lee Thompson's thriller *Cape Fear* compares with most of his Hitchcock music. In the main-title theme, Herrmann introduces a dramatic four-note melodic idea that recurs throughout the film—an ominous series of brass tones that descend through the octave. These tones suggest the menacing presence of Max Cady (Robert Mitchum). Cady is stalking the family of his defense attorney (Gregory Peck), whose purposely botched defense of the dangerous Cady caused him to be imprisoned. The score overall is taut and compelling, filled with tensely dramatic chords.

Martin Scorsese so revered this score that, when he decided to remake *Cape Fear* in 1991, he hired Elmer Bernstein to rearrange Herrmann's music from the original film. In doing so, Bernstein illustrated how superior Herrmann's work is to most of the newer film music of the 1990s.

Herrmann's other 1962 score is also one of his most romantic. F. Scott Fitzgerald's *Tender Is the Night* was made into a handsomely produced film by veteran director Henry King, who had earlier made *The Snows of Kilimanjaro*, which includes another eloquent score by Herrmann. This time, Herrmann's creativity was impaired somewhat by the use of a title song composed by Sammy Fain and Paul Francis Webster. Although it is tuneful, Herrmann refused to include this song in his background score. Overall, the romantic qualities in Herrmann's music suggest that he excelled in a genre far different from the thrillers with which he is so often associated.

SHORT CUTS ■■■■ André Previn. One of the most dramatic scores of 1962 was André Previn's lushly orchestrated music for MGM's expensively mounted remake of *The Four Horsemen of the Apocalypse*. Despite the many deficiencies of this film, the main-title theme, with a pounding drumbeat accompanying the full orchestra, creates a powerful impact. The other principal musical idea is a rhapsodic love theme, with a solo violin sounding above sustained orchestral chords.

■■■■ Bronislau Kaper. MGM's other mammoth 1962 movie was another remake, *Mutiny on the Bounty*. Like *Four Horsemen*, it required a big orchestral score. The main theme is a magnificent musical tapestry that conjures up the drama of the sea, sailing ships, and the expectancy of setting sail for the South Pacific as Captain Bligh prepares an expedition to find the tropical breadfruit plant and take specimens of it back to England.

Although the film itself is thrown off course by Marlon Brando's bizarre interpretation of Fletcher Christian as an English dandy, Kaper's score remains a work of superbly dramatic eloquence, with a terrifically dynamic accompaniment for the storm sequence, plus a lyrically exotic melody for the scenes on Tahiti. The melody is called "Love Song from *Mutiny on the Bounty* (Follow Me)," with words by Paul Francis Webster. One of the most memorable uses of this theme occurs when a group of Tahitian natives sings it as a native chant in a cappella style.

■ ■ ■ ■ **Jerry Goldsmith.** Jerry Goldsmith, who had been writing film music since 1957, began to show significant signs of artistic growth with the scores for films made by Universal in 1962. He demonstrated a remarkable ability to adapt his style to whatever genre seemed appropriate for the film at hand. For example, in *Lonely Are the Brave*, a compelling drama of a cowboy (Kirk Douglas) at odds with modern technology, Goldsmith's music seems to emulate the Western style of Elmer Bernstein's *Magnificent Seven*, whereas in *Freud*, one of his most dissonant scores to date, he chose to flavor the film with Herrmannesque sustained brass chords accompanied by faster moving strings. This score, for which he received his first Oscar nomination, is uncannily vague in terms of tonality. It seems to mirror the atonal works of Arnold Schoenberg, which emanated from the time when Sigmund Freud was upsetting the medical community in Vienna with his revolutionary theories about the subconscious.

■ ■ ■ ■ **Franz Waxman.** Nearing the end of his career, Franz Waxman contributed fine scores for the 1962 films *Taras Bulba* and *Hemingway's Adventures of a Young Man*. The former is distinguished by a romantic large-scale orchestra score, which flavors this Nikolai Gogol story of a Cossack family. Especially memorable is the scene in which the Cossacks gather a fighting force as they ride en masse to the city of Dubno. The "Ride to Dubno" music begins softly, but soon grows to a wild, full-orchestra tumult.

The *Hemingway* score is smaller scaled, but has some compelling dramatic moments, including the theme for Billy Campbell (Dan Dailey), whose alcoholic character is musically accompanied by a piece called the "D. T. Blues," featuring a bizarrely out-of-tune piano set against the harmony of strings. For the soundtrack recording, the piano part was played by John Williams, who at the time frequently found employment recording film scores by other composers.

■ ■ ■ **Henry Mancini.** Two of the scores that Henry Mancini composed in 1962 continued his collaboration with Blake Edwards. *Experiment in Terror* employs tense, stark background music; *Days of Wine and Roses* is an early example of the monothematic score, that is, a score built on a single melodic idea—that of the song Mancini wrote for the film with lyricist Johnny Mercer. This melancholy ballad went on to win for Mancini and Mercer their second consecutive Best Song Oscars. Throughout this engrossing drama, the melody is heard in a variety of tempos to accompany the story of Joe Clay (Jack Lemmon), who introduces his wife Kirsten (Lee Remick) to drink. Eventually they both become alcoholics. While Joe learns to handle his dependency through Alcoholics Anonymous, Kirsten refuses to accept her addiction. By the end of the film they have separated, with their small daughter in his custody. When he seeks her out in a cheap motel room, trying once more to convince her to seek help, the music contributes an almost heartbreaking poignancy to the scene.

Mancini also produced a memorable score for Howard Hawks's *Hatari!*, in which he accompanied the adventures of big-game hunters in Africa. Most notable is the music entitled "Baby Elephant Walk," which features a boogie-woogie bass accompanying a tune played on an electric calliope.

FOOTNOTE TO **1962.** In 1962, the first film based on the spy novels of Ian Fleming appeared. Although the music of *Dr. No* is credited to an English songwriter named Monty Norman, there is controversy about the authorship of the now-famous James Bond theme. Norman suggests that he wrote the tune and that John Barry (b. 1933) was called in at the last minute to fix it up in a jazzier arrangement. Barry counters that he basically took a guitar riff from one of the tunes he wrote for the 1960 English film *Beat Girls* and utilized it to create the theme that has appeared in almost every James Bond movie. The agreement reached at the time *Dr. No* was being finished stipulated that Norman would get composer credit for the theme and that Barry would be listed as its arranger. Whatever the truth is regarding the actual authorship, John Barry, once he got involved with the first Bond film, became associated with the sound of 007—in a popular series of films starring Sean Connery.

JOHN **A**DDISON: **T**OM **J**ONES. In 1963, the relatively obscure John Addison (b. 1920) became the third English composer to win an Oscar (after Brian Easdale in 1948 and Malcolm Arnold in 1957)—for *Tom Jones.*

The son of a British army colonel, Addison received his formal education at Wellington College, a respected school for sons of the military; this was not a musical education. He decided against a career in the military, and subsequently enrolled at the Royal College of Music in London, where he studied composition. After only one year, his studies were interrupted by the war. As a tank commander he was wounded in a battle at Caen, where his unit was wiped out. He later became a member of XXX Corps and was involved in Operation Market Garden, a tragically flawed campaign in which the Allies got bogged down in the winter of 1944–45. This operation became the subject of *A Bridge Too Far* (1977), which fittingly has a score by John Addison.

After the war he received a degree and settled into a career as a teacher of composition at the Royal College of Music. Although film scoring held little interest for him then, a chance meeting with a war buddy, Roy Boulting, led to his first film score, which was written for the Boulting Brothers' production of *Seven Days to Noon* (1950).

During the 1950s, Addison divided his composition time between writing film scores and composing concert pieces. In 1959, not only was his ballet score for *Carte blanche* performed at the prestigious Edinburgh Festival, but also he composed his score for the film version of *Look Back in Anger*, produced by the newly formed Woodfall film company, which was spearheaded by playwright John Osborne and director Tony Richardson.

John Addison.

Photo by Gay Goodwin Wallin

In the film version of *The Entertainer* (1960), Addison constructed the score by adapting the songs he had written for the stage production. Subsequent Woodfall film productions included *A Taste of Honey* (1961) and *The Loneliness of the Long Distance Runner* (1962), both of which feature Addison's music. These projects served as a prelude for the film that would elevate all these creative people to celebrity status: the 1963 movie based on Henry Fielding's bawdy novel *Tom Jones*.

Although the novels of Henry Fielding (1707–54) have been widely read for more than two centuries, until the Woodfall production, no film adaptation of his work had ever been attempted. Part of the problem may have been the lusty sexual humor in Fielding's stories, which satirize eighteenth-century society and its social conventions. The new openness of the cinema in the early 1960s convinced the makers of *Tom Jones* that they could adapt this story for the screen without emasculating its substance. The finished film proved them to be right: *Tom Jones*, as directed by Tony Richardson from John Osborne's script, and with John Addison's richly textured musical score, became the movie sensation of 1963. All three of these individuals were rewarded on Oscar night in early 1964, when *Tom Jones* collected a total of four Oscars, including Best Picture, Best Direction, Best Screenplay, and Best Music Score.

What ultimately makes *Tom Jones* work as a film is that Addison played along so totally with Richardson's freewheeling directorial style. Richardson allowed Addison to try novel ideas, such as the combination of an out-of-tune piano with a harpsichord for the opening silent sequence. After establishing the main theme, a rapid-paced idea full of repeated notes, Addison introduced the film's love theme, a lilting idea for piano in the style of a waltz. In addition to the score's two primary themes, there is a jaunty idea for saxophone, guitar, and various woodwinds, which appears several times. There is also a comical reference to the hymn "O God Our Help in Ages Past." Overall, Addison's music is an eclectic mixture of styles, but it works wonderfully in this rollicking film.

Tom Jones, with Susannah York, Hugh Griffith, and Albert Finney.

There would be further film adaptations of eighteenth-century novels, including *The Amorous Adventures of Moll Flanders* (1965), based on Daniel Defoe's *Moll Flanders* and directed by Terence Young, the first James Bond director; and *Joseph Andrews* (1977), based on the Fielding novel, which Richardson himself directed. Despite the physical beauty of these productions, and despite John Addison's witty music for them, they do not compare favorably with *Tom Jones*, which remains a cinematic romp.

After winning the Oscar, Addison moved on to many prestigious film productions. For the Hitchcock film *Torn Curtain* (1966), he wrote a replacement score for the Bernard Herrmann music that was thrown out, and he also did the scores for several more films directed by Tony Richardson. In recent years, Addison has settled in the United States, where he has found work scoring television features, as well as theme music for programs such as the CBS series "Murder, She Wrote."

ALFRED NEWMAN: HOW THE WEST WAS WON.

By 1963, few Hollywood producers were inclined to utilize the talents of composers who had been around since the early days of the talkies. Fortunately, when MGM launched its wide-screen production of *How the West Was Won*, the second Cinerama film to feature a continuous scenario rather than a travelogue format, Alfred Newman was chosen to do the scoring. The movie covers several generations of pioneers who braved the elements to move westward across the American frontier. The resultant score is definitely old-school in its design, but still makes a powerfully dramatic contribution to this episodic but entertaining film.

Newman's main theme is a heroic melody, which is first stated by French horns, with support by the full orchestra. This is followed by a variety of themes, both new and borrowed. Debbie Reynolds, one of the film's stars, sings a number of songs, including "Home in the Meadow," with a melody based on the English folk song "Greensleeves." Additionally, there is a lot of choral singing, provided by the Ken Darby Singers. For the initial reserved-seat showings of this film Newman and Darby collaborated on two extended choral pieces, an overture and an entr'acte, in which such old American songs as "Shenandoah," "I'm Bound for the Promised Land," and "Battle Hymn of the Republic" are incorporated. Several references are also made to "When Johnny Comes Marching Home"; it is used in the film's central episodes, which are devoted to the Civil War. This score is a collage of many parts, which fit together nicely to make a stirring musical portrait of the American West.

SHORT CUTS ■■■■ Bernard Herrmann.

Herrmann wrote powerful music for *Jason and the Argonauts*, his fourth and last score for the production team of Charles Schneer and Ray Harryhausen. To accompany this grand mythological fantasy, Herrmann employed a huge brass section, which is heard most splendidly in the majestic main-title theme, with an accompaniment of woodwinds, harp, cymbals, and pounding drums. (Herrmann used no orchestral strings at all in his scoring of this film.) This music is yet another fine example of the composer's fertile imagination let loose on a cinematic fantasy that demanded colorful scoring.

■■■■ **Dimitri Tiomkin.** As a follow-up to his exciting music for *The Guns of Navarone*, Dimitri Tiomkin was hired in place of Miklos Rozsa to score Samuel Bronston's epic, *Fifty-five Days at Peking*, an entertaining if highly fictionalized account of the Boxer Rebellion in China. Amid much spectacular pageantry and battle music, Tiomkin contributed a beautifully melancholy love theme for the American major (Charlton Heston) and the Russian baroness (Ava Gardner), heard both as an instrumental waltz and as the melody of the song "So Little Time," which, along with the score, was nominated for an Oscar.

■■■■ **Miklos Rozsa.** Miklos Rozsa, underemployed as a film composer during the 1960s, produced only his fourth score of the decade in 1963 when he composed the memorable music for MGM's multistar drama *The V.I.P.s*, for which he returned to the expressive style of scoring that he had used so effectively in such earlier films as *Lydia* and *Madame Bovary*. The main-title theme of *The V.I.P.s* is a sweepingly romantic piece played by soaring strings and French horns. For Margaret Rutherford, who won an Oscar in a hilarious supporting role as a dotty duchess, Rozsa wrote in a rare comical vein. This theme, which features a recorder playing a jaunty tune accompanied by harpsichord, is one of his cleverest bits of orchestration. This music also has a decidedly Scottish flavor, with a middle section that sounds like an imitation of bagpipes.

■■■■ **Riz Ortolani and Nino Oliviero.** The year's most unexpected success, both as movie and as theme music, is the Italian documentary *Mondo Cane*, with a musical score by Riz Ortolani (b. 1926) and Nino Oliviero. When the film was released in America with a narration that was dubbed into English, a vocal rendition of one of the background themes, entitled "More," with English lyrics by Norman Newell, was recorded for the English sound track. "More" was nominated for an Academy Award and became the top song of the year, with a stint on the *Billboard* charts of twenty-five weeks, for eight of which the song was number one. This song helped the film reach a wide film-going audience that might otherwise have ignored it.

■■■■ **Elmer Bernstein.** Although the scoring of some of the films Elmer Bernstein worked on is sparse, including Martin Ritt's *Hud* and Robert Mulligan's *Love with the Proper Stranger*, he once again had a rich scoring opportunity with Hall Bartlett's mental hospital drama *The Caretakers*. Beginning with a brassy main-title theme that evokes his earlier jazz-flavored scores, such as for *Sweet Smell of Success*, this score has quite a variety of styles; at times it is reminiscent of *Summer and Smoke*, at other times it has the gentler sound of *To Kill a Mockingbird*. The most noteworthy scoring effect is the use of string harmonics in a bit of the nursery tune "Twinkle, Twinkle, Little Star." Altogether, this is an effective scoring achievement.

Besides *The Caretakers*, Bernstein had another interesting musical opportunity with *The Great Escape*. The main theme is a jaunty march tune, which begins simply and gradually builds up until it reaches a heroic level. In the later stages of the film, in which several American and British POWs dig their way out of a German prison camp, Bernstein capitalized on the opportunity to produce some rhythmically charged chase music.

■■■■ **Jerry Goldsmith.** Of Jerry Goldsmith's six scores for 1962 films, *Lilies of the Field* deserves mention for its clever orchestration, which includes harmonica, banjo, and strings played in the manner of country music. For this touching story of Homer Smith, an itinerant black man (Sidney Poitier) who gets conned into building a chapel for a group of nuns in a desert area of Arizona, Goldsmith borrowed the old spiritual "Amen," which is heard several times in the film. It provides moments of humor, as when the nuns are taught to sing the word "amen" repeatedly while Homer sings a text about Jesus. Although Poitier's singing voice was dubbed by famed black singer and choral director Jester Hairston, he looks very believable in the musical scenes. The "Amen" melody is also used as background scoring; a banjo, a harmonica, and other solo instruments are heard in melodic variations on the tune.

■ ■ ■ **André Previn.** The film version of the hit musical *Irma la Douce* is a bit of a curiosity. Billy Wilder decided to discard the songs from the stage version and instead hired André Previn to compose a background score that would incorporate bits of the musical's song melodies. The result, about 90 percent original music, is some of the most tuneful work of Previn's career. The main-title theme is in the style of a cancan, filled with boisterous rhythmic vivacity, while Irma's theme is a charming waltz for accordion, flute, and strings. The originality of this score might lead one to ponder why Previn's work won an Oscar in the category Scoring of Music—Adaptation or Treatment.

FOOTNOTE TO 1963. The most unusual-sounding background score of the year consisted of electronically produced bird sounds, which were utilized in providing a sonic atmosphere for Alfred Hitchcock's chilling movie *The Birds*. Bernard Herrmann served as a sound consultant on the film, but refrained from writing musical backgrounds. Ordinarily, the avoidance of music in a thriller would be a mistake, but in this film the eeriness of the bird sounds conveys a great deal of tension.

LAURENCE ROSENTHAL: BECKET. Although Laurence Rosenthal's total output in forty years of film work includes fewer than twenty scores, much of this music is outstanding. Such is the case with his score for *Becket*, which towers over most of the other film music of 1964.

Rosenthal, who was born in 1926, scored his first films *Yellowneck* in 1955 and *Naked in the Sun* in 1957, followed by the film version of Lorraine Hansberry's acclaimed play *A Raisin in the Sun*. This highly regarded film led directly to Rosenthal's second major score, for the film version of William Gibson's brilliant stage play about the young Helen Keller (Patty Duke) and her teacher Anne Sullivan (Anne Bancroft), *The Miracle Worker* (1962). To accompany Duke's wondrous performance, Rosenthal created mood music of extraordinary beauty. Although it is used sparsely in the film, his musical contribution is a strong factor in the film's emotional impact.

A golden opportunity for Rosenthal came with the film adaptation of Jean Anouilh's *Becket*, which director Peter Glenville planned as a wide-screen spectacle. Two vivid portrayals are at the center of the film: Richard Burton as Thomas à Becket, and Peter O'Toole as King Henry II of England.

Although Anouilh's play is basically a two-character study of love and conflict, the film version took a much more lavish approach. Screenwriter Edward Anhalt envisioned the film as a grand pageant set against actual English locales. In order to bring the twelfth century to life, the production was shot on location, in some of the very places where Becket and King Henry had spent time. The film remains what the play had been: a drama of two friends who are pulled apart by conflicting loyalties. After Henry appoints Thomas as Chancellor, the two remain close friends; but when Henry decides, almost on a whim, to make Thomas the Archbishop of Canterbury, Thomas resists the idea because he feels that he will be serving God first and Henry second. When Henry appoints him anyway, a breach in their friendship occurs that culminates in Thomas's assassination.

The film begins with the end of the story, after Thomas's death. When Henry comes to Canterbury to do public penance, he first submits to a lashing, and then becomes absorbed in memories.

The music for the opening credits gives a strong indication of the nature of Rosenthal's score—an ingenious combination of medieval and modern elements. The medieval part consists of copious quoting of Gregorian chant melodies. A Latin text is heard right at the outset of the main-title music, with brass chords adding a modern harmonic background. At the end of the credits the cellos sound the closing "Pie Jesu" section of the "Dies irae," from the Gregorian funeral mass. As Henry approaches the cathedral, there is a brass fanfare, followed by male voices singing the beginning verses of the "Dies irae," again with a modernistic counterpoint of sustained violins,

Becket, with Peter O'Toole as King Henry II (left) and, Richard Burton as Thomas à Becket (right).

woodwind tones, and timpani. Throughout the film this juxtaposition of elements is present in the score, much of which was derived from Rosenthal's incidental music for the Broadway version. While many other film scores have featured quotations of the "Dies irae," few have used Gregorian chant so amply or so creatively.

Certain parts of the score are free of Gregorian quotations. Among the more noteworthy of these is the fast-paced piece that occurs early in the flashbacks, when Thomas and Henry as young men are frolicking through a village during a thunderstorm. It is here that Rosenthal first introduces Thomas's principal musical motif: a three-note idea in the horns that returns periodically throughout the film.

For the scene of Thomas's martyrdom, Rosenthal's music includes several musical elements, including a male choir in the singing of a chant, plus tremolo strings that suggest danger. Brass instruments are then heard in a soft instrumental rendition of the beginning of the "Dies irae." As the knights arrive and slay Thomas with their swords, the three-note motif is sounded defiantly by the horns and trumpets.

MALCOLM ARNOLD: *THE CHALK GARDEN.* After winning an Oscar for *The Bridge on the River Kwai*, Malcolm Arnold continued to score films until the end of the 1960s. Of his later works none is more emotionally conceived than his music for Ronald Neame's film version of the Enid Bagnold play *The Chalk Garden.* A picturesque country home outside of London is the setting for this engrossing story of a troubled teenager named Laurel (Hayley Mills), who resents her mother's remarriage and lives with her grandmother, Mrs. St. Maugham (Edith Evans). After the mysterious Miss Madrigal (Deborah Kerr) is hired to be the girl's governess, the mischievous Laurel clandestinely tries to find out the secrets of this woman's past.

Arnold's score features two primary ideas, one for each of the story's two main characters. Madrigal is represented by a romantic-style theme for strings, French horns, and harp that is based on a gently rising melodic pattern; Laurel is accompanied by a six-note motif consisting of pairs of semitones. These two ideas both appear during the opening credits and thereafter are intertwined as the relationship of Madrigal and her young charge develops. The most ingenious use of music occurs in an extended scene in which Laurel sneaks into Madrigal's room and removes an artist's case. As she smuggles the case outdoors to examine its contents, the six-note motif is used repeatedly, in a briskly paced setting for woodwinds and muted trumpets, with a dash of dissonant harmony included. This motif often occurs as musical punctuation, such as in the opening scene. As Miss Madrigal and another applicant for the governess position await an interview with Mrs. St.. Maugham, Laurel suddenly appears, accompanied by a loud statement of the six-note pattern.

SHORT CUTS. The 1964 film year featured two major musical films: the movie version of Lerner and Loewe's Broadway triumph *My Fair Lady* and Walt Disney's film of *Mary Poppins.* André Previn adapted the score for *My Fair Lady*, with Marni Nixon providing the singing voice for Audrey Hepburn. Richard M. Sherman (b. 1928) and his brother Robert B. Sherman (b. 1925) wrote the Oscar-winning score for *Mary Poppins*, which included "Chim Chim Cher-ee" (which also won the Oscar as Best Song), plus the jaunty

"Jolly Holiday" and the riotous "Supercalifragilisticexpialidocious." This is one of the best scores ever written for a Disney film.

■■■■ **Bernard Herrmann.** After a productive ten-year collaboration, the Herrmann-Hitchcock team came to a bittersweet end with the poorly received *Marnie*. Nevertheless, this film offers a lyrically inspired score. The principal melodic idea is a nine-note motif that is centered around a single tone and built above a series of chords which contain an unresolved harmonic quality. This entire musical pattern is extended through repetition at successively lower pitch levels. The end result is both romantic and mysterious, with a musical flow that avoids a clear sense of tonal direction. The only other time that Bernard Herrmann achieved such an expressive level of eloquence in his work for Hitchcock was in *Vertigo*.

■■■■ **André Previn.** The Warner Bros. thriller *Dead Ringer*, featuring Bette Davis in a dual role (and her former costar Paul Heinreid as director), contains an extremely dramatic score by André Previn. The main theme, which foreshadows the film's murder plot, begins with a French horn fanfare, followed by a minor-key theme played by solo harpsichord accompanied by horns and strings. Throughout the film, the tinkly sounds of the harpsichord punctuate this story of two sisters; while Margaret has lived in luxury, her twin sister Edith has slaved to make a living as a bar owner. When reunited by chance after a long separation, Edith enacts a deadly revenge on her sister. Previn's inspired music often raises this film above the level of formulaic melodrama.

■■■■ **Greek Music.** Greek music got another shot in the arm from a pair of films released in 1964. Although Jules Dassin's *Topkapi* did not duplicate the box-office success of his earlier *Never on Sunday*, the tuneful score by Manos Hadjidakis is every bit as good as its predecessor. Michael Cacoyannis's *Zorba the Greek*, with a galvanic performance by Anthony Quinn, got American audiences to snap their fingers in time with the infectious dance music of Mikis Theodorakis (b. 1926).

■■■■ **Dimitri Tiomkin.** Dimitri Tiomkin invaded Miklos Rozsa territory again in 1964 with his music for Samuel Bronston's *Fall of the Roman Empire*. Although both the film and its score seemed overblown when the film was released, time has been kind to both; Tiomkin's music has a grand sweep to it, with several loud brass fanfares, majestic organ chords, and even bits of Italian folk songs played on mandolins.

■■■■ **Elmer Bernstein.** One of the most publicized movies of 1964 was Joseph E. Levine's film version of Harold Robbins's steamy novel *The Carpetbaggers*. Although this expensively mounted film lacks dramatic credibility, the score by Elmer Bernstein succeeds in creating a swingy, bluesy atmosphere for the story, set in Hollywood of the 1930s. Noteworthy is the brassy main theme, which (like so many of Bernstein's other scores) has a sound reminiscent of that of *The Man with the Golden Arm*, with an insistently driven rhythmic background propelling the music forward. A catchy blues tune in the film features both saxophone and muted trumpet.

A better film is George Roy Hill's *World of Henry Orient*, in which two teenage girls become obsessed with Henry Orient (Peter Sellers), a very avant-garde pianist. In the film's most hilarious scene, Orient is seen in action in the midst of playing an absolutely wild piano concerto. The scene, which is a parody of many twentieth-century concert stunts that have included bizarre and totally unexpected sound effects, features music by Elmer Bernstein that is suitably unrestrained.

■■■■ **The Beatles.** In Richard Lester's *Hard Day's Night*, the Beatles burst upon the silver screen to the delight of millions of young fans. Among the memorable tunes performed by the Fab Four in this black-and-white film are "I Should Have Known Better," "If I Fell," "And I Love Her," and "Can't Buy Me Love." In many ways this was a landmark film; not only did it elevate the Beatles to even greater fame, but it paved the way for more films featuring rock stars. Although many such films were made, including some featuring the Beatles themselves, none would ever be quite as refreshing as *A Hard Day's Night*, an almost perfect marriage between rock music and the cinematic medium.

MAURICE JARRE: DOCTOR ZHIVAGO. Three years after scoring *Lawrence of Arabia*, Maurice Jarre received further acclaim for his music for David Lean's next film, the wide-screen MGM version of Boris Pasternak's celebrated novel *Doctor Zhivago*, for which the author was awarded the Nobel Prize for Literature in 1958.

Although the book was officially banned in the Soviet Union, an Italian publisher in Milan received a smuggled copy of the manuscript in 1957 and printed an Italian translation. An English-language version followed shortly thereafter. The novel is centered on a Russian physician and poet, who got caught up in the revolution, became separated from his wife and family, and wound up writing poetry in the company of a woman named Lara, until they too became separated.

The screenplay by Robert Bolt is a brave attempt to render a complex and episodic story in a cinematic form. Bolt decided that, in order to condense the novel, he had to use the flashback technique. Thus, he developed the idea of Yuri Zhivago's brother, a respected Soviet official, trying to find the daughter to whom Lara had given birth shortly after Yuri's death. Bolt remained faithful to the basic plot of the novel.

There was some softening of Lara's character (encouraged by Lean), to make her more sympathetic. Whereas in the novel she seems to be initially enamored of Kamarovsky, who has taken her as his mistress, in the film she is raped by him and then tries to shoot him.

Likewise, the character of Yuri is somewhat more passive in the film than in the novel. This may have to do with Omar Sharif's performance, which plays on the same melancholy level throughout. In any case, Bolt's reconstructed version of the story pays increased attention to the triangular relationship of Yuri (Omar Sharif) and the two women in his life, his wife, Tonya (Geraldine Chaplin) and his lover, Lara (Julie Christie). Given the passivity of the main character, the events that unfold around Zhivago seem like personal misfortune. He is both a witness to history and a victim of the time in which he lives. Ultimately, one does not come away from the film caring about him very much; this weakens the film as a whole.

The film was originally slated to premiere in March 1966, but MGM executive Robert O'Brien, after seeing some footage, decided to move up the film's release date to have it qualify for the 1965 Oscars. Because of the schedule change, Maurice Jarre had only six weeks to complete the musical score. David Lean's biographer, Stephen Silverman, states that what eventually became "Lara's Theme" was originally supposed to be a borrowed tune, but the "old Russian melody" that Lean had in mind turned out not to be an old tune at all; since this tune was still under copyright, Jarre was instructed to create his own theme.[19]

Lean invited Jarre to Spain—where part of the film was shot—to observe the reconstruction of Moscow, and then showed him some of the raw footage. Jarre went back to his hotel room and wrote a theme. When he played it for Lean, he was disappointed in the director's reaction. He described the subsequent events as follows:

> I rushed back to my room and wrote another piece of music. He said it was too sad. After a time, I wrote a third theme. He said it was too fast. I was beginning to get very depressed when David suggested, "Maurice, forget about Zhivago, forget about Russia. You go with your girlfriend to the mountains, because I know you like mountains, and you think about it and write a love theme for her."[20]

Jarre took Lean's advice, spent one weekend in the Santa Monica mountains, and wrote his fourth theme the following Monday. This theme, which turned out to be exactly the kind of music Lean was looking for, consists of a lilting waltz theme that begins with a four-note ascending melodic pattern—the tune that has become known as "Lara's Theme." Whenever the theme appears in the film, it clearly identifies with Lara and with Yuri's thoughts of her.[21]

Jarre has stated that there is no Russian folk music in the score. He did, however, incorporate the melody of the old Russian anthem "God Save the Czar" into the overture and he also used a Russian Orthodox melody, the "Kontakion," for the burial of Yuri's mother. The revolutionary anthem, "The Internationale," is sung by a crowd of people gathered in the street outside the restaurant where Yuri is dining with Tonya. In that same scene Lara is seen dancing with Komarovsky (Rod Steiger) to the tune of two Russian-style waltzes that Jarre wrote specifically for the film.

Doctor Zhivago, with Julie Christie as Lara.

The composer's other original thematic material, besides "Lara's Theme" and the waltzes, includes a jaunty tune used for traveling sequences, such as the scene in which Tonya and Yuri arrive at the cottage at Varykino. It is in a minor key, but yet has a folklike quality that makes it sound optimistic rather than overly somber.

There is other minor-key music in the score, for the scenes of war in which Yuri gets involved as a physician, with Lara as his nurse. The central portion of *Doctor Zhivago*, in which the war scenes are shown, is the least melodious part of the film. The music compounds the visual bleakness by conveying a sense of tragedy. The score reflects the hardships that are imposed on the Russian people by the dual agonies of war and revolution.

There are a few happier moments in the film; most of these include renditions of "Lara's Theme," with a lush orchestration that was performed for the soundtrack by an expanded MGM studio orchestra, to which were added twenty-four balalaika players. The score also calls for a forty-voice choir, plus several nontraditional instruments, including a samisen (a Japanese flat-backed lute), a koto, a six-foot gong, an organ, a novachord, an electric sonovox, a harpsichord, an electric piano, a tack piano, and a zither. Jarre also had a prototype of the Moog synthesizer brought in by truck to add an enhanced bass sound to his score. In all, there were 110 instrumentalists—the largest orchestra ever assembled up to that time in Hollywood for the performance of a film score.[22]

Doctor Zhivago was shown in theaters around the world for more than a year and became the second most successful film in MGM history (after *Gone with the Wind*). Much of the credit for the film's box-office success lies with its music. The MGM Records soundtrack album was released in January 1966, and by the end of 1967 it had sold two million copies. The soundtrack album remained on the charts for a total of 157 weeks.[23] The popularity of *Zhivago* was further enhanced by the song "Somewhere, My Love," a vocal version of "Lara's Theme" with lyrics by Paul Francis Webster. Ray Conniff's recording of the song became one of the biggest hits of 1966.

Despite the popularity of the film, Maurice Jarre had some misgivings about the final result. When the film was trimmed to its final running length of 197 minutes, many of the cues he had written were dropped. (Several bits of his music not in the film as it now exists may be heard on the Rhino CD, which includes virtually everything Jarre wrote for the film.) The finished film also spotlights "Lara's Theme" a bit too frequently, an idea that Jarre disdains; but what cannot be argued is the impact that this theme has had. Except for the music by John Williams for *Jaws* and *Star Wars*, no recent film composition has become as widely known as "Lara's Theme."

MUSIC FOR EPICS. The lavish film version of Irving Stone's novel *The Agony and the Ecstasy*, with Charlton Heston as Michelangelo, has its moments, but the film's story seems overly burdened by the ongoing clash between the artist and Pope Julius (Rex Harrison). One of the film's saving graces is its music, which is the combined work of Alex North and Jerry Goldsmith. North did a fine job of creating a background score for the main body of the film. This background score consists of pseudo-Baroque orchestrations, with brass fanfares accompanied by organ, and with harpsichord often providing a basso continuo effect. Better than the actual film is a short prologue in which the camera escorts the viewer around Vatican City and Florence to observe the art of Michelangelo in breathtaking close-ups. Goldsmith produced a beautifully understated musical accompaniment for this guided tour, with string trills providing a sweet sound for some of the shots. When the statues of David and Moses are shown, the music builds up in intensity to become wonderfully dramatic.

Another fine dramatic score is that by Alfred Newman for George Stevens's flawed film about Jesus, *The Greatest Story Ever Told*. For the most part, Newman's music stays in the background, with a lyrical string melody that is used as a recurrent theme. For the raising of Lazarus, Newman wrote a wondrous choral piece. However, because of an overruling decision by the director, the "Hallelujah Chorus" from Handel's *Messiah* was used instead of most of Newman's original theme. Those who heard Newman's composition in the recording sessions lamented the loss of this music; one can only hope that someday it will be restored. Other musical borrowings (also insisted upon by Stevens) include parts of Verdi's *Requiem*, which are heard during the "Via Dolorosa" sequence in which Jesus (Max von Sydow) carries the cross.

SHORT CUTS ■■■ **Bronislau Kaper.** Bronislau Kaper composed an epic score for Richard Brooks's ambitious filming of Joseph Conrad's *Lord Jim*, with Peter O'Toole in the title role. In the heroic main theme, the horns introduce a rising melodic line that suggests Jim's noble character (an interesting concept, in view of Jim's act of cowardice in the opening scene of the film). This theme builds up in the film's opening credits, with soaring strings and blaring trumpets. Elsewhere in the score, Kaper made use of the metallic sounds of the Javanese gamelan orchestra to provide an exotic effect appropriate for the Southeast Asian locales of the story.

■■■ **Henry Mancini.** Following several years of successes with swingy, up-tempo modern scores for Blake Edwards's comedies, Henry Mancini got the opportunity to do a period piece for Edwards's elaborate film *The Great Race*. The score features a collage of styles, including a Dixieland opening theme, the charming tune "The Sweetheart Tree," and several other songs in which the old silent comedies are gently satirized by the sounds of an out-of-tune piano. Mancini even incorporated a piano-roll version of "The Sweetheart Tree" in his score.

■■■ **Jerry Goldsmith.** On a much smaller scale is Goldsmith's charming score for *A Patch of Blue*, in which a black social worker, Gordon (Sidney Poitier), attempts to help a young blind woman named Selena (Elizabeth Hartman), whose mother (Shelley Winters) treats her shabbily. The most memorable musical moment in the film comes when Selena, who falls in love with her new friend, gets help from him in stringing necklaces. The music cleverly coincides with the stringing of the beads. In addition to a piano, a flute, and a harmonica, Goldsmith used a type of woodblock to create knocking sounds which are synchronized with the beads sliding down the strings.

■■■ **Elmer Bernstein.** Elmer Bernstein scored two Western films in 1965. *The Sons of Katie Elder* has another rousing theme in the manner of *The Magnificent Seven*. In contrast, *The Hallelujah Trail* provided him with the opportunity to create a comic romp of a score. For this lavishly produced Western about a wagonload of booze being transported by the U.S. Army across Indian territory to Denver, Bernstein composed some of his most rhythmically buoyant music. The title theme is actually a choral piece with an exuberant vocal rendition of the word "hallelujah" juxtaposed over Bernstein's rhythmically syncopated Western-style music. One of the main instrumental themes consists of shifting rhythmic patterns, with quick beats in groups of 3s alternating with groups of 2s, using the formula 1–2–3, 1–2–3, 1–2, 1–2, in which there is always an accented 1.

■■■■ **Ernest Gold.** For Stanley Kramer's engrossing film of Katherine Anne Porter's *Ship of Fools*, Gold wrote a Viennese-style score, in which a variety of waltzes and other dances are played on screen by a trio consisting of violin, cello, and piano. The main-title theme is a clever combination of Spanish rhythms (reflecting the ship's embarkation from Mexico), in which Gold incorporated a syncopated rhythmic effect similar to the one Leonard Bernstein used in the song "America" (from *West Side Story*); that is, patterns of 3s alternate with patterns of 2s: 1–2–3, 1–2–3, 1–2, 1–2, 1–2, with accents on each 1. The pattern always adds up to six short beats in each measure, but the accents occur at differing intervals.

■■■■ **André Previn.** For Robert Mulligan's *Inside Daisy Clover*, set in the Hollywood of the 1930s, André Previn wrote an effective background score, including a catchy main theme which is first heard on a steam calliope (the teenage Daisy is discovered at an oceanside carnival and soon brought to a movie studio for a screen test). Previn wrote the song, "You're Gonna Hear from Me," for Daisy's screen test. In the film-within-a-film sequence in which Daisy is seen on screen singing this song (with lyrics by the composer's wife at the time, Dory Previn), the fanciful production is reminiscent of the glorious days of the kaleidoscopically choreographed Busby Berkeley dance numbers.

■■■■ **John Barry.** John Barry struck pay dirt again with his third James Bond score, the raucous music for *Thunderball*. He also scored *The Ipcress File*, the first of the spy thriller series featuring Michael Caine as Harry Palmer, and he wrote jaunty backgrounds for Richard Lester's film *The Knack ... and How to Get It*. His best work of the year, the melancholy score for *King Rat*, contains a mournful main theme consisting of a melody played by an English horn which alternates as solo with the oboe, while an accompanying four-note idea is repeatedly sounded on the cimbalom. All this is combined with arpeggiated chords which are provided by various instruments over a continuously rumbling tone on timpani.

■■■■ **Michel Legrand.** Michel Legrand received three Oscar nominations for his music for *The Umbrellas of Cherbourg*, which had already been nominated as Best Foreign Language Film the previous year. For Jacques Demy's charming love story, in which all the dialogue is sung in the manner of a contemporary opera, Legrand wrote a batch of catchy tunes, including the Oscar-nominated "I Will Wait for You," as well as "Watch What Happens."

J**ERRY** G**OLDSMITH**: A C**OMPOSER FOR** A**LL** S**EASONS.** In the ten-year span ending in 1966, Jerry Goldsmith demonstrated considerable skill as a film composer, working in a wide variety of musical styles that ranged from the folksy sound of *Lilies of the Field* to the modernistic *Freud*. His versatility is shown in the films he scored in the mid-1960s, including the Westerns *Rio Conchos* and *Stagecoach*; the thrillers *Seven Days in May* and *The Satan Bug*; the James Bond–inspired spy dramas *Our Man Flint* and *In Like Flint*; the World War II dramas *In Harm's Way* and *Von Ryan's Express*; and the lighthearted films *Take Her, She's Mine* and *The Trouble with Angels*. From 1963 on, Goldsmith has seldom composed fewer than four film scores per year, and in some years he has written as many as seven.

Photo by Thomas Jaehnig

Jerry Goldsmith.

Composing film scores was not Goldsmith's primary musical interest during his formative years. Born in Los Angeles in 1929, Jerrald Goldsmith studied piano with renowned composers such as Mario Castelnuovo-Tedesco, with the idea of becoming a concert pianist. His interests slowly turned to creating music rather than recreating it. With Castelnuovo-Tedesco, Goldsmith learned composition, theory, and counterpoint. After high school, he enrolled at Los Angeles City College, but soon started attending classes at the University of Southern California conducted by Miklos Rozsa, who for many years taught film-music composition there.

At age twenty-one and newly married, Goldsmith took a job at CBS as a clerk-typist in the music department. He was soon invited by Lud Gluskin, head of the department, to be a part of the studio musical workshop. This led to assignments in composing scores for radio series such as "Romance," "Escape," and "Suspense."

In 1955, Goldsmith moved into TV scoring, and began writing music for the CBS series "Climax," which was the first live dramatic program produced by CBS at its Los Angeles studios.[24] Since these scores were performed live, they required skill at improvisation. Goldsmith's keyboard talents allowed him to fill in as needed. By the time he quit CBS in 1960, he had already scored several episodes of "The Twilight Zone" and had also scored his first feature films. Through Alfred Newman, who became an admirer of many younger composers in Hollywood, Goldsmith received his first major scoring assignment in 1962 for the modern-day Western *Lonely Are the Brave*, which starred Kirk Douglas. This led to his scoring John Huston's *Freud*, which won for Goldsmith his first Oscar nomination. From that time on, he would have little difficulty in finding work in Hollywood.

As the 1960s progressed, Goldsmith received more prestigious films to score, and he became associated with several prominent directors, including John Huston, John Frankenheimer, John Sturges, Robert Wise, and especially Franklin J. Schaffner, whose first film, *The Stripper* (1963), had a Goldsmith score. Eventually, seven of Schaffner's fourteen films would have music by Goldsmith, including the Oscar-winning *Patton* (1970).

Three of the seven films released during 1966 with music by Goldsmith deserve special mention. The heroic music for John Guillermin's *Blue Max* has a soaring main theme in which the melodic line keeps climbing ever higher. This score has a grand sound that resembles the orchestral sonorities of Richard Strauss's tone poems. That is perhaps no accident since, according to Tony Thomas, the film was pretracked with Strauss's *Also Sprach Zarathustra* (an interesting musical usage, considering that Stanley Kubrick would have the same idea just two years later when he was filming *2001: A Space Odyssey*).

Goldsmith's Oscar-nominated score for Robert Wise's film *The Sand Pebbles* is an immensely brooding score, with a theme which is one of the few songlike melodies to emanate from a Goldsmith score, and the only one to become a chart-topping hit (titled "And We Were Lovers," with lyrics by Leslie Bricusse). This melody, which is heard only instrumentally in the film, is associated with the relationship between an American sailor, Jake Holman (Steve McQueen), and a young teacher (Candace Bergen) who works at a mission in China with her father. Jake spends most of his time on board a U.S. gunboat, the *San Pablo* (from whence comes the movie's title, a nickname for the crew members). This theme, which has a wide-arching melody

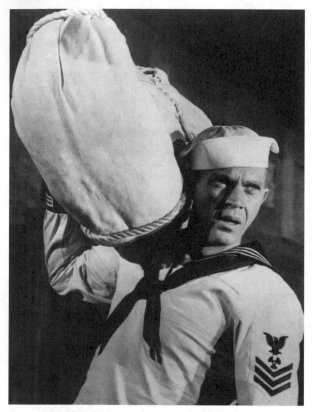

The Sand Pebbles,
with Steve McQueen.

that leaps up an octave at the outset, is used as a motif; its first five notes serve as the film's principal melodic idea. The somber opening music is based on a two-note pattern that recurs periodically. There is also an assortment of Oriental effects, including a plucked string instrument and several percussion instruments, especially ones made of wood which are struck to make a variety of clacking sounds.

Goldsmith's music for John Frankenheimer's *Seconds* is neither as grand as that of *The Blue Max* nor as exotic as that of *The Sand Pebbles*; yet it is among Goldsmith's most unique creations. During the weird opening-credit sequence (designed by Saul Bass), while distorted closeups of a human face are seen, a solo violin is heard, accompanied by low, growling string chords. As the title appears on the screen, a pipe organ is heard in a series of menacingly minor chords. Then a pounding beat, which accompanies a high violin melody, creates a funeral-march effect.

This film, in which a middle-aged man seeks a new beginning through experimental surgery, from which he emerges looking young and handsome (and played by Rock Hudson), is a trip into the macabre. Though not a pleasurable journey to witness, this man's solitary odyssey, marvelously photographed by James Wong Howe, makes for an engrossing film, with an immensely effective contribution by Goldsmith. The film suffers from being too pessimistic, but in light of its subject matter, Goldsmith's sound concept ingeniously creates an eerie effect that is quite unsettling.

The music in each of these films is at the center, even though there are long stretches in all three with no music at all. Goldsmith's approach is an obvious departure from the wall-to-wall ethic of the Golden Age since in the films with his scores there is such a large amount of open space. This tendency to avoid background scoring as musical wallpaper has continued in Goldsmith's work throughout his career, which, as of this writing, has extended through four decades. Jerry Goldsmith has expressed his philosophy regarding film scoring in these terms:

> My main interest in scoring is in examining the characters in a film and making comment on them, and I think you can only do that if you use music sparingly. *Patton*, for example, is a three-hour film, but it has only about thirty minutes of music. The longest score I have done is *The Sand Pebbles*, which has about an hour, or one-third of the running time. . . . The composer must wait for those moments in the picture where there is a scene so special, where there is something to be said that only music can say. Then the presence of music will bring that extra element you need, and, if it's done right, it will elevate the scene.[25]

That, in a nutshell, is the modus operandi of Jerry Goldsmith, a truly dedicated film composer.

BERNARD HERRMANN: *FAHRENHEIT 451.* There should have been two 1966 releases with music by Bernard Herrmann, but trouble behind the scenes of Hitchcock's *Torn Curtain* caused Universal officials to dump Herrmann's dark and brooding score. Hitchcock did not attempt to forestall this, and thereby caused the abrupt termination of one of the most creative collaborations in the history of cinema.

By midyear, Herrmann was already at work on another film, but he was now in England, where he would live for the remainder of his life. It was there that François Truffaut, a Hitchcock fan, engaged him to compose the music for his first English-language film, an adaptation of Ray Bradbury's futuristic novel *Fahrenheit 451.* The resultant score is light-years better than most contemporaneous film scoring, and one of the most creative efforts in Herrmann's career.

Using an orchestra of strings, harp, and metallic percussion, Herrmann accompanied this story of a bookless society with wondrous music, including the fire-truck theme, which consists of a steadily driven chordal idea based on a seven-beat metric pattern. For the scenes in which the firemen ignite piles of forbidden books, Herrmann composed music of a richly romantic quality. This music, which Herrmann entitled "Flowers of Fire," consists of several overlapping layers of violin lines accompanied by a variety of jingling percussion sounds provided by orchestra bells and celesta.

The final sequence, in which Montag (Oscar Werner) joins the outlawed book people in their hideaway in the woods, consists of a slow, sweetly lyrical accompaniment for strings, as various people walk through the snowy landscape reciting the books that they have memorized in an attempt to keep alive the literature that mankind has been denied. The film's closing chord, an inconclusively dissonant combination of juxtaposed tones, is a brilliant final touch.

SHORT CUTS ■■■■ **John Barry.** In 1966, John Barry proved that he could do other things besides James Bond pictures. His music for *Born Free* collected two Oscars, one for the song (with lyrics by Don Black), the other for the background score, which principally features the melody in a variety of tempos, with lots of intriguing African instruments used as atmospheric background.

■■■■ **Elmer Bernstein.** Meanwhile, Elmer Bernstein scored *Return of the Seven*, in which he reprised some of the themes from his 1960 score for *The Magnificent Seven*. His best work for 1966 was his Oscar-nominated music for George Roy Hill's film of the first portion of James Michener's sprawling novel *Hawaii*. The main theme of the *Hawaii* score is a soaring string melody built on a rising five-note motif. With exotic instruments used as flavoring, this score builds up at times to marvelously dramatic levels. It proved that Bernstein, although primarily devoted to smaller-scale films, could score an epic with both skill and artistry.

■■■■ **Francis Lai.** Francis Lai (b. 1932), a French counterpart of Henry Mancini, made a smashing debut on the international film-music scene with his score for Claude Lelouch's romantic drama *A Man and a Woman*. The film became one of the all-time foreign-film box-office hits in the United States. After winning the Academy Award for Best Foreign Language Film, the film's soundtrack became extremely popular, with a title tune that soared to the top of the *Billboard* charts in early 1967. The soundtrack eventually became the first album of a foreign-language film to sell a million copies.[26] Lai's pop-oriented score contains several memorable melodies, especially the title song, which is set in a changing meter that fluctuates periodically between groups of two and four beats. French singers Pierre Barouh and Nicole Croisille collaborated on a vocal-duet version of the tune, and also performed several other songs as background music for this stylishly filmed story of a lonely widow and widower who fall in love.

■■■■ **Alex North.** The most provocative film of 1966 was Mike Nichols's film version of Edward Albee's play *Who's Afraid of Virginia Woolf?* Alex North contributed a small-scale score with a subdued main theme that features a solo guitar and a harp over a background of strings. In striking contrast with the loud verbal abuse being unleashed by the actors, the music maintains an air of controlled melancholia.

■■■■ **Laurence Rosenthal.** One of the most charming scores of the year is Laurence Rosenthal's tuneful music for Peter Glenville's *Hotel Paradiso.* Performed by a chamber ensemble of fifteen players, the score features solo strings, woodwinds, trumpet, trombone, harp, piano, and percussion, in music that provides a humorous commentary. Rosenthal's main theme features a sprightly dancelike tune which is first introduced by clarinet and oboe over a rhythmically bouncy piano accompaniment. The score seems to have been inspired by the charming French music of Francis Poulenc; it succeeds in being a fittingly vivacious and comical background for this handsomely produced Gallic farce.

■■■■ **Franz Waxman.** Franz Waxman's towering music for Mark Robson's *Lost Command* represents a fitting musical valedictory for one of the most distinguished careers in the history of film music. Here is a score that is stylistically right out of the Golden Age but is done with consummate skill. It was Waxman's last contribution to film music (except for one TV movie score) before his death in 1967.

■■■■ **Georges Delerue.** French composer, Georges Delerue (1925–92), already renowned in Europe for his scores of such films as Truffaut's *Jules et Jim* (1961), gained recognition in 1966 for his period-flavored music for Fred Zinnemann's meticulously crafted (and Oscar-winning) version of Robert Bolt's play *A Man for All Seasons.* A number of Renaissance fanfares and dances were incorporated into Delerue's score, which helped his career to become more international in scope.

LALO SCHIFRIN: COOL HAND LUKE. Once Henry Mancini made such a hit with his *Breakfast at Tiffany's* score, composers with a background in jazz and popular music began to create a more contemporary film-music sound. Among these is Lalo Schifrin.

Born in Buenos Aires on June 21, 1932, Lalo Schifrin quickly demonstrated a talent for music. This is not surprising, considering that for thirty years his father was concertmaster and his uncle first cellist of the Buenos Aires Symphony Orchestra. Young Lalo was, in his own words, "steeped in classical music,"[27] but he felt rebellious in his teenage years and gravitated toward an interest in American jazz. He especially liked the music of Thelonious Monk, Charlie Parker, and Dizzy Gillespie. To please his family Schifrin studied classical composition, first with Argentinian

Photo by Gay Goodwin Wallin
Lalo Schifrin.

composer Juan Carlos Paz, and then at the Paris Conservatory, where he took classes with Olivier Messiaen. After graduation in 1952, he returned to Argentina, where he started writing scores for the theater and for television. At this time he began to develop a keen interest in films and their music. He would watch a film many times in order to listen to the score.[28]

Schifrin remained in Argentina until 1957, when he met Dizzy Gillespie, who was on a U.S. State Department tour of South America. After hearing Schifrin play the piano, Gillespie offered him a job. Schifrin came to the United States the following year to work as an arranger with Gillespie's band. In addition, Schifrin soon found jobs doing arrangements for Count Basie, Stan Getz, and Sarah Vaughan, among others. Tired of the traveling that was required of him in this affiliation, Schifrin soon gravitated toward Hollywood. Stanley Wilson, the head of Universal's TV music department, hired him to score episodes of such series as "The Alfred Hitchcock Show" and "The Virginian."

While still doing TV scores, Schifrin got his first chance to compose music for feature films. In 1965, he scored *Joy House* and *Rhino!* plus a TV movie called *See How They Run*. In 1967, he earned his first Academy Award nomination—for *Cool Hand Luke*.

Stuart Rosenberg's *Cool Hand Luke* is a wonderfully acted comedy-drama about a prison chain gang. Paul Newman stars as a troublesome convict whose behavior forces a guard (played by Strother Martin) to utter the famous words: "What we have here is a failure to communicate."

What we have with regard to the musical score is a far cry from the big orchestral sounds that emanated from theaters during the Golden Age.

Cool Hand Luke, with Paul Newman.

Schifrin establishes the nature of his score during the opening credits. The "Luke" theme is first played by two guitars, one of which lays down a rhythmically steady harmony line while the other adds a tuneful melodic pattern. Only toward the end of the credits do the strings join in, along with a few tones played on a solo harmonica. Later in the film, Schifrin makes use of the gospel song "Just a Closer Walk with Thee," played in a bluesy style by a piano and a rhythm section, with a rock beat. He also features the harmonica in a reprise of the "Luke" theme, and includes, at various times, a solo banjo, a flute, and a trumpet.

There are only a few places in the film where the instrumentation involves an orchestral combination. One is a tarring sequence, in which the convicts are resurfacing a road. There is a rustling sound in the violins, plus a rapidly repeated note on banjo, followed by brass chords. As the piece progresses, Schifrin brings in the xylophone, plus the harmonica once more. Another is a chase scene, following one of Luke's many attempts to escape. Here there is fast-sounding banjo music, with a rhythm section supplying a driving beat. Brass comes in, then harmonica and strings; but even in this sequence there is no long, extended use of full-orchestra timbres. Schifrin has almost completely decentralized the score, so that one becomes conscious of individual colors such as banjo or harmonica, rather than a massive orchestral sonority.

Schifrin obviously has the talent to create melody; the "Luke" theme is particularly tuneful, as is also a slow piece called "Arletta's Blues." The highlighting of solo instruments, however, makes this score a unique listening experience.

By the end of the 1960s, Schifrin would be recognized as one of the leading voices in film scoring, with about five scores per year. As of this writing, Schifrin has completed three decades of writing music for theatrical films and TV movies, and has amassed some 150 film credits.

Q**UINCY JONES: SCORING HOT AND COLD.** In addition to Lalo Schifrin, another young film composer with a jazz background who came into the limelight in 1967 is Quincy Jones.

In the Heat of the Night is a contemporary drama about two policemen, a white gum-chewing Southern police chief (Rod Steiger) and a black San Francisco detective (Sidney Poitier), who attempt to solve a murder in a small Mississippi town. The title song, with lyrics by Marilyn and Alan Bergman, and performed by Ray Charles, is a funky blues tune with a wailing electric organ background. Most of the other music also has a rhythm-and-blues style, and it features a number of noted Nashville artists, including a guitarist named Glen Campbell.

For Richard Brooks's grim version of Truman Capote's *In Cold Blood*, Jones's backgrounds are laced with percussion and dissonant orchestral effects, while still incorporating a variety of jazz elements. At the same time, there is an occasional lyrical element, as in the theme for the Clutter family, which is set in the style of a waltz. The most memorable theme is another waltz, written for one of the killers, Perry Smith (Robert Blake). It combines a lyrical melody with an offbeat instrumentation, including both acoustic and electric guitar, plus violins playing eerily high-pitched harmonics, with various bell-like tones in the background. In this score Jones used a real novelty: a set of bottles tuned to the various scale notes, which can be heard in Perry's theme and elsewhere. The most chilling part of the film brought about the score's most dramatic musical effect: prolonged pipe-organ chords, which are heard over a sustained low string tone, produce a disturbingly dissonant result during the flashback to the murder scene.

E**NNIO MORRICONE: THREE SPAGHETTI WESTERNS.** Italian composer Ennio Morricone (b. 1928) made quite an impact with his 1960s scores. He was unknown in the United States until the release of a trilogy of Western films made by Sergio Leone that starred Clint Eastwood as the "Man with No Name."

These three films, which were shot in Spain on a low budget during the mid-1960s, feature many violent deaths but little dialogue. The first, *A Fistful of Dollars*, a remake of Akira Kurosawa's *Yojimbo* (1961), was made while Clint Eastwood's TV series "Rawhide" was on a summer hiatus in 1964. *A Fistful of Dollars* soon became a huge hit in Italy and the rest of Europe, but did not play in America until two similar Westerns, *For a Few Dollars More* (1965) and *The Good, the Bad and the Ugly* (1966) were shot. Apparently all three were held up by legal entanglements.

By the time these films were released in the United States in 1967, Eastwood was already a big name in Europe. In Italy, where he became known as "Il Cigarillo" (after his cigar-chomping character in these movies), he was the top box-office draw.[29]

Much credit for the success of Leone's trilogy goes to the music. Morricone had already composed music for over a dozen films by the time he was hired to do *A Fistful of Dollars*. Though this composer had classical training, one aspect of his music that is immediately obvious in all three Leone films is their use of unusual instrumental sonorities. The main-title music of *Fistful*, for instance, is performed by solo guitar, with a melody that is whistled (by Alessandro Alessandroni). There had actually been earlier Western themes with a whistled melody [one notable example is Lionel Newman's theme from *The Proud Ones* (1956)], but Morricone's simplicity seemed so fresh that many later film scores would emulate this one.

Although the Western genre had been a staple of the American cinema since the early silent days, it was in the 1960s that European filmmakers began to show a reverence for the Old American West, but with a fresh perspective that extended to many aspects of the films, including their music. In the words of film historian Didier Deutsch, who, in turn, quotes Leone:

> Morricone did not blindly follow the traditional patterns set up by Hollywood. Instead, he developed a musical style which complemented Leone's own vision of the Old West as a rugged place in which gore and violence were the order of the day, and in which the good, the bad and the ugly sometimes were indistinguishable. . . . "Without pretending to copy what had been done before, Ennio applied himself to exploring new territories in scoring Western films. Instead of slavishly trying to reproduce the usual monotonous music heard in such films, he had the audacity to invent new ideas and use new sounds, like the cries of birds and animals, a modulated howling in *The Good, the Bad and the Ugly*, the musical watch in *For a Few Dollars More*, or the harmonica in *Once Upon a Time in the West* [1969]."[30]

The music for these films gradually emerged on a series of recordings, beginning with the original soundtrack of *A Fistful of Dollars*, which was released by RCA in 1967, followed shortly thereafter by the release of the soundtrack of *The Good, the Bad and the Ugly* on United Artists Records. Morricone's music gained further recognition through a studio recording, arranged and conducted by Hugo Montenegro, that consists of several tracks from each of the three films. Released in early 1968, this RCA album quickly became a bestseller.

With its vocal yells and grunts, *The Good, the Bad and the Ugly* theme seemed to redefine the sound of film music. Its raucous, brash, and rhythmically driven sound departed drastically from the folksy style of Dimitri Tiomkin's Western ballads and the exuberant full-orchestra sonorities of Elmer Bernstein. Morricone suddenly became the established master of Western film music and, although he would later branch out into other genres, his Western themes would remain his chief claim to fame.

NEW **DIRECTIONS IN FILM MUSIC.** Arthur Penn's stylish and trend-setting *Bonnie and Clyde* uses music sparingly, although there is a screen credit for an original score by Charles Strouse (b. 1929), who later became renowned for the Broadway musical *Annie*. The film's most noticeable music is the bluegrass hit "Foggy Mountain Breakdown," which is heard primarily in scenes of the bank-robbing gang being chased by the cops following their holdups. The original 1950 recording by the tune's composers, Lester Flatt and Earl Scruggs, was used.

Even more musical borrowings show up in Mike Nichols's hugely successful film *The Graduate*, which features Dustin Hoffman as Benjamin

Braddock, a recent college graduate, who has an affair with Mrs. Robinson (Anne Bancroft) and then falls in love with her daughter, Elaine (Katharine Ross). There are some catchy instrumental backgrounds by Dave Grusin (b. 1934), who was then in his first year as a film composer. More importantly, this film includes a number of previously composed songs by Paul Simon, whose recordings with his singing partner Art Garfunkel were incorporated into the film as a running, if somewhat detached, commentary. One new song by Simon that does comment topically on the film's plot is "Mrs. Robinson," which became a top-selling hit through a studio recording made after the film was completed.

After the success of *The Graduate*, which became one of the top boxoffice hits of the decade, film music would never be the same. The idea of using an entire score of songs as commentary was seen as a logical extension of both Dimitri Tiomkin's influence, which dates back to 1952's *High Noon*, and the impact of Bill Haley and the Comets' recording of "Rock around the Clock," which had been used as a teen anthem in *The Blackboard Jungle* in 1955. In films made after 1967, original scores were increasingly jeopardized by the producers' willingness to pay for the rights to include popular recordings of previously existing songs. As *The Graduate* demonstrated so effectively, this device is not necessarily bad, if used with discretion. However, many films in the years directly following *The Graduate*'s runaway success would prove to be musically inept, due to the priorities of film producers who looked for box-office gold rather than dramatic suitability.

Short Cuts ▪▪▪▪ Henry Mancini.

In 1967, Henry Mancini produced three excellent film scores, including *Gunn*, a theatrical version of the TV series "Peter Gunn," and two films starring Audrey Hepburn, *Two for the Road* and *Wait Until Dark*. The lilting title tune of the first of these two Hepburn films ranks as one of Mancini's best movie songs.

▪▪▪▪ **Fred Karlin.** One of the catchiest scores of 1967 is the tuneful music of Robert Mulligan's film version of Bel Kaufman's *Up the Down Staircase*, which marks the film-scoring debut of Fred Karlin (b. 1936). A native of Chicago, Karlin created some interesting new sonorities for this score by combining a number of soprano recorders (which are forerunners of the modern flute) with a rock-band instrumentation featuring electric organ and guitar, plus a rhythm section. The charm of Karlin's music provides a lighthearted counterpoint to some of the film's more melodramatic moments, most of which are set in a New York City high school where Miss Barrett (Sandy Dennis) struggles through her first year as an English teacher.

▪▪▪▪ **Frank De Vol.** Frank De Vol (or simply De Vol, as the film credits bill him) produced one of his most effective scores for MGM's violent World War II drama *The Dirty Dozen*. Amid lots of military-style drums, there is a main theme based on a four-note melodic motif, usually sounded by trumpets. For the scene in which the military misfits recruited by Major Reisman (Lee Marvin) erect their barracks, De Vol used a clever set of variations on "You're in the Army Now." During the film's climactic mission the music gets more tensely dramatic, with exciting full-orchestra sonorities.

De Vol is also responsible for the tuneful music of Stanley Kramer's well-acted but dramatically contrived *Guess Who's Coming to Dinner*. Most of the score consists of variations on the 1936 song "The Glory of Love," by Billy Hill, which was resurrected for this film.

■■■ **Richard Rodney Bennett.** Two of the 1967's most memorable scores were written by the English symphonic composer Richard Rodney Bennett (b. 1936), who had started scoring films a decade earlier but only began to gain recognition in the 1960s. John Schlesinger's beautifully photographed version of Thomas Hardy's *Far from the Madding Crowd* includes a score of remarkable subtlety, with a melancholy main idea consisting of a motif that rises boldly and then drops back down in pitch. Bennett used a variety of woodwinds for this motif, including English horn and oboe, plus solo violin. Though the film has lavish production values, this score concentrates on the characters of Bathsheba (Julie Christie) and the three men in her life by using the orchestra very sparingly. In view of the film's nineteenth-century setting, the score includes some surprisingly modern harmony.

For the third Harry Palmer movie, *Billion Dollar Brain*, which again starred Michael Caine, Bennett displayed an uncanny knack for creating an atmospheric score much different from the usual spy-movie backgrounds then in vogue. Adding to the novelty of his sometimes pulsing themes is the use of the *ondes martenot*. Although this electronic keyboard instrument would be featured almost regularly in later film scoring, especially in works by Elmer Bernstein and Maurice Jarre, its presence in this 1967 film score provides a tonal sonority that is unique for its time.

■■■ **Alfred Newman.** Alfred Newman collected his ninth Oscar (on his forty-fourth nomination!) for his dazzling arrangements of the Lerner and Loewe songs in Joshua Logan's *Camelot*. Despite the shortcomings in the vocal abilities of the film's stars, Richard Harris and especially Vanessa Redgrave, the brilliant background score, a good deal of which is based on Newman's original musical ideas, keeps this film from being a total failure.

■■■ **John Williams.** Another Oscar nominee was John Williams, who did lushly orchestrated arrangements of André Previn's songs for the popular but critically panned *Valley of the Dolls*. This was Williams's first appearance among the music nominees. Although he didn't win this time, he would eventually rival Alfred Newman in the total number of nominations and Oscars earned for both original scores and musical arrangements.

1968

J OHN BARRY: *THE LION IN WINTER.* Almost from the time John Barry first began scoring films, his name has been synonymous with the brash and brassy sounds of James Bond films. Yet his creative achievements in film music encompass much more, as a list of his Oscar-winning scores indicates. Thus far, he has won five Oscars—for the scores of *Born Free* (1966), *The Lion in Winter* (1968), *Out of Africa* (1985), and *Dances with Wolves* (1990), as well as the Best Song award for the title song of *Born Free*.

John Barry was born in York, England on November 3, 1933, the youngest of three children. His father ran a chain of eight movie theaters and his mother played the piano. At nine, he started piano lessons, at twelve, he began the study of harmony, counterpoint, and composition, and at age sixteen, he began playing trumpet.[31] He was also a projectionist at his father's cinema chain. He become serious about music composition while studying with Dr. Francis Jackson at York Minster. Military service soon followed, during which time he exhibited his trumpet-playing skills as a member of an army band.

Photo by Gay Goodwin Wallin

John Barry.

Following his discharge, he formed a rock-jazz group, called the John Barry Seven, in which he played lead trumpet. He also began composing pop tunes. His "What Do You Want?" was sung by Adam Faith and became a number-one hit, selling 50 thousand copies a day for a period. This led to a contract as musical director at EMI Records and also to his first film-scoring opportunity, for a teen exploitation film called *Beat Girl*, filmed in 1959 as a starring vehicle for Adam Faith.[32] He was first hired to write the songs Faith would sing in the film, but soon he was approached to do the background score as well. Despite the film's generally poor script, the musical results were so successful that EMI released the film's music on a soundtrack recording.

After a few more films, including some jazz backgrounds (which were mixed in with works by Johannes Brahms) for Bryan Forbes's *L-Shaped Room* (1963), his work on the "James Bond Theme" (the authorship of which remains disputed between Barry and Monty Norman) led to Barry's first major score, the second Bond film, *From Russia with Love* (1963).

When *Goldfinger* (1964), the third Bond film, elevated Barry's name to celebrity status, he began to get film-scoring opportunities outside the spy genre. In 1964, he also scored *Man in the Middle*, *Zulu*, and Forbes's *Seance on a Wet Afternoon*, for which he got to do an entirely symphonic score. In 1965, Barry wrote one of his best scores, the melancholy and brooding music for Forbes's *King Rat*; 1966 was the year of his Oscar-winning *Born Free*.

The first full flowering of John Barry's talent as a film composer came in 1968 with the inspired musical backgrounds for Anthony Harvey's film version of James Goldman's play *The Lion in Winter*. Goldman's screenplay retains the essential structure of his play, which is a series of family squabbles involving King Henry II of England and his family, who have gathered to spend the Christmas holiday of 1183 together. The problem of selecting Henry's successor is supposed to be addressed. Henry (Peter O'Toole) and his queen, Eleanor of Aquitaine (Katherine Hepburn), have different ideas on this delicate matter. The joke in both the play and the film adaptation is that absolutely nothing is resolved. After several verbal battles (and a few physical ones), Henry bids farewell at the end of the holiday season to Eleanor, who returns to her confinement at Chinon; all remains as before.

Barry's score begins with a gloriously dramatic background consisting of a rhythmically driven main theme for trumpets and strings, with a choral melody added after a few moments. The Latin text, the meaning of which is unfortunately not explained in the film (although a translation is listed on the soundtrack recording), hints of the dark cloud hanging over this family and the enmity that is felt, although in much of the film the hatred is so disguised by the royal family members that the viewer almost believes them when they speak lovingly to one another.

The most memorable musical moment in the film arrives early on, as Katharine is being brought by boat from Chinon, where she has been confined by Henry for the last ten years. Here Barry's music has an ethereal beauty that casts a spell over the scene, with a romantic-style theme played by strings, over which is juxtaposed another choral line, this time featuring angelic-sounding women's voices.

Following this preliminary music, the score takes a back seat to the dialogue. Barry's music returns in the latter part of the film, at the end of which there is a marvelous repetition of the score's dramatic opening music.

The Lion in Winter, with Katharine Hepburn as Eleanor of Aquitaine and Peter O'Toole as Henry II.

What is ultimately fascinating about Barry's score is his uncanny way of combining, in the main-title theme, a modernistic, steadily driven beat with a melodic pattern inspired by the sounds of medieval chant. Few scores have so successfully bridged the gap between ancient and modern techniques, while being constructed so skillfully and with such an inspired sense of melody. Barry richly deserved the Oscar he received for this score.

NINO ROTA: ROMEO AND JULIET. There were few dissenters regarding the merits of Franco Zeffirelli's breathtakingly beautiful production of Shakespeare's *Romeo and Juliet*. Zeffirelli's choice of two inexperienced teenagers for the title roles, Leonard Whiting and Olivia Hussey, caused some negative comment, but they looked so right for their parts that this filming of Shakespeare's play transcended other productions featuring more mature actors.

One of the most popular movie themes of the decade was the melancholy love theme for this film, by Italian composer Nino Rota (1911–79). After having scored several Italian films made by internationally renowned Federico Fellini, Rota began to get offers from other filmmakers, including Zeffirelli, who first hired Rota to write a boisterous score for his 1967 version of *The Taming of the Shrew*. Rota's music for *Romeo and Juliet* is subdued in style, with a smaller instrumentation than its predecessor. Romeo's theme is a slow-paced minor-key idea, first played by a solo English horn with strings. The love theme is first heard in the party scene at the Capulet home, where Romeo has gone incognito. When he first sees Juliet dancing with her family, the theme is sounded by a solo oboe over a background of tremolo strings. When Juliet looks at Romeo, several woodwinds take up bits of the melody; finally, the strings play it for a moment. The theme is also performed vocally as the melody of the song "What Is a Youth," as a young man sings it for the assembled party guests.

This theme later became enormously popular as the melody of the song "A Time for Us," with a new set of words written by Larry Kusik and Eddie

Snyder. Several recordings of the song were eventually released, along with three different soundtrack albums produced by Capitol Records. The first, which includes excerpts of both dialogue and music, became one of the top-selling albums of 1969. Its popularity led Capitol to take the unprecedented step of releasing a four-record set of the film's entire vocal and music tracks. In 1970, due to popular demand, a single-disc album of Rota's score was released.[33] Zeffirelli's *Romeo and Juliet* is unique in that no other Shakespearean film has ever spawned such a record-buying frenzy.

MARVIN HAMLISCH: *THE SWIMMER*. The most promising newcomer to the ranks of film composers in 1968 was Marvin Hamlisch (b. 1944), who was chosen by producer Sam Spiegel to score the film version of John Cheever's short story *The Swimmer*. This score is quite an accomplishment for such a young musician (although veteran arrangers Leo Shuken and Jack Hayes deserve credit for their expert orchestrations).

Hamlisch's evocative themes include a lyrical and melancholy main-title melody. This melody launches a story in which Ned Merrill (Burt Lancaster), clad only in bathing trunks, declares that he is going to swim home to his wife Lucinda via all of the swimming pools in the neighborhood (it is Westchester County, so there are lots of pools). When he at last reaches home, the place is empty, with broken window panes and no furnishings.

There are two other important melodic motifs in the score, which builds up in intensity through the last scene where Ned, broken both physically and emotionally, slumps onto the deserted doorstep while the wind and cold rain blow around him. All three of the score's primary melodic ideas are combined into one emotionally devastating final piece of music that reflects the hopelessness of Ned's situation.

SHORT CUTS ■■■■ Lalo Schifrin. Among the successful film music accomplishments of 1968 were two scores by Lalo Schifrin. *Bullitt* has a funky, jazz-inflected sound with an up-tempo main theme and several other numbers with a bluesy style plus a rock beat. *The Fox*, for which Schifrin received an Oscar nomination, is much more tuneful and has a very subdued instrumentation. The lovely main theme, which is also heard in a song entitled "That Night," is introduced by a solo flute with harp. Its melody line is based on a rising motif of six notes.

■■■■ Christopher Komeda. One of the most talked-about films of 1968 was Roman Polanski's version of Ira Levin's tale of modern witchery in Manhattan, *Rosemary's Baby*. Polish composer Christopher Komeda (1937–69), who had composed the music for several of Polanski's earlier films, did an effective score, including a main theme in the style of a lullaby, with Mia Farrow singing the "la–la–la's" that are heard on the soundtrack. The death the next year in a car crash of this talented musician deprived film music of a promising young artist.

■■■■ Maurice Jarre. The main theme for *Isadora*, a long but engrossing film, starring Vanessa Redgrave in a dazzling performance as the great dancer Isadora Duncan, is set in the style of a waltz. Its minor-key harmony qualifies it as one of the many film themes of the year (along with the main themes of *The Lion in Winter*, *Romeo and Juliet*, *The Odd Couple*, *The Fox*, and *Rosemary's Baby*) to make extensive use of minor chords. This trend would be short-lived, but its presence in the film music of 1968 is an unmistakable part of the year's most acclaimed scores.

■ ■ ■ ■ **Michel Legrand.** Still another minor-key tune is Michel Legrand's haunting main theme from *The Thomas Crown Affair*. Its vocal version, "The Windmills of Your Mind," became one of 1968's most memorable melodies, and also won for Legrand his first Oscar as a composer of movie songs. The lyricists for this tune, Alan and Marilyn Bergman, have contributed to a long string of award-winning movie songs. This would be only the first of many Oscar wins in their collaborative career, which has lasted, as of this writing, more than a quarter of a century.

■ ■ ■ ■ **Alex North.** Among the year's critical disappointments was the film version of Morris L. West's intriguing novel *The Shoes of the Fisherman*. Despite the film's deficiencies, Alex North's brilliant score remains one of his most accomplished works, with majestic brass fanfares for scenes set in the Vatican, where a new pope is being elected. Russian folk melodies were also incorporated in the music.

■ ■ ■ ■ **Jerry Goldsmith.** The most unusual film score of 1968 is Jerry Goldsmith's dissonant and percussive accompaniment for Franklin J. Schaffner's *Planet of the Apes*. There is scarcely a melodious moment in this score, but it nevertheless has a propulsively dramatic style. For this first of the *Apes* films Goldsmith richly deserved his Oscar nomination because of this score's uncompromising departure from film-music tradition.

■ ■ ■ ■ **The Elder Statesmen.** Dimitri Tiomkin wrote his final original film score in 1968, for the physically pretty but dramatically lame adaptation of George Bernard Shaw's *Great Catherine*. Even Peter O'Toole couldn't rescue this attempt at political satire.

With Max Steiner's retirement in 1965 and Franz Waxman's death in 1967, few of the film-scoring pioneers were still active by 1968. Alfred Newman had no scores in progress that year, and Bernard Herrmann's only film music came from France, by way of Truffaut's bizarre suspense thriller *The Bride Wore Black*.

About the only notable achievement in Hollywood by one of the masters was the emotionally stirring music by Miklos Rozsa for *The Power*, an entertaining sci-fi film made by MGM. Its tensely dramatic main theme starts out with a six-note idea, the first four tones of which bear a striking similarity to his theme from *The Killers* (and also the *Dragnet* motif). Adding to the colorfulness of this score is Rozsa's use of a Hungarian folk instrument, the cimbalom; the instrument can be glimpsed briefly during the opening credits, as a pair of arms are seen using mallets to produce rapidly repeated twangy tones based on the score's main motif.

F**OOTNOTE TO 1968.** A final comment concerns the ill-fated score by Alex North for *2001: A Space Odyssey*. After composing music for the first hour of the film, North was prepared to record his cues, but director Stanley Kubrick stopped him. Although North subsequently used some of his *Odyssey* themes in concert pieces, only in the early 1990s did Jerry Goldsmith, with the cooperation of North's widow, make the first-ever recording of this score. In many ways North's music resembles some of the classical pieces that wound up as replacements in the film.

Apparently Kubrick had grown so fond of the musical pieces he used as a temporary track while editing that he decided to keep them. Thus, when the film premiered, audiences thrilled to the sounds of the opening chords of Richard Strauss's tone poem *Also Sprach Zarathustra* and the lilting strains of Johann Strauss, Jr.'s *The Blue Danube*. These and several other previously composed pieces became *2001*'s "score." Perhaps without realizing it at the time, Kubrick was setting a dangerous precedent for future filmmakers, who would often hire composers to write original scores, then reject them in favor of preexisting music.

1969

JOHN WILLIAMS: *THE REIVERS*. When Mark Rydell's film version of William Faulkner's *Reivers* was released at the end of 1969, little did anyone connected with the film realize how significant its music was. Even though the score was nominated for an Oscar, its composer, John Williams, was not well-known.

Born on Long Island on February 8, 1932, John Williams is the son of a jazz drummer who played with the Raymond Scott Quintet and later became a Hollywood studio musician. John began studying piano at the age of eight, and decided early on that he wanted to become a concert pianist. When his family moved to the West Coast in 1948, John enrolled at Hollywood High School. There he met fellow student Barbara Ruick, who later became his first wife (and who was a movie starlet in the 1950s). He formed a band while still in high school, with Barbara as the vocalist.

Following high school, Williams enrolled at the University of California at Los Angeles to study music, but his education was interrupted by a three-year stint in the air force. After his discharge in 1954, he spent a year at Juilliard, where he studied piano with the renowned Rosina Lhevinne.

Returning to Los Angeles, Williams pursued composition studies with Mario Castelnuovo-Tedesco, the noted Italian composer who also taught Jerry Goldsmith, Henry Mancini, and Jerry Fielding, among others. He obtained work as a studio musician; his piano playing can be heard on the soundtracks of many 1950s films, especially those produced by Columbia, where he began working in 1956 under Columbia's music director, Morris Stoloff.

Then known as Johnny Williams, he moved to 20th Century-Fox, where he worked under Alfred Newman during the latter's last days as director of the Fox music department. He subsequently worked for Lionel Newman, who assumed the duties of director after his brother Alfred resigned. Williams played piano parts for film-music recording sessions, including the out-of-tune piano part for Franz Waxman's *Hemingway's Adventures of a Young Man* (1962).

By this time, Williams had already gained considerable experience as both composer and arranger. Between 1955 and 1965, he took a number of jobs, among which were arranging and conducting music for several popular singers, including Vic Damone, Patti Page, and Howard Keel. According to Tony Thomas, Williams got his first TV scoring opportunity in 1958. For the next few years, his name appeared on credits for episodes of "Wagon Train" and "M Squad," plus such sitcoms as "Gilligan's Island" and "Bachelor Father."[34] The turning point in his TV career seems to have been the original score for the CBS series "Checkmate," which ran from 1960 to 1962. A soundtrack album, issued by Columbia Records, contains twelve examples of his music for this series.

John Williams.

Photo by Thomas Jaehnig

By the time, he was writing music for "Checkmate," Johnny Williams had already scored three motion pictures, *Daddy-O*, *I Passed for White*, and *Because They're Young*. In 1965, Williams created his last music for television, the second of the two title themes that were used for the "Lost in Space" series. This delightfully up-tempo music is the first truly memorable theme that Williams penned.

It was in 1966 that Williams's film-scoring career began to take flight, with the scores of *The Rare Breed*, William Wyler's *How to Steal a Million*, *Penelope*, *Not with My Wife You Don't*, and the Universal remake of *The Plainsman*. The film-scoring opportunities were now coming on such a regular basis that he left TV series work behind. The next year, he earned his first Oscar nomination for the arrangements of André Previn's songs for *Valley of the Dolls*. The following year, he won his first Emmy award for the score of the NBC movie version of *Heidi*.

Although the soundtrack recording of *Valley of the Dolls* lists him as Johnny Williams, the Emmy citation was announced as John T. Williams (the "T" stands for "Towner," his middle name). By 1969, he had dropped the middle initial. His three film scores for that year consisted of the tense music for Mark Robson's *Daddy's Gone a-Hunting*, the charming arrangements of Leslie Bricusse's songs for *Goodbye, Mr. Chips*, and the richly orchestrated Americana score for Mark Rydell's delightful film version of William Faulkner's last novel, *The Reivers*.

From the opening moments of *The Reivers*, Williams's evocative music enhances Faulkner's nostalgic story of the four-day adventures of the three reivers (or thieves, as the narration of Burgess Meredith helpfully explains), in the summer of 1905. The film begins in the town of Jefferson, Mississippi, on the day when a train arrives bearing a brand new Winton Flyer; this car has been purchased by Boss McCaslin (Will Geer), the grandfather of young Lucius (Mitch Vogel). Two of Boss's employees, Boon Hogganbeck (Steve

The Reivers, with Steve McQueen.

McQueen) and Ned (Rupert Crosse), take advantage of the absence of Lucius's parents and Boss, who have left Jefferson for a few days to attend a family funeral. Soon after they leave, Boon decides to take Lucius on a joy-ride in the new car. Along the way to Memphis they discover that Ned has hidden out in the rumble seat.

The main-title music consists of a pair of themes; although they contrast in style, they are both in $\frac{3}{4}$ time. The first consists of a fast-paced melody sounded by strings, while the other, a more lilting tune, is first played by a solo harmonica. Both melodic ideas are then presented in a more fully orchestrated style, with extra sounds thrown in for flavoring, including guitar and orchestra bells.

There are two other principal themes, the first of which for the Winton Flyer—represented by a soaring waltz tune. It is first heard when the townspeople gather at the train station to get their first look at the car. When Boss pulls the cover off the automobile, Williams's theme sounds, with tremolo strings followed by full orchestra. The remaining melodic idea is a boisterous theme that is first heard as Ned swipes the car from Boon and drives it recklessly through town, and later, when Boon, Ned, and Lucius take off on their trip to Memphis. This rambunctious music is peppered with clever instrumental insertions, including banjo and Jew's harp.

These themes, with their preponderance of waltzlike rhythms, contribute an air of nostalgia for the Old South at the turn of the century and also celebrate the romance of the early automobile, which is seen in Jefferson as a real novelty.

BURT BACHARACH: *BUTCH CASSIDY AND THE SUNDANCE KID.* In the continuing trend away from symphonic backgrounds, Hollywood embraced the score by Burt Bacharach (b. 1929) for George Roy Hill's *Butch Cassidy and the Sundance Kid*, which was a radical departure from the Waxman/Newman/Rozsa brand of music. As wonderfully made as this film is, with terrific performances and with atmospheric photography that at times gives the film the look of old sepia-tinted photographs, the film's music is somewhat questionable, in view of the disparity between the score's modern, pop-oriented style and the late-nineteenth-century setting of this film. The jaunty song "Raindrops Keep Fallin' on My Head" was written for a scene in which Butch (Paul Newman) spins around on a bicycle, performing a variety of stunts, and also carries Etta Place (Katharine Ross) on the handlebars. The song, as performed by B. J. Thomas, is undeniably charming, and perhaps helps to account for the success of the film, which went on to win several Oscars, including two for Bacharach (for the song and the score).

SHORT CUTS ■■■■ **John Barry.** Following his Oscar for *The Lion in Winter*, John Barry continued to prove his versatility with one of the best of his James Bond scores, the music for *On Her Majesty's Secret Service*, and with the haunting harmonica theme of John Schlesinger's *Midnight Cowboy*. Although Barry's music in *Midnight Cowboy* often had to take a back seat to the songs of Harry Nilsson and a number of rock songs used in the film, his contribution greatly enhanced this film.

■■■■ **Michael J. Lewis.** Thanks to John Barry's overcrowded schedule, Bryan Forbes's film of *The Madwoman of Chaillot* introduced a new name in film scoring: Michael J. Lewis (b. 1939). Apparently, Barry recommended Lewis personally to Forbes, who took a chance on him. Lewis created a first film score that is marvelously atmospheric. There are two main themes, the haunting "Aurelia's Theme" (for Katharine Hepburn's character, the madwoman who attempts to foil a plot by several anarchists to blow up Paris), and the lovely "Irma's Theme," for the pretty barmaid (played by Forbes's wife, Nanette Newman). The melody for Aurelia is particularly memorable, with a mandolin line that boldly rises through the octave (starting with the pitches A–D–A), then turns around and comes back down. A repeated pattern of six tones is heard several times as part of a long, lyrical line. At the film's conclusion this theme gradually builds up to a gorgeous statement for full orchestra.

■■■■ **Ennio Morricone.** Italian composer Ennio Morricone continued to crank out Western scores, including the music for *Once upon a Time in the West*, starring Henry Fonda and Charles Bronson, which many consider to be director Sergio Leone's best film. Morricone's music incorporates the style of the "Man with No Name" trilogy, in which Clint Eastwood starred. The main-title theme is performed by a solo voice, and other themes are either whistled or played on a solo harmonica. In many ways this is one of Morricone's finest scores.

■■■■ *Easy Rider.* Instead of an original score, the music in Dennis Hopper's *Easy Rider* basically consists of a series of prerecorded tracks by such popular rock groups as Steppenwolf, The Byrds, and the Jimmie Hendrix Experience. There are additional songs by Bob Dylan and Roger McGuinn, including the latter's "Ballad of Easy Rider." Sales of the soundtrack album topped the million mark. The success of this film, with its rock soundtrack, would lead to many imitators in the years ahead.

■■■■ **John Green.** For the vivid recreation of the dance-marathon contests of the Great Depression in Sydney Pollack's film version of the Horace McCoy novel *They Shoot Horses, Don't They?*, Pollack hired John Green to provide a background score of period songs, which included Green's own "Body and Soul" and "Out of Nowhere." Green's arrangements incorporate a number of such songs, while providing atmospheric scoring for this ultimately depressing story of a number of desperate people who compete for prizes by dancing almost nonstop for over thirty hours.

POSTLUDE

PASSING THE TORCH. A look back at the 1960s reveals the gradual passing of the torch from the film-music pioneers of Hollywood's Golden Age to a younger generation of composers. Not only did Max Steiner, Dimitri Tiomkin, and Bronislau Kaper retire from film scoring during the 1960s, but death claimed Franz Waxman in 1967, and Alfred Newman survived only two months into the start of the next decade. Of the Hollywood veterans who did remain active through the '60s, neither Miklos Rozsa nor Bernard Herrmann were given many scoring opportunities.

Film music changed drastically during the 1960s, from a symphonic idiom to a more modernistic, popular style. Henry Mancini, John Barry, and Michel Legrand, all of whom possessed an affinity for pop tunes, jazz, and rock sounds, were now the leading trendsetters for the film-music art. Despite this stylistic metamorphosis, symphonic film scoring was not completely gone. Composers such as Elmer Bernstein and Jerry Goldsmith demonstrated in their music a versatility which set the stage for a remarkable mixture of styles that can be found in the film music of the 1970s.

Endnotes

1. David Ewen, *All the Years of American Popular Music* (Englewood Cliffs, NJ: Prentice-Hall, 1977), p. 615.

2. David Cook, *A History of Narrative Film*, (New York: W. W. Norton & Co., 1981), p. 425.

3. André Previn, *No Minor Chords: My Days in Hollywood* (New York: Doubleday, 1991), p. 86.

4. Tony Thomas, *Film Score: The Art and Craft of Movie Music* (Burbank, CA: Riverwood, 1991), p. 239.

5. Ibid, pp. 239–40.

6. Tony Thomas, *The Great Adventure Films* (Secaucus, NJ: Citadel, 1976), p. 222.

7. Henry Mancini, *Did They Mention the Music?* (Chicago: Contemporary Books, 1989), pp. 3–4.

8. Ibid., p. 75.

9. Ibid., p. 63.

10. Ibid., p. 70.

11. Ibid., p. 71.

12. Ibid., p. 82.

13. Ibid., p. 98.

14. Miklos Rozsa, *Double Life* (New York: Wynwood, 1989), p. 193.

15. Ibid., p. 195.

16. Steven M. Silverman, *David Lean* (New York: Harry M. Abrams, 1989), pp. 142–43.

17. Tony Bremner, Liner notes for the studio recording of *Lawrence of Arabia*, with Bremner conducting the Philharmonia Orchestra, on a Silva Screen Digital Film Scores CD, FILMCD 036.

18. Derek Elley, ed., *The Chronicle of the Movies* (Toronto: B. Mitchell, 1991), p. 236.

19. Thomas, *Film Scores*, pp. 298–300.

20. Silverman, p. 167.

21. Maurice Jarre, Liner notes for the 30th Anniversary Edition of the *Doctor Zhivago* soundtrack, on a Rhino Movie Music CD, R2 71957.

22. Ibid.

23. Ibid.

24. Joseph Murrells, *Million Selling Records* (New York: Arco, 1984), p. 217.

25. Thomas, *Film Scores*, p. 287.

26. Ibid., p. 292.

27. Murrells, p. 217.

28. Tony Thomas, *Music for the Movies* (South Brunswick, NJ.: A. S. Barnes and Co., 1973), pp. 214–15.

29. Ibid., p. 216.

30. Francois Guerif (trans. Lisa Nesselson), *Clint Eastwood: The Man and His Films* (New York: St. Martin's Press, 1984), p. 8.

31. Didier Deutsch, Liner notes for the *Ennio Morricone: The Legendary Italian Westerns* CD, vol. II of *The Film Composers Series* on RCA, No. 9974-2-R.

32. Tom Soter, "License to Score," *Starlog*, o. 199 (February 1994), p. 41.

33. Pete Walker, Liner notes for the soundtrack of *Beat Girl*, released on a Play It Again CD, PLAY 001.

34. Murrells, p. 275.

35. Thomas, *Film Score*, p. 326.

6

1970–79

The Revival of the Symphonic Film Score

PRELUDE

After the turbulent 1960s, in which the Vietnam war divided Americans into opposite camps, the 1970s began as a time of reconciliation; but even before the American pullout from Southeast Asia was completed, further division was caused by the troubled presidency of Richard Nixon, which ended amid controversy with his resignation in August 1974, two years after the fateful Watergate incident.

POPULAR MUSIC. In the world of popular music no single performer or group dominated the 1970s to the extent that the Beatles had ruled the preceding decade. Pop musicians who came into prominence in the 1970s include Stevie Wonder, John Denver, Elton John, Barry Manilow, Billy Joel, and Linda Ronstadt. The king of rock-'n'-roll, Elvis Presley, enjoyed a late burst of fame with several stage appearances, plus the TV show "Aloha from Hawaii via Satellite," which aired in 1973; but years of reckless living took their toll, and Elvis died suddenly on August 16, 1977. His death sent shock waves through the media; in the years following his untimely death, rumors persisted that he was still alive and living in seclusion.

A new musical novelty came on the scene in the 1970s with the arrival of the disco craze. A factor in the rise of disco music was the film *Saturday Night Fever* (1977), for which the Bee Gees recorded a number of catchy songs, including "Stayin' Alive" and "Night Fever." The success of the double-disc soundtrack album from *Saturday Night Fever*, which broke all existing records for film-album sales, caused a ripple effect; much of the popular music in the late 1970s contained the disco sound, including songs sung by such performers as Donna Summer and the Village People.

TELEVISION. Prior to the 1970s, most TV viewers had access to only three networks; but with funding from major corporations, the Public Broadcasting Service became an entity in 1970. Although the ratings of PBS shows were lower than those of shows on the commercial networks, the broadcast of such programs as "Masterpiece Theatre" and Kenneth Clark's "Civilisation" caused a significant change in viewing habits.

Another auspicious debut occurred when Home Box Office (HBO) first presented an uncut, uncensored movie on a paying basis in Wilkes-Barre, Pennsylvania, on November 8, 1972 to 365 subscribers. Within five years, HBO's operation would expand to include five hundred cable systems in forty-six states and Puerto Rico.[1]

Meanwhile, the commercial networks were still presenting more sixties-style family programs. But there were signs of change in TV's portrayal of the American family. In 1971, CBS decided to pull the plug on its folk-style sitcoms such as "The Beverly Hillbillies" and "Green Acres." A ground-breaking new show had already arrived, Norman Lear's caustically funny "All in the Family," which featured Carroll O'Connor as the loud-mouthed, biased Archie Bunker. Never before had a TV-sitcom character behaved in such an obnoxious manner. In the years directly following this phenomenal success, Lear produced two spin-offs: "Maude" (1972–78), featuring Bea Arthur in a reprise of her role as Edith Bunker's outspoken (and frequently divorced) cousin, and "The Jeffersons." He also introduced "Sanford and Son" (1972–77), starring Redd Foxx as a curmudgeonly junk dealer. Although it was not the first all-black sitcom, "Sanford" proved to be the first to achieve a huge success in the ratings. Two shows that made their first network appearances in 1970 stretched the concept of "family." In "The Mary Tyler Moore Show" (1970–77), a TV newsroom was the setting for comical exchanges between Mary Richards (Moore) and her fellow workers, who served as surrogate family members. "The Odd Couple" (1970–83), based on the Neil Simon hit play and film, starred Tony Randall and Jack Klugman as Felix and Oscar, two divorced men whose attempt to share an apartment led to comic complications.

Some TV dramas of the 1970s also emphasized traditional family values. NBC led the way with a pair of wholesome family sagas, "The Waltons" (1972–81), in which viewers relived the Great Depression, and "Little House on the Prairie" (1974–83), which dealt with the hardships of life on the frontier in the 1870s. Both shows had their share of heartaches as well as heart-warming moments.

Television showings of major films continued to gain momentum. The high ratings for the telecast of *Ben-Hur* in 1971 led to TV broadcasts of other blockbuster movies. *The Godfather* reached TV in 1974, two years after its record-breaking run in theaters, and *Gone with the Wind* appeared in 1976.

A new phenomenon in 1970s television was the advent of the mini-series. The first such program to be spread over several nights was "Rich Man, Poor Man," based on Irwin Shaw's novel. This twelve-hour, six-night saga made ratings history in 1976. It was soon overshadowed by one of the most memorable events in the history of TV, the week-long showing of Alex Haley's "Roots" in 1977. "Roots" remains the most popular TV series in history; an estimated 100 million people watched its concluding episode.[2]

Television news departments increased their ability to bring into the nation's living rooms history as it happened. Such events as the Kent State tragedy of May 4, 1970, and the Moon landing of Apollo 14 on February 5, 1971, were witnessed while they happened. When President Nixon went to China for four days in 1972, the events were carried around the world via satellite. The most watched news-related TV programming of the decade involved the Watergate hearings, which were conducted by members of the U.S. Senate in 1973 and watched by millions on live TV. By the end of the decade, ABC started a pair of programs that would enhance TV's journalistic capabilities. "Twenty/Twenty," which made its debut on June 6, 1978, carried news stories in a manner similar to "Sixty Minutes." Eventually, all the networks would carry at least one prime-time newsmagazine program. The other ABC innovation in the late '70s occurred when the Iranians were holding fifty-three Americans hostage in Teheran. Following the late news, ABC broadcast nightly updates of the developing situation in a program called "The Iran Crisis: America Held Hostage." News correspondent Frank Reynolds was the original host of this program; but when Ted Koppel sat in for him after three weeks, a new star was born. After the release of the hostages ABC would launch the popular "Nightline" series with Koppel as host.

MOVIES. The number of Americans attending movie theaters had begun an almost steady decline with the evolution of network TV. By 1970, fewer than eighteen million people were going to the movies each week, as compared to sixty million in 1950.[3]

A new style of movie theater came into being in the 1970s. Whereas movie houses had traditionally been located in downtown areas, theaters were now being opened either in or near shopping malls. In order to boost attendance theater owners tried to make more viewing choices available, and thus was born the concept of the multiplex. By the end of the decade, these buildings had evolved from spaces with two or three screens to theaters with six or more separate viewing areas.

The ways and means by which movies were released also underwent significant changes. The typical big-budget movies of the 1960s, such as *West Side Story* and *My Fair Lady*, were first shown in limited release. Showings were limited to only a few screens, often with only reserved-seat tickets sold. This practice began to fade toward the end of the decade, and by 1970, few films were released this way. The concept of saturation booking was adopted, with the idea that, even if critics disliked a film, it might already have made a great deal of money by the time the reviews were printed because the film was being shown simultaneously on a thousand or more screens. The wide release of movies not only made the existence of the new multiscreen cinemas financially lucrative, but TV advertising of new films was increasingly used to lure viewers to leave their homes. In many cases almost as much was spent on publicity as on production.

To reach a wider, and often younger, audience, certain types of movies, such as the disaster film, were made in greater numbers. Although films with elaborate fires, earthquakes, and violent storms had been popular in the 1930s, a new cycle of expensively mounted films with spectacular destruction scenes took hold. The 1970 *Airport* began to point in that direction, but the film that really put disasters back into movies was Irwin Allen's *Poseidon Adventure*, which became the hottest ticket at the box office during the 1972 Christmas season. Long lines formed at mall cinemas everywhere to see an ocean liner being capsized by a huge tidal wave.

One of the most phenomenally successful genres in the 1970s was the tough-cop movie, the popularity of which was ably abetted by Clint Eastwood, the decade's number-one box-office star. Eastwood's movie fame had begun when he played the "Man with No Name" in Sergio Leone's spaghetti Westerns of the 1960s. Eastwood shrewdly found a niche in the 1970s by trading in his Stetson for a .44 magnum. With the R rating to protect them, the three movies Eastwood made in the 1970s in which he played tough San Francisco cop Harry Callahan are violent and gritty examples of moviemaking. From *Dirty Harry* (1971) to *Magnum Force* (1973) and *The Enforcer* (1976), Eastwood's soft-spoken character became one of the decade's most enduring images.

The most acclaimed male actors of the decade were those who appeared in the two *Godfather* films. Al Pacino, James Caan, Robert Duvall, and Robert De Niro all rose to movie stardom on the basis of their roles in Francis Ford Coppola's Mafia masterpieces. The top female star of the 1970s was Barbra Streisand, whose hit films *The Way We Were* (1973) and *A Star Is Born* (1976) were enhanced by songs she performed. Among the other popular female stars of the '70s were Jane Fonda, who won Oscars in 1971 and 1978 (for *Klute* and *Coming Home*, respectively), and Diane Keaton, who won an Oscar for Woody Allen's *Annie Hall* (1977).

More than the movie stars themselves, the films of the 1970s revealed the rise of important directors, including several who had learned the techniques of filmmaking while enrolled in college. Chief among these was Francis Ford Coppola, who got his Master of Fine Arts degree at UCLA in 1967. He subsequently turned his thesis, an original screenplay, into the film *You're a Big Boy Now* (1966) and went on to direct the acclaimed *Godfather* films. Another director who rose to prominence was Martin Scorsese, who made the critically acclaimed *Mean Streets* (1973), and then directed one of the decade's most controversial films, *Taxi Driver* (1976).

Two directors who specialized in comedies made a lasting impression. Mel Brooks had two hits in 1974, *Blazing Saddles* and *Young Frankenstein*; Brooks used his gift for parody, often laced with ribald humor, to create films of high hilarity. Although Woody Allen has never enjoyed the commercial success of Brooks, his *Bananas* (1971), *Sleeper* (1973), and *Love and Death* (1975), indicate his genius for satire. With *Annie Hall* (1977) Allen became one of the few directors to win an Oscar for directing a comedy.

Among all the film directors of the 1970s, Steven Spielberg was the most successful. Although his first film, *The Sugarland Express* (1974) was only a modest hit, *Jaws* (1975) made him the most recognized director in movies. Spielberg's next film, *Close Encounters of the Third Kind* (1977), based on his own script, added even more luster to his fame.

With the gradual corporate takeover of the movie industry, which had begun in the 1960s with the buyout of Paramount by Gulf and Western, many composers, songwriters, and arrangers found it increasingly difficult to find work. Not only were musical films no longer box-office draws, but the few that were made in the '70s were usually film adaptations of Broadway hits, such as *Fiddler on the Roof* (1971) and *Cabaret* (1972), or were based on rock musicals, such as *Jesus Christ Superstar* (1973), *Grease* (1978), and *Hair* (1979).

The scoring of dramatic and comedy pictures in the 1970s was still often left to such talented individuals as Elmer Bernstein, Jerry Goldsmith, and John Williams. Williams achieved something akin to superstardom for his scores of the decade's two top box-office hits, *Jaws* (1975) and *Star Wars* (1977). For older moviegoers, Williams's richly orchestrated music seemed to bring back the days of Erich Korngold, while for younger viewers, the sound of a full orchestra on a film's soundtrack was a real novelty.

With the passing of Alfred Newman in early 1970, the last of the original pioneers of film scoring was gone. Scores by such masters as Miklos Rozsa and Bernard Herrmann were heard infrequently. When Herrmann died suddenly at the end of 1975, only Rozsa remained as a living link to the glorious days of the studio music departments. The few movies that Rozsa and Herrmann scored in the 1970s resulted from the interest that such young filmmakers as Brian De Palma and Martin Scorsese had in their work. It was for these two directors that Bernard Herrmann scored *Obsession* and *Taxi Driver*, respectively, the films that marked the end of his illustrious career as perhaps the most ingenious of all film composers.

European composers, especially those from France and Italy, found continued employment in the 1970s with a number of successful film projects. Besides Michel Legrand, Francis Lai, and Georges Delerue, Philippe Sarde (b. 1945) joined the ranks of French-born film composers, while the Italians Nino Rota and Ennio Morricone continued to score both foreign and English-language films. Morricone demonstrated a productivity that rivaled that of Max Steiner during his years at RKO.

Advances in electronic instruments made the 1970s the first decade during which film music could be recorded with synthesizers. Through this new technology, the sound of an orchestra could be simulated by electronic means, creating opportunities for such musicians as Giorgio Moroder (b. 1940), the first composer to win an Oscar for a synthesized score (*Midnight Express*, 1978). By the end of the decade, the recording of film music by electronic means began to catch on in such a big way that few composers could afford to ignore the impact of this technological development.

HENRY MANCINI: FROM *DARLING LILI* TO *THE NIGHT VISITOR*. The film-composing projects Henry Mancini accepted in 1970 suggest that his career was at a crossroads. In his next five scores Mancini began to branch out from the sophisticated comedies for which he was best known. Each of these scores reveals a different aspect of his musical personality.

Blake Edwards's *Darling Lili* is a lavish musical, which stars Julie Andrews as a Mata Hari–like German spy, who masquerades as an English music-hall performer during World War I. An American flying ace (Rock Hudson) falls in love with her, and complications ensue. The spy story weights the film down, but the music compensates nicely, especially the catchy tune "Smile Away Each Rainy Day," and the wonderfully melancholy Oscar-nominated song "Whistling Away the Dark," one of Mancini's finest songs. Julie Andrews's rendition of the song is beguiling; most of the melodic line is set in the lower range of her voice, an area that was never showcased until this song (and was not much used again until Mancini's *Victor/Victoria* score of 1982). Although Mancini had been writing songs for motion pictures throughout the 1960s, the score of *Darling Lili* was his first for a musical. He was greatly assisted by lyricist Johnny Mercer, with whom he had a long-term collaboration.

There are three main themes in Mancini's score for Martin Ritt's *Molly Maguires*. The first, a lovely melody with a folk-music quality, is played on an ocarina (also known as a "sweet potato"), a globe-shaped instrument with a

The Molly Maguires, with Samantha Eggar and Richard Harris.

whistle mouthpiece. The ocarina has a quasi-flute sound, but without the flute's expansive pitch range and pure-sounding overtones. This tune is accompanied by an Irish harp, which plays repeated sets of three-note figures. Also featured in this piece, which accompanies the film's opening precredit sequence showing the miners going about their daily tasks, is the button accordion, also known as the "concertina."

The main-title theme is a rousing marchlike tune for horns and strings, which is also used in scenes depicting the miners' struggles to improve their working conditions. The third theme is a lovely ballad for the relationship of Mary (Samantha Eggar), who runs a boarding house, and the Pinkerton detective (Richard Harris), who has gone undercover to learn of the Mollys' terrorist activities.

For Tom Gries's film *The Hawaiians*, Mancini did extensive research into Oriental instruments. Not wanting to duplicate Elmer Bernstein's epic score for *Hawaii*, Mancini approached this continuation of Michener's saga in a different way, with music that emphasizes the Oriental ancestry of the Hawaiian Islanders. As a result, the score contains one of the largest gatherings of Oriental instruments ever assembled for an American-made film, including the *cheng* (a Chinese zither), the *hsun* (a Chinese ocarina), the koto and bass koto, the Chinese flute, the *santure* (an oriental cimbalom), and the *hichriki* (a Japanese oboe), along with lots of drums. When heard in combination with conventional orchestral sounds, these instruments provide the score with an authentically ethnic flavor.

The soaring main theme, which is built on a gradually rising pitch pattern, is a conventionally melodious tune of no special distinction, but the other music in the score is ingeniously devised, with melodic patterns made up of pentatonic scale steps. Especially noteworthy is the tune called

"Auntie's Theme," which features the entire group of Oriental instruments, with a rising motif plucked on the strings of the koto.

Mancini's fourth score of 1970 was written for Vittorio De Sica's *Sunflower*, a love story set against the background of World War II. A young Italian married couple (Sophia Loren and Marcello Mastroianni) become separated when he goes off to war and fails to come back. Years later, after she learns that he disappeared in Russia, she goes to find him. When she does manage to locate him, she finds that he has married the young Russian woman who nursed him back to health following an almost fatal injury.

The *Sunflower* score combines Italian and Russian elements. The Italian music for the early courtship scenes is tuneful. The Russian flavor is conveyed by the use of balalaikas, the strumming sounds of which blend in nicely with the conventional orchestration. There are two principal melodic ideas that are melancholy in character and involve the use of the minor scale. Despite the film's limited release, this score received an Oscar nomination.

In late 1970, Mancini worked on the most unique score of his entire film career. *The Night Visitor*, which was directed by Laslo Benedek, features some of Ingmar Bergman's stockpile of actors, including Max von Sydow, Liv Ullmann, and Per Oscarsson. This film is the downbeat story of an inmate who plots to escape from an asylum for one night to seek revenge on the people who had him committed.

The score consists of short bits of music performed on a variety of woodwinds and keyboards; only seventeen instruments are involved in the instrumentation. There are a dozen woodwinds in all, with instruments of both high and low range. Especially noticeable are the low timbres of bass clarinet and contrabassoon, which convey a very menacing effect. Combined with these sounds are five keyboards: an electronic organ, two pianos, and two harpsichords, with one piano and one harpsichord tuned a quarter-tone lower than the other. Mancini had used this out-of-tune effect once before, in his eerie music for *Wait Until Dark*. In *The Night Visitor* he found a second opportunity to explore some most unusual harmonic sonorities. This score, which is remarkably sparse in terms of melodic materials, is somewhat reminiscent of Bernard Herrmann's scoring for some of his Charles Schneer–Ray Harryhausen fantasies, in which growling woodwinds are heard in scenes involving the various creatures and monsters. *The Night Visitor* illustrates a creative side of Mancini's musical personality that was regrettably overshadowed by the more tuneful style that made him one of the most successful film composers.

FRANCIS LAI: *LOVE STORY.* The big film-music success story of 1970 is French composer Francis Lai's Oscar-winning music for Arthur Hiller's *Love Story*, an old-fashioned, romantic movie with tragic overtones that became a huge box-office hit. Erich Segal's screenplay, which was turned into a best-selling novel before the release of the film, helped Ryan O'Neal and Ali MacGraw to attain stardom. Oliver (O'Neal) shocks his wealthy, conservative family by falling in love with Jenny (MacGraw), a young Italian woman from a lower-middle-class background. After Oliver defiantly marries her, she soon becomes ill with cancer; the film becomes an extended tear-jerker, as Oliver has to face her imminent death.

Love Story has attractive settings, nice performances, and tuneful music. When the movie was released, its main melodic idea, a minor-key love theme with a lot of repeated notes, became an enormous hit in a commercial recording, with Henry Mancini duplicating the original soundtrack's piano part.

Francis Lai is capable of composing genuinely memorable themes (as in the Claude Lelouch films *A Man and a Woman* and *Live for Life*). However, the main theme he wrote for *Love Story* is not very original; it came along when melancholy, minor-key themes were in vogue. It bears more than a superficial resemblance to the melodic outline of Michel Legrand's 1968 Oscar-winning song "The Windmills of Your Mind" (from *The Thomas Crown Affair*). This theme gets a thorough workout in the course of the film, which includes a scene in which it is played on harpsichord with a rock beat. The balance of Lai's score consists of catchy tunes that use strings, again often combined with either piano or harpsichord, and also with a rock beat. There is no attempt to develop motifs; they simply fill in as window dressing, and rarely contribute to the emotional content of the film.

SHORT CUTS ■■■ Alfred Newman.

Alfred Newman's final film composition, written for George Seaton's popular adaptation of the Arthur Hailey best-selling novel *Airport*, is memorable. Newman's music is one of the best things about this entertaining, if not very original, film about a plane in danger because a crazed man on board has a bomb in his suitcase. The score's main theme is a dramatically charged idea that helps to underline the romance and suspense of the film's multicharacter story.

■■■ Jerry Goldsmith.

Perhaps the most Oscar-worthy of 1970's nominated scores is Jerry Goldsmith's music for Franklin J. Schaffner's Oscar-winning film *Patton*. Although the score takes up less than a half-hour of this three-hour film, its main march theme is one of Goldsmith's most memorable creations. With a clever accompanying trumpet effect that consists of repeated sets of three notes, the melody begins with a repeated pair of notes that uses the descending fourth. The same interval is found in the main themes of both *Lawrence of Arabia* and *Born Free*, but the rhythmic motion of the *Patton* theme distinguishes it from the other two. Its overall effect has been described by Tony Thomas in these terms:

> The main theme, a jaunty march, captured the bravura of the American general; but it was a particular device that made its mark in this score—a solo trumpet fanfare in triplets which echoed across the screen, fading out, and used to pinpoint Patton's thoughts on the history of warfare and his belief that he had lived in previous times. It is both heroic and slightly eerie, and skillfully underlines an important aspect of the famous soldier's character.[4]

■■■ M*A*S*H.

Johnny Mandel composed a catchy title tune for *M*A*S*H*, the irreverent Korean War comedy that catapulted director Robert Altman into the limelight. The original version of the film includes a choral arrangement of Mandel's theme known as the song "Suicide Is Painless." When 20th Century-Fox released a slightly reedited version of the film, an instrumental version of the tune by Ahmad Jamal was featured in place of the song. The two differing versions of the title music may be found on alternate versions of the film's soundtrack.[5]

■■■ Maurice Jarre.

One of Maurice Jarre's most memorable scores was composed for David Lean's epic film *Ryan's Daughter*, set in a small village in Northern Ireland in 1916. The triangular love story, which includes the marriage of young Rosie Ryan (Sarah Miles) to the local school-teacher (Robert Mitchum) and her subsequent adulterous affair with a wounded British soldier (Christopher Jones), may seem dwarfed by the sheer size of this film, with its expensively mounted scenes; but Jarre's jaunty background music keeps the film from sinking under its own weight. Most memorable is "Rosie's Theme," a lilting tune that rhythmically bounces along, with an occasionally lavish orchestration.

■■■■ **Leonard Rosenman.** Leonard Rosenman contributed two unusual scores in 1970, the first, a daringly different effort on behalf of *A Man Called Horse*, which consists of lots of Native American flutes and drums, plus some tribal chanting. The other was the more conventionally melodious but bizarre music for *Beneath the Planet of the Apes*, the first of four film sequels to the 1968 *Planet of the Apes*. The most unique musical moment in this score occurs when a choir sings a pseudo-liturgical piece in celebration of a nuclear bomb that is worshipped as a holy relic.

MICHEL LEGRAND: *SUMMER OF '42.* When Michel Legrand won an Oscar for his original score for Robert Mulligan's *Summer of '42*, he became the second Frenchman in a row to win the coveted award. This illustrates the increasingly international nature of filmmaking during the 1960s and '70s, when Oscars were being won by foreigners, such as the French composers Maurice Jarre and Francis Lai, and the Englishmen John Addison and John Barry.

By the time Legrand joined the ranks of the foreign-born Oscar winners, he had already accomplished a great deal as a musician. His father, Raymond Legrand, was a noted conductor, arranger, and pianist. When Michel (born February 24, 1932) was five, he began to study the piano. Five years later, he was enrolled at the Paris Conservatory, where he remained until the age of twenty. During that time he advanced as a pianist and also studied composition with Nadia Boulanger, who had taught such distinguished American composers as Aaron Copland and Walter Piston.

At the age of twenty, Legrand became a piano accompanist for a number of classical instrumental soloists. He also found employment for two years as Maurice Chevalier's regular pianist. This connection brought him opportunities outside the realm of classical music. In addition, he had an interest in jazz, which had been ignited when he heard American jazz artist Dizzy Gillespie, whose band played in Paris in 1947. Legrand soon became known as an arranger/conductor of popular music.

In 1954, Columbia Records released an album of Legrand arrangements, entitled *I Love Paris*, which became a top seller and launched a recording career that resulted in almost fifty albums. One of the highlights of his work for Columbia Records was the 1956 album *Castles in Spain*, in which Legrand conducted his own orchestra in a variety of Spanish-flavored works.

By this time, Legrand had already begun his film-scoring career, with several movies made in France. Starting with *Beau fixe* in 1953, Legrand composed scores for over fifteen films within a decade. In 1963, he scored his first English-language film, David Swift's *Love Is a Ball*, and by the end of the decade he was hired by directors on both sides of the Atlantic.

Michel Legrand.

Courtesy of David Sneed,
F Sharp Productions, Ltd.

Legrand's most fortunate experiences as a film composer in the 1960s resulted from a fruitful collaboration with French director Jacques Demy, who hired Legrand to score his first film, *Lola* (1961). Three years later, they collaborated on *The Umbrellas of Cherbourg*, which became a huge hit in Europe after winning the 1964 Palme d'Or at the Cannes Film Festival. In this unique film there is no spoken dialogue. Instead, this bittersweet love story features the recitative operatic technique for all the dialogue scenes, plus a number of tuneful songs, including "Watch What Happens" and "I Will Wait for You." *Umbrellas* was nominated as a foreign-language film in the 1964 Oscar race; a year later, when it qualified in the other categories, it received four nominations—for the screenplay (Demy), for the original score (Legrand and Demy), for the musical arrangements (Legrand), and for the song "I Will Wait for You" (music by Legrand, French lyrics by Demy, and English lyrics by Norman Gimbel).

His subsequent film projects included scores for both English-language and French films. Among these are most of Jacques Demy's later films, beginning with a second operatic film, *The Young Girls of Rochefort* (1968). Despite a lovely score, this film did not impress critics as much as its predecessor. Legrand also scored a number of American films, including Norman Jewison's *Thomas Crown Affair* (1968), for which he was nominated for best score. He won an Oscar for the film's beguiling song "The Windmills of Your Mind." Following this, Legrand received Oscar nominations for his movie songs "What Are You Doing the Rest of Your Life?," from Richard Brooks's *Happy Ending* (1969), and the title song of *Pieces of Dreams* (1970). Both songs feature lyrics by Marilyn and Alan Bergman. He also created one of his finest film scores, the fetching music for Serge Bourguignon's *Picasso Summer* (1969). Although this film was a box-office dud, its theme song, "Summer Me, Winter Me," which was recorded by several popular artists, became another in the growing canon of Legrand's memorable movie songs.

In 1971, he scored Jacques Demy's *Donkey Skin*; this was followed by Joseph Losey's intriguing film of L. P. Hartley's novel *The Go-Between*, which contains a single theme based on a four-note motif that goes through a series of ten variations as the film progresses, in a chamber orchestra setting that features two solo pianos. The film is dramatically propelled by this music, one of Legrand's most classical attempts at film scoring, with the element of sequential repetition in its melody that often occurs in the music of Baroque composers. Legrand's third noteworthy score of that year is one of his rare efforts on behalf of a made-for-TV movie, *Brian's Song*, the touching story of Brian Piccolo (James Caan) of the Chicago Bears football team and his losing battle with cancer. The film won ten Emmy nominations, including drama, special effects, and music score. The film itself won an Emmy, but Legrand watched while John Williams collected an Emmy for his brilliant score for the TV remake of *Jane Eyre*.

Screenwriter Herman Raucher, drawing on memories of his own adolescence, wrote the script for *Summer of '42*, about three teenage boys seeking their first sexual experiences while spending a summer on an island off the New England coast during World War II. Hermie, Oscie, and Benjie (Gary Grimes, Jerry Houser, and Oliver Conant) lie on the dunes contemplating ways to meet girls. Nearby, a lonely young woman (Jennifer O'Neill) passes the time while awaiting letters from her husband, who is

Summer of '42, with Jerry Houser, Oliver Conant, and Gary Grimes.

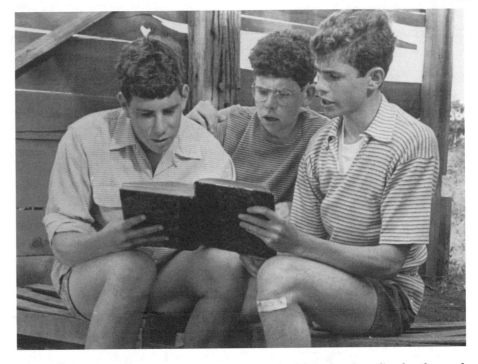

away at war. Eventually she receives word of her husband's death, and Hermie gets his initiation into adulthood as she turns to him for comfort.

Setting a tone of sweet melancholy for this movie of nostalgic remembrance is Michel Legrand's haunting background theme, which is based on a simple minor-key idea of four notes. As in many other Legrand movie scores, there is a lot of repetition of this basic idea, to the exclusion of all else. The attractiveness of the melody, plus Legrand's emotionally moving string arrangements contributed to the music's success. The score was awarded an Oscar; to date, this is the only one of Michel Legrand's original film scores to be so honored.

BERNARD HERRMANN: A RESURGENCE. After a three-year absence from movie work, Bernard Herrmann contributed music to three films. The first of these, *The Night Digger* (known by the title *The Road Builder* in Great Britain where it was filmed) deals with the relationship between the lonely Maura (Patricia Neal) and the much younger Billy Jarvis (Nicholas Clay). Maura lives with an elderly blind woman named Edith Prince (Pamela Brown), who is completely dependent on her. Though Maura is Edith's adopted daughter, the two do not have a warm relationship. When Edith hires Billy to do some handiwork, Maura becomes physically attracted to him. She eventually runs away with him, but only after marrying him does she realize how unbalanced he is (though the viewer has already learned that he is a serial killer of young women).

As is customary in a Herrmann score, the instrumentation of *The Night Digger*'s music is a study in the use of selective orchestral colors. Designed predominantly for strings and harp, this score features two solo instrumental "voices": a solo harmonica is used for Billy and the viola d'amore musically portrays Maura. Each voice has a separate motif; the harmonica idea consists of tones that ascend the scale; the viola motif is built on a five-note descending pattern. As the relationship between Maura and Billy develops, these two musical ideas are bound together in a powerfully emotional way.

Herrmann's music for the English-language version of *The Battle of Neretva* is not on the exalted level of his preceding score, but it contains the most ambitious orchestration that Herrmann ever used. Its primary musical idea is a somber minor-key march, which at the film's conclusion is transformed into a victory theme.

An interesting aspect of the *Neretva* score is the borrowing of previously composed materials. In his book *A Fire at Heart's Center*, Steven C. Smith points out two borrowings: a bit of the discarded score for Hitchcock's *Torn Curtain*, and also a melody from his clarinet quintet entitled *Souvenirs de voyage* (1967). Also in the *Neretva* score is still another borrowing: the music entitled "Pastorale" on the soundtrack of this film is identical with the music in *Fahrenheit 451* that is identified as "The Garden."[6]

The music for Sidney Gilliat's *Endless Night* is the least interesting of the three Herrmann scores, but for the first time Hermann employed the Moog synthesizer, which he subsequently used for two other suspense-film scores, Brian De Palma's *Sisters* (1973) and Larry Cohen's *It's Alive* (1974). With the advent of Robert Moog's invention in the late 1960s, many film composers began to take advantage of its tonal possibilities.

WALTER CARLOS: A CLOCKWORK ORANGE. One musician who also used the Moog synthesizer as a potent factor in film scoring during 1971 is Walter Carlos (b. 1939). When Stanley Kubrick adapted Anthony Burgess's futuristic fable *A Clockwork Orange*, he hired Carlos to concoct an electronic score based on familiar concert pieces. The first borrowed music is Rossini's Overture to *The Thieving Magpie*, which is featured in two scenes. It is first heard during the opening sequence, when Alex (Malcolm MacDowell) and his three fellow Droogs indulge in "the old ultra-violence" by brawling with a rival gang. This music is heard again when Alex, goaded on by his three friends, attempts to rape an artist in her studio. When she resists, he kills her with a giant phallic sculpture. Another Rossini piece, from the *William Tell Overture* (and better known as the "Lone Ranger" theme), is used for the speeded-up sex scene involving Alex and two girls he encounters at a record store.

The most frequently heard borrowed music in *A Clockwork Orange* comes from Beethoven's Symphony no. 9 in D Minor, opus 125, which is used as part of Alex's behavioral reconditioning. Although Alex has been a big fan of Beethoven, whom he calls "Ludwig van," after being brainwashed in a rehabilitation center, he throws up every time he hears the "Ode to Joy" theme. In the course of the film both Carlos's electronic arrangement and the original Beethoven orchestration are heard.

The best borrowing is the use of "Singin' in the Rain" by Arthur Freed and Nacio Herb Brown, which Alex routinely sings as he goes about his rapacious business. Toward the end of the film, after being brutally beaten by his former fellow gang members, Alex is taken in by a crippled man, who at first displays kindness toward him. When the man hears Alex singing this song while soaking in a bathtub, he realizes that Alex is the same person who raped and killed his wife, and left him without the use of his legs. Finally, the Gene Kelly recording of "Singin' in the Rain," from the 1952 MGM musical film of the same name, is played during the closing credits; its inclusion provides *A Clockwork Orange* with an ironically cheerful conclusion.

While there are lapses in Kubrick's direction of this futuristic scenario (he seems to have reveled in the display of nudity and violence, which earned this film an X-rating when it was released), his use of music is ingenious.

SHORT CUTS ■■■ Police Films with Jazz Scores.

In William Friedkin's Oscar-winning film *The French Connection*, Gene Hackman introduces the character of Jimmy "Popeye" Doyle, based on the real-life police investigator Eddie "Popeye" Egan who goes after a group of French criminals suspected of smuggling cocaine into New York. The film's razzle-dazzle style, with a classic chase scene, required a lively musical score; with the contributions of jazz artist Don Ellis (1934–78), an often throbbing big-band sound was achieved. When the adventures of "Popeye" Doyle were continued in the 1975 film *The French Connection II*, Ellis again supplied an energetic jazz score.

Another police film, which was almost as successful in 1971 as the first *French Connection* film, was Don Siegel's *Dirty Harry*, in which Homicide Inspector Harry Callahan of the San Francisco Police Force tracks a serial killer named Scorpio. *Dirty Harry* also benefits from a jazz-inflected score, this time by Lalo Schifrin.

A third crime fighter, private eye John Shaft, became a popular cinematic figure in *Shaft*, the first of three films featuring Richard Roundtree. Isaac Hayes (b. 1942) received an Oscar for his up-tempo title song and a nomination for his pulsating, jazzy, rhythmically driven background score.

■■■ Richard Rodney Bennett.

One of 1971's most lavishly produced films is Franklin J. Schaffner's film adaptation of Robert Massie's fascinating book *Nicholas and Alexandra*. Although this film lasts for three hours, and requires some knowledge of Russian history to follow the melodramatic plot concerning the sinister Rasputin and the Bolshevik Revolution of 1917, it is a feast for the eyes; with Richard Rodney Bennett's lush score, it is also a treat for the ears.

Bennett used both Russian folk-song materials and original melodic ideas in his score. The theme for the four daughters of the royal couple is based on a five-note motif that has the simplicity of folk music; the main theme is a somber march that is first heard in a heroic style, but later returns as a funereal accompaniment when it becomes evident that the royal family is to be annihilated. For scenes with Czar Nicholas and his devoted wife, Bennett created a lyrical theme built on a seven-note pattern that is repeated at successively lower pitch levels. Occasionally, this theme swells to a full-orchestra statement in which the melody takes on a very emotional quality. This is an altogether fine score, one which richly deserved the Oscar nomination it received.

■■■ Jerry Goldsmith.

The Mephisto Waltz, the title of which comes from a virtuosic piano piece by Franz Liszt, tells of a dying concert pianist (Curt Jurgens) who joins a Satanic cult in an attempt to extend his life by possessing the body of an unsuspecting acquaintance (Alan Alda). Liszt's music, which is periodically played by the dying pianist, is tied to the film's demonic possession theme in that Mephisto (Mephistopheles), one of the seven chief devils of medieval demonology, tempted the aging Faust to sell his soul in exchange for the restoration of his youth, in Goethe's tragedy. In this film Goldsmith's often bizarre variations of Liszt's music include some dazzling string orchestrations.

FOOTNOTE TO 1971. The year ended with the sad news of the death of film-music pioneer Max Steiner on December 28. Although he had stopped composing for films in 1965, Steiner never really wanted to retire. According to Tony Thomas:

> The decline toward the end of his life came about with the decline in the productivity of Hollywood in general and with a shift in the tastes of the newer producers, many of whom were propelled by the notion of using music more for its promotional value than its dramatic content. Steiner was also gradually defeated by his declining health, especially his failing eyesight, which were factors he never wanted to admit.[7]

Steiner's death represents an irreversible break with the Golden Age of Hollywood, which had inspired not only some of his most memorable film scores, but also works of other pioneers who would live on in retirement. Among those who remained creatively silent during the 1970s were Dimitri Tiomkin and Bronislau Kaper. Two other composers, Hugo Friedhofer and David Raksin, each contributed only a pair of scores (for films released in 1971 and 1972). Friedhofer subsequently wrote the music for two short subjects, whereas Raksin composed two scores for made-for-TV movies.

Such a waste of talent is a reflection on the state of film music in the 1970s, wherein a good score seems to have been the exception rather than the rule, though a few film directors still cared about the role a score could play in enhancing the dramatic essence of a film. As we shall see, some emerging filmmakers would help to keep the art of film scoring alive, if not altogether well, as the 1970s continued.

NINO ROTA: *THE GODFATHER*. The year 1972 can be identified by a single film, Francis Ford Coppola's extraordinary adaptation of Mario Puzo's novel *The Godfather*. The film's earnings surpassed those of each of the previous box-office champions *Gone with the Wind* and *The Sound of Music* in less than six months.[8]

Although some of the music in *The Godfather* was contributed by the director's father, Carmine Coppola (1910–91), who had for many years played flute under Arturo Toscanini in the NBC Symphony, the bulk of the score was composed by famed Italian composer Nino Rota (1911–79). The choice of Rota to create a pseudo-Italian atmosphere for the first *Godfather* film was an inspired one, since this composer had been associated with some of the finest Italian filmmakers to emerge in the wake of World War II, including Federico Fellini and Luchino Visconti.

Film music was far from Nino Rota's mind during his formative years. A native of Milan, Rota was a child prodigy, whose mother played the piano and whose paternal grandfather was the pianist/composer Giovanni Rinaldi (Rota's full given name is Giovanni Rota Rinaldi). At nine, he began studying the piano with his mother; within a year, he composed his first pieces. By the age of eleven, he had already written an oratorio, *L'infanzia di San Giovanni Battista*, which was performed in Milan and Lille in 1923. That year, he entered the Milan Conservatory, and within two years, he began studying harmony and counterpoint privately with

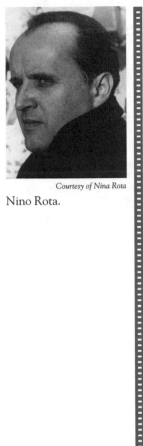

Courtesy of Nina Rota

Nino Rota.

Ildebrando Pizzetti. He then moved on to Rome, where he studied with Alfredo Casella and received a diploma in composition at the Accademia di Santa Cecilia in 1930. Further studies followed, including a stint in the United States. He was invited by the Curtis Institute of Music to come to Philadelphia, where he continued his musical training under Rosario Scalero (composition), Fritz Reiner (conducting), and music history (Johann Beck). In 1937, he received a degree in letters at Milan University upon the completion of his thesis, which concerned composer/theorist Gioseffo Zarlino and the Italian Renaissance.

Rota then began a teaching career with a one-year stint at the Taranto Music School, where he taught music theory in 1937–38. In 1939, he joined the faculty of the Bari Conservatory as a teacher of harmony. Later, he taught composition there, and in 1950, he became the director of the school. While maintaining his teaching career, Rota, a creative artist with varied interests, became known in Italy as a composer of operas and ballet scores. Of his ten operas the best known is *Il cappello di paglia di Firenze* (1946), which is based on Eugène Labiche's comic play *The Italian Straw Hat*. He also created many choral works, plus a large number of instrumental pieces for either solo piano or small ensembles. In addition, he wrote three symphonies (in 1939, 1943, and 1957) and several concertos, for harp (1948), trombone (1968), cello (1973), and bassoon (1977). His final work, a piano concerto, was completed shortly before his death on April 10, 1979.[9]

Rota composed his first film score in 1933 for a movie entitled *Treno popolare*. His next film assignments occurred during World War II, when he wrote scores for six Italian films. Between 1946 and 1949, Rota completed scores for over twenty films, including the British films *The Glass Mountain* and *The Hidden Room*.

The first major film director to utilize Rota's talents was Federico Fellini, who embarked on an extraordinary series of semiautobiographical movies, beginning with *The White Sheik* (1952), for which he first hired Nino Rota. The two worked together on fifteen films; this is one of the most outstanding examples of creative collaboration in the history of the cinema. Four of the movies won Oscars for Best Foreign Language film; *La strada* (1954; U.S. release, 1956), *The Nights of Cabiria* (1957), *8½* (1963), and *Amarcord* (1974). Not only was *La strada* highly regarded, but Rota's charming background score, based principally on a single songlike theme, became known through recordings by popular artists such as Mantovani. Every subsequent Fellini film was a major cinematic event, and Rota's music played a large part in the success of these films.

The key to Rota's approach to Fellini's films is the utter simplicity of his style. There is always a strong melodic element at work, with sometimes a meager amount of orchestration. The *La strada* theme, for instance, features strings with a solo trumpet. But often, a Rota melody is memorable because of its rhythmic vivacity. An example of this is *Il Bidone* (*The Swindle*, 1955), with a sprightly syncopated rhythmic idea that permeates most of the film's musical backgrounds. There is also a more sentimental melody, and often the up-tempo idea and the sentimental tune are cleverly juxtaposed.

A significant year for Rota was 1960, with Fellini's sensational *La dolce vita* and Visconti's *Rocco and His Brothers*. Another exceptional year was 1963, with Fellini's *8½* and Visconti's *Leopard*.

Although Rota's scores for English-language films may have been few and far between, there were some significant ones, including his lush score for King Vidor's *War and Peace* (1956). Subsequently, Italian director Franco Zeffirelli engaged Rota for his pair of Shakespearean films, *The Taming of the Shrew* (1967) and the award-winning *Romeo and Juliet* (1968), which benefitted from Rota's melancholy love theme.

When Puzo's novel *The Godfather* was purchased by Paramount in 1966, only a twenty-page draft existed. After Puzo finished the book, it became a publisher's dream, with sales of a half million copies in hardcover and ten million in paperback.[10]

Paramount production head Robert Evans thought the story needed a director of Italian background, so Francis Ford Coppola, fresh from winning an Oscar for coauthoring the *Patton* screenplay, was assigned the directorial position. When casting began, Marlon Brando agreed to a screen test for the key role of Don Vito Corleone; from the moment studio executives saw him with his cheeks stuffed with Kleenex, they knew he was right for the role. The casting of the other important roles was a painstaking task, with Al Pacino eventually winning out over several competitors for the part of Don Vito's youngest son, Michael. James Caan, though of German–Jewish heritage, had grown up in an Italian neighborhood of New York City, and thus brought authenticity to his role of Sonny, Don Vito's oldest son.

With the casting completed, filming began in March 1971, a full year before the film opened. *The Godfather* cost Paramount six million dollars to make, and most of it was shot on sites around New York City. Altogether, 120 locations were used in the course of the production, which was atmospherically photographed by Gordon Willis.

With filming completed, Nino Rota commenced the scoring. The choice of Rota might have been a simple one to make, in view of Coppola's desire

The Godfather, with Al Pacino.

for authenticity, since he felt that only an Italian composer could authen-ticate the truly Italianate quality.

There are three principal themes in the score, all of them in minor keys. The first has echoes of *La Strada* in its use of the solo trumpet. Set in a slow triple meter, this theme, known as the "Godfather Waltz," is first heard as the film's title is shown over a black background. Later, this melody is sounded by such other instruments as clarinet and oboe over a background of strings. One of the nicest touches is the way Rota combines two instru-ments in parallel thirds for the closing part of the theme, in which the melodic pattern climbs the scale in a stepwise manner.

The second prominent theme, a darker-colored melody, accompanies the often violent comings and goings of this Mafioso family, with the orchestral strings prominently featured. This theme almost resembles a funeral march in its steady, slow-paced rhythm. It is first heard in the scene following the gunning down of Don Vito in the streets, in which Michael arrives home from a day with his girlfriend Kay (Diane Keaton) and learns of the shooting. Soon thereafter, it is heard again when Michael enters the hospital to visit his father and senses there is something wrong. This theme, like the waltz music, returns several times, including the scene in which Michael proposes to Kay. At the end of the film, during the closing credits, it is played by strings in an emotionally stirring statement.

The third theme, identified on the soundtrack as the "Love Theme," is first heard when Michael arrives in Sicily after his dastardly killing of the New York police captain and a rival gang leader who had conspired to kill Don Vito. Michael becomes smitten with the lovely Appollonia, a cafe owner's daughter, and soon proposes marriage. As he is escorting her on a walk, chaperoned by most of her family, a mandolin can be heard in a strumming version of this poignant melody, with a guitar as the sole accompaniment. The music is heard again on Michael's wedding night. This theme later be-came a popular song, thanks to lyrics by Larry Kusik that were added after the film became a box-office hit. As "Speak Softly Love," this theme is the most recognized music associated with *The Godfather*.

Besides Nino Rota's original background themes, there are several additional pieces of music in the film. These include a number of dance tunes by Carmine Coppola that are played at the wedding reception of Michael's sister Connie (Talia Shire) and Carlo (Gianni Russo) in the movie's opening scenes. Bits of songs are also used in the film, including the familiar "Mona Lisa" and "Have Yourself a Merry Little Christmas," the not-too-well-known Irving Berlin piece "All of My Life," and the old Frank Sinatra hit "I Have but One Heart"—an appropriate choice for the singer Johnny Fontane (Al Martino), since Puzo patterned this character after Sinatra himself.

In an early scene the Corleone family's consigliere, Tom Hagen (Robert Duvall), flies to Hollywood to pressure a movie producer (John Marley) to hire Johnny Fontane for an upcoming war movie. A swing version of Louis Alter's "Manhattan Serenade" is heard in the background of this sequence.

One of the most ingenious uses of music in the film occurs during the baptism scene, in which Michael and Kay, now married, become god-parents for Connie's baby. During this sequence, which is intercut with scenes of Michael's henchmen preparing for and carrying out the killing of rival Mafia family members, there is a continuous musical background of organ music while the priest recites a series of short Latin prayers, followed by the English words of the baptismal vows. Although the music used in this scene is not limited to one single piece, most of it consists of bits of the Passacaglia in C Minor by J. S. Bach. This violent but brilliantly edited scene is one of many memorable moments in *The Godfather* that resulted in the film becoming a huge box-office hit.

In the Oscar balloting for 1972, *The Godfather*, with ten nominations, won for Best Picture, Brando won for Best Actor, and both Puzo and Coppola were awarded statues for the screenplay. When the nominations were originally announced, there was an additional eleventh citation for *The Godfather*'s original score; but in a rare instance of the weird maneuvering by members of the Motion Picture Academy, the nomination was withdrawn after it was learned that parts of Rota's score, including the love theme, had been used in a 1958 Italian film called *Fortunella*.[11] In light of other borrowed ideas used by film composers over the years, this treatment of *The Godfather*'s score seems in retrospect to have been needlessly harsh. The fact of its Oscar rejection seems even sillier in light of the subsequent awarding of the Oscar for the score of *The Godfather Part II* in 1974, in which Nino Rota incorporated much of the music written for the first film.

JERRY GOLDSMITH: *THE OTHER*. Although Thomas Tryon adapted his own novel *The Other* for the screen, the film, directed by Robert Mulligan, ultimately falls short of capturing the mysterious mood of the novel. Yet *The Other* is still a worthwhile viewing experience, thanks largely to Jerry Goldsmith's lyrical main theme, a haunting tune that is first heard during the opening credits. It is begun with the sound of whistling, and then is completed by a solo flute, with a background of strings and harp.

The story, which takes place during the summer of 1935, centers around twin brothers, Niles and Holland (played by twins Chris and Martin Udvarnoky), who live with their recently widowed mother and their grandmother on a farm in Connecticut. At first the viewer is not sure where Holland is, since it appears that Niles, with the encouragement of his grandmother, plays "the game" in order to be with his brother, who has apparently died by falling down a well. Goldsmith's theme is ingeniously used throughout the film as a signal that Holland is present. He can be heard whistling the beginning of the main theme, and in one scene he is seen playing it on his harmonica, which Niles is later seen carrying in his tin can of precious possessions. Niles just pretends to be with Holland. Unfortunately, Niles fantasizes too hard, and soon Holland becomes more than just a memory, as several people, including the boys' mother and grandmother, meet a terrible fate. The music presents a compelling argument for Niles's possession by his dead brother's spirit, with Goldsmith's haunting theme that periodically reappears as either a whistled tune or as a harmonica solo, against a lyrical string-orchestra background.

DELIVERANCE: "DUELING BANJOS." The most popular film music of 1972 comes from John Boorman's memorable version of James Dickey's novel *Deliverance*, in which four Atlanta businessmen go canoeing down a river. What starts out as a weekend adventure turns to tragedy as the four encounter a pair of sadistic mountain men.

In the first part of his book, Dickey describes a scene where Lewis, one of the four men, plays his guitar while a young albino named Lonnie tries to match Drew's notes on a banjo. As Drew attempts increasingly more complicated licks on his guitar, Lonnie keeps right up with him until the two become engaged in a furiously competitive musical number.[12] Though in the novel Dickey describes the piece Drew plays as "Wildwood Flower," in the film, which Dickey himself adapted, the music is known as "Dueling Banjos." This piece was thought to be an old folk tune until Arthur Smith, nicknamed "Guitar Boogie," after a tune he recorded in 1945, proclaimed that he was its composer.

> It was thought to be traditional, but composer/guitarist Arthur Smith said "somebody heard the tune on and off since he [sic] wrote it in 1955 and figured it was non-copyright, and just put his name on an arrangement of it for the movie."[13]

Arthur Smith recorded the tune for MGM Records in 1955 under the title "Feuding Banjos." Seven years later, this music was recorded as a duet with Marshall Brickman playing the banjo while Eric Weissberg performed the other part on an acoustic guitar. This version was included on an album entitled *Folk Blues*, which featured Weissberg, Brickman, and other members of the Tarriers. Other versions of the tune, now entitled "Dueling Banjos," emanated from the 1960s, including a recording by a bluegrass group known as the Dillards.[14]

Apparently, it was James Dickey himself who suggested to John Boorman that "Dueling Banjos" be used in the film. Dickey recommended it after hearing the tune on the radio, and subsequently Eric Weissberg was contacted for the movie's soundtrack. "They asked me if I could play that song and they wanted a guitar and a banjo, so I called Steve Mandell. . . . We went to this office and auditioned. We must have played it 25 ways—sad, slow, fast."[15] Weissberg and Mandell passed the test and were hired by the film's producers to go on location in Clayton, Georgia: "He [Boorman] wanted to shoot the scene to the music, because it was a pivotal scene in the beginning of the picture. . . . We must have recorded ten different closely related versions of the song."[16] After instructing the two actors in mimicking the moves on their instruments for two days, Weissberg and Mandell went to Atlanta, where they recorded the tune. In the film, when Lonnie (Billy Redden) and Lewis (Ronnie Cox) are seen handling the banjo and guitar, respectively, it is actually a studio performance by Weissberg and Mandell that is heard. Boorman was so delighted with the results of this scene that he invited Weissberg and Mandell to record further versions of "Dueling Banjos" to be used as background music in the film. This tune wound up being the only music featured in *Deliverance*.

After the film's debut, Warner Bros. released the Weissberg–Mandell recording as a single in January 1973. Within one month, the tune reached the Top Ten, and it claimed the number-one spot for ten weeks.[17]

SHORT CUTS ■ ■ ■ ■ John Williams. Survival is also the crux of Ronald Neame's *Poseidon Adventure*, the first in a string of disaster movies produced by the prolific Irwin Allen. Paul Gallico's story about an ocean liner capsized by a mountainous tidal wave centers on a group of survivors who must climb to the bottom of the ship in hope of being rescued. John Williams's Oscar-nominated score was dubbed at such a low level that it can barely be heard. The music consists mostly of brooding, sustained harmonies without much of a melodic profile. It is far removed from some of the grandiose scores that Williams would later compose.

Also nominated for Best Score of 1972 was Williams's singularly unusual music for Robert Altman's *Images*. This story of a woman (Susannah York), who experiences a series of traumatic events, most of which are imagined, is accompanied by one of the composer's most unique scores, with little in the way of melody, but lots of atmospheric bits of instrumental coloration.

More readily accessible than either of these scores is John Williams's rousing music for Mark Rydell's *Cowboys*, in which a rancher played by John Wayne recruits a group of schoolboys to lead a cattle drive. The score, which is often reminiscent of Williams's earlier music for Rydell's *Reivers*, consists of one principal theme, a vigorous melody that has a marchlike quality most of the time, but occasionally appears in a more subdued orchestral setting, complete with harmonica and guitar, instruments that Williams had earlier used for *The Reivers*. A bit of borrowed music occurs when one of the boys plays his guitar as they are camped under the stars. The tune he is playing comes from the second movement of a Vivaldi guitar concerto (Concerto in D Major, RV 93).

■ ■ ■ ■ **John Addison.** One of the year's best films is Joseph L. Mankiewicz's *Sleuth*, based on the play by Anthony Shaffer. John Addison received an Oscar nomination for his clever background score, which begins with a short medley of themes that accompanies the opening credits. Principal among the score's themes is a jaunty minor-key idea that features several melodic skips and a fast-paced rhythmic background. Another interesting melody is a lilting waltz for strings that represents the unseen Marguerite, wife of mystery writer Andrew Wyke (Laurence Olivier). The film's other principal theme represents Marguerite's lover, Milo Tindle (Michael Caine), who has been invited to spend an afternoon at the Wykes' country home while she is away. Milo's theme features the harpsichord in a playful tune based on a five-note pattern; from time to time this theme also features such instruments as saxophone and flute, with pizzicato strings in the background. In the course of the trick-filled scenario, Addison's score serves as an additional character, since it comments on the attempts by Andrew and Milo to outsmart each other. Although there are long stretches of *Sleuth* without background scoring, when musical commentary is apt, Addison's score makes its witty presence felt.

■ ■ ■ ■ **Richard Rodney Bennett.** One of 1972's most distinctive film scores is Richard Rodney Bennett's melancholy background for Robert Bolt's *Lady Caroline Lamb*, a colorfully produced story of the ill-fated romance of Lord Byron (Richard Chamberlain) and Lady Caroline (Sarah Miles). For Caroline there is a lyrically conceived theme for solo viola that represents her unpredictable nature, whereas the marital theme is more subdued.

■ ■ ■ ■ **Charlie Chaplin.** Charlie Chaplin's lyrical score for *Limelight* was 1972's Oscar-winning music, an unusual choice since this score had been composed twenty years earlier, when the film was originally scheduled to be released. Because of the circumstances surrounding Chaplin's departure from the United States in 1952, just as *Limelight* was being released, most theater owners refused to screen the film. As a result, the picture failed to qualify for Oscar eligibility that year. With Chaplin's triumphant return to the United States in 1972 to receive an honorary Oscar, several of his films were given theatrical showings.

Like the music for such earlier Chaplin films as *Modern Times*, *Limelight*'s music is built around one central theme, an often soaring melody that lingers in the mind long after the film has ended. The disqualification of Nino Rota's *Godfather* score opened the door for Chaplin to get a much belated recognition for his unconventional musical talent.

1973

MARVIN HAMLISCH: *THE WAY WE WERE AND THE STING*. At the Forty-Sixth Annual Academy Awards, on April 2, 1974, Marvin Hamlisch became the first composer ever to sweep all three music categories.

Born in New York City on June 2, 1944, Hamlisch demonstrated an uncanny sense of perfect pitch at the age of four by playing on the piano a tune he had just heard on the radio.[18] At age seven, he became the youngest student to be admitted to the prestigious Juilliard School in New York. Although his early training was primarily as a pianist, with several New York recitals to his credit, by the age of fourteen he decided to concentrate on composition. Hamlisch's first song "What Did You Give Santa for Christmas?" had lyrics by Howard Liebling, who later became his brother-in-law. At fifteen, Hamlisch and Liebling collaborated on the song "Sunshine, Lollipops and Rainbows," which became Hamlisch's first hit.[19]

While attending Juilliard from 1951 to 1964, Marvin received his basic education at P.S. 9 and at the Professional Children's School. He later enrolled at Queens College, where he graduated cum laude with a B.A. in music. While in college, Hamlisch was already finding regular employment as a rehearsal pianist for the "Bell Telephone Hour" and as the musical assistant and vocal arranger for two Broadway productions, *Fade Out Fade In* and *Funny Girl*.

Hamlisch's introduction to film music occurred in 1968. While playing the piano at a party for movie producer Sam Spiegel, Hamlisch learned that the producer was looking for a composer for his new film *The Swimmer*. Within a matter of days, Hamlisch composed several themes, showed them to Spiegel, and was hired to do the score. The final product was filtered through the experienced hands of arrangers Leo Shuken and Jack Hayes, with the latter conducting the score for the film's soundtrack; it became one of the year's most talked-about film scores. Hamlisch, who was still attending Queens, received permission to submit his score as a class project instead of the required string quartet.[20] Almost immediately, Hamlisch obtained more film work, including the catchy score for Woody Allen's directorial debut, *Take the Money and Run* (1969). This was followed two years later by the delightful music for Allen's *Bananas*, which includes some unique instrumentation, with a hilariously nutty conglomeration of bizarre woodwind and percussion effects.

Marvin Hamlisch.

Photo by Gay Goodwin Wallin

Hamlisch developed a working relationship with Jack Lemmon that would eventually lead to his writing scores for six films, including *The April Fools* (1969), *The War between Men and Women* (1972), and *Save the Tiger* (1973), for which Lemmon won an Oscar. Hamlisch also scored Lemmon's directorial debut, *Kotch* (1971), which starred the actor's long-time costar Walter Matthau as a septuagenarian; Hamlisch composed a melodious tune for the film, in the Henry Mancini manner, called "Life Is What You Make It," which even had lyrics by Mancini's frequent collaborator, Johnny Mercer. The song was nominated for an Academy Award, Hamlisch's first such honor.

By the time he was hired by producer Ray Stark to score Sydney Pollack's film *The Way We Were*, about the ill-fated marriage of campus radical Katie Morosky (Barbra Streisand) and college athlete and aspiring writer Hubbell Gardiner (Robert Redford), Hamlisch had already scored twelve films, plus incidental music for the 1970 Broadway musical *Minnie's Boys*, about the Marx Brothers.

In addition to the score of *The Way We Were*, Hamlisch was also assigned to compose a song for Streisand to sing. Although he was instructed to compose in a minor key, to reflect the rocky relationship of the story's two main characters, Hamlisch had other ideas: "If I'd written in a minor mode, it might have told you too much in advance . . . that Streisand and Redford were never going to get together. So, I wrote a melody that was sad, but also had a great deal of hope in it."[21]

Since *The Way We Were* was planned as a straight dramatic film and not as a musical, Streisand did not want to sing the song in the film. Besides, when she first heard the song, she felt it was too simple for her type of voice; Hamlisch and the entire cast and crew urged her to do it.[22] After Streisand relented and recorded the song, it was used over the opening credits, during the film's closing scene, and it also figures prominently in the background score as the theme for the stormy romance.

The Way We Were became one of the biggest box-office successes of the year, thanks to the popularity of the title song, which was released as a single by Columbia Records in November 1973 and was rated the top hit of 1974. Two albums were released with Streisand's version of the song. One of these, the official soundtrack album, became quite popular; it also included Hamlisch's instrumental arrangements of the title tune as well as other bits of his original score.

The Sting, with Robert Shaw and Paul Newman.

The Sting, released in 1973, reunited Paul Newman and Robert Redford with George Roy Hill, the director of *Butch Cassidy and the Sundance Kid*. Within weeks, *The Sting* began setting box-office records. It won seven Oscars, including one for Best Picture, another for Hill, and a third for Hamlisch's arrangements of ragtime pieces by Scott Joplin.

Although David Ward set his script in the 1930s instead of at the turn of the century, when the ragtime craze was at its peak, Hill thought the ragtime sound would contribute just the right flavor to the story of two con artists who construct an elaborate scam to fleece a powerful New York racketeer, whose men have killed a close friend of Johnny Hooker (Redford). Hooker enlists the aid of Henry Gondorff (Newman) in setting up a complicated betting operation, to get Doyle Lonnegan (Robert Shaw) to unload a half-million-dollar bet and then swindle him out of his money.

The Sting is often credited for the 1970s ragtime revival, but actually, the revival was already ongoing when the film went into production. George Roy Hill, himself a trained musician, discovered rags in 1972 after hearing one of his sons play Scott Joplin recordings.[23] *The Sting* was in production at the time, and as Hill directed the scenes, he heard Joplin's music in his head. He even constructed montages where the ragtime tunes were used to give the film a lighthearted and nostalgic flavor.

Hamlisch had worked as a rehearsal pianist for a Broadway musical that Hill had directed. Not only did Hamlisch wind up as pianist for the film, but he also arranged some of Joplin's music for a small ragtime ensemble, patterned after the type of group for which Joplin himself had arranged some of his own music.

Three Joplin pieces in the film were arranged by Hamlisch: "Solace," "Gladiolus Rag," and "Pineapple Rag." Hamlisch also performed "The Entertainer" and "Solace" as piano solos for the movie's soundtrack. Additional arrangements by Gunther Schuller, which had already been recorded with the New England Ragtime Ensemble, were used for the film. These include "The Entertainer," "Easy Winners," "Pineapple Rag," and "Ragtime Dance." Besides all the borrowed Joplin tunes, there is some original music in *The Sting* that Hamlisch composed from scratch; three tracks on the soundtrack album are credited to Hamlisch. The Oscar citation, in the category of "Original Song Score and/or Adaptation," seems odd since Hamlisch relied as much on Schuller's arrangements as on his own. Even before Hamlisch won his three Oscars, his recording of "The Entertainer" was released as a single, with electrifying record sales.

JERRY GOLDSMITH: *PAPILLON*. For Franklin J. Schaffner's film version of *Papillon*, based on a book by Henri Charriere about the author's adventures as an escaped convict, the lyrical score was composed by Jerry Goldsmith. It was later revealed that Charriere had invented some incidents to flesh out the details of his life. The film's screenplay further fictionalized his story by augmenting the role of Louis Dega, a fellow prisoner on Devil's Island. With Steve McQueen as Charriere, whose chest tattoo of a butterfly gave him the nickname "Papillon" (French for "butterfly"), and with Dustin Hoffman as Louis, this grim film has stunning performances.

Music is barely present until the second half of the film. After the opening credits, which contain no music at all, the film follows the day-to-day life of Papillon as a prisoner in a French penal colony. As he, Louis, and a third prisoner escape in a small boat, Goldsmith's score begins in earnest, with some surging music. The three arrive on Honduras, and the music becomes turbulent as they are chased by hostile soldiers. Papillon eludes his pursuers and is given shelter by members of an Indian tribe; the score becomes much more romantic as he becomes involved with a young tribal woman.

Periodically through the latter stages of the film there is a single recurrent theme, a melancholy waltz tune that features accordion, flute, and strings, often with a harpsichord used as harmonic background. This lyrical theme, one of Goldsmith's most haunting melodies, adds an emotional quality that would otherwise be sorely lacking in the film.

BY BORROWING POSSESSED: *THE EXORCIST*. The year's most talked-about film, William Friedkin's *Exorcist*, created a box-office sensation when it arrived at the end of December 1973. With a screenplay by William Peter Blatty, who adapted his own runaway bestseller, this film about demonic possession inspired many lurid horror films. The story concerns Regan MacNeil (Linda Blair), an adolescent girl in Washington, D.C., whose bizarre behavior leads her mother (Ellen Burstyn) to conclude that she has indeed been possessed by the Devil.

Friedkin had originally considered commissioning an original score from Bernard Herrmann, but Herrmann apparently found the story distasteful and declined. The music that wound up in the film is a pastiche of previously recorded music in the manner that Stanley Kubrick had already demonstrated in such films as *2001: A Space Odyssey* and *A Clockwork Orange*.

According to the closing credits, among the musical works that Friedkin borrowed for *The Exorcist* are some avant-garde pieces by Krzystof Penderecki, Hans Werner Henze, George Crumb, and Anton Webern, plus pieces by Mike Oldfield and David Borden, and by a group called Beginnings. Five different works by Penderecki are cited, while David Borden is listed for Study No. 1 and Study No. 2; only single titles are included for each of the remaining composers. There is also a listing for film composer Jack Nitzsche (b. 1937), who is credited with "Additional Music."

The most remarkable thing about all of these musical borrowings is that, with one single exception, none of them are featured very extensively in the actual film. Friedkin envisioned an aural concept in which the sounds of Regan's satanic voice (provided by Mercedes McCambridge) should be given plenty of volume, along with sound effects for Regan's shaking bed and various crashing sounds. In stark contrast with the loudness of the scenes in Regan's bedroom, the rest of the film is amazingly quiet. When music is present at all, it is usually for only a few seconds at a time.

The only piece allowed much soundtrack time in this visually powerful film is "Tubular Bells," which emanates from an album released earlier that year in which English musician Mike Oldfield (b. 1953) put on a one-man show featuring the overdubbing of eighty separate instrumental tracks on more than two dozen instruments.[24] Friedkin extracted a short excerpt of Oldfield's original composition and patched it into the film's soundtrack as a recurring musical motif. In its original version, the Oldfield album became one of 1973's biggest hits, but after the release of *The Exorcist*, the movie version of "Tubular Bells" became an even greater success when released as a single in early 1974.

SHORT CUTS ■■■■ *American Graffiti.* In addition to *The Exorcist*, many of 1973's movies include almost no original music. George Lucas's nostalgic *American Graffiti*, which includes a vivid reenactment of the midsummer rites of teenagers cruising the main streets of a northern California town in the early 1960s, includes a soundtrack based on the popular songs of the era. The music in the film is heard on car radios, as the characters in the story, played by such future stars as Richard Dreyfuss and Harrison Ford, spend most of their time in their souped-up automobiles. Forty-one hit songs of the 1950s and '60s were included in the film, beginning with the rock-'n'-roll anthem "Rock around the Clock," in the classic recording by Bill Haley and the Comets, and followed by a host of other rock classics. A double-record album was released in August 1973; it became one of the best-selling recordings of the year.[25]

■■■■ **Bernard Herrmann.** In *Sisters*, Brian De Palma devised a chilling tale of Siamese twins who undergo surgical separation, in the course of which one dies. The surviving twin, Danielle (Margot Kidder), becomes schizophrenic and takes murderous revenge on both her unfortunate sister's lover and the doctor who performed the surgery. Herrmann's music, which conveys some echoes of his famous Hitchcock scores for *Psycho* and *Vertigo*, uses repeated ostinato figures and growling low string and woodwind sonorities. A four-note French horn motif opens the title music, which contains some chilling sounds provided by a synthesizer. The murder scenes contain various truly frightening musical sounds; at other times, the score has a more subdued quality.

RICHARD RODNEY BENNETT: *MURDER ON THE ORIENT EXPRESS*. When the production team of John Brabourne and Richard Goodwin filmed Agatha Christie's *Murder on the Orient Express*, no expense was spared in adapting this story for the screen, with exotic locales, elaborate period costuming, and an international cast of over a dozen renowned actors. The role of Hercule Poirot went to Albert Finney, who put on a great deal of makeup and a thick French accent in order to portray the finicky Belgian detective. With an intriguing plot dealing with a murder that takes place while the Orient Express is stopped because of an avalanche, the film became one of the most acclaimed of the year and a major box-office hit. The score is the work of Richard Rodney Bennett.

Bennett, who was born in England in 1936, went to Paris in 1957 to become a student of renowned French composer and conductor Pierre Boulez.[26] Through Boulez's influence, Bennett expressed his preference for a musical style that incorporates the new serial techniques of Schoenberg, while not abandoning centuries of harmonic tradition. He also scored his first films during this period, the most distinguished of which were Stanley Donen's *Indiscreet* (1958), a sophisticated romantic comedy with Cary Grant and Ingrid Bergman, and Guy Hamilton's *Devil's Disciple* (1959), a handsomely produced adaptation of the George Bernard Shaw play. *Indiscreet*, on which Bennett shares billing with Kenneth V. Jones as co-composer, has a charming main theme built on a four-note motif that moves only by semitones. Although this theme is tuneful and decidedly tonal in its harmony, it indicates Bennett's interest in exploring the complete range of chromatic tones within the octave.

Following his Paris studies, he became increasingly involved in composing music for the opera house and concert hall. Bennett received international recognition for his film music, thanks to the acclaimed 1967 John Schlesinger film *Far from the Madding Crowd*, for which Bennett received his first Oscar nomination. In the wake of these successes, Bennett, like Miklos Rozsa, continued to divide his creative time between symphonic works and background music for the movies. By the time Bennett was hired for *Murder on the Orient Express*, he had already scored over two dozen movies and had been Oscar-nominated twice.

To evoke the period of *Murder on the Orient Express*, which is set for the most part in 1935, Bennett created a nostalgia-flavored main theme with the sound of a high-society orchestra playing a love ballad. This theme is first heard during the opening credits; a dramatic fanfare for full orchestra leads directly into the theme, which features a solo piano accompanied by strings. This tuneful piece recurs several times during the course of the film.

A second prominent theme represents the train itself. Cinematographer Geoffrey Unsworth brilliantly captures the moment when the Orient Express, with all passengers aboard, is being readied for its departure from the Istanbul station. As the camera closes in on the front of the engine, a spotlight is suddenly turned on, and the engine is bathed in light, accompanied by a brilliantly orchestrated chord that is filled with sounds of bells and tremolo strings. This leads directly to the train theme, which begins slowly

Murder on the Orient Express,
with Albert Finney
(as Hercule Poirot)
interrogating the
occupants of the train car.

when the train begins to move; as the train accelerates, so does the music. The theme itself is a charming waltz; its lilting idea for strings is heard in counterpoint against a contrasting melodic pattern featuring a solo French horn. At the film's conclusion these two principal themes appear simultaneously, with one juxtaposed over the other.

Following the opening credits, a montage sequence is presented, in which we learn of the kidnapping and killing of a small girl in the year 1930. The facts of the case are presented in a series of newspaper headlines, with Bennett's music providing a sinister and foreboding sound in the background. Although it is not clear until the conclusion of the film how this murder ties in with the killing of the American businessman Mr. Ratchett (Richard Widmark), which occurs while the train is en route, there are musical parallels between the opening montage and later scenes that involve the discovery of Ratchett's body and Poirot's subsequent investigation. The eeriness of Bennett's murder music is in stark contrast with the romanticism of his two principal themes.

This is an utterly charming score, one that holds the viewer's attention during some stretches where the film has little or no dialogue. Bennett received his third Oscar nomination for this score.

FRANCIS FORD COPPOLA FILMS. In 1974, Francis Ford Coppola directed two of the five Oscar-nominated films. *The Conversation,* which won that year's Palme d'Or at the Cannes Film Festival, is an intriguing film concerning a surveillance expert (Gene Hackman) who gets too involved in a case. The periodic saxophone playing by this character features a catchy jazz tune by David Shire (b. 1937).

Coppola's other 1974 effort is the Oscar-winning film *The Godfather Part II.* With sequel fever running rampant during the 1970s, almost every popular film begat some sort of follow-up. However, *The Godfather Part II* is that rarest of rarities: a film that is even better than its predecessor.

Split between scenes of the young Don Vito coming to the United States from Sicily and scenes of Michael continuing in his father's Mafia-boss footsteps, this film is extraordinarily complex but stylistically rich, with many unforgettable scenes. Nino Rota reprised some of his themes from the first film and added several new ones, with the help of Carmine Coppola. Ironically, there are more borrowings from the previous film than there were in *The Godfather*'s music, but this time the Academy members didn't object. Rota and the senior Coppola both collected Oscars.

SHORT CUTS ■ ■ ■ ■ **Jerry Goldsmith.** Among 1974's praiseworthy scores is Jerry Goldsmith's moody background for Roman Polanski's *Chinatown*, a richly textured period melodrama set in Los Angeles during the late 1930s. The slow-moving trumpet theme provides a romantic backdrop for this dark tale of corruption and moral decay, which features a classic performance by Jack Nicholson as private detective J. J. Gittes.

■ ■ ■ ■ **Michel Legrand.** In keeping with the breakneck speed and acrobatic nature of the action in Richard Lester's *Three Musketeers*, Michel Legrand produced a lively score. Following the dramatic main-title theme, featuring pounding drums and repeated brass chords, there are several supremely melodic moments in the score. Chief among these is the marchlike theme associated with the rambunctious D'Artagnan (Michael York); this idea, which prominently features trumpets and other brass instruments, is heard quite prominently in one of the film's many dueling scenes, in which D'Artagnan and the three Musketeers fight a group of soldiers in a laundry. As the skirmish continues, Legrand's music maintains a furiously fast pace, with swirling strings added above the brass melody.

■ ■ ■ ■ **Nelson Riddle.** Another period piece with notable music is Jack Clayton's elaborate version of F. Scott Fitzgerald's *Great Gatsby*. Nelson Riddle, whose orchestral arrangements effectively backed up Frank Sinatra, Nat "King" Cole and others during the 1950s, when they were all under contract to Capitol Records, put together an effective collage of songs from the 1920s for this film, with Irving Berlin's "What'll I Do" serving as the primary melodic ingredient. Additionally, there are two Charleston numbers, for party scenes at the Gatsby estate, where the guests dance with unbridled fervor. Riddle's arrangements, which won him a well-deserved Oscar, added a much-needed spark to this long and rather uninvolving film.

■ ■ ■ ■ **Henry Mancini.** One of Henry Mancini's supreme achievements as a film composer comes from 1974, with Philip Kaufman's grim but fascinating *White Dawn*, based on the true story of three sailors who are shipwrecked in northern Canada, and are rescued by an Eskimo tribe that lives on Baffin Island. As the three adapt to the ways of the natives, Mancini's music makes up for the sparseness of dialogue by maintaining a lyrical mood that elevates the story until its downbeat conclusion, when the superstitious natives kill all three sailors.

A lullaby, sung in the film by a native woman, was recorded on location and used by Mancini for scenes in which the Eskimos and their three guests are hunting for food. Although the melody is not by Mancini himself, his ingenious orchestral arrangements of this tune provide some of the most memorable musical moments of the year.

■■■■ **John Williams.** For *The Sugarland Express*, Steven Spielberg's first film, John Williams created a fetching theme for solo harmonica that was recorded for the soundtrack by the renowned Dutch artist Toots Thielemans. For the big-budget disaster film *The Towering Inferno* Williams created a soaring main theme whose melody has upward-reaching leaps that evoke the awesome height of the office building where most of the film's story takes place.

■■■■ **John Morris.** A pair of crazy comedy films by Mel Brooks left audiences in stitches during 1974. Both *Blazing Saddles*, an often hilarious parody of old Westerns, and *Young Frankenstein*, a deliriously goofy takeoff on the old Universal horror films, were scored by John Morris (b. 1926). Of the two, *Saddles* is by far the raunchier; the loud and raucous title song, in which Morris tried to satirize Western ballads from the 1950s, is sung in the film by Frankie Laine. In *Young Frankenstein*, by contrast, Morris's solo violin theme, which recurs throughout the film, is a lovely piece of music that creates a romantic atmosphere to counteract the silliness of Gene Wilder and Marty Feldman, who camp things up mightily as Dr. Frankenstein and his assistant Igor.

■■■■ **Miklos Rozsa.** The heroic music for *The Golden Voyage of Sinbad* represents a welcome return to film scoring for Miklos Rozsa, who spent the three previous years away from the medium. His colorful *Sinbad* score also marks a return to the realm of fantasy films with which he had been associated during the early 1940s. There are several noteworthy features in Rozsa's score, which begins with a dramatic brass fanfare that gradually builds to a brilliant proclamation by trumpets and cymbals. This leads directly to the score's main theme, a soaringly romantic idea built on a six-note motif that is principally sounded by strings. Several dramatic secondary themes appear in the score as Sinbad (John Phillip Law) encounters a number of fantastic adversaries, including a six-armed statue that is magically brought to life by an evil wizard (Tom Baker).

Although this *Sinbad* suffers by comparison with such earlier adventure films as *The Seventh Voyage of Sinbad*, Rozsa's brilliantly orchestrated music greatly enhances the stop-motion visual effects of Ray Harryhausen. No other composer in the 1970s demonstrated as artistically as Miklos Rozsa the grandiose sounds that had played such a prominent role in film music during Hollywood's Golden Age.

DAVID SHIRE: *FAREWELL, MY LOVELY* AND *THE HINDENBURG.* A composer whose works have not received the attention that they deserve is David Shire, who to date has composed more than eighty film scores, including more than forty for made-for-TV movies and miniseries. He has also composed significantly for theatrical features, including scores for two 1975 films that contain some of his most accomplished work. Neither *Farewell, My Lovely* nor *The Hindenburg* was a box-office blockbuster, despite the presence in both of some of Hollywood's big-name stars and some elaborate production values. Both of these films and their scores are worth a closer look, as is the career of this gifted composer.

Photo by Gay Goodwin Wallin

David Shire.

Born in Buffalo in 1937, Shire is the older of the two sons of Irving Daniel Shire, who was the leader of a society dance band and was also a pianist and piano teacher. David Shire remembers that, while attending Buffalo's public schools between 1942 and 1955, he was "saturated in the sounds of Gershwin, Kern, Rodgers, and Cole Porter."[27]

Although Shire's formal training at the piano began in 1944 with a concentration on classical music, he learned how to play popular songs on the keyboard from his father. While still in high school, Shire took lessons in theory and composition with Stanley King. He also played in his father's band at weddings and parties, and worked as a cocktail pianist at Buffalo hotels. He even formed a combo that performed at high school dances. After graduating in 1955 from the Nichols School, Shire enrolled at Yale, where he first majored in English but soon switched to music. While making spending money by forming a progressive jazz group that played at various eastern colleges, he also found time to collaborate with classmate Richard Maltby, Jr., on the composition of college musicals. From one of these productions, a musical version of *Cyrano de Bergerac*, comes the song "Autumn," which Barbra Streisand included on her album *People*, recorded in 1964 while she starred on Broadway in *Funny Girl*.

Shire eventually moved to New York, where he earned a living by playing the piano, accompanying and coaching singers, and arranging and conducting. He became involved with various Off-Broadway musicals, including *The Fantasticks*, for which he spent a year as pianist, and *The Sap of Life* (1961), for which he composed the songs. His connection with Streisand formally began when he played as the pit pianist for *Funny Girl* from 1964 to 1966. During that time he also served on a part-time basis as assistant conductor for the show.

Shire's first background score was written for "The Final War of Ollie Winter," which was broadcast as a dramatic special on CBS.[28] He worked with Barbra Streisand again as assistant musical director and arranger for two of her TV specials, "Color Me Barbra" and "Belle of 14th Street." These experiences led to his becoming a composer for two TV series, "The Virginian" and "McCloud." He also composed the score for the two-hour TV movie *McCloud: Who Killed Miss USA?*, which launched the series, starring Dennis Weaver, in the fall of 1970.

By the end of the 1960s, Shire had already gotten a taste of writing film music. His first assignments were as the composer of songs, on which he worked with his college chum, Richard Maltby. He was lucky in that his first film song, the title tune of *I'd Rather Be Rich*, was not only sung by Robert Goulet and Andy Williams in the film, but was recorded by Williams and also by Pearl Bailey. Shire collaborated with Maltby on a pair of Broadway musicals, *How Do You Do, I Love You* (1968) and *Love Match* (1970); he also composed incidental music for Peter Ustinov's play *The Unknown Soldier and His Wife* (1967).

By lucky chance, when Shire was in Los Angeles in 1970 to supervise the pre-Broadway tryout of *Love Match*, he was introduced to Stanley Wilson, head of Universal's music department. Wilson, who apparently had already heard some of the music Shire had written for TV, signed him as a contract composer at Universal Studios. Shire's first motion picture score was for Andrew V. McLaglen's *One More Train to Rob* (1971), a

Western that starred George Peppard. By the time Francis Ford Coppola hired him to score *The Conversation* in 1974, Shire had already scored twenty films, nine of which were theatrical releases.

Next came Shire's most important score to date, the rhythmically charged backgrounds for Joseph Sargent's exciting thriller *The Taking of Pelham One Two Three*. Melodically, this is one of the few film scores ever to make use of the twelve-tone row concept of Arnold Schoenberg. The main theme, which consists of the basic row divided into four groups of three tones, is accompanied by a hard-driving rhythmic ostinato that involves two tones that are repeated over and over.[29] *Pelham's* score provides a tense musical atmosphere for this compelling film.

For Philip Marlowe fans, the 1975 version of Raymond Chandler's *Farewell, My Lovely* is a visual treat, with a painstakingly realistic recreation of Los Angeles in the 1940s. As an added bonus, Robert Mitchum seems perfectly cast in the lead role. When Marlowe proclaims that he's tired of all of the chasing around that goes with the job of being a private eye, one can sense the fatigue in his voice.

David Shire's score is a bluesy confection, with a hauntingly memorable main theme that features solos on the trombone and alto sax. This slow-paced music, with the smooth sounds of its melodic solos, provides an atmospheric background for the film, which can be regarded as one of the best adaptations of a Chandler work to reach the screen.

Farewell, My Lovely,
with Robert Mitchum.

The Hindenburg was a dramatic misfire that abused its promising source material, the nonfiction book by Michael M. Mooney, who speculated that the 1937 explosion of the Hindenburg might have been caused by a bomb planted on the airship by one of the German crew members. Although the film uses this theory as its basic premise, screenwriter Nelson Gidding has fleshed out the story with a highly fictional script that lacks the book's historical credibility.

After an opening newsreel about the famous airship, the film's credits are superimposed over a series of colorful shots of the Hindenburg floating amid the clouds, accompanied by Shire's main theme, a soaring idea that features a solo trumpet and strings. A quickly paced six-note figure in the woodwinds frequently occurs as a rhythmic and melodic counterpoint to the main idea. As the orchestration builds up, the title music achieves a sense of noble eloquence.

Elsewhere in the film, a nervous melodic idea that features pairs of semitones accompanies scenes in which various American and German diplomats attempt to prevent an act of sabotage aboard the airship. In addition to the instrumental score, a catchy song entitled "There's a Lot to Be Said for the Fuhrer" is featured in a scene in which two passengers (played by Peter Donat and Robert Clary) provide entertainment aboard the ship.

Music is almost totally absent from the climactic scene, in which the ship explodes and comes crashing down to the ground. Following this tragic moment, which is shown in black and white, the film returns to color for the closing scene, in which the airship is again seen in its once-proud state, while Chicago newsman Herb Morrison's famous radio broadcast of the disaster is heard. Shire's main theme returns, with the trumpet again sounding the soaring tones of the melodic line, while the film's closing credits are shown. David Shire's dramatically inspired score remains one of the few memorable aspects of this formulaic disaster film.

JOHN WILLIAMS: JAWS. Steven Spielberg's *Jaws*, with an Oscar-winning score by John Williams, became the first movie to gross over 100 million dollars.[30]

Several factors may be cited for the success of this film. Peter Benchley's suspenseful book *Jaws* was a huge best-seller; Benchley subsequently coauthored the screenplay with Carl Gottlieb. The aggressive producing team of Richard Zanuck and David Brown clearly targeted the mass audience by launching a huge advertising campaign. *Jaws* became the first film to open in wide release, with showings on more than four hundred screens. An outstanding trio of actors were cast as the men who battle the deadly shark. Roy Scheider was altogether convincing as the local sheriff who hates the water but goes out into the deep anyway. Robert Shaw, as the elder fisherman, gave one of his typically colorful portrayals. As the young ichthyologist, Richard Dreyfuss, appearing in an early leading role, dominated practically every scene he was in. Additionally, director Steven Spielberg and editor Verna Fields helped to mold this film.

To create an undertone of suspense, John Williams used the now-famous two-note motif that features an ascending semitone. This pattern begins almost inaudibly in the lowest sounding instruments of the orchestra, and

Jaws, with Roy Scheider, Robert Shaw, and Richard Dreyfuss.

slowly grows in volume until it becomes part of a rhythmically driven ostinato pattern, upon which various melodic lines are juxtaposed. The end result is a main theme that conveys both excitement and danger. Throughout the film, the two-note motif is used as an early warning of the shark's appearances. In one scene, where some kids try to scare a crowd of swimmers into believing that the shark is nearby, the two-note idea is not used; but moments later, when this foolish prank turns into the real thing, the motif makes its presence felt.

For the scene in which tourists arrive on Amity Island, Williams used a Baroque-style piece in a lighthearted mood that is in striking contrast with the rest of the score. For the scenes at sea in which the three hunters search for their monstrous prey, the music becomes aggressively dramatic.

Perhaps Williams engages the viewer's attention by using a hodgepodge of musical styles, but this approach is undeniably effective. No one who has ever seen *Jaws* is likely to forget its music.

JACK NITZSCHE: ONE FLEW OVER THE CUCKOO'S NEST. Jack
Nitzsche wrote an unusual score for Milos Forman's Oscar-winning adaptation of Ken Kesey's *One Flew over the Cuckoo's Nest*. Two original musical themes dominate this film. This idea is set in a mental hospital located in the Pacific Northwest. The first is an oddly orchestrated tune that includes the sounds of a musical saw, which is heard as main-title music and also as the theme for the supposedly catatonic Indian, Chief Bromden (Will Sampson), who befriends McMurphy (Jack Nicholson), a newly arrived inmate in the all-male ward that is overseen by Nurse Ratched (Louise Fletcher). The other significant Nitzsche tune is a sweet-sounding piece entitled "Medication Waltz," which accompanies scenes of the patients stepping up to a counter to receive their daily dosages. The soothing strains of the synthesized string arrangement of this lilting melody appropriately act as a musical sedative.

One other piece of music that is heard prominently in *Cuckoo's Nest* is the 1920s film theme "Charmaine," which is used as source music. A muzak-style recording of the piece is played by the nurses to provide a relaxed atmosphere in the ward. The inclusion of this tune provokes more irritation than enjoyment because the viewer is led to reject this sedative effect as an attempt by Nurse Ratched to manipulate the men's behavior.

The film's closing scene is also its most memorable musical moment, as Chief Bromden rips a huge water basin off of its pedestal and smashes it through a wall. As he breaks free of his incarceration and runs across a field, the music includes rhythmic instruments to convey an Indian effect, while the score's main theme builds up to a triumphant statement.

Cuckoo's Nest emerged as the most critically acclaimed film of 1975 and went on to accomplish a rare sweep of the Academy Awards, with the film, the director, and Nicholson and Fletcher all winning Oscars. Jack Nitzsche received a nomination for his music but lost out to John Williams for his celebrated score for *Jaws*.

SHORT CUTS ■ ■ ■ ■ Jerry Goldsmith. Among the best film scores
of 1975 is Jerry Goldsmith's dramatic tour de force on behalf of John Milius's *Wind and the Lion*, a highly fictionalized account of an actual incident that took place in Morocco during the Theodore Roosevelt administration. The film stars Sean Connery as the Raisuli, a Berber chieftain who

kidnaps an American widow (Candace Bergen) and her small son. This act sets off an international incident in which Roosevelt (Brian Keith) becomes involved. There is an inevitable hint of romance between the captor and his beautiful captive, which is made all the more potent by one of Goldsmith's most rapturous love themes. The score is largely built on two principal themes. The first is an opening fanfarelike idea that alternates between the first and fifth tones of the scale. The heroic main theme also employs a rising fifth as part of its soaring melodic line. With its energetic musical backgrounds *The Wind and the Lion* earned for Goldsmith a richly deserved Oscar nomination.

■ ■ ■ ■ **Alex North.** Alex North's Oscar-nominated music for Richard Brooks's *Bite the Bullet*, a rousing film about a 700-mile horse race set in the American West during the first decade of the twentieth century, is typical of his later works: bits of jaunty melodic material are featured in a very original orchestration, with lots of brass and percussion. North's primary melodic motif consists of a three-note idea that includes an ascending fifth, as in the pattern C–G–G. His music incorporates bits of two old songs about horses, "Goodbye, Old Paint" and "Camptown Races," the latter of which is used in an extremely boisterous manner as the contestants move into the final stages of the race.

■ ■ ■ ■ **Leonard Rosenman.** In Stanley Kubrick's visually brilliant adaptation of William Thackeray's *Barry Lyndon*, composer Leonard Rosenman based most of the score on borrowed thematic materials, including the saraband movement from the Suite in D Minor by Handel, originally written for harpsichord. In addition to this music, which is heard during the opening credits and in several later sequences, Rosenman included pieces by Mozart, Schubert, Vivaldi, Paisiello, and J. S. Bach. The minor-key tonality of Handel's saraband is especially significant, since it casts an air of melancholy over the film as it details the rise and fall of Lyndon (Ryan O'Neal), an opportunistic rogue who climbs the social ladder but falls back down at the end.

There is also some traditional English and Irish music in the film. The tune "British Grenadiers," for instance, is used for one of the scenes in which Barry is marching into battle. The Chieftains, a celebrated Irish folk-music ensemble, was also enlisted to perform some of the Irish tunes in the film, including a few composed by Sian O Riada. Rosenman received an Oscar for his arrangements, which work well within the context of this film. He even added a few moments of original scoring, but they take a back seat to the use of borrowed materials.

BERNARD HERRMANN: REQUIEM FOR A MUSICAL HEAVYWEIGHT. The year 1975 ended with the sad news of the sudden death of Bernard Herrmann on December 24, hours after he completed the recording sessions for Martin Scorsese's *Taxi Driver*. Three months prior to his work on *Taxi Driver*, Herrmann completed a brilliant score for Brian De Palma's *Obsession*. Columbia allowed the film to sit on the shelf for a year until they could figure out a way to market it properly.

Thus, as 1976 began, the last two films with Bernard Herrmann's music were eagerly anticipated by the many fans who mourned the loss of this most ingenious of film composers. When these films did emerge, few serious devotees of film music were disappointed with the results of Herrmann's last efforts.

In *Obsession*, which owes a great deal to Hitchcock's *Vertigo*, a New Orleans businessman, Michael Courtland (Cliff Robertson), mourns the loss of his wife (Genevieve Bujold) and daughter, Amy, who have been abducted and then are supposedly killed in a tragically bungled police ploy to catch the kidnappers. Sixteen years later, he becomes obsessed with a young woman (Genevieve Bujold, again) who strongly resembles his late wife. He learns that she is actually Amy, and that she has been deceived by his business partner, LaSalle (John Lithgow), who had engineered the kidnapping as part of a plot to swindle him. Michael kills LaSalle in self-defense and he and Amy are tearfully reunited.

Herrmann suggested to De Palma the intercutting device that is seen during the opening credits: shots of the church in Florence where Michael had first met his wife alternate with a series of old family photos. The music for these recurring shots alternates between repeated pairs of ominous brass chords accompanied by pipe organ and softer music provided by the distant sounds of voices and harp. The latter music creates a sighing effect through the use of one of the score's principal motifs, a melodically descending two-note pattern.[31]

In the opening scene Herrmann's score includes a romantic waltz theme for the moment when Michael dances with his wife, while also holding their young daughter in his arms. In the scenes following the abduction, Michael is seen delivering the ransom money to a prearranged location. As he boards a ferry, the music features the score's third principal theme, in which a rhythmically driven brass figure (in dotted rhythm) accompanies the organ, heard in a melodically descending idea.

All these thematic elements play significant roles in the film; the two-note idea of the opening credits is particularly important, but the other two ideas also return in a meaningful way. Late in the film a second abduction apparently occurs, and Michael has to employ the same means for delivering the ransom money that he had utilized earlier. But this second sequence is condensed in time, and the music, which also features the earlier rhythmic idea, is set in a slightly faster pace than before.

In the closing scene at the airport, in which Michael and Sondra are reunited, the waltz music from the opening scene is heard again, but this time, instead of the actors spinning around the room, now they are standing still, with the camera creating the idea of waltzlike movement. As we see the two seemingly engaged in a dizzying circular dance, it is actually the inventive camerawork of cinematographer Vilmos Zsigmond that creates the waltzing effect.

If *Obsession* is a fitting valedictory to Herrmann's film music career, the score of *Taxi Driver* stands only slightly below that level. This film, devised by Paul Schrader from his own experiences as a cab driver in Detroit while suffering from both depression and insomnia, is a bleak portrait of urban life. The protagonist, Travis Bickle (Robert De Niro), is an ex-marine who has difficulty sleeping. He takes a night shift as a cab driver in New York City, hoping that this job will help burn off the anxiety that is building up inside him. Instead, the work only exacerbates the problem. We hear Travis's voice as he records in his daily journal his thoughts about the squalid conditions that he sees, the amoral behavior of his customers, and his gradually

Taxi Driver, with Robert De Niro.

increased sense of frustration and rage. We watch with intended discomfiture as he buys an armory of weapons and seeks out a victim. When Travis is rejected in his efforts to establish a romantic relationship with Betsy (Cybill Shepherd), who works in the campaign headquarters of a presidential candidate, he directs his rage at the candidate and plans to assassinate him. When that fails, Travis next turns on the pimp (Harvey Keitel) who controls the teenaged Iris (Jody Foster), whom Travis has befriended. In a horrific bloodbath, Travis kills not only the pimp but several others; in the process he is wounded. In a wild twist of fate, Travis not only survives but becomes a much-publicized hero for rescuing Iris. The film ends with the unsettling feeling that Travis might again go over the edge.

Instead of the gloriously orchestrated symphonic score that accompanies *Obsession*, the music of *Taxi Driver* is primarily influenced by jazz. The principal theme features an alto sax in a lyrical but melancholy blues tune that recurs periodically as Travis drives around; it appears prominently when he first sees Betsy inside the campaign office. Apparently, Herrmann was not comfortable with the jazz idiom that Scorsese wanted for the score. Christopher Palmer, acting as Herrmann's assistant, was instructed by the composer to find a suitable theme that could be adapted. Palmer chose a tune from a score that Herrmann had written for the English stage. Thus, the first four bars of "As the Wind Bloweth," from *The King of Schnorrers*, became the first segment of the *Taxi Driver* theme.[32]

The film's opening music, heard during the credits, is a two-note melodic idea heard over sustained chords with a percussive accompaniment. This theme, which increases in volume as drums and cymbals repeatedly sound, suggests the anger that eventually drives Travis to the brink of madness.

One can find fault with certain aspects of Herrmann's orchestration, especially in the latter stages of the film, where heavy rumbles on timpani, together with repeated glissandos on the harp, rather blatantly underscore Travis's disintegrating mental condition. But *Taxi Driver*'s music contains a hauntingly memorable theme, with its lyrical saxophone melody that accompanies Travis's nocturnal odyssey-turned-nightmare.

Almost fourteen months after Herrmann's death, he became the first film composer in the history of the Oscars to be posthumously nominated twice in the same year. The twin citations for 1976's *Obsession* and *Taxi Driver* represent the only scores by Herrmann to receive nominations since *Anna and the King of Siam* in 1946. He received only three other nominations—for his first two scores, *Citizen Kane* and *The Devil and Daniel Webster* (which won for him his only Oscar), and for *The Magnificent Ambersons*. Where were the votes for the Hitchcock scores and the Charles

Schneer–Ray Harryhausen fantasy films? And what about such classics as the scores for *The Ghost and Mrs. Muir* and *Fahrenheit 451*?

When Herrmann died at the age of sixty-four, his career was in turn-around, following his discovery by Brian De Palma, Larry Cohen, and Martin Scorsese. He was scheduled to score two other films—De Palma's *Carrie* and Herbert Ross's *Seven-Per-Cent Solution*. The fifty film scores Herrmann did complete stand as the legacy of a temperamental genius whose works continue to inspire film composers working today.

IN **HERRMANN'S WAKE.** The two films scheduled to be scored by Bernard Herrmann before his untimely death contain notable music by other composers. Brian De Palma hired Italian composer Pino Donaggio (b. 1941) for *Carrie*, the first film adaptation of a Stephen King novel. Donaggio, who had previously composed an eerie score for Nicholas Roeg's bizarre thriller *Don't Look Now* (1974), carried on in a Herrmannesque manner by creating a main theme that has a lullaby quality, whereas the final scenes of mayhem have much more melodramatic background music.

Herbert Ross's colorful film *The Seven-Per-Cent Solution* features one of John Addison's best scores since his Oscar-winning *Tom Jones*. The screenplay was adapted by Nicholas Meyer from his own novel about Sherlock Holmes's attempt to shake off his cocaine addiction by seeking help from Sigmund Freud. In the opening credits, four melodic ideas are introduced: a six-note motif associated with Holmes that is played on a solo violin; a robust Spanish-style melody in triple meter; a fast-paced minor-key gypsy tune that uses the cimbalom; and a lyrically tuneful love theme.

Once Holmes (Nicol Williamson) and Watson (Robert Duvall) arrive in Vienna to meet Dr. Freud (Alan Arkin), the score takes on a triple-meter rhythm for a while, with waltz music providing an appropriately Viennese atmosphere. In the duel scene between Holmes and Baron Von Leinsdorf (Jeremy Kemp), the music is excitingly rhythmic; the same holds true for a hallucination scene involving Holmes.

SHORT CUTS ■■■■ **Bill Conti.** *Rocky* brought instant fame to Sylvester Stallone, who both wrote and starred in the engaging story of a losing boxer who finally manages to go the distance. The attention-getting trumpet fanfare by Bill Conti (b. 1942), heard at the outset as the enormous letters of the film's title float across the screen from right to left, is one of 1976's most memorable movie-music moments.

■■■■ **Jerry Goldsmith.** The year's Oscar-winning effort in the Original Score category is Jerry Goldsmith's dynamic music for Richard Donner's *Omen*. Although this is a big-budget horror film in which a number of people are killed in hideous ways (and never the same way twice!), Goldsmith's eerie music keeps the tension at a high level throughout. The score is largely founded on a choral piece entitled "Ave Satani," which earned a nomination as Best Song. Repeated ostinato patterns in the low strings propel the melodic patterns of Goldsmith's often dissonant melodic and harmonic ideas, which owe at least some of their inspiration to Carl Orff's dramatic choral work *Carmina burana*.

Though not as effective as his music for *The Omen*, Goldsmith's brilliantly orchestrated backgrounds for Michael Anderson's sci-fi film *Logan's*

Run resulted in one of the year's better scores. One noteworthy aspect of this music is its use of electronics in connection with the domed city in which the first part of the movie takes place. As Logan (Michael York) first sets foot outside the dome, the music takes on a more romantic atmosphere, with heroic fanfares sounded by trumpets. A beautiful love theme shows up in the latter stages of the film, when Logan and Jessica (Jenny Agutter) return to the city to free everyone else from captivity.

■■■■ **Laurence Rosenthal.** Irvin Kershner's *Return of a Man Called Horse* represents one of the few theatrical films of the 1970s to have a score by Laurence Rosenthal. This well-made sequel to the 1970 film *A Man Called Horse* again stars Richard Harris as John Morgan, the English aristocrat who became a member of a Sioux tribe after being captured while on a hunting trip. In the second film Morgan comes to the aid of his tribe, which faces extinction at the hands of white men. For this film, Rosenthal created a wonderfully atmospheric score, with a lyrical main-title theme for strings, French horn, and harp that achieves an aura of grandeur. The title theme is also part of a majestic rhythmically driven piece that accompanies a buffalo hunt. Altogether, this is a wonderful score, and one of the best ever conceived for a Western.

■■■■ **John Morris.** Another 1976 score that should have been nominated for an Oscar is John Morris's clever music for Mel Brooks's riotously funny *Silent Movie*. Without any dialogue, except for a single emphatic "No!" spoken by famous mime Marcel Marceau (a nice gag!), this film soars merrily along on the wings of Morris's melodies, some of which are in the style of silent-era film music. The music underscores literally everything in a cartoonish sort of way, while keeping the merriment at a high level.

■■■■ **John Barry.** For the ill-fated remake of *King Kong*, both the film and John Barry's often-thrilling, lavishly orchestrated backgrounds attempt to create a dramatic impact commensurate with that of the 1933 original film; but when Kong and his captive, Dwan (Jessica Lange) are alone in the jungle, and later when the story moves from the remote island to New York City, something goes desperately wrong with the new version. The oddest moments in Barry's score come from the tuneful but rather disorienting love theme, based on a four-note motif, which seems to belong to some other film. However, the best part of the score accompanies an early scene in which the natives prepare a human sacrifice to Kong. Here Barry's rhythmically propelled music adds greatly to the excitement.

■■■■ **Michael Small.** Unlike John Barry's music, which often pushes itself into the foreground, the film scores of Michael Small (b. 1939) have tended to make their presence felt in an almost subliminal manner. After some subtly effective work on behalf of Alan J. Pakula's *Parallax View* in 1974, Small created another low-key score for John Schlesinger's exciting *Marathon Man*, in which Dustin Hoffman becomes the unwitting victim of a former Nazi dentist, played to the menacing hilt by Laurence Olivier. The dentist's question "Is it safe?" became an instant classic movie line.

■■■■ **Leonard Rosenman.** Leonard Rosenman deserves mention for his work on Hal Ashby's beautifully mounted portrait of Woody Guthrie,

Bound for Glory, starring David Carradine. A cache of Guthrie songs were adapted for the film, most of which are nicely sung by Carradine himself, who leaves a lasting impression as the itinerant ballad singer. When Rosenman collected a second consecutive Oscar for his arrangements, he saw fit to remind the audience at the Academy Award ceremony that he also composed music! Perhaps the point was well taken, since he contributed some lyrical original scoring to this memorable film.

JOHN WILLIAMS: CELESTIAL ENCOUNTERS. It was due to the friendship of George Lucas and Stephen Spielberg that John Williams was hired to compose one of the all-time classics of film music: the thrilling symphonic background for George Lucas's *Star Wars*. According to Charles Lippincott, who wrote the liner notes for the original soundtrack release:

> Two years ago around the time *Jaws* was being completed, director Steven Spielberg introduced George Lucas to composer John Williams and told Williams about *Star Wars*. Steven's recommendation to George began to see fruition in December 1975 when George started discussing his film with John and gave him a script to read.[33]

George Lucas relates a similar story in his liner notes to the rerecording of the *Star Wars* trilogy that was released in 1990:

> When it came time to choose a composer, I asked around, and Steven Spielberg told me about John Williams. He raved about Johnny, a wonderful jazz composer who also has an amazingly thorough understanding of symphonic music. Many film composers can write small orchestral pieces or various kinds of indigenous scores, but there are few with the talent to create the full-on, old-fashioned movie score for a large orchestra that I envisioned.[34]

As a result of Spielberg's recommendation, John Williams came to a project that made motion picture history and that generated the most often recorded and performed film music ever composed.

As Lucas indicates in his 1990 liner notes, what he had in mind for *Star Wars* was a musical background that would create the same kind of atmosphere that the scores of Erich Wolfgang Korngold had accomplished in the swashbuckling epics that had starred Errol Flynn. As Lippincott again points out:

> George felt that since the picture was so original and so highly different in all of its physical orientations—creatures unknown, places unseen, and noises unheard of—that the music should be on a fairly familiar emotional level. He didn't want electronic or concrete music. Rather, he wanted a dichotomy to his visuals, an almost 19th Century romantic, symphonic score against these yet unseen sights.[35]

Thus, John Williams created a score that helped a younger generation of filmgoers gain an appreciation for the sweepingly romantic scores of the Golden Age.

The film begins with the classic opening logo music (plus CinemaScope extension) of Alfred Newman. This is followed by the inscription "A long time ago, in a galaxy far, far away. . . ." The time and place of the story are mythic rather than futuristic; thus, the presentation of music anchored in the traditions of the nineteenth century seems justified.

This inscription is followed by the announcement of the title:

**STAR
WARS**

Episode IV
A NEW HOPE

As the title appears, Williams's heroic-sounding opening fanfare segues directly into the film's most famous theme, a soaring melody that begins with a triplet rhythm and goes on to introduce higher tones in the scale. The first eight tones of this theme bear a striking resemblance to the beginning of Korngold's main theme of *Kings Row*. Whether intended or not, the similarity of the two themes seems an appropriate homage to the earlier genius. In any case, as this theme continues, a written explanation of the story appears on the screen, moving into the distance three-dimensionally as the lines of print travel toward the top of the screen. As this superscription fades from view, the opening chase scene commences as part of the same shot. An enormous Imperial spacecraft gives chase to a smaller vehicle bearing Princess Leia (Carrie Fisher), whose rebel army is trying to withstand a threat by the military forces of the Galactic Empire. At this point the second important motif is introduced, a menacingly dramatic three-note idea that is used to identify the Empire.

Other motifs in the score are soon introduced: the theme for Princess Leia, which begins with two pairs of repeated tones; and a pattern of four rising pitches, which is used as the motif for Ben Kenobi (Alec Guinness), who is actually retired Jedi knight Obi-Wan Kenobi. Princess Leia has been desperately attempting to contact this knight for help in her struggle to free the galaxy from the tyrannical Imperial rulers.

There are also several other subsidiary motifs in the score, which is constructed according to the leitmotif concept established by Richard Wagner in his operas during the 1860s and '70s. This concept influenced the film-scoring technique of both Max Steiner and Erich Wolfgang Korngold. As we have already seen, both Steiner and Korngold used separate melodic motifs to identify the various characters in the films that they scored. The practice reached its zenith in the late 1930s; Korngold's *Anthony Adverse* and Steiner's *Gone with the Wind* are classic examples of the technique. Although this approach to scoring decreased somewhat after 1950, Miklos Rozsa applied it many times, especially in his expansive score for *Ben-Hur*.

In this sense, the scoring represents not so much a return to the use of symphonic sound, as a return to the use of the leitmotif as a basic procedural device for film music. Williams thereby demonstrated that the techniques of the 1930s could still serve the film composers of the 1970s.

If *Star Wars* was not a showcase for film-music innovation, *Close Encounters of the Third Kind* was altogether a different matter. While completing his score for *Jaws*, John Williams was already formulating ideas for this score, based on an early draft of the script by Steven Spielberg himself. According to Spielberg:

> [Williams] actually started work on musical ideas two years before *Close Encounters* was finalized, basing his impressions on the unfinished script and [on] dinner conversations we would have twice a week. In many instances,

> John wrote his music first, while I put the scenes to it much later. . . . John found himself composing to blank leader months before the effects were finished and cut in. This was a challenge to both of us, but it liberated John to score freely . . . and inspired me in reconstructing certain visuals to the final music.
>
> John became more than just a composer for hire. He was a creative collaborator in all phases of post production, spending every day for fifteen weeks in the mixing studio and editing rooms.[36]

Spielberg felt strongly that one of the primary musical ingredients in the film needed to be composed before certain key scenes were shot. This was the motif that Spielberg envisioned as a musical greeting to be used by the aliens. In one of the central scenes, a team of ufologists, which has been charting the strange appearances of long-lost World War II airplanes in the Sonora Desert of Mexico and a cargo ship in the sands of the Gobi Desert, arrives in India to witness a huge crowd of people chanting a strange bit of music based on a repeated pattern of five notes. In the following scene, Lacombe (François Truffaut) plays a tape recording of this music for a gathering of fellow scientists, while he explains the use of hand gestures devised by the Hungarian composer Zoltan Kodaly to teach pitch perception. It appears that this combination of five pitches, in the pattern D–E–C–C–G, with the second C down an octave from the first, is some sort of message being transmitted to Earth from outer space. This same musical motif also appears to be haunting several residents of Muncie, Indiana, who have had close encounters with unidentified flying objects (UFOs), including Roy Neary (Richard Dreyfuss); Jillian Guiler (Melinda Dillon); and Jillian's five-year-old son Barry (Cary Guffey), who repeatedly plays the five-tone pattern on his toy xylophone.

To select this bit of music, John Williams spent a long time plotting out a variety of different pitch patterns. According to Fred Karlin:

> John Williams tried over 250 different five-note motifs before arriving at the one used as the "communication" motif for the spaceship. Williams initially leaned more toward a seven-note motif, but Spielberg was concerned that the longer motif might sound too much like a melody, or at least the beginning of a melody rather than the unfinished sound of a short motif.[37]

Several other important melodic motifs were composed for the score. Among the principal ones is a rising two-note pattern used to represent the natural monument known as Devil's Tower, a flat-topped mountain in Wyoming with a shape that spooks several people who have had encounters with the visitors from space. This motif is usually accompanied by a pair of sustained chords played softly by strings, with harp and wordless female voices; it first appears in an early scene where little Barry is seen mounding up dirt into the shape of Devil's Tower.

A second idea, the "Encounter" motif, consisting of an ascending three-note pattern, is associated with the encounters that the humans have been experiencing. Heard several times in the film, this idea is eventually developed into an emotion-charged romantic theme. Another idea, the "Danger" motif, built on a four-note pattern that resembles the beginning of the "Dies irae," the Gregorian chant melody from the *Mass of the Dead*, is the most rhythmically driven music in the score, and occurs in certain scenes to create a feeling of danger or excitement.

All of these motifs can be heard in a scene in which several residents of Muncie, having already experienced a UFO sighting, reassemble at the same

Close Encounters of the Third Kind, with Cary Guffey.

site on the following night. What begins as a hopeful encounter turns into a traumatic event when Roy, Jillian, and others recognize Army helicopters, which have been summoned to prove that evidence of a supposed alien visitation could actually be caused by man-made machinery.

Another scene in which several of the musical motifs converge is the dramatic sequence in which Roy and Jillian, after having learned of the existence of Devil's Tower, travel to Wyoming, only to discover that the army has ordered an evacuation of the area due to a supposed gas leak. After they evade military personnel, they speed through barricades in Roy's rented station wagon and drive past cattle that lie lifeless by the side of the road. It is at this point that they approach something in the distance that intrigues them. They get out of the station wagon and walk toward this object. As they climb the hill, we finally see what has them mesmerized: Devil's Tower begins to come into camera range. Williams's "danger" motif is sounded repeatedly, and the music swells up to a full-orchestra proclamation of the "encounter" motif in a moment of soaringly romantic music. The music then becomes quieter, with another reference to the two-note Devil's Tower motif, again with wordless voices heard in the background.

Yet another melodic idea, the "army" motif, consisting of a minor-key five-note pattern, is used for scenes involving the army's operation to establish a rendezvous point with the aliens at the base of Devil's Tower.

The final reels of *Close Encounters* contain almost nonstop scoring. First comes the musical conversation between the U.S. Army's computer and the alien spaceship, in which Williams's five-note "communication" motif is played by two instruments—a solo oboe for the computer and a tuba for the spacecraft. After this ingenious musical moment, viewers get their first glimpses of the friendly aliens, who are just as curious about Earth's inhabitants as the humans are about them. In the closing scenes all the primary musical motifs of the score are combined in a symphonic way, with one additional musical interpolation: the Disney song "When You Wish upon a Star" from *Pinocchio.* At Spielberg's request, Williams inserted a slow-moving version of this melody into the orchestral music that accompanies Roy as he enters the mother ship. As he looks around in wonder, the Disney tune begins to sound.

When the mother ship ascends into the night sky, the film's credits begin to appear on the screen. As the ship continues its ascent, soaring music is heard. Here the grandest of all statements of the primary motifs of the score comes together, with a majestic rendering of the five-note motif, which is expanded into a grandiose orchestral theme.

There are actually two versions of the film. In 1980, three years after the original release, Spielberg released a "Special Edition." Apparently motivated by a desire to refine the film and also to give a glimpse of the interior of the mother ship, Spielberg inserted a new scene of Roy inside the ship. Another added scene is the one in the Gobi Desert, where the cargo ship is discovered (this was shot for the original film but not used). Besides adding scenes, Spielberg also removed from the film some bits of dialogue plus a lengthy section in which Roy builds a likeness of Devil's Tower.

As a result of these alterations, parts of the score had to be rewritten. Whereas the Disney melody was relegated to a subtly sounded moment in the original closing-credits sequence, in the "Special Edition" it is featured more prominently. Regrettably missing from the changed version of the closing credits is the repeated use of the five-note "communication" motif, which in the original version brings the film to a beautifully serene close.

In the orchestral suite that Williams arranged after *Close Encounter*'s release in 1977, the original ending appears; it has been included on several recordings of the music, including those by Williams and by such conductors as Charles Gerhardt and Zubin Mehta.

Although John Williams has scored films for more than twenty years since the original release of *Star Wars* and *Close Encounters*, no other films have drawn from him such a high degree of musical inventiveness and creativity. In the 1977 Oscar race, both scores were nominated; not only did the *Star Wars* music win the prize, but it remains the best-known film score of Williams's career.

JERRY GOLDSMITH: FROM MACARTHUR TO DAMNATION ALLEY.

Among Jerry Goldsmith's scores for 1977 films is the rousing music for Joseph Sargent's *MacArthur*. With its bold main theme for trumpets and its repeated use of strongly accented low tones, achieved by hitting directly on the bass strings of a piano, the *MacArthur* score is a worthy companion to Goldsmith's earlier music for *Patton*. In fact, Goldsmith later arranged a concert piece called "The Generals March," which includes both of these themes.

A more lyrical Goldsmith score accompanies Franklin J. Schaffner's often-absorbing film based on Ernest Hemingway's unfinished last novel *Islands in the Stream*. A haunting main theme permeates the score, with swirling woodwind figures heard as an ongoing accompaniment. These figures occasionally emerge as primary melodic patterns in the strings; throughout the film they convey a sense of the sea that surrounds the Caribbean island on which most of this film is set. The main theme speaks eloquently for Tom (George C. Scott), a painter who becomes reunited with his three sons from former marriages.

George P. Cosmatos's disaster movie *The Cassandra Crossing* featured Sophia Loren as a passenger on a doomed train. Goldsmith's music alternates between a lyrical main theme and some extremely jarring dissonant music for the scenes involving the attempts by a passenger (played by Richard Harris) to save the people on the train.

Another Goldsmith score of interest is his dramatic music for the post–nuclear-war drama *Damnation Alley*, in which a few survivors head across the ruins of America toward Albany, where they believe there are other survivors. Although the film is little more than a futuristic road movie, the music provides a much needed lyrical quality, especially for scenes with Dominique Sanda and Jan-Michael Vincent, two of the survivors.

SHORT CUTS.

Some of 1977's top films have no background scores, as is the case with Woody Allen's Oscar-winning *Annie Hall*. Others use borrowed music, as does Herbert Ross's entertaining ballet film *The Turning*

Point, which contains excerpts from works by Prokofiev, Tchaikovsky, Henryk Wieniawski, and Chopin. The film's compiled score, which also includes an excerpt from Duke Ellington's ballet *The River*, was performed for the soundtrack by the Los Angeles Philharmonic.

■■■■ **Miklos Rozsa.** Despite an interesting cast that includes John Gielgud, Ellen Burstyn, and Dirk Bogarde, Alain Resnais's *Providence*, the French director's only English-language film, is chiefly of interest because of Miklos Rozsa's main theme, a rather mournful piece in the style of a funeral march, which is heard during the film's opening credits. Later, this music is transformed rhythmically into a melancholy theme entitled "Twilight Waltz," which is heard both as a solo piano piece and as a work for piano and string ensemble. There is much more thematic material in this lovely score, some of it quite dramatic in nature.

■■■■ **Laurence Rosenthal.** One of 1977's better scores is Laurence Rosenthal's exotic background for *The Island of Dr. Moreau*, based on the H. G. Wells story of a crazed doctor (Burt Lancaster), who performs weird experiments that turn his imprisoned patients into part-man–part-animal. Rosenthal's intriguing score includes some very dissonant music for the main theme, which has a recurring trumpet motif. There is also a beautiful love theme for the young shipwrecked man (Michael York), who falls in love with a native girl (Barbara Carrera).

■■■■ **John Addison.** Richard Attenborough's ambitious film *A Bridge Too Far*, based on Cornelius Ryan's book about Operation Market Garden (an Allied operation intended to shorten World War II by the taking of several bridges in Holland), boasts of a rousing score by John Addison, who actually participated in the campaign as a British soldier in XXX Corps. In addition to the dramatically stirring main march theme there is a rambunctious piece called "March of the Paratroopers." This is altogether one of Addison's best scores, with just the right amount of patriotic music to flavor this expertly crafted and beautifully photographed film.

■■■■ **Angela Morley.** For the British film *The Slipper and the Rose*, based on the Cinderella story, the lovely songs, including the Oscar-nominated "He Danced with Me/She Danced with Me," were composed by the Sherman Brothers, of *Mary Poppins* fame. The lilting orchestral arrangements were done by Angela Morley, who with this film began to use her own name for the screen credits, instead of the pseudonymous "Wally Stott." She became one of the first women to identify herself as a film composer.

■■■■ *Saturday Night Fever.* John Badham's *Saturday Night Fever*, which elevated John Travolta to stardom, concerns a young hardware store employee who desires to win a local disco contest. The scenes in the nightclub are beautifully choreographed, with a large number of 1970s pop hits heard on the soundtrack, along with several songs that were written for the film (and performed on the soundtrack) by the Bee Gees. David Shire added some bits of original background music; but the most memorable musical moments come from the various disco tunes, such as the jazzed-up classical piece called "A Fifth of Beethoven," one of several previously composed tunes incorporated into the film. All in all, *Saturday Night Fever* includes a potpourri of musical styles. Its success clearly signaled that there would be many more films with a disco beat on the horizon.

JERRY GOLDSMITH: FROM COMA TO MAGIC. Jerry Goldsmith has been one of the most steadily employed film composers ever since his first Oscar nomination in 1962. Each of his 1978 film scores is noteworthy.

Michael Crichton's intriguing film version of Robin Cook's medical thriller *Coma* features Genevieve Bujold as Dr. Susan Wheeler, a young surgical resident, who works at Boston Memorial Hospital. She becomes suspicious when several patients, after undergoing routine surgical procedures, lapse into irreversible comas. In her ensuing investigation, she winds up in danger when she learns that the head of surgery at Boston Memorial is actually in the business of selling body parts of comatose patients. Her fiancé, Dr. Mark Bellows (Michael Douglas), eventually comes to her rescue.

Basically an old-fashioned thriller, albeit with a contemporary scientific twist, *Coma* is noteworthy for the absence of Goldsmith's score in the first part of the film. In fact, not a single note of music occurs until the moment when Susan discovers that she is being watched; this occurs exactly forty-nine minutes into the film. From that moment on, Goldsmith's music provides an ingenious background played by strings, with four pianos and timpani. Much of the impact of the score stems from the unusual timbre of the piano sound, derived by directly hitting and plucking the strings. This timbre, together with some unusual echo effects, produces a great deal of tension. The end result is not very melodious, but the film benefits enormously from Goldsmith's unusual piano-and-string sonorities.

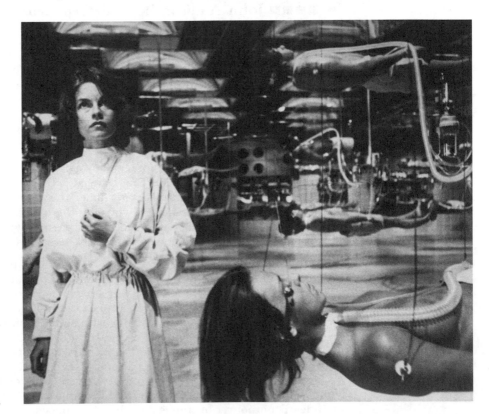

Coma, with
Genevieve Bujold.

Peter Hyams's *Capricorn One* begins with a farfetched idea but then becomes a first-rate chase film. Three astronauts, prepped for a manned mission to Mars, become involved in a fraudulent TV transmission that actually emanates from an abandoned airplane hangar in Mexico. After learning that their lives are going to be forfeited, two are caught in an attempted escape, but the third, Charles Brubaker (James Brolin), is helped by an investigative reporter (Elliott Gould) who stumbles onto the hoax. Goldsmith's main theme is a jagged rhythmic idea with a strangely patterned group of accents that seem to avoid a steady meter; a lyrical second idea is used in quiet moments with Brubaker's wife (Brenda Vaccaro) and their small son. In the closing credits, these two ideas are combined in a majestic final piece of music.

Damien—Omen II, the first of two sequels to *The Omen*, continues the story of Damien the Antichrist, who has grown from a small child to a teenager enrolled in a military academy. Goldsmith's music for this film is almost as effective as that of its predecessor. As in the first film there is a choral background, which is advertised on the soundtrack album as "A Black Mass." Continuing the satanic nature of *The Omen*'s choral music, this work is dutifully dark-hued and pulsating stuff, with a lot of grinding low-string sonorities for the many violent scenes in which people are gruesomely killed. By the end of this film, one might surmise that the *Omen* movies are not so much about the son of Satan as about the variety of ways in which violent deaths can occur. Like *The Omen*, this film ultimately becomes rather silly, but the music succeeds in lending it a very sinister aura.

Irwin Allen's film *The Swarm* was one of the year's major disappointments. With a publicity buildup regarding the impending threat of killer bees on the rampage, the actual death scenes in this film are totally without suspense. Because the menace consists of tiny insects which are rather difficult to see, the scenes in which people are attacked become ludicrous when slow-motion photography extends their length. Without any real visual terror, the film depends almost totally on its music. Fortunately, Goldsmith found a way to convey the horror that the visuals lack by employing a string orchestra which produces a great deal of tension through a simulated buzzing effect that occurs whenever the bees are seen. This is a clever score that should have been attached to a better film.

Number five in the chronology of Goldsmith's 1978 scores is Franklin J. Schaffner's *Boys from Brazil*, adapted from an intriguing Ira Levin novel about Dr. Josef Mengele, the Nazi doctor who escaped from Germany after World War II and wound up in South America. As Dr. Mengele, Gregory Peck gives a commanding performance that is filled with menace, while Laurence Olivier, as the determined Nazi-hunter Ezra Lieberman, is compelling in a benign role. The score is permeated with the sound of the Viennese waltz, which fits the setting of the story since Lieberman's office is located in Vienna. Seldom has the waltz rhythm been used more effectively than in this film. Goldsmith's tuneful themes present a striking contrast to the sinister nature of this story, in which ninety-four young boys have been cloned from Hitler as a result of Mengele's experiments. The main waltz theme has an energetic flavor. Its generous use of strings and its brass sound recall the lavishly orchestrated tone poems of Richard Strauss. *The Boys from Brazil* secured for Goldsmith his eleventh Oscar nomination.

Goldsmith's final score for 1978 is Richard Attenborough's thriller *Magic*, based on William Goldman's story of Corky Withers, a mild-mannered ventriloquist (Anthony Hopkins) whose mind is taken over by that of his smart-alecky dummy, Fats. A rather menacing harmonica sound is heard throughout the film to give vent to Corky's disturbed condition, in which Fats begins to dominate him. In contrast to this music is a bluesy main theme for piano and strings, which creates a lyrical and melancholy mood. Goldsmith's music helps to humanize the not always likeable Corky.

JOHN WILLIAMS: FROM JAWS 2 TO SUPERMAN. Following the tremendous success of *Star Wars* and *Close Encounters of the Third Kind*, John Williams scored a diverse trio of films that were ranked among the most popular of 1978. *Jaws 2* suffers by having too many bratty teenagers and an excess of shark attacks. John Williams's score itself is every bit as effective as that of the original film, with the inevitable two-note shark motif again used to stir up tension.

Brian De Palma's lurid thriller *The Fury*, about two telekinetic teenagers, relies more on exploding bodies than on anything else. Despite the mayhem, Williams's moody minor-key main theme is a masterful creation, with a six-note motif that slowly rises in pitch, then returns back down the scale. The motif is later expanded into a full-bodied thematic statement, and is also used motivically (and with synthesizer) to indicate moments when one of the two teens (Andrew Stevens and Amy Irving) is experiencing telekinesis.

The best Williams score of the year is the one he wrote for Richard Donner's epic screen version of *Superman*, with Christopher Reeve as the Man of Steel. The main theme captures the heroic nature of the man from Planet Krypton with a rhythmically driven march theme consisting of a boldly rising melodic statement. The love theme, which is heard most prominently when Superman gives Lois Lane (Margot Kidder) a bird's-eye view of Metropolis, is a lyrically soaring idea that later became a song hit with the title "Can You Read My Mind?" There are many other musical themes in the film, including the comical accompaniment for Lex Luthor's slow-witted henchman Otis, played hilariously by Ned Beatty. Although Donner tried to cram too much into this production, Williams's score manages to keep pace with the film's many shifts in style.

SHORT CUTS ■■■■ Bill Conti. After his acclaimed music for *Rocky*, Bill Conti scored two films in 1978 that starred Sylvester Stallone, *F.I.S.T.* and *Paradise Alley*. Of these, the former music is the more interesting, with some dramatic symphonic scoring for the early scenes in which the labor problems of interstate truckers are vividly depicted. Conti also provided a lyrical jazz-inflected background for Paul Mazursky's Oscar-nominated film *An Unmarried Woman*. His most impressive work of the year was his lyrical score for John G. Avildsen's *Slow Dancing in the Big City*. Paul Sorvino plays a columnist in love with a ballerina (Anne Ditchburn) who has been warned to quit dancing. Naturally, the ballerina ignores her doctor's advice and goes on to perform in a ballet. Despite the pathos of this scene, Conti's rhapsodic score creates a highly emotional musical background.

■■■■ Stanley Myers. The Oscar-winning film of 1978, Michael Cimino's Vietnam War epic *The Deer Hunter*, incorporates different types of music, from Russian Orthodox chant to modern pop songs. English composer Stanley Myers (1939–93) left a lasting impression with a lyrical piece called "Cavatina" that recurs several times in this film. Australian guitarist John Williams provided a lovely solo for the melancholy melodic line of this haunting piece.

■■■■ **Ennio Morricone.** The Oscar-nominated scores for 1978, in addition to Goldsmith's *Boys from Brazil* and Williams's *Superman*, include two charming scores for films with the word "heaven" in their title. Terrence Malick's *Days of Heaven* features the first score by Ennio Morricone to receive an Oscar nomination. Having been passed over for his music in the Sergio Leone Westerns, not to mention the rest of his prodigious output (by 1978, he was already past the 200-film mark), Morricone finally received recognition for his melancholy backgrounds for this somber turn-of-the-century story. In the film two ne'er-do-wells (played by Richard Gere and Brooke Adams) from the sweatshops of Chicago take a train west and find work on a wheat farm. Morricone obviously reacted to the poetic vistas that were captured beautifully by Nestor Almendros, who won an Oscar for his cinematography. Also in the musical background of this film is a borrowed theme from Camille Saint-Saens's *Carnival of the Animals*. Originally entitled "The Aquarium," this haunting music accompanies the opening titles and also appears elsewhere in the film.

■■■■ **Dave Grusin.** *Heaven Can Wait*, a warm-hearted romantic comedy written by Warren Beatty and Elaine May and directed by Beatty and Buck Henry, is a remake of *Here Comes Mr. Jordan* (1941). Here Beatty portrays football player Joe Pendleton, a man taken from Earth prematurely after a biking accident that was not supposed to have been fatal. When the crash occurs, Dave Grusin's charming background score commences, with a tuneful piece built on a repeated four-note motif. Periodically throughout the film, the theme built on these notes is heard on a soprano saxophone, the instrument which Joe carries with him as he is taken to meet Mr. Jordan (James Mason), the archangel who helps Joe get back to Earth. Several times during the film, Joe is heard playing bits of "Ciribiribin" (although his attempts at this tune are a bit short of virtuosic).

■■■■ **Giorgio Moroder.** The Oscar-winning score of 1978 is a bit of a curiosity: the debut score for rock musician Giorgio Moroder. His synthesized music for Alan Parker's *Midnight Express* is one of the most memorable things about this excessively violent film in which Billy Hayes (Brad Davis), a young American, is arrested in Turkey for attempting to smuggle drugs. Throughout the grueling scenes that follow, as Billy tries to survive the atrocious conditions of a Turkish prison, Moroder's throbbing, rhythmically driven music keeps the film moving. Within the context of this unconventional type of score the electronic effects work well.

■■■■ **Nino Rota.** In *Death on the Nile*, the second Agatha Christie adaptation from the production team of John Brabourne and Richard Goodwin, Peter Ustinov plays Hercule Poirot. This film is good fun, as the Belgian supersleuth tries to figure out who killed a rich heiress during a cruise down the Nile. Although Nino Rota's music is used sparsely, his soaring main theme comes swelling up at the right moments, with a five-note rising idea played by horns. The music is somewhat reminiscent of such Giuseppe Verdi operas as *Aida*, which was probably Rota's intention. In any case, the symphonic style of this score is far removed from Rota's music for the Fellini films and the *Godfather* movies.

MIKLOS ROZSA: THRILLER AND FANTASY. In the late 1970s, Miklos Rozsa was the last link with the Golden Age of Hollywood. Although several other composers from the old studio days were still living, Rozsa was the only one still scoring films.

Rozsa's throbbingly vibrant score for Jonathan Demme's stylish thriller *Last Embrace* was one of his final masterworks. Like many young filmmakers before him, including Brian De Palma, Demme was in awe of Alfred Hitchcock, the acknowledged master of suspense. Demme's film, adapted by David Shaber from the novel *The Thirteenth Man* by Michael Teigh Bloom, is set in contemporary time, but is reminiscent in tone of the classic Hitchcock films of the 1940s. Like Gregory Peck's amnesiac character in *Spellbound*, Harry Hannan (Roy Scheider) suffers from nightmares and is paranoid. Riddled with guilt over the death of his wife, the innocent victim of a shooting in a restaurant, Harry spends time in a sanatorium. Once outside the institution weird things happen to him and he starts fearing for his life.

Harry discovers a young woman living in his apartment, which was apparently sublet during his absence. As in many a Hitchcock film, there is more to this woman than first meets the eye. As played by Janet Margolin, Ellie Fabian appears to be a dedicated young anthropologist; before long, her connection with Harry assumes a much darker aspect.

By the time Harry learns that his name is on a list of people descended from a Jewish consortium that long ago had run several brothels in New York, most of the other people on the list are dead. In a final confrontation at Niagara Falls, Ellie has the opportunity to kill him (she has already murdered another man); at the last moment her feelings cause her to hesitate, and Harry ultimately chases her through a series of tunnels until they wind up on the brink of the falls in a life-and-death struggle.

Rozsa's pulsating music captures both the suspenseful and the romantic elements of the plot, as the film leads the viewer from one tense moment to the next. Seldom has any filmmaker since Hitchcock shown paranoia as successfully as Demme, whose photographer Tak Fujimoto used a handheld camera to thrust the viewer into the action. In several scenes a sense of unease is conveyed as we see the world from Harry's viewpoint, with suspicious-looking people everywhere.

In many ways Rozsa's music, like the basic plot itself, is a throwback to the 1940s. The music includes string tremolos to heighten the tension of various scenes, plus lots of deep-sounding bass tones that add to the generally ominous mood. Melodically, the score is based on three primary ideas. The first is introduced immediately in the opening credits, during which Rozsa's music establishes a darkly romantic aura by means of a five-note motif that is inclined downward. Several repetitions of this motif occur through the use of a contrapuntal effect, typical of much of his work, wherein a melodic idea played by the upper strings is echoed by a similar idea in the lower strings. The melodic fabric thus includes several reiterations of a single idea as the music builds in intensity.

In the film's opening restaurant scene a second motif is heard for the first time; it is played by a strolling violinist who is an employee of the establishment. Later, after Harry is released from the sanatorium, this melody is heard again when he is reminded of his late wife as he returns to his apartment. It recurs in a late-night scene in which Harry wakes up screaming; as Ellie listens, he reconstructs for her the events that led up to the fatal shooting. This melody is heard yet another time when Harry visits the gravesite of his wife. A third motif, a four-note idea, is associated with Harry and the danger that surrounds him. In the tension-filled closing sequence, as Harry insistently drives Ellie to Niagara Falls to confront her about the killings, the score provides a rhythmically driven background based on this third idea. A further musical element is associated with a cryptic message given by Ellie to Harry, who is told that it was left for him at his apartment. This musical motif consists of a series of sustained chords that move up and down by semitone, with wordless voices added to evoke a feeling of mystery. As Harry and a concerned Jewish friend (Sam Levene) try to trace the origin of the message's Aramaic symbols, this bit of music is heard several times. Ultimately, Rozsa's music provides an emotional quality that elevates a routine melodrama to the level of a highly effective thriller.

Soon after completing work on the Jonathan Demme film, Rosza was enlisted by Nicholas Meyer to create the background score for the fantasy *Time after Time,* which Meyer based on his original script about H. G. Wells on the trail of Jack the Ripper. In Meyer's fanciful story, the Ripper escapes from 1893 London to the San Francisco of 1979, thanks to a time machine that Wells (Malcolm McDowell) has just unveiled for his friends, one of whom, John Stevenson (David Warner), has fatally slashed a prostitute earlier that evening on the way to Wells's home. Wells decides to go after him, and thus is propelled forward in time almost ninety years.

As Wells travels from 1893 to 1979 inside his machine, the soundtrack is filled with sound bits that indicate the passage of time. Included in this audio montage are fragments of period songs, including "Over There," along with news reports of key events—such as the Lindbergh flight, the rise of Hitler, World War II, the Korean War, the Kennedy and King assassinations, and the terrorist attack at the Munich Olympics. Meyer's inclusion of these details is used to help Wells conclude that his hoped-for future Utopia will not materialize.

Through Amy Robbins (Mary Steenburgen), who deals in foreign currencies at a San Francisco bank, Wells learns of Stevenson's whereabouts. Stevenson escapes after a confrontation with Wells in a hotel room, and is pursued by Wells onto the streets. Thinking that Stevenson has been fatally struck by a car, Wells returns to Amy, and the two spend a romantic evening together. He learns the next morning that Stevenson is still alive; now he must once again find him, to bring him back to justice.

Unlike *Last Embrace*, which has a generally dark and suspenseful tone throughout, *Time after Time* contains a mixture of styles, from thriller to science fiction to romance to comedy. The comic aspects of the film are perhaps the most unexpected. By following a nineteenth-century man into the twentieth century, Meyer found many little ways to highlight Wells's amazement with modern technology, such as his first traumatic ride in a taxi.

With such a rich variety of styles to accompany, Rozsa had a field day providing an appropriate musical accompaniment, and the result is one of his most masterful creations. Following the opening Warner Bros. logo, which includes the classic Max Steiner chords, Rozsa's main theme is

Time after Time, with Mary Steenburgen and Malcolm McDowell.

immediately introduced. A five-note motif is used to create a dramatic atmosphere. This motif is later used as part of the rhythmically driven music that accompanies the beginning of the scene in which Wells travels into the future; it is heard until a climactic chord occurs, following which the montage of songs and news items takes over.

There are several other prominent themes in the film. For the relationship of Amy and Herbert (the name by which she calls Wells), Rozsa composed a rhapsodic melody that begins with a rising interval of a seventh, then falls back down in pitch. Based on an eight-note pattern, this melody subsequently soars higher, in typical Rozsa fashion, with even larger upward leaps of a ninth. This theme is first heard as Amy and Herbert are walking in Golden Gate Park, on the way back to her apartment. Two other themes of note are each relegated to a single scene. When Stevenson runs out of the hotel to avoid being caught by H. G. (as Stevenson calls him), a piece entitled "Chase Fugue" begins, with a nervous idea in the strings, which is given a contrapuntal treatment. It soon grows from overlapping string lines to involve the entire orchestra in a dramatic musical statement.

During the next scene, in which Amy and Herbert are dining in a restaurant, a lyrical piece entitled "Time Machine Waltz" is played in the manner of piped-in music by piano and strings. Unfortunately, in the film it is difficult to hear this music, since it was dubbed at a terribly low volume level. After hearing the music on the soundtrack album, one regrets the reduction of this lovely piece to such an inaudible level.

There is more chase music in the film, for the late scene in which Stevenson, with Amy as his hostage, drives back to the museum where the time machine sits as part of an H. G. Wells exhibit. Wells, whose only knowledge of driving is based on having observed Amy driving her car, has no recourse except to give chase by attempting to commandeer her vehicle. This is a very effective scene, in that it manages to combine the basic tension of the chase with the comical idea of Wells trying to drive a car for the first time. The music helps to propel the scene forward, until they reach the museum, where Wells sends Stevenson, who has climbed into the time machine, into infinity. As the film ends, Amy realizes she would rather be back in 1893 with Wells than alone in San Francisco, and Wells manages to get her inside the machine just before it transports them back in time. The closing credits include majestic renderings of both the main motif and the love theme, as *Time after Time* comes to a satisfyingly romantic conclusion.

For younger audience members, this score was probably their first taste of Rozsa's richly orchestrated, romantically charged music. It is regrettable that, in the wake of this triumphal achievement, Rozsa would score only two more films before retiring.

JERRY GOLDSMITH: IN OUTER SPACE. Jerry Goldsmith scored two sci-fi films in 1979. The first of these is the often majestic score for the first theatrical feature based on the 1960s "Star Trek" TV series.

As directed by Robert Wise, *Star Trek—The Motion Picture* evolved into a rather ponderous film, largely based on one of the scripts from the series, in which the crew of the *Enterprise* solve the mystery of "V'ger," a tremendously powerful entity in the universe that has annihilated several Klingon space cruisers and is on a collision course with Earth.

The slow-moving first part of the film, in which the crew members of the *Enterprise* are gradually reunited, is rescued by Goldsmith's inspired music, largely based on the heroic main-title theme. This tune first appears in a fast march tempo; later, as the crew approaches the space station where the *Enterprise* is being made ready for its next mission, the theme reappears in a slower tempo, with brilliantly orchestrated chords.

Among the other musical highlights is the dramatically charged Klingon theme, in which electronic sounds have been added for dramatic effect. Some unusual string pizzicatos are also included in this music. For the character of Ilia (Persis Khambatta), a bald-headed female Deltan assigned to the *Enterprise* as technical adviser, Goldsmith composed one of his loveliest melodies, a rhapsodic theme for strings that invests this score with a much needed emotional quality.

Another 1979 science fiction film with a Jerry Goldsmith score is Ridley Scott's fascinating but gruesome *Alien*, in which members of the spacecraft *Nostromo* are endangered by an alien being that grows in embryonic form inside the bodies of humans. In contrast to scenes such as the one in which the alien bursts out of the chest of Kane (John Hurt), Goldsmith's music is a study in subtlety. The slow-paced main theme, which features a lyrical melody played by a solo trumpet, gives little indication of the traumatic scenes which follow. For the conclusion of the film, after Ripley (Sigourney Weaver), the *Nostromo*'s sole survivor, has successfully ejected the alien into space from the rescue craft, Goldsmith planned a return of his understated main theme. Though this music appears on the soundtrack album, it is not heard in the film. In its place one hears the lyrical strains of a slow-moving theme from Howard Hanson's *Romantic Symphony*. As lovely as Hanson's music is, this last-minute replacement of original scoring by borrowed music reinforces a trend that would unfortunately interfere with the efforts of many film composers in the years ahead.

VIVA VIVALDI! THREE SCORES IN THE BAROQUE STYLE. The music of Baroque composer Antonio Vivaldi was on display in three major films released in 1979. First was Robert Benton's Oscar-winning *Kramer vs. Kramer*, in which bits of Vivaldi's music, plus several pieces by the English composer Henry Purcell, were used as background music. The result is a tuneful accompaniment that features a pair of street players, a guitarist and a mandolinist, who are seen in a sequence in Central Park playing part of the first movement of Vivaldi's Concerto in C Major for Mandolin, Strings, and Harpsichord. Broadway composer John Kander, who helped make musical selections for the film, suggested that Purcell's music "might lend a more elegiac quality to some of the scenes."[38]

George Roy Hill's *Little Romance* also features Vivaldi's music as part of the background score. This time, however, a Vivaldi theme is part of a supposedly original score by Georges Delerue, who utilized the Vivaldi music for several sequences in this charming film about two precocious teenagers who leave Paris without informing anyone and wind up in Venice under the

Bridge of Sighs. Laurence Olivier plays an elderly con artist who encourages the youngsters to go to Venice; the girl's parents frantically alert the police, who launch a search for the pair (delightfully played by Diane Lane and Thelonious Bernard).

The Vivaldi tune that Delerue appropriated is from the slow movement of the Concerto in D Major for Guitar and Two Violins. In addition to this lyrically tuneful piece, Delerue actually composed some original themes in a Baroque style; most prominent among these is a sprightly, fast-paced theme that is used during the opening and closing credits. Apparently, the borrowing did not bother the members of the Motion Picture Academy, for they awarded Georges Delerue an Oscar for Best Original Score.

Vivaldi showed up a third time as part of the collage of music used for the background of Bob Fosse's *All That Jazz*, a semi-autobiographical film in which Roy Scheider plays Broadway director Joe Gideon, whose obsessive behavior, including nonstop drinking and smoking, eventually leads to a heart attack. A piece by Vivaldi, identified in the film's credits as Concerto in G, is heard in the film's opening scene, in which Joe puts a tape into a cassette player and listens to music while doing his morning thing—taking Alka-Seltzer and Dexedrine followed by a hot shower. As he finishes dressing, he looks into the mirror and exclaims "It's showtime, folks!" This ritual, with the Vivaldi music, occurs four times in the course of the film, with only minor variations in the visual formula.

All That Jazz also includes bits of original scoring by the film's music director, Ralph Burns, along with such borrowed music as George Benson's recording of "On Broadway"; Peter Allen's "Everything Old Is New Again"; and an updated version of the 1950s Everly Brothers hit "Bye Bye Love," which is transformed into the film's bizarre closing number, "Bye Bye Life," as sung by Ben Vereen while Joe undergoes open heart surgery.

SHORT CUTS ■■■■ *The Black Hole.* Another 1979 sci-fi film with a noteworthy score is Disney's *Black Hole*, which is loosely adapted from Jules Verne's *Twenty Thousand Leagues under the Sea*. In this version the Captain Nemo character, Dr. Hans Reinhardt (Maximilian Schell), commandeers the *Cygnus*, which hovers near the entrance to a black hole in space. The crew of the *Palomino* stumble across the *Cygnus* and find themselves captives of Dr. Reinhardt. John Barry, after years of scoring James Bond movies, created an arresting musical background for this visually stunning film. His main-title theme features a slow-paced but dramatically inclined melody for French horns, accompanied by an eerie repeated motif played by violins. The most noteworthy music in the film is a piece originally designed as an overture to be played in theaters before the start of the film. Set in the style of a dramatic march, Barry's heroic music features trumpets in a fanfarelike opening melody, which segues into a rhythmically driven theme played by strings and French horns. This same music returns late in the film as accompaniment for one of the climactic battle scenes.

■■■■ *The Amityville Horror.* Stuart Rosenberg's *Amityville Horror* is based on the supposedly factual book by Jay Anson, about a family that moves into a house possessed by demons. This is a potentially interesting film with an intriguing Oscar-nominated score by Lalo Schifrin, but the inclusion of such horror-movie effects as flickering lights, swarms of flies, and oozing mud weakens it. In Schifrin's music, the main-title theme begins with a repeated two-note descending figure; this pair of tones a semitone apart generates most of the melodic material in the score. The main theme suggests a lullaby, with a clever instrumentation that features children's voices singing a "la-la" effect, accompanied by quiet piano arpeggios and high violin harmonics.

■■■ *Manhattan.* Woody Allen's *Manhattan*, wonderfully shot in black and white by Gordon Willis, features a soundtrack made up entirely of George Gershwin's music. In addition to portions of the *Rhapsody in Blue*, there are several show tunes in lovely arrangements by Tom Pierson, which were recorded for the film by the New York Philharmonic under Zubin Mehta. This is one of the few Allen films with a lush musical background.

■■■ *10.* In Blake Edwards's *Ten*, a beautiful woman named Jenny (Bo Derek) becomes a major distraction for George (Dudley Moore), a successful Hollywood songwriter who is experiencing a midlife crisis. Despite the Oscar nomination for Henry Mancini's original score, the most noticeable music in *Ten* is Maurice Ravel's *Bolero*, which Jenny says is the best lovemaking music ever written. Henry Mancini arranged a shortened version of the piece, which made more people aware of Ravel's music than had ever heard it during the late French composer's lifetime.

■■■ *Apocalypse Now.* The strangest musical score of 1979 is that for Francis Ford Coppola's Vietnam War film *Apocalypse Now*, which Coppola and John Milius loosely adapted from Joseph Conrad's novella *Heart of Darkness*. As Captain Willard (Martin Sheen) goes upriver to find the renegade Colonel Kurtz (Marlon Brando), we hear a collage of sounds, including songs by the Doors, plus various electronic bits of music composed by Carmine Coppola. The director actually shares the screen credit for the music, which consists mostly of throbbing bass sounds. For the most part, the music has a muffled quality, without any direct melodic appeal. Lieutenant Colonel Kilgore (Robert Duvall) uses Richard Wagner's "Ride of the Valkyries" as inspiration for his troops when they parachute out of a plane over the Vietnamese jungle. As the plane flies over the green terrain, the soaring strains of Wagner's music provide an eerie serenade.

POSTLUDE

THE LAST HURRAH. While many film composers rose to prominence during the 1970s, this decade was the last hurrah for others such as Bernard Herrmann and the three godfathers of film music, Max Steiner, Alfred Newman, and Dimitri Tiomkin. Herrmann's death in 1975 came prematurely, in view of the impressive quality of works that he wrote during his last months for films directed by Brian De Palma and Martin Scorsese. The other three composers, however, had left the limelight by the beginning of the decade. Of these, only Alfred Newman was musically active to the end; his score for *Airport* was completed just before his death in 1970. As for Max Steiner, failing eyesight had forced his retirement sixteen years before his death in 1971. Dimitri Tiomkin, after composing his last original score in 1968, lived on in retirement until the end of the 1970s. The death of Tiomkin's first wife, the choreographer Albertina Rasch, appears to have convinced him that it was time to retire. As Tony Thomas indicates:

> With the death of his wife Albertina in 1968, Tiomkin seemed to sense that the Hollywood phase of his career was over. He moved to London where he

married a young Englishwoman, Olivia Patch, with whom he happily spent the remainder of his life.[39]

Tiomkin's death, on November 11, 1979, represents the end of the final chapter in the lives of the Hollywood music pioneers, who had established many of the techniques that would remain in force long after their departure from the scene. With their deaths the torch was now passed to members of a younger generation of musicians, who were largely trained in television, a medium that was virtually nonexistent when pioneers like Tiomkin first began working in film.

Endnotes

1. Ed Weiner et al., *The TV Guide TV Book* (New York: HarperCollins, 1992), p. 229.

2. Tim Brooks and Earle Marsh, *The Complete Directory to Prime Time Network TV Shows, 1946–Present,* 2d ed. (New York: Ballantine Books, 1988), p. 673.

3. Gene Brown, *Movie Time: A Chronology of Hollywood and the Movie Industry from Its Beginnings to the Present* (New York: Macmillan, 1995), pp. 201, 303.

4. Tony Thomas, *Film Score: The Art and Craft of Movie Music* (Burbank, CA: Riverwood, 1991), p. 288.

5. The original soundtrack of *M*A*S*H,* with the vocal rendition of the title theme, was released as a Columbia Records LP, OS 3520. The Ahmad Jamal instrumental version appears on another Columbia LP of the film's score, S-32753.

6. For a comparison, see the soundtrack of *Battle of Neretva* (Southern Cross Records LP, SCAR 5005, Side B, Band 3; also on CD No. SCCD-5055, Track 8); and the studio recording of *Fahrenheit 451* (Varese Sarabande CD, VSD-5551, Track 5).

7. Thomas, *Film Score*, pp. 59, 66.

8. Peter Biskind, *The Godfather Companion* (New York: HarperCollins, 1990), pp. 67–68.

9. Stanley Sadie, ed., *The Norton/Grove Concise Encyclopedia of Music* (New York: W. W. Norton & Co., 1988), p. 256.

10. Susan Sackett, *The Hollywood Reporter Book of Box Office Hits* (New York: Billboard Books, 1990), p. 222.

11. Charles Matthews, *Oscar A to Z: A Complete Guide to More Than 2,400 Movies Nominated for Academy Awards* (New York: Doubleday, 1995), p. 330.

12. James Dickey, *Deliverance* (New York: Houghton Mifflin Co., 1970), p. 69.

13. Joseph Murrells, *Million Selling Records* (New York: Arco, 1984), p. 376.

14. Ibid.

15. Craig Rosen, *The Billboard Book of Number One Albums* (New York: Billboard Books, 1996), p. 154.

16. Ibid.

17. Elston Brooks, *I've Heard Those Songs Before: The Weekly Top Ten Tunes for the Last Fifty Years* (New York: William Morrow and Co., 1981), pp. 356–57.

18. David Ewen, *American Songwriters* (New York: H. W. Wilson Co., 1987), p. 196.

19. Ibid.

20. Ibid., p. 197.

21. Gary Theroux and Bob Gilbert, *The Top Ten: 1956–Present* (New York: Simon and Schuster, 1982), p. 229.

22. Ewen, *American Songwriters*, p. 197.

23. George Roy Hill, Liner notes for the original soundtrack of *The Sting*, released on an MCA LP, MCA-390.

24. Murrells, p. 370.

25. Ibid., p. 359.

26. John Caps, "An Interview with Richard Rodney Bennett," *High Fidelity*, vol. 27, no. 6 (June 1977), p. 58.

27. Ewen, *American Songwriters*, p. 362.

28. Ibid.

29. For a thorough analysis, see the article by Doug Adams in *Film Score Monthly*, no. 68 (April 1996), pp. 18–20.

30. Sackett, *Box Office Hits*, p. 240.

31. Steven C. Smith, *A Heart at Fire's Center: The Life and Music of Bernard Herrmann* (Berkeley: University of California, 1991), pp. 342–43.

32. Ibid., p. 351.

33. Charles Lippincott, Liner notes for the original soundtrack release of *Star Wars* on a Twentieth Century Records double-LP set, 2T-541.

34. George Lucas, Liner notes for *John Williams Conducts John Williams: The Star Wars Trilogy*, on a Sony Classical CD, SK 45947.

35. Lippincott, *Star Wars* soundtrack liner notes.

36. Steven Spielberg, Liner notes for the original soundtrack release of *Close Encounters of the Third Kind*, on an Arista Records LP, AL 9500.

37. Fred Karlin, *Listening to Movies: The Film Lover's Guide to Film Music* (New York: Schirmer Books, 1994), p. 129.

38. Liner notes for the album that was advertised as the soundtrack of *Kramer vs. Kramer*, on a CBS Masterworks LP, no. M 35873. Although this album is entitled *Great CBS Masterworks Recordings of Baroque Favorites from "Kramer vs. Kramer,"* the only actual soundtrack performance included is the first track. The rest consists of recordings from the archives of Columbia Records.

39. Thomas, *Film Score*, p. 123.

7

1980–89

The Influence of Synthesized Sound

PRELUDE

Seldom has there been a time in American history when one man so dominated a decade as Ronald Reagan did the 1980s. Following the debacle of the Nixon administration and the problems that plagued Jimmy Carter in the White House, the arrival of the former Hollywood actor in the oval office helped to restore public confidence in the presidency.

NEW TECHNOLOGY. Yet the big story of the 1980s does not involve politics, but rather an overwhelming technological revolution. Computers came into wide use both in the workplace and in the home, where a variety of electronic devices became available for hookup to TV monitors. Meanwhile, the recording industry underwent its most momentous change in four decades with the introduction of laser technology, which led to development of the compact disc (CD). Another development was the videotape machine, which could both play and record programs such as movies. For a time the legality of copying from television was highly contested, but eventually the video industry resolved the legal obstacles. During the 1980s, electronics companies began the mass reproduction of movies on videotape. By the end of the decade the marketing of movies using the VHS system became a booming business, one that very much enhanced the profit margins of films. Satellite TV reception led to the creation of dozens of specialized networks and to the introduction of both cable and satellite dish companies that could connect viewers to the growing cornucopia of television channels.

In all these new technological formats, one common factor emerged: now more than ever before, almost everyone could watch movies. With more people watching movies, whether at home or at a theater, more people were listening to soundtracks. As the video industry made an ever-wider selection of films available, so also did the recording industry increase the production of both original soundtracks and studio rerecordings of film music. During the 1970s, George Korngold had already produced for RCA a series of recordings of classic film scores, including a pair of albums devoted to his father's works. In the '80s, many other companies began to realize the appeal of film music to a wider listening audience. Thus, small recording companies such as Varese Sarabande and Silva Screen gambled on the marketability of film music. Determined efforts by companies such as these have helped to make much of the film-music legacy available to the viewing public.

POPULAR MUSIC. The tragic shooting death of John Lennon on December 8, 1980, outside his apartment building in New York City, left a pall on the music scene. Several previously unpublished Lennon songs were subsequently released, including those in the *Double Fantasy* album, which became one of the top-selling albums of 1981.

For the most part, the popular music scene in the 1980s was dominated by Michael Jackson. The former child performer, who had risen to fame as the youngest member of the Jackson Five during the 1970s, catapulted to an unprecedented success as a solo performer with the *Off the Wall* album in 1980. Jackson's next album, *Thriller*, became one of the most successful albums of all time. It ranked as the top seller for both 1983 and 1984, during which time several songs from the album became number-one hits, including "Billie Jean," "Beat It," and the title song.

Although most of the popular music of the 1980s was directed at a youthful audience, occasionally a more mature message could be included in the lyrics. Such was the case with Paul McCartney's "Ebony and Ivory," a 1982 hit in which he and Stevie Wonder made a plea for racial harmony. Another song that called for peace was the 1985 hit "We Are the World," which Lionel Richie wrote with Michael Jackson. Quincy Jones, who produced Michael Jackson's solo albums, arranged the song and also brought in dozens of popular recording artists to participate. No performers' names were individually listed; instead the group of singers was simply announced as "USA for Africa." "We Are the World," which was released both as a single and as part of an album, ultimately raised $44 million for African aid.[1]

The decade witnessed the rise to prominence of several female performers. In fact, three recordings from 1981 with female lead vocalists sold more than any others released that year. The top seller was Olivia Newton-John's "Physical," followed by Kim Carnes's breathy rendition of "Bette Davis Eyes" and Diana Ross's duet with Lionel Richie on the latter's movie hit "Endless Love." By the middle of the decade, the popularity of these performers would be eclipsed by the rising fame of two other talented young women: Madonna and Whitney Houston. After first reaching the top of the charts with "Like a Virgin," released in 1984, Madonna recorded several songs that made the Top Ten during 1985: "Crazy for You"; "Angel"; and the song that seems to sum up her career, "Material Girl." Meanwhile, Whitney Houston jumped into the limelight with a pair of albums that included such hits as "Saving All My Love for You," "How Will I Know?," and a remake of the movie tune "The Greatest Love of All."

TELEVISION. The top-rated program of the early 1980s was CBS's prime-time soap opera "Dallas," which boasted ratings of historic magnitude following the creation of a cliffhanger at the end of its second season that involved the shooting of the villainous J. R. Ewing. The continuing popularity of "Dallas" led to the creation of such other prime-time soap operas as "Dynasty," "Knot's Landing," and "Falcon Crest." Viewers also got a steady dose of crime-fighting with such shows as "Magnum, P.I." (1980–88), "Hill Street Blues" (1981–87), and "Miami Vice" (1984–89). Of these, "Hill Street Blues" was the most innovative, with an excellent cast of actors and a gritty cinematic style.

The most successful sitcom of the 1980s was NBC's "Cheers," which began an eleven-season run in September 1982. Although this show caught on slowly, after three seasons it placed in the Top Ten in the Nielsen standings and remained one of the most-watched TV programs for the rest of the decade, despite growing competition from such newer comedy hits as "The Cosby Show," "The Golden Girls," and "Designing Women."

CBS, NBC, and ABC countered the ever-increasing number of cable TV networks with many fine made-for-TV movies and miniseries. Particularly memorable were Arthur Miller's *Playing for Time* (1980), with Vanessa Redgrave as a concentration-camp prisoner; *Crisis at Central High* (1981), with Joanne Woodward as a high school teacher in Little Rock during the 1957 desegregation battle; *The Day After* (1983), about a nuclear holocaust; and *The Burning Bed* (1984), with Farrah Fawcett as an abused wife. *The Thorn Birds* (1983) was a fine rendering of Colleen McCullough's novel; ABC's blockbuster adaptations of Herman Wouk's *Winds of War* (1983) and *War and Remembrance* (1988–89) gave viewers glimpses of World War II that reached beyond the scope of any single theatrical film. These and other lavishly produced miniseries offered a continuing threat to the box-office prospects of theatrical films.

MOVIES. Because of ongoing competition from television, movies in the 1980s often turned to rather sensational subjects, and dealt frankly with the problematic lives of real people. Between 1980 and 1982, the list of significant fact-based films included the award-winning *Raging Bull*, with Robert De Niro as boxer Jake La Motta; *Coal Miner's Daughter*, in which Sissy Spacek portrayed country singer Loretta Lynn; David Lynch's *Elephant Man*; Warren Beatty's *Reds*; and Richard Attenborough's *Gandhi*.

Box-office figures for the 1980s, however, reveal that the most popular movies were those that enabled viewers to escape reality. The most success-ful was Steven Spielberg's *E.T. the Extra-Terrestrial* (1982). Following close behind in popularity were the second and third installments of George Lucas's *Star Wars* trilogy, *The Empire Strikes Back* (1980) and *The Return of the Jedi* (1983). There were also the three movies in which Harrison Ford portrayed the intrepid archaeologist *Indiana Jones*. Conceived by George Lucas and directed by Steven Spielberg, these period films brought to younger audiences the flavor of the old 1930s serials, with heroic adventures and cliff-hanging perils.

Sequel fever, which had caught on in a big way in the 1970s, became an epidemic in the 1980s. Many box-office hits were automatically followed by sequels (the one significant exception being *E.T.*). In addition to the three *Star Wars* and *Indiana Jones* films, four *Star Trek* sequels and three follow-up films to the 1978 smash hit *Superman* were made. Other hit films that spawned successful sequels include *Airplane!* (1980), *Ghostbusters* (1984), and *Gremlins* (1984). Sequels that did amazingly well in the 1980s were

Rocky III (1982) and *Rocky IV* (1985), each of which made more money than the first two installments in the series, while *Aliens* (1986) also exceeded its 1979 predecessor in terms of box-office earnings.

Among the top male stars of the decade were several newcomers, including Eddie Murphy, Tom Cruise, Robin Williams, Kevin Costner, Mel Gibson, and William Hurt. Meanwhile, veterans Paul Newman and Dustin Hoffman both won Oscars for roles they played opposite Cruise. A new crop of muscle-bound actors began to emerge, with Sylvester Stallone leading the way, thanks not only to the *Rocky* films but also to three movies in which he played John Rambo, a distressed Vietnam veteran. The most surprising success story of the 1980s, however, was the rise of Arnold Schwarzenegger from titleholder in the Mr. Universe competition to box-office movie star. The transition began with *Conan the Barbarian* (1982) and its sequel *Conan the Destroyer* (1984), plus his mostly silent presence as *The Terminator* (1984). Many action-packed films followed, but the film that pleased fans most was *Twins* (1988), in which he proved that he could act alongside expert comedian Danny De Vito.

Meryl Streep led the list of actresses in the 1980s, with a series of acclaimed roles. In all, Streep was nominated six times between 1981 and 1989. With two Oscars and eight nominations accumulated by the end of the decade, she ranks, with Katharine Hepburn and Bette Davis, among the most honored actresses of all time. Not far behind Streep were Glenn Close and Jessica Lange, each of whom was nominated five times during the '80s, and Sissy Spacek, with four nominations. Among the newcomers were Kathleen Turner, Cher, Whoopi Goldberg, Melanie Griffith, and Holly Hunter.

One trend of actors in the 1980s was to work behind the camera. With *Ordinary People* (1980), Robert Redford became the first major box-office star to win an Oscar for direction. A year later, Warren Beatty won for directing *Reds*. Perhaps the most successful star to get the directing bug has been Ron Howard, who abandoned his acting career to become one of the most accomplished directors working in film.

A thumbnail sketch of 1980s films would not be complete without recognizing the talents of such filmmakers as Joel and Ethan Coen, Tim Burton, Jonathan Demme, David and Jerry Zucker, David Lynch, Lawrence Kasdan, Joe Dante, and James Cameron. In addition, several filmmakers from Australia left their mark on American films. They include Peter Weir, Bruce Beresford, and George Miller (who made all three *Mad Max* films).

Several young composers began to gain recognition for scoring films in the 1980s. James Horner, Michael Kamen, Randy Newman, Basil Poledouris, Howard Shore, and Alan Silvestri had already written film music before the '80s, but such other composers as Bruce Broughton, Danny Elfman, James Newton Howard, David Newman, Thomas Newman, and Hans Zimmer were newcomers. All of these composers as well as veterans such as John Barry, John Willams, and Jerry Goldsmith made significant contributions to the art of film music during a decade of tremendous technological advancement.

JOHN BARRY: *RAISE THE TITANIC* AND *SOMEWHERE IN TIME*. Following successful scores in the late 1960s (including the Oscar-winning *Born Free* and *The Lion in Winter*), Barry's film career declined somewhat during the next decade. In 1979, Barry began to show the level of creativity he had demonstrated during the '60s, with *Moonraker*, his first Bond film in five years, and especially with *The Black Hole*, the rousing overture of which remains among his most inventive creations. Of the five films he worked on in 1980, two in particular, *Raise the Titanic* and *Somewhere in Time*, exhibited his genius for establishing mood. Though both movies were roasted by critics, they include some of Barry's best work.

Based on the best-selling novel by Clive Cussler, *Raise the Titanic* is the fictional story of a U.S. military effort to locate the sunken ocean liner. A rare mineral, "byzanium," was supposedly buried with the ship—a mineral that, if retrieved by the wrong people, might have cataclysmic consequences.

The best part of the film is the prologue, in which historic black-and-white stills have been assembled into a visual history of the building of the Titanic. Accompanying this photo gallery is Barry's stirring main theme, which soars up the scale in a highly romantic way. Barry's theme captures both the heroic feeling that accompanies the making of this gigantic ocean liner and the excitement of the Titanic sailing across the Atlantic on its maiden voyage. This theme is not heard again until much later, when the sunken ship emerges amid a mountain of foam and spray. At first, after depth charges designed to raise the ship have been detonated and it begins to rise, amid much grinding noise, there is no music at all. As the smokestacks begin to appear above the waves, Barry's soaring music starts to sound. This stirring theme also appears as the ship is towed into New York harbor, and is heard one final time during the closing credits. The rest of Barry's score consists of much darker and more mysterious music; this includes the somber theme heard during the opening credits and the music which accompanies the undersea search for the Titanic. Luckily, Barry's career did not sink with *Raise the Titanic*, which lost more money than any other 1980 film with the exception of *Heaven's Gate*.

Somewhere in Time, which screenwriter Richard Matheson adapted from his novel *Bid Time Return*, can be considered only a minor flop, since it didn't cost nearly as much to make as *Raise the Titanic*. Shot primarily in and around the Grand Hotel on Mackinac Island, *Somewhere in Time* concerns a successful young playwright who falls in love with a woman's portrait, and then wills himself back almost seventy years in time to meet her. Jane Seymour plays an actress named Elise McKenna, who stays at a resort hotel during June 1912, while appearing in a play at a nearby theater. In 1980, Richard Collier (Christopher Reeve) visits this hotel while trying to overcome writer's block. He sees Elise's portrait in the hotel and learns that she is the same person (then elderly) who approached him eight years earlier, gave him a fancy pocket watch, and said "Come back to me"; he also learns that she died later that night. Among her possessions are a book about time travel, written by one of Richard's former professors, and a music box that plays Rachmaninoff's Rhapsody on a Theme by Paganini.

Encouraged to try time traveling by the professor, whom he visits, Richard determines to hypnotize himself into believing that he is back in 1912. In his room at the Grand Hotel, he puts away all reminders of 1980. After a fretful night, he awakens to discover that he is indeed back in June 1912. He finally meets the woman of his dreams, who approaches him and says the enigmatic words, "Is it you?" Before he can even introduce himself, her manager, William Robinson (Christopher Plummer), chases him away. The following afternoon, while Richard and Elise go rowing he hums the Rachmaninoff tune, which Elise loves but doesn't recognize. (Rachmaninoff's Rhapsody dates from 1934, and she and Richard are boating in 1912.)

Somewhere in Time,
with Jane Seymour
and Christopher Reeve.

Despite Robinson's further attempts to keep Elise and Richard apart, they meet again and become intimate. Their idyll ends with a sudden jolt, however, when Richard finds a 1979 penny in his pocket. At this moment, he is thrust back to 1980. He stays locked in his hotel room for days in a futile attempt to return to the past. When he is at last found, he is dying from malnourishment. Elise appears as in a vision; he embraces her, and the film ends with them joined for eternity.

The first use of background scoring comes at the end of the opening scene, in which the elderly Elise gives Richard the watch following the opening of his play. As she returns to her room at the Grand Hotel, a few moments of a lyrical theme by Barry are heard; this music continues until she arrives at her room and plays a phonograph. At this point, the Eighteenth Variation from the Rachmaninoff Rhapsody is heard, while Elise sits clutching the program from Richard's play. The scene then shifts ahead eight years to Richard's office in Chicago, where he is having difficulty in finishing his next play. He too is listening to the Rachmaninoff piece, which continues to play through this time change.

Of the original themes in John Barry's score, one stands out: a slow-paced lyrical idea that is first heard when Richard sees the portrait of Elise in the Grand Hotel. After learning that Elise is actually the old woman who gave him the watch eight years earlier, he returns to the portrait and becomes transfixed; this is when Barry's theme is first introduced. Its lyricism conveys the depth of Richard's feelings and lets the viewer know that the two principals are destined to meet. Some mysterious and somber music accompanies Richard's attempts to travel through time. Barry's lyrical theme returns after Richard succeeds in going back to the past, when he sees Elise in the distance. Isidore Mankovsky's ingenious camerawork features her reflection in a window, as Richard looks out across the hotel lawn. As the camera moves in toward the window, it becomes clear that the figure in the distance is indeed Elise. At this point the music starts up and continues as Richard walks toward her. This theme reappears when they spend their first afternoon together, and again that evening, during an intermission in her play, as she poses for the portrait that winds up in the hotel.

Later that evening, Robinson has Richard abducted and then tries to convince Elise that Richard has gone away. Barry's theme returns for a moment when she hears this news. The most prominent statement of Barry's lyrical idea occurs in the next scene, when Richard goes looking for Elise after escaping. Mankovsky's camera again catches her figure in the distance, as Richard sits dejectedly on a bench in front of the hotel. Elise cries "Richard!" and they run toward each other; as Barry's theme swells up to a beautifully lush statement. The music continues at a softer level when they are next seen in her hotel room, where they are about to consummate their relationship. At the end of the film, when Elise and Richard are reunited, the closing credits begin to appear as Barry's romantic theme returns once more, in a lush version that features pianist Roger Williams. There were few films made in the '80s that had such a vividly romantic musical atmosphere as *Somewhere in Time*.

JOHN WILLIAMS: *THE EMPIRE STRIKES BACK*. One of the most noteworthy films of 1980 was the second installment of the *Star Wars* trilogy, *The Empire Strikes Back*. Since all the principal characters of the first film return in *Empire*, the themes that John Williams devised for them are heard again. But there are also new musical materials added by Williams. Most significant among these is the dark-hued "Imperial March," which is associated with Darth Vader. In its employment of heavy brass and minor-key harmony, this music is in striking contrast with the brighter-tinted tones of the first film's themes. This dark quality is altogether appropriate for the second film, with its downbeat ending.

This film is the most dramatically compelling of the series. Not the least of its virtues is the addition of Yoda, the diminutive Jedi master who trains Luke to be a Jedi knight. Through the voice of Frank Oz, this often humorous character gives the film a much needed lift; Williams's lyrical theme also imbues Yoda with a sense of dignity and compassion.

Also new to the second film is the character of Lando Calrissian (Billy Dee Williams), an old friend of Han Solo, who is the administrator of Cloud City. For Lando and his celestial domain Williams created an up-tempo theme in the style of a march, in which many dotted rhythms are employed to propel the repeated-note melody. There are other new themes in *Empire*, including a dramatic idea for Boba Fett, the bounty hunter who is tracking Han Solo, plus a lyrical love theme for Han and Princess Leia, whose relationship develops considerably during the course of the second film.

Veteran screenwriter Leigh Brackett, who collaborated with Lawrence Kasdan on the insightful script, and director Irvin Kershner deserve credit for taking George Lucas's characters, who were basically comic-book heroes and villains in the first film, and developing their human qualities. With John Williams's Wagnerian method of assigning leitmotifs to every character, this film is musically accompanied in grand fashion; the composer received a well-deserved Oscar nomination.

JOHN MORRIS: *THE ELEPHANT MAN*. John Morris, who for many years worked as Mel Brooks's musical associate, stepped out of the comedy vein for David Lynch's *Elephant Man*, which was produced by Brooks's company Brooksfilms. The brilliant acting of John Hurt as the physically misshapen John Merrick, along with Freddie Francis's wonderful black-and-white photography, make this somber film worthwhile. Morris's main theme is set in the style of a melancholy waltz. First heard during the opening credits, it is played by flute and then by oboe, with an accompaniment of strings and harp. In the opening scene, which takes place at an English carnival, a portion of the waltz is heard in a calliopelike arrangement that features handbells and that was doubtlessly inspired by the setting. The kindly Dr. Treves (Anthony Hopkins) rescues Merrick, who is an attraction in a freak show, from this miserable environment, and Merrick gradually comes to accept the kindness of others.

Toward the end of the film the Adagio for Strings by Samuel Barber is heard. Merrick knows it is risky for him to sleep in a prostrate position, due to his impaired breathing, but he wants to experience the way a person would normally sleep. He attempts to emulate a painting on the wall of his room that depicts a woman lying down in bed. As the somber music continues, it becomes apparent that Merrick will not survive the night; the Barber theme becomes the Elephant Man's funeral music. Despite the interpolation of Barber's eloquent string piece, which would subsequently be used to create a funereal mood in Oliver Stone's *Platoon*, John Morris's evocative score was granted an Oscar nomination.

SHORT CUTS ■■■■ Philippe Sarde.

Particularly memorable is French composer Philippe Sarde's lovely score for *Tess*, Roman Polanski's meticulous adaptation of Thomas Hardy's novel *Tess of the d'Urbervilles*, with Nastassia Kinski conveying a youthful radiance in the title role. Sarde's lyrical themes recall English folk songs in their simple melodic quality. With a predominantly minor-key tonality, Sarde's themes effectively convey the melancholy mood of this tragic story, in which an innocent farm girl reluctantly succumbs to a man whom she thinks is her higher-born cousin, bears his child (who dies during infancy), and later becomes the wife of a minister's son. On their wedding night, when her husband learns of Tess's troubled past, there are tragic repercussions for all concerned. Sarde's evocative music, which consists primarily of a melancholy waltz theme, was justly honored with an Oscar nomination.

■■■■ John Corigliano.

Altered States has one of the most bombastic scores in memory. Composed by John Corigliano (b. 1938), whose father was the long-time concertmaster of the New York Philharmonic, this Oscar-nominated original score includes some incredibly grinding sounds for scenes accompanying Eddie Jessup (William Hurt, in his debut role), who discovers through a series of experiments a primeval form of existence. Combined with Ken Russell's often psychedelic visual imagery, Corigliano's music has a tremendous, if unsettling, impact.

■■■■ Michael Gore.

The Oscar for Best Original Score of 1980 went to the songs composed by film-music newcomer Michael Gore (b. 1951) for *Fame*, Alan Parker's musical film about a group of talented teenagers at the New York High School for the Performing Arts. Gore's music consists basically of vocal numbers that punctuate the film's plot, which follows several teenagers from the time they audition for admission to their graduation four years later. Especially noteworthy is the exuberant "Hot Lunch Jam" sequence, which begins as a dance number in the school cafeteria. The scene winds up out on the street, where dozens of teens stop traffic with their uninhibited dancing. Another impressive moment comes in the concluding scene, which features the entire cast in "I Sing the Body Electric," an elaborate production number that incorporates many musical styles, including symphonic music, rock-'n'-roll, and jazz.

Gore's music was composed in collaboration with several lyricists, including Dean Pitchford and Leslie Gore (the composer's sister). Other musical contributions were made by Irene Cara and Paul McCrane, who had lead roles in the film. Cara, in particular, conveyed a youthful enthusiasm in her solo performance of two songs, "Out Here on My Own" and the title song. Although Gore did not do much background scoring for this film, he would be hired later to provide purely instrumental scoring. The music of *Fame* is by far the picture's most memorable element.

■■■■ *Ordinary People.* The year's Oscar-winning film, Robert Redford's moving adaptation of Judith Guest's *Ordinary People*, has a simple form of musical accompaniment that features arrangements by Marvin Hamlisch of Johann Pachelbel's famed Canon in D. In an early scene, Conrad (Timothy Hutton), the troubled teenage son of Calvin and Beth (Donald Sutherland and Mary Tyler Moore), has been released from a mental hospital following a suicide attempt and is back in high school, where the choir is singing a vocal arrangement of the Pachelbel piece. This music subsequently shows up periodically in a piano version as Conrad spends time with a therapist (Judd Hirsch), who tries to convince the youth that the drowning death of Conrad's older brother was an accident for which he is blameless.

■■■■ *Raging Bull.* One of the most critically praised movies of the decade, Martin Scorsese's *Raging Bull*, is the astonishingly candid film biography of boxer Jake La Motta. For scenes in the ring, brilliantly photographed in black and white by Michael Chapman, Scorsese chose the "Intermezzo" from Pietro Mascagni's opera *Cavalleria rusticana* to create the appropriate mood. Although this music, with its lush string melody, might seem out of place for such a contemporary type of scene, it eventually becomes part of the dramatic fabric and elevates this film to a highly artistic level.

■■■■ **Dominic Frontiere.** One of the better scores of 1980 comes from one of the best films, Richard Rush's wildly comic *Stunt Man*. Dominic Frontiere (b. 1931) created a lively musical background for this film, in which Peter O'Toole plays Eli Cross, a dictatorial movie director who hires Lucky Cameron (Steve Railsback), whom the police are after, as a stunt man. Frontiere's main theme, a lively minor-key march, perfectly captures the excitement that attends the filming of a World War I action film, which is ostensibly what this movie is about. But *The Stunt Man* really concerns the difficulty in determining the dividing line between reality and fantasy.

■■■■ *The Shining.* As is typical of Stanley Kubrick's films from *2001* on, the score of *The Shining* consists mainly of previously composed materials. In this film, the borrowings include three pieces by Polish composer Krzystof Penderecki; György Ligeti's *Lontano*; and the third movement of Béla Bartók's Music for Strings, Percussion, and Celesta. Portions of this last piece accompany scenes in which little Danny (Danny Lloyd) pedals his way down the long corridors of the Overlook Hotel and encounters some bizarre phenomena, such as the repeated apparition of twin sisters (who have been dead for a long time). In addition, there is a synthesized arrangement by Wendy (nee, Walter) Carlos, played on electronic equipment by Carlos along with her associate Rachel Elkind, of the "Dies irae," from the Gregorian Mass of the Dead. The eerie sounds of this music, heard during the opening credits, convey a sense of foreboding that foretells the dire incidents to come. Kubrick's use of previously conceived music may be a questionable practice, but the "score" of *The Shining* is uncannily appropriate.

1981

DAVE GRUSIN: ON GOLDEN POND. The one musician with a jazz background who has maintained a steady pace in film scoring, since his debut in 1967, is Dave Grusin (b. 1934).

A native of Denver, he was raised in Littleton, Colorado, where his father, a watchmaker and a violinist, observed his talent and pushed him toward the piano. Despite his early accomplishments as a keyboardist, Grusin initially resisted the idea of becoming a career musician. Just before entering college, however, Grusin changed his mind and enrolled at Colorado University as a music major, where he began to show an interest in jazz, playing with young musicians such as Terry Gibbs and Johnny Smith. This interest was furthered when he later enrolled at the Manhattan School of Music. Once in New York, he worked as a pianist for singer Andy Williams, who took him along on his concert tours between 1959 and 1966. He began arranging some of Williams's material, and when Williams got a regular variety show spot on NBC in the fall of 1962, Dave Grusin became the second of several musicians to lead the studio orchestra. Grusin's stint, which lasted from 1963 to 1966, prepared him for a career in TV and film scoring that soon began to emerge. In 1967, he scored *Divorce American Style*, *Waterhole #3*, and *The Graduate*. In *The Graduate*, his instrumental background music alternated with the songs of Simon and Garfunkel. Following these efforts, Grusin got to do his first major score, the lyrical music for the memorable film version of Carson McCullers's *Heart Is a Lonely Hunter* (1968).

It would be a full decade before the Motion Picture Academy would honor him with a nomination for his work, but in the meantime, Grusin began to accumulate some impressive film-scoring credits for both theatrical films and TV movies, including *Winning* (1969); *The Friends of Eddie Coyle* (1973); *The Nickel Ride* (1974); and in 1975, *W.W. and the Dixie Dance-kings*, *The Yakuza*, and *Three Days of the Condor*. The last of these has been highly esteemed for its lyrical melodies, the most memorable of which is "Kathy's Theme," written for the character played by Faye Dunaway.

After this came several other scores, at the rate of about three per year. In 1978, Grusin received an Oscar nomination for the charming music for *Heaven Can Wait*, with a jaunty soprano saxophone melody associated with Joe Pendleton (Warren Beatty), the saxophone-playing football star. The following year, another nomination came Grusin's way, also for a movie with a sports milieu, the Zeffirelli remake of *The Champ*.

Despite Grusin's ongoing interest in jazz, occasionally a film assignment would come along that would invite a different way of thinking. Such is the case with Tony Bill's *My Bodyguard*, a little charmer of a film from 1980 in which Grusin composed some lovely background themes that were recorded by a chamber music ensemble. It is probably the most classical work that he has yet done, and one of his most memorable scores.

Dave Grusin.

Photo by Gay Goodwin Wallin

On Golden Pond, with Jane Fonda, Henry Fonda, and Katharine Hepburn.

In 1981, Grusin provided musical backgrounds for Sydney Pollack's *Absence of Malice*; Warren Beatty's *Reds* (which also includes a theme composed by Stephen Sondheim), and the most important, Mark Rydell's *On Golden Pond*, which received a lot of negative criticism at its release because of an excessive amount of sentimentality in Ernest Thompson's script (based on his own play). *Golden Pond* is noteworthy for the performances of Henry Fonda and Katharine Hepburn, both of whom won Oscars in the roles of Norman and Ethel Thayer and also because it is the film in which Jane Fonda finally got the chance to play opposite her father. Her role, although small, is pivotal. She plays the Thayers' daughter, Chelsea, who has remained close to her mother but has never developed a strong bond with her father. Toward the end of the film, as the father becomes reconciled with his offspring, one senses that the real-life Fondas are also bonding.

The main theme of the score is a lyrical idea first heard during the opening credits, where it is played by a piano alone, and then by piano accompanied by strings. One Grusin trait that became established with this score is a piano "flicker," a set of three or four notes that is sounded at the high end of the keyboard along with a lower-pitched chord. This intriguing touch provides an extra layer of melodic lyricism in moments when the music comes to a cadence point. Other than the slow-paced main theme, the most memorable part of the score is a piece entitled "New Hampshire Hornpipe," which is heard as Billy (Doug McKeon), the son of Chelsea's fiancé, takes the Thayers' motorboat out for a spin on the lake. Here Grusin comes closer to the jazz vein than in the rest of the score, which is predominantly in the harmonic tradition of the romantic scores of Hollywood's Golden Age. In the simplicity of its orchestration, the music of *Golden Pond* is reminiscent of such 1960s classics as Elmer Bernstein's music for *To Kill a Mockingbird* and Grusin's own score for *The Heart Is a Lonely Hunter*.

Like many other film composers before him, Grusin had a tendency to be something of a musical chameleon. Although his jazz roots are seldom concealed, in *Golden Pond* Grusin clearly demonstrates his ability to respond to both visual imagery and the strong emotions of a story's characters.

Besides continuing his career in film scoring as the 1980s progressed, Grusin also remained true to his jazz background by coproducing with Larry Rosen a number of jazz recordings, under the auspices of Grusin/Rosen Productions (GRP), an umbrella organization encompassing GRP Records, the label under which most of Grusin's later film soundtracks would be released. In addition to original soundtrack recordings, Grusin has recorded several samples of his film work for GRP Records. Chief among these is the album *Cinemagic*, which includes themes from *The Heart Is a Lonely Hunter*, *Three Days of the Condor*, *Heaven Can Wait*, *The Champ*, and *On Golden Pond*, along with tracks from two later film scores. This album is a well-crafted compilation of musical accomplishments from what Grusin himself calls "the 'filmic' side of my life."[2]

JOHN WILLIAMS: RAIDERS OF THE LOST ARK. As if to compensate for the failure of his 1979 film *1941*, John Williams worked diligently with Steven Spielberg to score the adventure film *Raiders of the Lost Ark*. Devised by executive producer George Lucas as a fond tribute to the cliff-hanging serials of the 1930s and '40s, *Raiders* sweeps the viewer into a breathless series of adventures, with Harrison Ford starring as Indiana Jones, a professor of archaeology who will stop at nothing to find a long-lost treasure.

Williams's music consists primarily of two themes, one of which, the "Raiders March," is heard whenever Jones is on the run from a hostile native tribe or is chasing after a bunch of Nazis. The other theme is associated with Marian (Karen Allen), an old flame of Indie's who turns up at a bar in a remote outpost in Mongolia. Williams incorporated several other themes into this thrilling adventure, which concerns the efforts of Jones and his Egyptian associates to beat the Nazis to the burial site of the Ark of the Covenant, which is thought to be entombed near one of the burial chambers of the Pharaohs. The almost nonstop action of *Raiders* obviously provided Williams with the inspiration to create a fast-paced musical background. Because of the popularity of the film, there would be two sequels, both enhanced by Williams's music.

RANDY NEWMAN: RAGTIME. One of the most promising newcomers on the film-scoring scene in the 1980s was Randy Newman (b. 1943), Alfred Newman's nephew, who contributed a charming score of upbeat tunes and sentimental melodies to *Ragtime*, Milos Forman's expert adaptation of E. L. Doctorow's brilliant novel about American life at the turn of the century. Although some of the book was jettisoned in the translation, what remains is wonderfully brought to life by an outstanding cast, which includes such veterans as Pat O'Brien as a detective and James Cagney (in his last film role) as Waldo Rhinelander, the New York police chief who attempts to remove a gang of black insurgents who have taken over the J. P. Morgan Library. As Coalhouse Walker, Jr., the ragtime-playing leader of the gang, Howard Rollins etched a memorable portrait of an angry black man who has been wronged by society. Several of Newman's fetching tunes are used for nightclub scenes in which Walker is playing piano with a dance band.

There is also the lovely Oscar-nominated song "One More Hour," which casts a melancholy aura over the film. With its mixture of real and fictional characters, *Ragtime* is a fascinating panorama that benefits greatly from Randy Newman's inspired melodic creations.

VANGELIS: *CHARIOTS OF FIRE.* The Oscar-winning film score of 1981 was Vangelis's synthesized keyboard music, which was composed for the year's Academy Award-winning film, *Chariots of Fire*, about two runners who compete in the Paris Summer Olympics of 1924. Despite some favorable reviews, this film did not appear destined for either box-office gold or Oscar glory; but the release of the soundtrack album precipitated a surprising amount of interest. By the time the Oscar nominations were announced in early 1982, the theme from *Chariots of Fire* was already popular. Notwithstanding competition from *Reds* and *Raiders of the Lost Ark*, this film won several awards.

The main theme of the score accompanies the film's parallel opening and closing scenes of a group of young men running along an English beach near Cambridge University. One of the runners, Harold Abrahams (Ben Cross), a bright but angry student who wants to use running to gain acceptance as a Jew in English society, is enrolled at Cambridge. Among other synthesized tunes in the score, is one called "Hymne," which Vangelis had actually created two years earlier for a recording entitled *Opéra sauvage.* This music is heard in an early scene where the other runner, a young Scottish preacher named Eric Liddell (Ian Charlson), is proving his terrific speed as a sprinter.

This beautifully photographed but slightly disjointed film, which brings the two primary characters together for only a few moments, lacks dramatic focus. The music itself is somewhat anachronistic in its use of synthesizers for a story that takes place in the 1920s. Despite the catchy nature of Vangelis's tunes, they seem slightly out of place in this film. Nonetheless, the popularity of this film's music virtually guaranteed the usefulness of synthesizers for creating musical backgrounds in movies of the 1980s.

SOME THINGS BORROWED, SOME THINGS NEW: *EXCALIBUR.* John Boorman's *Excalibur* is noteworthy for its prolific use of borrowed music. Based on Sir Thomas Malory's *Le morte d'Arthur*, Boorman's film is an immensely vivid cinematic version of the Arthurian legend. One of the borrowed pieces, the opening "O fortuna" chorus of Carl Orff's dramatic cantata *Carmina burana*, is featured in several scenes of Arthur and his knights riding into battle.

The most extensive utilization of borrowed music in the film is revealed in scenes involving the sword Excalibur. These moments are accompanied by "Siegfried's Funeral Music," which is taken from Act III of Richard Wagner's *Die Götterdämmerung*, the last of the monumental cycle of four operas known as *Der Ring des Nibelungen*. The first appearance of this music actually occurs at the very outset, as the Warner Bros. logo appears, followed by the announcement of the film's title. The second use occurs in the opening scene, in which Merlin (Nicol Williamson) is handed the sword by the Lady of the Lake. In the following battle scene, in which Arthur's father, Uther Pendragon (Gabriel Byrne), is wielding Excalibur, this theme is heard again. Further appearances of the Siegfried music occur when the young Arthur (Nigel Terry) pulls the sword from the stone into which Arthur's father had encased it, shortly before his death, and, toward the end of the film, as Arthur and Mordred (Robert Addie) fight to the death. This music shows up once more, during the closing scene, in which Perceval (Paul Geoffrey), acting upon Arthur's command, takes the sword back to the lake, where he tosses it to the Lady of the Lake. The Siegfried music continues to sound as the film's closing credits are flashed onto a black screen. Excerpts from two other Wagner operas are used briefly; these include the "Prelude" from *Parsifal* and the opening music from *Tristan und Isolde*. But it is the grandiloquent Siegfried music, with a succession of dramatic chords, that makes the most powerful impact.

Trevor Jones (b. 1949) was enlisted to compose an original score for *Excalibur*, including some lively dance pieces heard in banquet scenes. He also wrote music with an eerie vocal effect for a scene in which Uther employs a disguise devised by Merlin to gain admittance to an enemy's castle, where he makes love to the enemy's wife, who then becomes pregnant with Arthur. Jones's original music, plus the powerfully dramatic excerpts from works by Wagner and Orff, combine to form an eclectic but highly individual score, one that creates a memorable tonal background for this compelling version of the Arthurian saga.

SHORT CUTS ■■■■ Laurence Rosenthal.

Of the many adventure films released in 1981, one of the most colorful was *Clash of the Titans*, produced by Charles Schneer and Ray Harryhausen, who had been responsible for several Sinbad films and also for *Jason and the Argonauts*. Laurence Rosenthal was chosen to accompany the story of Perseus and his attempts to marry the fair Andromeda despite the interference of the gods. Rosenthal created a rousing score, with a soaring main brass theme for the heroic Perseus, who goes to extraordinary lengths to regain Andromeda. This theme reappears in the flying sequence in which Perseus tames the winged stallion Pegasus.

■■■■ Jerry Goldsmith.

After a rather unproductive year in 1980, Jerry Goldsmith returned to full stride in 1981 with five new scores, including portions of the TV miniseries *Masada*. In terms of theatrical releases, Goldsmith composed a throbbing score for Peter Hyams's futuristic *Outland*, plus a brilliantly conceived choral and orchestral background for *The Final Conflict*, the concluding film in the *Omen* trilogy. Although by the third film the screenwriters had just about run out of ways to kill people, Goldsmith's often majestic music keeps the film from floundering.

Goldsmith's best work of 1981 is the deceptively simple background for *Raggedy Man*, in which Sissy Spacek plays a mother of two who takes a job as a phone operator in a small Texas town during World War II. The lyrical main theme features a slow-paced melody based on a seven-note melodic pattern. This theme is first heard in a simple arrangement for flute and guitar. The harmonica is also used extensively in this charming score.

■■■■ Alex North.

The list of Oscar-nominated scores for 1981 includes Alex North's highly creative music for *Dragonslayer*. With this unusually modernistic score, North proved himself to be among the most unpredictable of film composers. The main theme includes a rhythmically lively melody played by woodwinds in their highest register. The score of *Dragonslayer* is one of the most offbeat and original ever composed for a sword-and-sorcery epic.

■■■ **John Carpenter.** One of the leading synthesizer score composers of the early 1980s was film director John Carpenter, who followed up his earlier *Halloween* and *The Fog* with an intriguing electronic score for *Escape from New York*. This clever but violent melodrama is set in 1997 and takes place in a futuristic prison, which, in fact, is the island of Manhattan. The plot concerns an attempt to rescue the president, who has been taken there as a hostage. Kurt Russell effectively plays Snake Plissken, the convict who is given a chance at freedom if he can successfully bring the president out of confinement. Carpenter, with his computer-programming associate Roger Howarth, created some ingenious synthesized sounds for this film. He also arranged a clever electronic version of Claude Debussy's piano piece "The Sunken Cathedral," which is heard as Snake's plane glides over the Hudson River and lands in the foreboding prison area.

■■■ **John Barry.** The year's sexiest score is the bluesy background by John Barry for Lawrence Kasdan's *Body Heat*, which has the flavor of film noir updated to the 1980s. For this intriguing film of adultery, deception, and murder, Kasdan elicited from Barry a haunting background theme, with a truly sensuous saxophone melody that captures the chemistry of the illicit lovers played by Kathleen Turner and William Hurt.

■■■ **Carl Davis.** Sexual attraction is also at the center of Karel Reisz's adaptation of John Fowles's intriguing novel *The French Lieutenant's Woman*, which benefited by the choice of English composer Carl Davis (b. 1936) for the background score. A lyrical solo violin theme contributes a much-needed emotional flavor to this slow-moving drama, which provides viewers with alternative endings. Curiously, Meryl Streep and Jeremy Irons are also shown as actors in the process of bringing Fowles's characters to life on the screen. Their affair parallels that of the nineteenth-century characters they are portraying.

■■■ *The Four Seasons.* Alan Alda's *Four Seasons* is another 1981 film that is notable for its use of borrowed music. Alda inserted the music of Antonio Vivaldi to add flavor to this episodic film, in which three couples are seen taking vacations together. Each vacation sequence takes place at a different time of year, and the music suitable to each segment is borrowed from one of Vivaldi's four violin concertos, known collectively as *The Four Seasons*. Each of the four seasonal segments into which the film is structurally divided is preceded by a beautifully photographed series of nature shots, over which the appropriate Vivaldi music has been juxtaposed.

BASIL POLEDOURIS: CONAN THE BARBARIAN. One of the most expensively produced films of the early 1980s was John Milius's action movie based on the stories by Robert E. Howard about Conan the Barbarian, a powerfully muscular warrior living in an unspecified ancient time. To bring the character to cinematic life, former bodybuilder Arnold Schwarzenegger was an ideal choice. Milius chose Basil Poledouris for the background score.

Kevin Mulhall's liner notes for the 1992 expanded CD release of the *Conan* soundtrack reveal the following about Poledouris:

> Knowing that music would play a key role in the film, Milius asked his friend Basil Poledouris to handle the scoring duties. Poledouris and Milius first hooked up on the campus of the University of Southern California in the late

1960s. Poledouris was originally enrolled in USC's music department (David Raksin was one of his professors), but he switched his major to film after one year. After earning his master's degree in Cinema, Poledouris attended the California State University in order to complete his musical training. Poledouris was something of an anomaly in film school—he could direct, write, edit and compose his own scores. But after a while, Poledouris decided he would rather stand in front of an orchestra than behind a camera.[3]

For Poledouris, who was born in Kansas City in 1945, the film school experience, plus his ongoing friendship with John Milius, helped to launch his film-composing career. In 1971, he received his first professional scoring opportunity as co-composer (with Richard Baskin) of the music for the TV movie *Congratulations, It's a Boy!*, for Spelling Productions. Poledouris's first score for a theatrical feature was the music for *Extreme Close-Up* (1973), which is primarily distinguished by the fact that it was written by Michael Crichton and directed by Jeannot Szwarc (of *Jaws 2* and *Somewhere in Time*).

When John Milius and Oliver Stone's script about Conan was put into production, Poledouris was already on the set. As a result, he had the visual style of the production in his mind while composing the score. In a 1982 interview with David Hutchison, Poledouris made some revealing comments about working with John Milius on this film:

> It was always in John's mind that *Conan* would be solid music—much like an opera, but without singing. Even the first three reels of the film is wall-to-wall music. From the first frame of reel one to the end of the wheel-of-pain sequence, somewhere in the middle of reel three, is one long cue without any break. I was terrified when I first realized that.[4]

The music at the beginning of *Conan* accompanies the following scenario: it commences with the forging of the sword; continues with the passing on

Conan the Barbarian, with Arnold Schwarzenegger.

of the sword, the passage of the riders of doom, the master being eaten by the dogs, and the beheading of Conan's mother; and finally comes to an end with the wheel of pain, to which Conan has been bound by heavy ropes. This opening music, entitled "Anvil of Crom" on the soundtrack, is the movie's principal theme. It features the brassy sound of twenty-four French horns in a dramatic intonation of the melody, while pounding drums add an incessantly driven rhythmic propulsion.

Poledouris's score includes a second principal melodic idea, entitled "The Riddle of Steel," which defines the emotional core of Conan's character. As the young warrior vows revenge for the brutal slaying of his parents, the music gives Conan's quest a stirring resonance. The first time this music is used, however, is when Conan's father is delivering a speech from atop a mountain. After his death, the music is transferred to Conan; this suggests that the son will carry on his father's leadership.[5]

When filming and editing were completed, Milius presented Poledouris with two videotapes of the finished film, one with a temporary musical track using excerpts from works by Wagner, Stravinsky, and Prokofiev, and the other without any music. It took Poledouris some time to get past the intimidation of having to write music that might compare favorably with these established masters of dramatic underscoring. He finally realized that Milius had simply wanted to show him what kinds of moods he was looking for. The temporary score may have been a starting point for Poledouris's music, but the final result is entirely his own work, which includes the choral music heard in several scenes. Milius used the "Battle on the Ice" sequence from Prokofiev's film music of *Alexander Nevsky* plus choral numbers from Carl Orff's *Carmina burana* as temporary tracks for several action sequences. Milius had wanted Poledouris to incorporate some of Orff's work into the score, but while *Conan* was in production, *Excalibur*, which includes the opening "O Fortuna" chorus of *Carmina burana*, was released. This persuaded Milius to abandon that idea and thus Poledouris was given the green light to compose an original chanting theme that was eventually performed for the soundtrack by members of the Chorus of Santa Cecilia in Rome, where the entire score was recorded.[6]

The chant pieces were based on an English text by Poledouris himself; these were then translated into Latin by Beth Lawson and Teresa Cortey. The final product, according to Poledouris, was used in an early scene as cheerleading music for the film's chief villain, Thulsa Doom (James Earl Jones). The English version of the text roughly corresponds to the following lines that Poledouris offered in his interview with David Hutchison:

> Steel.
> We seek things of steel.
> Riven from hell, driven by evil,
> We are dying in battle for Doom,
> For fated Doom.
>
> Farewell skies, farewell snow,
> Farewell earth, we are dying;
> We are dying for Doom,
> Dying for fated Doom.

Another chant is going on when Conan's mother is beheaded. John suggested a title for that one; John has a great gift for putting visual moments and concepts into words. Of that moment with the young Conan watching transfixed as his mother's head falls onto the white snow Milius says, "Conan is receiving the 'Gift of Fury'." The chant goes (again the English approximate):

> Doom approaches,
> Bringing the Gift of Fury
> Darkness reigns.[7]

Besides the appropriately dramatic music for the many action sequences, the exquisitely lovely "Wifeing" theme accompanies a scene between Conan and Valeria (Sandahl Bergman). Although this theme is first played softly by a solo oboe with a sustained string background, soon the entire string section repeats it in a lushly romantic statement that is emotion-filled. This melancholy music is consistent with the rest of *Conan*'s score. Poledouris's use of minor-key harmony sets this score apart from the Romantic period sound of scores for other films set in the past.

One other theme deserving comment is "The Orgy," which Poledouris's daughter Zoe had a hand in creating. According to Poledouris:

> I was working out the music at the piano, when my young daughter walked in and started playing along with me on the recorder. I couldn't get the tune out of my head, so when I was finishing that piece of music in Rome for the

recording session it was included. The orchestration of that sequence is particularly brilliant. I worked very closely with orchestrator Greig McRitchie and a lot of the build and excitement of the cue is in the instrumentation, like having the trumpets and trombones playing what the clarinets were doing only a few moments before.[8]

Poledouris completed two hours of nearly continuous music for a film that runs just under 130 minutes. Because this was the first large-scale orchestral score that he had attempted, his accomplishment in scoring *Conan the Barbarian* is considerable. Although there would be some further scores by Poledouris of a scope similar to that of *Conan the Barbarian* in the next few years, including the 1984 sequel *Conan the Destroyer*, plus several films by the Dutch filmmaker Paul Verhoeven, his monumental score for *Conan the Barbarian* remains one of the most spectacular film music achievements of the decade.

JOHN WILLIAMS: *E.T. THE EXTRA-TERRESTRIAL.* Steven Spielberg's *E.T. the Extra-Terrestrial* eclipsed all previous movies in terms of box-office earnings; this record would go unchallenged until Spielberg's own 1993 sensation *Jurassic Park*.

As opposed to most of Spielberg's earlier films, in which special effects sometimes overwhelm the human elements in the story, *E.T.* is that rarest of species, a science-fiction film in which emotions dominate over hardware. The deceptively simple idea of the film is a variation on the old "boy and his dog" formula of such pictures as *Lassie Come Home* and *Old Yeller*. When the alien E.T. becomes an ex-officio member of a fatherless family in a middle-class California suburb, the viewer is drawn in emotionally by the relationship that develops between E.T. and ten-year-old Elliott (Henry Thomas), who seems especially protective of this visitor from space. Elliott's older brother, Michael (Robert MacNaughton), and his younger sister, Gertie (Drew Barrymore), are also drawn to the friendly alien, but the transference of feelings between E.T. and Elliott makes their relationship special.

After a while, E.T. begins to succumb to ill effects from the Earth's atmosphere, and Elliott also experiences declining physical health. The film becomes a rescue story; the children undertake the task of protecting E.T. from scientists who have been keeping surveillance on their home; ultimately, they help him set up a transmitter so that he can contact his home planet. When the alien craft returns to rescue E.T., there is a tearful farewell between the alien and his newfound friends on planet Earth.

Williams's earlier effort on behalf of Spielberg's *Close Encounters of the Third Kind* had produced one of the classic scores of the 1970s, in which an alien visitation is treated as a mystical event. Five years later, Williams created an even more emotionally moving musical background for *E.T.* There are at least five melodic motifs in the score, all of which have a common musical thread: the use of the rising fifth. Although the music for the beginning credits includes some muted synthesizer sounds and is not very melodic in nature, the opening scene demonstrates a shift to a more conventional musical style, with a motif that begins with an ascending fifth ("do-sol"), before falling back down in pitch by a semitone. (This chromatically raised fourth-scale step is located between "fa" and "sol," and is prominently heard as the second tone of Leonard Bernstein's song "Maria"). The idea is first sounded as Elliott looks out at the starry night sky. The next musical idea to be introduced accompanies Elliott as he bikes to

E.T. the Extra-Terrestrial.

school. In this melodic pattern, the ascending fifth is built into a steadily moving line that again includes the raised fourth step of the scale. This idea is also utilized for several further biking scenes.

For E.T. himself, Williams created a seven-note motif that also starts with the rising fifth; the film's fourth idea, which is ultimately developed into the score's principal theme, grows out of an eight-note idea that once again begins with these two notes. This idea first appears in a scene in Elliott's room, when Michael and Gertie meet Elliott's new friend.

One further melody is introduced during the climactic bicycle chase, when Michael and his friends help Elliott take E.T. to the woods, to await the spaceship that will return E.T. to his own planet. In this melodic pattern, which is more a rhythmic fanfare than a fully developed theme, the rising fifth occurs as part of a nine-note idea. The concluding scene in the woods, where E.T. says his goodbyes to Elliott and his siblings, features a grandiose full-orchestra version of several melodic ideas, from the opening night-sky motif to E.T.'s theme and the romantic main theme. This scene remains one of the most touching moments of any film of the decade. John Williams richly deserved the Oscar he won for this inspiring score.

JERRY GOLDSMITH: *POLTERGEIST.* Released concurrently with *E.T.* was 1982's other summer blockbuster, *Poltergeist*, which includes one of Jerry Goldsmith's most potently dramatic scores. This tense ghost story was directed by Tobe Hooper but has the stamp of Steven Spielberg as original author, cowriter of the screenplay, and coproducer. A house in a suburban California neighborhood has been erected over an ancient burial plot. We soon learn that the graves were not actually moved; this explains the unsolicited presence of hostile spirits in the home of the Freeling family, whose youngest child, Carol Anne (Heather O'Rourke), is the first to acknowledge their presence when she talks to them via the TV set.

The TV screen provides the film's first images, in stark closeup, of soldiers on Iwo Jima, as we hear the "Star Spangled Banner." As the credits roll, Jerry Goldsmith's score begins with the theme for Carol Anne, which features a lyrical melody played by strings, accompanied by the sound of a wordless children's choir. As the poltergeists invade the home, Goldsmith's score takes on a much more dramatic style. During the course of this film, there is plentiful opportunity for musical commentary, and Goldsmith's score provides much of the film's impact. Especially dramatic is the scene in which a team of parapsychologists, led by a diminutive medium (Zelda Rubenstein), helps Diane Freeling (JoBeth Williams) retrieve Carol Anne, who has been taken hostage by the malevolent ghosts. Amid flickering lights and gusty winds, Goldsmith's music adds even more impact to the already emotionally gripping scene.

S HORT CUTS ■■■■ **James Horner.** In addition to *E.T.* and *Poltergeist*, two futuristic films inspired some of 1982's most memorable soundtrack sounds. For *Star Trek II: The Wrath of Khan*, James Horner furnished a heroic main theme with a boldly rising melodic motif sounded by French horns. Although Horner came to the second *Star Trek* film with relatively few previous film-scoring experiences, his emotion-charged music helped establish him as a rising young star of film music in the 1980s.

■■■■ **Vangelis.** The other noteworthy 1982 film with a science-fiction premise is Ridley Scott's *Blade Runner*, which is set in the Los Angeles of 2019. While Decker (Harrison Ford) searches throughout the city for four remarkably human-looking robots called replicants, who have escaped from an Offworld facility, the synthesized score by Vangelis creates a dreamlike atmosphere. Since *Blade Runner* takes place in the future, the electronic sounds seem more fitting in this film than in *Chariots of Fire*.

■■■■ **Dave Grusin.** One of 1982's most outstanding films, Sydney Pollack's delightful *Tootsie*, features a catchy and tuneful background score by Dave Grusin, including the melody of a title song, and also the tune of "It Might Be You," which was one of the year's Oscar-nominated songs.

■■■■ **Marvin Hamlisch and Jack Nitzsche.** Other 1982 Oscar-nominated scores include Marvin Hamlisch's melancholy but lyrical music for *Sophie's Choice*, plus the part-synthesized rock score by Jack Nitzsche for Taylor Hackford's film *An Officer and a Gentleman*, the music of which is predominantly based on the melody of the Oscar-winning song "Up Where We Belong."

■■■■ **Ravi Shankar and George Fenton.** The final scoring nominee was the subdued background music of Richard Attenborough's Oscar-winning film, *Gandhi*. For this film, music was used sparingly; yet this long but engrossing drama features a combination of Indian sounds and more traditionally European ones. Attenborough engaged the services of Ravi Shankar (b. 1920), who had composed the music for the *Apu* trilogy of famed Indian director Satyajit Ray, plus the score of Ralph Nelson's *Charly* (1968). The sitar music by Shankar contributes an authentic Indian flavor to much of *Gandhi*; the balance of the score is the work of newcomer George Fenton (b. 1950).

■■■ **Philippe Sarde.** Jean-Jacques Annaud's *Quest for Fire* includes an almost wall-to-wall score by Philippe Sarde. This highly unusual film, about the daily life of a prehistoric tribe, features a primitive type of speech that was especially invented for the film. Sarde's music fills in the gaps with a sometimes dissonant but lyrical background.

■■■ **Henry Mancini.** In Blake Edwards's *Victor/Victoria*, Julie Andrews plays an out-of-work actress in Berlin of the 1930s who, to get a job, does a drag act in reverse. This movie, basically a reworking of a 1933 German film, features a Henry Mancini score that includes six original songs which are used as stage material by various cast members, especially Andrews, whose stage character of Victoria is thought by her audience to be a man. Despite the 1950s feel of the songs, Mancini won an Oscar in the about-to-be-deleted category called "Original Song Score and Its Adaptation, or Adaptation Score."[9]

■■■ **Miklos Rozsa.** Finally, 1982 marks the end of the illustrious film-composing career of Miklos Rozsa. With Carl Reiner's *Dead Men Don't Wear Plaid*, the final Rozsa score pays homage to the film noir style that Rozsa had helped establish in the 1940s. Reiner, who produced the movie and coauthored the screenplay with the film's star Steve Martin, wanted to incorporate footage from old 1940s films, several of which had Rozsa's music to begin with. Thus, it seemed necessary to hire Rozsa to blend the old with the new. The score is an incredibly dramatic affair that utilizes all the typical 1940s trappings; this includes the theremin, which was Rozsa's signature instrument in both *Spellbound* and *The Lost Weekend*. In sheer musical terms the score of *Dead Men Don't Wear Plaid* stands as one of Rozsa's supreme scoring accomplishments. Both the wonderfully tense main theme and the lyrically inspired love theme are reprised in the glorious music that accompanies the closing credits.

Regrettably, this project took a heavy toll on the composer. Rozsa developed back trouble during the final preparations for the recording sessions, which were subsequently conducted by Lee Holdridge. Rozsa soon thereafter decided to end his outstanding career as a film composer.

BILL CONTI: *THE RIGHT STUFF.* Many American film composers have received their first scoring opportunities because of their previous work in Hollywood either as instrumentalists (e.g., John Williams) or as arrangers (e.g., Henry Mancini and Hugo Friedhofer). For Bill Conti, whose score for *The Right Stuff* won an Oscar, the road to fame as a movie composer came from going east instead of west—all the way to Rome.

Born on April 13, 1942, in Providence, Rhode Island, Conti was raised in a musical family. From his father, an accomplished pianist, sculptor, and painter, Conti received his first lessons in piano at the age of seven. In his early teens, the family moved to Florida because of his father's health. In high school he organized a rock-'n'-roll group and also played in the high school marching band and symphony orchestra.[10] Since his family could not afford to send him to college, Conti took a high school counselor's advice and applied for a scholarship on the bassoon. (There is usually money available for a good bassoonist since there are so few contenders.) The only problem was that until his high school graduation he

Photo by Gay Goodwin Wallin

Bill Conti.

had never played the bassoon. Rather than letting that technicality stand in his way, Conti taught himself the instrument over the summer of 1960 and managed to pass an audition at Louisiana State University (LSU).[11]

As a music major at LSU Conti became very active in musical groups. Not only did he play the bassoon in the university symphony orchestra, but he also became the staff arranger for the marching band. In addition to these activities he found time to play jazz piano in local clubs in Baton Rouge to help finance his college education. By the time he graduated, Conti had become more interested in composing than in performing. He took his portfolio of arrangements to New York and passed another audition, which led to three years at the Juilliard School of Music as a composition major. It was at this time that he came into contact with several top American composers, including Vincent Persichetti, Roger Sessions, and Luciano Berio. He received both a bachelor's degree and a master's degree from Juilliard.

Conti, already married to a young dancer whom he had met at LSU, decided to go to Italy because of the influence of another of his teachers, Hugo Weisgall, who was going there himself. With Rome as their home base, the Contis adjusted to living on a shoestring while Bill got work playing in clubs with a jazz trio that he had formed. Over the next five years Conti continued to live and work in Italy. To make ends meet, he accepted jobs ghostwriting scores for spaghetti Westerns. It was through these low-budget films that Conti learned the craft of motion-picture scoring. In 1969, he received a credit for the score of *Candidate for a Killing*, which starred Anita Ekberg; three years later, he met film director Paul Mazursky, who would be most influential in turning Conti's attentions to Hollywood.

When Mazursky went to Italy to direct location scenes for *Blume in Love* (1973), he needed someone who could arrange bits of classical themes for a small orchestra that was to play background music for the scenes with Steven and Nina (George Segal and Susan Anspach), who have gone to Venice for their honeymoon. As the couple sit in an outdoor café sipping espresso, the orchestra plays portions of several pieces, including the "Dance of the Hours" from Amilcare Ponchielli's opera *La Gioconda*, "Largo al factotum" from Gioacchino Rossini's *Barber of Seville*, the first movement of Mozart's *Eine Kleine Nachtmusik*, a Viennese waltz by Rudolf Sieczynski, and two traditional Italian songs.

Although Mazursky did not credit Conti for his work on *Blume in Love*, he offered Conti a job scoring his next film, *Harry and Tonto* (1974). The success of this film, which earned for Art Carney the Oscar as Best Actor, led to Conti's being hired for Paul Mazursky's next two films, *Next Stop, Greenwich Village* (1976) and *An Unmarried Woman* (1978). In between these two films Conti scored a movie about a down-on-his-luck boxer who wants to go the distance against the heavyweight champion. Since the script was written by the then unknown Sylvester Stallone, who insisted that he be allowed to star in the film, *Rocky* was not expected to be a box-office hit. Even its director, John G. Avildsen, had not previously met with much success, although *Joe* (1970) had received critical praise. *Rocky*'s two producers, Robert Chartoff and Irwin Winkler, had great faith in the project and wisely decided on a limited release of the film. Their game plan worked better than expected. When the film opened in New York and Los Angeles in December 1976, it received glowing reviews. Two months later, *Rocky* walked off with ten nominations, including one for Bill Conti's song "Gonna Fly Now." After *Rocky* won the Oscar as Best Picture, movie-goers everywhere wanted to see the film. Although Conti did not personally receive an Oscar for his work on *Rocky*, its huge success led to other projects, including numerous films directed by John G. Avildsen, among which were *Slow Dancing in the Big City* (1978), *The Formula* (1980), and several *Karate Kid* films.

Conti's connection with Sylvester Stallone continued; he worked on Stallone's next three films: *Paradise Alley* (1978); *F.I.S.T.* (1978), for which he created one of his most dramatic scores; and *Rocky II* (1979). Conti ultimately scored a total of four Rocky films, in each of which he used the same trumpet fanfare at the beginning, as the title rolls across the screen. Other noteworthy films with music by Conti were *The Seduction of Joe Tynan* (1979); *Gloria* (1980); *Victory* (1981); and even a James Bond film, *For Your Eyes Only* (1981), the title song of which won Conti a second Oscar nomination.

The most ambitious project of Bill Conti's career came when Philip Kaufman hired him to score the film version of *The Right Stuff* (1983), Tom Wolfe's nonfictional book about the efforts to put man in space. This lengthy film recounts the history of the American space program from its

The first seven astronauts, as portrayed (left to right) by Scott Glenn, Scott Paulin, Charles Frank, Fred Ward, Lance Henriksen, Dennis Quaid, and Ed Harris in *The Right Stuff*.

inception in the 1950s to the successful orbital flights of John Glenn and Gordon Cooper in the early 1960s. It is framed by scenes with Chuck Yeager (Sam Shepard), who is first seen in his successful attempt to break the sound barrier in 1947, and is later shown narrowly escaping death in the crash of an NF-104, in which he is trying to set another speed record. For people who lived through the 1960s, the scenes of Alan Shepard (Scott Glenn), Gus Grissom (Fred Ward), John Glenn (Ed Harris), and Gordon Cooper (Dennis Quaid) going into space provide a vivid reminder of the days when America's Mercury program attempted to surpass the Russians to gain a predominant position in space exploration.

Not only is *The Right Stuff* brilliantly scripted (by Kaufman) and photographed (by Caleb Deshanel), but Bill Conti's soaring patriotic music adds considerably to the film's impact. The score is based on two principal themes. The first, a glorious march, is initially presented during the opening credits. Although both the melody and the rhythm of this music bear an uncanny resemblance to a march theme in Alexander Glazunov's ballet score *The Seasons*, the fanfarelike ambiance contributes a stirring, heroic quality to the film's music. The second theme, for woodwinds and strings, is less martial in style; it is heard as Yeager successfully breaks the sound barrier on October 14, 1947. One of the scenes prominently featuring the opening march theme occurs when the seven original astronauts are first seen wearing their space suits. It is also heard toward the end of the film during the twenty-two-orbit flight of Gordon Cooper on May 15, 1963.

For the earlier three-orbit flight of John Glenn on February 20, 1962, Kaufman preempted Conti's music in favor of fragments of the "Mars," "Jupiter," and "Neptune" movements from Gustav Holst's orchestral suite *Planets*. Although each of these three excerpts has a strong emotional content, there is a sense of familiarity about them which may detract from their effectiveness in this film. Also curious is Kaufman's choice of an Eskimo melody, as arranged by Henry Mancini for his score of *The White Dawn*, which accompanies the scene of Glenn floating around the Earth in orbit.

Although *The Right Stuff* was not a huge box-office hit, it managed to eke out eight Oscar nominations, including citations for Best Picture and Best Original Score. Of the four Oscars that *The Right Stuff* won, three have to do with sound (Best Sound, Best Sound Effects Editing, and Best Original Score); the fourth award was for Best Film Editing. This is the only score for which Bill Conti has been given accolades by the Academy, but he has achieved recognition in a different way: since 1977 he has been a regular fixture at the Academy Awards ceremony as conductor of the orchestra.

JERRY GOLDSMITH: FROM *UNDER FIRE* TO *TWILIGHT ZONE: THE MOVIE*.

In the twenty years following his first Oscar nomination in 1962 (for *Freud*), Jerry Goldsmith became perhaps the most consistently creative and accomplished composer in Hollywood, and was nominated for many more awards. Though he has won only one Oscar (for *The Omen*), no one has demonstrated better than Goldsmith the ability to adapt his style to fit a particular film.

He received his fourteenth Oscar nomination for the music of *Under Fire*, a story of journalists covering a series of political upheavals in South America. The Spanish style of the music is enhanced by the sounds of the solo guitar, which was recorded for the soundtrack by popular recording artist Pat Metheny.

Even better than *Under Fire* is Goldsmith's music for *Psycho II*, a much-belated sequel to Alfred Hitchcock's 1960 classic. In this follow-up, Norman Bates (Anthony Perkins) is released at long last from a mental hospital, but he teeters on the edge of insanity. Instead of the all-strings accompaniment created by Bernard Herrmann for the original film, Goldsmith opted for a normally voiced orchestration. While the results may not be as unique as those of Herrmann, Goldsmith's slow-paced themes are nonetheless melodically intriguing.

Goldsmith's best score of the year is his powerful music for *Twilight Zone: The Movie*, which consists of four separate stories and a prologue. The most effective section, both musically and dramatically, is the final one, entitled "Nightmare at 20,000 Feet," in which a passenger on an airplane (John Lithgow) thinks someone is trying to rip off one of the plane's wings. With pulsating rhythms, Goldsmith's music helps to create an unsettling effect.

SHORT CUTS ■■■■ John Williams. *The Return of the Jedi* made almost as much money as the original *Star Wars*. While lacking the sheer energy of the first film and the probing characterizations of *The Empire Strikes Back*, *Jedi* has many action-filled moments, and brings this trilogy to a satisfactory close. John Williams received yet another Oscar nomination for his efforts, which include several new themes, most notably the jaunty music for the diminutive Jawas.

■■■■ **Michael Gore.** Michael Gore followed his award-winning music of *Fame* with a charming background score for James L. Brooks's film version of Larry McMurtry's *Terms of Endearment*. Gore's music features one principal theme, a lyrical melody for piano and strings, which is heard periodically throughout this story of two women, Aurora (Shirley MacLaine) and her daughter Emma (Debra Winger). The film covers Emma's entire life span, from her birth to her tragic death from cancer. The shift in tone from comedy to drama toward the end of the film may be a bit unsettling, but the performances and the music are so strong that they carry this film over its rough spots.

■■■■ **Maurice Jarre.** Although Maurice Jarre's earlier film music was usually performed by a full symphony orchestra, with Peter Weir's *Year of Living Dangerously* he began to have his scores realized on electronic equipment. In the wake of the success of such electronic scores as Giorgio Moroder's *Midnight Express* and Vangelis's *Chariots of Fire*, many moviemakers wanted their films to include synthesized sounds. Thus, Jarre's score for *Living Dangerously* was performed on electronic instruments by Spencer Lee, in collaboration with Jarre himself. The finished product appears only sporadically in the film, which is set in Jakarta at the time of an Indonesian civil war in 1965. Many sequences lack music, due to director Weir's attempt to create a documentarylike atmosphere. There is, however, the use of a Javanese gamelan effect at different points in the film, including the opening credits, and a later sequence in which the metallic gamelan sound is mixed with synthesized tones. Jarre's score is somewhat undercut by the borrowed use of a theme from Vangelis's 1979 recording *Opéra sauvage*, heard in a romantic scene in which Guy (Mel Gibson) is out driving with Jill (Sigourney Weaver) after curfew. This music reappears in a later scene in which Jill goes out in the rain to be with Guy again.

■ ■ ■ **James Horner.** Following the success of *Star Trek II*, James Horner was offered the scoring for several other sci-fi films. Although Peter Yates's *Krull* is overly reminiscent of such earlier movies as *Star Wars*, Horner created a melodically rich score for this elaborate film. There are three main ideas in *Krull*'s music; these include a brilliant brass fanfare, a heroic march theme for French horn and strings, and a lyrical love theme first introduced by cellos, with celesta and piano accompaniment.

Equally dramatic but less melodic is Horner's score for *Brainstorm*, Douglas Trumbull's somewhat disjointed film about an electronic company's latest invention, a virtual-reality device consisting of audio tapes that give listeners powerful sensations when they wear specially designed headsets. A boys' choir provides an eerie accompaniment to much of the film, whereas low grinding chords punctuate several scenes, especially one in which one of the company's inventors (Louise Fletcher) uses the new equipment to record brain waves of her own fatal heart attack.

■ ■ ■ **Elmer Bernstein.** John Landis's *Trading Places* is an often hilarious film in which wealthy executive Louis Winthorpe (Dan Aykroyd) and street hustler Billy Ray Valentine (Eddie Murphy) find their lifestyles exchanged as part of a bet between Louis's two elderly bosses Randolph and Mortimer Duke (Ralph Bellamy and Don Ameche). The bet concerns the relative importance of heredity and environment in the formation of a man's character and position in life. If Billy Ray rises to the top of the business world, it will prove Mortimer's assertion about environment.

The Billy Wilderesque tone of *Trading Places* reveals the greed of the 1980s; still, the film is quite endearing, thanks largely to Elmer Bernstein's clever arrangements of various classical pieces. From the opening overture to Mozart's *Marriage of Figaro*, the score progresses through several Mozart works, plus pieces by Mendelssohn and others.

1984

R**ANDY NEWMAN: *THE NATURAL.*** Alfred Newman, as head of 20th Century-Fox's music department for twenty years, was the creator of some of the most memorable scores ever written for movies. Most of his seven younger brothers worked in Hollywood during the Golden Age and stayed around during the 1950s and '60s. Both Emil (d. 1984) and Lionel (d. 1989) contributed memorable film scores. A third brother, Robert (1903–82), was a studio executive, whereas Marc Newman (d. 1980) was a Hollywood agent. Irving Newman, who dedicated himself to medicine rather than music, became the personal physician to many well-known film personalities.[12] Irving was also the father of Randy Newman, who became one of the most noted film composers in Hollywood in the 1980s, thanks to the charming score of *Ragtime* (1981) and his heroic music for Barry Levinson's film *The Natural* (1984).

Randy Newman was born in Los Angeles. His family relocated frequently because of his father's military service as an army doctor; between 1944 and 1946, they lived in three Southern cities—New Orleans; Mobile; and Jackson, Mississippi. In 1950, they returned to Los Angeles, where his father set up practice. With so many musicians in the family, young Randy was encouraged to study the piano at the age of seven; five years later, he began studying music theory. By the age of fifteen, Randy was already composing songs. He was also visiting the film studios to watch his uncles

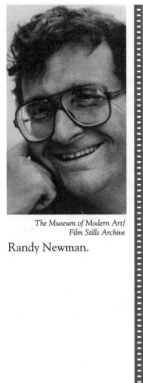

*The Museum of Modern Art/
Film Stills Archive*

Randy Newman.

in action. He became personally acquainted with many of his uncle Alfred's scores by hearing them in recording sessions.

While attending University High School in Los Angeles, one of his songs was recorded by Gene McDaniels. When Randy was seventeen, Lenny Waronker, son of the founder of Liberty Records, helped Randy land a job with Metric Music, a subsidiary of Liberty Records, as a staff composer, with a monthly salary of $150. After graduating from high school, Randy enrolled at UCLA, where he was a music major, concentrating in theory and composition. Although he completed all of his coursework for a bachelor's degree, he failed to get a diploma because he did not fulfill the requirement to have one of his pieces performed.

At this point, Newman decided to became a full-time songwriter. He gained recognition when Judy Collins included his song "I Think It's Going to Rain Today" on her 1967 album *In My Life*. Thirty other singers, including Peggy Lee, soon recorded this song, which became Newman's first big hit. Two years later, he made his first album, *Randy Newman Creates Something New under the Sun*, which was only a modest success. He began to make a name on the *Billboard* charts with such later albums as *Randy Newman Live*, *Sail Away*, and *Good Old Boys*.

In 1969, he was hired by Norman Lear to compose the score for *Cold Turkey*, a satire about a small-town minister (Dick Van Dyke), who convinces his community to give up smoking for thirty days in order to win a cash prize. When the film proved to be a turkey upon its release in 1971, Newman did not attempt another film score for a decade. During the late '70s, he obtained his first gold record for his album *Little Criminals* (1977), from which comes the song that is most often identified with him, "Short People," whose lyrics were deemed by some to be offensive. Newman's next album, *Born Again* (1979), did poorly in the United States. His recordings would not achieve hit status again until the 1983 release of his album *Trouble in Paradise*, which features the tune "I Love L.A."

In 1981, he was coaxed back into composing film music by director Milos Forman, who solicited Newman to contribute a period-flavored score for *Ragtime*. With the success of *Ragtime*, Randy Newman's fame spread beyond the pop-music scene. That same year, a cabaret revue entitled *Maybe I'm Doing It Wrong: A Musical Celebration of the Songs of Randy Newman* opened Off Broadway. A year later, an expanded version of this show, with twenty-three songs, opened at the Astor Place Theatre.

Newman's next film-scoring project—the music for Barry Levinson's film version of the Bernard Malamud novel *The Natural*—would prove to be even more successful than his memorable music for *Ragtime*. Roy Hobbs (Robert Redford), a talented young pitcher, is shot by an unstable woman upon his arrival in Chicago to play baseball in 1923. The story then jumps ahead to 1939, when Hobbs, now an outfielder, arrives at the home park of the New York Knights (a fictional National League team). His batting prowess quickly becomes the talk of baseball, and the Knights, the "losingest" team in baseball, suddenly becomes the league's hottest club.

In a tie-breaker at the end of the season, Roy, who has just been released from a hospital where he was treated for internal bleeding stemming from the shooting, goes to the plate for one final time; he produces a powerful swing that sends the ball flying right into a light tower, winning the pennant for the Knights. (It is here that the book and the movie differ. In the

The Natural, with
Robert Redford.

novel, Malamud suggests that Roy is too injured to be able
to hit the ball well, and thus at the crucial moment he
strikes out.)

Randy Newman's melodically rich score is absent during the opening credits, but starts with the film's first
scene, which shows Roy as a youth tossing a baseball with
his father. Here the first prominent theme, featuring a gentle melody for flute accompanied by harp, is introduced.

After the death of Roy's father, we see the boy looking
out a window as lightning strikes a tree. The next scene
features Roy chopping down the tree and carving a bat out
of some of its wood. As he engraves the name "Wonderboy"
on the bat and includes the insignia of a lightning bolt, the
music features a pair of motifs; the first has a gently rising
scale pattern played by low woodwinds, while the second
begins with a boldly rising pair of tones played by French
horns. This second motif is always associated with heroic
moments in the film, such as the scene where Roy, now a
rising baseball star, clouts a towering home run which hits
the clock by the scoreboard. In its rhythmic movement,
this motif has a forward momentum which consists of a
short sixteenth note quickly moving up in pitch to a much
longer note.

The score's most memorable theme is introduced rather
late in the film, when Roy gets together with his childhood
sweetheart, Iris (Glenn Close), for the first time since he left
home sixteen years earlier. As he leaves her apartment, she
watches from her window, with a soft statement of a seven-
note melodic idea sounding in the background. This motif,
which boldly rises before returning back down the scale
again, plays a significant role in the film's climactic scene,
in which Roy hits his final home run. As sparks fly from the
light tower and the entire stadium is plunged into darkness,
the theme soars gloriously in a full-orchestra statement.

One other notable melody appears only once, in an early
scene where Roy, en route to Chicago in 1923, is lured into
pitching against the world's greatest hitter, the Slammer
(Joe Don Baker), as a wager between Roy's elderly mentor and the conniving sportswriter Max Mercy (Robert Duvall). When the Slammer takes a
called third strike, the music sounds a repeated four-note idea that has a
bright, Coplandesque quality.

The closing scene mirrors the film's opening, only now it is Roy as the
father who tosses a baseball with his son. Here the score's opening strain is
appropriately repeated.

In the final credits, all the main motifs of Newman's score are brought
back for a last time, in an orchestral arrangement that brings the film to a
close on a very positive note. Randy Newman richly deserved the Oscar
nomination he received for his efforts on behalf of this film, which is one of
the most emotionally satisfying of the year.

MAURICE JARRE: A PASSAGE TO INDIA AND DREAMSCAPE. One
of the irritating aspects of the Academy Awards is the all-too-frequent

tendency for the Oscar to be given to a composer on the basis of a score that isn't one of his better accomplishments. Such is the case with Maurice Jarre's music for *A Passage to India*, David Lean's beautifully crafted final film, which is based on E. M. Forster's novel about the clash between cultures in India during the 1920s. Despite a catchy main theme which is identified with Adela (Judy Davis), a young Englishwoman who travels to India with Mrs. Moore (Peggy Ashcroft), her fiancé's mother, this score, which contains only about twenty minutes of music, is a relatively minor effort. The lavish orchestration includes the *ondes martenot* (which Jarre had also used in Lean's *Lawrence of Arabia*), but melodically, this score is very derivative of the music Jarre composed for one of the director's earlier films, *Ryan's Daughter*.

Far more original is Jarre's electronic score for *Dreamscape*, a thriller which involves a young man (Dennis Quaid) who has the psychic ability to enter other people's dreams. The performance of Jarre's music was accomplished through the efforts of Craig Huxley, who has functioned as a synthesizer programmer for a variety of film scores and also for such recordings as Michael Jackson's *Thriller* and Quincy Jones's *Ai no corrida*.

SHORT CUTS. The year 1984 was the high-water mark of movie theme-song popularity, with five of the year's top tunes emanating from films. *Purple Rain*, the debut film of the artist formerly known as Prince, brought forth the year's number-one song, "When Doves Cry"; three other movies also benefited from the popularity of their title songs, *Against All Odds*, *Footloose*, and *Ghostbusters*. Not far behind, in terms of its record sales, was Stevie Wonder's "I Just Called to Say I Love You," the Oscar-winning song that was first heard in Gene Wilder's *Woman in Red*.

It seems that 1984 was also the year that electronic realization of film music really caught on. In addition to Maurice Jarre's *Dreamscape*, there were several other scores in which synthesizers were used.

■■■■ **Jack Nitzsche.** Arguably the best synthesized score of 1984 was by Jack Nitzsche for John Carpenter's *Starman*, in which Jeff Bridges plays an alien who crashes to Earth. He then clones the body of the dead husband of Jenny Hayden (Karen Allen). Jenny is forced into helping the alien, but then falls in love with him. Nitzsche's main theme is a romantic idea that includes a synthesized choral effect. It is used most prominently in the scene where he carries Jenny's lifeless body out of the fiery wreckage after their car collides with an oil tanker, and again in the closing scene, where an alien spacecraft has arrived at a rendezvous point so that he can go safely back to his own planet.

■■■■ **Jerry Goldsmith.** Jerry Goldsmith also turned to synthesizers for the throbbing score of Michael Crichton's futuristic *Runaway*, in which Tom Selleck plays a cop chasing robots that have gone bad. This score has dramatic moments but doesn't match the quality of Goldsmith's earlier work. Far better is his music for Joe Dante's *Gremlins*, a tongue-in-cheek thriller about a small town turned upside down by a rapidly multiplying army of small but deadly creatures. In this score Goldsmith incorporates a synthesizer effect along with the strings for the lyrical main theme, a slow-paced melody that gives the film an eloquence it would otherwise lack. The score's other principal theme, the catchy "Gremlin Rag," is hinted at a number of times during the latter stages of the film, and finally gets a full-fledged performance during the closing credits.

■■■■ **John Williams.** At the top of the box-office listings was Steven Spielberg's *Indiana Jones and the Temple of Doom*. Despite some excessively gory effects, much of this film is supremely entertaining, especially the opening scenes, which are paced at a breakneck speed. Perhaps the single cleverest touch comes at the very outset, when the film's credits are shown while an American singer (Kate Capshaw) renders Cole Porter's "Anything Goes" in Chinese at a Shanghai night club. John Williams's score includes robust themes, plus several reprises of the "Raiders March" from *Raiders of the Lost Ark*.

■■■■ **Howard Shore.** A folklike quality permeates the music of Robert Benton's *Places in the Heart*, which features a score made up of old tunes such as "Cotton-Eyed Joe," "Ida Red," "La Golondrina," "Mexicali Rose," and "In the Sweet Bye and Bye." Howard Shore is credited with producing and adapting the materials used in the film, with such folk-music artists as Doc Watson, Merle Watson, and the Texas Playboys recording the music. The most affecting scene is the last one, which is set in Bethel Community Church in Waxahachie, Texas. The choir is singing "Blessed Assurance" while a communion basket is being passed in the congregation, which includes all the characters in the film, several of whom have died before this scene takes place. Benton, who based this film on memories of his grandmother, intended this scene to be symbolic of the continuation of life. It is a magical moment in one of the finest films of the decade.

■■■■ *Amadeus.* Milos Forman's lavishly produced Oscar-winning version of Peter Shaffer's play *Amadeus* doesn't include a single note of original score. Yet the music of Mozart, as performed by Sir Neville Marriner with the Academy of St. Martin in the Fields orchestra, provided one of the year's most musically satisfying listening experiences at the movies.

Popular Music in Films. Filmmaking had become very costly by the mid-'80s, with production costs and advertising fees pushing up the average film budget to over $30 million. With so much money at stake, many producers used music to help promote their films. The interference of producers who had little appreciation for music made the job of scoring films difficult. Movie soundtracks and commercially released soundtrack recordings increasingly featured songs performed by popular artists. While new songs were still being composed for new films, previously recorded hits were often inserted with the result that, though composers were hired, they frequently found themselves with diminished scoring opportunities.

In John Hughes's *The Breakfast Club*, Keith Forsey is credited with the background score and with co-composing several songs, including "Fire in the Twilight" (performed by Wang Chung), "Heart Too Hot to Hold" (sung by Jesse Johnson and Stephanie Spruill), and "Didn't I Tell You" (featuring the voice of Joyce Kennedy). The soundtrack also includes performances of two songs by others: "Don't You (Forget about Me)," by Simple Minds, and "We Are Not Alone," by Karla DeVito, Robby Benson, and Steve Goldstein. The song that ultimately helped *Breakfast Club* at the box office was "Don't You (Forget about Me)" which placed as number sixteen on the *Billboard* list of 1985's top 100 songs.[13]

Joel Schumacher's *St. Elmo's Fire* features three actors who had earlier appeared in *Breakfast Club*, namely Emilio Estevez, Judd Nelson, and Ally Sheedy. The film was scored by David Foster (b. 1949), who composed most of the music used in the film, including the love theme, which is also heard as the melody of the song "Just for a Moment," with lyrics by Cynthia Weil. Foster also cowrote with singer John Parr the song entitled "St. Elmo's Fire (Man in Motion)," which became a huge hit and ended up as number eleven on the *Billboard* list of 1985's top 100 songs.[14] Other vocals heard in *St. Elmo's Fire* include "This Time It Was Really Right," cowritten by Foster with Jon Anderson (who also did the vocals); "If I Turn You Away," by Foster and Richard Marx (vocals by Vicki Moss); "Stressed Out (Close to the Edge)," by Foster, Jay Graydon, Stephen A. Kipner, and Peter Beckett (vocals by Airplay); and "Saved My Life," by Foster, Fee Waybill, and Steve Lukather (vocal by Waybill). The soundtrack also includes two additional songs, "Shake Down," by Billy Squire, who sang it in the film; and "Young and Innocent," by John and Dino Elefante, who performed their tune under the name Elefante.

What really complicates the business of scoring a film with such a motley assortment of musical materials is the necessity of giving credit where credit is due. Therefore, at the end of a film such as *St. Elmo's Fire*, all the songs are listed separately, with composers, arrangers, and so on, and with licensing information included. Thus, some new positions were created for musicians in the world of film music, including the music supervisor, who would coordinate the entire project and would also, according to Fred Karlin, act as a liaison between the filmmakers and the composer.[15]

One of the most familiar names in the music business in the 1980s was Phil Ramone, who acted as music supervisor on Taylor Hackford's 1985 film *White Nights*. Although the film contains a scoring credit for Michel Colombier (b. 1939), most of the music used in *White Nights* consists of a number of songs by various composers, which were sung on the soundtrack by such artists as Phil Collins, Robert Plant, and Roberta Flack. Two bestselling songs were included in *White Nights*. The first was "Say You, Say Me," recorded by Stevie Wonder, who also wrote both the music and the lyrics; this lyrical tune won the Oscar in the Original Song category. The other hit song from the film was Stephen Bishop's "Separate Lives," which he had written in 1982. At that time, Hackford couldn't get studio backing for the film, the project fell into limbo, and Bishop abandoned the song. When Hackford eventually got the film made, Phil Collins and Marilyn Martin were hired to perform the song.[16] This tune, which was also nominated for an Oscar, finished the year as the third most popular song of 1985, right behind Lionel Richie's "Say You, Say Me," which was in second place on the *Billboard* list.[17]

The popularity of songs such as those heard in *The Breakfast Club*, *St. Elmo's Fire*, and *White Nights* stands as evidence of the rampant use of popular musical materials in films. Of the top five box-office films of 1985, only one failed to have at least one song interpolated into the background music: the year's Oscar-winning film *Out of Africa*, which finished the year in fifth place in terms of box-office receipts. The top four films of 1985, in order of their earnings, are listed below, with their musical interpolations, including the artists who recorded them:

Back to the Future: "The Power of Love" and "Back in Time," (Huey Lewis and the News); "Time Bomb Town" (Lindsey Buckingham); "Heaven Is One Step Away" (Eric Clapton); "Dance with Me, Henry" (Etta James); "Earth Angel" (Harry Waters, Jr.); and "Johnny B. Goode" (Mark Campbell).

Rambo: First Blood Part II: "Peace in Our Life" (Frank Stallone).

Rocky IV: "Burning Heart" (Survivor); "Heart's on Fire" (John Cafferty), and others.

The Color Purple: "Miss Celie's Blues" (Tata Vega).

With the exception of *The Color Purple*, these films include songs that became chart-topping hits. "The Power of Love" ended 1985 as the ninth most popular song of the year and received an Oscar nomination.[18]

The opportunities for composing a purely instrumental film score were dwindling, thanks to the interference of producers who were looking for megabuck profits. The good news is that this attitude, although widespread, did not completely destroy symphonic film music. In fact, there are many fine examples of film scoring in movies released in 1985.

BRUCE BROUGHTON: FROM SMALL SCREEN TO BIG SCREEN. For many years prior to becoming a composer of feature films, Bruce Broughton (b. 1945) had gained recognition for scores written for some of TV's most watched series, including *Dallas,* for which he received an Emmy in 1983. That same year he made the transition to the silver screen with his music for the futuristic fantasy *The Ice Pirates*. In 1985, Broughton earned the esteem of his peers with a pair of film scores, for one of which he gained an Oscar nomination. The Academy Award citation came for his lively music for Lawrence Kasdan's old-fashioned Western epic *Silverado*, which benefited greatly from the energetic contributions of Kevin Kline, Scott Glenn, Danny Glover, and Kevin Costner. Broughton's score is built around two primary melodic ideas. The first is a heroic theme for French horns that employs a five-note motif consisting of ascending perfect fifths. This theme is heard during the opening credits, and later is used in a scene in which the four gunslingers ride toward the town of Silverado. The other idea is a gentle tune for the settlers, who have come by wagon train only to find a hostile cattle rancher (Brian Dennehy), who wants them off the land. These themes form the nucleus of a score that helps to elevate this lengthy and episodic film, which is a bit top-heavy with action-movie clichés.

Broughton earned a Grammy nomination for his interesting score of Barry Levinson's *Young Sherlock Holmes*, about the youthful Sherlock Holmes and John Watson, who get involved in their first sleuthing adventure while enrolled at a private boys' school. The lively main theme, in a minor key, features piccolo and then flute above a steady rhythmic bass. In a curious parallel to the ritual scenes in *Indiana Jones and the Temple of Doom* (1984), Holmes (Nicholas Rowe) and Watson (Alex Cox) discover a hidden underground temple where a human sacrifice is about to take place. During this scene, a choral piece reminiscent of "O Fortuna," the opening chorus of Carl Orff's *Carmina burana*, is chanted as dramatic tribal music by those gathered for this grim ritual. This rhythmically driven piece, which utilizes a seven-beat metric pattern, consists of several layers of vocal and instrumental sound that come together in a harmoniously blended fashion. This score has an even more ingenious quality than the music of *Silverado*.

S HORT CUTS ■■■■ **John Barry.** For the atmospheric score of Sydney Pollack's *Out of Africa*, based on Danish writer Isaak Dinesen's experiences in Africa as co-owner of a farm, John Barry returned to the venue with which he had been so successful when he scored *Born Free* in 1966. Barry's languid main theme once again demonstrates his keen ability to set forth a lyrical melodic line that flows above long-sustained chords. Although there is nothing innovative about this score, it works well within the context of Pollack's film, which also features a fine performance by Meryl Streep as the writer. The film went on to collect eleven Oscar nominations, and took home seven gold statues, including Best Picture, Best Director, and Best Original Score, at the 1985 Academy Awards. For Barry this marked his third scoring award, and his first since *The Lion in Winter* (1968).

■■■■ **Quincy Jones.** Steven Spielberg's *Color Purple*, beautifully adapted from Alice Walker's novel, also collected eleven Oscar nominations, including one for the bluesy score supervised by Quincy Jones, who co-produced the film and coordinated the work of eleven other musicians.

■■■■ **Georges Delerue.** Among the other Oscar-nominated scores was Georges Delerue's somber music for Norman Jewison's bleak but well-acted film *Agnes of God*. Employing more dissonance than usual, Delerue utilized chant melodies and wordless choral backgrounds to add a religious flavor to this tragic story of a young nun accused of murdering a baby to whom she has mysteriously given birth.

■■■■ **Maurice Jarre.** Maurice Jarre received the remaining nomination for the synthesized music of Peter Weir's *Witness*. Using an ensemble of nine musicians, Jarre's moody backgrounds provide a brooding accompaniment for this unusual story of a Philadelphia cop, John Book (Harrison Ford), who is hiding in an Amish community in rural Pennsylvania, while recovering from a bullet wound and trying to solve a murder. The most memorable musical moment occurs when Book helps the men of the village erect a barn. To accompany this scene, Jarre employed a Baroque-period device known as "passacaglia," in which a steadily repeated bass pattern is overlaid with several melodic lines that are combined harmonically as the piece continues.

■■■■ **Alan Silvestri.** Among the other scoring highlights of 1985 is the exuberant score by Alan Silvestri for Robert Zemeckis's *Back to the Future*. High schooler Marty McFly (Michael J. Fox) finds himself transported by means of a souped-up DeLorean back to 1955, where he meets two young people whom he recognizes as his own parents. There is one principal melodic motif in this score, an energetic nine-note idea that is heard numerous times. Although Silvestri's contribution is a bit repetitive, its rhythmic vitality keeps the final reels of the film moving at breakneck speed, as Marty attempts to return to 1985 with the help of Doc Brown (Christopher Lloyd), the inventor of this automotive time machine. *Future* contains several rock songs, including two featuring Huey Lewis and the

News, but the underscore amounted to a large-scale work. A ninety-eight-piece orchestra was used for the soundtrack recording sessions.

■ ■ ■ **Jerry Goldsmith.** Of Goldsmith's five new scores, the music for Ridley Scott's *Legend* was by far the most memorable. Unfortunately, only European filmgoers saw the film with Goldsmith's music; the version released in the United States, which was delayed until 1986, features an electronic score by Tangerine Dream. The lyricism of Goldsmith's score, with its impressionistic harmony, is reminiscent of Maurice Ravel's ballet *Daphnis et Chloe*, especially the lovely "Dress Waltz," which begins softly with a solo flute, a harp, and sustained strings. Slowly the music builds to a sensuously full orchestration, with wordless voices added for coloristic effect. This is one of Goldsmith's most inventive scores, a work that was regrettably denied a chance to be heard in theaters. Fortunately, a CD of this score appeared on the Silva Screen label in 1992. [19]

■ ■ ■ **Henry Mancini.** Arguably one of the worst films of 1985 was the sci-fi film *Lifeforce*. Despite its lurid subject matter, which concerns an alluring but vamperlike woman from outer space who fatally infects all with whom she has intimate contact, Mancini wrote an ingenious score. The main theme features a steadily driven rhythmic accompaniment, on top of which is layered a string idea with lots of repeated notes that propel the music forward. This score again demonstrates that, away from the blatant physical comedy of Blake Edwards's films, Mancini could excel as a composer of inspired dramatic music.

ENNIO MORRICONE: *THE MISSION*. To call Ennio Morricone one of the most prolific of all film composers is almost to understate the productivity of this acclaimed Italian musician. With some four hundred film scores to his credit, Morricone has surpassed everyone, including Max Steiner; as of this writing he is still active.

As recognizable as many of his film scores are, Morricone's film-music style remains something of a mystery. Like Jerry Goldsmith, Morricone has perfected the art of being a musical chameleon. Although he became internationally renowned for his scores for the Sergio Leone Western trilogy starring Clint Eastwood as the "Man with No Name," Morricone is much more than a Western composer. In his native Italy, where he was born in 1928, Morricone has collaborated with many leading directors, including Pier Paolo Pasolini (*120 Days of Sodom*, 1975), Elio Petri (*Investigation of a Citizen above Suspicion*, 1970), Gillo Pontecorvo (*The Battle of Algiers*, 1965), and Bernardo Bertolucci (*1900*, 1977). Morricone received training in classical music at the Conservatory of Santa Cecilia in Rome, where he studied composition with Goffredo Petrassi. His subsequent career has encompassed many aspects of music, including original symphonic compositions, arrangements for popular stage performers, and musical scores for the theater and film.

Morricone has written over fifty works for chamber groups, symphony orchestra, solo voice, and choral ensembles. In addition, he has worked as an arranger with Charles Aznavour, Mario Lanza, Paul Anka, and others. It was his work in the Italian theater that steered him in the direction of film. After working with director Luciano Salce on a number of plays, Morricone was hired by Salce to compose his first film score, the music

The Museum of Modern Art/
Film Stills Archive

Ennio Morricone.

for the 1961 film *Il federale*. Three years and over a dozen film scores later, Morricone composed the music for Sergio Leone's *Fistful of Dollars*.

Although *A Fistful of Dollars* was not shown in the United States until three years after its initial release, Morricone's score became immediately popular with European filmgoers. When Leone started working on a sequel, *For a Few Dollars More*, Morricone was automatically hired. The third film in the series, *The Good, the Bad and the Ugly*, became the biggest hit of the three, and its bizarrely orchestrated theme, with raucous voices, became Morricone's first American hit theme in early 1968. Leone and Morricone worked together several more times, but by this time Morricone was being hired by major directors from several countries.

The first American director to hire Morricone was Don Siegel, for whom he scored *Two Mules for Sister Sarah* in 1970. Of the few Morricone scores written for English-language films, several are noteworthy; these include the ones for: John Boorman's *Exorcist II: The Heretic* (1977); Terrence Malick's *Days of Heaven* (1978), which won for Morricone his first Oscar nomination; and John Carpenter's remake of *The Thing* (1982).

Morricone's versatility makes it problematic to recognize his style. According to Harlan Kennedy, who interviewed him in 1991:

> Indeed, it's hard to define the Morricone style at all. *Eclectic* is an understatement for music whose mood can encompass the lyrical (*The Mission*), the bellicose (*The Battle of Algiers*), the grotesque (*The Good, the Bad and the Ugly*) or the plaintive (Bertolucci's *Tragedy of a Ridiculous Man*). And his equally eclectic instrumentation leaves no sonic source untapped, from the routine repertoire of brass, strings and percussion to the screams, bells and whistles of Leone's *Dollar* trilogy or the weird scratching and plumbing noises for Petri's *Investigation of a Citizen above Suspicion*. . . . Every acoustic gewgaw is grist to his mill; every period of musical history may be ransacked for inspiration.[20]

Kennedy then assesses Morricone as a film composer:

> If Morricone has achieved anything single-handedly as a film composer, it's the perfection of a fusion between the classical composing methods of the Steiners or Korngolds and the eclecticism that has informed music culture since the 1960s and that is typified by the pile-on-the-pop-songs brand of movie score.[21]

In this interview Kennedy posed a question regarding the purpose of film music, to which Morricone replied: "Music in a film must not add emphasis but must give more body and depth to the story, to the characters, to the language that the director has chosen. It must, therefore, say all that the dialogue, images, effects, etc., cannot say."[22]

Morricone also has an unwavering attitude about the role of the composer in writing film music:

> [M]y scores have always [been], and will always be, written by me. I have never needed collaborators to write for me. On the contrary, this revolts me. The great classic musicians in the history of musical composition have never had such need. This habit of not writing one's own music is a negative practice of composers who are lazy, incapable, or who take on too much work. In my opinion, it is an immoral system because it takes advantage of creative qualities of others for one's own exclusive purposes.[23]

When asked by Kennedy about the unusual instrumentation of some of his scores, Morricone gave the following response:

> Some of Leone's Westerns (but also those of other directors) have need of underlining a character's quirks. I do only what I think is correct. For the rest, a composer has the obligation to "invent and capture" noises, the musical sounds of life.[24]

Roland Joffé's film, *The Mission*, his first directorial project since the award-winning picture *The Killing Fields* (1984), is based on an original script by Robert Bolt, who had previously worked with David Lean on *Lawrence of Arabia* and *Doctor Zhivago*. When Morricone first saw the film, he was initially reluctant to score the picture.

> After having seen *The Mission* the first time without music, I liked it and it moved me to such a point that I thought of not writing the music for it. Roland Joffé, Fernando Ghia and David Puttnam are my witnesses. But they later convinced me to write the sound track.[25]

Once Morricone was convinced that he could have a positive impact on *The Mission*, he embarked on the study of musical practices of South America around 1750. There are native drums and flutes in the score, plus a choir that provides both a native type of chanting and the traditional choral sound of Catholic service music. This bilateral vocal sound reflects the story, which concerns the efforts by Jesuit missionaries to build missions in the jungles of South America and to convert members of the local tribes to Christianity.

The film also depicts the horrible deaths that many of the Jesuits suffered as a result of their bold and sometimes foolhardy efforts. In the film's opening scene, one of the missionaries is strapped to a huge cross and tossed into the raging waters of a river, the current of which pulls him downstream until he meets his martyrdom by going over a waterfall.

One of Bolt's principal characters is Father Gabriel (Jeremy Irons), who uses his musical abilities to charm the natives. Knowing their fascination with music, he sits on a cliff overlooking a jungle vista and plays a plaintive oboe tune. Although a tribal chieftain comes along, grabs the instrument, and breaks it in two, several others of the local Guarani tribe soon learn to trust the priest. Eventually, he and his fellow missionaries erect a small chapel and formally begin their conversion efforts.

The film's other leading character is Rodrigo Mendoza (Robert De Niro), a slave trader and mercenary who, in a jealous rage, kills his brother in a duel over a woman they both love. Looking for atonement, Rodrigo soon comes under the influence of Father Gabriel, who convinces him that he can receive God's forgiveness if he accepts a harsh penance. Thus begins a grueling journey in which Rodrigo is tied to a heavy burden and made to drag it uphill to the mission. Once he manages to make the climb, he breaks down; at this point Father Gabriel suggests that this troubled man join the religious order.

The characters of Gabriel and Mendoza are only incidental to Bolt's main theme, which is based on a series of events that actually took place in the South American jungle in the mid-eighteenth century. In the film, a local trader, jealous of the mission's productivity, connives with a cardinal to have the mission shut down. In a political arrangement whereby the territory is ceded from Spain to Portugal, the mission is ordered to be closed. Once the Jesuits, especially Rodrigo, refuse to abandon their work, a bloody confrontation takes place in which the mission is burned and the priests are killed. In the final scene, some surviving native children leave the ruins of the mission and go by boat back into the jungle. The not-too-subtle message of the

The Mission, with
Robert De Niro.

film is that the intrusion of European Christians brought suffering and
death to the native tribes. This message is hammered home from the very
beginning of the film, when the cardinal (Ray McAnally) reads, in a voice-
over, the contents of a letter being written to the pope in which he explains
the dreadful events which we then witness.

There are three main thematic ideas in Morricone's score. The first,
heard during the opening titles, features a many-times-repeated pattern of
four notes which move slowly and steadily within a confined pitch range.
While this music continues, the Jesuits, led by Father Gabriel, climb the
rocky terrain to reach the high plateau where they plan to build a mission.
The second musical idea comes when Gabriel plays his oboe to attract the
natives' attention. This beautifully lyrical piece features a freely flowing
melody played by a solo oboe with a string accompaniment. The third and
most intriguing piece of music is first heard in a scene where the cardinal
is being escorted by boat upriver to the mission of San Carlos. Here there
are several layers of music; first there is a plaintive melody played by the
solo flute; then there are deeply resonant sounds of native drums, plus
sustained sounds provided by strings. Added to all this is the chanting of a
repeated melodic idea that is sounded as a series of individually accented
tones by a choir of treble voices. The deliberate rhythmic movement of this
chanted idea is in marked contrast to the more fluid rhythm of the flute
melody. Together with the drums and sustained strings, these layers of
sound produce a haunting musical passage.

This chanting theme occurs two more times: as the armed mercenaries approach the mission, the music persists; it even continues while gunfire is exchanged. At the end of the battle sequence, when the last of the priests has fallen and the mission is set ablaze, the music occurs again, but dies down until all we hear is the drumbeats that accompany this theme. These drumbeats then fade gradually until there is total silence.

Morricone's emotion-filled music contributes a memorably heroic quality to this film. Not only is the score of *The Mission* one of Morricone's master-pieces, but it brought this composer long-overdue recognition.[26]

JERRY **G**OLDSMITH: *H*OOSIERS. David Anspaugh's *Hoosiers* is a film about a former college basketball coach who is reduced to taking a high school coaching job in a small town in Indiana. The basketball team develops under the disciplined guidance of dedicated coach Norman Dale (Gene Hackman), whose love for the sport shines through in the way his kids play.

Jerry Goldsmith's Oscar-nominated score at first appears to be just another ordinary sports-movie effort, with rhythmically charged music to accompany the playing scenes. Closer inspection reveals several original touches in Goldsmith's score, which has four principal themes. The first theme, based on a repeated pattern that uses the first and fifth notes of the scale, is a heroic melody which is initially played by a solo trumpet. This theme appears in various guises in the early part of the film, including a scene where Coach Dale talks to a fellow teacher (Barbara Hershey) on her family farm. Here the theme is transformed into a slow and lyrical idea.

As the basketball scenes commence, the score begins to include a steadily repeated drumming effect that persists through most of the film's remaining scenes. Three other themes, which are introduced in the course of the team's games, all have a rousing, dramatic impact. Of these, the one that is particularly worth mentioning has a seven-beat metric pattern, in a grouping of 2 + 2 + 3. This highly energetic idea is preceded by one of the other themes; by the end of the film they are all included together as the team faces the postseason playoffs. In the scene that showcases the championship game, as the winning basket is scored during the final seconds, one of the these three themes is heard amid the roar of the crowd. The noises gradually fade and the music takes over, with a heroic rendition of the opening trumpet idea. In the closing credits all four of Goldsmith's themes are presented as an emotion-filled musical epilogue.

SHORT **C**UTS. Among the other Oscar-nominated scores of 1986, James Horner's pulsating music for James Cameron's *Aliens* is almost tuneless; Leonard Rosenman's score for *Star Trek IV: The Voyage Home* includes a rousing main theme set in the style of a march, but is not as effective as either the Goldsmith score for the first *Star Trek* film or the James Horner scores for *Star Trek II* and *Star Trek III*.

■■■■ **Herbie Hancock.** The year's Oscar-winning score is a real oddity: Herbie Hancock's music for Bertrand Tavernier's *Round Midnight*, an almost plotless film about a black American tenor saxophone player, Del (Dexter Gordon), who goes to Paris in 1959 and hangs out with other fine jazz players. Hancock himself appears as a piano player with a small combo that performs in the club where Del hangs out. There really isn't much of a "score" in this film; instead, there are several performances of jazz pieces, including the title tune (by Thelonious Monk), "Body and Soul" (by Johnny Green), "As Time Goes By" (by Herman Hupfeld), "How Long Has This Been Going On?" (by George and Ira Gershwin), and "Fair Weather" (by Bud Powell). There are three original Hancock compositions: "Berangere's Nightmare"; "Still Time"; and "Chan's Song (Never Said)," in which Bobby McFerrin is featured as vocalist. McFerrin's versatile voice also produces a trumpetlike wordless sound in the title tune that is quite listenable. This may not be great movie music, but the pieces played in *Round Midnight* provide a veritable feast for jazz enthusiasts.

■■■■ **Richard Robbins.** Although Richard Robbins (b. 1940) wrote some charming original music for James Ivory's adaptation of E. M. Forster's novel, *A Room with a View*, much of the score is based on a pair of operatic arias by Giacomo Puccini. The first of these, "O mio babbino caro," from *Gianni Schicchi*, is heard during the opening credits and in the first scene, where Charlotte (Maggie Smith) and her young traveling companion Lucy (Helena Bonham-Carter) first look out of their hotel room window in Florence. Later, while Charlotte and Lucy are still vacationing in Italy, "Chi il bel sogno di Doretta," from *La Rondine*, is heard. Both arias feature the lovely operatic sounds of soprano Kiri te Kanawa, whose recordings were borrowed for this film. Robbins's original music includes a minor-key waltz, heard in one of the early scenes set in Florence. The combination of solo mandolin and pizzicato strings adds to the charm of this theme. Elsewhere, Robbins wrote music for a number of short cues that feature predominantly strings, woodwinds, and harp. The effect of these cues is generally subdued but always appropriate for Forster's tale of romantic yearning.

■■■■ **Georges Delerue.** With *Platoon*, director Oliver Stone launched a trilogy of movies about the Vietnam War. Georges Delerue received credit for an original score, which consists of some short bits of music for flute and strings, accompanied by eerie high-pitched sounds made with a woodblock. Overall, music is used sparsely in *Platoon*; most of the music heard in this gritty film stems from Samuel Barber's Adagio for Strings, parts of which appear several times. The most extensive use of Barber's melancholy work comes at the end of the film, as the wounded Chris (Charlie Sheen) is taken by helicopter out of the jungle. Barber's slow-paced music provides a distinctly funereal mood that adds a tinge of sadness to this wrenching visual reconstruction of the Vietnam War.

■■■■ **Giorgio Moroder and Harold Faltermeyer.** *Top Gun* qualifies as the loudest movie of 1986, with a raucous soundtrack that features several songs by Giorgio Moroder with lyrics by Tom Whitlock. These include "Danger Zone," sung in the film by Kenny Loggins; "Lead Me On"; and the year's Oscar-winning song, "Take My Breath Away," which was recorded for the film by the group Berlin. This song helped make *Top Gun* the year's biggest box-office hit and also pushed the sales of the film's soundtrack album to spectacular levels, with a total of seven million copies. Moroder's insistently rhythmic tunes were worked into the visually exciting flying sequences by the score's composer Harold Faltermeyer (b. 1952). Faltermeyer, who had previously composed a rhythmically charged electronic score for *Beverly Hills Cops* (1984), again used eletronics to create a pulsating musical background.

■ ■ ■ ■ **The Emergence of Women Film Composers.** In a field that had been almost completely male-dominated throughout Hollywood's Golden Age, a composer who in the 1970s had gone by the name of "Wally Stott" had revealed her true identity—Angela Morley. Not long thereafter, Shirley Walker (b. 1945) began to work as an orchestrator and conductor. Among the scores that she worked on in 1986 is Michael Convertino's music for *Children of a Lesser God*, which features Walker's work as co-orchestrator and conductor of the soundtrack recording.

Rachel Portman, who was born in England in 1960, created her debut score for the British film *Sharma and Beyond* in 1986, which was barely released in the United States. Within a few years, she would be moving on to some major film projects, through her association with directors Mike Leigh and Beeban Kidron.

The second woman to emerge as a film-music composer in 1986 was Carly Simon (b. 1945). Already one of America's most popular singing stars, Simon also became known as a songwriter. She got a chance to score a major movie for her film-music debut, Mike Nichols's *Heartburn*. Her score is largely based on the song "Coming Around Again," which is heard several times in the course of the film, with Carly Simon herself as the vocalist. Simon composed this song to form an intriguing bit of counterpoint with the children's song "Itsy Bitsy Spider." When sounded together, these two tunes produce a delightful contrapuntal effect. Although her scoring efforts were ignored by the Oscar voters in 1986, Simon's work on *Heartburn* showed much promise.

JOHN WILLIAMS: *EMPIRE OF THE SUN*. Following *The Color Purple*, Steven Spielberg returned to John Williams for the score of his next film, *Empire of the Sun*, based on the autobiographical novel by J. G. Ballard. This was the eighth time that John Williams had the opportunity to provide music for a Spielberg film.

Ballard's story is a fictionalized account of the author's childhood, which was spent in China and which included four years of internment in a Japanese prison camp during World War II. The main character, Jim Graham (whose name is derived from Ballard's first and middle names), is played by Christian Bale, who gives a buoyant performance as the young British boy from an affluent background in Shanghai who becomes separated from his parents in the confusion of the Japanese invasion, and must fend for himself.

The story of *Empire of the Sun* bears some similarities to Spielberg's most phenomenal success of the 1980s, *E.T.* In both films the chief protagonist is a child who has been separated, either emotionally or physically, from his family and has to rely on his own instincts. The difference between Elliott and Jim lies in their emotional makeup. Whereas Elliott's feelings are awakened by his caring for the lost alien, Jim's are shut down by the horrible realities of war.

John Williams approached the scoring of *Empire* in a way that is much different from his work for *E.T.* Whereas in the earlier film the emotionally rich music underscores Elliott's feelings for his new friend, in *Empire* the music avoids an overt emotional style, since Jim's feelings are utterly blocked. The score therefore has a rather understated facade, with one of the most subtle underscores of Williams's career. One of its chief attributes is a beautiful choral effect, which stems from Jim's choirboy experience.

Although there is no music in the opening credits, the film's initial images of objects floating in a river are accompanied by the singing of a boys' choir. Then we see the church where Jim and his fellow choristers are rehearsing a traditional Chinese song called "Suo Gan," which is presented as a beautifully lyrical piece with Jim as the soprano soloist. This tune was arranged by John McCarthy, and was recorded for the film by the Ambrosian Junior Choir, with James Rainbird as soloist.

This vocal music is carried over into the following scene, which begins with a closeup of the shiny hood ornament mounted on a deluxe model car. Jim is riding in the back seat as the family chauffeur brings him home from school. We next hear a Chopin mazurka which his mother plays on the grand piano in the Graham's expansive living room. Williams's first original thematic idea is introduced in the following scene, in which Jim's mother is at his bedside at night. A short statement of this lyrical idea is presented by a solo flute with strings in the background. An arrangement of the Chopin mazurka for piano and strings, combined with Williams's own music, then occurs when the family is en route to a costume party. As Jim looks out the car window at crowds in the street, we hear wordless music for treble voices with strings.

When Jim wanders away from the party and sees a wrecked plane, there is more ethereal music, with voices and strings. When he then spots the Japanese soldiers who are encamped nearby, weird music is sounded on a Japanese flute, accompanied by some rumbling on the timpani. In the chaos of the next day, as Jim and his parents attempt to leave Shanghai, there is tense music, but the crowd noises soon overwhelm the background scoring. There is no music from the time Jim is separated from his parents until his arrival at a detention camp located near an airstrip. At this point the first musical idea of the score is presented in a fully developed statement that begins with a solo piano, which is soon joined by the sound of strings. As Jim walks toward an airplane that some men are working on, the theme begins to build in strength. Jim, who is perpetually infatuated with planes, puts his hands on the fuselage. This attracts the attention of three pilots,

Empire of the Sun, with Christian Bale.

who return Jim's salute. The theme reaches its climactic moment while the addition of a wordless choral sound provides a beautifully ethereal effect.

The screen immediately fades to black, and the next scene picks up the story in 1945. Williams's theme, which has played through the time change, continues to sound as a Japanese boy, who is holding a model plane, runs toward a barbed-wire fence that encloses a prisoners' compound. Jim becomes the protégé of Basie (John Malkovich), a camp hustler; Jim's adventures as a teenage entrepreneur of bartered goods are accompanied by Williams's next theme, a jauntily paced idea that provides a bit of levity to what is otherwise a grim scene of human suffering. The wonder of Williams's music is that it transcends the scenes of human misery to form a lighthearted commentary on Jim's ability to adapt to his difficult circumstances.

Basie wants Jim to check out the terrain beyond the barbed-wire fence to see if the area is mined, and in exchange, Jim will get to bunk in Basie's American compound. When Jim returns triumphantly to the Americans' bunkhouse, the men line up in formation and salute him, to the accompaniment of "The British Grenadiers," which is heard in an arrangement for concert band.

"Suo Gan" makes another appearance as music for a scene in which Jim watches three Japanese pilots preparing for a kamikaze flight. As they sing a Japanese melody, Jim sings his church song once more. At first, we hear only Jim's voice, but then the choral version heard earlier, with organ accompaniment, is brought back to provide background music for the next part of the scene, in which Jim salutes the pilots as they take off.

Moments later, when one of the Japanese planes bursts into flame in midair, Jim observes an air attack by a squadron of B-51s. As he climbs to the roof of a tall building to observe the attack, he excitedly shouts, "Cadillac of the skies!" At this point, Williams's first theme is brought back, in an ethereal version in which voices join in with the orchestra.

Still later, the prisoners have been moved out of the camp to a place used as an open-air storage facility for confiscated goods. There is a stunningly photographed moment when Jim sees something; his gaze is transfixed on the object, and soon a closeup of the hood ornament of the Graham's car comes into focus, accompanied by the sounds of a ghostly piano. This music serves as a reminder of Jim's mother. The next day Jim awakens to find the camp deserted except for Mrs. Victor (Miranda Richardson), a fellow prisoner, who has died during the night. As he discovers her lifeless body, he sees a flash in the sky and thinks her soul has gone to Heaven; in actuality, he is witnessing the bomb blast at Hiroshima. The music in this scene again features wordless voices added to the instrumentation.

Jim finds a huge container of food rations that has been dropped from a plane. At this point the first musical theme returns in a glorious fullorchestra statement. When Jim angrily leaves Basie, one of whose cronies has shot the Japanese boy whom Jim has befriended, he bikes back to the internment camp, which is now occupied by American soldiers. As Jim rides into the camp, Williams's score features a new theme, a choral piece, set to a Latin text featuring the words "Exsultate justi" ("Let the just exult"), which is sung at a lively pace by a boys' choir. In the film's final scene, dozens of lost children are claimed by their parents. "Suo Gan" is heard once more when Jim's mother finds him. At first reluctant to embrace her, he finally rests his head on her shoulder and closes his eyes.

During the closing credits "Exsultate justi" is heard for a second time, with woodwinds, strings, and harp. As closing music for the film, this is an unusual finish, considering the brilliantly orchestrated final pieces that Williams had composed for such earlier films as *Star Wars* and *Raiders of the Lost Ark*. Not only is this the most choral of all of Williams's scores, but also it is one of the most melodically eloquent.

A MULTICULTURAL SCORE: *THE LAST EMPEROR*. In 1987, a year of relatively few outstanding film scores, two John Williams scores were nominated for the Oscar (in addition to *Empire of the Sun* he was cited for his exuberant music for the satanic comedy *The Witches of Eastwick*). Although either of these scores might have been chosen, the music award went to the score of the year's runaway winner of nine Oscars, Bernardo Bertolucci's *Last Emperor*. This lavishly-produced film is based on the life of Pu Yi, the last emperor of China, who was ousted by revolution. Though it has the advantage of having been filmed in such authentic locations as Beijing's Forbidden City, the central character is never very well-defined, and the resultant film is ponderously slow-moving.

The score is a multicultural mix by three composers: Japanese musician Ryuichi Sakamoto (who also has a role in the film); American singer/songwriter David Byrne (of Talking Heads fame); and Chinese composer Cong Su. Byrne scored the film's principal melodic idea, a slow-moving, lyrical melody that features a solo violin accompanied by drums and a repeated xylophone motif (with Byrne himself performing all the parts), and Sakamoto did the orchestral scoring for some of the more elaborate scenes, including a royal coronation. Su was brought in to provide a single musical cue, which features Oriental sounds played by the composer himself. The musical materials are basically Oriental in style, with much reliance on the pentatonic scale. The music seems appropriate if not particularly memorable, with the exception of Byrne's haunting violin theme, which casts a melancholy aura over the film.

P ETER MARTIN AND BORROWED CLASSICAL THEMES: *HOPE AND GLORY*. One of 1987's most memorable films is John Boorman's *Hope and Glory*, the director's autobiographical memoir of his childhood in England during World War II. As in Spielberg's *Empire of the Sun*, the horrors of World War II are revealed through the innocent eyes of a child; but, whereas Jim Graham sees a world of deprivation and death in the Japanese internment camp, Bill Rohan (Sebastian Rice Edwards) observes the war from his own front yard in a London suburb, as the German air raids begin. Once his father goes off to war, Bill is left at home with his mother and two sisters. When several bombs fall onto neighboring homes on their street, Bill and his older sister observe the flaming aftermath with a kind of raucous excitement; at one point they hold hands and dance around. Bill's adventures at school are also the source of some comical moments, especially when the kids have a practice drill and go running merrily for the bomb shelter. Later in the film, Bill's grandfather drives him to school, and Bill and his fellow classmates shout for joy when they discover that the school has been bombed during the night.

This surprisingly lighthearted but emotionally affecting portrait of Boorman's family is accompanied by a pastiche of familiar songs and voices, beginning with Glenn Miller's "In the Mood," which is played during the opening credits. Since Bill comes from a musical family, there is much classical music featured, including a Chopin prelude and a bit of a quartet played by Bill's mother and her three sisters, who were all trained to be string players. Music by Richard Wagner, Edward Elgar, and Henry Purcell is used in the course of the film. There are also a few moments of original background scoring, by English composer Peter Martin, who contributed some sentimental music for strings that accompanies such scenes as the one in which Bill's mother takes her two youngest children to the train station to have them shipped off to safer quarters, but at the last minute, realizes that she can't bear to be separated from them. Martin's music, along with the many borrowings, helps to bring this affectionate memoir of John Boorman's wartime experiences to vivid cinematic life.

SHORT CUTS ■■■■ **George Fenton and Jonas Gwangwa.** Richard Attenborough's *Cry Freedom* has a score with an ethnic flavor, produced by the combined talents of two composers. George Fenton and South Africa native Jonas Gwangwa collaborated on this Oscar-nominated score that includes much chanting, with the use of tribal drums and hand-clapping. The result is often rhythmically driven music, with very subdued underscoring. One particularly memorable theme features a series of slow-moving chords with a woman's voice providing a wordless melodic line.

■■■■ **Ennio Morricone.** The final nominee was the often heroic music by Ennio Morricone for Brian De Palma's handsomely produced crime film *The Untouchables.* The most noteworthy part of this score is the dramatic music for the confrontation scene between U.S. Treasury agents and the bootleggers at the Canadian border. Overlapping trumpet lines add such coloristic brilliance that the music almost overwhelms the scene. Nonetheless, the score of this big-screen version of the classic 1950s TV series is one of Morricone's finest works.

■■■■ **Basil Poledouris.** Among the noteworthy action/adventure films of 1987 was Paul Verhoeven's ultraviolent *RoboCop*, with its pulsating, dramatic score by Basil Poledouris, which utilizes mostly minor keys. The music features one principal theme, which is identified with a Detroit police officer (Peter Weller) who is mortally wounded and then transformed by advanced technology into a robotically enhanced crime-fighter. This theme, which is built on a repeated five-note motif, is forcefully sounded by French horns. Throughout the film synthesized effects are heard in combination with a large-scale orchestration to provide a thrilling musical background.

■■■■ **Jerry Goldsmith.** Franklin J. Schaffner's *Lionheart* includes a score of epic proportions by Jerry Goldsmith, who combined synthesizer-generated tones with standard orchestral sounds to create a sometimes ethereal musical background for this fictional story that takes place in 1212, during the Children's Crusade. Most of the thematic ideas in Goldsmith's richly textured score grow out of a three-note motif introduced at the outset of the film. This motif, which begins with a rising fifth, is expanded into a theme for Robert Nerra (Eric Stoltz), a young knight who seeks to join the army led by Richard the Lionhearted. A prominent secondary idea is Mathilda's theme, a folklike melody in fast tempo for trumpet and French horns, which is associated with one of the female crusaders. Though released to relatively few theaters, *Lionheart* contains one of Jerry Goldsmith's most memorable achievements.

■ ■ ■ ■ **Carter Burwell.** One of the weirdest scores of 1987 was written by Carter Burwell (b. 1955) for the delightful offbeat comedy *Raising Arizona*, by Joel and Ethan Coen. Accompanying the misadventures of former prison inmate H.I. (Nicolas Cage) and his wife, a former law-enforcement officer (Holly Hunter), is a score filled with raucous vocal sounds and many unusual instrumental effects. Burwell's music fits this unconventional film perfectly.

■ ■ ■ ■ **Alex North.** Alex North scored John Huston's final film, *The Dead*, based on a section of James Joyce's *Dubliners*. North's music is a melancholy Irish-inflected accompaniment written for a small instrumental ensemble, in which the Irish harp is prominently featured. North's other 1987 score was written for Barry Levinson's *Good Morning, Vietnam*, which includes several hilarious scenes of Adrian Cronauer (Robin Williams) as an unconventional radio disc jockey. At the end of the film, North's music adds a poignant note when Cronauer gets transferred out of Vietnam. As he travels in a military vehicle, he observes the besieged Vietnamese along the route; North's dramatically compelling accompaniment, with powerful string chords, provides a thoughtful conclusion to this otherwise comic film.

■ ■ ■ ■ **Borrowings from Puccini.** A number of filmmakers borrowed from the operatic melodies of Giacomo Puccini in the mid-1980s. Two Puccini arias are heard on the soundtrack of James Ivory's 1986 film *A Room with a View*, and several Puccini tunes grace the background score of Norman Jewison's delightful *Moonstruck*, in which a pretty Italian widow, Loretta (Cher), gets engaged to a proper Italian gentleman (Danny Aiello), but soon becomes romantically involved with his younger brother Ronny (Nicolas Cage). After making love to the strains of the duet from the closing moments in Act I of Puccini's *La Boheme*, Loretta and her new lover attend a performance of the opera at the Metropolitan Opera House in Lincoln Center. The score is based on several melodies from *La Boheme*, especially "Musetta's Waltz," from Act II of the opera, which is heard midway through the film as several couples look in wonder at the full moon and get romantic feelings. A recording of the original operatic number is heard during the film's closing scene, as Ronny proposes to Loretta and the entire family rises in a toast. The charming arrangements of Puccini's music were handled by Dick Hyman (b. 1927), who came to fame with his recording of Kurt Weill's "Moritat" in the 1950s and later worked on several Woody Allen films, including *Zelig* (1983) and *Radio Days* (1987). The opening and closing credits feature Dean Martin's recording of Harry Warren's 1953 movie hit "That's Amore" (originally written for *The Caddy*).

Adrian Lyne's *Fatal Attraction* also uses the music of Puccini since Alex (Glenn Close) seems to have a special fondness for *Madama Butterfly*. In the early part of the film, Dan (Michael Douglas) foolishly lets himself get sexually involved with Alex. He goes to her apartment, and she plays a recording of the opera while she fixes some drinks. The discarded original ending of the film parallels the end of Puccini's opera, with Alex taking her life as does Cio-Cio San in the last scene of *Butterfly*. Filmmakers of the 1980s seem to have considered the music of Puccini's Italian operas to be a perfect complement for American movie love scenes.

1988

ALAN SILVESTRI: *WHO FRAMED ROGER RABBIT?* Two genres, the 1940s detective thriller and the animated cartoon, come together in Robert Zemeckis's ingenious movie *Who Framed Roger Rabbit?*, in which live actors interact with cartoon characters through the use of a dazzling array of special effects. Private eye Eddie Valiant (Bob Hoskins) is hired by R. K. Maroon (Alan Tilvern), whose company produces animated films featuring Roger Rabbit, to keep an eye on Roger's sexy wife, Jessica. Soon thereafter, Roger is accused of a murder. Eddie must not only save Roger's life, but also rescue the entire population of Toontown, where all the Hollywood cartoon actors (the "Toons") live, from the greedy hands of the evil Judge Doom (Christopher Lloyd).

As outlandish as this premise might seem, *Roger Rabbit* is a lively and entertaining film, thanks to the creative work of many people, including composer Alan Silvestri who had worked on Zemeckis's two preceding films, *Romancing the Stone* and *Back to the Future.*

The art of film composing might once have seemed to be beyond the scope of this musician, whose background was mainly in pop music and jazz. Born in New York in 1950, Alan Silvestri began his musical career as a drummer during his high school years. He subsequently took up the guitar and received a music degree at the Berklee School in Boston. He played the guitar with a number of bands and went on the road with Wayne Cochran and the CC Riders. The promise of a recording contract lured Silvestri to Los Angeles; when that offer turned out to be a false hope, he wound up unemployed.[27]

In 1976, through his connection with a West Coast musician, Silvestri, though inexperienced, was offered his first film score for *The Amazing Dobermans*, a second sequel to the 1972 sleeper hit *The Doberman Gang.* This led to several other films featuring Silvestri's music which were made over the next few years, plus five seasons of the TV series "CHiPs," which ended its run on NBC in 1983.

Silvestri's next scoring assignment would change the composer's life. As Frank Sponitz explains: "His career seemed to have hit a dead end when he got a call to score a short scene in *Romancing the Stone.* Director Bob Zemeckis was so pleased with the result, he had Silvestri finish the movie."[28] Next came the biggest hit of 1985, *Back to the Future*, which Zemeckis handed to Silvestri based on his previous success.

Once *Back to the Future* was finished, Zemeckis approached Silvestri about his next film. According to Randall Larson, Silvestri was called in even before the film was shot:

> *Who Framed Roger Rabbit* is a film he was actually involved with for almost two years before its premiere, having been first called in by Zemeckis in October 1986 to pre-score source music cues heard from bands, pianos and other instruments actually seen on screen and which therefore had to be composed or orchestrated beforehand. Silvestri worked on the movie on and off through the next year, and in December 1987, he became attached to post-production full time. By then, the film's rough editing was finished enough for him to time, compose and record his original score, an assignment which wasn't completed until early June 1988, a scant two weeks before the film's opening date.[29]

Silvestri explains that he intentionally avoided the sort of mickey-mousing that has traditionally been associated with animated films. He

Photo by Gay Goodwin Wallin

Alan Silvestri.

admits that he attempted to support all the characters in the film as if they were real people, and that he used the music to emphasize the dramatic situation:

> The filmmakers' intention was that the animation be so beautifully integrated into the picture that you never had this feeling that it was a real-life film with cartoon characters intruding. . . . We did everything from playing everyone cartoony to playing everyone very straight, in a traditional kind of under-scoring way. . . . There's something inherently schizophrenic in cartoon mentality. The characters suddenly just *do* things! They'll be talking with someone and suddenly their eyes will bug out. Sometimes, the music needed to support something like that, and sometimes, it felt wrong to do that. I was really just following the picture and seeing what kind of emotional support it needed at any given time.[30]

The opening of *Roger Rabbit* features a movie within a movie: the animated short "Somethin's Cooking," an A. K. Maroon Cartoon, which is in the process of being filmed. In the scenario, Roger Rabbit is baby-sitting for Baby Herman and trying unsuccessfully to keep the tyke out of trouble.

Roger and Eddie (Bob Hoskins) in *Who Framed Roger Rabbit?*

© *Touchstone Pictures and Amblin Entertainment, Inc.*

Unlike most cartoons, which are drawn to the already composed score, "Somethin's Cooking" was created differently. In Silvestri's own words:

> Traditionally, music for cartoons is recorded first and then the cartoons are drawn to the music. . . . That was *not* the case in this film, so it presented a challenge both in the writing and especially in the performing of the music. The tempo was all over the place, and the London Symphony had to do very precise cartoon music, hitting endless bits of action, but having to do it in sync with the picture and still have it look like the cartoon was drawn to the music. It was a bit of a twist on that situation and it took us all time to make that adjustment.[31]

One of the film's most impressive bits is the duck duet that occurs when Eddie enters a private nightclub. On stage, Donald Duck and Daffy Duck are playing on back-to-back pianos a frantic version of Liszt's *Hungarian* Rhapsody no. 2. Apparently Zemeckis wanted the pianos, which are real and not drawn, to be actually playing the music. Silvestri solved this problem by using a Yamaha Synclavier, which can make the keys move in the manner of the old player piano. Again in Silvestri's words:

> We took the piece of music and had it played into the computer's memory banks . . . extensively editing it so that we could create this four-handed version that would play on two pianos. A man named Jim Cooper invented an interface between the Synclavier and the Morantz Player Piano mechanism. The special effects guys in London took the upright pianos and replaced the mechanisms with Morantz mechanisms. We were then able to lock the Synclavier up to the cameras and the playback machines and through MIDI [Musical Instrument Digital Interface], trigger the keys on both pianos live to the playback music.[32]

As far as the film's setting and scenario are concerned, Silvestri approached the score from the standpoint of incorporating 1940s jazz sounds. Combined with the orchestral cues, which were recorded by the London Symphony, a five-piece ensemble was used to add period flavor in certain scenes. Again in Silvestri's own words:

> We wanted to incorporate this jazz aspect into the score, but we still needed the orchestra's strength and the emotional range. . . . It was all mixed together, the jazz segued in and out of the out-and-out orchestral scoring. There would be a chase and we would be playing be-bop, and suddenly, we would go into high-adventure underscore, and then back into be-bop![33]

Designing themes for the various characters led Silvestri to create a variety of melodic ideas, which he discusses as follows:

> Roger has his own tuney-little theme. . . . Eddie Valiant, the down-on-his-luck detective, has a very nostalgic '40-ish ballad-type of theme [featuring a solo trumpet]. Judge Doom has an ominous-sounding, conventional bad-guy theme, and his henchmen, the weasels, have a more frantic kind of thematic material. All through the picture, these different thematic elements are constantly being used and combined to keep the presence of the characters alive, musically.[34]

Roger Rabbit's music presented challenges that few film composers have had to face. Compounding the difficulties was the fact that when Silvestri composed much of the score, the animated special effects were not yet completed; thus he had to imagine what the final print of the film would look like. Silvestri succeeded in meeting these challenges and creating an inspired musical accompaniment.

DANNY ELFMAN: *BEETLEJUICE*. Danny Elfman wrote an exceedingly clever score for Tim Burton's wild comedy *Beetlejuice*. Set in rural New England, this offbeat film begins with the accidental deaths of Adam and Barbara Maitland (Alec Baldwin and Geena Davis) in an automobile accident. After dying, the couple discover that they are continuing to inhabit their large home as ghosts. Unfortunately, the house is being sold to a city couple with a teenage daughter, Lydia (Winona Ryder), who has a penchant for wearing black. In their attempts to rid the house of the new owners, the Maitlands consult a book called the *Handbook for the Recently Deceased* and soon hire the services of a bio-exorcist named "Betelgeuse" (Michael Keaton), who is known by the nickname "Beetlejuice."

Elfman's approach to this supernatural fantasy resulted in a score of striking originality. The opening-title music incorporates a bit of the calypso tune "Day-O." It begins with a rambunctious minor-key theme that features a fast-repeated "oompah" beat. This leads to a fast-moving clarinet idea, which is followed by strings and then by a menacing melody played by trombones. This music appears to have a pseudo-horror-film background, with an ever-pulsing rhythmic flavor. The rest of Elfman's score cleverly follows the film's unpredictable plot, which features many action-filled scenes that occur whenever one of the Maitlands attempts to leave the house, only to land in a bizarre desertlike terrain populated by strange monsterlike creatures. Adam is playing calypso music on a cassette player at the beginning of the film, and references to this music occur throughout the picture. Two Harry Belafonte recordings are featured: in one scene Lydia's family and invited dinner guests get up and start dancing to the strains of "Day-O"; "Jump in Line (Shake, Shake Señora)" is used in the final scene, as Lydia happily dances with Adam and Barbara, who are reconciled to the fact that they must share their home with Lydia's family.

HANS ZIMMER: *RAIN MAN*. One of 1988's most charming scores is from the year's top box-office film, Barry Levinson's *Rain Man*. This engaging movie won honors for Best Picture, Best Actor (Dustin Hoffman), Best Director, and Best Original Screenplay. German composer Hans Zimmer (b. 1957), composed a rhythmically jaunty musical accompaniment.

In the film, Tom Cruise plays Charlie Babbitt, a fast-talking car salesman in California who returns to Ohio for his father's funeral and learns that the estate has been willed to a brother that Charlie didn't even know he had. When he finds his brother Raymond (Dustin Hoffman) in a mental institution, Charlie sneaks him out and attempts to take him to California until he can figure out a way to get half of the inheritance money. Charlie soon learns that his brother is autistic, and has a great fear of airplanes and trains. Thus begins a cross-country trip in the family's old 1949 Buick roadster, the only thing Charlie's father left him. Charlie also learns that his brother is amazingly adept with numbers, and can win big money at the Las Vegas casinos, even though Raymond has no appreciation for his own arithmetical capabilities.

For this road movie, which epitomizes the time-honored cliché about two people thrown together by chance and continuing on their journey in tandem, Hans Zimmer got his first chance to score a picture by himself after several years of working as an assistant to English film composer Stanley Myers. Although much source music is used as background, Zimmer contributed a catchy original theme that features a minor-key tune played by flutes, with an accompanying rock beat. This theme, which is heard periodically as the two brothers head West, includes a rhythmic drive that sets a lively pace. Zimmer's music earned him his first Oscar nomination.

S**HORT** C**UTS** ■ ■ ■ ■ **John Williams.** Among the other scoring nominees for 1988 is John Williams's music for Lawrence Kasdan's memorable film version of Anne Tyler's *Accidental Tourist*. Principally based on a six-note motif that features solo piano, strings, and winds, Williams's lyrical music provides dramatic substance for this melancholy story that centers on the emotional reawakening of Macon Leary (William Hurt), whose feelings have been shut down by the senseless killing of his adolescent son. With his marriage to Sarah (Kathleen Turner) in limbo, Macon is drawn into a relationship with a woman named Muriel (Geena Davis), whom he meets at a pet shop.

Although most of the score is kept at a low dynamic level, by the end of the film, when Macon is forced to choose whether to resume his marriage to Sarah or to be with Muriel, his decision is musically resolved by a gloriously romantic final statement of Williams's theme. When Macon sees Muriel standing in front of a Paris hotel he breaks out in a big smile, with accompanying music that beautifully underscores this emotional moment.

■ ■ ■ ■ **George Fenton.** Stephen Frears's *Dangerous Liaisons*, based on Christopher Hampton's play, which, in turn, was based on the celebrated novel by Choderlos de Laclos, is set in prerevolutionary France. George Fenton received his third Oscar nomination for his bits of original score, which were blended with such borrowed materials as themes by Vivaldi, J. S. Bach, Handel, and Gluck. During the opening credits, Fenton's main theme is introduced, with a fast-paced minor-key theme featuring strings and trumpets. This soon fades and is replaced by the sounds of Vivaldi as the scheming Marquise de Merteuil (Glenn Close) is seen at her makeup table. In the course of the film, the Marquise offers her friend and former lover, the Vicomte de Valmont (John Malkovich), a challenge that involves the sexual conquest of two young women. If he succeeds, he can have renewed intimacy with the Marquise herself. While Valmont puts his nefarious plans into motion, there is much scurrying about, with letters and keys being surreptitiously handed back and forth. During a central episode of the film, in which Valmont orchestrates a complex web of deception, Bach's Concerto in A Minor for Four Harpsichords creates a rhythmically driven pace, with its fast-moving lines for strings and keyboards.

■ ■ ■ ■ **Maurice Jarre.** Maurice Jarre received an Oscar nomination for his scoring of Michael Apted's *Gorillas in the Mist*, which contains an ingenious mix of conventional orchestration and electronic sounds. For the film, Jarre assembled what is identified as "The Maurice Jarre Electronic Ensemble," a group of nine keyboard-proficient musicians, including several who had worked with Jarre on such earlier scores as *The Year of Living Dangerously*, *Witness*, and *Fatal Attraction*. Jarre's tuneful backgrounds are heard during the African scenes in which Dian Fossey (Sigourney Weaver) bravely climbs up the rocky terrain to the region in which endangered mountain gorillas live. One particularly memorable scene is the one where Fossey first spots a gorilla; here the sounds of a solo cello are combined with electronic music to convey the wonder of the moment.

Another notable Jarre score is featured in Paul Mazursky's amusing *Moon over Parador*, in which an actor (Richard Dreyfuss) is conned into impersonating a South American dictator. Here Jarre used a large-scale symphonic approach, with a Latin-inflected rhythm. The buoyant main-title theme is an exhilarating tune that employs quintuple meter ($\frac{5}{4}$ time).

■ ■ ■ **Dave Grusin.** The year's Oscar-winning score was the catchy music by Dave Grusin for Robert Redford's *Milagro Beanfield War*, a film about the attempts of some local villagers in a small New Mexico town to resist the machinations of land developers, who are buying up land in order to build a country club. There are several melodious tunes in Grusin's score, which relies heavily on waltz meter ($\frac{3}{4}$ time). The main-title theme features a melody played on the concertina; another theme is sounded by a solo guitar and strings.

■ ■ ■ **Trevor Jones.** One of 1988's most controversial films was Alan Parker's *Mississippi Burning*, in which two FBI agents investigate the 1964 deaths of three civil rights workers in Mississippi. The agents, Gene Hackman and Willem Dafoe, dash about in search of evidence to implicate local authorities, who are thought to be involved in the killings. Much of Trevor Jones's score is made up of pounding drums, with bits of melody on guitars. The result is not very tuneful, but it does propel the action of this violent, well-acted movie that succeeds as a crime drama, but is less successful as history.

■ ■ ■ **James Horner.** Among James Horner's five new movie projects in 1988 is the score for Ron Howard's fantasy/adventure *Willow*, which includes a richly symphonic background. Walter Hill's *Red Heat*, which deals with a Russian drug dealer, features Horner's highly dramatic main-title theme with a choir singing in Russian. In *Red Heat* Horner effectively emulates the choral style of Prokofiev's film music.

■ ■ ■ **Mark Isham.** One of 1988's better scores is the melodious work by Mark Isham for Alan Rudolph's period film *The Moderns*, which is set in Paris during the 1920s. Isham's main theme features a solo violin in a lyrical, slow-paced melody, accompanied by a small ensemble that includes piano, cello, marimba, acoustic bass, and sustained chords played on an electronic keyboard. Isham created some other charming tunes for the film, including a lyrical piece for violin and piano called "La valse moderne." Throughout the film the violin playing of Sid Page is an asset that greatly enhances the effectiveness of Isham's tunes.

■ ■ ■ **Carly Simon.** Mike Nichols's *Working Girl* was scored by Carly Simon, who created a memorable song, "Let the River Run," which won for her the Oscar as Best Original Song. Additional bits of instrumental scoring occur in the film, along with interpolated songs by the Pointer Sisters ("I'm So Excited") and Chris De Burgh ("Lady in Red").

JAMES HORNER: *FIELD OF DREAMS.* In 1989, James Horner began his second decade as a film composer by writing the wistful Oscar-nominated music for Phil Alden Robinson's *Field of Dreams* (also nominated for best picture), a charming baseball-themed fantasy. Like veterans John Williams, Elmer Bernstein, and Jerry Goldsmith, Horner began his film-music career by creating scores for films of dubious distinction.

Photo by Gay Goodwin Wallin

James Horner.

Born in Los Angeles in 1953, James Horner spent much of his youth in England, where he was enrolled at the Royal College of Music. Thereafter he returned to the United States and obtained a bachelor's degree in composition at the University of Southern California and a master's degree at UCLA.[35] While working on his Ph.D., Horner began teaching music theory. A chance contact with an official of the American Film Institute (AFI) significantly changed the direction of Horner's career. In a 1982 interview, Horner made the following comment about his connection with the AFI and his early regard for film music:

> I had up until that time looked down at film music. . . . I looked at myself as a classical composer. I was asked to do an AFI film, *The Drought*. I said, what the hell. I fell in love with the film, like a stroke of lightning. I suddenly knew what I wanted to do—write film music. I did another six or seven AFI films, learned about Roger Corman, bothered him until he gave me a job, stopped working on my PhD, resigned from UCLA, left academia, and began working on film music, which I am doing to this day.[36]

Horner's Hollywood career began with a series of scores written for films produced by New World Pictures, a small company run by Gene and Roger Corman. Despite the low-budget limitations of such movies as *The Lady in Red*, *Battle Beyond the Stars*, and *Humanoids from the Deep*, these films afforded Horner the opportunity to hone his film music skills, so that by the early 1980s, he was prepared for better things to come.

Indeed, better things did come! First, Oliver Stone invited him to write the score for *The Hand* in 1981. This was followed shortly thereafter by a replacement score for Michael Wadleigh's *Wolfen*, for which he wrote almost an hour of music in twelve days. After several other films, producer Harve Bennett asked Horner to do the score for *Star Trek II: The Wrath of Khan*. With this score Horner joined the ranks of major film composers. Ever since, he has been one of the most sought-after musicians working in the film medium.

Horner's list of film-scoring credits for the 1980s includes a roster of more than forty feature films. Among these are some of the most popular movies of the decade, including the second and third movies in the *Star Trek* series; *Aliens* (1986); and films directed by Ron Howard, such as *Cocoon* (1985) and *Willow* (1988).

Whether epic or small-scale, the quality of Horner's film music has been pretty consistent over the years. Unfortunately, one aspect of his work that has caused grumbling among some film-music aficionados concerns the use of similar musical ideas in several of his scores. For instance, the opening descending-scale pattern heard at the beginning of *Aliens* (1986) resembles a motif he later used in *Patriot Games* (1992). If this can be considered a weakness in Horner's work, it is not very different from the instances of melodic, harmonic, or rhythmic similarity that can be found in scores by most of the renowned composers of Hollywood's Golden Age. If Horner has consciously borrowed from himself, he also follows in the time-honored tradition of such renowned composers as J. S. Bach, Vivaldi, and Handel, all of whom were known to recycle entire movements of music in later works.

A landmark in Horner's career is the part-synthesized, part-orchestral score that he created for *Field of Dreams*, which Robinson, the director, adapted from the 1982 novel *Shoeless Joe*, by W. P. Kinsella. The story is a fantasy about baseball, memories, and second chances.

Following other recent films with baseball themes, such as *The Natural*, *Bull Durham*, and *Eight Men Out*, *Field of Dreams* tells of Ray Kinsella (Kevin Costner), who converts part of his Iowa cornfield into a ballfield, his "field of dreams," in response to a mysterious voice that calls to him, saying, "If you build it, he will come." Sometime after completing the baseball diamond, the youthful Shoeless Joe Jackson (Ray Liotta), who had been banned from major league baseball following the notorious Black Sox scandal of 1919, arrives and asks if he can bring some of his friends. Soon there are eight players on the field, all dressed in old-fashioned White Sox uniforms. Ray, his wife (Amy Madigan), and their young daughter Karin (Gaby Hoffman) are at first the only ones who can see the mysterious visitors. In response to another message and an apparition, Ray brings Terrence Mann (James Earl Jones), a writer and former peace advocate, now in seclusion, and the youthful Archie Graham (Frank Whaley), whose entire major league career consisted of a half inning without an at-bat and who is now an elderly doctor (played by Burt Lancaster), back to his Iowa ballfield, where other former greats have now assembled. Archie finally gets his chance to play and score a run. When Karin Kinsella falls off the bleachers, Archie is transformed into the elderly Doc Graham, who then treats Karin.

Later, Shoeless Joe points to the catcher on the diamond, and repeats the words, "If you build it, he will come." Ray realizes that he is looking at his own father as a youth. As father and son share a bonding moment, the camera backs away to reveal a solid line of cars approaching the farm. It seems that little Karin, who had proclaimed that people would come from all around to see their field of dreams, is about to have her prediction become a reality.

With a story that induces the suspension of disbelief similarly to the way in which Frank Capra's *It's a Wonderful Life* coaxes the viewer into accepting the existence of angels, *Field of Dreams* benefits greatly from the "ghostly" music that Horner devised. Whenever Ray hears a mysterious voice or sees a vision, there are soft sounds provided by a synthesizer, with the addition of distant piano tones.

Thematically, Horner's score is built around one principal theme, with a few other subordinate ideas thrown in from time to time. The score's main melodic idea, which is introduced during the opening credits, is a slow-moving lyrical tune that features a solo French horn accompanied by sustained tones on a string synthesizer, with a few deep-sounding electronic "thuds" added for dramatic emphasis. This melody does not appear again until after the field is finished. As Ray looks frustratedly out the window at the falling snow, a purely electronic rendition of the tune is heard. Electronic effects are featured again when the theme returns, in the scene where Shoeless Joe makes his first appearance and Ray meets him. As the two begin to play ball, a solo piano version of the melody is introduced.

Much later, after Ray brings Terrence Mann and young Archie Graham back to his Iowa farm, Terrence states author W. P. Kinsella's idea that people will come to see baseball because this game is a part of our past, and that baseball reminds us of all that was good. As his eloquent speech continues, Horner's theme grows from a soft statement by the French horn to a much more heroic version that features a solo trumpet and strings.

When Ray recognizes the young catcher as his own father, the French horn and strings play an emotionally charged version of Horner's theme, which grows to even greater emotional heights when the miraculously

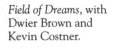

Field of Dreams, with
Dwier Brown and
Kevin Costner.

reconciled Kinsellas, father and son, silently toss a baseball back and forth.
The theme continues playing, into the closing credits.

In addition to the "ghost" motif and the principal melodic idea, Horner's
music also contains a catchy tune for high woodwinds (mostly flute and
piccolo) accompanied by a gentle rock beat that occurs in a scene in which
Ray reads up on Terrence Mann at the local library. A melancholy-sounding
minor-key idea is heard in the scene in which Doc Graham tends Karin after
her fall. A sustained melody sounded by violin and flute, accompanied by a
repeated arpeggio figure, creates a lyrical effect.

There are a few interpolations of borrowed music in the score. For instance, a recording by Duke Ellington of Billy Strayhorn's "Lotus Blossom"
is heard in one of the baseball scenes involving the ghostly White Sox.
Field of Dreams is a joyous celebration of the great American pastime and is
also a wondrous demonstration of wish fulfillment. With a musical score that
manages to be at the same time both nostalgic and mystical, *Field of Dreams*
is an extremely touching film.

Horner's musical contribution to *Field of Dreams* not only earned him
a second scoring nomination, but it helped him acquire more significant
film-music projects, such as Edward Zwick's moving Civil War drama *Glory*,
which was released at the end of 1989. This film vividly portrays the true-
life story of the all-black Massachusetts Fifty-Fourth Regiment, which
tragically was wiped out in a suicidal charge on Fort Wagner, on the out-
skirts of Charleston, South Carolina, on July 18, 1863. Horner contributed
an ethereal score with the sounds of voices, provided by the Boys Choir of
Harlem. Unconventional in terms of instrumentation, Horner's music adds
considerable impact to this powerful and somber film.

PATRICK DOYLE: *HENRY V*. The year 1989 marks the auspicious film-music debut of Patrick Doyle (b. 1953), who both acted in and scored Kenneth Branagh's vividly cinematic version of Shakespeare's *Henry V*. A native of Scotland, Doyle was working as an actor, a composer, and a music director with the Renaissance Theater Company in England when he first met Branagh. When Branagh announced plans to direct a film of *Henry V*, Doyle auditioned to do the score. Branagh liked his rough sketches and commissioned him to do the original background music.

The score of *Henry V* is sometimes darkly dramatic, at other times sweetly lyrical. The most memorable musical moment comes at the end of the Battle of Agincourt, which takes place during a driving rainstorm. Doyle, who also plays the role of Court, stands on the muddy battlefield and begins to sing a Latin song called "Non nobis, Domine." Soon all the men are singing, and after a couple of verses, the orchestra joins in. This music, which builds to a powerfully emotional climax, is used as a touching eulogy for those who have fallen in battle. One casualty that is singled out is a slain adolescent (Christian Bale), whose body the king carries over his shoulders back to the campsite as the music continues.

This version of the Shakespearean play, which is much grittier than Laurence Olivier's handsome 1940s adaptation, emerged as a fine film that demonstrates a spectacularly creative flair. Both Branagh and Doyle achieved wondrous things with this film, which represents the beginning of a long and fruitful artistic collaboration.

JOHN WILLIAMS: *BORN ON THE FOURTH OF JULY*. In 1989, John Williams earned Oscar nominations for two very contrasting films. Whereas *Indiana Jones and the Last Crusade* allowed Williams to rely on his action/adventure type of scoring, Oliver Stone's *Born on the Fourth of July* inspired him to create a melancholy score with a richly textured string instrumentation, plus the sound of a solo trumpet. Tim Morrison of the Boston Pops Orchestra achieved celebrity status because of the lyrical trumpet solos that he recorded for this film; there was even a video featuring Morrison playing the main theme that was shown on TV cable music channels. A fanfarelike trumpet idea, built on a four-note motif that moves within a very confined melodic space, leads to an emotionally charged theme that moves slowly but forcefully.

The film features such familiar tunes as Henry Mancini's "Moon River" (for the high school prom scene) and some rock songs that were popular during the Vietnam war. Stone used Williams's music to establish the basic mood of this biographical film, which is centered on Ron Kovic (Tom Cruise), who went to Vietnam as a patriotic marine but came home crippled and disillusioned. His subsequent odyssey through the troubled waters of America during the latter part of the Vietnam war is often painful to watch, but Williams's poignant and sometimes powerful music creates a compelling tonal picture of the chaos caused by this controversial war.

SHORT CUTS ■■■■ Alan Menken. The Oscar-winning music in 1989 was the tuneful score by Alan Menken for the Disney studio's *Little Mermaid*. After a long dry spell during which few memorable scores were created for their animated feature films, Disney producers wisely decided to return to the musically rich style of *Snow White* and *Cinderella* for this colorfully drawn adaptation of the Hans Christian Andersen fairy tale. Although some regrettable liberties were taken with Andersen's moral fable, Menken's songs, with the inspired lyrics of Howard Ashman, are melodically and rhythmically inspired. The Oscar-winning song "Under the Sea," one of the film's highlights, is sung during an underwater concert, with all sorts of cleverly drawn instruments partaking in the festivities. For Menken this score was the first of many that would usher him into the ranks of the most awarded composers in film history.

■■■ **Alan Silvestri.** One score that was unaccountably missing from the list of Oscar nominees in 1989 was Alan Silvestri's dramatic music for James Cameron's elaborate underwater sci-fi film *The Abyss.* The film ultimately resembles Spielberg's *Close Encounters of the Third Kind* in that mysterious aliens show up and prove to be friendly. Silvestri's majestic chords, with full orchestra and choir, provide a thrilling sound for the final portion of this film.

■■■ **Danny Elfman.** One of the musical highlights of 1989 is the pulsating score by Danny Elfman for Tim Burton's dark but fascinating version of *Batman.* The main theme, a bold, rhythmically driven minor-key idea featuring low brass instruments, sets the tone for this, the first of several Warner Bros. films based on the famed comic-book action hero.

■■■ **Jerry Goldsmith.** Among other action films of the year with memorable music is *Star Trek V: The Final Frontier.* Goldsmith's symphonic score, which is partially based on themes he composed for the first *Star Trek* film a decade earlier, contributes a great deal of dramatic energy.

The 'burbs, in which Tom Hanks suspects his suburbanite neighbors of being devil worshippers, features one of Goldsmith's most ingenious scores, a work of considerable dramatic force that emphasizes the darker aspects of the story, as a counterpoint to the film's broad humor.

■■■ **Elmer Bernstein.** Following a first excursion into a small, chamber-music kind of scoring for *Da* in 1988, Elmer Bernstein contributed a gentle score for Jim Sheridan's touching biographical film *My Left Foot,* in which Daniel Day-Lewis gives an Oscar-winning performance as Christy Brown, the Irish painter and writer who suffered from cerebral palsy. The *ondes martenot* provides an eerie sound for the melody of the score's main theme, which is accompanied by a small ensemble and features a string quartet, a few woodwinds, a piano, and a harp. Although the music is used somewhat sparsely, some of the film's most affecting moments occur when Bernstein's music provides a lyrical accompaniment.

In contrast with his subtle music for *My Left Foot* is Bernstein's turbulent orchestral score for *Slipstream*, a British film that starred Bill Paxton and Mark Hamill. Hamill's gruff appearance may be a shock to those who remember him only as Luke Skywalker. Regrettably, this futuristic action film was not released to theaters in the United States.

■■■ **Ennio Morricone.** Of the foreign composers who wrote for American films in 1989, Ennio Morricone distinguished himself with an emotionally moving score for Brian De Palma's powerful but depressing

Casualties of War. Morricone's use of strings and wordless voices provides a lyrical contrast to the wrenching scenes of this Vietnam war drama in which a young soldier (Michael J. Fox) witnesses the brutal rape and murder of a young Vietnamese woman by members of his outfit.

Morricone also wrote sublimely lyrical music for Giuseppe Tornatore's autobiographical *Cinema Paradiso,* which won the Oscar as best foreign-language film. Of the score's three principal themes, the first is the tuneful main-title theme, which begins with solo piano, and then is joined by a clarinet and strings. The second idea, which is associated with the principal character Toto as a young boy, features a solo violin in a jaunty tune that moves stepwise up the scale, before descending back. Additionally, there is a love theme (with a melody composed by the composer's son, Andrea), which is introduced by soprano saxophone with strings.

■■■■ **Maurice Jarre.** In Peter Weir's *Dead Poets Society,* French composer Maurice Jarre combined electronic sounds, conventional orchestration, and the sound of bagpipes for this story of impressionable young students at a private boys' academy. The stirring main theme, which is heard most prominently in the concluding scene when the boys salute Mr. Keating (Robin Williams) by standing on top of their desks and proclaiming Walt Whitman's words "O captain, my captain," provides an emotional charge for the movie's ending.

■■■■ **Georges Delerue.** A romantic score by another French composer, Georges Delerue, for Herbert Ross's film of the play *Steel Magnolias* adds an eloquent beauty to this heavily sentimental story of several women in a small Louisiana town. Delerue's main theme provides a lyrical background for the final scene, where Annelle (Daryl Hannah) goes into labor during the town's annual Easter egg hunt. The melody features a solo flute, with harp and strings, plus a solo harmonica, as the credits begin to appear.

■■■■ **Philippe Sarde.** Still a third French composer, Philippe Sarde, composed a lyrical symphonic background for Jean-Jacques Annaud's nature film *The Bear.* With a bear cub and a giant grizzly as the two main characters, *The Bear* contains very little dialogue, and thus Sarde's music provides a much-needed dramatic atmosphere. While the lyrical minor-key main theme closely resembles the melody of Tchaikovsky's "Barcarolle" (also known as "June," part of a set of twelve pieces known as *The Seasons*), there are several other tuneful themes. Sarde's score stands beside his earlier score for Annaud's *Quest for Fire* as one of his finer film-music achievements.[37]

POSTLUDE

AN EMPHASIS ON YOUTH. Many changes came about in the world of film music during the 1980s. Motion picture scores were being created increasingly by younger musicians, who could manage the frantic schedules imposed on them by demanding filmmakers. Many of these younger composers were drawn to the rapidly advancing field of electronic technology, which became a standard part of the film-music vocabulary in the 1980s. Patrick Doyle (b. 1955), Cliff Eidelman (b. 1964), Elliot Goldenthal (b. 1954), all scored their first feature films in 1988 or 1989; all three have gone on to highly creative careers in film music.

Endnotes

1. Fred Bronson, *Billboard's Hottest Hot 100 Hits* (New York: Billboard Books, 1991), p. 301.

2. Dave Grusin, Liner notes for the *Cinemagic* LP, on the GRP label, GR 1037.

3. Kevin Mulhall, Liner notes for the CD rerelease of the *Conan the Barbarian* soundtrack, on Varese Sarabande, VSD-5390.

4. David Hutchison, "Music for a Barbarian," *Starlog*, no. 62 (September 1982), p. 24.

5. Ibid.

6. Ibid.

7. Ibid., pp. 24–25.

8. Ibid., pp. 25, 65.

9. With the continuing decline of film musicals, this category disappeared for lack of eligible candidates. After 1985, there was only one slate of score nominees; this change in rules again allowed the unfair practice of pitting scores of songs (such as those of 1980's *Fame*) against original background scores. This condensing of the scoring nominees remained intact until a 1995 ruling resulted in the creation of two separate categories: Original Score, Drama—and Original Score, Comedy or Musical.

10. Harvey Siders, "Bill Conti," *BMI: The Many Worlds of Music*, issue 2, 1977, p. 35.

11. Ibid.

12. Ephraim Katz, *The Film Encyclopedia*, 2d ed. (New York: HarperCollins, 1994), p. 1005.

13. Bronson, p. 299.

14. Ibid.

15. Fred Karlin, *Listening to Movies: The Film Lover's Guide to Film Music* (New York: Schirmer Books, 1994), p. 49.

16. Bronson, pp. 299–300.

17. Ibid., p. 299.

18. Ibid.

19. James Fitzpatrick, Liner notes for the *Legend* soundtrack, with Jerry Goldsmith's score, which was released on CD by Silva Screen, FILMCD 045. There was also an earlier release, but this one is a more complete version, with over seventy minutes of music and with better sound quality.

20. Harlan Kennedy, "The Harmonious Background," *American Film*, vol. XXVII, no. 2 (February 1991), p. 40.

21. Ibid.

22. Ibid., p. 41.

23. Ibid.

24. Ibid.

25. Ibid., p. 46.

26. Jon Burlingame, "A Biography of Ennio Morricone," Program of the 1994 Career Achievement Award Tribute Dinner, presented by the Society for the Preservation of Film Music, March 18, 1994.

27. Randall Larson, "Alan Silvestri's Tunes for Toons," *Starlog*, no. 135 (October 1988), p. 19.

28. Frank Sponitz, Introduction to "Dialogue on Film: Alan Silvestri," *American Film*, vol. XVI, no. 8 (August 1991), p. 14.

29. Larson, p. 19.

30. Ibid.

31. Ibid., p. 20.

32. Ibid.

33. Ibid.

34. Ibid.

35. Tom Sciacca, "James Horner: New Melodies for the Starship 'Enterprise'," *Starlog*, no. 63 (October 1982), p. 23.

36. Ibid.

37. According to the liner notes included with the original soundtrack, the main theme of this score "is inspired by Eastern European Jewish folklore. Much as Tchaikovsky used it before, Sarde does now."

8

1990–97

Into the 1990s

PRELUDE

Since the days of the nickelodeons, the motion picture has evolved from a primitive series of silent black-and-white images to a highly sophisticated art form, with multicolored cinematography accompanied by a carefully synchronized and digitally recorded soundtrack. In the 1990s, this ever-changing process continues to have an impact not only on film, but also on the media in general.

POPULAR MUSIC. In the world of popular music, the 1990s may be remembered as the decade of rap music, a rhythmically driven, melodically minimal, and often scatological creation of mostly young, angry, urban black performers. An indication of the popularity of this music is the inclusion of a rap-influenced musical score in one of 1995's major films, *Dangerous Minds*, which utilizes throbbing rap rhythms to flavor this story set in an inner-city high school.

One of the biggest successes among mainstream recording artists in the 1990s is Whitney Houston, whose movie debut as costar of the 1992 thriller *The Bodyguard* was enhanced by the soundtrack album, which had unprecedented sales of fifteen million copies.[1]

Madonna, whose early films were critically reviled, gave an alluringly sexy performance as Breathless Mahoney in *Dick Tracy* (1990). Her rendition of Stephen Sondheim's "Sooner or Later" in this film helped to propel the song to an Oscar. Since then, her most significant film role has been that of Evita Peron in Alan Parker's lavish film adaptation of Andrew Lloyd Webber's stage musical *Evita* (1996), with lyrics by Tim Rice.

Other rock stars who have made significant contributions to films are Bruce Springsteen, whose Oscar-winning song "Streets of Philadelphia" helped the AIDS drama *Philadelphia* become one of 1993's more prestigious films; and Bryan Adams, who cowrote (with Michael Kamen) and sang "(Everything I Do) I Do It for You" in *Robin Hood—Prince of Thieves* (1991) and "Have You Ever Really Loved a Woman?" in *Don Juan DeMarco* (1995).

Both Michael Jackson and his younger sister Janet have made musical contributions to 1990s films. Michael's rendition of "Will You Be There?" helped make *Free Willy* a sleeper in 1993, and Janet's "Again," which was featured that year in her film debut *Poetic Justice*, became a number-one hit on the *Billboard* charts.[2]

Although recordings of film music represent only a small percentage of the total repertoire of music available on CDs, there have been several other big sellers in addition to the *Bodyguard* soundtrack, including the many recordings of music from Disney films. Since the release of *The Little Mermaid* in 1989, the scores written by Alan Menken for the animated films *Beauty and the Beast* (1991), *Aladdin* (1992), and *Pocahontas* (1995) have been highly successful. Elton John's recording of the songs for *The Lion King* (1994) has sold more than eight million copies.[3]

Compilation discs of period songs have also continued to propel the sales of movie soundtrack albums. Just as *American Graffiti* (1973) featured a host of popular rock songs of the 1950s, Robert Zemeckis's *Forrest Gump* (1994) includes dozens of songs from the '50s through the '80s that were chosen for the purpose of creating a musical portrait of America during the life and times of this film's unlikely hero. The resultant double-disc soundtrack album became one of the most popular releases of 1994.

A wave of nostalgia hit the popular music world in 1993 with the release of Nora Ephron's sentimental film *Sleepless in Seattle*. Its soundtrack of old romantic standards became one of the year's biggest successes, with sales topping the seven million mark. Especially noteworthy are the renditions by Jimmy Durante of "As Time Goes By" and "Make Someone Happy." The biggest hit from this film is Victor Young's 1951 song "When I Fall in Love," originally featured in *One Minute to Zero*, and performed in the new film by Celine Dion and Clive Griffin. This marks the third time around for this popular ballad, which had been an earlier hit for both Nat "King" Cole (1957) and the Lettermen (1961).

Meanwhile, another old tune, "Can't Help Falling in Love" (based on Giovanni Martini's "Plaisir d'amour"), which had been updated successfully by Elvis Presley in his 1961 film *Blue Hawaii*, got another facelift in 1993 when it was turned into a jaunty rock song for the soundtrack of *Sliver* (1993). The new version, sung by the popular group UB40, became one of the year's biggest hits. This old tune, incidentally, is the same one that Aaron Copland had borrowed back in 1949 for his score of William Wyler's film *The Heiress*.

TELEVISION. If TV has taught us anything, it is probably that what goes around, comes around. The success of such sitcoms as *Seinfeld and Frasier* on NBC indicates that sharply written shows with a variety of oddball characters always seem to find an audience. Other shows, such as ABC's *Home Improvement* and *Roseanne*, suggest that there is still room on TV for traditional two-parent families. The single-parent sitcoms, such as ABC's *Grace under Fire*, portray the anxiety of modern living that has struck a sympathetic chord in viewers. In the case of NBC's *Friends*, the "family" of the 1990s has taken on a new meaning, with a set of characters whose lives intertwine in interesting and comical ways.

The success of the multiple-character medical dramas *ER* and *Chicago Hope* indicates that viewers are still attracted by the dramatic potential of TV shows with a hospital setting. Crime and legal dramas remain popular, thanks to such strongly acted shows as *NYPD Blue* and *Law and Order*.

MOVIES. Although there doesn't seem to be one prevailing trend in the movies of the 1990s, there has been a tendency for redundancy. With the success of the *Die Hard* and *Lethal Weapon* movies, violent action films with spectacular visual effects seem to have a permanent place at the multiplex. Sequel fever runs rampant and originality takes a backseat to the striving for box-office gold.

There have been a few films with original ideas in the 1990s, including movies made by Joel and Ethan Coen, who have gained a reputation for uncommonly creative work with such pictures as *The Hudsucker Proxy* and *Fargo*. There will always be box-office bonanzas like *Jurassic Park*, *Independence Day*, and *Titanic*, but the good news is that small-budget independent films like *Dead Man Walking* and *Leaving Las Vegas* continue to remind moviegoers of the film medium's creative potential.

As for the role of the film composer, thus far the movies of the1990s indicate that occasionally a strong score is still called for. Regrettably, a score is sometimes thrown out by a producer who feels that the music is wrong for his particular movie. There is probably no major composer working in film who has not had the disconcerting experience of being paid for a score that is then rejected. Even so, many talented musicians continue to prosper.

Film music remains a thriving art form, despite the hugely complicated and often stressful film projects that are being made. Indeed, the film composer still gets called on to "save the picture."

JOHN **B**ARRY: *DANCES WITH WOLVES*. Kevin Costner's Oscar-winning *Dances with Wolves* marked the popular actor's directorial debut; it also marked the return to film scoring of John Barry, after an almost two-year absence due to illness. Based on a book by Michael Blake, a North Carolina native who spent years reading about the ongoing struggles of native Americans, *Wolves* is a fictional story about a Union soldier who joins one of the Sioux tribes during the Civil War.

As a reward for an act of bravery, Lieutenant John Dunbar (Kevin Costner) chooses a Western post, because he wants to see the prairie and experience frontier life. Assigned to Fort Sedgwick, he makes the last part of his journey with a wagonload of supplies that have been anxiously awaited by the soldiers at the isolated site. When he finds Fort Sedgwick deserted, Dunbar decides to stay in seemingly total isolation.

In the days that follow, Dunbar scouts the region but he finds few signs of human life in the area. He has his faithful horse Cisco, and he begins to bond with a wolf that he names "Two Socks," because of his white paws.

Dunbar encounters a small band of Sioux Indians who are encamped nearby. He peacefully goes to their camp and becomes friendly with Kicking Bird (Graham Greene), the medicine man of the tribe. On the way to the camp, he rescues a young white woman, who has lived as an Indian, and

Dances with Wolves, with
Kevin Costner.

has recently been widowed. A relationship soon
develops between him and this woman, who is
called "Stands with a Fist" (Mary McDonnell).

Dunbar, who is dubbed "Dances with Wolves" by
the Indians, gradually adopts their lifestyle and
even hunts buffalo with them. Soon he is betrothed
to the young widow. This idyllic existence is threatened when a regiment of U.S. cavalry attacks the
tribe and Dunbar is taken prisoner. Eventually, he
escapes and goes away with his new bride to make
a life in the wilderness.

John Barry's score serves as a catalyst to bring
the many moods of *Wolves* together. At a relatively
early stage of production, Costner sent Barry almost
four hours of rough footage, from which Barry extracted enough ideas to begin composing a vast
symphonic panorama. According to Jon Burlingame:
"His comeback score is the longest and in many
ways the most complex work of his 31-year film
career. . . . Barry interwove fifteen separate themes
into a virtual symphony, performed by a 91-piece
orchestra and a twelve-voice choir."[4]

John Barry himself describes how the scoring
project got started almost a full year before the
film's release:

> He [Costner] sent me an assembly of about four hours, from which I started
> to work on themes, . . . I recorded about twenty minutes of material with just
> a piano, solo flute, percussion, and some voices, to give the smell and the
> tone of what the whole score would be. It had the romantic quality that
> Costner wanted, the Indian themes, the feeling of adventure.[5]

Barry goes on to discuss his musical approach to the film, indicating
that rather than research the period or the Indian music, he preferred to
capture the emotions of the story and reflect on the characters.

> Though it's a big score, in a strange way it had to be very simple. . . . Dunbar
> is a simple, decent man, and the story has a kind of purity to it. . . . I
> approached the whole score from John Dunbar's point of view—his obser-
> vations of the Sioux tribe. . . . As he says in the movie, "All of the things I've
> ever heard and ever been told about these people are totally wrong." And so,
> musically, it's his assessment of the dignity and graciousness of these
> people.[6]

Barry's score includes at least five clearly identifiable themes. The first
and most prominent is the slow-paced trumpet tune that is heard over the
opening credits. This melody, the "John Dunbar Theme," which is always
associated with the young adventurer, receives its most developed statement when Dunbar first arrives with the supply wagon at Fort Sedgwick.
While the provisions are being unloaded, the strings take up this theme in
tones of longer duration than those that Barry employed during the opening
credits. This slow-moving pace conveys a sense of peaceful resolve that
Dunbar has at last found a home. Later, when he discovers dead deer in a
neighboring pond, the harmonica presents a lyrical version of the theme.

Two traveling themes are included in the score. The first is a leisurely paced melody that accompanies Dunbar's arrival at Fort Hays, his last stop before Fort Sedgwick, as he rides into the settlement in search of the fort's commanding officer. The second traveling theme is then introduced as the wagon rolls over the endless expanse of prairie. Barry's music for this sequence is faster-paced; the melody is a buoyant idea played by violins, with lower strings and French horns in the background. This theme conveys a sense of adventure, as Dunbar discovers the beauties of the West. In a field of tall grass, while Cisco feeds on some of the tastier shoots, Dunbar feels the grass in his hands while he listens to the wind. The music suggests that this voyage is like the great explorations of the first Europeans to set foot on American soil. Barry has brought Dunbar's emotions to life with music that is both optimistic and heroic.

For Two Socks, Barry utilized a gently lyrical waltzlike theme that is played by a solo flute accompanied by sustained string chords. Yet another idea is incorporated into the score when Dunbar alerts the Sioux that the buffalo have returned to the region. French horns provide a slowly rising melodic line that conveys a sense of noble dignity. As the music again suggests, the buffalo hunt is one of the prime adventures in the life of the Sioux, who depend on the buffalo for both food and clothing.

With a score that helps to portray Native Americans as people of simple needs, whose emotions are the same as any other group of ordinary people, *Dances with Wolves* succeeds—where many other films have attempted but failed—in telling a story in which the Indians are the true heroes.

DANNY ELFMAN: *EDWARD SCISSORHANDS*. For Tim Burton's film *Edward Scissorhands*, Danny Elfman wrote a charming score. This very original movie about young Edward (Johnny Depp), who is the robotic creation of an elderly and reclusive scientist (Vincent Price), includes a main theme in the style of a minor-key waltz. The bell-like tones of the celesta are heard prominently in this score, along with the wordless singing by a fifteen-voice boys' choir (performed by the Paulist Choristers of California).

One of the most memorable musical sequences occurs when Edward, adjusting to his new home in suburbia, trims the neighborhood bushes into wildly creative shapes, gives the local dogs new "hairdos," and finally goes to work on the housewives. When he trims the hair of the sexy neighbor Joyce (Kathy Baker), the music starts out as a tango, segues into a fast-paced *moto perpetuo* for strings, and then returns to the tango idea.

RANDY NEWMAN: *AVALON AND AWAKENINGS*. Randy Newman's Oscar-nominated musical background for Barry Levinson's autobiographical film *Avalon* describes in loving detail the daily life of his family in the late 1940s.

The story centers around Levinson's grandfather, Sam Krichinsky (Armin Mueller-Stahl), who leaves Poland in 1914 to join his brothers in Baltimore. Following World War II, Sam's son Jules (Aidan Quinn) goes into business with his cousin (Kevin Pollack) to sell appliances, including TV sets. Although leisurely paced and lacking any real dramatic focus, *Avalon* is a touching glimpse of an ordinary family and the problems they face. Television serves as a symbol for aspects of modern life that have contributed to the breakup of the family unit. When Sam's family rushes from the table to watch Milton Berle on TV, it is apparent that dinner conversation doesn't exist anymore.

Throughout the film there is a slow-paced piano theme, in the style of a minor-key waltz. This tuneful musical idea, which is sometimes heard with a flowing string accompaniment, provides an emotional quality for this charming, nostalgic film.

Although Newman's other 1990 score, a lyrical effort for Penny Marshall's emotionally moving *Awakenings*, failed to receive a nomination, in many ways it is superior to his *Avalon* music. This is especially true in the scenes that take place in the hospital ward where Dr. Sayer (Robin Williams) has energized a group of catatonic patients through the use of the drug L-dopa. Particularly touching is the scene where Leonard (Robert De Niro), who is gradually losing his mobility and slowly regressing to his prior state, is embraced by Paula (Penelope Ann Miller), the young woman who has become his friend. She begins to dance with him to the simple strains of a slow piano theme by Newman, which is played by one of the other patients (enacted by saxophonist Dexter Gordon, who had previously starred in *Round Midnight*).

There are two other prominent themes in the *Awakenings* score, both of which employ $\frac{3}{4}$ meter. The opening title tune is a melancholy waltz theme in A minor; the other theme is a more optimistic-sounding piece in A major. Both employ a relatively simple instrumentation that involves a solo flute, a piano, and strings.

SHORT CUTS ■■■■ **John Williams.** John Williams's music for *Home Alone*, for which he received his twenty-fourth scoring nomination, provides a Yuletide flavor for the hit comedy in which young Macaulay Culkin appears as little Kevin, who is accidentally left behind when his entire family rushes off to the airport to board a plane for Paris. To enhance the Yuletide setting of the story, Williams incorporates bits of several carols into the score, along with the melody of his original song "Somewhere in My Memory," which was nominated as Best Song. The celesta and sleigh bells are featured in the minor-key opening music which segues into an instrumental rendition of this song. Elsewhere there is rambunctious music, especially in the early scene where Kevin's family awakens to discover that the power has gone off, delaying their departure. While they rush about madly, the music captures the mania of the moment with a wildly fast musical accompaniment.

■■■■ **Maurice Jarre.** Maurice Jarre received his eighth scoring nomination for the hugely popular *Ghost*, which features, in addition to Jarre's electronic background effects, some romantic string music, and a revival of Alex North's 1955 tune "Unchained Melody." Not only is the song featured in an updated version of the hit 1960s recording by the Righteous Brothers, but Jarre also employed the theme instrumentally for the closing scene in which Molly (Demi Moore) and the spirit of her lover Sam (Patrick Swayze) communicate through a medium (Whoopi Goldberg). The score also includes a romantic-style original string theme, which is featured in an extended version during the closing credits.

■■■■ **Elmer Bernstein.** In 1990, Elmer Bernstein returned to the jazz style that had made him so popular in the '50s. For *The Grifters*, which has an intriguing tinge of film noir, Bernstein created a sprightly background theme for keyboards, woodwinds, and a few strings. He also continued in his Irish vein with another lyrical score produced in the Emerald Isle, this time for Jim Sheridan's film *The Field*.

Photo by Suzannah Gold

Alan Menken.

ALAN MENKEN: *BEAUTY AND THE BEAST*. Walt Disney's *Beauty and the Beast* is the only animated film ever to receive a Best Picture nomination. Its melodious score was done by Alan Menken, who previously distinguished himself as the composer of Disney's *Little Mermaid*.

For Menken, the road that led to fame as a Disney composer was a slightly winding one. The second of three children, Alan began studying the piano at age six in New Rochelle, New York, where he grew up. He obtained a college degree in music in the early 1970s at New York University; afterward, he played the piano in various nightclubs in Manhattan and also accompanied dance classes at New York's Hebrew Arts Center. One of the young dancers he accompanied subsequently became his wife.

But piano playing did not entirely satisfy Menken, who really wanted to compose. He enrolled for special classes at the Lehman Engel Musical Theatre Workshop. Engel (1910–82), who composed incidental music for several Broadway stage productions and conducted many studio recordings of Broadway scores for Columbia Records, introduced Menken to the man who would help him forge a songwriting career: Howard Ashman (1950–91), who had come to New York to write plays. A creative partnership was born. Although their first Off-Broadway collaboration, *God Bless You, Mr. Rosewater* (1979), was a flop, their next project was the highly successful musical adaptation of Roger Corman's low-budget film *The Little Shop of Horrors*. With book, lyrics, and stage direction by Ashman and music by Menken, *Little Shop* became an instant hit when it opened at the Orpheum Theatre on the Lower East Side of Manhattan on July 27, 1982.[7] The show became one of the longest-running Off-Broadway shows in history, with 2,209 performances.[8]

David Geffen, who had coproduced the stage version, decided to bring this show to the screen in 1986. Ashman adapted his own libretto, and Menken arranged the music. With a cast of such popular comic actors as Rick Moranis, Steve Martin, John Candy, and Bill Murray, *Little Shop of Horrors* became one of the more popular films of the year, and a new song added to the score, "Mean Green Mother from Outer Space," was awarded an Oscar nomination.

Following the success of *Little Shop*, David Geffen introduced Menken and his partner to Jeffrey Katzenberg, chairman of the Walt Disney company, who wanted to produce new animated versions of classic fairy tales. Ashman proposed the idea that Sebastian, the musically knowledgeable crab of the undersea kingdom in *The Little Mermaid*, should have a Jamaican accent. This led to the calypso style of music that made some of the *Mermaid* songs, including the Oscar-winning "Under the Sea," so utterly charming.

Ashman played a major role in shaping the story of the team's next project, an animated version of the classic fairy tale *Beauty and the Beast*. To appeal to children, Ashman had a candelabrum, a teapot, and a clock become a chorus of vaudevillians. With the delightful vocal participation of Jerry Orbach as Lumiere, Angela Lansbury as Mrs. Potts, and David Ogden Stiers as Cogsworth, these three characters add a dimension of fun to this

Dancing under the stars in
Beauty and the Beast.

essentially dark tale of a young prince transformed into an ogre, who can never regain his former handsome appearance unless someone falls in love with him before the last petal falls from a glass-encased rose.

With the creation of these characters, Menken was inspired to compose some of his cleverest melodies. The film's showstopper is "Be Our Guest," which Lumiere introduces as Belle (the beauty) prepares to dine at the Beast's castle. She has voluntarily agreed to stay in exchange for the release of her father, who has earlier been held captive there. Set in a style reminiscent of a Broadway musical production number, "Be Our Guest" provides the film with a toe-tapping rhythm.

The film's Oscar-winning tune is the title song, a lilting ballad that is heard twice. In the midsection of the movie it is sung by Mrs. Potts; for the closing credits a more contemporary-sounding version was recorded by Celine Dion and Peabo Bryson. The Dion–Bryson version became a chart-topping hit, with twenty weeks on the *Billboard* list. Two other scenes provide Menken and Ashman the opportunity to create large-scale musical numbers. "Belle," the opening song in the film, is presented in an operatic-style scene in which almost all the dialogue is sung in the manner of recitative, while Belle sings a lyrically composed melody every now and then. The other song is the hilarious "Gaston," sung by the muscular Gaston, who practically tears an inn apart while singing his tune. Set in the meter of a waltz, "Gaston" has some of Ashman's cleverest lyrics and one of Menken's most buoyantly rhythmic tunes.

For Belle and the Beast's only romantic scene together, and their only opportunity to interact musically, Menken and Ashman provided "Something There," a song that allowed the characters' voices, Paige O'Hara and Robbie Benson, to blend their singing in a duet. It works wonderfully; Benson, in fact, shocked many filmgoers with his richly resonant baritone, which is a far cry from the breathy-sounding voice he had revealed in his previous on-screen film appearances.

With *Beauty and the Beast*, Menken and Ashman completed the second of a proposed series of animated film scores. Sadly, Howard Ashman succumbed to AIDS on March 14, 1991, a full eight months before the film's national release. Before Ashman's death, he and Menken had commenced work on the score of *Aladdin*; he was replaced by Tim Rice. Menken would also collaborate with Stephen Schwartz, the composer of *Godspell*, for the music of *Pocahontas*. Menken has also created the song score for a live-action musical called *Newsies*, and has done the background score for a nonmusical film, the comedy *Life with Mikey*. As of this writing, Menken has won eight Oscars, including four for the scores of Disney animated films.

JAMES NEWTON HOWARD: *THE PRINCE OF TIDES*.

The most noteworthy work in 1991 by James Newton Howard was his lush score for Barbra Streisand's dramatically compelling version of Pat Conroy's family chronicle *The Prince of Tides*. The main theme of this score is a haunting idea built on three ascending tones. Howard's scoring may be a bit top-heavy with harp glissandos, but the sheer attractiveness of the thematic material makes the Oscar nomination well-deserved.

Among Howard's other film scores of 1991, the music for *Dying Young* also contains some tuneful themes, many of which were recorded for the film by soprano saxophonist Kenny G. Lawrence Kasdan's *Grand Canyon* features Howard's music rather sparsely, but when most of the story's principal characters arrive at the natural wonder of the film's title, the music takes over to provide an emotionally upbeat conclusion to the film. A brilliantly brassy fanfare theme, with a wordless chorus, is heard as the camera scans the breathtaking scenery of the Arizona landmark.

MICHAEL KAMEN: *ROBIN HOOD—PRINCE OF THIEVES*.

One of the most popular scores to date of the English-born Michael Kamen (b. 1948) is the alternately heroic and romantic music for *Robin Hood—Prince of Thieves*, one of the biggest hits of 1991. Kamen's score contains a brassy fanfare for trumpets and horns, and an up-tempo theme for horns which features rhythmically driven repetitions of two notes. This theme has the flavor of a march, and is appropriate for the many action scenes.

Although Kevin Costner sounds a bit too American to be totally convincing in the role of the legendary English bandit, with the help of R. J. Lange and singer Bryan Adams, Kamen created a beautiful love theme for Robin and Maid Marian (Mary Elizabeth Mastrantonio), which is first played softly by harp and strings. At the conclusion of the film Adams's vocal version of the theme, "(Everything I Do) I Do It for You," is heard over the end credits. The modernistic arrangement used here is at odds with the medieval time period of the film; but nonetheless, the song became a huge hit, with a twenty-two-week stay on the *Billboard* charts, for seven of which weeks the song was in the number-one position.[9]

Like James Newton Howard, Michael Kamen began to get scoring offers on a regular basis, once he became involved with a hit film. This may account for Kamen's unusually productive year in 1991, when he worked on six films. While most of his film music accompanies contemporary action pictures in the *Die Hard* mold, the lyricism of the *Robin Hood* score indicates that he is equally at home with films in a historical setting.

ELMER BERNSTEIN: FROM RAMBLING ROSE TO OSCAR. Elmer Bernstein's music for Martha Coolidge's *Rambling Rose* bears striking similarities to his earlier score for *To Kill a Mockingbird*. Like *Mockingbird* in its nostalgic feeling for the 1930s, *Rambling Rose*, a period piece set in the South during the Depression, is a story of remembrance, with a lyrical musical accompaniment provided by a small orchestral ensemble.

For *A Rage in Harlem*, Bernstein returned to the jazz idiom he had used so successfully in the 1950s and '60s, and also in his brilliantly rhythmic score for *The Grifters* in 1990. For *Cape Fear*, Bernstein didn't compose original music; instead he was commissioned by Martin Scorsese to rework the vibrant Bernard Herrmann score from the original 1962 version of this chillingly melodramatic story. The result is quite powerful, and a vivid reminder of the brilliance of both Herrmann and Bernstein.

The most ingenious of Bernstein's efforts in 1991 was the score for John Landis's *Oscar*, in which a big-time gangster (Sylvester Stallone) promises his dying father (Kirk Douglas) that he is going to give up his life of crime. The movie is framed by the aria "Largo al factotum," from Rossini's opera *The Barber of Seville*, which was recorded for the soundtrack by operatic baritone Earle Patriarco. During the opening credits a clay figure of a barrel-chested baritone stands at the side of a stage singing the Rossini song as a red curtain rises to reveal the film's credits. This same song also accompanies the closing credits, with Patriarco again doing the singing. For the underscoring in the film Bernstein arranged various bits of Rossini's music. These add a jaunty flavor to this amusing story, which provided Stallone with one of his few successful roles other than Rocky and Rambo.

SHORT CUTS ■■■■ **John Williams.** John Williams contributed an atmospheric, Oscar-nominated score for Oliver Stone's monumental *JFK*, and then another exciting action/adventure score for Steven Spielberg's lavishly produced *Hook*. For *JFK*, trumpeter Tim Morrison, who had played for *Born on the Fourth of July*, again provided a lyrical solo melodic line on Williams's brooding main theme. After a slow start, *Hook* soars, thanks to Williams's heroic music. The film follows the adventures of an older Peter (Robin Williams) as he rediscovers his youth in Neverland. As a change of pace from *Hook*'s rambunctious action music, John Williams also contributed the gentle Oscar-nominated song "When You're Alone," which is sung in the film by one of Peter's children.

■■■■ **Jerry Goldsmith.** For *Sleeping with the Enemy*, in which an attractive young woman named Laura (Julia Roberts) fakes her own death to get away from her abusive husband (Patrick Bergin), Jerry Goldsmith wrote a lyrical score. The cleverest use of music occurs when the husband plays his record of the "Dies irae" theme from the last movement of Hector Berlioz's *Symphonie fantastique* for an early love-making scene. Because of this vivid memory, when Laura's new boyfriend asks her if they can listen to some mood music, she replies that it's OK to play anything but Berlioz.

■■■■ **Ennio Morricone.** A real-life gangster role is at the center of Barry Levinson's *Bugsy*, with Warren Beatty in his finest hour as an actor as Bugsy Siegel, who gambles all his ill-gotten wealth on a casino in Las Vegas. Ennio Morricone's Oscar-nominated music, a combination of rhythmically driven and lyrical themes, is one of his better scores for an American-made film.

■■■■ **George Fenton.** George Fenton received his fourth Oscar nomination for his dramatic score of Terry Gilliam's *Fisher King*. This score contains several renditions of the Burton Lane–Ralph Freed song "How about You?," which was originally composed for MGM's *Babes on Broadway*.

■■■■ **Hans Zimmer.** For Mike Nichols's *Regarding Henry*, Hans Zimmer reduced his orchestration to chamberlike proportions for the story of a high-powered lawyer (Harrison Ford) who loses his memory after being shot in the head, and becomes a much nicer person. The accompanying music combines synthesized sounds with piano and solo clarinet, plus the unique vocal contribution of Bobby McFerrin, to provide a subdued but often tuneful background.

JERRY GOLDSMITH: *BASIC INSTINCT.* After Elmer Bernstein and Maurice Jarre, whose film-scoring careers began in 1951, the composer still active in the '90s with the greatest longevity is Jerry Goldsmith. As of 1997, when he began his fifth decade as a film composer, Goldsmith has completed more than 170 film scores, plus several others written for television movies and miniseries. The remarkable thing about this composer is that, despite the limited time allotted him to complete his film scores, there has been such a high degree of originality and stylistic variety in his work.

For the most part Goldsmith's music for Paul Verhoeven's *Basic Instinct* provides a mysterious background for this sexually explicit thriller, which involves a police search for a female ice-pick killer. Two melodic ideas are prominently featured; the first appears during the opening credits and is based on a six-note motif that includes much use of chromatic tones. Against a minor-key background of harp and strings, this idea is first sounded by various pairs of woodwinds, including clarinets, flutes, and oboes; the violins then play the melody in a romantic extension of the title theme. This music segues into the film's opening scene, which graphically shows a couple in the midst of lovemaking. A sudden tenseness in the music accompanies the moment when the woman, whose face is obscured by her hair, takes an ice pick and stabs her partner.

The main-title theme also appears in scenes involving police detective Nick Curran (Michael Douglas) and Catherine Tramell (Sharon Stone), a wealthy writer of murder mysteries, who is the prime suspect in the stabbing death. This music effectively suggests Nick's physical attraction to Catherine, despite his growing suspicion of her.

The second prominent theme, consisting of the tones of a minor triad, first appears in the scene where Nick and his partner, Gus (George Dzundza), drive to Catherine's beach house to question her. This theme is thereafter heard in several scenes in which Nick is driving around San Francisco, where the film's story is set. The most dramatic appearance of the theme accompanies Nick's chase of Catherine, who is driving at a recklessly fast speed through the hilly city. Underlying this second idea in several scenes is a rhythmically driven motif played on the bass keys of a piano keyboard. In the scene where Nick is almost killed by a speeding car driven by

Basic Instinct,
with Michael Douglas
and Sharon Stone.

Catherine's jealous friend Roxy (Leilani Sarelle), this motif gradually builds to a furious level and is sounded at one point by French horns in a frenzied manner, with pulsating and shifting rhythmic patterns.

The music of *Basic Instinct*, which is often enhanced by synthesizer-generated percussion effects, provides a richly atmospheric background for this stylish but lurid film. The overreliance on sexuality plus an ambiguous ending which leaves the question of Catherine's guilt unresolved, work against *Basic Instinct*, but Goldsmith's music remains one of the truly distinctive scores of the 1990s.

Among Goldsmith's other scores in 1992, the one for *Medicine Man* is distinguished by a combination of rhythmically charged music and a slower-paced lyrical theme. The fast-moving music accompanies an American research scientist, Dr. Rae Crane (Lorraine Bracco), into the rain forest of Brazil. Her assignment is to assist Dr. Robert Campbell (Sean Connery), who thinks he has found a cure for cancer amid the exotic species of insects. As Dr. Campbell and "Dr. Bronx" (his nickname for her) sail through the air on a system of ropes and pulleys to examine the jungle foliage at close range, Goldsmith's lyrical cello theme creates a beautifully romantic mood.

In Steve Miner's *Forever Young*, Mel Gibson plays a pilot who is put to sleep in 1939 as part of a cryogenics experiment, and is accidentally left in a comatose state until being discovered fifty years later by two young children. As in *Medicine Man*, there is a distinct stylistic split between dramatic and lyrical backgrounds in Goldsmith's score. For the early scene in which the experiment is carried out, a rhythmically driven French horn theme is accompanied by a fast-moving repeated ostinato figure. Later in the film, a tuneful soprano saxophone theme is associated with the relationship between Danny McCormick (Mel Gibson) and his childhood sweetheart Helen (Isabel Glasser), who he thought had died fifty years earlier. In the film's tearjerking final scene he finds her still alive. At this point the saxophone theme returns in a romantically impassioned style.

In my 1995 interview with Goldsmith, one question had to do with his longevity as a film composer and what has kept him going. His reply was simply, "I love what I'm doing." He also intimated that if a film pleased him, he could find something musical to say.[10] Although what Goldsmith has to say musically may vary from one film to another, there is little doubt that his basic instinct for finding the right musical sound for a film is as strong as it has ever been.

TREVOR JONES AND RANDY EDELMAN: THE LAST OF THE MOHICANS.

One of the best scores of 1992 was the combined work of Trevor Jones and Randy Edelman (b. 1947) for Michael Mann's brilliantly filmed wide-screen version of James Fenimore Cooper's novel *The Last of the Mohicans*. The division of the composing duties between two different musicians might have resulted in a mishmash, but happily, the efforts of the two men seem enough alike so as not to draw undue attention to their differences. Jones was assigned the principal thematic work, which includes a slow minor-key main theme that is heard during the opening credits, with violins sounding a slow-moving idea over a sustained accompaniment punctuated by throbbing drum sounds.

The most memorable musical moment occurs in the scene, scored by Jones, where Hawkeye (Daniel Day-Lewis) is kissing Cora (Madeleine Stowe). As a folk-style violin is sounding a rapid-paced repeated idea, the music starts to build up; high violins add the score's main theme over the top of this repeated motif, while low strings provide a sustained harmonic background. This music and the scene it accompanies are as sensuous as anything in the year's most sensationalistic film, *Basic Instinct*, and never once in this intimate scene does either character remove a single article of clothing. Edelman's contribution, meanwhile, consisted of some dramatic underscoring that helped to maintain the film's intensity.

SHORT CUTS ■■■■ Alan Menken.

The delightful song score of Disney's *Aladdin* by Alan Menken, who seems to have the Midas touch with each new animated film project, was the inevitable Oscar winner. Menken had a double win for *Aladdin* (the score plus the song "A Whole New World").

■■■■ Mark Isham. Mark Isham received his first Oscar nomination for the folksy music of Robert Redford's lovingly produced version of Norman Maclean's memoir *A River Runs through It*. The main theme, played by a solo violin with guitar and sustained string accompaniment, is very pretty in its gentle use of dotted rhythms. When heard in connection with Robert Redford's spoken narration, this music helps to create a moving portrait of the strait-laced Norman (Craig Sheffer), his reckless brother Paul (Brad Pitt), and the love for fly-fishing which they have inherited from their father, a Presbyterian minister (Tom Skerritt), while growing up in Montana.

■■■■ **Richard Robbins.** Another music nomination went to Richard Robbins, who was honored for the first time as the composer of the Merchant-Ivory film *Howards End*, a beautifully photographed film translation of the E. M. Forster novel. In addition to Robbins's subdued, romantic-styled melodies, the score includes two borrowed themes by Percy Grainger, "Bridal Lullaby" and "Mock Morris," plus an abridged version of the first movement of Beethoven's Symphony no. 5.

■■■■ **Hans Zimmer.** Another outstanding 1992 film score is Hans Zimmer's music for John G. Avildsen's film *The Power of One*. The choral chanting provides an emotionally involving background for this anti-apartheid drama set in South Africa. This score is doubly significant in that it afforded Zimmer the opportunity to work in an "African" style two years before he did the background music for the Disney film *The Lion King*.

■■■■ **Women in Film Music.** The year 1992 denotes an important step forward for women in film music. British composer Rachel Portman contributed some tuneful themes to her first American film, Beeban Kidron's *Used People*, while Anne Dudley (b. 1956) added atmospheric background scoring to Neil Jordan's award-winning hit *The Crying Game*. Shirley Walker, a talented arranger and conductor (and sometimes part-composer) of others' film scores, achieved her first solo project, a highly dramatic score for John Carpenter's *Memoirs of an Invisible Man*.

PATRICK DOYLE: MUCH ADO ABOUT NOTHING. Following *Henry V* and *Dead Again* (1991), Patrick Doyle began his third scoring project with Kenneth Branagh, for a film version of Shakespeare's delightful comedy *Much Ado about Nothing*. Basically a story of romantic longing, deception, and premarital discord, *Much Ado* was filmed entirely on location at the Villa Vignamaggio in Tuscany, where the film's cast and crew spent two months in 1992. In adapting the play Branagh tightened Shakespeare's florid prose somewhat, but still managed to retain much of the original language, including two sets of lyrics for songs, composed by Doyle, that figure prominently in the story. The first of these, "Sigh No More, Ladies," is a lyrical ballad that occurs in Act II of the play. In the movie it is sung by one of the attendants of Don Pedro (Denzel Washington). Don Pedro has come to Messina with several of his soldiers to vacation at the villa of Leonato, the governor of the region. The other song, "Pardon, Goddess of the Night," is a melancholy ballad sung at the funeral of Hero (Kate Beckinsale), the governor's daughter, who has supposedly taken her own life.

Because of Shakespeare's inclusion of two sets of song lyrics, Doyle had an unusual opportunity in creating an original musical score for this film. It was agreed that not only the songs but also some dance music for a masked ball should be composed before the filming started, so that the actors could hear the music while the cameras rolled. According to Doyle:

> Ken and I discussed preparing in advance many of the music cues required for "play-back" purposes on the set. . . . By the end of the rehearsal week, all

the actors had learnt the melody and harmonies for "Sigh No More, Ladies," and the small strolling band of players had learnt their dance tunes for "The Masked Ball."[11]

Finding an appropriate melody for the remaining song became the most difficult part of the score's composition. As Doyle explains: "The melody for 'Pardon, Goddess of the Night' proved to be the most elusive as each time I presented Ken with what I though he was searching for, I was sent back to the 'Drawing Board.' After much hair pulling, I was fifth time lucky."[12]

With the songs already in place prior to the filming, Doyle was later able to add the underscore by adapting the melodies of these two vocal pieces. The resulting musical score features some brilliantly orchestrated arrangements of these materials, plus the addition of a few new themes written specifically as instrumental backgrounds. Chief among the additional melodic ideas is a short fanfare with a series of upward leaps, first an octave, then a seventh. Another added melody is an energetic theme that has the flavor of a march, although Doyle employed a metric scheme that alternates between patterns of four beats and patterns of three.

Another romantic plot involves Benedick (Kenneth Branagh), one of Don Pedro's faithful soldiers, and the governor's niece, Beatrice (Emma Thompson). Although Benedick and Beatrice carry on a continual verbal feud, it becomes apparent that these two are really perfectly matched.

For the final sequence of the film Branaugh transformed "Pardon, Goddess of the Night" into a rousing march that accompanies the two sets of lovers as they prepare for their double wedding. "Sigh No More, Ladies" returns as a rollicking dance tune that involves the entire assemblage of people at the governor's villa. As the camera backs away to reveal several groups of people spinning around in circles with hands joined, the "Sigh No

Much Ado about Nothing, with Emma Thompson and Kenneth Branagh.

More" theme becomes gradually more majestic. This uninhibited merry-making brings the film to a joyous conclusion.

Last to be composed but first to be heard in the score is the film's overture, a vivacious arrangement of the score's principal themes, which is similar to the music at the end of the film.

With the score of *Much Ado*, the Doyle–Branagh collaboration can be regarded as an artistic entity almost as viable as that of Williams and Spielberg, or Herrmann with Welles, and also with Hitchcock. Subsequent to *Much Ado*, Branagh began working on a new adaptation of *Mary Shelley's Frankenstein*, and once again Patrick Doyle would be called in to compose the music; thus this highly creative partnership would continue to flourish.

In the wake of his work on *Much Ado*, Doyle found almost immediate employment on three additional film-scoring projects. For the movie version of Stephen King's *Needful Things*, directed by Fraser C. Heston (son of Charlton Heston), Doyle created a dark and brooding score. There are several choral passages in the film, including one that occurs toward the melodramatic ending, where the police officer (Ed Harris) declares that shopowner Leland Gaunt (Max von Sydow) is actually the Devil. At this point, Doyle's score includes the "Dies irae" melody from the Gregorian Mass for the Dead. There is at times a hint of playfulness in the music, which underscores the prankish way in which the Devil causes the residents of Castle Rock to go berserk in various ways.

Doyle's third score in 1993 is a lyrical background for the charming fantasy film *Into the West*, a film which regrettably did not find an audience upon its brief theatrical release. Doyle's music has a decidedly Irish flavor, and even includes a solo vocal number that was recorded for the soundtrack by the composer's sister, Margaret Doyle.

The final work among Patrick Doyle's four 1993 scores marks a real departure from the Shakespearean films and fantasies with which he had earlier been associated. For *Carlito's Way*, Brian De Palma's gritty portrait of drug dealers and mob lawyers in the 1970s, Doyle created a score that combines Latino sounds with jazz harmonies and rhythms, while still finding space for lyrical moments, in the scenes between Carlito (Al Pacino) and his girlfriend (Penelope Ann Miller).

ELMER BERNSTEIN: *THE AGE OF INNOCENCE* AND *THE GOOD SON*. With his Oscar-nominated music for Martin Scorsese's acclaimed film version of Edith Wharton's novel *The Age of Innocence*, Elmer Bernstein returned to the kind of lyrical scoring that had brought him to the heights of his profession in the early 1960s, when he wrote such masterworks as *Summer and Smoke* and *To Kill a Mockingbird*.

The Age of Innocence is a story of thwarted love in the upper crusts of New York society of the 1870s. This world of gaslit streets and formal dances held in the ballrooms of stately mansions is evoked by the magnificent cinematography of Michael Ballhaus. Newland Archer (Daniel Day-Lewis) is betrothed to the docile May Welland (Winona Ryder), when he meets the intriguing noncomformist Countess Ellen Olenska (Michelle Pfeiffer), who has just returned to New York from Europe.

The score of *Innocence* is rhythmically coordinated since all of the principal themes heard in the film are set in waltz time.[13] The main-title music begins with a melancholy tune in C minor, featuring a six-note motif that is used to generate most of the other melodic ideas in the score; one of these ideas is the theme for the countess, which is a retrograde (backward) version of the first four notes of the basic motif. One melodic idea seems cut from different cloth; it appears as the theme for Mrs. Mingott (Miriam Margolyes), the elderly matriarch of the Archer family. Set in a major key, this theme bears a resemblance to the "Sky Symphony," the lilting waltz theme from Victor Young's score of *Around the World in Eighty Days*.

In addition to Bernstein's original music, *Innocence* contains some borrowed excerpts from Gounod's *Faust*; the *Radetzky* March by Johann Strauss, Sr.; and two waltzes by Johann Strauss, Jr., *Emperor* Waltz and *Tales from the Vienna Woods*.

Although Bernstein's orchestration for *Innocence* includes the *ondes martenot*, the wavy sounds of this electronic keyboard instrument are used only sparingly. However, one of Bernstein's other 1993 scores, written for Joseph Ruben's film *The Good Son*, features the *ondes* very prominently, especially in the main-title music. After an opening statement by solo piano of the score's principal melodic idea, which begins with four rising pitches, the *ondes*, accompanied by strings, provides a hauntingly beautiful musical moment. The lyricism of this music is in strange contrast to the film's story of two boys, one of whom (Macaulay Culkin) exhibits homicidal tendencies, while his cousin (Elijah Wood) tries in vain to warn the boy's parents.

JOHN WILLIAMS: JURASSIC PARK AND SCHINDLER'S LIST. Two of 1993's most exceptional films represent a continuation of the phenomenally successful Williams–Spielberg collaboration. Although *Jurassic Park* did not impress the critics the way *Schindler's List* did, this action/adventure film, based on Michael Crichton's best-selling novel of a fantasy island with live prehistoric animals, became one of the most popular films in history, with a soaring John Williams score that contains, among several melodic ideas, a heroic trumpet theme that repeatedly utilizes ascending fifths.

Williams's music for *Schindler's List* makes use of the descending fifth for its poignant main theme, beautifully recorded for the soundtrack by violinist Itzhak Perlman. In view of the grimness of this story of the Jewish plight in Poland during World War II, Williams wisely refrained from creating a score that would generate an excess of dramatic flavoring. Instead, his slow and somber music creates an air of dignity and quiet resignation. As the film gradually unfolds, the heroic actions of Oskar Schindler (Liam Neeson) in rescuing over a thousand Jewish people by employing them in his factory stand as a noble gesture against the horrific and systematic killing of the millions of Jews in the death camps. Williams, in his music, greatly assisted Spielberg in bringing this story to vivid cinematic life. Both the film and Williams's score were honored with Oscars.

SHORT CUTS ■ ■ ■ ■ Oscar Nominations. The other Oscar nominees for Best Original Score of 1993 were Dave Grusin's unique piano backgrounds for *The Firm*; James Newton Howard's pulsating, rhythmically driven score of *The Fugitive*; and Richard Robbins's intriguing excursion into minimalism, *The Remains of the Day*. Of these three, the Robbins score is the most tuneful and subdued, with a rhythmic, slow-paced string theme that accompanies several scenes. Howard's *Fugitive* contains the most dramatic score of the three, although it lacks melodic interest. Grusin's music for *The Firm* is clever up to a point, with knocking sounds (produced on the frame of the piano) added to the keyboard tones;

but in some of the chase sequences, an orchestrated sound might have provided a more interesting palette of musical colors than those the solo piano can produce.

■■■■ **Randy Edelman.** Randy Edelman composed an emotionally stirring score for *Gettysburg*, which, despite its four-hour-plus length, is one of the best war films ever made. Edelman's soaring main theme, even with the anachronistic sounds of synthesizers included in the orchestration, succeeds in creating a tone of heroic nobility for this in-depth portrait of the three days in early July 1863 when the Union and the Confederate armies converged upon Gettysburg.

■■■■ **Danny Elfman.** For Danny Elfman, 1993 was a change-of-pace year, in which he wrote an emotionally involving score for the post-Civil War drama *Sommersby*. His other effort of the year, for Tim Burton's animated film *The Nightmare before Christmas*, is reminiscent of his earlier scores for Burton films, but it is distinguished by having several vocal numbers, in some of which Elfman himself provided the lyrical singing voice of Jack, the principal character.

■■■■ **Zbigniew Preisner.** One of the newer names on the film-music horizon in 1993 was that of Polish-born Zbigniew Preisner, who contributed a charming score to the exquisitely filmed *The Secret Garden*. Especially memorable is the theme heard as Mary (Kate Maberly) finds the hidden door to the garden and opens it. Wordless voices provide an additionally lyrical flavor to this simple, yet effective, theme. Preisner also deserves recognition for his trio of scores for the color-coded trilogy of symbolic films, *Blue*, *White*, and *Red*, which were directed by Krzysztof Kieslowski. *Red*'s music, which primarily consists of a bolero rhythm pattern played by strings, is particularly memorable.

■■■■ **Hans Zimmer.** There are some charming ideas in Hans Zimmer's Jamaican-influenced music for Jon Turteltaub's *Cool Runnings*. Also, Tony Scott's violent *True Romance* has a unique main theme, played by nine marimbas. The catchiness of this tune provides a strange counterpoint to the frequent bloodletting of this Quentin Tarantino–scripted film.

■■■■ **Shirley Walker and Rachel Portman.** Of women in film scoring, the steadiest workers during 1993 were Shirley Walker and Rachel Portman. Walker continued to function as an orchestrator and a conductor of other composers' works. Portman produced four new scores in 1993, including the delightfully jaunty music of *Benny & Joon*. Noteworthy is the scene in the park in which Sam (Johnny Depp) does a Chaplinesque pantomime, with Portman's catchy background theme gradually accelerating in pace as the visual antics pick up in intensity. Among her other 1993 scores, the music of *The Joy Luck Club* has memorably lyrical moments.

■■■■ *Untamed Heart.* Special mention should be made of the score for Tony Bill's touching romantic drama *Untamed Heart*. Although Cliff Eidelman was given screen credit, and though the Varese Sarabande soundtrack recording includes his themes for the main and end titles, in the final version of the film, Roger Williams's piano-and-orchestra recording of the 1948 song "Nature Boy" is heard at the beginning of the film, and Nat "King" Cole's chart-topping vocal version of the song is included during the closing credits.[14] These changes were no doubt authorized by the film's producers to coordinate the film's music with the scene in which Adam (Christian Slater) plays his recording of the song for Caroline (Marisa Tomei), and again, with the scene at the film's conclusion, after Adam's tragic death due to a damaged heart, when Caroline sits alone in his apartment playing the recording once more.

Eidelman's original theme music has a lyrical quality, if not the exact tune of "Nature Boy." This situation points up the fact that, in Hollywood, many films get changed at the last minute. At times, those changes may require significant rescoring of the music; at other times, the producers may decide to make an insertion of borrowed materials, as in *Untamed Heart*. Whether the original composer will be consulted on the musical revisions is open to question. As Aaron Copland found out when he attended a screening of *The Heiress*, it is never to be assumed that all of one's music will wind up in the final version of the film.

■ ■ ■ **Michael Nyman.** One final 1993 score that should be mentioned is Michael Nyman's music for Jane Campion's award-winning film *The Piano*. Although Nyman's music earned praise in some circles for his ingenious piano solo creations, which were actually played in the film by its mute heroine (Holly Hunter), the modernism of this music, with its unusual harmonic progressions, seems utterly at odds with the nineteenth-century setting of the film. The music actually fares better apart from the film, in a version of the score simply called The Piano Concerto, which Nyman arranged for a 1994 recording.[15] Here the haunting main minor-key theme achieves a beauty that renders it one of the more noteworthy musical creations to emanate from a film score in recent years.

HANS ZIMMER: *THE LION KING.* When *The Little Mermaid* became an enormous hit in 1989, the Disney company began to realize that the audience for animated films was not purely limited to small children escorted by their parents. As Walt Disney himself had understood from the time he began making fully animated features in the late 1930s, audiences of all ages could enjoy magical stories of brave knights, beautiful princesses, and the triumph of good over evil, with a few songs thrown in to brighten the mood. Indeed, music seems to have been a key to the success of such animated classics as *Snow White*, *Pinocchio*, and *Cinderella*.

When TV came along, animation became more and more relegated to the TV networks on Saturday mornings. Especially after the disappointing box-office returns of Disney's *Sleeping Beauty* in 1959, animated films would never be the same. Such 1960s films as *101 Dalmatians* almost jettisoned the song scores that had helped to make earlier Disney efforts so popular. This aversion to musical treatment of classic children's stories continued almost unabated through the '70s and '80s, until the arrival of *The Little Mermaid*, for whose music Alan Menken won a pair of Oscars.

Despite the serious tone of the story, Disney producers contemplated the possibilities of *The Lion King* as a musical film, in the mold established by *The Little Mermaid*. Following upon the even bigger success of *Beauty and the Beast* in 1991, an Alan Menken score was considered just the right thing. However, when the musical decisions needed to be made, Menken declined any involvement with *The Lion King* because of his interest in scoring another Disney animated film, *Pocahontas*.

Lion King producer Don Hahn and other Disney executives then consulted Tim Rice, the lyricist who had replaced Howard Ashman on *Aladdin* after Ashman's death. According to Rice: "They asked me who I wanted to work with, . . . and I said, 'Elton John would be great, but you won't get him.' But they did."[16]

Once Elton John signed on to compose the songs, another musician had to be found to handle the background scoring. At this point the problem of the authenticity of the film's African setting arose. In order to learn what Africa was really like, the *Lion King*'s writers decided to embark on a two-week expedition, which proved to be quite enlightening. According to Ari Posner: "They snapped photos, drew sketches, slept in tents, and generally grew to appreciate the sights and sounds of their real-life setting."[17] It was at this point that Hans Zimmer came into the project because of his experience with African music.

Born in Frankfort, Germany, in 1957, Hans Zimmer grew up in several different places, including Switzerland and England. He was introduced to the piano at the age of three, and soon thereafter his family began taking him to classical concerts. At age six, he started piano lessons, but these were soon curtailed since he wanted to make his own music rather than practice someone else's pieces.

During his youth, Zimmer played in rock bands and did not pursue any further musical training. However, he had acquired a considerable expertise with synthesizers; so when he took a job at Edel Air in England as a jingle writer, he began making synthesizer programs for others. At this time Hans Zimmer met Stanley Myers, best known as the composer of the score for Michael Cimino's *Deer Hunter*. According to Zimmer: "I was his assistant, and thanks to him I really learned to appreciate all the various aspects of orchestral music. Actually, all the films Stanley did not have the time to work on, I would begin for him."[18]

Zimmer received his first screen credit as co-composer of Jerzy Skolimowski's *Moonlighting* (1982). Between then and 1988, Zimmer and Myers shared the composing credits on over a dozen films, of which the best known is Stephen Frears's *My Beautiful Laundrette* (1985). In 1988, Zimmer was offered his first solo scoring assignment, for Chris Menges's antiapartheid drama *A World Apart*, which won several awards at Cannes.

One of the people who was the most impressed with Zimmer's work on *A World Apart* was the wife of film director Barry Levinson. According to Zimmer: "Barry Levinson's wife saw *A World Apart*, bought the CD and played it to her husband, who then asked me to work on *Rain Man*!"[19]

Rain Man became 1988's top-grossing film, won several Oscars including Best Picture, and also succeeded in gaining for Hans Zimmer his first Oscar nomination. In fact, he has the unique distinction of having composed the scores for two successive Academy Award-winning films since *Driving Miss Daisy* took home the Oscar for Best Picture of 1989.

After this pair of films, Zimmer could almost pick and choose his film-music assignments. He took on another film about apartheid, John G. Avildsen's 1992 drama *The Power of One*; for this film, Zimmer built on the core of knowledge about African music that he had absorbed while doing *A World Apart*. With its chanted themes, *The Power of One* contains one of the most distinctive scores of the early 1990s, and led to Zimmer's being chosen to do the original score for *The Lion King*.

Hans Zimmer.

Courtesy of Chasen & Co.

The first question that Zimmer had to deal with concerned the *Lion King*'s upbeat opening number. According to Disney's chief animator, Peter Schneider, "It was Hans who really gave us the key to this movie."[20] Co-director Roger Allers agrees with this assessment:

> The turning point was when Hans did his treatment of "Circle of Life." We had built the sequence with all the animals going to Pride Rock, music at the front, and then dialogue with Rafiki. Then we went to Hans and he played the song on its own and we were blown away by it.[21]

Zimmer's treatment of Elton John's material was unanimously approved. In fact, it was decided that the dialogue in the opening scene was not necessary, because the music could speak for itself. According to Peter Schneider: "The physical sound, the Africanization of the piece, made it work for everybody. And it gave us the style and a fundamental sense of the movie. . . . It even changed the look of the film."[22]

How did Hans Zimmer feel about tampering with the work of such an established musical legend as Elton John? The composer has the following to say on the subject: "I could be really careful or I could just go, like, completely nuts. And that's pretty much what I did. I threw in all those choirs. I changed the rhythm, put big modulations in them suddenly."[23]

Although Elton John approved of most of Zimmer's arrangements of his songs, he had one objection, concerning the comical treatment of "Can You Feel the Love Tonight?" Apparently the Disney animators had turned this song into a comic number by having it performed by Pumbaa and Timon, the friends of Simba, the lion cub. After a screening at Elton John's home, he spoke out against this approach. He explained that he had written this as a love song, and it should be kept in a romantic style. The filmmakers agreed, and the original intentions of this song were restored to the film.[24] In addition to his arrangements of the Elton John songs, Hans Zimmer contributed over an hour of underscore to *The Lion King*. When the film had been edited enough for Zimmer's original music to be inserted, he had a mere three weeks to produce the score. In that short time, he managed to compose sixty-five minutes of music.

One of the people who greatly assisted Zimmer on *The Lion King* was African singer and songwriter Lebo M., who had been given credit for his lyrics to the vocal music written by Zimmer for *The Power of One*. Lebo M. assisted Zimmer in completing the vocal arrangements for both the Elton John–Tim Rice songs and the choral music by Zimmer that was incorporated into the original score. Because of the large amount of vocal music written for the film, many other people were involved in doing the vocal arrangements; these included Andrae Crouch, Mark Mancina, Bobbi Page, Bruce Fowler, Mbongeni Ngema, and Nick Glennie-Smith. The end result was an African flavor that greatly enhanced *The Lion King*'s overall sound.

Almost as difficult as writing and arranging the music for the new Disney film was the task of recording it, which entailed trips to England and South Africa to record the choral sounds that Zimmer wanted to incorporate in the film. Elton John's performances of three of his songs were recorded in London, with a gospel choir made up of members of the London Symphony Choir brought in to provide background vocals. The choral passages included in Zimmer's original score were recorded in Mmabatho, South Africa, whereas the orchestral arrangements of Zimmer's music, which were handled by Bruce Fowler and Nick Glennie-Smith (who conducted), were recorded in Los Angeles. A total of five venues were used in recording *The Lion King*'s music, including two each in Los Angeles and London.

Throughout the film, the music is woven almost seamlessly into the story, so that, unlike film musicals of old, there is hardly a moment when this film stops moving. For example, the opening scene, in which there are several shots of various animals being summoned to the official presentation of Simba, son and heir to the kingdom ruled by Mufasa, starts out with Zimmer's music, which includes a lovely background choral effect. This segues directly into the Elton John–Tim Rice song "Circle of Life," which accompanies the rest of the scene.

At the conclusion of this song the film's title is flashed onto the screen and then the story begins to unfold. Scar, Mufasa's brother, gripes about how unfair life is, since he has no chance to become king as long as Simba lives. After a confrontation between Scar and Mufasa there is a panoramic sweep of the horizon, with a distant storm approaching. Here again, a choral background provides an atmospheric effect for one of the principal themes in Zimmer's score, a slow-moving melody that builds up to a level of heroic proportions as the melodic line leaps upward, with an instrumentation of flute and strings. In the following scene Simba gets a lesson from his father about the circle of life; about how everything occurs for a reason; and about the necessity for the king to assume responsibility, no matter how powerful he is. Here another theme is introduced, a minor-key melody that features the exotic sounds of panpipes accompanied by strings and wordless voices.

Simba's father, in *The Lion King*.

© *Disney Enterprises, Inc.*

Both melodic ideas figure prominently in the score, which is sometimes used with subtlety behind the dialogue. At other times, as in the stampede during which Scar lets Mufasa fall from a cliff to his death, the music becomes dramatic, with pounding percussion added to the instrumentation.

Zimmer's music is skillfully woven into the film to enhance the emotions of the story and to keep the rhythm of the movie flowing. Unlike the typical wall-to-wall cartoon scores used in some of the older Disney classics, Zimmer's score often fades out to allow the dialogue to work by itself. In this respect the approach to the music in *The Lion King* is no different from that of most live-action films. The approach works wonderfully here, helping to give the drawn figures on the screen the dimensions of live beings. Seldom have the animal characters in a Disney film projected such a sense of humanity as do the characters in this story. Of course, the employment of such fine actors as James Earl Jones and Jeremy Irons for the voices of Mufasa and Scar helped a great deal, but Zimmer contributed greatly to the sound of *The Lion King* with his richly atmospheric score.

With its African flavor, which Zimmer helped to achieve through the use of choral chanting, *The Lion King* became one of the most critically acclaimed films of 1994, and also the most financially successful, with a box-office total of $306 million.[25] *The Lion King*'s composers took home Academy Awards; Elton John and Tim Rice won for Best Song ("Can You Feel the Love Tonight?") and Hans Zimmer for Best Original Score.

A**LAN** S**ILVESTRI**: F**ORREST** G**UMP**. Alan Silvestri's fine work on behalf of *Forrest Gump* won for him an Oscar nomination. This is a melodically rich score, with at least eight discernible themes. The two most noteworthy ideas are the lyrical "Forrest" theme and the contrasting, fast-paced "Running" motif. The first of these, which is presented during the opening credits while a lone white feather is seen floating through space, is a lilting idea for solo piano and strings with some gently syncopated rhythms. The "Running" theme, which is heard for the first time when little Jenny yells "Run, Forrest, run," is built on a three-note idea that incorporates a descending fifth (D–G–G), which is repeated numerous times. This motif is heard again when the adult Forrest (Tom Hanks) reminisces about his football days in college, and later still when Forrest becomes a cross-country runner. There is also a love theme, which is associated with Forrest's long-time friendship with the adult Jenny (Robin Wright), and a sentimental melody that is connected with Forrest's mother (Sally Field).

J**AMES** H**ORNER**: L*EGENDS OF THE* F*ALL AND* C*LEAR AND* P*RESENT* D*ANGER*. James Horner's eloquent music enhances Edward Zwick's *Legends of the Fall*, a beautifully filmed saga of a Montana rancher and his three sons, all of whom love the same woman. Like Silvestri's *Forrest Gump*, this is a melodically rich score, one that seems cut from the same cloth as many of the John Barry scores of the 1980s. The first theme includes a slow-paced melody that describes the land itself, a wide expanse of prairie upon which Major Ludlow (Anthony Hopkins) has erected a home. For the Ludlow family Horner composed a waltzlike theme, the first five notes of which are reminiscent of Georges Auric's *Moulin Rouge* melody. *Legends*' epic score, which has many other melodious elements, including a catchy fiddle theme in waltz time, continually elevates Zwick's melodramatic film.

Horner also contributed a heroic main theme for the third film adaptation of Tom Clancy's Jack Ryan thrillers, *Clear and Present Danger*. During the action scenes, Horner again included some of the slap-handed piano chords that he used in both his *Sneakers* and *The Pelican Brief* scores.

SHORT CUTS ■■■■ Jerry Goldsmith.

Among the veterans, Jerry Goldsmith did several new film scores in 1994. The best of the lot is his flavorful music for *The River Wild*, which is musically distinguished by its use of variations on the old English song "The Water Is Wide." The borrowed theme is treated quite eloquently at times in this melodrama. Goldsmith's score for *IQ* is a minor but charming effort, with a set of clever variations of the nursery tune "Twinkle Twinkle, Little Star."

■■■■ Thomas Newman.

Thomas Newman received Oscar nominations for two very contrasting works. For the beautifully made *Little Women*, he created a noble main theme for trumpet and strings; his music for the engrossing prison drama *The Shawshank Redemption* is often subdued but always appropriate.

■■■■ Randy Newman.

Another Newman who did distinctive work in 1994 is Randy Newman, whose scores for *The Paper* and for *Maverick* contain tuneful themes. *The Paper* is especially noteworthy as one of Newman's first excursions into the jazz vein since his score for *Ragtime*. *Maverick*, on the other hand, has a Coplandesque flavor, especially in its Western-style main theme for trumpet and strings.

■■■■ Elliot Goldenthal.

A first-time Oscar nominee for music composed in 1994 was Elliot Goldenthal, who was cited for his dramatic music for the violent and bloody *Interview with the Vampire*. Among the more memorable musical moments is a theme entitled "Madeleine's Lament." This theme includes one of the score's primary melodic motifs, a three-note idea that begins with a descending semitone followed by a descending fourth (A♭–G–D). This motif is played by violins in an emotionally charged statement in which the pattern is used several times. Another noteworthy musical idea is "Lestat's Tarantella," a minor-key theme for harpsichord and strings associated with Tom Cruise's character. Goldenthal incorporated a number of other intriguing ideas, including a funeral march and a waltz theme, into this atmospherically rich score.

■■■■ Ennio Morricone.

Another vampire film is Mike Nichols's *Wolf*, which benefits from one of Ennio Morricone's finest scores. An ominous mood is established during the opening credits by a series of sustained chords that move slowly down in pitch. A fast-moving, rhythmically syncopated melodic figure, based on the repeated use of three adjacent pitches, is interwoven to add an element of tension. Gradually, a melodic idea emerges, based on a four-note pattern. Later, a solo saxophone accompanied by strings introduces a romantic theme for the relationship of Will (Jack Nicholson) and Laura (Michelle Pfeiffer). Although *Wolf* descends to the level of formulaic melodrama in the last reel, it is buoyed considerably by Morricone's music.

■■■■ Patrick Doyle.

Yet a third 1994 film of the horror/fantasy genre is Kenneth Branagh's fascinating but flawed version of *Mary Shelley's Frankenstein*, in which Branagh plays the monster-maker and Robert De Niro plays the hideously sewn-together creature who is given life through the mad doctor's experiments. Patrick Doyle graced this film with a dramatic and emotion-filled score, as he had done for *Needful Things*. The romantic theme, heard in the love scenes between the doctor and his bride (Helena Bonham-Carter), is built on a five-note idea that keeps on sounding in the lower strings, while a lyrical melody for violins is introduced above it. This compelling score, the fourth in the ongoing Doyle–Branagh collaboration, is a fine example of the high quality of music that can result from a creative partnership in which the composer is given artistic license.

▪▪▪ **David Arnold.** Another very effective score is the surgingly romantic music by newcomer David Arnold for Roland Emmerich's elaborate science-fiction film *Stargate*. Choral backgrounds occur frequently to buoy this emotionally charged music, which keeps the film dramatically compelling even when it isn't coherent.

▪▪▪ **James Newton Howard.** James Newton Howard continued to demonstrate his considerable creative talent with a melodically rich score for Lawrence Kasdan's epic Western film, *Wyatt Earp*. There are at least seven distinct themes in this symphonically conceived score, which begins with a French horn theme for Wyatt (Kevin Costner) consisting of a five-note motif that includes two boldly ascending leaps. The music for the climactic shootout at the O. K. Corral is built around a five-beat rhythmic pattern that is somewhat reminiscent of the "Mars" movement of Gustav Holst's orchestral suite *The Planets*. Throughout this three-hour-plus saga, Howard's dramatically compelling music heightens the film's impact.

▪▪▪ **Howard Shore.** Among Howard Shore's 1994 film-scoring projects are Tim Burton's *Ed Wood*, in which the theremin is incorporated into the purposefully bizarre orchestration, and Robert Benton's *Nobody's Fool*. One of the year's finest films, *Nobody's Fool* includes a jaunty main-title tune for various woodwinds (including clarinet and a wooden flute), plus guitar and strings. In its utter simplicity the theme seems exactly right for this almost plotless portrait of Sully Sullivan (Paul Newman), whose hard-luck life in a small, economically depressed New York State town finally changes, thanks to unforeseen circumstances involving members of his estranged family. Buoyant rhythms and the lyrical woodwind tune are significant features of this charming score.

MICHAEL KAMEN: MR. HOLLAND'S OPUS. The classically trained Michael Kamen became involved in rock before turning to film scoring; as he put it, he is a "classical musician who has gone astray."[26]

Michael Kamen, who was born in New York City in 1948, played the oboe while enrolled at the High School of Music and Art, and then moved on to Juilliard, where he majored in performance. Despite his classical training, Kamen formed the New York Rock and Roll Ensemble, for which he wore many hats, acting as writer, keyboardist, singer, and oboist. According to Kamen himself, this group actually performed some of his orchestral arrangements in concert with the New York Philharmonic and the Boston Pops.[27] Not completely satisfied to be a rock musician, Kamen decided to try writing an original ballet score. This, combined with the opportunity in 1976 to compose his first film score, for the Sean Connery thriller *The Next Man*, eventually led to an extremely varied career.

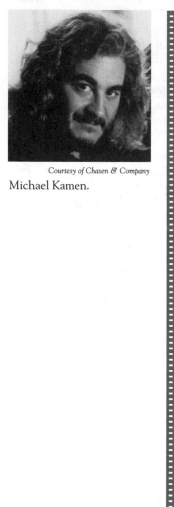

Courtesy of Chasen & Company

Michael Kamen.

According to Kamen: "Then I became music director for David Bowie, which gave me my first taste of stadium rock 'n' roll. And for the next several years I wrote many ballet scores for companies in New York and Europe. . . . And then I started working with Pink Floyd."[28]

In the late 1970s, Kamen kept up a musical juggling act by producing albums for Pink Floyd while writing ballet scores for the Joffrey Ballet, the Alvin Ailey company, and even the ballet company of Milan's La Scala Opera. In addition, he continued to score such films as *Between the Lines* and *Stunts* (both 1977).

Kamen's career began to blossom with the 1982 film version of Pink Floyd's 1979 album *The Wall*, which had featured Kamen's arrangements. For Alan Parker's film adaptation of the album, Kamen served as music director. A year later, while continuing to work with Pink Floyd in London, he received a call from Los Angeles which led to his creation of the brooding music for David Cronenberg's adaptation of Stephen King's story *The Dead Zone*. Kamen recalls working on this score:

> I flew back to London where I wrote the entire score in ten days, pounding on a piano through the night with the windows wide open. Very early one morning a distraught looking neighbor in a nightgown rang my doorbell. She was trembling as she said, "Please, please stop playing the piano. . . . You're scaring me and my family to death, we're having nightmares, we can't sleep. . . . Please stop." I knew then that I must have been doing something right![29]

Indeed, there was plenty right with that score, which helped *The Dead Zone* become one of the best-reviewed film adaptations of any Stephen King novel. Two years after this, Kamen received another fortuitous assignment, the music for Terry Gilliam's fascinating *Brazil*. This score came about through Kamen's friendship with percussionist Ray Cooper, who had a small role in the film and also helped Gilliam produce it.

Although *Brazil* received a lot of attention because of a controversy over its final release print, which was trimmed by Universal over Gilliam's objections, it did not fare well at the box office. Still, several critics rated the film as one of the best of 1985, and Kamen soon found himself in demand as a film composer.

Kamen's first major box-office hit came in 1987, with the violent action-comedy *Lethal Weapon*, which paired Mel Gibson with Danny Glover for the first time. For the score, director Richard Donner not only enlisted Kamen, but brought in guitarist Eric Clapton and saxophonist David Sanborn. Together, the three musicians collaborated on a sometimes dramatic, sometimes jazzy background score. When Warner Bros. decided upon sequels in 1990 and 1993, respectively, Donner again utilized the combined talents of these three diverse musicians.

Another hit series of violent action films with Michael Kamen's music came with the *Die Hard* movies, with Bruce Willis as New York City cop John McClane. The original 1988 *Die Hard* was one of the sleeper hits of the year since Willis had been known primarily as a comic actor in the TV series *Moonlighting*. Director John McTiernan used Willis's offbeat style to perfect effect, and with Kamen's dramatic musical backgrounds, the film packed an exciting punch. Although the 1990 sequel, *Die Hard 2: Die Harder*, did not live up to the original in terms of excitement, it still provided some lavishly staged thrills; again Kamen produced an appropriately fast-paced score. Still a third film in the series, *Die Hard with a Vengeance*, was released in 1995. This time the action took place in New York City, and

Willis shared screen time with a sidekick played by Samuel L. Jackson. The action scenes were again stunningly designed, with Kamen's music helping set the pace.

In all of the *Die Hard* films, the use of classical melodies was intermixed with Kamen's own scoring. The closing scene of the first *Die Hard* includes repeated references to the choral finale of Beethoven's Symphony no. 9, whereas the ending of *Die Hard 2* features the concluding portion of Sibelius's tone poem *Finlandia*. The third *Die Hard* film was originally scored using themes from Brahms's Symphony no. 1 combined with part of Beethoven's Ninth; but after the soundtrack was recorded, changes were made and these classical excerpts were replaced. A cleverly orchestrated set of variations on "When Johnny Comes Marching Home" was inserted into both the big robbery sequence and the final scene, and was also used in the end credits.

Kamen's longest score to date is his symphonic background for the 1991 *Robin Hood—Prince of Thieves*, which required the efforts of sixteen different orchestrators, including Kamen himself and the veteran Jack Hayes. Kamen provided a rousing score for the 1993 Disney remake of *The Three Musketeers*, which also required a large number of orchestrators.

Kamen's best work of 1995 came at the very end of the year, with the Christmas-time release of the sentimental *Mr. Holland's Opus*. Richard Dreyfuss plays Glenn Holland, a composer who gets sidetracked into teaching and finds himself tied to the same job for thirty years, while helping his wife raise their deaf son. Some critics scoffed at this film, but it struck a sympathetic chord with viewers, many of whom could relate to the experiences of this dedicated high school teacher.

Musically, *Holland* is a collage of original scoring, excerpts from pieces by Bach and Beethoven, and a large-scale symphonic piece that is played in the film's climactic scene: Glenn is the guest at his surprise retirement party, which is attended by the entire school population and many of Mr. Holland's former students. For the occasion the school orchestra has prepared a performance of their teacher's work, "An American Symphony," which he had begun as a young man out of college and had only recently completed, after a life of dedication to his students.

Director Stephen Herek, who had worked with Kamen on *The Three Musketeers*, collaborated with the composer even before filming of *Holland* began. In the director's own words:

> For many weeks prior to shooting the film we talked about musical ideas and philosophies—how music touches our lives—how it touches other people's lives and how people and life influence music. Much like a novel that has diverse characters and plot twists, one idea melding into another, a musical composition contains the same life rhythms. We talked about the different people that Mr. Holland meets in the film and how they affected his life. This led to Michael writing themes for different characters as well as for incidents in the film that deeply affected Mr. Holland.[30]

Herek goes on to say that the symphony written by Mr. Holland takes the listeners on a musical journey through his life. When the work is performed in the closing scene, viewers are reminded musically of all the events of the film. Again in Herek's words:

> This "Opus" written before the movie was shot became the life force for the shooting of the movie and the themes provided the underscoring of the movie later. When you watch the movie and listen to the music you can see and

© Interscope Communications, Inc.

Mr. Holland's Opus,
with Richard Dreyfuss
and Alicia Witt.

hear how the final musical score plays much like a symphony that takes you on an emotional ride through Mr. Holland's life.[31]

As Herek points out, the themes heard in the "American Symphony" were composed before the filming began, so that when Kamen added the underscore, he could utilize the many musical ideas from Mr. Holland's big piece. In the very beginning of the film, Kamen presents two of the musical ideas of his "opus." While sitting at a piano in their apartment, with his wife nearby, Glenn plays some bits of a work he is composing. The first tune is part of "Cole's Theme," which is later associated with their son, named for John Coltrane. Following this, as Glenn imagines what the final orchestration will sound like, we hear the triumphant final portion of the work, based on a five-note idea that is associated with Mr. Holland himself. This melody helps to define the nature of his work as a teacher, a role he accepts reluctantly at first, but eventually with great dedication. The next theme heard, also based on a five-note pattern, is linked with Iris (Glenne Headly), Mr. Holland's devoted wife. When Cole is born, the score features a fuller version of Cole's theme, and later, when Glenn is encouraging a talented student named Rowena (Jean Louisa Kelly) to pursue her dream, we hear the sounds of a solo cello playing Rowena's theme.

Since all these themes were created for the work heard in the film's closing scene, the more intently viewers listen to the score during the film, the more they are likely to derive from the performance of the "American Symphony." In this work, Iris's theme is heard first, followed by Cole's theme and then by the Rowena melody. Between the first and second theme is a dramatic episode, set in a minor key, in which we hear music of conflict. This section seems to suggest Glenn's inner struggle to accept his teaching job. As he becomes resigned to this means of earning a living, the music moves on to the other themes. The symphony culminates in a bold and brassy statement of the five-note idea that was heard at the beginning of the film, but now this idea is fleshed out, with pounding drums added to the orchestral mix.

Kamen's concept for the "American Symphony" is a bit eclectic, with a rock beat thrown in to reflect Holland's assorted musical tastes and experiences. As a composer's creative work, Mr. Holland's "opus" includes a considerable amount of dramatically effective music. His opus brings this film's episodic and sentimental story of a musician's professional odyssey to an emotionally satisfying conclusion.

Earlier in 1995, Kamen scored *Circle of Friends,* a seriocomic coming-of-age story set in Ireland during the 1950s. Although period songs, such as "Bo Weevil," were used to establish the time frame of the story, Kamen provided an Irish-flavored score, with a fully orchestrated sound for some of the cues, while in others the Chieftains, a popular Irish group, were enlisted to perform Kamen's themes. Especially delightful is the piece entitled "Air–You're the One," in which Kamen's gentle tune is played by a combination of wooden flute, tin whistle, and harpsichord.

Shortly after *Circle of Friends* came the release of *Don Juan DeMarco*. The Spanish-flavored score by Kamen is principally distinguished by the song "Have You Ever Really Loved a Woman?," on which he shared the composing credits with Bryan Adams and R. J. Lange, who had previously collaborated with him on songs for both *Robin Hood* and *The Three Musketeers*. This catchy romantic ballad is not only heard vocally in the film, with Adams as the singer, but is also incorporated into the background scoring, with guitars, castanets, and maracas used to provide a Spanish style.

TWO CATEGORIES OF FILM SCORES.

As yet another attempt to improve the Motion Picture Academy's awarding process, in 1995 the Academy's Board of Governors decided to split the music scoring nominations into two separate categories—Original Dramatic Score and Original Musical or Comedy Score—with five nominees in each. Two John Williams scores were nominated: *Nixon* as a dramatic score and *Sabrina* for a comedy. James Horner also became a double nominee; his Scottish-derived score for Mel Gibson's *Braveheart* and his heroic score for Ron Howard's *Apollo 13* were both nominated for Original Dramatic Score. Patrick Doyle became a first-time nominee for *Sense and Sensibility* (and should have been nominated again for his charming music for *A Little Princess*). The score that won in the drama category was Luis Bacalov's gently tuneful music for the delightful Italian film *The Postman* (*Il Postino*).

In the Original Musical or Comedy Score category, besides Williams's *Sabrina*, Mark Shaiman became a first-time honoree for his melodious score of Rob Reiner's *American President*. The cousins Randy and Thomas Newman were also cited for their work on *Toy Story* and *Unstrung Heroes*, respectively. The winner in this category was Alan Menken, for Disney's *Pocahontas*. As a bonus, Menken also took home an Oscar for the song "Colors of the Wind." With these two awards Menken reached a total of eight Oscars, which he collected in the space of only seven years. Although this new split awarding system has the built-in flaw of lumping together comedy and musical scores, it seems to indicate an increased awareness by the Academy of the importance of music in films.

SHORT CUTS ■■■■ Jerry Goldsmith.

Though he wasn't nominated for any of the scores he wrote for films released in 1995, Jerry Goldsmith proved with his music for *First Knight*, *Congo*, and *Powder* that his creative energies were still intact. Jerry Zucker's *First Knight* regrettably left out the magical elements of the Arthurian legend by eliminating Merlin and any mention of the sword Excalibur, but Goldsmith's often heroic music has some glorious choral moments. For the section known as "Arthur's Farewell," there is a lyrical piece of music featuring a choir singing a Latin text, the dramatic nature of which comes across in a powerful manner. The score begins with a brightly colored brass fanfare; it also includes a wonderfully romantic main theme and a lovely melody for Guinevere.

Although *Congo* is essentially a compendium of stock jungle-movie clichés, it contains some beautiful background scoring, with vocal arrangements by Lebo M., who had already proved valuable to Hans Zimmer on both *The Power of One* and *The Lion King*. *Powder* includes some synthesized sounds mixed in with a romantic-style orchestration for this story of a troubled teenager with some very special powers.

■■■■ **John Williams.** Of John Williams's two nominated scores, *Nixon* demonstrates the composer's keen talent for adding incisive music to dramatic films with a modern setting. As in his earlier *Born on the Fourth of July* and *JFK* scores, trumpeter Tim Morrison enhances Williams's main theme by providing several lyrical solo passages. For *Sabrina*, Williams created a pleasantly old-fashioned romantic score, written mostly for piano and strings. As a nod to the earlier version of Samuel Taylor's play, filmed by Billy Wilder in 1954, the French song "La Vie en Rose" (music by R. S. Louiguy, English lyrics by Mack David) was again incorporated as background music.

■■■■ **John Barry.** Despite dramatic lapses and a ludicrous change in Hawthorne's ending, *The Scarlet Letter* benefits from John Barry's exquisite score, which includes a memorable slow-paced main theme. The quality of this music is all the more impressive since Barry was called in at the last minute to write a replacement for a rejected Elmer Bernstein score.

■■■■ **Maurice Jarre.** One of 1995's most romantic scores is Maurice Jarre's lilting music for the beautifully photographed *A Walk in the Clouds*. The theme for Victoria (Aitana Sanchez-Gijon) includes a soaring melody for strings. Classical guitarist Liona Boyd provides a series of charming solos for Jarre's catchy themes. There is also a Spanish rhythmic flavor in the harvest music, for which Jarre combined metrical groups of threes and twos in alternating patterns, as follows: 1–2–3, 1–2–3, 1–2, 1–2, 1–2. The same rhythmic pattern prevails in one of the two melodious songs written for the film by guitarist Leo Brouwer, with lyrics by the film's director, Alfonso Arau.

■■■■ **Miklos Rozsa.** On July 27, 1995, there was a press release from Los Angeles concerning the death of Miklos Rozsa at age eighty-eight. Although he had not composed a single movie score during the last fourteen years of his life, this Hungarian-born, classically trained composer remained the last living musical link to the Golden Age of Hollywood. Rozsa continually demonstrated in his work, which includes ninety film scores over a period of forty-five years, a marvelous insight for the motion picture medium. There are few other film musicians whose works reveal such a keen understanding of the role that music can play in underscoring the emotions of a film.

1996

E LLIOT GOLDENTHAL: *MICHAEL COLLINS*. Rarely does a film composer work on a score while the film is in production. An exception is Sergei Prokofiev, with his music for *Alexander Nevsky*. A more recent example of such a collaborative effort is the score by Elliot Goldenthal for Neil Jordan's *Michael Collins*. Although Goldenthal, a Brooklyn native, might seem an odd choice as composer for a film about the founder of the Irish Republican Army, the result was a major film score.

Before scoring his first film in the 1970s, Goldenthal had already demonstrated a keen ability to compose in a variety of genres and styles. Following a public school education in his native Brooklyn, Goldenthal attended the Manhattan School of Music, where his principal composition teacher was John Corigliano. During his seven years at the Manhattan School, Goldenthal also studied under Aaron Copland. Goldenthal has given the following acknowledgement of his teachers and their influence:

I studied with John Corigliano offically and Aaron Copland I was very close to, sort of as an unofficial teacher, and knew him for many years. Just being in New York and being exposed to so many different schools and approaches to music was very formative in how I turned out and my development so far.[32]

Another composer who influenced Goldenthal was Leonard Bernstein, to whom Goldenthal was introduced by Copland. Goldenthal's work *Shadow Play Scherzo* was written in honor of Leonard Bernstein's seventieth birthday.

Goldenthal's youthful training at the piano helped him get playing jobs while in high school and college. One group with which he played was a blues band that toured the country for a while. It was this experience that brought him into contact with many of the divergent types of American popular music, including ragtime, blues, and various jazz styles.

Following his college years, Goldenthal gravitated toward the West Coast, where he eventually got an opportunity to score some low-budget films.

Perhaps due to the influence of Corigliano, Copland, and Bernstein, Goldenthal's composing interests have always been diversified. While still lacking recognition as a film composer, Goldenthal created several works for the concert hall among which are the *Pastime Variations* for chamber orchestra, the Concerto for Trumpet and Piano, and the award-winning oratorio *Juan Darién*, based on a children's story by the Uruguayan writer Horacio Quiroga. Goldenthal also wrote many scores for plays and ballets.

A recording of *Juan Darién* proved to be Goldenthal's calling card in Hollywood. According to Goldenthal: "It [*Juan Darién*] was a tape that a lot of Hollywood directors listened to. My agent, Sam Schwartz, had the tape, he didn't expect much of it, but many directors listened to it, and they heard an alternative type of a thing that turned them on a lot."[33] Two film scores resulted from *Juan Darién*: for *Pet Semetary* and the highly acclaimed *Drugstore Cowboy*, both of which films were released in 1989. They led to some high-profile film projects, beginning with *Alien* 3 (1992) and *Demolition Man* (1993). It was *Interview with the Vampire* (1994) that brought Goldenthal into contact with director Neil Jordan.

While Jordan was shooting *Michael Collins* in and around Dublin, he invited Goldenthal to Ireland to discuss the music. Goldenthal remembers "many a drunken, poetic night in Dublin," at which time the style of the film's music was discussed.[34] The composer admits that the basic problem to be resolved regarding the music of *Michael Collins* had to do with the Irish flavor. ". . . he [Jordan] felt he wanted the music to be more dramatic as opposed to Irishy, . . . There were Celtic themes that were both traditional and invented that sort of informed the score."[35] The resultant score is founded on two primary ideas. The first of these is heard at the very outset of the film, which is set during the Easter Uprising of 1916. Here, a minor-key idea is used to delineate the film's dramatic essence. Beginning with the tones of a minor triad, sounded in ascending fashion, this theme returns periodically throughout the film. In its first appearance this melancholy idea is sounded by Irish singer Sinead O'Connor, who sings an unidentified Gaelic text. A choir also joins in the singing, accompanied by a large-scale orchestration, which features a wood flute and Uilleann pipes. This theme grows to a dramatic climax as the conflict between the Irish rebels and English troops escalates.

Elliot Goldenthal.

Michael Collins, with
Julia Roberts, Liam Neeson,
and Aidan Quinn.

The score's other principal musical idea is a lilting tune called "Kitty's Waltz." This theme, heard on a piano, with string accompaniment, is associated with the character of Kitty Kiernan (Julia Roberts), who befriends both Michael (Liam Neeson) and his best friend, Harry Boland (Aidan Quinn). Whenever Kitty is seen with either of these men, the theme is heard very softly in the background. At one point the theme is sounded more prominently, with a trumpet playing the melodic line.

A basic problem with the film's score, as heard in the film, is its low volume level. The waltz theme, despite its melodic tunefulness, is barely audible in the first scene in which it appears. It is only on the soundtrack recording that the beauty of Goldenthal's music can be properly appreciated. Another problem with the score is its fragmentation. Because of the pace established by Jordan, the film moves very quickly through the early history of the Irish rebellion, in which there are several graphic scenes of violence. The music seldom has a chance to establish a mood for more than a few seconds at a time. Only in the intermittent romantic moments is there a break from the film's hectic pacing.

Despite these complications, Goldenthal's score is a major work. Perhaps the single most memorable musical moment comes at the film's conclusion, after Collins is fatally shot. In a mock newsreel, shot in black and white, the funeral of Michael Collins is shown as an occasion of national mourning, with diplomats from around the world gathered to pay their last respects. During this scene Goldenthal's music becomes brilliantly ceremonial, with a full-orchestra set of dramatic chords, which are repeated several times.

Besides Goldenthal's original themes, two borrowed melodies are prominently featured. The traditional Irish tune "She Moved through the Fair," is sung by Sinead O'Connor, and "Macushla," a turn-of-the-century song by Dermot MacMurrough and Josephine V. Rowe, is sung by tenor Frank Patterson, accompanied by the Café Orchestra.

The music for *Michael Collins* provides an effective musical portrait for the turbulent times in which the IRA came into being. Elliot Goldenthal's original score richly deserves the Oscar nomination that it received.

MARK ISHAM: *FLY AWAY HOME.* One of the most charming films of 1996 is Carroll Ballard's *Fly Away Home*, a scenically photographed movie about a Canadian artist and inventor, Tom Alden (Jeff Daniels), who helps to rescue a family of baby geese when their nest is disturbed by a bulldozer near his farm.

The character of Alden derives from Bill Lishman, whose autobiography was used as the basis for the screenplay. The film's scenario is loosely based on an actual event that made headlines, when Lishman flew his own motorized glider in order to lead a flock of geese to a warmer climate for the winter. In the film Tom has a daughter, Amy (Anna Paquin), who comes to Ontario to live with her father following the accidental death of her mother, from whom Alden has been long divorced. When Amy finds goose eggs, she brings them into a barn and then raises the geese after they are hatched. When Tom observes that the geese follow Amy around, he decides to teach her to fly his glider, so that the two of them together can lead the geese southward to spend the winter.

Mark Isham's often folksy score is a perfect musical accompaniment for this offbeat story. Although some of the music is played by an eighty-piece orchestra, Isham focuses primarily on the sounds of solo instruments. Chief among these is a violin, which sounds one of the score's principal themes, a soaring idea that begins with three rising tones (G–C–G) that lead to a fourth, which is down a semitone in pitch. This pattern is used several times in a scene in which Amy first observes her father trying to fly in a glider of his own design. As he sails through the air, Isham's music captures the feeling of a man floating in air, with no concern for the earth below.

Also prominently featured in the score are a solo cello and a clarinet. The cello is combined in unison with a solo female voice in the scene in which Amy first discovers the goose eggs. Later, when the geese begin to hatch, the solo cello is heard again, accompanied by repeated piano tones. A catchy tune for clarinet and violin over a rhythmic background is heard while Amy playfully runs about, with the geese obediently following her.

Another significant musical aspect of *Fly Away Home*'s music is an original song composed by Isham for the film. With the title "10 Thousand Miles," this gentle, folk-style melody, sung by Mary Chapin Carpenter, appears twice. It is first heard during the opening credits, as Amy is seen in a car with her mother. No noises are heard when the car crash occurs; the song provides an ironic counterpoint to the tragic nature of the scene. A second appearance of this music occurs as Amy, in her homemade plane, is in the final stages of guiding the geese toward a lakeside destination in North Carolina. The melody of "10 Thousand Miles" is first heard instrumentally in this scene. A solo cello and a soprano saxophone, plus rippling piano tones, are featured in the song, which continues as Carpenter's voice is heard once more.

The music for *Fly Away Home* is one of Mark Isham's best achievements thus far in a film-composing career that has spanned almost two decades. This score represents the second time that Isham has worked with Carroll Ballard, who gave him his first film-scoring assignment, the music of the 1983 film *Never Cry Wolf.* Despite Ballard's leisurely pace in film-making, there appears to be a meaningful collaboration in the offing between this director and Mark Isham, a composer who has clearly responded to the poetic imagery of Ballard's films.

GABRIEL YARED: *THE ENGLISH PATIENT.* One of 1996's most memorable scores is the slowly paced, brooding music by Gabriel Yared (b. 1949) for one of the year's most critically acclaimed films, Anthony Minghella's *English Patient.*

Adapted by Minghella from the novel of the same name by Michael Ondaatje, *The English Patient* is the somber but beautifully photographed story of a Hungarian nobleman, Count Almasy (Ralph Fiennes), whose ill-fated love affair with Katharine (Kristin Scott Thomas), a married British woman, at the outset of World War II, is told in flashbacks by the count, who has been horribly burned in a plane crash, and now lies dying in the ruins of an Italian monastery. As he responds to the kindness of his dedicated nurse Hana (Juliette Binoche), the count, who is mistakenly believed to be English, regains his memory. Thus begins the series of reminiscences that make up a large part of the film.

Yared, who worked closely with the director during the production of this film, created a score that incorporates a number of diverse elements. Hungarian folk melodies are heard periodically, in performances featuring Marta Sebestyen and an ensemble known as Muzsikas. There is also much solo piano music, which is taken from J. S. Bach's *Goldberg Variations.* The piano music is associated with Hana, who at one point sits at a damaged piano in the monastery and plays the beginning of the Bach work.

Among Yared's musical ideas are two principal themes; a solo clarinet is featured in the score's melancholy main idea, and a large string orchestra plays an emotional love theme that conveys the tragic consequences of the count's affair with Katharine. Yared's score serves as a catalyst to amalgamate the diverse elements of this story; his music forms part of a moving portrait of several people, brought together by circumstance, whose lives are shattered as the tragic consequence of war. Of the nine Oscars that were awarded this unusual film, one deservingly went to Yared in the Original Dramatic Score category.

SHORT CUTS ■■■■ **Blockbuster Films.** The year 1996 was one of box-office blockbusters, in view of the success of Brian De Palma's *Mission: Impossible,* Roland Emmerich's *Independence Day,* Jan De Bont's *Twister,* Charles Russell's *Eraser,* Ron Howard's *Ransom,* John Woo's *Broken Arrow,* Stuart Baird's *Executive Decision,* Rob Cohen's *DragonHeart,* and Michael Bay's film *The Rock.* In most of these films, special-effects wizardry is on display in lavish doses. What is not especially evident in these blockbusters is any sense of stylistic originality. Whether a recycled TV series, a film remake, or a more spectacular version of earlier movies of a similar nature, these films suffer from a lack of creative thinking.

The same criticism, in general, may be leveled at the musical scores of these nine films. A sad reflection on the state of film music in the 1990s is the fact that one of the most memorable musical moments in all of 1996's films occurs when the original *Mission: Impossible* theme of Lalo Schifrin appears during the opening credits of De Palma's updated version of the popular TV series. The adrenaline rush of Schifrin's rhythmically driven theme captures the imagination in a way that none of the other music in the new film can equal, despite the efforts of Danny Elfman to create a lively and suspenseful background for the densely plotted scenario of De Palma's film.

Although it can be argued that there are some glorious moments in scores such as those of David Arnold for *Independence Day* and Mark Mancina for *Twister*, these scoring efforts reflect a hurry-up-and-get-it-done attitude on the part of filmmakers, who are giving composers increasingly tight schedules. In one specific instance, the music by James Horner for *Ransom* came about after the rejection of an earlier score written by Howard Shore. With *Ransom* locked into a mid-November release date, the final score for this film was literally thrown together at the last minute.

Of the scores for these blockbusters, the most memorable are those by Jerry Goldsmith for *Executive Decision* and by Randy Edelman for *Dragon-Heart*. Goldsmith's four decades of experience in film have made him one of the most insightful of film composers. In *Executive Decision*, Goldsmith set his main theme in a seven-beat meter. The alternating groups of three and four pulses that make up the seven-beat pattern help to create a keen sense of anticipation concerning the action that is yet to come.

The heroic melodies of Edelman's score for *DragonHeart* form one of this medieval adventure film's chief pleasures. Although the dragon is an impressive bit of filmmaking magic, it is Edelman's music that creates a flavor of excitement. This is one of the composer's best efforts since his memorable *Gettysburg* score.

■■■■ **Rachel Portman.** The Oscar winner in the Original Musical or Comedy Score category was Rachel Portman's charming music for Douglas McGrath's adaptation of Jane Austen's *Emma*. Although this film is the most comically light-hearted of the various film adaptations of Austen novels to reach the screen in the 1990s, Portman's lyrical score emphasizes the serious and romantic sides of Emma Woodhouse's personality. Ever eager to meddle in the lives of her friends, Emma (Gwyneth Paltrow) ultimately fails in her well-intentioned plotting, but succeeds in getting a husband for herself, the honorable Mr. Knightly (Jeremy Northam). The main-title theme is a slow-paced waltz tune for flute, strings, and harp, whereas several other melodies have a buoyant dance-like quality, with harmonies founded on such old-English folk tunes as "Greensleeves."

■■■■ **Wojciech Kilar.** Another classic novel that received a fine film adaptation in 1996 is Jane Campion's *Portrait of a Lady*, based on the Henry James novel. Polish composer Wojciech Kilar (b. 1932), already known for the music of *Bram Stoker's Dracula*, created a highly emotional score. The music heard during the opening credits features a minor-key theme played by two flutes with a deeply resonant string accompaniment. The theme for Isabel Archer (Nicole Kidman) is a melancholy string piece, whereas the music for her arrival in Florence is a more cheerful major-key idea which features a solo oboe. Additionally, there are several compositions by Franz Schubert incorporated into the film. Taken together, the score for *The Portrait of a Lady* creates a rich musical tapestry for this story of love and deceit.

■■■■ **Shakespearean Films.** Patrick Doyle created another fine Shakespearean score, for Kenneth Branagh's four-hour film based on the entire text of *Hamlet*. Although neither this film nor Doyle's music is ultimately as successful as were their counterparts for Branagh's 1989 adaptation of *Henry V*, there are many inspired moments. Especially memorable is the closing music, "In Pace," a funereal elegy based on Doyle's themes for Hamlet and Ophelia, with a Latin text sung by Placido Domingo.

In *Looking for Richard*, a part-documentary, part-adaptation of *Richard III*, Al Pacino explores various perceptions concerning the modern world's view of Shakespeare's plays. Howard Shore was assigned the task of creating a series of musical portraits. In response to Pacino's attempt to find out who each of the play's major characters really is, Shore's music delves deeply inside each one. He created a brilliantly symphonic accompaniment for orchestra and chorus, with a series of Latin texts by Elizabeth Cotnoir, often translated from the Shakespearean originals. The most dramatically compelling portrait is that of Richard himself; it is brooding, dark-tinged music, with more than a touch of menace. The other portraits are also musically somber, with an emphasis on minor-key harmony, and the resonant sounds of a pipe organ added for dramatic effect.

■■■■ *Shine*. For Scott Hicks's *Shine*, which is based on the life of Australian pianist David Helfgott, composer David Hirschfelder, who previously scored the 1992 film *Strictly Ballroom*, wove several classical melodies into his score. The bulk of the borrowed music heard in the film comes from Rachmaninoff's Piano Concerto no. 3 in D Minor, which young David desires to play, over the objections of his teacher. This music, which is referred to in the film as the "Rach 3," provided Hirschfelder with melodic material for much of his background scoring.

There is also some original scoring in *Shine*. The principal theme in Hirschfelder's score is a melancholy idea for woodwinds and violins accompanied by string orchestra, with rhythmically driven patterns on harp and piano added as a background flavoring. *Shine*'s music is ultimately a *potpourri* of elements, both new and borrowed; all of the film's musical elements combine to furnish a portrait of a talented but troubled musician.

■■■■ **James Horner.** One of 1996's noteworthy independently made films is Lee David Zlotoff's *Spitfire Grill*, about a young woman Percy Talbott (Alison Elliott), recently released from prison, who comes to a small New England town to work in a café. Her presence proves unsettling to many of the town's residents, who are afraid of her. James Horner created a lyrical score that is reminiscent of Elmer Bernstein's music for *To Kill a Mockingbird*. The resemblance is not coincidental, since Bernstein's *Mockingbird* music was used to accompany *The Spitfire Grill*'s theatrical trailer. However, Horner's small-scale orchestration provides a charming musical accompaniment that achieves a style of its own. Prominently featured are a solo violin and French horn, which are heard in unison in the score's principal theme. The piano and guitar are also featured, along with such woodwinds as clarinet and flute, to create a sometimes folksy but always lyrically inspired background for this melancholy film.

■■■■ **Alan Menken.** One last 1996 film score that should be mentioned is Alan Menken's often operatic music for the Disney animated film of Victor Hugo's *Hunchback of Notre Dame*. Menken combined elements of solo song, choral music, and symphonic underscoring to make an entertaining version of Hugo's starkly dramatic story. If the final product is not true to the mood of the novel, the Disney film still manages to be a supremely satisfying film entertainment, with one of the year's best musical scores. Ironically, this is the first of Menken's scores for a Disney film that failed to earn an Academy Award.

Danny Elfman.

DANNY ELFMAN: FROM MEN IN BLACK TO GOOD WILL HUNTING.

For many moviegoers, Danny Elfman is probably best known for his association with director Tim Burton—specifically, for his *Batman* music. Despite his success as a film composer, Elfman's musical background is quite unconventional.

Elfman, who was born in Los Angeles in 1953, never received a formal education in music. During his early years, he learned about film music by going to the movies. Elfman has stated that his familiarity with film scores made him quite conscious of different composers' styles: "By the time I was fifteen, I could listen to movies and say, 'That's a Goldsmith score, that's a Korngold score, that's an Alfred Newman score.'"[36]

While in high school, within a few months, Elfman taught himself to play the violin well enough to join a musical group called Grand Magic Circus, which also included his older brother, Richard, who played conga drums. The success of this group led to a period of touring that induced the younger Elfman to quit high school. In 1973, after an extended stay in West Africa, Danny joined his brother in an avant-garde new group with the African-inspired name "The Mystic Knights of the Oingo Boingo." This unique eight-member ensemble has been described as follows:

> [This group] was an avant-weird theatrical troupe. . . . There were costumes, backdrops, film clips, and props; gorilla outfits; ten-foot dinosaurs; music from every known style; and story lines, including a show-length history of the world ending in Earth's destruction at the hands of space people.[37]

In 1979, Danny Elfman reorganized this group as a more conventional type of rock band. With the shortened name of Oingo Boingo, new members joined a few from the Mystic Knights. In addition to Elfman, who provided lead vocals, guitar, and handled songwriting responsibilities, the group included Steve Bartek (guitar), who would later orchestrate most of Elfman's films. This group's music has been described as "complex, precision played" and "funhouse-kinetic."[38] Although Oingo Boingo never achieved a wide fame outside of the Los Angeles area, their albums provided listeners with alternative rock. Seven albums were released between 1981 and 1990, the first of which was *Only a Lad*.

Richard Elfman, who had moved into filmmaking, directed his first film, *Forbidden Zone*, in 1980; its music, written by Danny Elfman, is predominantly in rock style and includes songs performed by the Mystic Knights of the Oingo Boingo.

Danny Elfman was approached by director Tim Burton, who was a fan of Oingo Boingo; the result was Elfman's first orchestral film score, the catchy, light-hearted music of *Pee Wee's Big Adventure* (1985). With the popular success of this movie, Elfman and Burton maintained an artistic collaboration that has led to seven films as of this writing. Whereas *Beetlejuice* (1988) also features a comical score, Burton's dark version of *Batman* (1989), with Michael Keaton as the mysterious Caped Crusader of Gotham City, includes a rhythmically pulsating orchestral background.

With his score of *Batman*, Elfman gained recognition as a major film composer. Thus far, he has scored thirty films. His music for three of the biggest box-office hits of 1997 demonstrates his keen sense of originality.

Barry Sonnenfeld's *Men in Black* is a unique combination of sci-fi, thriller, and comedy. Tommy Lee Jones portrays Agent K, who works for a secretive government enterprise, whose agents, the "Men in Black," monitor and police alien activity on Earth. Will Smith plays Agent J, a New York City cop who is recruited as a replacement for K's aging partner. Together, Agents K and J must save the planet from destruction at the hands of a hostile alien force.

Since *Men in Black* is a very fast-paced film, with an extremely imaginative script, Danny Elfman's job was to write music that would complement this picture's unique style. Rather than a wall-to-wall score, Elfman's music provides mostly brief but effective moments of clever musical commentary. One of the few places in the film that includes an extended musical accompaniment occurs during the opening credits, which are shown during a scene in which the camera follows a large horsefly in closeups, as it flies over the terrain, including a busy freeway. To accompany this bizarre photographic series of shots, Elfman created first a slow, four-note motif played on string basses, then a celestial effect, with high strings and harp, plus metallic percussion. As the credits continue, the score's dramatic, minor-key main theme is introduced, with an accompanying rock beat; this music continues until the horsefly has a fatal collision with the windshield of a pickup truck. At this point the film's action commences; aboard the truck are some Mexicans who are entering the United States illegally. As Agent K well knows, one of them is an extra-terrestrial in disguise. There is a moment of frantic music as the alien charges an investigating policeman. Agent K zaps the creature at the last instant; this is accompanied by a dynamic musical punctuation.

The music in the remainder of the film follows the pattern of this scene closely; some cues last for thirty seconds or less. One important short cue is the heroic music that Elfman wrote for the scene in which Agent J is introduced, as he dons his new black suit and sunglasses.

The longest continual use of music occurs in the final portion of the film, when another alien, who has taken over the body of a farmer, attempts to steal the galaxy, a tiny orblike pendant, which must be returned to its owners or else Earth will be destroyed. Throughout the final scenes Elfman's music includes lots of pounding and grinding brass-and-percussion effects. There is relatively little melody in the entire score since what is needed is a steady background beat to accompany the swift visual action.

Les Mayfield's *Flubber*, an updated version of the 1961 Disney film *The Absent-Minded Professor*, features Robin Williams as Professor Brainard, who saves Medfield College from financial ruin by inventing a buoyant substance called flubber (short for flying rubber). Although this film is a bit overladen with mechanical devices, including a cute robot named Weebo (who speaks with a woman's voice), Elfman has created a charming score.

There are three primary melodic elements, all of which appear in the music that accompanies the opening credits. The first of these is a five-note piano motif that includes two short tones followed by three longer ones. The second is a rising motif for saxophones, which figures prominently in the mambo music heard later on. The third melodic element is the film's most developed theme, a soaring idea that begins with a six-note motif.

The orchestration contains several ingenious elements. The piano motif, which is sometimes heard in combination with orchestra bells, vibraphone, and celesta, conveys a celestial sound for scenes in which Brainard takes his car for a flubberized flight. There is also a theremin effect, plus various other electronic sounds, which collectively add a great deal of fun to this often entertaining film.

A highlight of *Flubber* is the scene in which Weebo lets the flubber out of its protective canister. We then see a dance number patterned after a classic Busby Berkeley routine. The flubber separates into a number of dancing shapes, including a lead couple and a chorus line. The music for this scene, built on the saxophone motif heard earlier, includes lots of Latin percussion effects. The scene's clever visuals, plus Elfman's exuberant score, give the film a much-needed lift.

A third 1997 film with Danny Elfman's music is Gus Van Sant's *Good Will Hunting*, based on an original screenplay by two of the film's actors, Matt Damon and Ben Affleck. Elfman wisely refrained from overscoring this emotionally affecting drama, in which Will (Damon), a brilliant young man, receives therapy from a psychologist (Robin Williams again!), who helps Will overcome the lingering effects of childhood abuse. There is a slow-paced main theme, which features an oboe, a wood flute, and strings, plus a steel-string guitar and a wordless choral background. This wistful music creates a mood of sweet melancholy until the film's conclusion, when the music becomes more upbeat, as Will takes charge of his life and goes after Skylar (Minnie Driver), the girl he loves.

J OHN WILLIAMS: FROM ROSEWOOD TO AMISTAD. Four disparate films with music by John Williams were released in 1997—a clear indication that this multitalented composer is still at the top of his form.

For John Singleton's *Rosewood*, Williams created a folk-flavored musical accompaniment. There are three principal themes: First is a noble idea that suggests the black residents of Rosewood, the small Florida town that was torn apart by racial hated in 1923. There is also a bluesy theme for piano and steel-string guitar, and a folklike melody that features, at different times, harmonica and fiddle.

For *The Lost World: Jurassic Park*, Steven Spielberg's long-awaited sequel to his 1993 blockbuster about an exotic theme park populated with prehistoric animals, Williams created a variety of dramatically charged themes. The most important of these is a chordal idea played by strings above the repeated beating of drums. This theme, which is based on a five-note idea, is heard whenever the two teams of investigators search the ruins of the park for any surviving animals. In its orchestration, Williams has cleverly imitated the music from such classic jungle pictures as *King Kong*.

An even better score accompanies Jean-Jacques Annaud's *Seven Years in Tibet*, which relates the real-life story of Heinrich Harrer, an Austrian mountain climber, who escaped from an Indian detention camp during World War II and wound up in Lhasa, the Tibetan capital, where he became the friend and mentor of the young dalai lama. Despite critical scoffs, which came after news stories revealed that Harrer had belonged to the SS unit of the Nazi party, *Tibet* is an intriguing film, with a charismatic performance by Brad Pitt as Harrer.

Williams's score consists of three primary themes. The first, a melancholy idea, which begins with a five-note pattern, is utilized extensively throughout the score. Providing a solo musical voice in this theme is the cello, which was beautifully recorded for the soundtrack by Yo-Yo Ma. A second musical idea, also melancholy in nature, is first heard during the opening scene, when Heinrich leaves his pregnant wife at a train station, in Vienna, en route to the Himalayas. The third prominent idea is a melody of Asian character, based on a pentatonic (five-note) scale which is associated with the dalai lama. Whenever the solo cello or the orchestral strings sound this idea, there is an uphill slide in pitch that provides an Oriental quality.

Williams also scored Spielberg's *Amistad*, a vivid cinematic retelling of events that occurred in the pre–Civil War era. The film begins with a mutiny aboard the schooner La Amistad, which is being used for the illegal transport of Africans to America. The remaining crew members are instructed to sail back to Africa, but the ship winds up off the coast of Connecticut. Once the mutineers are charged for murder and piracy, the film's lengthy legal proceedings are depicted.

As the film's title is shown, a woman's solo voice is heard in a melancholy melody based on a simple three-note motif that is later identified with the head of the mutiny, a proud young African known as Cinque (Djimon Hounsou). In a scene in the jail where the Africans are imprisoned during their trial, Cinque and a fellow prisoner look at pictures in a Bible. Here Williams's theme is eloquently played by a solo flute and harp.

When ex-President John Quincy Adams (Anthony Hopkins) is approached to help defend the Africans, a theme of noble character is heard, with the lyrical trumpet tones of Tim Morrison, who played Williams's themes in such earlier films as *Born on the Fourth of July* and *JFK*. This music is also played at length during the climactic scene in which Adams pleads eloquently before the Supreme Court.

Many scenes in *Amistad* are accompanied by a choir of voices. When the chained prisoners are being led past the townspeople to their place of confinement, the singing is accompanied by flute and drums. Elsewhere, there are moments when the singing is totally without instrumental background. Although *Amistad*'s music, like that of *Schindler's List*, is sometimes of an understated nature, Williams has succeeded in dramatizing the emotions of this vivid historical drama in an eloquent manner.

JAMES **H**ORNER: *T*HE *D*EVIL'S *O*WN AND *T*ITANIC. Both of Horner's scores for films released in 1997 include an Irish flavor. In Alan J. Pakula's film *The Devil's Own*, several folk instruments, including the wood flute, the uilleann pipes, and the Irish harp, provide a Celtic sound. The film's most prominent theme is actually presented in the opening credits as a song in which Horner's melody is sung in Gaelic by Irish singer Sara Clancy. This melancholy tune, which bears the name "There Are Flowers Growing upon the Hill," features tones of a minor scale that rise in thirds. Horner's idea has the qualities of a folk theme, with an accompaniment of harp and wood flute. At the end of the film this song is heard again, but this time in English.

Another prominent melodic idea is associated with Brad Pitt, who plays Frankie Maguire, a member of the Irish Republican Army who has come to America to meet an arms supplier. As a house guest of a New York City policeman (played by Harrison Ford), Frankie masquerades as Rory Devaney, but soon his cover is revealed. Frankie's theme is a folklike melody played by wood flute and steel-string guitar. Various drums, including the bodhran, are also featured in this flavorful score.

Horner also worked on 1997's most celebrated film, James Cameron's *Titanic*, a fictional story of young love, set aboard the doomed ocean liner.

Again, Horner turned to Irish folk instruments to add an ethnic coloration. As in *The Devil's Own*, there is also a considerable use of synthesized sounds. Four melodic ideas are featured in *Titanic*'s score. One is a folk-style melody associated with Rose, whose memories of the fateful voyage form the basis of the story. Horner introduces Rose's theme with a wordless female voice in unison with wood flute. The uilleann pipes also present this melody at one point. There is a jaunty theme that utilizes dotted rhythms; this melody is associated with the more than 1,300 passengers aboard the gigantic ocean liner, many of whom are seen boarding at Southampton for the maiden voyage aross the Atlantic. For the ship itself Horner created a soaring melody that is often presented by French horns and strings. Finally, there is the film's love theme, for the ill-fated romance of young Rose (Kate Winslet) and Jack Dawson (Leonardo Di Caprio), a penniless young artist who wins his passage in a poker game. The melodic line of this theme, which primarily moves stepwise around a central tone, is also included in Horner's song "My Heart Will Go On," which is heard at the film's conclusion. The film score, set against Cameron's awesome visual production, adds both an emotional quality and a sense of excitement to this undeniably impressive movie.

SHORT CUTS ■■■ Jerry Goldsmith.

Three diverse dramas of 1997 contain scores by Jerry Goldsmith. Of these, the best film is Curtis Hanson's critically acclaimed *L. A. Confidential*, an absorbing crime drama set in the early 1950s. Against a setting of police corruption, Goldsmith's background score presents a rather bluesy mood. The main theme, for trumpet and strings, is based on a four-note motif that includes tones that slowly rise in pitch. With its minor-key tonality and jazz harmonies, this theme is used extensively; but, it is often displaced by such '50s recordings as Kay Starr's "Wheel of Fortune" and Dean Martin's "Christmas Blues."

Goldsmith's forceful score for Wolfgang Petersen's tense thriller *Air Force One* is one of this film's major assets. The main theme, a marchlike idea, is first presented as a dramatic fanfare for French horns. Later, it forms the basis for a soaring theme played by trumpets and strings. In its rising tones, this theme signals the heroics of President James Marshall (Harrison Ford), who tries to foil the takeover of the presidential plane by Russian terrorists.

The most effective of Goldsmith's 1997 scores is the often heroic music for Lee Tamahori's tale of survival *The Edge*, set in the wilds of Alaska. While a billionaire (Anthony Hopkins) and a fashion photographer (Alec Baldwin) battle both a bear and each other after the crash of their plane, Goldsmith's soaring themes add a tone of eloquence to an otherwise formulaic story.

■■■ Alan Silvestri.

For *Contact*, his first film since the hugely successful *Forrest Gump*, director Robert Zemeckis again solicited a musical score from Alan Silvestri. The result is a lyrical, sometimes ethereal, accompaniment for a sci-fi film that deals with an extraterrestrial civilization that is trying to make contact with the inhabitants of Earth. The tinkly sounds of the celesta are heard in the film's opening scene, as little Ellie explores the skies with the help of her father. As the adult Ellie (Jodi Foster) continues to ponder the existence of life on other planets, Silvestri's main theme is introduced. A rising four-note motif forms the basis of a lyrical melody sounded by piano and strings. Electronic sounds are also featured in this music, which is one of Silvestri's finest film scores to date.

■ ■ ■ ■ **The Newman Legacy.** In 1997, music by the three active Newmans could be heard at cinema multiplexes. Randy Newman's score for *Air Force One* was replaced just weeks prior to the film's release; however, his charming songs for the animated film *Cats Don't Dance* proved again, as in *Toy Story* (1995), his ability to score effectively films aimed at children.

Meanwhile, music by Thomas Newman was featured in two major 1997 dramas, Jon Avnet's *Red Corner* and Costa-Gavras's *Mad City*. The latter film is particularly enlivened by Newman's uniquely percussive instrumentation, with lots of metallic sounds blended with several types of drums.

Lastly, Thomas Newman's older brother David Newman contributed a wonderfully vibrant orchestral background score to the colorfully animated *Anastasia*. Although this musical film includes songs by Lynn Ahrens (lyrics) and Stephen Flaherty (music), the elder Newman composed some enchanting original music. Especially memorable is a marchlike theme heard in the film's prologue, in which the royal Romanov family is briefly profiled. Then tumultuous music is heard as the revolution is depicted along with the death of Rasputin, the mad monk. In the course of the film Newman's scoring incorporates bits of Flaherty's tunes but still manages to introduce several original melodic ideas. The end result is quite brilliant, especially with the more than ninety orchestral players and thirty choral voices used to record his score.

The recent successes of these three composers all reflect the grand film-music achievements of Alfred Newman (Randy's uncle and Thomas's and David's father). Since Alfred Newman's bluesy urban theme of *Street Scene* was introduced in 1931, every decade has had a film score by the Newman family. Together, the ongoing work by the three younger Newmans virtually guarantees a continuation of the Newman name as a potent force in film scoring for years to come.

POSTLUDE

IN **SUMMARY.** **D**ecember 28, 1995 marks a century that films had been shown to the paying public. The year 1997 marks the seventieth anniversary of the the first talkie, *The Jazz Singer*. Since that auspicious occasion, thousands of films with carefully synchronized musical scores have been shown on theater screens around the world. Movies have also become a staple item for both local TV stations and networks, many of which are beamed via satellite to the farthest reaches of the planet. Thanks to the mushrooming videotape and laser-disk industries, movies have even become available for rental or purchase. With all of these viewing opportunities, more people than ever before watch movies. A vast number of film-music recordings have been released on LP records, CDs, and audio cassettes, meaning that viewers also have direct access to film music. It is unfortunate that such pioneering film composers as Max Steiner and Alfred Newman did not live long enough to profit from the phenomenal popularity of film scores. Since film music written today easily reaches a much wider audience than ever before, it is to be hoped that the filmmakers of the future will give the coming generations of film composers opportunities to create scores as memorable as those of the godfathers.

Viewers today generally take the presence of a prerecorded musical score for granted and seldom question how the music got there—though they complain to the theater management when the sound is either too loud or too soft. Relatively few moviegoers listen intently to the musical score; yet some filmgoers have expressed their candid opinions on film music. Max Steiner probably summed it up best in his unfinished autobiography, with the following comments about film music:

> There is a tired old bromide . . . that a good film score is one you don't hear. What good is it if you don't notice it? However, you might say that the music should be heard and not seen. The danger is that the music can be so bad, or so good, that it distracts and takes away from the action.[39]

Steiner's statement points out the important role that the invisible musical score has always played in the creation of the film experience. In his view, a careful balance must ultimately be maintained between the images shown in a film and the emotions viewers feel as they watch. When the images and the score do not mesh in exactly the right way, the film may suffer. This places a heavy burden upon the composer, who often shoulders the blame when the finished film doesn't impress the viewer.

When a filmmaker has the insight to choose a talented composer to provide the best possible film music, the results can be worthwhile for both the film and its music. The late Fred Zinnemann made an insightful comment about film music when he was planning *Five Days One Summer* (1982). In the notes which he prepared for Elmer Bernstein to consider, Zinnemann wrote: "The music should add to the interior dimension of the film."[40] It is indeed an interior, invisible quality that music is called upon to provide. No one, including Zinnemann, may have ever been able to explain exactly what that invisible quality is, but with the instincts of a gifted composer at work, the music that reaches the ears of moviegoers is capable of greatly enhancing the viewing experience.

One positive development for which this century will be remembered is the evolution of the motion picture from a primitive, silent peep show to a technologically advanced art form, with a digitally recorded musical score— a part of the film that may be invisible to the eye but is nonetheless vividly real. The aim of this book has been to give readers a better understanding of some of the complexities of film music, so that whenever they view a movie, they will have a heightened awareness of the intricate role played by music in the total film experience. Perhaps future film composers will be better appreciated for their efforts than were many of the unsung heroes of film music's first century, during which so many composers, including several who regrettably have not received mention here, labored long and lovingly on behalf of the motion picture. Hopefully, film composers will someday receive the same visible recognition now granted to the writers, producers, and directors of films, despite the invisibility of the music.

Endnotes

1. Michael Cader, ed., *1996 People Entertainment Almanac* (New York: Little, Brown and Co., 1995), p. 124.

2. Susan Sackett, *Hollywood Sings! An Inside Look at Sixty Years of Academy Award–Nominated Songs* (New York: Billboard Books, 1995), p. 307.

3. Cader, p. 124.

4. Jon Burlingame, "John Barry," *Premiere*, vol. 4, no. 4 (December 1990), p. 66.

5. Ibid.

6. Ibid.

7. Stanley Green, *Broadway Musicals Show by Show* (Milwaukee: Hal Leonard Books, 1985), p. 262.

8. Sackett, *Hollywood Sings*, p. 277.

9. Ibid., p. 298.

10. Interview with Jerry Goldsmith, Toledo, March 11, 1995.

11. Patrick Doyle, Liner notes for the *Much Ado about Nothing* soundtrack, an Epic Soundtrax CD, EK 54009.

12. Ibid.

13. Conversation between the author and Elmer Bernstein at the 1994 conference of the Society for the Preservation of Film Music, Los Angeles, March 17–20, 1994. On March 18, following Bernstein's presentation on his Western scores, including *The Magnificent 7*, he met informally with several conference attendees. When asked whether the choice of waltz time for the themes of *The Age of Innocence* was intended or accidental, Bernstein replied that the choice was indeed predetermined, in view of the milieu of the story, which is set amid the parties and dinner gatherings of New York's elite in the 1870s.

14. The Varese Sarabande CD release of *Untamed Heart*, VSD-5404, contains a footnote referring to the identifying titles for the first and last tracks, which reads: "not included in the final version of the film."

15. Michael Nyman's Piano Concerto, with Kathryn Stott, pianist, and the Royal Liverpool Philharmonic Orchestra, released on an Argo CD, no. 443 382-2.

16. Ari Posner, "The Mane Event," *Premiere*, vol. 7, no. 11 (July 1994), pp. 82.

17. Ibid.

18. Liner notes for the *Beyond Rangoon* soundtrack CD, Milan 35725-2.

19. Ibid.

20. Posner, p. 84

21. Ibid.

22. Ibid., p. 86.

23. Ibid.

24. Ibid.

25. Gene Brown, *Movie Time: A Chronology of Hollywood and the Movie Industry from Its Beginning* (New York: Macmillan, 1995), p. 409.

26. Phone interview with Michael Kamen, August 22, 1997. Mr. Kamen offered me informative insights on his progression from classical oboist to film composer.

27. Liner notes for the *Brazil* soundtrack CD, Milan 35636-2.

28. Fred Karlin, *Listening to Movies* (New York: Schirmer Books, 1994), p. 252.

29. Michael Kamen, Liner notes for the soundtrack of *The Dead Zone*, a Milan CD, no. 35694-2.

30. Stephen Herek, Liner notes for the soundtrack of *Mr. Holland's Opus*, a London CD, no. 452 065-2.

31. Ibid.

32. Lucas Kendall, "Elliot Goldenthal," Interview in *Film Score Monthly*, nos. 41/42/43 (January/February/March 1994), p. 14

33. Ibid.

34. Mary Campbell, "A Composer Who Can Handle Batman, Beowulf, or Ballet," *The Flint Journal*, 29 December 1996, p. F4.

35. Ibid.

36. Karlan, p. 250.

37. Wayne Jancik and Tad Lathrop, *Cult Movies* (New York: Simon and Schuster, 1955), p. 209.

38. Ibid.

39. Tony Thomas, *Film Score: The Art and Craft of Movie Music* (Burbank, California: Riverwood Press, 1991), pp. 71–72.

40. Karlin, p. 15.

Bibliography

The following list represents the major sources used in writing this text. This list includes written sources; it does not include interviews that the author held with various film composers.

   To assist the reader, the bibliographic entries have been divided into two categories: books (including general reference works; biographies and autobiographies; general histories of film; books on film music; and works on such subjects as television, film genres, and specific films) and articles from periodicals. Because some periodicals, such as *Film Score Monthly*, have included so many film-music articles, including interviews with composers, only the most essential ones have been included in this list.

   Additionally, liner notes for film-music recordings have included much relevant information on composers and their scores. Especially helpful have been the recordings in the RCA "Classic Film Scores" series. Although liner notes are not included in the bibliography, their importance to the writing of *The Invisible Art of Film Music* must be acknowledged.

BOOKS

Anderson, Gillian B., *Music for Silent Films, 1894–1929: A Guide*. Washington, D.C.: Library of Congress, 1988.

Ash, Russell, *The Top Ten of Everything*. New York: Dorling Kindersley, 1994.

Barrios, Richard, *A Song in the Dark: The Birth of the Musical Film*. New York: Oxford University Press, 1995.

Baxter, John, *Sixty Years of Hollywood*. South Brunswick, NJ and New York: A. S. Barnes, 1973.

Berger, Arthur, *Aaron Copland*. New York: Oxford University Press, 1953.

Biskind, Peter, *The Godfather Companion*. New York: HarperCollins, 1990.

Bohn, Thomas W., and Richard Stromgren, *Light and Shadows: A History of Motion Pictures*. Port Washington, NY: Alfred Publishing Co., 1975.

Bookbinder, Robert, *The Films of the Seventies*. Secaucus, NJ: The Citadel Press, 1982.

Bookspan, Martin, and Ross Yockey, *André Previn: A Biography*. New York: Doubleday, 1981.

Bradley, Edwin M., *The First Hollywood Musicals: A Critical Filmography of 171 Features, 1927 through 1932*. Jefferson, NC.: McFarland & Co., 1996.

Bridges, Herb, and Terryl C. Boodman, *Gone with the Wind: The Definitive Illustrated History of the Book, the Movie, and the Legend.* New York: Simon and Schuster, 1989.

Brode, Douglas. *The Films of the Eighties.* Secaucus, NJ: The Citadel Press, 1990.

———, *The Films of the Fifties.* Secaucus, NJ: The Citadel Press, 1976.

———, *The Films of the Sixties.* Secaucus, NJ: The Citadel Press, 1980.

———, *Lost Films of the Fifties.* Secaucus, NJ: The Citadel Press, 1988.

Bronson, Fred, *Billboard's Hot 100 Hits.* New York: Billboard Books, 1991.

Brooks, Elston, *I've Heard Those Songs Before: The Weekly Top Ten Tunes for the Last Fifty Years.* New York: William Morrow, 1981.

Brooks, Tim, and Earle Marsh, *The Complete Directory to Prime Time Network TV Shows; 1946–Present.* 4th ed. New York: Ballantine Books, 1988.

Brown, Gene, *Movie Time: A Chronology of Hollywood and the Movie Industry from Its Beginning.* New York: Macmillan, 1995.

Brown, Royal S., *Overtones and Undertones: Reading Film Music.* Berkeley: University of California Press, 1994.

Burkhart, Jeff, and Bruce Stuart, *Hollywood's First Choices.* New York: Crown Publishers, 1994.

Burlingame, Jon, *TV's Biggest Hits: The Story of Television Themes from "Dragnet" to "Friends."* New York: Schirmer Books, 1996.

Buxton, Frank, and Bill Owen, *The Big Broadcast: 1920–1950.* New York: Viking, 1972.

Cader, Michael, ed.-in-chief. *1996 People Entertainment Almanac.* New York: Little, Brown and Co., 1995.

Capra, Frank, *The Name above the Title.* New York: Macmillan, 1971.

Case, Brian, and Stan Britt, *The Harmony Illustrated Encyclopedia of Jazz.* 3rd ed. Revised and updated by Chrissie Murray. New York: Harmony Books, 1986.

Castleman, Harry, and Walter J. Podrazik, *Watching TV: Four Decades of American Television.* New York: McGraw-Hill, 1982.

Cawkwell, Tim, and John M. Smith, eds., *The World Encyclopedia of Film.* New York: World Publishing, 1972.

Cook, David, *A History of Narrative Film.* New York: W. W. Norton, 1981.

Copland, Aaron, *Copland on Music.* New York: W. W. Norton, 1963.

———, What to Listen for in Music, rev. ed. New York: Mentor, 1957.

Crowther, Bosley, *The Great Films: Fifty Golden Years of Motion Pictures.* New York: G. P. Putnam's Sons, 1967.

D'Arc, James, and John W. Gillespie, *The Max Steiner Collection.* Provo, UT: Brigham Young University, 1996.

David Lean's Film of "Doctor Zhivago." New York: Alsid Distributors, 1965.

De Forest, Lee, *Father of Radio: The Autobiography of Lee De Forest.* Chicago: Wilcox and Follett, 1950.

Dobrin, Arnold, *Aaron Copland: His Life and Times.* New York: Thomas Y. Crowell, 1967.

Duchen, Jessica, *Erich Wolfgang Korngold*. London: Phaidon Press, 1996.

Elley, Derek, ed., *The Chronicle of the Movies: A Year-by-Year History from "The Jazz Singer" to Today*. Toronto: B. Mitchell, 1991.

Ewen, David, *All the Years of American Popular Music*. Englewood Cliffs, NJ: Prentice-Hall, 1977.

——, *American Composers Today*. New York: H. W. Wilson, 1949.

——, *American Songwriters*. New York: H. W. Wilson, 1987.

——, *Composers Since 1900: A Biographical and Critical Guide*. New York: H. W. Wilson, 1969.

——, *Composers Since 1900: First Supplement*. New York: H. W. Wilson, 1981.

——, *The World of Twentieth Century Music*. Englewood Cliffs, NJ: Prentice-Hall, 1968.

Finler, Joel W., *The Hollywood Story*. New York: Crown Publishers, 1988.

Francillon, Vincent J., and Stephen C. Smith, comps. and eds., *Film Composers Guide*. 2nd ed. Los Angeles: Lone Eagle Publishing Co., 1994.

Frischauer, Willi, *Behind the Scenes of Otto Preminger*. New York: William Morrow, 1974.

Gabler, Neal, *An Empire of Their Own: How the Jews Invented Hollywood*. New York: Anchor Books, 1988.

Geduld, Harry M., *The Birth of the Talkies: From Edison to Jolson*. Bloomington, IN: Indiana University Press, 1975.

Glinsky, Albert Vincent, *The Theremin in the Emergence of Electronic Music*. Unpublished doctoral dissertation. New York: New York University, 1992.

Goldner, Orville, and George E. Turner, *The Making of King Kong*. South Brunswick, NJ and New York: A. S. Barnes, 1975.

Green, Stanley, *Hollywood Musicals Year by Year*. Milwaukee: Hal Leonard, 1990.

Guerif, François, *Clint Eastwood: The Man and His Films*. New York: St. Martin's Press, 1984.

Hamlisch, Marvin, with Gerald Gardner, *The Way I Was*. New York: Charles Scribner's Sons, 1992.

Hirschhorn, Clive, *The Hollywood Musical*, 3rd impression, revised and updated. New York: Crown Publishers, 1983.

Hofmann, Charles, *Sounds for Silents*. New York: DBS Publications, 1970.

Holden, Anthony, *Behind the Oscar: The Secret History of the Academy Awards*. New York: Simon and Schuster, 1993.

Hollis, Richard, and Brian Sibley, *The Disney Studio Story*. New York: Crown Publishers, 1988.

Jancik, Wayne, and Tad Lathrop, *Cult Rockers*. New York: Simon and Schuster, 1995.

Jewell, Richard, with Vernon Harbin, *The RKO Story*. New Rochelle, NY: Arlington House, 1982.

Kalinak, Kathryn, *Settling the Score: Music and the Classical Hollywood Film*. Madison: University of Wisconsin Press, 1992.

Karlin, Fred, *Listening to Movies*. New York: Schirmer Books, 1994.

Karney, Robyn, ed., *Chronicle of the Cinema*. New York: Dorling Kindersley, 1995.

Katz, Ephraim, *The Film Encyclopedia*, 2nd ed. New York: HarperCollins, 1994.

Knight, Arthur, *The Liveliest Art*, rev. ed. New York: Macmillan, 1978.

Lambert, Gavin, *GWTW: The Making of Gone with the Wind*. Boston: Atlantic Monthly Press, 1973.

Larkin, Rochelle, *Hail, Columbia*. New Rochelle, NY: Arlington House, 1975.

Lloyd, Ann, ed., *70 Years at the Movies*. New York: Crescent Books, 1988.

McBride, Joseph, ed., *Film Makers on Film Making: The American Film Institute Seminars on Motion Pictures and Television*. 2 vols. Boston: Houghton Mifflin, 1983.

MacGowan, Kenneth, *Behind the Screen*. New York: Dell Publishing Co., 1965.

Machlis, Joseph, *Introduction to Contemporary Music*, 2nd ed. New York: W. W. Norton, 1979.

McNeil, Alex, *Total Television: A Comprehensive Guide to Programming from 1948 to the Present*, 3rd ed. New York: Penguin Books, 1991.

Maltin, Leonard, *The Disney Films*, abridged and updated. New York: Popular Library, 1978.

——, ed., *Leonard Maltin's Movie Encyclopedia*. New York: Plume, 1995.

——, ed., *Leonard Maltin's 1997 Movie & Video Guide*. New York: Signet, 1996.

Mancini, Henry, with Gene Lees, *Did They Mention the Music?* Chicago: Contemporary Books, 1989.

Manvell, Roger, ed., *International Encyclopedia of Film*. New York: Crown Publishers, 1972.

Matthews, Charles, *Oscar A to Z: A Complete Guide to More Than 2,400 Movies Nominated for Academy Awards*. New York: Doubleday, 1995.

Michael, Paul, ed., *The American Movies Reference Book: The Sound Era*. Englewood Cliffs, NJ: Prentice Hall, 1969.

Miller, Frank, *Casablanca: 50th Anniversary*. London: Virgin Books, 1993.

Monaco, James, and the editors of Baseline, *The Encyclopedia of Film*. New York: Perigee Books, 1991.

Morehead, Philip D., with Anne MacNeil, *The New American Dictionary of Music*. New York: Dutton, 1991.

Morella, Joe, Edward Z. Epstein, and John Griggs, *The Films of World War II*. Secaucus, NJ: Citadel Press, 1973.

Moses, Robert, and Beth Rowen, eds., *1996 Information Please Entertainment Almanac*. Boston: Houghton Mifflin, 1995.

Murrells, Joseph, *Million Selling Records: From the 1900s to the 1980s*. New York: Arco Publishing Co., 1984.

Nestyev, Israel V., *Prokofiev*. Translated by Florence Jonas. Stanford: Stanford University Press, 1960.

The New York Times Directory of the Film. New York: Arno Press, 1971.

Norman, Barry, *The Story of Hollywood.* New York: New American Library, 1987.

Palmer, Christopher, *The Composer in Hollywood.* London: Marion Boyars, 1990.

——, *Dimitri Tiomkin: A Portrait.* London: T. E. Books, 1984.

Peyser, Joan, *Bernstein: A Biography.* New York: William Morrow, 1987.

Pratley, Gerald, *The Cinema of David Lean.* London: The Tantivy Press, 1974.

Preminger, Otto, *Preminger: An Autobiography.* Garden City, NY: Doubleday, 1977.

Prendergast, Roy M., *Film Music: A Neglected Art*, 2nd ed. New York: W. W. Norton, 1992.

Previn, André, *No Minor Chords: My Days in Hollywood.* New York: Doubleday, 1991.

Quigley, Martin, Jr., and Richard Gertner. *Films in America 1929–1969.* New York: Golden Press, 1970.

Quirk, Lawrence J., *The Great War Films: From "The Birth of a Nation" to Today.* Secaucus, NJ: The Citadel Press, 1994.

Robertson, Patrick, *Guinness Film Facts and Feats*, new ed. Middlesex, England: Guinness Superlatives, 1985.

Robinson, David, *Chaplin: His Life and Art.* New York: McGraw-Hill, 1985.

Robinson, Harlow, *Sergei Prokofiev: A Biography.* New York: Viking, 1987.

Robinson, Paul, *Bernstein.* New York: Vanguard, 1982.

Rosen, Craig, *The Billboard Book of Number One Albums: The Inside Story behind Pop Music's Blockbuster Records.* New York: Billboard Books, 1996.

Rozsa, Miklos, *Double Life.* London: Midas Books, 1982. New York: Wynwood Press, 1989.

Sackett, Susan, *The Hollywood Reporter Book of Box-Office Hits.* New York: Billboard Books, 1990.

——, *Hollywood Sings!: An Inside Look at Sixty Years of Academy-Nominated Songs.* New York: Billboard Books, 1995.

Sadie, Stanley, ed., *The Norton/Grove Concise Encyclopedia of Music.* New York: W. W. Norton, 1988.

Sennett, Ted, *Warner Brothers Presents: The Most Exciting Years—from "The Jazz Singer" to "White Heat."* New York: Castle Books, 1971.

Shipman, David, *Cinema: The First Hundred Years.* New York: St. Martin's Press, 1993.

——, *The Story of Cinema.* New York: St. Martin's Press, 1982.

Silverman, Stephen M., *David Lean.* New York: Harry M. Abrams, 1989.

Smith, Stephen C., *A Heart at Fire's Center: The Life and Music of Bernard Herrmann.* Berkeley: University of California Press, 1991.

The Story of the Making of "Ben-Hur." New York: Random House, 1959.

Theroux, Gary, and Bob Gilbert, *The Top Ten: 1956–Present*. New York: Simon and Schuster, 1982.

Thomas, Tony, *Film Score: The Art & Craft of Movie Music*. A revised and expanded edition of *Film Score: The View from the Podium*. Burbank, CA: Riverwood Press, 1991.

———, *The Films of the Forties*. Secaucus, NJ: Citadel Press, 1975.

———, *The Great Adventure Films*. Secaucus, NJ: Citadel Press, 1976.

———, *Harry Warren and the Hollywood Musical*. Secaucus, NJ: Citadel Press, 1975.

———, *Music for the Movies*. South Brunswick, NJ and New York: A. S. Barnes, 1973.

Tietyen, David, *The Musical World of Walt Disney*. Milwaukee: Hal Leonard, 1990.

Tiomkin, Dimitri, and Prosper Buranelli, *Please Don't Hate Me*. New York: Doubleday, 1959.

Vaines, Colin, *Anatomy of the Movies*, 2nd ed. New York: Macmillan, 1981.

van Gelder, Peter, *That's Hollywood: A Behind-the-Scenes Look at 60 of the Greatest Films Ever Made*. New York: HarperCollins Publishers, 1990.

Von Gunden, Kenneth, and Stuart H. Stock, *Twenty All-Time Great Science-Fiction Films*. New Rochelle, NY: Arlington House, 1982.

Walker, John, ed., *Halliwell's Filmgoer's & Video Viewer's Companion*, 12th ed. New York: HarperCollins, 1997.

Weiner, Ed, and the editors of TV Guide, *The TV Guide TV Book*. New York: HarperCollins Publishers, 1992.

Welles, Orson, and Peter Bogdanovich, *This Is Orson Welles*. New York: HarperCollins Publishers, 1992.

Wiley, Mason, and Damien Bona, *Inside Oscar*, 10th anniversary ed. New York: Ballantine Books, 1996.

Wilson, Arthur, comp. and ed., *The Warner Bros. Golden Anniversary Book*. New York: Dell, 1973.

Zinman, David, *50 Classic Motion Pictures: The Stuff That Dreams Are Made of*. New York: Crown Publishers, 1970.

Zinnemann, Fred, *A Life in the Movies: An Autobiography*. New York: Charles Scribner's Sons, 1992.

ARTICLES

Ahrens, Dennis, "John Williams Strikes Back! or, The Soundtrack Continues," *Starlog*, no. 37 (August 1980): 29–30.

Behlmer, Rudy, "Erich Wolfgang Korngold," *Films in Review* 18, no. 2 (February 1967): 86–100.

Bernstein, Elmer, "What Ever Happened to Great Movie Music?," *High Fidelity* 22, no. 7 (July 1972): 55–58.

Burlingame, Jon, "John Barry," *Premiere* 4, no. 4 (December 1990): 65–66.

Caps, John, "An Interview with Richard Rodney Bennett," *High Fidelity* 27, no. 6 (June 1977): 58–62.

Clement, Thom, "Composer Elmer Bernstein: Scoring Fantasy Films," *Starlog*, no. 103 (February 1986): 68–71.

Cook, Page, "Bernard Herrmann," *Films in Review* 18, no. 7 (August–September 1967): 398–412.

———, "Franz Waxman," *Films in Review* 19, no. 7 (August–September 1968): 415–30.

Dobroski, Bernie, and Claire Greene, "Pass the Popcorn: An Interview with John Williams," *The Instrumentalist* 38, no. 12 (July 1984): 6–9.

Doeckel, Ken, "Miklos Rozsa," *Films in Review* 16, no. 9 (November 1965): 536–48.

Haun, Harry, and George Raborn, "Max Steiner," *Films in Review* 12, no. 6 (June–July 1961): 338–51.

Hirsch, David, "Composer of the Fantastic," *Starlog*, no. 172 (November 1991): 56–60, 72.

———, "Music for RoboCop," *Starlog*, no. 62 (November 1993): 58–63.

Horton, Robert, "Miklos Rozsa: Music Man," *Film Comment* 31, no. 6 (November– December 1995): 2–4.

Houston, David, "Miklos Rozsa," *Starlog*, no. 31 (February 1980): 47–49.

Hutchison, David, "Music for a Barbarian," *Starlog*, no. 62 (September 1982): 24–25, 65.

Jacobs, Jack, "Alfred Newman," *Films in Review* 10, no. 7 (August–September 1959): 403–14.

Kendall, Lukas, "Interview: Elliot Goldenthal," *Film Score Monthly*, no. 41/42/43 (January/February/March 1994): 14–16.

Kennedy, Harlan, "The Harmonious Background," *American Film* 16, no. 2 (February 1991): 39–46.

Kolodin, Irving, "The Wide Screen World of Bernard Herrmann," *Saturday Review* 3, no. 11 (March 6, 1976): 35–38.

Kreuger, Miles, "The Birth of the American Film Musical," *High Fidelity* 22, no. 7 (July 1972): 42–48.

Larson, Randall, "Alan Silvestri: Tunes for Toons," *Starlog*, no. 135 (October 1988): 19–23, 44.

Lyons, Len, "Michel Legrand: Pianist, Songwriter, Film Composer," *Contemporary Keyboard* 3, no. 10 (October 1977): 20, 51.

Pirani, Adam, "J. G. Ballard: Abandoned Worlds, Fantasy Landscapes," *Starlog*, no. 126 (January 1988): 28–31, 58.

Sciacca, Tom, "James Horner: New Melodies for the Starship 'Enterprise,'" *Starlog*, no. 63 (October 1982): 22–23.

Sheff, Victoria, "Lalo Schifrin: Profile," *BMI Music World* (Winter 1989): 53–55.

Siders, Harvey, "Bill Conti," *BMI: The Many Worlds of Music*, Issue 2 (1977): 35.

Simels, Steve, and Gerald Carpenter, "Elmer Bernstein: The Dean of American Movie Music," *Stereo Review* 58, no. 9 (September 1993): 73–75.

Soter, Tom, "License to Score," *Starlog*, no. 199 (February 1994): 41–45.

Spotnitz, Frank, "Dialogue on Film: Alan Silvestri," *American Film* 16, no. 8 (August 1991): 14–17.

Stearns, David Patrick, "They Don't Get No Respect: The Tough, Unglamorous World of the Movie Composer," *A & E Monthly* 9, no. 2 (February 1994): 51–54.

Thomas, Tony, "David Raksin," *Films in Review* 14, no. 1 (January 1963): 38–41.

———, "Hugo Friedhofer," *Films in Review* 16, no. 8 (October 1965): 496–502.

Windeler, Robert, "André Previn: Who Wants Me in May 1978?," *Stereo Review* 27, no. 3 (September 1971): 48–57.

Yakir, Dan, "The Men Who Score in Hollywood," *A & E Monthly* 10, no. 11 (November 1995): 34–37.

Filmography

The following listing includes 570 films that are commented upon in the text. Those whose titles appear in boldface receive more extensive coverage. For each film the following information is included: the year of release, the director, the composer, the studio that released the film, recordings of the film's music, and video releases, including those on video tape (VHS) and those in laser disk format (LD).

For the studio listings, the following abbreviations have been used:

AA = Allied Artists	DW = DreamWorks	PR = Paramount
AE = Avco Embassy	EL = Eagle Lion	RKO = RKO Films
AF = Alive Films	EM = Embassy	RP = Republic
AFD = Associated Film Distribution	FL = FineLine	SG = Samuel Goldwyn
	FS = Fox Searchlight	SZ = Selznick
AI = American International	GR = Gramercy	TS = TriStar
	LA = Landau	20th = 20th Century-Fox
BS = Belgoskino Studios	LO = Lopert	
	MGM = Metro-Goldwyn-Mayer	UA = United Artists
BV = Buena Vista		UMC = UMC Pictures, Inc.
CC = Cinecom	MI = Mier	
C5 = Cinema 5	MOS = Mosfilm	UN = Universal
CL = Claridge	MR = Miramax	USG = U.S. Government
CO = Columbia	NG = National General	WB = Warner Bros.
CR = Cinerama	NLC = New Line Cinema	WP = World Pictures

For the recording listings, the following procedure has been used. If an original score (or actual soundtrack) album has been released, an asterisk appears. For those films which have had a compact disc (CD) release of the original score, the symbol "CD*" appears. In cases where there has been an LP (33⅓ rpm) soundtrack album of the score but no CD reissue, "LP*" appears. Studio remakes of original scores are marked with a plus sign, as in "LP+" or "CD+." Recordings of movie themes or excerpts of film scores are marked with an "x," as in "LPx" or "CDx." Since some films (such as *Gone with the Wind* and *Ben-Hur*) have generated a large number of different recordings, only the most recent releases are indicated. In other cases there have been few, if any, recordings; thus, the listing indicates whether an LP or CD with music from a particular film has ever been released.

This list includes some items that have had only limited releases, and others that have been available only as imports. Because many film-music recordings are issued and withdrawn within the space of a few years, it is impossible to give a completely accurate list of available recordings. It is suggested that this list be used as a basic guide to the existence of film music in the LP and CD formats. In many cities there are collector shops with extensive stockpiles of film-music LPs and CDs. Additionally, there are mail-order businesses. Since many film-music albums are often collectible in both LP and CD formats, prices may vary widely. Price guides for sound-track LPs and CDs have been published (copies of which may be found in some public-library reference collections). Publications such as *Film Score Monthly* often include lists of recordings available for sale and/or trade.

Title	Year	Director	Composer	Studio	Recordings	Video
A ••••						
Abyss, The	1989	J. Cameron	A. Silvestri	20th	CD*x	VHS LD
Accidental Tourist, The	1988	L. Kasdan	J. Williams	WB	CD*	VHS LD
Adventures of Don Juan, The	1949	V. Sherman	M. Steiner	WB	CDx	VHS LD
Adventures of Robin Hood, The	1938	M. Curtiz/ W. Keighley	E. Korngold	WB	CD+x	VHS LD
Affair to Remember, An	1957	L. McCarey	H. Friedhofer	20th	CD*	VHS LD
Age of Innocence, The	1993	M Scorsese	E. Bernstein	CO	CD*x	VHS LD
Agnes of God	1985	N. Jewison	G. Delerue	CO	CD*x	VHS LD
Agony and the Ecstasy, The	1965	C. Reed	A. North/ J. Goldsmith	20th	CD*	VHS LD
Air Force One	1997	W. Petersen	J. Goldsmith	CO	CD*	VHS LD
Airport	1970	G. Seaton	A. Newman	UN	CD*x	VHS LD
Alamo, The	1960	J. Wayne	D. Tiomkin	UA	CD*x	VHS LD
Alexander Nevsky	1938	S. Eisenstein	S. Prokofiev	MOS	CD*+	VHS LD
Alien	1979	R. Scott	J. Goldsmith	20th	CD*x	VHS LD
All about Eve	1950	J. Mankiewicz	A. Newman	20th	CDx	VHS LD
All That Jazz	1979	B. Fosse	R. Burns/et al.	CO/20th	CD*	VHS LD
All the King's Men	1949	R. Rossen	L. Gruenberg	CO		VHS LD
Altered States	1980	K. Russell	J. Corigliano	WB	CD*	VHS LD
American Graffiti	1973	G. Lucas	various	UN	CD*	VHS LD
Amistad	1997	S. Spielberg	J. Williams	DW	CD*	
Amityville Horror, The	1979	S. Rosenberg	L. Schifrin	AI	LP*	VHS LD
Anastasia	1956	A. Litvak	A. Newman	20th	CD*x	VHS LD
Anastasia	1997	D. Bluth	D. Newman	20th	CD*	VHS LD
Anatomy of a Murder	1959	O. Preminger	D. Ellington	CO	CD*	VHS LD
Anna and the King of Siam	1946	J. Cromwell	B. Herrmann	20th	CDx	VHS
Anthony Adverse	1936	M. LeRoy	E. Korngold	WB	CD+x	VHS LD
Apartment, The	1960	B. Wilder	A. Deutsch	UA	LP*	VHS LD
Apocalypse Now	1979	F. F. Coppola	C. Coppola/ F. F. Coppola	UA	CD*	VHS LD
Around the World in Eighty Days	1956	M. Anderson	V. Young	UA	CD*x	VHS LD
Auntie Mame	1958	M. DaCosta	B. Kaper	WB	LP*	VHS LD
Avalon	1990	B. Levinson	R. Newman	TS	CD*	VHS LD
Awakenings	1990	P. Marshall	R. Newman	CO	CD*	VHS LD
B ••••						
Back to the Future	1985	R. Zemeckis	A. Silvestri	UN	CD*x	VHS LD
Bad and the Beautiful, The	1952	V. Minnelli	D. Raksin	MGM	CD*x	VHS LD
Bad Seed, The	1956	M. LeRoy	A. North	WB	LP*/CDx	VHS LD
Bambi	1942	D. Hand	F. Churchill/ E. Plumb	RKO	CD*x	VHS LD

Title	Year	Director	Composer	Studio	Recordings	Video
Barretts of Wimpole Street, The	1957	S. Franklin	B. Kaper	MGM		VHS LD
Barry Lyndon	1975	S. Kubrick	L. Rosenman	WB	CD*	VHS LD
Basic Instinct	1992	P. Verhoeven	J. Goldsmith	TS	CD*x	VHS LD
Batman	1989	T. Burton	D. Elfman	WB	CD*x	VHS LD
Battle of Neretva, The	1971	V. Bulajic	B. Herrmann	AI	CD*x	VHS
Bear, The	1989	J.- J. Annaud	P. Sarde	TS	CD*	VHS LD
Beauty and the Beast	1991	G. Trousdale/ K. Wise	A. Menken	BV	CD*x	VHS LD
Becket	1964	P. Glenville	L. Rosenthal	PR	LP*	VHS LD
Beetlejuice	1988	T. Burton	D. Elfman	WB	CD*x	VHS LD
Beneath the Planet of the Apes	1970	T. Post	L. Rosenman	20th	LP*	VHS LD
Beneath the 12-Mile Reef	1953	R. Webb	B. Herrmann	20th	CDx	VHS LD
Ben-Hur	1959	W. Wyler	M. Rozsa	MGM	CD*+x	VHS LD
Benny & Joon	1993	J. Chechik	R. Portman	MGM	CD*	VHS LD
Best Years of Our Lives, The	1946	W. Wyler	H. Friedhofer	RKO	CD+	VHS LD
Big Country, The	1958	W. Wyler	J. Moross	UA	CD*+x	VHS LD
Billion Dollar Brain	1967	K. Russell	R. R. Bennett	UA	LP*/CDx	
Bill of Divorcement, A	1932	G. Cukor	M. Steiner	RKO	CDx	VHS
Bird of Paradise	1932	K. Vidor	M. Steiner	RKO	CDx	VHS
Bite the Bullet	1975	R. Brooks	A. North	CO	CD*	VHS LD
Black Hole, The	1979	G. Nelson	J. Barry	BV	LP*/CDx	VHS LD
Black Swan, The	1942	H. King	A. Newman	20th		VHS
Blazing Saddles	1974	M. Brooks	J. Morris	WB	LPx	VHS LD
Blue Max, The	1966	J. Guillermin	J. Goldsmith	20th	CD*	VHS LD
Body Heat	1981	L. Kasdan	J. Barry	WB	CD*x	VHS LD
Bonnie and Clyde	1967	A. Penn	C. Strouse	WB	LP*	VHS LD
Born Free	1966	J. Hill	J. Barry	MGM	LP*/CDx	VHS LD
Born on the Fourth of July	1989	O. Stone	J. Williams	UN	CD*x	VHS LD
Boys from Brazil, The	1978	F. J. Schaffner	J. Goldsmith	20th	CD*	VHS LD
Brainstorm	1983	D. Trumbull	J. Horner	MGM/UA	CD*	VHS LD
Breakfast at Tiffany's	1961	B. Edwards	H. Mancini	PR	CD*x	VHS LD
Bride of Frankenstein, The	1935	J. Whale	F. Waxman	UN	CD+x	VHS LD
Bridge on the River Kwai, The	1957	D. Lean	M. Arnold	CO	CD*x	VHS LD
Bridge Too Far, A	1977	R. Attenborough	J. Addison	UA	LP*/CDx	VHS LD
Broadway Melody, The	1929	H. Beaumont	N. H. Brown	MGM	LP*/CDx	VHS LD
Bugsy	1991	B. Levinson	E. Morricone	TS	CD*x	VHS LD
'burbs, The	1989	J. Dante	J. Goldsmith	UN	CD*	VHS LD
Butch Cassidy and the Sundance Kid	1969	G. R. Hill	B. Bacharach	20th	CD*	VHS LD

C····

Title	Year	Director	Composer	Studio	Recordings	Video
Caine Mutiny, The	1954	E. Dmytryk	M. Steiner	CO	LP*/CDx	VHS LD
Cape Fear	1962	J. Lee Thompson	B. Herrmann	UN	CDx	VHS LD
Capricorn One	1978	P. Hyams	J. Goldsmith	WB	CD*x	VHS LD
Captain from Castile	1947	H. King	A. Newman	20th	LP*/CDx	VHS LD
Captains Courageous	1937	V. Fleming	F. Waxman	MGM	CDx	VHS LD
Caretakers, The	1963	H. Bartlett	E. Bernstein	UA	CD*	VHS
Carpetbaggers, The	1964	E. Dmytryk	E. Bernstein	PR	LP*	VHS LD

Title	Year	Director	Composer	Studio	Recordings	Video
Carrie	1952	W. Wyler	D. Raksin	PR		VHS LD
Carrie	1976	B. De Palma	P. Donaggio	UA	CD*	VHS LD
Casablanca	1943	M. Curtiz	M. Steiner	WB	CD*x	VHS LD
Cassandra Crossing, The	1977	G. P. Cosmatos	J. Goldsmith	AE	CD*	VHS
Casualties of War	1989	B. De Palma	E. Morricone	CO	CD*x	VHS LD
Chalk Garden, The	1964	R. Neame	M. Arnold	UN		VHS
Champion	1949	M. Robson	D. Tiomkin	UA		VHS LD
Charge of the Light Brigade, The	1936	M. Curtiz	M. Steiner	WB	CDx	VHS LD
Chariots of Fire	1981	H. Hudson	Vangelis	WB	CD*x	VHS LD
Chinatown	1974	R. Polanski	J. Goldsmith	PR	CD*x	VHS LD
Cimarron	1931	W. Ruggles	M. Steiner	RKO		VHS
Cinema Paradiso	1989	G. Tornatore	E. Morricone	MR	CD*x	VHS LD
Citizen Kane	1941	O. Welles	B. Herrmann	RKO	CD+x	VHS LD
Clash of the Titans	1981	D. Davis	L. Rosenthal	MGM	LP*/CDx	VHS LD
Clockwork Orange, A	1971	S. Kubrick	W. Carlos	WB	CD*	VHS LD
Close Encounters of the Third Kind	1977	S. Spielberg	J. Williams	CO	CD*x	VHS LD
Cobweb, The	1955	V. Minnelli	L. Rosenman	MGM	LP*	LD
Coma	1978	M. Crichton	J. Goldsmith	MGM	CD*	VHS LD
Comancheros, The	1961	M. Curtiz	E. Bernstein	20th	CD+	VHS
Come and Get It	1936	H. Hawks/ W. Wyler	A. Newman	UA		VHS LD
Conan the Barbarian	1982	J. Milius	B. Poledouris	UN	CD*x	VHS LD
Constant Nymph, The	1943	E. Goulding	E. Korngold	WB	CDx	
Contact	1997	R. Zemeckis	A. Silvestri	WB	CD*	VHS LD
Cool Hand Luke	1967	S. Rosenberg	L. Schifrin	WB	LP*/CDx	VHS LD
Cowboys, The	1972	M. Rydell	J. Williams	WB	CD*x	VHS LD
Cry Freedom	1987	R. Attenborough	G. Fenton/ J. Gwangwa	UN	CD*	VHS LD
Cyrano de Bergerac	1950	M. Gordon	D. Tiomkin	UA		VHS LD

D....

Damien—Omen II	1978	D. Taylor	J. Goldsmith	20th	CD*	VHS LD
Damnation Alley	1977	J. Smight	J. Goldsmith	20th	CDx	VHS
Dances with Wolves	1990	K. Costner	J. Barry	Orion	CD*x	VHS LD
Dangerous Liaisons	1988	S. Frears	G. Fenton	WB	CD*	VHS LD
Darling Lili	1970	B. Edwards	H. Mancini	PR	LP*x	
Days of Heaven	1978	T. Malick	E. Morricone	PR	LP*	VHS LD
Days of Wine and Roses	1962	B. Edwards	H. Mancini	WB	CDx	VHS LD
Day the Earth Stood Still, The	1951	R. Wise	B. Herrmann	20th	CD*x	VHS LD
Dead Men Don't Wear Plaid	1982	C. Reiner	M. Rozsa	UN	CD*x	VHS LD
Dead Poets Society	1989	P. Weir	M. Jarre	BV	CD*x	VHS LD
Dead Ringer	1964	P. Henreid	A. Previn	WB	LP*	VHS LD
Death on the Nile	1978	J. Guillermin	N. Rota	PR	CD*	VHS LD
Deception	1946	I. Rapper	E. Korngold	WB	CDx	VHS
Deliverance	1972	J. Boorman	E. Weissberg	WB	CD*	VHS LD
Desire under the Elms	1958	D. Mann	E. Bernstein	PR	LP*	VHS LD
Devil and Daniel Webster, The	1941	W. Dieterle	B. Herrmann	RKO	CDx	VHS LD
Devil's Own, The	1997	A. Pakula	J. Horner	CO	CD*	VHS LD
Dial M for Murder	1954	A. Hitchcock	D. Tiomkin	WB	CDx	VHS LD
Diary of Anne Frank, The	1959	G. Stevens	A. Newman	20th	LP*	VHS LD

Title	Year	Director	Composer	Studio	Recordings	Video
Dirty Dozen, The	1967	R. Aldrich	F. De Vol	MGM	CD*x	VHS LD
D.O.A.	1950	R. Maté	D. Tiomkin	UA		VHS LD
Doctor Zhivago	1965	D. Lean	M. Jarre	MGM	CD*x	VHS LD
Dodsworth	1936	W. Wyler	A. Newman	UA		VHS LD
Don Juan	1926	A. Crosland	W. Axt/ D. Mendoza	WB		VHS LD
Double Indemnity	1944	B. Wilder	M. Rozsa	PR	CDx	VHS LD
Double Life, A	1947	G. Cukor	M. Rozsa	UN	CDx	VHS
Dragonslayer	1981	M. Robbins	A. North	PR	CD*x	VHS LD
Dreamscape	1984	J. Ruben	M. Jarre	20th	CD*	VHS LD
Duel in the Sun	1946	K. Vidor	D. Tiomkin	SZ	CDx	VHS

E•••••

Title	Year	Director	Composer	Studio	Recordings	Video
East of Eden	1955	E. Kazan	L. Rosenman	WB	CDx	VHS LD
Easy Rider	1969	D. Hopper	R. McGuinn/ et al.	CO	LP*	VHS LD
Edge, The	1997	L. Tamahori	J. Goldsmith	20th	CD*	VHS LD
Edward Scissorhands	1990	T. Burton	D. Elfman	20th	CD*x	VHS LD
Egyption, The	1954	M. Curtiz	A. Newman/ B. Herrmann	20th	CD*	VHS LD
El Cid	1961	A. Mann	M. Rozsa	AA	CD*+x	VHS LD
Elephant Man, The	1980	D. Lynch	J. Morris	PR	CD*	VHS LD
Elmer Gantry	1960	R. Brooks	A. Previn	UA	LP*x	VHS LD
Emma	1996	D. McGrath	R. Portman	MR	CD*x	VHS LD
Empire of the Sun	1987	S. Spielberg	J. Williams	WB	CD*x	VHS LD
Empire Strikes Back, The	1980	I. Kershner	J. Williams	20th	CD*+x	VHS LD
English Patient, The	1996	A. Minghella	G. Yared	MR	CD*	VHS LD
Escape from New York	1981	J. Carpenter	J. Carpenter/ A. Howarth	AE	CD*	VHS LD
Escape Me Never	1947	P. Godfrey	E. Korngold	WB	CDx	VHS
E.T. the Extra- Terrestrial	1982	S. Spielberg	J. Williams	UN	CD*x	VHS LD
Excalibur	1981	J. Boorman	T. Jones	Orion	CD*x	VHS LD
Exodus	1960	O. Preminger	E. Gold	UA	CD*x	VHS LD
Exorcist, The	1973	W. Friedkin	M. Oldfield/ et al.	WB	LP*	VHS LD

F•••••

Title	Year	Director	Composer	Studio	Recordings	Video
Fahrenheit 451	1966	F. Truffaut	B. Herrmann	UN	CDx	VHS LD
Fall of the Roman Empire, The	1964	A. Mann	D. Tiomkin	PR	CD*x	VHS LD
Fame	1980	A. Parker	M. Gore	MGM	CD*	VHS LD
Farewell, My Lovely	1975	D. Richards	D. Shire	AE	LP*/CDx	VHS
Farewell to Arms, A	1957	C. Vidor	M. Nascimbene	20th	CD*	VHS
Far from the Madding Crowd	1967	J. Schlesinger	R. R. Bennett	MGM	CD*x	VHS LD
Field of Dreams	1989	P. A. Robinson	J. Horner	UN	CD*	VHS LD
55 Days at Peking	1963	N. Ray	D. Tiomkin	AA	CD*x	VHS LD
Firm, The	1993	S. Pollack	D. Grusin	PR	CD*x	VHS LD
First Knight	1995	J. Zucker	J. Goldsmith	CO	CD*x	VHS LD
Five Graves to Cairo	1943	B. Wilder	M. Rozsa	PR	CDx	
Flame and the Arrow, The	1950	J. Tourneur	M. Steiner	WB	CDx	VHS LD
Flubber	1997	L. Mayfield	D. Elfman	BV	CD*	VHS LD
Fly Away Home	1996	C. Ballard	M. Isham	CO		VHS LD

Title	Year	Director	Composer	Studio	Recordings	Video
Forbidden Planet	1956	F. Wilcox	L. Baron/ B. Barron	MGM	CD*x	VHS LD
Forever Amber	1947	O. Preminger	D. Raksin	20th	CD*x	VHS LD
Forever Young	1992	S. Miner	J. Goldsmith	WB	CD*x	VHS LD
Forrest Gump	1994	R. Zemeckis	A. Silvestri	PR	CD*x	VHS LD
For Whom the Bell Tolls	1943	S. Wood	V. Young	PR	CD+x	VHS LD
Fountainhead, The	1949	K. Vidor	M. Steiner	WB	CDx	VHS LD
Four Horsemen of the Apocalypse, The	1962	V. Minnelli	A. Previn	MGM	LP*x/CDx	VHS
Four Seasons, The	1981	A. Alda	A. Vivaldi	UN		VHS LD
Fox, The	1968	M. Rydell	L. Schifrin	CL	LP*	
French Connection, The	1971	W. Friedkin	D. Ellis	20th		VHS LD
French Lieutenant's Woman, The	1981	K. Reisz	C. Davis	UA	CD*	VHS LD
Freud	1962	J. Huston	J. Goldsmith	UN	LP*	
Friendly Persuasion	1956	W. Wyler	D. Tiomkin	AA	CD*x	VHS LD
From Here to Eternity	1953	F. Zinnemann	G. Duning	CO	LPx	VHS LD
Fury, The	1978	B. De Palma	J. Williams	20th	CD*	VHS LD

G.....

Title	Year	Director	Composer	Studio	Recordings	Video
Gandhi	1982	R. Attenborough	G. Fenton/ R. Shankar	CO	LP*	VHS LD
Gettysburg	1993	R. F. Maxwell	R. Edelman	NLC	CD*x	VHS LD
Ghost	1990	J. Zucker	M. Jarre	PR	CD*x	VHS LD
Ghost and Mrs. Muir, The	1947	J. Mankiewicz	B. Herrmann	20th	CD*+x	VHS LD
Giant	1956	G. Stevens	D. Tiomkin	WB	CD*x	VHS LD
Godfather, The	1972	F. F. Coppola	N. Rota	PR	CD*x	VHS LD
Godfather, Part II, The	1974	F. F. Coppola	N. Rota/ C. Coppola	PR	CD*x	VHS LD
Golden Voyage of Sinbad, The	1974	G. Hessler	M. Rozsa	CO	LP*/CDx	VHS LD
Gone with the Wind	1939	V. Fleming	M. Steiner	MGM	CD*+x	VHS LD
Good, the Bad, and the Ugly, The	1967	S. Leone	E. Morricone	UA	CD*x	VHS LD
Goodbye, Mr. Chips	1939	S. Wood	R. Addinsell	MGM	CDx	VHS LD
Good Earth, The	1937	S. Franklin	H. Stothart	MGM		VHS LD
Good Morning, Vietnam	1987	B. Levinson	A. North	BV		VHS LD
Good Son, The	1993	J. Ruben	E. Bernstein	20th	CD*	VHS LD
Good Will Hunting	1997	G. Van Sant	D. Elfman	MR	CD*	
Gorillas in the Mist	1988	M. Apted	M. Jarre	UN	CD*x	VHS LD
Graduate, The	1967	M. Nichols	D. Grusin/ P. Simon	EM	CD*	VHS LD
Grand Canyon	1991	L. Kasdan	J. N. Howard	20th	CD*x	VHS LD
Grand Illusion	1938	J. Renoir	J. Kosma	WP		VHS LD
Grapes of Wrath, The	1940	J. Ford	A. Newman	20th		VHS LD
Great Dictator, The	1940	C. Chaplin	C. Chaplin	UA	CDx	VHS LD
Great Escape, The	1963	J. Sturges	E. Bernstein	UA	CD*x	VHS LD
Greatest Show on Earth, The	1952	C. B. DeMille	V. Young	PR	CDx	VHS LD
Greatest Story Ever Told, The	1965	G. Stevens	A. Newman	UA	CD*	VHS LD
Great Gatsby, The	1974	J. Clayton	N. Riddle	PR	LP*	VHS LD

Title	Year	Director	Composer	Studio	Recordings	Video
Great Race, The	1965	B. Edwards	H. Mancini	WB	CD*x	VHS LD
Gremlins	1984	J. Dante	J. Goldsmith	WB	CD*x	VHS LD
Guns of Navarone, The	1961	J. Lee Thompson	D. Tiomkin	CO	CD*x	VHS LD

H....

Title	Year	Director	Composer	Studio	Recordings	Video
Hallelujah Trail, The	1965	J. Sturges	E. Bernstein	UA	LP*/CDx	VHS LD
Hamlet	1996	K. Branagh	P. Doyle	CO	CD*	VHS LD
Hangover Square	1945	J. Brahm	B. Herrmann	20th	CDx	
Hatari!	1962	H. Hawks	H. Mancini	PR	CD*x	VHS LD
Hawaii	1966	G. R. Hill	E. Bernstein	UA	LP*/CDx	VHS LD
Hawaiians, The	1970	T. Gries	H. Mancini	UA	LP*x	
Heartburn	1986	M. Nichols	C. Simon	PR	CDx	VHS LD
Heaven Can Wait	1978	W. Beatty/ B. Henry	D. Grusin	PR	CDx	VHS LD
Heiress, The	1949	W. Wyler	A. Copland	PR	CDx	VHS
Hemingway's Adventures of a Young Man	1962	M. Ritt	F. Waxman	20th	CD*x	
Henry V	1946	L. Olivier	W. Walton	UA	CD+x	VHS LD
Henry V	1989	K. Branagh	P. Doyle	SG	CD*x	VHS LD
High and the Mighty, The	1954	W. Wellman	D. Tiomkin	WB	LP+/CDx	
High Noon	1952	F. Zinnemann	D. Tiomkin	UA	CDx	VHS LD
Hindenburg, The	1975	R. Wise	D. Shire	UN	LP*	VHS LD
Home Alone	1990	C. Columbus	J. Williams	20th	CD*	VHS LD
Hook	1991	S. Spielberg	J. Williams	TS	CD*x	VHS LD
Hoosiers	1986	D. Anspaugh	J. Goldsmith	Orion	CD*x	VHS LD
Hope and Glory	1987	J. Boorman	P. Martin	CO	CD*	VHS LD
Hotel Paradiso	1966	P. Glenville	L. Rosenthal	MGM	LP*	VHS
Howards End	1992	J. Ivory	R. Robbins	Sony	CD*	VHS LD
How Green Was My Valley	1941	J. Ford	A. Newman	20th	CD*x	VHS LD
How the West Was Won	1963	J. Ford/et al.	A. Newman	MGM	CD*x	VHS LD
Humoresque	1946	J. Negulesco	F. Waxman	WB	CD+x	VHS LD
Hunchback of Notre Dame, The	1996	G. Trousdale/ K. Wise	A. Menken	BV	CD*x	VHS LD
Hurricane, The	1937	J. Ford	A. Newman	UA	LPx	VHS LD

I......

Title	Year	Director	Composer	Studio	Recordings	Video
I Confess	1953	A. Hitchcock	D. Tiomkin	WB		VHS LD
Images	1972	R. Altman	J. Williams	CO		
In Cold Blood	1967	R. Brooks	Q. Jones	CO	LP*	VHS LD
Indiana Jones and the Temple of Doom	1984	S. Spielberg	J. Williams	PR	CD*x	VHS LD
Informer, The	1935	J. Ford	M. Steiner	RKO	CDx	VHS LD
Inside Daisy Clover	1965	R. Mulligan	A. Previn	WB	LP*	VHS LD
Interview with the Vampire	1994	N. Jordan	E. Goldenthal	WB	CD*	VHS LD
In the Heat of the Night	1967	N. Jewison	Q. Jones	UA	CD*	VHS LD
Irma la Douce	1963	B. Wilder	A. Previn	UA	CD*	VHS LD
Island of Dr. Moreau, The	1977	D. Taylor	L. Rosenthal	AI	LP*/CDx	VHS
Islands in the Stream	1977	F. Schaffner	J. Goldsmith	PR	CD*	VHS LD
It's a Wonderful Life	1946	F. Capra	D. Tiomkin	RKO	CDx	VHS LD
Ivanhoe	1952	R. Thorpe	M. Rozsa	MGM	CD+x	VHS LD
I Want to Live	1958	R. Wise	J. Mandel	UA	LP*	VHS LD

Title	Year	Director	Composer	Studio	Recordings	Video
J ••••••						
Jane Eyre	1944	R. Stevenson	B. Herrmann	20th	CD*+x	VHS LD
Jason and the Argonauts	1963	D. Chaffey	B. Herrmann	CO	CDx	VHS LD
Jaws	1975	S. Spielberg	J. Williams	UN	CD*x	VHS LD
Jazz Singer, The	1927	A. Crosland	L. Silvers	WB	LP*/CDx	VHS LD
Jezebel	1938	W. Wyler	M. Steiner	WB	CDx	VHS LD
JFK	1991	O. Stone	J. Williams	WB	CD*	VHS LD
Johnny Belinda	1948	J. Negulesco	M. Steiner	WB	CDx	VHS
Journey to the Center of the Earth	1959	H. Levin	B. Herrmann	20th	CD*x	VHS LD
Juarez	1939	W. Dieterle	E. Korngold	WB	CDx	VHS
Julius Caesar	1953	J. Mankiewicz	M. Rozsa	MGM	CD+x	VHS LD
Jungle Book, The	1942	Z. Korda	M. Rozsa	UA	CDx	VHS LD
Jurassic Park	1993	S. Spielberg	J. Williams	UN	CD*x	VHS LD
K •••••						
Kentuckian, The	1955	B. Lancaster	B. Herrmann	PR	CD+	VHS
Killers, The	1946	R. Siodmak	M. Rozsa	UN	CDx	VHS
King Kong	1933	M. Cooper/ E. Schoedsack	M. Steiner	RKO	CD+x	VHS LD
King Kong	1976	J. Guillermin	J. Barry	PR	CD*x	VHS LD
King of Kings	1961	N. Ray	M. Rozsa	MGM	CD*x	VHS LD
King of the Khyber Rifles	1953	H. King	B. Herrmann	20th	CDx	
King Rat	1965	B. Forbes	J. Barry	CO	CD*x	VHS
Kings Row	1942	S. Wood	E. Korngold	WB	CD+x	VHS LD
Knights of the Round Table	1953	R. Thorpe	M. Rozsa	MGM	CD*x	VHS LD
Knight without Armor	1937	J. Feyder	M. Rozsa	UA	CDx	VHS
Kramer vs. Kramer	1979	R. Benton	A. Vivaldi/ H. Purcell	CO	LP*	VHS LD
Krull	1982	P. Yates	J. Horner	CO	CD*	VHS LD
L •••••						
L.A. Confidential	1997	C. Hanson	J. Goldsmith	WB	CD*	
Lady Caroline Lamb	1972	R. Bolt	R. R. Bennett	UA	LP*/CDx	VHS
Last Embrace	1979	J. Demme	M. Rozsa	UA	CD*	VHS
Last Emperor, The	1987	B. Bertolucci	D. Byrne/ et al.	CO	CD*	VHS LD
Last of the Mohicans, The	1992	M. Mann	T. Jones/ R. Edelman	20th	CD*	VHS LD
Laura	1944	O. Preminger	D. Raksin	20th	CD*x	VHS LD
Lawrence of Arabia	1962	D. Lean	M. Jarre	CO	CD*+x	VHS LD
Legend [European version]	1985	R. Scott	J. Goldsmith	UN	CD*	VHS
Legends of the Fall	1994	E. Zwick	J. Horner	TS	CD*	VHS LD
Letter from an Unknown Woman	1948	M. Ophuls	D. Amfitheatrof	UN		VHS LD
Lieutenant Kijé	1934	A. Feinzimmer	S. Prokofiev	BS	CD+	
Lifeforce	1985	T. Hooper	H. Mancini	TS	CD*x	VHS LD
Life with Father	1947	M. Curtiz	M. Steiner	WB	CDx	VHS
Lili	1953	C. Walters	B. Kaper	MGM	LP*/CDx	VHS
Lilies of the Field	1963	R. Nelson	J. Goldsmith	UA	CD*	VHS
Limelight	1952	C. Chaplin	C. Chaplin	CO	CDx	VHS
Lionheart	1987	F. J. Schaffner	J. Goldsmith	Orion	CD*	VHS LD
Lion in Winter, The	1968	A. Harvey	J. Barry	AE	CD*x	VHS LD

Title	Year	Director	Composer	Studio	Recordings	Video
Lion King	1994	R. Allers/ R. Minkoff	H. Zimmer	BV	CD*x	VHS LD
Little Foxes, The	1941	W. Wyler	M. Willson	RKO		VHS LD
Little Mermaid, The	1989	J. Musker/ R. Clements	A. Menken	BV	CD*x	VHS LD
Little Romance, A	1979	G. R. Hill	G. Delerue	Orion	CD*x	VHS LD
Logan's Run	1976	M. Anderson	J. Goldsmith	MGM	CD*x	VHS LD
Looking for Richard	1996	A. Pacino	H. Shore	FS	CD*	VHS LD
Lord Jim	1965	R. Brooks	B. Kaper	CO	LP*x	VHS
Lost Horizon	1937	F. Capra	D. Tiomkin	CO	CD+	VHS LD
Lost Weekend, The	1945	B. Wilder	M. Rozsa	PR	LP*/CDx	VHS LD
Lost World: Jurassic Park, The	1997	S. Spielberg	J. Williams	UN	CD*	VHS LD
Louisiana Story	1948	R. Flaherty	V. Thomson	LO	LP+	VHS
Love in the Afternoon	1957	B. Wilder	F. Waxman	AA		VHS
Love Is a Many-Splendored Thing	1955	H. King	A. Newman	20th	CDx	VHS LD
Love Story	1970	A. Hiller	F. Lai	PR	LP*/CDx	VHS LD
Lust for Life	1956	V. Minnelli	M. Rozsa	MGM	CD*	VHS LD
Lydia	1941	J. Duvivier	M. Rozsa	UA	CDx	VHS

M....

Title	Year	Director	Composer	Studio	Recordings	Video
MacArthur	1977	J. Sargent	J. Goldsmith	UN	CD*x	VHS LD
Madame Bovary	1949	V. Minnelli	M. Rozsa	MGM	LP*/CDx	VHS LD
Madwoman of Chaillot, The	1969	B. Forbes	M. J. Lewis	WB	LP*/CDx	VHS LD
Magic	1978	R. Attenborough	J. Goldsmith	20th	CDx	VHS LD
Magnificent Ambersons, The	1942	O. Welles	B. Herrmann	RKO	CD+x	VHS LD
Magnificent Seven, The	1960	J. Sturges	E. Bernstein	UA	CD+x	VHS LD
Man and a Woman, A	1966	C. Lelouch	F. Lai	AA	CD*x	VHS
Manhattan	1979	W. Allen	G. Gershwin	UA	CD*	VHS LD
Man Who Knew Too Much, The	1956	A. Hitchcock	B. Herrmann	PR	CDx	VHS LD
Man with the Golden Arm, The	1955	O. Preminger	E. Bernstein	UA	LP*/CDx	VHS LD
Marnie	1964	A. Hitchcock	B. Herrmann	UN	CDx	VHS LD
Marty	1955	D. Mann	R. Webb	UA		VHS LD
Mary Shelley's Frankenstein	1994	K. Branagh	P. Doyle	TS	CD*	VHS LD
M*A*S*H	1970	R. Altman	J. Mandel	20th	CD*	VHS LD
Medicine Man	1992	J. McTiernan	J. Goldsmith	BV	CD*x	VHS LD
Men in Black	1997	B. Sonnenfeld	D. Elfman	CO	CD*	VHS LD
Mephisto Waltz, The	1971	P. Wendkos	J. Goldsmith	20th	CD*	VHS
Michael Collins	1996	N. Jordan	E. Goldenthal	WB	CD*	VHS LD
Midnight Cowboy	1969	J. Schlesinger	J. Barry	UA	CD*x	VHS LD
Midnight Express	1978	A. Parker	G. Moroder	CO	CD*	VHS LD
Milagro Beanfield War, The	1988	R. Redford	D. Grusin	UN	CDx	VHS LD
Mildred Pierce	1945	M. Curtiz	M. Steiner	WB	CDx	VHS LD
Mission, The	1986	R. Joffe	E. Morricone	WB	CD*x	VHS LD
Mississippi Burning	1988	A. Parker	T. Jones	Orion	CD*	VHS LD
Mr. Holland's Opus	1995	S. Herek	M. Kamen	BV	CD*x	VHS LD
Mr. Smith Goes to Washington	1939	F. Capra	D. Tiomkin	CO		VHS LD

Title	Year	Director	Composer	Studio	Recordings	Video
Moderns, The	1988	A. Rudolph	M. Isham	AF	CD*x	VHS LD
Modern Times	1936	C. Chaplin	C. Chaplin	UA	LP*/CDx	VHS LD
Molly Maguires, The	1970	M. Ritt	H. Mancini	PR	CD*x	VHS
Moon and Sixpence, The	1942	A. Lewin	D. Tiomkin	UA		VHS
Moon over Parador	1988	P. Mazursky	M. Jarre	UN	CD*x	VHS LD
Moonstruck	1987	N. Jewison	D. Hyman	MGM	CD*	VHS LD
Most Dangerous Game, The	1932	E. Schoedsack/ I. Pichel	M. Steiner	RKO		VHS LD VHS LD
Moulin Rouge	1952	J. Huston	G. Auric	UA	CDx	VHS LD
Mrs. Miniver	1942	W. Wyler	H. Stothart	MGM	CDx	VHS LD
Much Ado about Nothing	1993	K. Branagh	P. Doyle	SG	CD*x	VHS LD
Murder on the Orient Express	1974	S. Lumet	R. R. Bennett	PR	CD*x	VHS LD
Mutiny on the Bounty	1962	L. Milestone	B. Kaper	MGM	CD*x	VHS LD
My Left Foot	1989	J. Sheridan	E. Bernstein	MR	CD*x	VHS LD
Mysterious Island	1961	C. Endfield	B. Herrmann	CO	CD*x	VHS LD

N....

Title	Year	Director	Composer	Studio	Recordings	Video
Naked City, The	1948	J. Dassin	F. Skinner/ M. Rozsa	UN	CDx	VHS LD
Natural, The	1984	B. Levinson	R. Newman	TS	CD*	VHS LD
Needful Things	1993	F. Heston	P. Doyle	NLC	CD*	VHS LD
Never on Sunday	1960	J. Dassin	M. Hadjidakis	UA	CD*x	VHS
Nicholas and Alexandra	1971	F. J. Schaffner	R. R. Bennett	CO	LP*	VHS LD
Night Digger, The	1971	A. Reid	B. Herrmann	MGM	CD*x	
Night of the Hunter, The	1955	C. Laughton	W. Schumann	UA	LP*	VHS LD
Night Visitor, The	1971	L. Benedek	H. Mancini	UMC	CD*x	VHS
Ninotchka	1939	E. Lubitsch	W. Heymann	MGM		VHS LD
Nixon	1995	O. Stone	J. Williams	BV	CD*	VHS LD
Nobody's Fool	1994	R. Benton	H. Shore	PR	CD*	VHS LD
Noche de los Mayas, La	1939	C. Urueta	S. Rivueltas	MI	CD+	
North by Northwest	1959	A. Hitchcock	B. Herrmann	MGM	CD*+x	VHS LD
Notorious	1946	A. Hitchcock	R. Webb	RKO	CDx	VHS LD
Now, Voyager	1942	I. Rapper	M. Steiner	WB	CDx	VHS LD
Nun's Story, The	1959	F. Zinnemann	F. Waxman	WB	CD*x	VHS LD

O....

Title	Year	Director	Composer	Studio	Recordings	Video
Obsession	1976	B. De Palma	B. Herrmann	CO	CD*	VHS LD
Of Mice and Men	1939	L. Milestone	A. Copland	UA	CDx	VHS
Old Man and the Sea, The	1958	J. Sturges	D. Tiomkin	WB	CD*x	VHS
Omen, The	1976	R. Donner	J. Goldsmith	20th	CD*x	VHS LD
Once upon a Time in the West	1969	S. Leone	E. Morricone	UA	CD*x	VHS LD
One-Eyed Jacks	1961	M. Brando	H. Friedhofer	PR	LP*x	VHS LD
One Flew over the Cuckoo's Nest	1975	M. Forman	J. Nitzsche	UA	CD*	VHS LD
On Golden Pond	1981	M. Rydell	D. Grusin	UN	LP*/CDx	VHS LD
On the Beach	1959	S. Kramer	E. Gold	UA	LP*x	VHS LD
On the Waterfront	1954	E. Kazan	L. Bernstein	CO	CD+x	VHS LD
Ordinary People	1980	R. Redford	M. Hamlisch	PR		VHS LD
Oscar	1991	J. Landis	E. Bernstein	BV	CD*x	VHS LD

Title	Year	Director	Composer	Studio	Recordings	Video
Other, The	1972	R. Mulligan	J. Goldsmith	20th	CDx	VHS
Our Daily Bread	1934	K. Vidor	A. Newman	UA		VHS LD
Our Town	1940	S. Wood	A. Copland	UA	CDx	VHS
Out of Africa	1985	S. Pollack	J. Barry	UN	CD*x	VHS LD

P•••••

Title	Year	Director	Composer	Studio	Recordings	Video
Papillon	1973	F. J. Schaffner	J. Goldsmith	AA	CD*x	VHS LD
Paradine Case, The	1947	A. Hitchcock	F. Waxman	SZ	CDx	VHS
Passage to India, A	1984	D. Lean	M. Jarre	CO	CD*x	VHS LD
Patch of Blue, A	1965	G. Green	J. Goldsmith	MGM	CD*x	VHS
Patton	1970	F. J. Schaffner	J. Goldsmith	20th	LP*/CD+x	VHS LD
Perri	1957	N. Kenworthy/ R. Wright	P. Smith	BV		
Pete Kelly's Blues	1955	J. Webb	R. Heindorf	WB	LP*	VHS LD
Peyton Place	1957	Mark Robson	F. Waxman	20th	LP*/CDx	VHS
Phantom of the Opera, The	1943	A. Lubin	E. Ward	UN	LP*	VHS LD
Piano, The	1993	J. Campion	M. Nyman	MR	CD*x	VHS LD
Picnic	1955	J. Logan	G. Duning	CO	CD*x	VHS LD
Picture of Dorian Gray, The	1945	A. Lewin	H. Stothart	MGM		VHS LD
Place in the Sun, A	1951	G. Stevens	F. Waxman	PR	CDx	VHS LD
Places in the Heart	1984	R. Benton	H. Shore	TS	LP*	VHS LD
Planet of the Apes	1968	F. J. Schaffner	J. Goldsmith	20th	CD*	VHS LD
Platoon	1986	O. Stone	G. Delerue	Orion	CD*x	VHS LD
Plow That Broke the Plains, The	1936	P. Lorenz	V. Thomson	USG	CD+	
Plymouth Adventure	1952	C. Brown	M. Rozsa	MGM	CDx	VHS
Poltergeist	1982	T. Hooper	J. Goldsmith	MGM	CD*x	VHS LD
Portrait of a Lady, The	1996	J. Campion	W. Kilar	GR	CD*	VHS LD
Poseidon Adventure, The	1972	R. Neame	J. Williams	20th		VHS LD
Power, The	1968	B. Haskin	M. Rozsa	MGM	CD*	
Power of One, The	1988	J. G. Avildsen	H. Zimmer	WB	CD*	VHS LD
Pride and the Passion, The	1957	S. Kramer	G. Antheil	UA	CD*	VHS LD
Prince and the Pauper, The	1937	W. Keighley	E. Korngold	WB	CDx	VHS LD
Prince and the Showgirl, The	1957	L. Olivier	R. Addinsell	WB	CDx	VHS LD
Prince of Players	1955	P. Dunne	B. Herrmann	20th	CDx	
Prince of Tides, The	1991	B. Streisand	J. N. Howard	CO	CD*x	VHS LD
Prisoner of Zenda, The	1937	J. Cromwell	A. Newman	UA	CDx	VHS LD
Private Lives of Elizabeth and Essex, The	1939	M. Curtiz	E. Korngold	WB	CD+x	VHS
Providence	1977	A. Resnais	M. Rozsa	C5	CD*x	VHS
Psycho	1960	A. Hitchcock	B. Herrmann	PR	CD*+x	VHS LD
Psycho II	1983	R. Franklin	J. Goldsmith	UN	CD*	VHS LD
Pygmalion	1938	A. Asquith/ L. Howard	A. Honegger	MGM		VHS LD

Q•••••

Title	Year	Director	Composer	Studio	Recordings	Video
Quest for Fire	1982	J.-J. Annaud	P. Sarde	20th	LP*	VHS LD
Quiet Man, The	1952	J. Ford	V. Young	RP	CD+x	VHS LD
Quo Vadis	1951	M. LeRoy	M. Rozsa	MGM	CD+x	VHS LD

Title	Year	Director	Composer	Studio	Recordings	Video
R •••••						
Raggedy Man	1981	J. Fisk	J. Goldsmith	UN	CD*	VHS LD
Raging Bull	1980	M. Scorsese	P. Mascagni/ et al.	UA		VHS LD
Ragtime	1981	M. Forman	R. Newman	PR	LP*	VHS LD
Raiders of the Lost Ark	1981	S. Spielberg	J. Williams	PR	CD*x	VHS LD
Rain Man	1988	B. Levinson	H. Zimmer	UA	CD*	VHS LD
Raintree County	1957	E. Dmytryk	J. Green	MGM	CD*	VHS LD
Raise the Titanic	1980	J. Jameson	J. Barry	AFD	CDx	VHS LD
Raising Arizona	1987	J. Coen	C. Burwell	20th	CD*	VHS LD
Raisin in the Sun, A	1961	D. Petrie	L. Rosenthal	CO	CDx	VHS LD
Razor's Edge, The	1946	E. Goulding	A. Newman	20th	CDx	VHS LD
Rebecca	1940	A. Hitchcock	F. Waxman	UA	CD+x	VHS LD
Rebel without a Cause	1955	N. Ray	L. Rosenman	WB	CDx	VHS LD
Red House, The	1947	D. Daves	M. Rozsa	EL	CDx	VHS
Red Pony, The	1949	L. Milestone	A. Copland	RP	CD+	VHS LD
Red Shoes, The	1948	M. Powell/ E. Pressburger	B. Easdale	EL	CDx	VHS LD
Regarding Henry	1991	M. Nichols	H. Zimmer	PR	CD*	VHS LD
Reivers, The	1969	M. Rydell	J. Williams	NG	CD*x	VHS
Return of a Man Called Horse, The	1976	I. Kershner	L. Rosenthal	UA	LP*	VHS
Return of the Jedi	1983	R. Marquand	J. Williams	20th	CD*+x	VHS LD
Rhapsody in Blue	1945	I. Rapper	R. Heindorf/ M. Steiner	WB	LP*	VHS LD
Richard III	1956	L. Olivier	W. Walton	LO	CD+x	VHS LD
Right Stuff, The	1983	P. Kaufman	B. Conti	WB	CD*x	VHS LD
River Runs through It, A	1992	R. Redford	M. Isham	CO	CD*	VHS LD
Robe, The	1953	H. Koster	A. Newman	20th	CD*x	VHS LD
Robin Hood—Prince of Thieves	1991	K. Reynolds	M. Kamen	WB	CD*x	VHS LD
RoboCop	1987	P. Verhoeven	B. Poledouris	Orion	CD*	VHS LD
Romeo and Juliet	1968	F. Zeffirelli	N. Rota	PR	CD*x	VHS LD
Room with a View, A	1986	J. Ivory	R. Robbins	CC	CD*x	VHS LD
Rosemary's Baby	1968	R. Polanski	C. Komeda	PR	LP*/CDx	VHS LD
Rosewood	1997	J. Singleton	J. Williams	WB	CD*	VHS LD
Round Midnight	1986	B. Tavernier	H. Hancock	WB	CD*	VHS LD
Ryan's Daughter	1970	D. Lean	M. Jarre	MGM	CD*x	VHS LD
S •••••						
Sabrina	1995	S. Pollack	J. Williams	PR	CD*x	VHS LD
Samson and Delilah	1950	C. B. DeMille	V. Young	PR	CD*x	VHS LD
Sand Pebbles, The	1966	R. Wise	J. Goldsmith	20th	LP*/CDx	VHS LD
Saturday Night Fever	1977	J. Badham	D. Shire/et al.	PR	CD*	VHS LD
Sayonara	1957	J. Logan	F. Waxman	WB	LP*/CDx	VHS LD
Scaramouche	1952	G. Sidney	V. Young	MGM	CDx	VHS LD
Scarlet Letter, The	1995	R. Joffe	J. Barry	BV	CD*x	VHS LD
Schindler's List	1993	S. Spielberg	J. Williams	UN	CD*x	VHS LD
Scott of the Antarctic	1948	C. Frend	R. Vaughan Williams	EL	CD+	VHS
Sea Hawk, The	1940	M. Curtiz	E. Korngold	WB	CD+x	VHS LD
Seconds	1966	J. Frankenheimer	J. Goldsmith	PR		
Secret Garden, The	1993	A. Holland	Z. Preisner	WB	CD*	VHS LD
Separate Tables	1958	D. Mann	D. Raksin	UA		VHS

Title	Year	Director	Composer	Studio	Recordings	Video
Seven-Per-Cent Solution, The	1976	H. Ross	J. Addison	UN	CDx	VHS LD
7th Voyage of Sinbad, The	1958	N. Juran	B. Herrmann	CO	CD*x	VHS LD
Seven Years in Tibet	1997	J.-J. Annaud	J. Williams	TS	CD*	
Shadow of a Doubt	1943	A. Hitchcock	D. Tiomkin	UN		VHS LD
Shaft	1971	G. Parks	I. Hayes	MGM	CD*	VHS
Shane	1953	G. Stevens	V. Young	PR	CDx	VHS LD
Shanghai Gesture, The	1942	J. von Sternberg	R. Hageman	UA		VHS LD
Shine	1996	S. Hicks	D. Hirschfelder	FL	CD*	VHS LD
Shining, The	1980	S. Kubrick	W. Carlos	WB	CD*	VHS LD
Ship of Fools	1965	S. Kramer	E. Gold	CO	LP+	VHS LD
Shoes of the Fisherman, The	1968	M. Anderson	A. North	MGM	LP*/CDx	VHS
Silent Movie	1976	M. Brooks	J. Morris	20th	LP*	VHS LD
Silverado	1985	L. Kasdan	B. Broughton	CO	CD*x	VHS LD
Since You Went Away	1944	J. Cromwell	M. Steiner	UA	CDx	VHS LD
Singing Fool, The	1928	L. Bacon	L. Silvers	WB	LP*/CDx	VHS LD
Sisters	1973	B. De Palma	B. Herrmann	AI	CD*x	VHS
Sleeping Beauty	1959	C. Geronimi	G. Bruns	BV	CD*x	VHS LD
Sleeping with the Enemy	1991	J. Ruben	J. Goldsmith	20th	CD*	VHS LD
Sleuth	1972	J. Mankiewicz	J. Addison	20th	LP*/CDx	VHS LD
Slipper and the Rose, The	1977	B. Forbes	A. Morley	UN	LP*	
Snake Pit, The	1948	A. Litvak	A. Newman	20th		VHS
Snow White and the Seven Dwarfs	1937	B. Sharpsteen	L. Harline/et al.	RKO	CD*x CD*	VHS LD
Some Came Running	1958	V. Minnelli	E. Bernstein	MGM	CD*	VHS LD
Some Like It Hot	1959	B. Wilder	A. Deutsch	UA	CD*x	VHS LD
Somewhere in Time	1980	J. Szwarc	J. Barry	UN	CD*x	VHS LD
Song of Bernadette, The	1943	H. King	A. Newman	20th		VHS LD
Song to Remember, A	1945	C. Vidor	M. Rozsa/ M. Stoloff	CO		VHS LD
Son of Fury	1942	J. Cromwell	A. Newman	20th	CD*x	VHS
Spartacus	1960	S. Kubrick	A. North	UN	CD+x	VHS LD
Spellbound	1945	A. Hitchcock	M. Rozsa	UA		VHS LD
Spiral Staircase, The	1946	R. Siodmak	R. Webb	RKO	CD*+x	VHS LD
Spirit of St. Louis, The	1957	B. Wilder	F. Waxman	WB	CD*	VHS
Spitfire Grill, The	1996	L. Zlotoff	J. Horner	CO	CDx	VHS LD
Stagecoach	1939	J. Ford	R. Hageman	UA	LP+/CDx	VHS LD
Star Is Born, A	1937	W. Wellman	M. Steiner	UA	CD*x	VHS LD
Star Trek—the Motion Picture	1979	R. Wise	J. Goldsmith	PR	CD*x	VHS LD
Star Trek IV: The Voyage Home	1986	L. Nimoy	L. Rosenman	PR	CD*x	VHS LD
Star Trek II: The Wrath of Khan	1982	N. Meyer	J. Horner	PR	CD*x	VHS LD
Starman	1984	J. Carpenter	J. Nitzsche	CO	CD*x	VHS LD
Star Wars	1977	G. Lucas	J. Williams	20th	CD*x	VHS LD
Steel Magnolias	1989	H. Ross	G. Delerue	TS	CD*	VHS LD
Sting, The	1973	G. R. Hill	S. Joplin/ M. Hamlisch	UN	CDx	VHS LD
Strangers on a Train	1951	A. Hitchcock	D. Tiomkin	WB	CD*+x	VHS LD

Title	Year	Director	Composer	Studio	Recordings	Video
Streetcar Named Desire, A	1951	E. Kazan	A. North	WB	CD*+x	VHS LD
Street Scene	1931	K. Vidor	A. Newman	UA	CDx	VHS
Stunt Man, The	1980	R. Rush	D. Frontiere	20th	LP*	VHS LD
Summer and Smoke	1961	P. Glenville	E. Bernstein	PR	LP*	VHS LD
Summer of '42	1971	R. Mulligan	M. Legrand	WB	CD*x	VHS LD
Summer Place, A	1959	D. Daves	M. Steiner	WB	LP+/CDx	VHS LD
Sunflower	1970	V. De Sica	H. Mancini	AE	LP*/CDx	
Sunset Boulevard	1950	B. Wilder	F. Waxman	PR	CDx	VHS LD
Superman	1978	R. Donner	J. Williams	WB	CD*x	VHS LD
Suspicion	1941	A. Hitchcock	F. Waxman	RKO	CDx	VHS LD
Swarm, The	1978	I. Allen	J. Goldsmith	WB	LP*	VHS
Swimmer, The	1968	F. Perry	M. Hamlisch	CO	LP*	VHS LD

T •••••

Title	Year	Director	Composer	Studio	Recordings	Video
Taras Bulba	1962	J. Lee Thompson	F. Waxman	UA	CD*x	VHS LD
Taxi Driver	1976	M. Scorsese	B. Herrmann	CO	CD*x	VHS LD
Ten Commandments, The	1956	C. B. DeMille	E. Bernstein	PR	CD*x	VHS LD
Tender Is the Night	1962	H. King	B. Herrmann	20th		
Terms of Endearment	1983	J. L. Brooks	M. Gore	PR	CD*x	VHS LD
Tess	1980	R. Polanski	P. Sarde	CO	LP*	VHS LD
That Hamilton Woman	1941	A. Korda	M. Rozsa	UA	CDx	VHS LD
These Three	1936	W. Wyler	A. Newman	UA		VHS LD
They Shoot Horses, Don't They?	1969	S. Pollack	J. Green	CR	LP*	VHS LD
Thief of Bagdad	1940	L. Berger/et al.	M. Rozsa	UA	LP+/CDx	VHS LD
Thing from Another World, The	1951	C. Nyby	D. Tiomkin	RKO	CDx	VHS LD
Things to Come	1935	W. Menzies	A. Bliss	UA	CDx	VHS
Third Man, The	1950	C. Reed	A. Karas	SZ	CDx	VHS LD
Three Musketeers, The	1974	R. Lester	M. Legrand	20th	CD*	VHS
Time after Time	1979	N. Meyer	M. Rozsa	WB	CD*x	VHS LD
Titanic	1997	J. Cameron	J. Horner	20th/PR	CD*	
To Kill a Mockingbird	1962	R. Mulligan	E. Bernstein	UN	CD*+x	VHS LD
Tom Jones	1963	T. Richardson	J. Addison	UA/LO	LP*	VHS LD
Top Gun	1986	T. Scott	H. Faltermeyer	PR	CD*	VHS LD
Towering Inferno, The	1974	J. Guillermin	J. Williams	20th/WB	LP*/CDx	VHS LD
Trading Places	1983	J. Landis	E. Bernstein	PR		VHS LD
Treasure of the Sierra Madre, The	1948	J. Huston	M. Steiner	WB	CDx	VHS LD
Trouble with Harry, The	1955	A. Hitchcock	B. Herrmann	PR	CDx	VHS LD
Twilight Zone: The Movie	1983	J. Landis/et al.	J. Goldsmith	WB	LP*/CDx	VHS LD
2001: A Space Odyssey	1968	S. Kubrick	various	MGM	CD*	VHS LD

U •••••

Title	Year	Director	Composer	Studio	Recordings	Video
Umbrellas of Cherbourg, The	1965	J. Demy	M. Legrand	LA	CD*x	VHS
Uninvited, The	1944	L. Allen	V. Young	PR	CDx	VHS LD
Untamed Heart	1993	T. Bill	C. Eidelman	MGM	CD*	VHS LD
Untouchables, The	1987	B. De Palma	E. Morricone	PR	CD*x	VHS LD
Up the Down Staircase	1967	R. Mulligan	F. Karlin	WB	LP*	VHS

Title	Year	Director	Composer	Studio	Recordings	Video
V ●●●●●						
Vertigo	1958	A. Hitchcock	B. Herrmann	PR	CD*+x	VHS LD
Victor/Victoria	1982	B. Edwards	H. Mancini	MGM	CD*x	VHS LD
Vikings, The	1958	R. Fleischer	M. Nascimbene	UA	CD*x	VHS
V.I.P.s, The	1963	A. Asquith	M. Rozsa	MGM	LP*	VHS
W ●●●●●						
Walk in the Clouds, A	1995	A. Arau	M. Jarre	20th	CD*	VHS LD
Walk on the Wild Side	1962	E. Dmytryk	E. Bernstein	CO	CD*x	VHS
Way We Were, The	1973	S. Pollack	M. Hamlisch	CO	CD*	VHS LD
White Dawn, The	1974	P. Kaufman	H. Mancini	PR	CDx	VHS LD
White Witch Doctor	1953	H. Hathaway	B. Herrmann	20th	CDx	
Who Framed Roger Rabbit?	1988	R. Zemeckis	A. Silvestri	BV	CD*x	VHS LD
Who's Afraid of Virginia Woolf?	1966	M. Nichols	A. North	WB	CD+x	VHS LD
Wind and the Lion, The	1975	J. Milius	J. Goldsmith	MGM	CD*x	VHS LD
Witness	1985	P. Weir	M. Jarre	PR	CD*x	VHS LD
Wolf	1994	M. Nichols	E. Morricone	CO	CD*x	VHS LD
Working Girl	1988	M. Nichols	C. Simon	20th	CD*	VHS LD
World of Henry Orient, The	1964	G. R. Hill	E. Bernstein	UA		VHS LD
Wuthering Heights	1939	W. Wyler	A. Newman	UA	CDx	VHS LD
Wyatt Earp	1994	L. Kasdan	J. N. Howard	WB	CD*	VHS LD
Y ●●●●●						
Year of Living Dangerously, The	1983	P. Weir	M. Jarre	MGM/UA	CD*x	VHS LD
Young Bess	1953	G. Sidney	M. Rozsa	MGM	CD*x	VHS
Young Frankenstein	1974	M. Brooks	J. Morris	20th	LP*x	VHS LD
Young Lions, The	1958	E. Dmytryk	H. Friedhofer	20th	CD*	VHS LD
Young Sherlock Holmes	1985	B. Levinson	B. Broughton	PR	LP*/CDx	VHS LD

General Index

Index of Titles

Index of Names

(Film-score composers are given in bold.)